AMERICA'S
TEST KITCHEN

ALSO BY AMERICA'S TEST KITCHEN

Cooking for One

The Complete One Pot

How Can It Be Gluten Free Cookbook Collection

Meat Illustrated

The Complete Summer Cookbook

Bowls

Vegetables Illustrated

The Side Dish Bible

Foolproof Fish

100 Techniques

Easy Everyday Keto

Everything Chocolate

The Perfect Pie

How to Cocktail

Spiced

The Ultimate Burger

The New Essentials Cookbook

Dinner Illustrated

America's Test Kitchen Menu Cookbook

Cook's Illustrated Revolutionary Recipes

Tasting Italy: A Culinary Journey

Cooking at Home with Bridget and Julia

The Complete Diabetes Cookbook

The Complete Slow Cooker

The Complete Make-Ahead Cookbook

The Complete Mediterranean Cookbook

The Complete Vegetarian Cookbook

The Complete Cooking for Two Cookbook

Just Add Sauce

How to Braise Everything

How to Roast Everything

Nutritious Delicious

What Good Cooks Know

Cook's Science

The Science of Good Cooking

The Perfect Cake

The Perfect Cookie

Bread Illustrated

Master of the Grill

Kitchen Smarts

Kitchen Hacks

100 Recipes: The Absolute Best Ways to Make the True Essentials

The New Family Cookbook

The America's Test Kitchen Cooking School Cookbook

Mediterranean Instant Pot

The Cook's Illustrated Baking Book

The Cook's Illustrated Cookbook

The America's Test Kitchen Family Baking Book

America's Test Kitchen Twentieth Anniversary TV Show Cookbook

The Best of America's Test Kitchen (2007–2021 Editions)

The Complete America's Test Kitchen TV Show Cookbook 2001–2021

Cook It in Your Dutch Oven

Vegan for Everybody

Sous Vide for Everybody

Air Fryer Perfection

Multicooker Perfection

Food Processor Perfection

Pressure Cooker Perfection

Instant Pot Ace Blender Cookbook

Naturally Sweet

Foolproof Preserving

Paleo Perfected

The Best Mexican Recipes

Slow Cooker Revolution Volume 2: The Easy-Prep Edition

Slow Cooker Revolution

The America's Test Kitchen D.I.Y. Cookbook

THE COOK'S ILLUSTRATED ALL-TIME BEST SERIES

All-Time Best Brunch

All-Time Best Dinners for Two

All-Time Best Sunday Suppers

All-Time Best Holiday Entertaining

All-Time Best Appetizers

All-Time Best Soups

COOK'S COUNTRY TITLES

Big Flavors from Italian America

One-Pan Wonders

Cook It in Cast Iron

Cook's Country Eats Local

The Complete Cook's Country TV Show Cookbook

FOR A FULL LISTING OF ALL OUR BOOKS

CooksIllustrated.com

AmericasTestKitchen.com

PRAISE FOR AMERICA'S TEST KITCHEN TITLES

"Here are the words just about any vegan would be happy to read: 'Why This Recipe Works.' Fans of America's Test Kitchen are used to seeing the phrase, and now it applies to the growing collection of plant-based creations in *Vegan for Everybody*."

THE WASHINGTON POST ON *VEGAN FOR EVERYBODY*

"True to its name, this smart and endlessly enlightening cookbook is about as definitive as it's possible to get in the modern vegetarian realm."

MEN'S JOURNAL ON *THE COMPLETE VEGETARIAN COOKBOOK*

"This is a wonderful, useful guide to healthy eating."

PUBLISHERS WEEKLY ON *NUTRITIOUS DELICIOUS*

"Another flawless entry in the America's Test Kitchen canon, *Bowls* guides readers of all culinary skill levels in composing one-bowl meals from a variety of cuisines."

BUZZFEED BOOKS ON *BOWLS*

Selected as the Cookbook Award Winner of 2019 in the Health and Special Diet Category

INTERNATIONAL ASSOCIATION OF CULINARY PROFESSIONALS (IACP) ON *THE COMPLETE DIABETES COOKBOOK*

"Diabetics and all health-conscious home cooks will find great information on almost every page."

BOOKLIST (STARRED REVIEW) ON *THE COMPLETE DIABETES COOKBOOK*

"*The Perfect Cookie* . . . is, in a word, perfect. This is an important and substantial cookbook. . . . If you love cookies, but have been a tad shy to bake on your own, all your fears will be dissipated. This is one book you can use for years with magnificently happy results."

THE HUFFINGTON POST ON *THE PERFECT COOKIE*

"The sum total of exhaustive experimentation . . . anyone interested in gluten-free cookery simply shouldn't be without it."

NIGELLA LAWSON ON *THE HOW CAN IT BE GLUTEN-FREE COOKBOOK*

"The book's depth, breadth, and practicality makes it a must-have for seafood lovers."

PUBLISHERS WEEKLY (STARRED REVIEW) ON *FOOLPROOF FISH*

"Offers a real option for a cook who just wants to learn some new ways to encourage family and friends to explore today's sometimes-daunting vegetable universe. This is one of the most valuable vegetable cooking resources for the home chef since Marian Morash's beloved classic *The Victory Garden Cookbook* (1982)."

BOOKLIST (STARRED REVIEW) ON *VEGETABLES ILLUSTRATED*

"If you're a home cook who loves long introductions that tell you why a dish works followed by lots of step-by-step hand holding, then you'll love *Vegetables Illustrated*."

THE WALL STREET JOURNAL ON *VEGETABLES ILLUSTRATED*

"A one-volume kitchen seminar, addressing in one smart chapter after another the sometimes surprising whys behind a cook's best practices. . . . You get the myth, the theory, the science, and the proof, all rigorously interrogated as only America's Test Kitchen can do."

NPR ON *THE SCIENCE OF GOOD COOKING*

"The 21st-century *Fannie Farmer Cookbook* or *The Joy of Cooking*. If you had to have one cookbook and that's all you could have, this one would do it."

CBS SAN FRANCISCO ON *THE NEW FAMILY COOKBOOK*

"Some 2,500 photos walk readers through 600 painstakingly tested recipes, leaving little room for error."

ASSOCIATED PRESS ON *THE AMERICA'S TEST KITCHEN COOKING SCHOOL COOKBOOK*

"The go-to gift book for newlyweds, small families, or empty nesters."

ORLANDO SENTINEL ON *THE COMPLETE COOKING FOR TWO COOKBOOK*

"Some books impress by the sheer audacity of their ambition. Backed by the magazine's famed mission to test every recipe relentlessly until it is the best it can be, this nearly 900-page volume lands with an authoritative wallop."

CHICAGO TRIBUNE ON *THE COOK'S ILLUSTRATED COOKBOOK*

"It might become your 'cooking school,' the only book you'll need to make you a proficient cook, recipes included. . . . You can master the 100 techniques with the easy-to-understand instructions, then apply the skill with the recipes that follow."

THE LITCHFIELD COUNTY TIMES ON *100 TECHNIQUES*

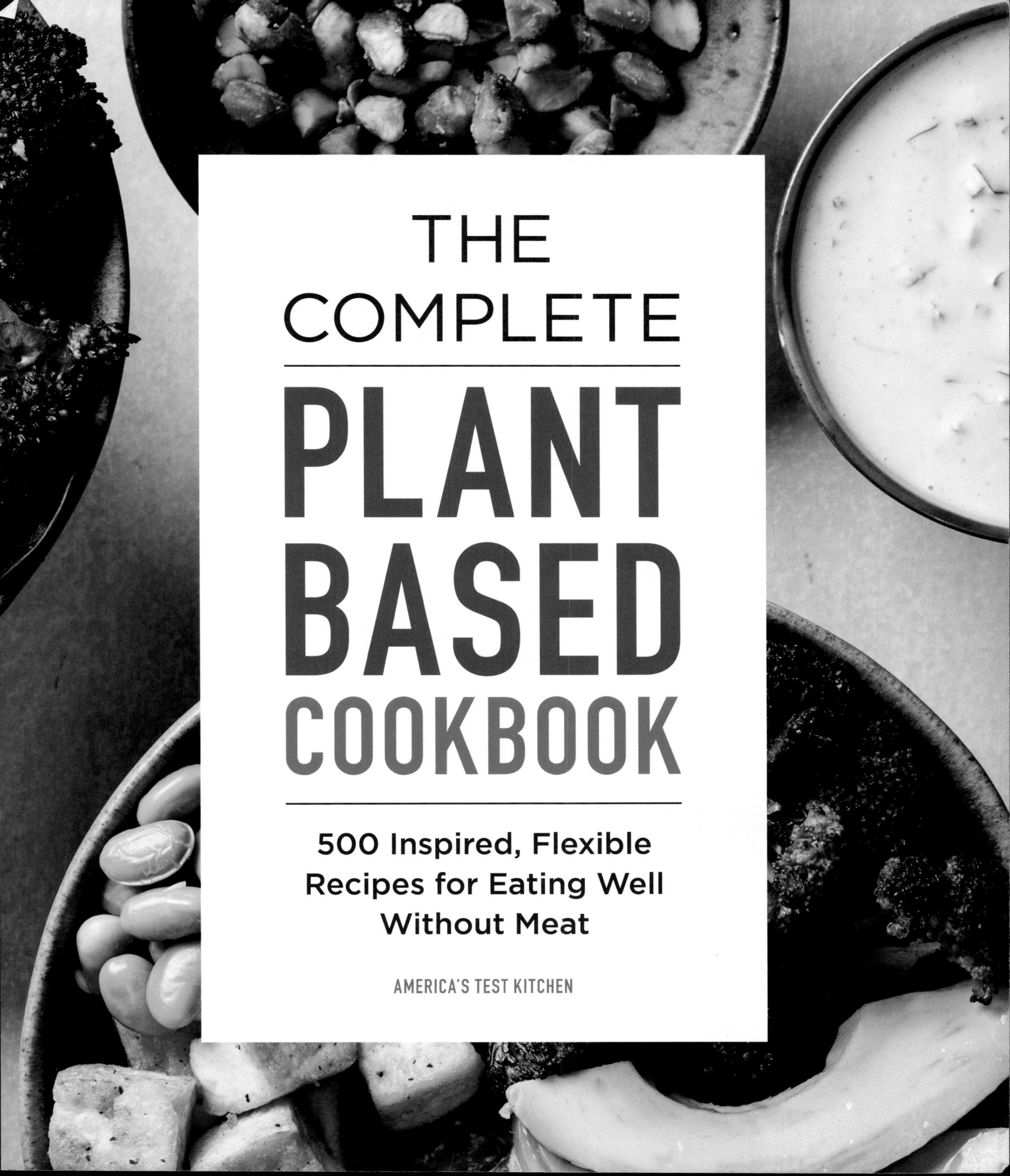

THE COMPLETE

PLANT

BASED

COOKBOOK

500 Inspired, Flexible
Recipes for Eating Well
Without Meat

AMERICA'S TEST KITCHEN

Library of Congress Cataloging-in-Publication Data

Names: America's Test Kitchen (Firm), editor.
Title: The complete book of plant-based cooking :
    500 inspired, flexible recipes for eating well without
    meat / America's Test Kitchen.
Description: Boston, MA : America's Test Kitchen,
    [2020] | Includes index.
Identifiers: LCCN 2020034726 (print) | LCCN 2020034727
    (ebook) | ISBN 9781948703369 (hardcover) |
    ISBN 9781948703376 (ebook)
Subjects: LCSH: Vegetarian cooking. | LCGFT: Cookbooks.
Classification: LCC TX837 .C683 2020 (print) |
    LCC TX837 (ebook) | DDC 641.5/636--dc23
LC record available at https://lccn.loc.gov/2020034726
LC ebook record available at https://lccn.loc.gov/2020034727

AMERICA'S
TEST KITCHEN ®

AMERICA'S TEST KITCHEN
21 Drydock Avenue, Boston, MA 02210

Manufactured in the United States of America
10 9 8 7 6 5 4 3 2 1

Distributed by Penguin Random House Publisher Services
Tel: 800.733.3000

Pictured on front cover **Baja-Style Cauliflower Tacos (page 98)**

Pictured on back cover **Green Goodness Salad with Tofu (page 146); Classic Pancakes (page 47); Red Lentil Kibbeh (page 291); Coconut Ice Cream (page 389); Eggplant and Kale Soup (page 69); Grilled Portobello Burgers (page 104)**

Front cover photography by **Carl Tremblay**
Front cover food styling by **Chantal Lambeth**

Editorial Director, Books **Adam Kowit**

Executive Food Editor **Dan Zuccarello**

Deputy Food Editor **Stephanie Pixley**

Executive Managing Editor **Debra Hudak**

Senior Editors **Valerie Cimino, Joseph Gitter, Nicole Konstantinakos, Sara Mayer**

Associate Editor **Camila Chaparro**

Test Cook **Samantha Block**

Assistant Editors **Tess Berger, Kelly Cormier, Sara Zatopek**

Additional Editorial Support **Octavia Pidoux**

Design Director **Lindsey Timko Chandler**

Deputy Art Directors **Courtney Lentz and Janet Taylor**

Photography Director **Julie Bozzo Cote**

Photography Producer **Meredith Mulcahy**

Senior Staff Photographers **Steve Klise and Daniel J. van Ackere**

Staff Photographer **Kevin White**

Additional Photography **Carl Tremblay and Joseph Keller**

Food Styling **Catrine Kelty, Chantal Lambeth, Ashley Moore, Marie Piraino, Elle Simone Scott, Kendra Smith, Sally Staub, Daniel J. van Ackere, Kevin White**

PHOTOSHOOT KITCHEN TEAM

Photo Team and Special Events Managers **Allison Berkey and Timothy McQuinn**

Lead Test Cook **Eric Haessler**

Assistant Test Cooks **Hannah Fenton, Jacqueline Gochenouer, Gina McCreadie, Christa West**

Senior Manager, Publishing Operations **Taylor Argenzio**

Imaging Manager **Lauren Robbins**

Production and Imaging Specialists **Tricia Neumyer, Dennis Noble, Amanda Yong**

Copy Editor **Cheryl Redmond**

Proofreader **Ann-Marie Imbornoni**

Indexer **Elizabeth Parson**

Chief Creative Officer **Jack Bishop**

Executive Editorial Directors **Julia Collin Davison and Bridget Lancaster**

CONTENTS

WELCOME TO AMERICA'S TEST KITCHEN

This book has been tested, written, and edited by the folks at America's Test Kitchen, where curious cooks become confident cooks. Located in Boston's Seaport District in the historic Innovation and Design Building, it features 15,000 square feet of kitchen space including multiple photography and video studios. It is the home of *Cook's Illustrated* magazine and *Cook's Country* magazine and is the workday destination for more than 60 test cooks, editors, and cookware specialists. Our mission is to empower and inspire confidence, community, and creativity in the kitchen.

We start the process of testing a recipe with a complete lack of preconceptions, which means that we accept no claim, no technique, and no recipe at face value. We simply assemble as many variations as possible, test a half-dozen of the most promising, and taste the results blind. We then construct our own recipe and continue to test it, varying ingredients, techniques, and cooking times until we reach a consensus. As we like to say in the test kitchen, "We make the mistakes so you don't have to." The result, we hope, is the best version of a particular recipe, but we realize that only you can be the final judge of our success (or failure). We use the same rigorous approach when we test equipment and taste ingredients.

All of this would not be possible without a belief that good cooking, much like good music, is based on a foundation of objective technique. Some people like spicy foods and others don't, but there is a right way to sauté, there is a best way to cook a pot roast, and there are measurable scientific principles involved in producing perfectly beaten, stable egg whites. Our ultimate goal is to investigate the fundamental principles of cooking to give you the techniques, tools, and ingredients you need to become a better cook. It is as simple as that.

To see what goes on behind the scenes at America's Test Kitchen, check out our social media channels for kitchen snapshots, exclusive content, video tips, and much more. You can watch us work (in our actual test kitchen) by tuning in to *America's Test Kitchen* or *Cook's Country* on public television or on our websites. Download our award-winning podcast *Proof*, which goes beyond recipes to solve food mysteries (AmericasTestKitchen. com/proof), or listen to test kitchen experts on public radio (SplendidTable.org) to hear insights that illuminate the truth about real home cooking. Want to hone your cooking skills or finally learn how to bake—with an America's Test Kitchen test cook? Enroll in one of our online cooking classes. And you can engage the next generation of home cooks with kid-tested recipes from America's Test Kitchen Kids.

Our community of home recipe testers provides valuable feedback on recipes under development by ensuring that they are foolproof. You can help us investigate the how and why behind successful recipes from your home kitchen. (Sign up at AmericasTestKitchen.com/recipe_testing.)

However you choose to visit us, we welcome you into our kitchen, where you can stand by our side as we test our way to the best recipes in America.

facebook.com/AmericasTestKitchen
twitter.com/TestKitchen
youtube.com/AmericasTestKitchen
instagram.com/TestKitchen
pinterest.com/TestKitchen

AmericasTestKitchen.com
CooksIllustrated.com
CooksCountry.com
OnlineCookingSchool.com
AmericasTestKitchen.com/kids

GETTING STARTED
A PLANT-BASED PRIMER

INTRODUCTION

Plant-based eating is capturing the attention of home cooks everywhere for its emphasis on health and sustainability. But "plant-based" is a somewhat nebulous and still-evolving term. Does it refer to a structured diet? Does it mean that something is vegan or vegetarian? Is it a marketing hook used to capture our attention? In short, yes. "Plant-based" can mean any of these things, depending on its context.

Here at America's Test Kitchen, we've already jumped into the world of plant-centric cooking, with books including *The Complete Vegetarian Cookbook* and *Vegan for Everybody*. With this new guide, we prove how easy it is to build a bridge between those two camps to move back and forth between them with ease, depending on your lifestyle and your taste preferences. *The Complete Plant-Based Cookbook* takes the next step in the evolution of plant-based eating as we see it. Our plant-forward philosophy means moving vegetables, grains, beans, and legumes to the center of the plate and eliminating or minimizing animal products, all with the end goal of achieving a healthier, sustainable everyday diet.

We all know instinctively that eating your vegetables is not only virtuous but also imperative for good health. We also know that many home cooks are highly interested in incorporating more vegetables and fewer animal products into their meals but aren't able or willing to make the jump to adopting a long-term vegan diet. And it can be hard to bring the whole family on board with one family member's eating goals. This cookbook satisfies the whole spectrum when it comes to eating plant-based. While every recipe can be prepared vegan, the recipes also include options for dairy-based ingredients and eggs whenever possible. For example, our recipe for Carrot Cake Pancakes (page 49) calls for either plant-based milk or dairy milk in the ingredient list. We've tested both options in the recipe and the results are equally delicious and successful, but the choice of which ingredient to use is up to you.

This is the crux of where we believe the wave of plant-based eating is heading. More and more people—not just strict vegetarians or vegans—are following a vegetable-focused but flexible diet. Sure, many who eat exclusively plant-based are doing so for ethical, environmental, and/or health reasons, but concepts like "meatless Mondays" and "mostly vegan" have also made it perfectly acceptable to eat a cheeseburger for dinner one night and a cauliflower steak the next. With this broad segment of home cooks in mind, we committed to covering as much ground as possible when developing our recipes, with chapters ranging from brunch to dessert.

In these pages, we equip you with all the information you need to produce satisfying, nutritious, and varied meals. We also demystify the complicated and rapidly expanding world of nondairy products and plant-based meats. When we first published *Vegan for Everybody*, oat milk was a new product and there were only a few nondairy yogurts available. Since then, the nondairy section of the grocery store has exploded into an unwieldy and complicated jumble of oat, soy, almond, coconut, pistachio, hemp, and pea protein products (among others). We tasted as many different brands of nondairy milk, yogurt, and creamer as we could find to provide you with guidance. Similarly, we entered the arena of plant-based meat and emerged with some winning cooking tips and recipes that everyone in your household will appreciate. We suggest starting with our Plant-Based Beef Tacos (page 100).

Think of *The Complete Plant-Based Cookbook* as your guidebook to exploring the plant-based cooking universe. We've included recipes that are easy makeovers of comfort food that you and your family will love, recipes that rethink the way we cook and eat vegetables, and naturally plant-based recipes inspired by traditional dishes from around the world. Try serving Loaded Meaty Nacho Dip (page 348) at your next game-day gathering, Cashew e Pepe e Funghi (page 165) when the craving for a lusciously creamy pasta strikes, or our take on Misir Wot (page 293), an Ethiopian red lentil stew, when you want to wake up your palate. So whether you've been eating plant-based for decades or are just starting out, we hope this book will help you to evolve your food boundaries, embrace something new, and ensconce plants squarely at the center of your plate.

—**STEPHANIE PIXLEY,** Deputy Food Editor

THE PLANT-BASED KITCHEN

The simplest way to begin setting up a plant-focused kitchen is to start making more room in your refrigerator and pantry (not to mention on your plate) for produce. You really don't need any special equipment, appliances, or storage items. Here's how to set yourself up for success.

STORAGE SMARTS

Once you bring all your colorful fresh ingredients home from the supermarket, how do you store them to keep them at their peak until you cook them? While there are many products sold as "produce keepers"—bags and containers promising to extend the life of fresh produce—we found them to be unnecessary. We tested several of these products, storing strawberries and spinach and placing them in the refrigerator alongside the same items left in their original packaging. After checking the produce every other day for two weeks, we discovered that the "protected" produce spoiled at the same rate as that in the original packaging, and in some cases even faster. Far more important is where in the kitchen you store your produce and when you wash it. You're better off controlling refrigerator temperature and storing produce strategically.

IN THE REFRIGERATOR

We often think of a refrigerator as having a single temperature—ideally at or below 40 degrees to comply with FDA guidelines for food safety—but every refrigerator has its own microclimates, with warmer, cooler, and more humid zones. When we monitored one of our refrigerators in the test kitchen, we found that the temperature ranged from 33 degrees to 43 degrees. You can make this temperature variation work to your advantage by knowing your own refrigerator and storing produce where it will fare best.

Cold Zone: Back, Top to Middle The top and middle shelves at the back of the refrigerator were normally the coldest; we found that temperatures in this zone dipped as low as 33 degrees. These areas are best for foods other than produce, such as tofu, yogurt, and miso.

Moderate Zone: Front, Middle to Bottom The areas at the front of our refrigerator, from the middle to the bottom shelves, were the most moderate, with temperatures that registered at least 37 degrees. Produce that is sensitive to chilling injury should be placed in this zone, including berries, lemons, limes, oranges, and melons. Avocados fit into this category as well. While avocados may be ripened on the counter or in the refrigerator, chilling them slows down the production of ethylene gas (the gas that triggers ripening in many fruits and vegetables) and, therefore, the ripening process. So they ripen more slowly but more evenly in the fridge.

Humid Zone: Crisper Drawer Crispers provide a humid environment that helps keep produce with a high water content from shriveling and rotting; in our refrigerator, the crisper's temperature mirrored the moderate temperature at the front of the fridge. If the humidity is too high, water can build up on fruits and vegetables and hasten spoilage. If your drawer has vents, regulate humidity by adjusting them; the more air that's allowed to pass in and out of the drawer, the less humid the environment. Virtually all vegetables do best in the crisper drawer, including artichokes, asparagus, beets, broccoli, cabbages, carrots, cauliflower, celery, chiles, cucumbers, eggplant, green beans, leafy greens, leeks,

lettuce, mushrooms, peppers, radishes, scallions, summer squash, sugar snap peas, turnips, and zucchini. We also store corn in the drawer. The sugar in corn begins to convert to starch from the moment the ears are picked; though this conversion is much slower in the supersweet varieties sold these days, storing corn in the refrigerator will slow the process even more. To store fresh herbs, remove twist ties, wrap them in paper towels, and place them in a plastic bag in the drawer.

Anywhere in the Fridge Apples, cherries, and grapes are not prone to chilling injury and can be stored anywhere in the fridge (including its coldest zones), provided the temperature isn't cold enough to freeze them.

ON THE COUNTER

Fruits that continue to ripen once harvested are called climeractic fruits; these include apricots, avocados, bananas, kiwis, mangos, nectarines, papayas, peaches, pears, plums, and tomatoes. Because they continue to ripen off the plant, they are often picked for transport before they're fully ripe. They develop their peak flavor, texture, and aroma when left at room temperature (away from heat and direct sunlight). With the exception of avocados, in the cold environment of the refrigerator they can fail to ripen properly and may discolor. However, once fully ripe, some climacteric fruit, including avocados, kiwis, pears, and even tomatoes, should be refrigerated in the front of the fridge to halt further ripening and to preserve their quality.

IN THE PANTRY

Long-keeping produce, including garlic, onions and shallots, potatoes and sweet potatoes, and winter squash, should be kept at cool room temperature away from light to prolong their shelf life.

WHEN TO WASH PRODUCE

Generally, it's best to wash produce just before you use it. Moisture promotes the growth of mold and bacteria, which causes spoilage. If you do wash it ahead of time, make sure to dry it thoroughly before storing it. One exception to this rule is fresh berries. While damp berries turn mushy faster than dry berries, we've learned that cleaning these fruits as soon as you bring them home destroys mold spores, ensuring their quality for a longer period of time. If you don't plan to eat your berries for a few days, we suggest washing them in a bowl with

---

PLANT POWER

ETHYLENE GAS

The ripening process in many fruits is controlled by ethylene, a colorless, odorless gas produced in minute quantities by the plant and its fruit. If ethylene gas is allowed to build up too much in a closed environment, it will activate enzymes that break down the cell walls of produce, speeding moisture loss and spoilage. But you can also harness ethylene to your advantage when it comes to ripening climeractic fruit. For example, unripe pears stored in a tightly closed paper bag to capture the gas they emit will ripen more quickly than those left in a bowl on the counter. Placing an already ripe, ethylene-emitting banana in the bag with the pears will cause the pears to ripen even faster. (Paper bags are moderately porous and allow a small amount of oxygen to enter, helping the pears produce enzymes that prevent them from spoiling as they ripen. Don't try to ripen fruit in plastic bags; it will spoil first.) Furthermore, we discovered that storing potatoes with an apple boosts the storage life of the potatoes by almost two weeks, because the tiny amount of ethylene gas emitted by the apple suppresses changes in the potatoes' cells that cause sprouts to form.

3 cups of water and 1 cup of distilled white vinegar. Drain them in a colander and rinse them under running water. Place the berries in a salad spinner lined with three layers of paper towels, and spin for 15 seconds or until the berries are completely dry. Then you can store the berries in a loosely covered paper towel–lined container at the front of the fridge.

PRODUCE PACKAGING

Often produce packaging has a function beyond simple convenience. For example, though they appear solid, the bags in which many greens are now sold are made of a polymer that allows ethylene to pass through freely, staving off spoilage. Other types of packaging often feature small perforations or other openings (such as the bags in which celery is sold); here, too, the intent is to allow ethylene to escape while allowing enough moisture to escape to prevent rot but not so much that the produce dries out.

THE PLANT-POWERED PANTRY

We regularly rely on a number of store-bought pantry items (both shelf-stable and refrigerated) to create satisfyingly delicious plant-based meals. Certain ingredients, such as coconut oil, can add buttery richness, while others are chock-full of umami, which enriches and deepens savory flavors (page 6). Common items like olives, capers, or other pickled condiments can bring briny saltiness to a dish. Such pantry staples pack a big flavor punch and bring complex depth while allowing the primary flavors of the main ingredients to still shine through. Other items may be less familiar to you if you are new to cooking plant-based dishes. Here's a rundown of how we use them.

Miso: Chances are you've sipped miso soup (dashi broth mixed with miso paste) at the start of a Japanese meal. Miso paste is a condiment made from fermented soy-beans, grains like rice or barley, salt, and koji mold, and comes in a range of colors, from milder, sweeter white miso (our favorite for its versatility) to more intense red and brown misos. In recipe development, we used Hikari Organic White Miso. We deploy miso in a variety of recipes to impart salty, nutty, intensely savory flavors, including French Onion Soup (page 66) and Cashew e Pepe e Funghi (page 165).

Nutritional yeast: Nutritional yeast is yeast that has been deactivated with heat to remove its leavening qualities and then dried into a flaky yellow powder. This umami powerhouse brings uniquely nutty, "cheesy" flavors to foods, including Vegan Parmesan Substitute (page 27), Cheez Sauce (page 26), Umami Croutons (page 143), and Creamy Polenta (page 270).

Soy sauce/tamari: Made from fermented soybeans, salt, water, and sometimes roasted grains (wheat, rice, or barley), soy sauce is one of the oldest food products in the world. Tamari, or shoyu, is Japanese soy sauce, which is generally gluten-free, but read the label carefully to be sure. While it's a frequent entry in ingredient lists for recipes of Asian origin, soy sauce can be used in a wide range of preparations to add both neutral seasoning and deep savoriness. In recipe development, we used Kikkoman Soy Sauce.

Tomatoes and tomato products: There's a reason that vine-ripened tomatoes taste so good. They have more umami than commercially grown tomatoes, which are typically picked green and ripened with ethylene gas. We've found that cherry and grape tomatoes are reliably sweet year-round. And when cooking plant-forward dishes, don't even think about getting rid of the seeds and pulp, which are packed with glutamates, natural flavor-enhancing compounds that contribute to umami. We also stock sun-dried tomatoes and canned tomato products, particularly tomato paste. These products have little moisture, so their umami is concentrated.

Mushrooms, dried and fresh: Drying mushrooms concentrates their umami content, so look to pantry-friendly dried mushrooms to boost the savory flavor of stocks and soups, as in our Umami Broth (page 22). Earthy shiitake mushrooms are one of the most potent sources of umami, particularly in their dried form, as are morels and porcinis, but even fresh mushrooms of any variety will provide some savory oomph.

Fermented black beans: Salted, fermented soybeans can be found in Asian grocery stores and are used in Chinese dishes like our Vegan Mapo Tofu (page 84) to give deep savoriness, a hint of sweetness, and a touch of fermented funk. These glutamate-packed nuggets are also the not-so-secret ingredient in our Umami Broth (page 22), adding mysterious depth of flavor that mimics the complexity of beef broth. Try adding them to braised vegetable dishes as well.

SNEAKY THINGS THAT MIGHT NOT BE VEGAN

Reading and understanding ingredient labels is your best defense against inadvertently purchasing nonvegan products. Be on the alert for nonvegan ingredients including casein, whey, and lactose (all dairy-derived), albumin (from eggs), and gelatin (from animal bones).

Sugar: If you're a strict vegan, purchase organic. Most conventional sugars (granulated, brown, confectioners', and molasses) are filtered through animal bone char as part of the production process. Some companies use granular carbon instead, but it's impossible to be sure. Likewise, be on the lookout for convenience foods where sugar lives, such as sandwich bread, condiments, jams and jellies, chocolate, and so on.

Pasta and noodles: Eggs can hide in dried and fresh pasta of all shapes and varieties.

Wine: Egg whites or other animal products may be used to remove tiny particles that filtration doesn't capture. Many producers use nonanimal products such as bentonite clay. If this is a concern, ask the store clerk.

Store-bought puff pastry: It's an unbeatable convenience product that we love to take advantage of. Many commercial varieties are vegan, using vegetable oils, but some use butter.

Seaweed: The concept of umami was originally discovered by a Japanese scientist who attributed this unique taste sensation to kombu, the kelp-like seaweed that's a primary component of Japanese dashi broth. Seaweeds like kombu, nori, and wakame are rich sources of glutamates and add umami depth to soups and sauces and can even be used to imitate anchovies, as in our Anchovy Substitute (page 23), made from nori and miso. We also have a great seaweed snacking chip, Sesame Nori Chips, on page 354.

Kimchi: There are many different kinds of this pungent, spicy, crunchy, funky Korean condiment, but all involve salting and fermenting vegetables—napa cabbage most commonly—traditionally with gochugaru (Korean hot pepper flakes) and often some type of seafood product like fish sauce or anchovies. However, vegan kimchi is commonly available, so read the labels. Try kimchi in our Hash Brown Omelet with Kimchi (page 34) or as an addition to Tofu Pad Thai (page 177) or Vegetable Fried Rice with Broccoli and Shiitake Mushrooms (page 246).

Plant-based fats: Many of our preferred cooking fats are naturally plant-based, such as extra-virgin olive oil and vegetable oils. In place of butter in both savory and sweet recipes, our go-to fat is refined coconut oil, which has virtually no taste or aroma. It's particularly useful for baking recipes where we might typically have used a solid saturated fat like dairy butter. In recipe development, we used Spectrum Naturals Organic Refined Coconut Oil, Nutiva Organic Refined Coconut Oil, and Crisco Organic Refined Coconut Oil. In general, we avoided using plant-based butters as cooking fats. There is a wide range of these products available, of varying degrees of quality. They are made from such a wide variety of ingredients that we couldn't count on them to perform reliably or consistently in all applications in place of dairy butter. We tested both yellow cake and chocolate chip cookies made with several different brands of plant-based butters, and the differences among them in terms of flavor, texture, and appearance were significant and not always acceptable.

UMAMI BOMBS

"Umami" translates from Japanese as "deliciousness," but this fifth taste sensation of the five basic tastes (along with sweet, sour, bitter, and salty) is aptly described as "savoriness" or "meatiness." Certain amino acids and nucleotides present in food create a deep, complex intensity of flavor that leaves you wanting more. Umami is often associated with meats or cheeses, but it was actually first identified in relation to seaweed. Glutamate—the primary amino acid associated with umami flavor—and other umami-producing nucleotides like inosinate and guanylate are common and naturally occurring substances found in many plant-based products, including mushrooms, ripe tomatoes, olives, nutritional yeast, fermented black beans, and soy. In addition, some food preservation techniques, including fermentation, aging, and drying, can increase the amount of umami an ingredient contains. Fermenting vegetables and grains breaks down their proteins, making the umami-rich glutamates more available to our taste buds, and drying vegetables or other foods concentrates the glutamates in the food. That's why

COCONUT OIL AND ITS USES

Coconut oil is made by extracting oil from the meat of coconuts, and it is sold in two forms, both of which are solid at room temperature: refined, which has virtually no taste or aroma, and unrefined (also called virgin), which retains a strong coconut flavor. Although both perform in the same way, we generally wanted a neutral-tasting fat for both savory and sweet cooking, so we used refined coconut oil.

Note that when our recipes call for coconut oil, we mean room-temperature, solid oil; we specify melted when necessary. If your kitchen is warmer than room temperature (around 75 degrees), the coconut oil will liquefy. Don't store coconut oil in the refrigerator, though, as it becomes extremely hard, breaking off in shards and becoming difficult to manipulate in doughs and batters. There's no need to refrigerate it, as coconut oil keeps at room temperature for up to a year.

Coconut oil is a great substitute for dairy butter because, like butter, it's a saturated fat and can be used both solid and melted, so it's versatile in a wide variety of cooking applications. When used in baked goods, coconut oil lubricates and coats the flour granules with fat, limiting gluten development, which occurs when flour meets liquid and which makes baked goods chewy. So using coconut oil results in light and fluffy Savory Drop Biscuits (page 47), delicately flaky Spiced Sweet Potato Scones with Chocolate and Pepitas (page 45), and ultratender pie and tart doughs. Unlike butter, which contains 16 to 18 percent water, coconut oil is 100 percent fat, so sometimes we needed to adjust the liquid in a recipe to compensate.

miso lends a punch of savoriness to soups, dressings, and sauces, and it's why dried mushrooms and sun-dried tomatoes are a more potent source of umami than the fresh versions. Combining some of these ingredients can have a synergistic effect, creating veritable umami bombs. We've developed some of our own umami bombs to flavor our recipes, including our Umami Broth (page 22), Umami Croutons (page 143), Vegan Parmesan Substitute (page 27), Cheez Sauce (page 26), and Anchovy Substitute (page 23).

PLANT PROTEIN POWER

One of the greatest concerns for someone new to plant-based eating may be getting enough protein. But the reality is that our bodies do not require meat to achieve this goal. Although animal foods are certainly the most protein-dense foods, many plant foods are rich in protein, and a well-rounded plant-based diet can meet your nutritional needs.

Proteins are always present in food as part of a "package," bundled with various other things that may be good for the body (such as fiber, nutrients, and omega-3 fatty acids) or not so good (such as saturated fats). Proteins themselves are made up of smaller molecules called amino acids, which are found in different combinations across a range of foods. Our bodies depend on 20 different amino acids to function properly. Many of these are considered nonessential amino acids, meaning the body can synthesize them on its own. Nine of these, however, are classified as essential amino acids, and they must be consumed through food because the body does not produce them.

In the standard American diet, animal-based foods are relied upon as primary protein sources. While these high-protein foods tend to contain all of the essential amino acids and many essential nutrients, on the downside, they often include high levels of unhealthy fats and sometimes added sodium. They are also very costly to produce from both an economic and an environmental perspective.

However, all of the proteins and essential amino acids that a body needs can be found in a well-balanced plant-based diet. Tofu and tempeh in particular are concentrated protein sources, and several plant foods, including quinoa, soy, and chia seeds, contain all of the essential amino acids. What's more, several essential nutrients found primarily in animal-based foods (such as vitamin B_{12}, calcium, and vitamin D) are regularly used to fortify plant-based foods, including nondairy milks and yogurts, nutritional yeast, and tofu.

According to Harvard Medical School, you can calculate your RDA (Recommended Daily Allowance) for protein by multiplying your weight in pounds by 0.36. So for a 150-pound person, that translates into about 54 grams of protein per day. This is a general guideline that varies depending on gender, age, activity level, and other individual needs or conditions. If you have concerns, you should speak to a registered dietician about your nutritional and dietary needs.

To give you some examples of translating that RDA into practice, the following amounts of food each contain about 7 grams of protein: ½ cup cooked chickpeas, ¼ cup (1 ounce) almonds, 2 tablespoons peanut butter, 8 ounces soy milk or dairy milk, 6 ounces dairy yogurt, 1 extra-large egg, and 1 ounce animal protein. But protein "hides" in many places you might not expect: 1 cup of cooked green peas contains about 8 grams of protein—as does 1 cup of cooked whole-wheat pasta. Even vegetables contain protein: 4 ounces of raw brussels sprouts contains 4 grams of protein; 4 ounces of raw mushrooms, spinach, or corn contains 3 grams of protein; and 4 ounces of raw asparagus, avocado, beets, cauliflower, or sweet or white potatoes contains 2 grams of protein.

HIGH-PROTEIN PLANT FOODS

Here's a quick reference to some of the most protein-dense plant foods. For complete nutritional information for all of the recipes in this book, see page 398.

LEGUMES

Soybeans (edamame) contain all nine essential amino acids. Tempeh is a source of vitamin B_{12}. Tofu is an excellent source of calcium and iron. Lentils are an excellent source of iron.

Beans: Black, cannellini, kidney, pinto	½ cup cooked = 8 g
Chickpeas	½ cup cooked = 7 g
Edamame	½ cup cooked = 7 g
Lentils	½ cup cooked = 9 g
Peanuts	½ cup = 19 g
Peas (English/garden)	½ cup cooked = 4 g
Tempeh	½ cup chopped = 17 g
Tofu (firm)	½ cup chopped = 10 g

Chickpeas

TREE NUTS

Almonds in particular contain calcium. Walnuts contain high levels of antioxidants and are the only nut that is an excellent source of omega-3 fatty acids.

Almonds	¼ cup = 7.5 g
Cashews, hazelnuts	¼ cup = 5 g
Pecans	¼ cup = 2.5 g
Pine nuts	¼ cup = 4.5 g
Pistachios	¼ cup = 6.5 g
Walnuts	¼ cup = 4 g

SEEDS

Chia seeds contain all nine essential amino acids.

Chia seeds	2 Tbs. = 3.5 g
Pepitas	2 Tbs. = 5 g
Sesame seeds	2 Tbs. = 4 g
Sunflower seeds	2 Tbs. = 3 g

GRAINS AND CEREALS

Whole grains tend to be higher in protein than their refined counterparts, with more iron and B vitamins. Oats in particular are high in iron. Brown rice is high in calcium. Quinoa contains all nine essential amino acids.

Barley (pearl)	½ cup cooked = 2 g
Buckwheat	½ cup cooked = 3 g
Bulgur	½ cup cooked = 2 g
Farro	½ cup cooked = 4 g
Freekeh	½ cup cooked = 4 g
Millet	½ cup cooked = 3 g
Oats (quick)	½ cup cooked = 3 g
Pasta	
Refined wheat	½ cup cooked = 3 g
Whole wheat	½ cup cooked = 4 g
Polenta	½ cup cooked = 2 g
Quinoa	½ cup cooked = 4 g
Rice	
Black, brown, wild	½ cup cooked = 3 g
Red	½ cup cooked = 4 g
White	½ cup cooked = 2 g
Wheat berries	½ cup cooked = 4 g

Nutritional information calculated using ESHA Food Processor Nutrition Analysis software.

PLANT-BASED MEAT

Meat alternatives have come a long way from first-generation frozen veggie burgers. Plant-based meats are now common sights in supermarket refrigerated cases and on restaurant menus from fast-food joints to upscale establishments. These modern substitutes are trying (and sometimes succeeding) to replicate the look, texture, taste, and cooking attributes of meat. They use a variety of plant-derived proteins, including pea protein and soy protein, plus fats, binders, vegetable purees, and seasonings. Many closely match the protein level, fat content, and calorie count of ground beef and have added B vitamins (and added sodium).

Plant-based beef is currently the most prevalent choice, though new categories, including pork and seafood, are being brought to market. In tastings of plant-based beef cooked as burgers, our favorite was Impossible Burger from Impossible Foods, a soybean-based product that we found remarkably similar to beef in taste, texture, and performance. Impossible Burger achieves a distinctly "iron-y" and "mineral-y" flavor and beefy red color through its use of an ingredient called heme protein. Heme is a type of iron-containing molecule; the most familiar example is hemoglobin, which makes blood red. The "leghemoglobin" (the "leg" prefix referring to its legume source) of heme protein performs similarly to animal-based heme by influencing the Maillard reaction—the chemical reaction between proteins and sugars that leads to the complex savory flavors we associate with browned meat. This use of plant-based heme in Impossible Burger is also responsible for its ability to mimic a beef burger's appearance of medium-rare doneness: a slightly red center. The use of coconut oil in the Impossible Burger also contributes to its authentic appearance: little flecks of coconut oil embedded throughout look and feel similar to the bits of fat in uncooked ground beef. As the meat cooks, the coconut oil flecks melt and help distribute aroma and flavor in much the same way beef fat does.

PLANT POWER

PEA PROTEIN
Easily digested and absorbed by the body, non-allergenic, high in protein and rich in iron, and containing all nine essential amino acids, pea protein is entering the mainstream grocery store. Its emulsifying and binding properties make it the protein of choice for the Beyond Meat brand of products, as well as some plant-based dairy products, commercial baked goods, and energy bars. Pea protein powder or concentrate is made by drying yellow peas and then grinding them into flakes. The oil is removed, the defatted flakes are ground into flour, and the protein is isolated from the flour for combining with other ingredients.

Although Impossible Burger was our clear favorite, it currently has limited availability nationwide (although this is changing quickly). Our runner-up was Beyond Meat (both the Beyond Meat Beyond Burger patties and the Beyond Meat Beyond Beef, which is packaged as bulk ground meat), made from pea protein. Beyond Meat products are available in many major grocery chains. As burgers, their exteriors didn't brown quite as well as the Impossible Burger and their interiors retained a slightly purplish tint, but their textures were very similar to ground beef. Beyond Meat also has a slightly smoky flavor that some tasters found artificial. We tested our recipes with both brands, and they work well with either. We encourage you to seek out both brands, or other brands depending on availability in your area, and try them in our Double Smashie Burgers (page 101) and Weeknight Meaty Chili (page 76) to see what you and your family like.

| MEDIUM-RARE | MEDIUM | WELL DONE |

HOW TO COOK A PERFECT PLANT-BASED BURGER

We cooked our way through dozens of plant-based burger patties and learned that cooking a perfect plant-based burger isn't as straightforward as just swapping plant-based ground beef into any given burger recipe. Here are some helpful tips.

DISCOVERY	SO . . .
Plant-based burgers lose their internal pinkness more rapidly and cook more quickly than beef. While the color change does reflect cooking progress, gradations of color and texture in a plant-based patty won't match those of a beef patty.	Rely on internal temperature rather than visual cues. Start checking for doneness earlier than you would with a beef burger.
Plant-based burgers cooked to medium-rare (125 degrees) yield burgers with pasty, mushy interiors. On the flip side, cooking them to well done (160 degrees) yields a bouncy, chewy texture.	Aim for cooking patties to medium doneness: 130–135 degrees.
Plant-based burgers retain moisture remarkably well and do not dry out, constrict, or shrink significantly during cooking.	When shaping plant-based burgers, it's not necessary to add an indentation to counteract shrinkage. After cooking, plant-based burgers do not need to rest to recirculate juices.
Plant-based burgers brown nicely, but they develop less fond than ground beef and have a tendency to stick in traditional skillets.	Cook plant-based burgers in a well-oiled nonstick skillet.

DIRECTIONS

You can cook any number of burgers using this method. If cooking two burgers, use a 10-inch nonstick skillet; if cooking up to four burgers at a time, use a 12-inch nonstick skillet. Increase the amount of oil as needed.

Gently shape 4 ounces plant-based beef into lightly packed ball, then flatten into ¾-inch-thick patty. Sprinkle patty all over with ⅛ teaspoon salt and pinch pepper. Heat 1 teaspoon vegetable oil in 8-inch nonstick skillet over medium-high heat until just smoking. Transfer patty to skillet and cook until well browned on first side, 1 to 2 minutes. Flip patty, top with cheese, if using, and continue to cook until browned on second side and meat registers 130 to 135 degrees, 1 to 2 minutes. Serve burger on toasted bun with your favorite toppings.

FROM COWS TO COCONUTS: DEMYSTIFYING DAIRY

Not that long ago, if you wanted nondairy "milk," soy milk and canned coconut milk were your only readily available commercial options. These days, it's impossible to keep track of the ever-expanding choices: In addition to milks made from soybeans, coconuts, and almonds, we tasted milks derived from oats, cashews, macadamia nuts, pistachios, hazelnuts, flaxseeds, hemp, sesame seeds, and peas. But while you may have a favorite plant-based milk for your morning coffee or a favorite plant-based yogurt to mix with fruit, how will it perform when used for cooking or baking? And what about the other plant-based dairy products popping up in the refrigerator case, such as creamers and cheeses? (For our take on plant-based butter, see page 6.)

To find out, we conducted blind side-by-side taste tests of a wide range of unsweetened milks, creamers, and yogurts currently available to understand the differences in flavors and textures. We then selected several brands—ones we liked and ones we disliked—and tested them in specific recipes where they figured prominently to see how they fared. The ones that performed the best we then used for additional recipe development. We were pleasantly surprised to learn that many of these plant-based dairy products on the market performed interchangeably with traditional dairy products in our favorite dishes. We have noted in specific recipes where they are not interchangeable, and we did find in some cases that specific categories of products worked better in certain recipes.

PLANT-BASED MILKS

Using plant-based milks for cooking can be intimidating, and with good reason. There is a huge range of options made from diverse ingredients, and tasting a sampling of them in the test kitchen demonstrated that there are significant differences in flavor and mouthfeel. Here are a few suggestions for using plant-based milks in recipes:

Oat milk, thanks to its higher natural sugar content, tastes great in baked goods (or our Crunchy Cinnamon French Toast, page 50, and Carrot Cake Pancakes, page 49) and also brings more browning to baked goods because of those sugars. Its relatively sweet flavor, however, can feel out of place in savory dishes.

Almond milk is neutral in flavor and is our preferred choice for savory cooking, but it can make sweet dishes taste slightly salty.

Soy milk is fairly neutral tasting, but in a mildly flavored dish, a slightly beany taste may be detectable.

Coconut milk can be used in both savory and sweet applications, although we did find in testing that it can lead to pale and gummy baked goods.

Commercial **rice milk** is generally too thin and watery to use in cooking or baking. See page 25 for our homemade rice milk, which is thicker than commercial varieties.

There can also be large nutritional differences not only between types of plant milks (for example, soy versus coconut), but also within the same type of plant milk from brand to brand, sometimes amounting to a three-fold difference in calorie, protein, or fat content per serving between brands. Soy milk has the highest protein content per cup (similar to that of cow's milk), followed by nut milks, whereas coconut milk contains no protein. Oat milks tend to be the most calorie rich, with much of that coming from their higher carbohydrate content, but several nut milks provide comparable calories per serving (with most of the energy coming from fat and protein). Some plant-based milks are also fortified with minerals and vitamins similar to cow's milk—most commonly calcium and vitamins A, D, E, and occasionally B_{12} as well. The bottom line is that if you are concerned about nutrient intake, read nutrition labels carefully, and don't assume that almond milk is almond milk is almond milk. Compare brands to find what works for you.

Brands we used for recipe development: Oatly Original Plant-Based Beverage, Silk Unsweetened Almond Milk, So Delicious Organic Unsweetened Coconut Milk, Silk Unsweetened Organic Soymilk.

PLANT-BASED YOGURTS

Plant-based yogurts have also exploded in recent years in terms of availability, variety of main ingredients (made from nuts, grains, and legumes), and styles, from thicker Greek-style yogurt options to thinner drinkable yogurts. Just as with plant-based milks, the nutritional content of these products differs significantly based on their primary ingredient (for example, coconut-based yogurts have less protein than nut-based yogurts) and from brand to brand, so read labels if nutrient intake is a concern. In addition to the primary ingredient, many plant-based yogurts have active bacterial cultures, thickeners, and in some cases, acidifiers to provide the tang we associate with dairy yogurt. Just as with dairy yogurt, all of these ingredients contribute to different textures and flavors in the final product. While the yogurts we chose for recipe development had what we felt was the closest texture to and flavor of dairy yogurt for eating straight from the container, we also discovered that even our least favorite options worked exceedingly well when made into a sauce with some citrus juice and herbs (as in our Herbed Yogurt Sauce, page 90) or when baked into muffins (as in our Cherry, Orange, and Rosemary Muffins, page 44). So even if you try a new plant-based yogurt and don't love it straight out of the container, you've got lots of delicious options to use it up. We even preferred to use plant-based yogurts as a substitute for dairy sour cream, rather than any of the plant-based sour cream options that are currently available.

Brands we used for recipe development: So Delicious Coconut Milk Unsweetened Plain Yogurt, 365 Brand Unsweetened Almond Milk Non-Dairy Yogurts, Blue Diamond Almondmilk Plain Unsweetened Yogurt Alternative.

PLANT-BASED CREAMERS

Plant-based creamers are a comparatively recent addition to the alternative dairy market. Some of them are sweetened or flavored, designed to be used in your favorite coffee drinks, while others are plain and can be used in recipes in place of dairy half-and-half or heavy cream. We tasted plant-based creamers made from almonds, cashews, coconuts, oats, soy, and pea protein. What distinguishes these products from regular plant-based milk is their fat content, which is higher than that of milks (many products include coconut cream or add oils to increase the fat content), as well as emulsifiers and thickeners, such as guar gum, to provide a thicker, more viscous consistency. While they can add richness to beverages and baked goods—all the varieties we tested worked beautifully in our scone recipes (pages 44–46)—one area where they didn't work well was whipping. For our favorite plant-based whipped topping, see our Coconut Whipped Cream on page 378.

Brands we used for recipe development: Forager Project Organic Dairy-Free Half and Half (Cashew Milk Coconut Cream), Califia Farms Unsweetened Dairy-Free Almond Milk Creamer (Almond and Coconut Cream).

PLANT-BASED CHEESE

Cheese is arguably one of the most challenging savory foods to replicate without using dairy. The main obstacles we found when trying plant-based cheeses were availability and consistency across brands. The plant-based cheese world is still an emerging one, unlike the plant-based meat and milk categories, which have both more established brands and greater nationwide availability of high-quality products.

While developing the recipes for this book, we tasted several plant-based cheese brands and products in the test kitchen, and we were underwhelmed by many, finding their flavors to be excessively sour and their consistency to be waxy, pasty, or grainy. While there were some promising products that we did enjoy, they are relatively new to the market and not yet close to nationwide distribution. Given this limited availability, we did not feel we could recommend them. Based on our research, though, we believe that your vegan cheese options will expand for the better in the near future.

On the issue of consistency, we looked at plant-based cheese in terms of cooking with it rather than eating it out of hand. Whereas with dairy cheese, all brands of mozzarella or all brands of cheddar perform basically the same way when melting, vegan versions of mozzarella or cheddar vary greatly. Since they didn't perform consistently or predictably in ways that we'd typically expect cheese to perform, we avoided using plant-based cheese in our recipes. Instead, we looked to other ingredients to replicate certain qualities of cheese. For example, white vinegar and mustard can provide the tanginess that we associate with cheese, while miso and nutritional yeast can add a savory nuttiness that typifies aged cheeses. We used some of these plant-based pantry staples to create our Vegan Parmesan Substitute (page 27), Cashew Ricotta (page 26), and Cheez Sauce (page 26). And in some cases, we found that a toasted bread-crumb topping gave us the satisfying crunchy,

CANNED COCONUT MILK AND CREAM

Coconut products can be confusing. Canned coconut milk and cream are not interchangeable with the coconut milk or coconut creamer available in cartons with all the other dairy milk alternatives. The latter products are much more diluted and are specifically designed to replace dairy milk and dairy cream, whereas the canned products are thicker and perform a key role in curries and other dishes such as our Banana Ice Cream (page 390).

Canned coconut milk is made by steeping shredded coconut in water and then pressing it to yield a creamy, coconut-flavored liquid; no sugar is added. When you open a can of coconut milk, you may find that it's separated—there will be a more solid mass of coconut cream above the watery liquid. Some recipes, particularly desserts, require using just the coconut cream, while others, such as curries, call for shaking the can and using the integrated coconut-milk mixture. If your recipe calls for just the solid coconut cream, to make the separation distinct, you must refrigerate the cans of coconut milk for 24 hours. Then, you can skim away the thick cream more easily. (If you don't want to waste the remaining thin liquid in the can, try using it in place of water in hot breakfast cereals or adding it to smoothies.) You may also find canned products labeled as "coconut cream," which are entirely this thick cream. Coconut cream whips up just like dairy whipped cream; it's amazingly delicious in our Tropical Fruit Pavlova (page 379).

We specify in our recipes when canned coconut products are required. In recipe development, we used Aroy-D Coconut Milk.

One last caveat: Do not confuse canned coconut milk or canned coconut cream with cream of coconut, which contains thickeners, emulsifiers, and added sugar.

toasty qualities we were looking for (see our Farro and Broccoli Rabe Gratin, page 268).

We do encourage you to try some plant-based cheeses straight out of the package, to see what you like. Try topping tacos with shredded Monterey Jack, adding a slice of mozzarella to a sandwich, or spreading cream cheese on a bagel. If you find one that you enjoy, then try making a simple grilled cheese to see how it melts in comparison to the dairy version of that cheese.

SUPERSTARS OF THE PLANT WORLD

We reimagined taken-for-granted vegetable stalwarts to move them squarely to the center of the dinner plate in versatile ways you may never have considered. And then we also experimented with ways to cook with some plant-based ingredients and some methods that were new to the test kitchen.

THE VEG-CENTRIC PLATE

Call them superstars or call them workhorses. In our kitchen, they are one and the same. Here are just a few of the vegetables we couldn't imagine doing without when following a plant-based way of eating.

CRAFTY CARROTS

Carrots aren't just a salad component or virtuous snack. Cooking them (without browning) until their cell walls break down and they release their sugars let us make a smooth, spicy Carrot-Habanero Dip (page 348). Browning and caramelizing them for our Roasted Carrots and Shallots with Chermoula (page 196) put them at the center of the plate as a main course. And Carrot Cake Pancakes (page 49) are both comforting and fast enough to serve for breakfast anytime.

Buffalo Cauliflower Bites with Vegan Ranch Dressing

CAULIFLOWER IS STILL KING

You can grill it and top it with a vibrant green herb sauce for Cauliflower Steaks with Salsa Verde (page 200), cook whole heads in a robust tomato sauce for Pan-Roasted Cauliflower with Capers and Pine Nuts (page 197), use the whole head both raw and cooked to make a main-course Roasted Cauliflower Salad with Golden Raisins and Almonds (page 134). Fry up florets to make Buffalo Cauliflower Bites with Vegan Ranch Dressing (page 364), and take advantage of their unique fiber content to make perfectly smooth Creamy Curried Cauliflower Soup (page 56).

KALE HAS COMPANY

Our substantial Crisp and Creamy Kale Salad (page 139) uses kale both raw and roasted, and we love our version of Kale Caesar Salad (page 140), but loads of other greens make hearty, healthy meals, too: Green Shakshuka (page 226), with Swiss chard and spinach; Sicilian White Beans and Escarole (page 298); and Green Gumbo (page 83), with collard greens and spinach, just to name a few.

DON'T QUASH SQUASH

Squash can also be turned into Chile-Rubbed Butternut Squash Steaks with Ranch Dressing (page 229) as well as roasted in cubes and put into Freekeh Salad with Butternut Squash, Walnuts, and Raisins (page 269), treated like noodles for Spaghetti Squash with Fresh Tomato Sauce (page 331), and pureed for elegant Butternut Squash Tartlets with Almonds, Pomegranate, and Mint (page 366).

SWEET SPUDS

Satisfying sweet potatoes are for more than just roasting: we use them in Vindaloo-Style Sweet Potatoes (page 223) and Sweet Potato Curry with Eggplant, Chickpeas, and Herb Chutney (page 224). We stuff them into Black Bean and Sweet Potato Tacos (page 99), whir them into Sweet Potato Hummus (page 344), and even bake them into brunch-worthy Spiced Sweet Potato Scones with Chocolate and Pepitas (page 45).

LENTILS CAN BE LOVELY

Poor lentils have an outdated image as brown and boring. In the test kitchen, we love green lentils, particularly the tiny green lentilles du Puy, which hold their shape beautifully and which we use in Lentils with Roasted Broccoli and Lemony Bread Crumbs (page 288) and Thai Red Curry with Lentils and Tofu (page 294). And gorgeous red lentils break down a bit when cooked and have a sweeter taste, so we used those attributes to their best advantage in developing our Red Lentil Kibbeh (page 291), Misir Wot (page 293), and vibrant Red Lentil Soup with North African Spices (page 63).

VEG SCIENCE

We made some unexpected culinary discoveries while creating the recipes in this book, which prompted us to delve into some of the scientific aspects of why plants behave the way they do in the kitchen.

CASHEWS

This nut is truly indispensable in the plant-based kitchen. Creams made from soaked and ground nuts and water are commonly used as a base for vegan cheeses and sauces. We made creams from nine different raw nuts—almonds, cashews, peanuts, pecans, walnuts, hazelnuts, pistachios, macadamia nuts, and Brazil nuts (all but the pecans and walnuts were blanched)—to see which had the best texture. All but one produced purees that were "gritty," "grainy," "foamy," and/or "chalky." The cashew cream, however, had a consistency so velvety that one taster called it "pure satin." That's because cashews are uniquely low in fiber, which resists breaking down, and high in starch, the particles of which suspend evenly in liquid and provide body. We make Cashew Ricotta (page 26) to use in Thin-Crust Pizza with Mushrooms and Cashew Ricotta (page 112) and Cashew Ricotta Tartlets with Celery-Olive Topping (page 365). We use our cashew-based Vegan Parmesan Substitute (page 27) in lots of recipes throughout this book. And we roasted cashews before blending them into a velvety, cheesy sauce for Cashew e Pepe e Funghi (page 165). We even developed a Pumpkin Cashew Cheesecake (page 386).

POTATOES

Potatoes consist mainly of starch and moisture, and the more you work cooked potatoes (for example, whipping them in a blender), the more likely the starch molecules are to burst and release an excess of starch, which turns

Meaty Loaded Nacho Dip

the spuds unpleasantly gluey. Boiling potatoes and then whipping them in the blender to within an inch of their life is a major no-no when it comes to fluffy mashed potatoes, but breaking this kitchen rule turned out to be the right starting point for developing a delicious vegan Cheez Sauce with the pleasingly gooey aspects of dairy cheese. We use it on Double Smashie Burgers (page 101) and Philly-Style Broccoli Rabe, Portobello, and Cheez Sandwiches (page 88) and as a component in Meaty Loaded Nacho Dip (page 348).

OYSTER MUSHROOMS

Mushrooms have long been a popular meat alternative because they're an excellent source of glutamates, molecules packed with savory umami flavor. Plus, their cell walls are made of a heat-stable substance called chitin, so instead of breaking down when cooked, they retain a satisfying meat-like chew. Oyster mushrooms have a woodsy flavor and naturally chewy texture, and for our Cashew e Pepe e Funghi (page 165), we sautéed them until they developed the deep golden-brown, crisp-chewy, craveable texture of bacon.

Chocolate-Espresso Tart

that aquafaba can replace egg whites and give structure and fluffy crumb to plant-based baked goods such as our Cherry, Orange, and Rosemary Muffins (page 44). We also use it to make meringues for our Tropical Fruit Pavlova (page 379). This wonder liquid doesn't stop there, though, lending thicker, fuller body to savory dishes, such as Pasta e Ceci (page 163) and Spicy Braised Chickpeas and Turnips with Couscous (page 283). To measure aquafaba, start by shaking the unopened can of chickpeas to distribute the starches in the liquid. Drain the chickpeas through a fine-mesh strainer over a bowl, whisk the aquafaba, and then measure. A 15-ounce can should give you ½ to ¾ cup aquafaba.

COFFEE WHIP

When we were developing the recipes in this book, Dalgona coffee, a specialty coffee drink from South Korea in which instant coffee, sugar, and water are whipped together and then poured on top of hot milk, began sweeping the Internet. We skipped the milk and worked just with the coffee foam in the test kitchen. When instant coffee is whipped with sugar and water, the protein in the coffee granules whips up in a similar way as the protein in egg whites would. The air bubbles that form are aided by the sugar, which acts as sort of a "glue" or stabilizer. We whipped our coffee mixture to a billowy, glossy, meringue-like foam that could be piped or dolloped just like whipped cream. It's perfect for topping desserts like our Chocolate-Espresso Tart (page 382).

WATER GANACHE

The classical way to make ganache is to combine chocolate and cream into a smooth emulsion (since cream is mostly water, it's a fat-in-water emulsion). Baking recipes often warn against letting any water drip into chocolate when melting it, or it will seize and turn grainy. But this catastrophe is more about the proportion of water in the emulsion than the water itself. In the correct proportions, by adding more water to the chocolate by weight, the fat in the chocolate will turn the emulsion smooth without the need for cream. And with no dairy to mask the flavor, a water ganache is intensely chocolaty. Our water ganache is also perfectly silky, setting up beautifully at room temperature and slicing like a dream. We used it in our rich Chocolate-Espresso Tart (page 382), but it's also just right for filling cake layers.

JACKFRUIT

Although it's related to the tiny fig, the jackfruit is the world's largest tree fruit, weighing up to 80 pounds. When ripe, this tropical fruit is soft and creamy and eaten just like any other fruit. However, immature green jackfruit is altogether different and is treated differently in the kitchen. It's vegetal in flavor; firm, dense, and very fibrous in texture; and when cooked, it uncannily mimics shredded pork or chicken. For this reason, the unripe fruit has long been widely used in many Asian cuisines as a meat substitute. It's readily available in Asian markets, canned in water or brine (don't buy the kind packed in syrup, which is ripe and sweet). We took advantage of this ingredient to create our Jackfruit Tinga Tacos (page 99).

AQUAFABA

Aquafaba is the starchy liquid in canned chickpeas. This liquid—more so than the liquid from other types of canned beans—whips to create a stable foam. Though the science behind this is still being researched, we know that chickpeas contain saponins, compounds that can create a soap-like foam when shaken. This means

HOW TO BUILD A PLANT-BASED MEAL

Taking meat off the plate and putting plants front and center can be an adjustment at first. But thanks to the small-plates restaurant trend and the general globalization of how we eat, our thinking about what deserves to be an "entrée" and what should be relegated to a "side dish" has changed considerably. Although this list is far from comprehensive, here are some of our favorite recipe-pairing ideas and serving suggestions to help you get started with building your own colorful plant-based meals.

Tofu Frittata with Mushrooms

ADD CRUSTY BREAD AND A GREEN SALAD

Tofu Frittata with Mushrooms (page 30)

Classic Tuscan White Bean Soup (page 61)

Lentil and Escarole Soup (page 63)

Eggplant and Kale Soup (page 69)

Italian Vegetable Stew (page 80)

Pot-Roasted Whole Cauliflower with Tomatoes and Olives (page 202)

Mediterranean Braised Green Beans (page 207)

Greek Stewed Okra with Tomatoes (page 213)

White Bean and Mushroom Gratin (page 299)

Cranberry Beans with Fennel, Grapes, and Pine Nuts (page 284)

Fire-Roasted Tomato and Fennel Soup (page 313)

SERVE OVER A BED OF GRAINS

See pages 254–255 for how to cook simple grains such as rice, quinoa, farro, wheat berries, and barley.

Chickpea Curry (page 74)

Grilled Vegetable Salad (page 150)

Tofu Salad with Vegetables (page 152)

Thai Red Curry with Cauliflower (page 201)

Walkaway Ratatouille (page 204)

Madras Okra Curry (page 212)

Green Shakshuka (page 226)

Greek Stewed Zucchini (page 234)

Black-Eyed Pea Salad with Peaches and Pecans (page 280)

SERVE PASTA OR NOODLES PLUS A VEGETABLE

MAKE BEANS THE CENTER OF THE PLATE

MAKE VEGETABLES THE CENTER OF THE PLATE

Cauliflower Steaks with Salsa Verde

Roasted Carrots and Shallots with Chermoula (page 196) + Basmati Rice Pilaf with Currants and Toasted Almonds (page 238)

Mexican-Style Spaghetti Squash Casserole (page 230) + Orange-Jicama Salad with Sweet and Spicy Peppers (page 141)

Summer Vegetable Gratin (page 233) + Tuscan White Bean and Fresh Corn Salad (page 298)

PAIR A FEW SMALL DISHES TO MAKE A MEAL

Scallion Pancakes with Dipping Sauce (page 117) + Sweet Chili Glazed Tofu (page 303) + Gingery Swiss Chard (page 227)

Roasted Smashed Potatoes (page 218) + Stuffed Mushrooms (page 363) + Tomato, Olive, and Basil Skewers (page 358)

Lavash with Romesco, Tomatoes, and Spinach (page 113) + Smoky Shishito Peppers with Espelette and Lime (page 359) + Chickpeas with Garlic and Parsley (page 283)

Summer Rolls with Tofu and Spicy Almond Butter Sauce (page 92) + Skillet-Roasted Brussels Sprouts with Gochujang and Sesame Seeds (page 194)

Hash Brown Omelet with Kimchi (page 34) + Thai-Style Tofu and Basil Lettuce Cups (page 307)

Beet Muhammara (page 351) + Stuffed Grape Leaves (page 366) + pita bread

Bruschetta with Smashed Minty Peas, Chile, and Lemon Zest (page 362) + Cranberry Beans with Fennel, Grapes, and Pine Nuts (page 284) + Spinach with Garlic and Lemon (page 221)

Baja-Style Cauliflower Tacos (page 98) + Avocado-Grapefruit Salad (page 129) + Braised Zucchini (page 234)

Buddha Bowl with Cauliflower, Sweet Potatoes, and Avocados

ONE-DISH MEALS

BUILDING-BLOCK RECIPES

Traditional Vegetable Broth

Makes 2 quarts

This robust broth has deep, balanced flavor and multidimensional sweetness. We caramelized plenty of onions, scallions, and garlic, plus carrots and celery in modest amounts, until we had some flavorful fond on the bottom of the pot. Cauliflower, while nontraditional, added a nutty complexity that tasters loved, while a single plum tomato provided bright acidity. Bay leaves and thyme contributed herbal notes. The fond is important for the flavor and color of the stock, so be sure to let it form on the bottom of the pot in step 1. To avoid a cloudy broth, simmer it gently (don't boil), and don't press on the solids when straining. You will need at least a 7-quart Dutch oven for this recipe.

- 3 onions, chopped
- 2 celery ribs, chopped
- 2 carrots, peeled and chopped
- 8 scallions, chopped
- 15 garlic cloves, peeled and smashed
- 1 teaspoon vegetable oil
- 1 teaspoon table salt

- 3 quarts water
- 1 head cauliflower (2 pounds), cored and cut into 1-inch florets
- 1 plum tomato, cored and chopped
- 8 sprigs fresh thyme
- 3 bay leaves
- 1 teaspoon black peppercorns

1. Combine onions, celery, carrots, scallions, garlic, oil, and salt in large Dutch oven or stockpot. Cover and cook over medium-low heat, stirring often, until golden brown fond has formed on bottom of pot, 20 to 30 minutes.

2. Stir in water, cauliflower, tomato, thyme sprigs, bay leaves, and peppercorns, scraping up any browned bits, and bring to simmer. Partially cover pot, reduce heat to gentle simmer, and cook until stock tastes rich and flavorful, about 1½ hours.

3. Strain stock gently through fine-mesh strainer (do not press on solids). (Stock can be refrigerated for up to 4 days or frozen for up to 2 months.)

Slow-Cooker Vegetable Broth

Makes 3 quarts

Cooking time: 9 to 11 hours on low or 6 to 8 hours on high

The slow cooker gently coaxes out the subtle flavors of vegetables while providing a nearly hands-off preparation method. For this broth, the ingredients are similar to our Traditional Vegetable Broth, with a base of onions, scallions, carrots, and celery along with a generous dose of garlic, cauliflower for complexity, and tomato for acidic balance. Although we wanted to be able to dump all the vegetables into the cooker raw, we found that we

needed the additional flavor that developed from first browning the aromatics, but it's a quick step with a big payoff. To avoid a cloudy broth, don't press on the solids when straining. You will need a 4- to 7-quart slow cooker for this recipe.

- 1 tablespoon vegetable oil
- 3 onions, chopped
- 4 scallions, chopped
- 2 carrots, peeled and chopped
- 2 celery ribs, chopped
- 15 garlic cloves, peeled and smashed
- 3 quarts water, divided
- ½ head cauliflower (1 pound), cored and cut into 1-inch florets
- 1 tomato, cored and chopped
- 8 sprigs fresh thyme
- 1 teaspoon black peppercorns
- ½ teaspoon table salt
- 3 bay leaves

1. Heat oil in 12-inch skillet over medium heat until shimmering. Add onions, scallions, carrots, celery, and garlic and cook until vegetables are softened and lightly browned, 8 to 10 minutes. Stir in 1 cup water, scraping up any browned bits; transfer to slow cooker.

2. Stir remaining 11 cups water, cauliflower, tomato, thyme sprigs, peppercorns, salt, and bay leaves into slow cooker. Cover and cook until broth is deeply flavored and rich, 9 to 11 hours on low or 6 to 8 hours on high.

3. Strain broth through fine-mesh strainer into large container, without pressing on solids. (Broth can be refrigerated for up to 4 days or frozen for up to 2 months.)

Vegetable Broth Base

Makes about 1¾ cups base; enough for 7 quarts broth

The ultimate in homemade convenience, this broth base is actually a concentrated paste of vegetables and herbs, which is turned into broth by stirring portions of it into boiling water. And the concentrate can be stored in the freezer; since it doesn't freeze rock-hard, you can easily scoop out the amount you need directly from the container. For the best balance of flavors, measure the prepped vegetables by weight. The coarseness of the kosher salt aids in grinding the vegetables. To make 1 cup of broth, stir 1 tablespoon of fresh or frozen broth base into 1 cup of boiling water. If particle-free broth is desired, let the broth steep for 5 minutes and then strain it through a fine-mesh strainer.

- 2 leeks, white and light green parts only, chopped and washed thoroughly (2½ cups or 5 ounces)
- 2 carrots, peeled and cut into ½-inch pieces (⅔ cup or 3 ounces)
- ½ small celery root, peeled and cut into ½-inch pieces (¾ cup or 3 ounces)
- ½ cup (½ ounce) fresh parsley leaves and thin stems
- 3 tablespoons dried minced onions
- 2 tablespoons kosher salt
- 1½ tablespoons tomato paste
- 3 tablespoons soy sauce

1. Process leeks, carrots, celery root, parsley, minced onions, and salt in food processor, scraping down sides of bowl frequently, until paste is as fine as possible, 3 to 4 minutes. Add tomato paste and process for 1 minute, scraping down sides of bowl every 20 seconds. Add soy sauce and continue to process 1 minute longer.

2. Transfer mixture to airtight container and tap firmly on counter to remove air bubbles. Press small piece of parchment paper flush against surface of mixture and cover. Freeze for up to 6 months.

Umami Broth

Makes 4 quarts

To develop a vegan broth with an intense flavor that approached stocks made from meat and bones, we experimented with various umami-packed ingredients, including seaweed, miso, tomato paste, and mushrooms. While we liked a combination of dried shiitake mushrooms—which contain some of the highest levels of glutamates—alongside nutritional yeast, white miso, and soy sauce, the resulting broth still lacked a certain depth of flavor. Adding fermented black beans—a Chinese ingredient used to boost savoriness in sauces and stir-fries like Vegan Mapo Tofu (page 84)—did the trick. Tasters felt that these salty, bitter, sweet, and funky umami powerhouses added a "mysterious" depth that perfectly complemented the other ingredients. This is perfect in our French Onion Soup (page 66). Fermented black beans can be found at Asian markets or online; if you are unable to find them, omit them. Do not substitute black bean paste (which generally has other flavorings) or

standard canned black beans. We prefer straining through a double layer of cheesecloth for a clearer broth, though there will still be some sediment. This recipe can be halved.

- 4 quarts water
- ½ cup nutritional yeast
- ¼ cup fermented black beans
- 3 tablespoons soy sauce
- 2 tablespoons white miso
- 1 tablespoon onion powder
- 1 tablespoon garlic powder
- ¾ ounce dried shiitake mushrooms, rinsed and chopped coarse

1. Combine all ingredients in large pot. Bring to boil, then cover, reduce heat to low, and simmer for 30 minutes.

2. Strain broth through fine-mesh strainer lined with double layer of cheesecloth. (Broth can be refrigerated for up to 4 days or frozen for up to 1 month.)

Fish Sauce Substitute

Makes about 1¼ cups

Like soy sauce, fish sauce is both a condiment and an ingredient and is full of glutamates that enhance flavor in food. But while soy sauce is vegan, made from fermented soybeans and grains, fish sauce is made from anchovies. So we developed a swap that mimicked the savory qualities of fish sauce so that we wouldn't have to sacrifice flavor in our favorite Southeast Asian dishes. Made with soy and dried shiitakes, this adds lots of umami depth to dishes including Thai Coconut Soup with Tofu (page 72) and Tofu Pad Thai (page 177).

- 3 cups water
- 3 tablespoons table salt
- 2 tablespoons soy sauce
- ¼ ounce dried sliced shiitake mushrooms

Simmer all ingredients in large saucepan over medium heat until mixture is reduced by half, 20 to 30 minutes. Strain liquid and let cool completely. (Fish sauce substitute can be refrigerated for up to 2 months.)

Anchovy Substitute

Makes ¼ cup

Anchovies play a subtle but unmistakably helpful supporting role in many recipes, and when we were developing recipes for this book, we missed the savory, funky umami qualities that anchovies brought to Creamless Creamy Green Goddess Dressing (page 128), Kale Caesar Salad (page 140), and more. So we developed this vegan substitute, finding that we could use 1 teaspoon anchovy substitute to replace either 1 anchovy fillet or ½ teaspoon anchovy paste. If you can't find nori powder, you can grind 1 sheet of toasted nori in a spice grinder to a fine powder (do not use snack-size sheets).

- ¼ **cup white miso**
- 1 **teaspoon nori powder**

Combine miso and nori powder in small bowl. (Anchovy substitute can be refrigerated for up to 2 months.)

Vegan Pesto

Makes ¾ cup (enough for 1 pound pasta)

Our goal in creating a dairy-free green pesto was to heighten the fresh basil flavor and subdue the harshness of the garlic so these two elements would be balanced. We started by toasting whole garlic cloves in their skins to develop their sweetness. Then we bruised the basil in a plastic bag with a meat pounder (you could also use a rolling pin) to bring out its aromatic oils. Toasted pine nuts and olive oil contribute lots of buttery richness. In place of dairy Parmesan (which you

can use if you prefer), we added a smaller quantity of our umami-rich Vegan Parmesan Substitute. If serving this with pasta, be sure to reserve some of the pasta cooking water to thin out the pesto and add creaminess as needed once it's been mixed with the pasta. Two cups of fresh basil leaves weigh about 2 ounces. Basil usually darkens in pesto, but you can boost the green color by adding the optional parsley. If you don't have Vegan Parmesan Substitute on hand, you can substitute a mixture of 2 tablespoons toasted pine nuts, 2 teaspoons nutritional yeast, and ⅛ teaspoon salt. This recipe can easily be doubled.

- 3 **garlic cloves, unpeeled**
- 2 **cups fresh basil leaves**
- 2 **tablespoons fresh parsley leaves (optional)**
- ¼ **cup pine nuts, toasted**
- 3 **tablespoons Vegan Parmesan Substitute (page 27) or ¼ cup grated dairy Parmesan cheese**
- ¼ **teaspoon table salt**
- 7 **tablespoons extra-virgin olive oil**

1. Toast garlic in 8-inch skillet over medium heat, stirring occasionally, until fragrant and skins are just beginning to brown, about 5 minutes. Remove garlic from saucepan and let cool, about 5 minutes. Once cool enough to handle, peel garlic and

mince. Place basil and parsley, if using, in heavy-duty quart-size zipper-lock bag; pound with flat side of meat pounder or a rolling pin until all leaves are bruised.

2. Process bruised herbs, pine nuts, Parmesan, salt, and toasted and minced garlic in food processor until smooth, scraping down sides of bowl as needed, about 1 minute. With processor running, slowly add oil until incorporated, about 30 seconds. Transfer pesto to bowl and season with salt and pepper to taste. (Pesto can be refrigerated for up to 3 days or frozen for up to 3 months. To prevent browning, press plastic wrap flush to surface, or top with thin layer of olive oil.)

Crispy Tempeh

Makes 1 cup

Many recipes in this book explore the versatility of tempeh as part of a plant-based meal, from hash to stir-fries to steaks to sandwiches. Here we turn tempeh into a condiment or topping of sorts: a crunchy, crumbly umami bomb that will be the star of any dish it's sprinkled on, including Rainbow Salad with Crispy Tempeh (page 131) and Moroccan Tempeh Salad (page 151). After crumbling the tempeh slabs into small pieces, a simple two-step preparation method of boiling in soy sauce–seasoned water followed by frying tempered its slight bitterness and transformed its overall neutral flavors into anything but.

- 3 **tablespoons soy sauce**
- 8 **ounces tempeh, crumbled into ¼-inch pieces**
- 1 **cup peanut or vegetable oil, for frying**

1. Bring 4 cups water and soy sauce to boil in large saucepan. Add tempeh, return to boil, and cook for 10 minutes. Drain tempeh well and wipe saucepan dry with paper towels.

2. Set wire rack in rimmed baking sheet and line with triple layer paper towels. Heat oil in now-empty dry saucepan over medium-high heat until shimmering. Add tempeh and cook until golden brown and crisp, about 12 minutes, adjusting heat as needed if tempeh begins to scorch. Using wire skimmer or slotted spoon, transfer tempeh to prepared sheet to drain, then season with salt and pepper to taste. Serve immediately.

Almond Butter

Makes 2 cups

Almond butter couldn't be easier to make, and it's a versatile pantry staple in a plant-based diet. One of our favorite recipes that uses it is our Sautéed Grape and Almond Butter Toast (page 36). It can also be used to make savory sauces, as in our Summer Rolls with Tofu and Spicy Almond Butter Sauce (page 92), or to add a toasty, buttery flavor to baked goods such as our Trail Mix Cookies (page 380).

    4 cups (1¼ pounds) whole almonds
    ½ teaspoon table salt

1. Adjust oven rack to middle position and heat oven to 375 degrees. Spread almonds in single layer on rimmed baking sheet and toast until fragrant and darkened slightly, 5 to 10 minutes, rotating sheet halfway

through cooking. Transfer baking sheet to wire rack and let cool, about 20 minutes.

2. Transfer almonds to food processor, add salt, and process almonds to smooth paste, 5 to 7 minutes, scraping down sides of bowl as needed. Season almond butter with salt to taste. (Almond butter can be refrigerated or stored at room temperature for up to 2 months; stir to recombine before serving.)

Almond Milk

Makes about 4 cups

Cooking time (for slow cooker): 3¼ hours on low

Typically, homemade almond milk starts by soaking the almonds for at least 8 hours or up to a full day, but using a slow cooker or an electric pressure cooker greatly sped up the process, allowing us to skip soaking altogether in favor of slow cooking for a few hours or pressure cooking for just 1 minute. Afterward, we simply drained the almonds, processed them with fresh water in a blender (4 cups of water gave our milk the best flavor and texture), and then poured the mixture through a cheesecloth-lined fine-mesh strainer to separate the milk from the pulp. Since the pulp still contained a great deal of milk, we squeezed it in the cheesecloth until no liquid remained. We found that sugar helped to round out the flavor; however, if you're cooking with this milk, we recommend omitting it.

    1¼ cups whole blanched almonds
     2 tablespoons sugar (optional)
     ⅛ teaspoon table salt

1. Place almonds in slow cooker or electric pressure cooker and add water to cover by 1 inch.

2A. To slow cook Cover slow cooker and cook on low heat setting until almonds are softened, 2 to 3 hours.

2B. To pressure cook Lock lid in place and close pressure release valve. Select high pressure cook function and cook for 1 minute. Turn off pressure cooker and quick-release pressure. Carefully remove lid, allowing steam to escape away from you.

3. Drain almonds and rinse well. Process almonds and 4 cups cold water in blender until almonds are finely ground, about 2 minutes. Set fine-mesh strainer lined with triple layer of cheesecloth in 4-cup liquid measuring cup. Transfer mixture to prepared strainer and press to extract as much liquid as possible. Pull edges of cheesecloth together and firmly squeeze pulp until liquid no longer runs freely; discard pulp. Stir in sugar, if using, and salt until completely dissolved. (Almond milk can be refrigerated for up to 4 days; stir to recombine before serving.)

Soy Milk

Makes about 4 cups

Soy milk is as creamy and rich as almond milk or oat milk but has a more neutral flavor than either of those. We think our homemade soy milk is far superior to store-bought. Dried soybeans are available at Asian markets, in well-stocked supermarkets, and online. The longer you soak the soybeans, the richer the milk will be. We found that sugar and vanilla helped to round out the flavor; however, if you're cooking with this milk, we recommend omitting them.

½ cup dried soybeans, picked over and rinsed

2 teaspoons sugar (optional)

½ teaspoon vanilla extract (optional)

⅛ teaspoon table salt

1. Place soybeans in bowl and add water to cover by 2 inches. Soak soybeans at room temperature for at least 1 hour or up to 24 hours. Drain and rinse well.

2. Bring soaked soybeans and 4½ cups water to simmer in medium saucepan. Gently simmer, partially covered, over medium-low heat until soybeans are tender, 30 to 40 minutes. Carefully transfer to blender. Add sugar, if using; vanilla, if using; and salt and process until mostly smooth, about 3 minutes.

3. Set fine-mesh strainer lined with triple layer of cheesecloth in 4-cup liquid measuring cup. Transfer mixture to prepared strainer and let drain, stirring occasionally, until liquid no longer runs freely and mixture is≈cool enough to touch, about 30 minutes. Pull edges of cheesecloth together and firmly squeeze pulp until liquid no longer runs freely; discard pulp. Transfer milk to airtight container and refrigerate until well chilled, about 1 hour. Serve. (Soy milk can be refrigerated for up to 4 days; stir to recombine before serving.)

Oat Milk

Makes about 4 cups

Oat milk is inexpensive to make and also supereasy, so we love keeping it on hand to bake with, to add to smoothies, and to just drink straight from the fridge. Oat milk is great if you have sensitivities to soy or nuts, and it's gluten-free if you make it with gluten-free oats. Quick-cooking rolled oats can be substituted, if necessary; do not substitute steel-cut oats. Avoid

squeezing the oat pulp too firmly; it will cause the milk to be starchy. The oil helps to reduce the amount of foam that forms while processing; do not omit it. We found that sugar and vanilla helped to round out the flavor; however, if you're cooking with this milk, we recommend omitting them.

1 quart water

¾ cup old-fashioned rolled oats

2 teaspoons sugar (optional)

¾ teaspoon vegetable oil

½ teaspoon vanilla extract (optional)

⅛ teaspoon table salt

Process water; oats; sugar, if using; oil; vanilla, if using; and salt in blender until coarsely ground, about 10 seconds, scraping down sides of blender jar as needed. Set fine-mesh strainer lined with triple layer of cheesecloth in 4-cup liquid measuring cup. Transfer mixture to prepared strainer and let drain, stirring occasionally, until liquid no longer runs freely, about 5 minutes. Pull edges of cheesecloth together and firmly squeeze pulp until liquid no longer runs freely; discard pulp. Transfer milk to airtight container and refrigerate until well chilled, about 1 hour. Serve. (Oat milk can be refrigerated for up to 4 days; stir to recombine before serving.)

VARIATION

Oat Milk with Ginger and Turmeric

Add 1 teaspoon grated fresh ginger and ¼ teaspoon ground turmeric to blender with water.

Rice Milk

Makes 4 cups

Commercial rice milk is usually too thin and watery to make use of in cooking, but this version is a different story. We discovered that how you handle the rice matters. We first tried using soaked rice, but the milk was too thick and tasted cooked. After much testing, we found that there was no need to presoak the rice and that we needed far less than expected. Adding all of the rice to the blender at the beginning along with the other ingredients delivered a milk with a creamy texture and fresh flavor. The blender pureed everything, but we strained the milk just in case a few granules were left behind. The oil helps to reduce the amount of foam that forms while processing; do not omit it. We found that sugar and vanilla helped to round out the flavor; however, if you're cooking with this milk, we recommend omitting them.

1 quart water

2 tablespoons long-grain white rice, rinsed

2 teaspoons sugar (optional)

¾ teaspoon vegetable oil

½ teaspoon vanilla extract (optional)

⅛ teaspoon table salt

1. Bring water; rice; sugar, if using; oil; vanilla, if using; and salt to simmer in large saucepan. Cover and simmer over low heat until rice is very tender, about 12 minutes.

2. Carefully transfer rice mixture to blender and process until opaque and smooth, about 1 minute. Strain rice mixture through fine-mesh strainer into bowl, stirring mixture as needed to extract as much liquid as possible; discard solids. Let cool to room temperature, about 30 minutes. Transfer milk to airtight container and refrigerate until well chilled, about 1 hour. Serve. (Rice milk can be refrigerated for up to 4 days; stir to recombine before serving.)

VARIATION
Brown Rice Milk
Substitute long-grain brown rice for white rice and increase simmering time in step 1 to about 25 minutes.

Almond Milk Yogurt

Makes about 3 cups
To promote the fermentation required in making yogurt, we elected to use probiotic capsules, since typical yogurt starter cultures are often sourced from dairy products. You can find the probiotic capsules and the agar-agar (a vegan alternative to gelatin) at your local natural food store. The flavor of your yogurt may vary depending on the brand of probiotic used; we developed this recipe using Renew Life Ultimate Flora Critical Care 50 Billion probiotic capsules. Do not substitute agar-agar flakes for the agar-agar powder.

1¾ teaspoons agar-agar powder
¼ cup water
3 cups almond milk
1 50-billion probiotic capsule

1. Adjust oven rack to middle position. Sprinkle agar-agar over water in small bowl and let sit until softened, about 10 minutes.

2. Heat milk in large saucepan over medium-low heat until just simmering. Add softened agar-agar and cook, whisking constantly, until fully dissolved. Transfer mixture to bowl and let cool, stirring occasionally, until mixture registers 110 degrees, about 20 minutes.

3. Twist open probiotic capsule and whisk contents into cooled milk mixture; discard capsule's casing. Cover bowl tightly with plastic wrap, place in oven, and turn on oven light. Let yogurt sit undisturbed for at least 12 hours or up to 24 hours. (Yogurt will not thicken while sitting.)

4. Refrigerate yogurt until completely chilled and set, about 4 hours. Process yogurt in blender until smooth, about 30 seconds. (Yogurt can be refrigerated for up to 1 week.)

Cashew Ricotta

Makes about 1 cup
Cashew ricotta is creamy, dreamy, and easy to make. Cashews are uniquely low in fiber among nuts, so they break down into a smooth texture more readily, and they're high in starch, which gives our ricotta body. The hardest part is simply waiting, since you need to soak the raw cashews for at least 8 hours before processing them with the other ingredients. Cashew Ricotta is endlessly versatile in the plant-based kitchen: We use it as the sauce base for Penne with Red

Pepper Pesto (page 158), to fill Cashew Ricotta Tartlets with Celery-Olive Topping (page 365), to top Thin-Crust Pizza with Mushrooms and Cashew Ricotta (page 112), and even to make Pumpkin-Cashew Cheesecake (page 386).

1 cup raw cashews
2 tablespoons extra-virgin olive oil
2 teaspoons lemon juice, plus extra for seasoning
¼ teaspoon table salt

1. Place cashews in bowl and add water to cover by 1 inch. Soak cashews at room temperature for at least 8 hours or up to 24 hours. Drain and rinse well.

2. Process cashews, ¼ cup water, oil, lemon juice, and salt in food processor until smooth, about 2 minutes, scraping down sides of bowl as needed. Adjust consistency with additional water as needed. Season with salt, pepper, and extra lemon juice to taste. (Ricotta can be refrigerated for up to 1 week.)

Cheez Sauce

Makes about 2 cups
You'll have a hard time believing that this sauce is vegan. We experimented with many ingredient options when developing this recipe, but tasters found all versions to be not cheesy enough. Then we tried something unorthodox: We whirred boiled potatoes in the blender at high speed to release as much of their starch as possible. While this would make awful mashed potatoes, the sticky mixture was ideal for a cheese-like sauce. We blended in carrot for color, nutritional yeast and mustard powder for funky flavor depth, vegetable oil for fluidity, and vinegar for tang—and ended up with this pleasing yellow-orange sauce with a mild flavor and ultracreamy

texture. We enjoy it as a topping for our Double Smashie Burgers (page 101). And the nacho cheese sauce in our Meaty Loaded Nacho Dip (page 348) builds on this sauce, with more vegetable oil for greater dipping fluidity, more vinegar for brighter acidity, and chipotle chiles in adobo for spicy zing.

- 12 **ounces russet potatoes, peeled and cut into 1-inch pieces**
- 1 **small carrot, peeled and cut into ½-inch pieces (⅓ cup)**
- 2 **tablespoons vegetable oil**
- 1½ **tablespoons nutritional yeast**
- ½ **teaspoon distilled white vinegar**
- 1 **teaspoon table salt**
- ⅛ **teaspoon mustard powder**

1. Bring 2 quarts water to boil in large saucepan over high heat. Add potatoes and carrot and cook until tender, about 12 minutes; drain in colander.

2. Combine cooked vegetables, ⅓ cup water, oil, nutritional yeast, vinegar, salt, and mustard powder in blender. Pulse until chopped and combined, about 10 pulses, scraping down sides of blender jar as needed. (You will need to stop processing to scrape down sides of blender jar several times for mixture to come together.) Process mixture on high speed until very smooth, about 2 minutes. Serve. (Sauce can be refrigerated in airtight container for up to 3 days; reheat in microwave, stirring every 30 seconds, until glossy and pourable. Adjust consistency with hot water as needed.)

Vegan Parmesan Substitute

Makes about 1 cup
To satisfy our cravings for the salty, nutty, savory punch that grated Parmesan adds to many dishes, we developed this rich-tasting dairy-free substitute, which you will find called

for in many recipes throughout this book. Toasted cashews contribute sweetness, pine nuts bring savoriness, nutritional yeast brings that desired umami quality, and green olives add a salty brininess. This winning combination even has a texture similar to that of the crystalline bits in high-quality aged Parmesan.

- ¾ **cup raw cashews**
- 3 **tablespoons nutritional yeast**
- 2 **tablespoons raw pine nuts**
- 1 **tablespoon chopped green olives, patted dry**
- ¾ **teaspoon table salt**

1. Adjust oven rack to middle position and heat oven to 275 degrees. Process cashews, nutritional yeast, pine nuts, olives, and salt in food processor until finely ground, about 1 minute, scraping down sides of bowl as needed.

2. Spread mixture on rimmed baking sheet in even layer. Bake until mixture is light golden and dry to the touch, about 20 minutes, stirring mixture and rotating pan halfway through baking.

3. Let mixture cool completely, about 15 minutes. Break apart any large clumps before serving. (Parmesan substitute can be refrigerated for up to 1 month.)

Vegan Mayonnaise

Makes about 1 cup
Aquafaba, the liquid found in a can of chickpeas, gives this egg-free mayo volume and emulsified body. It's devoid of off-flavors or textures that don't resemble mayonnaise, which was not the case when we tried creating vegan mayo with soy milk, tofu, cashews, or miso. We also like Just Mayo store-bought mayonnaise; it tastes significantly better than any of the other store-bought mayos we tasted, which ranged from rancid to too acidic in flavor and from slimy to foamy in texture.

- 2⅔ **ounces aquafaba (⅓ cup) (page 16)**
- 1½ **teaspoons lemon juice**
- ½ **teaspoon table salt**
- ½ **teaspoon sugar**
- ½ **teaspoon Dijon mustard**
- 1¼ **cups vegetable oil**
- 3 **tablespoons extra-virgin olive oil**

1. Process aquafaba, lemon juice, salt, sugar, and mustard in food processor for 10 seconds. With processor running, gradually add vegetable oil in slow steady stream until mixture is thick and creamy, scraping down sides of bowl as needed, about 3 minutes.

2. Transfer mixture to bowl. Whisking constantly, slowly add olive oil until emulsified. If pools of oil form on surface, stop addition of oil and whisk mixture until well combined, then resume adding oil. Mayonnaise should be thick and glossy with no oil pools on surface. (Mayonnaise can be refrigerated for up to 1 week.)

CHAPTER 1
BRUNCH

■ FAST (45 minutes or less total time)
Photos: Almond Granola with Dried Fruit; Blueberry Muffins; Black Beans on Toast with Tomato and Avocado

Tofu Frittata with Mushrooms

Serves 6 to 8

Why This Recipe Works Simpler and more substantial than omelets and less fussy than quiche, frittatas are a longtime test kitchen favorite, so naturally we were delighted to discover that we could make an extraordinary version with tofu instead of eggs. Silken tofu, with its creamy texture, seemed like the obvious starting point, but it actually proved too wet. Instead, we found that firm tofu became perfectly smooth and "eggy" when we processed it. For additional structure to balance the frittata's softness, we added some chickpea flour. Unlike wheat flour or cornstarch, the chickpea flour added heft and structure without making the frittata pasty; plus, it heightened the savory flavor profile. Turmeric gave the frittata a pleasing eggy color, and garlic powder provided umami flavor depth. After sautéing mushrooms and aromatics until deeply caramelized, we stirred the tofu puree into the vegetables and baked the frittata until it was set throughout and lightly golden. Given a 5-minute rest in the pan, the frittata slid right out and sliced into neat wedges. Do not use silken, soft, or extra-firm tofu in this recipe.

- 28 ounces firm tofu, drained and patted dry
- 3 tablespoons extra-virgin olive oil, divided
- 1¼ teaspoons table salt, divided
- ½ teaspoon ground turmeric
- ½ teaspoon garlic powder
- ⅛ teaspoon pepper
- ¼ cup chickpea flour
- 8 ounces cremini mushrooms, trimmed and sliced thin
- 2 shallots, minced
- 1 garlic clove, minced
- 1 teaspoon minced fresh thyme
- 1 tablespoon minced fresh parsley

1. Adjust oven rack to middle position and heat oven to 350 degrees. Process tofu, 1 tablespoon oil, 1 teaspoon salt, turmeric, garlic powder, and pepper in food processor until smooth, about 30 seconds, scraping down sides of bowl as needed. Add chickpea flour and process until well combined, about 15 seconds.

2. Heat remaining 2 tablespoons oil in 12-inch ovensafe nonstick skillet over medium-high heat until shimmering. Add mushrooms and remaining ¼ teaspoon salt and cook until mushrooms have released their liquid and are beginning to brown, 5 to 7 minutes. Stir in shallots and cook until mushrooms are well browned, 5 to 7 minutes. Stir in garlic and thyme and cook until fragrant, about 30 seconds.

3. Off heat, stir in tofu mixture and spread into even layer. Transfer skillet to oven and bake until center is set and surface is slightly puffed, dry, and lightly golden, 30 to 35 minutes, rotating skillet halfway through baking.

4. Being careful of hot skillet handle, remove skillet from oven and let frittata sit for 5 minutes. Using spatula, loosen frittata from skillet and slide onto cutting board. Sprinkle with parsley, cut into wedges, and serve.

Tofu Rancheros with Avocado

Serves 4

Why This Recipe Works Tofu rancheros with warm corn tortillas nestled alongside makes for a hearty, zesty way to start the day. This plant-based version of huevos rancheros replaces the eggs with supple squares of firm tofu. Similar to a poached egg, the tofu achieved a creamy, silky interior texture while still holding its shape during cooking. The backbone of any rancheros dish is really the sauce, so for maximum flavor with little effort, we roasted canned diced tomatoes with brown sugar, lime juice, onion, green chiles, garlic, and chili powder. Roasting on a sheet pan allowed moisture to quickly evaporate and a nice char to form on the vegetables. We seared the tofu while the sauce cooked for a beautiful golden color. Finishing the sauce and tofu together on the stovetop allowed the flavors to meld. We supercharged the toppings by adding a vibrant salad of avocado, cilantro, and scallions. If you would like to use eggs and cheese in your rancheros, see the variation. Use a heavyweight rimmed baking sheet for this recipe, as flimsy sheets will warp in the 500-degree oven.

- 2 (28-ounce) cans diced tomatoes
- 4 teaspoons lime juice, divided, plus lime wedges for serving
- 1 tablespoon packed brown sugar
- 1 onion, chopped
- ½ cup chopped canned green chiles
- ¼ cup extra-virgin olive oil, divided
- 2 tablespoons plus ½ teaspoon chili powder, divided
- 4 garlic cloves, sliced thin
- 14 ounces firm tofu, halved lengthwise, then cut crosswise into twelve ½-inch-thick slabs
- ¼ teaspoon table salt
- ⅛ teaspoon pepper
- 1 cup fresh cilantro leaves
- 4 scallions, white parts sliced thin, green parts cut into 1-inch pieces
- 1 avocado, halved, pitted, and diced
- 8 (6-inch) corn tortillas, warmed

Tofu Rancheros with Avocado

5. Transfer roasted tomato mixture to now-empty skillet and stir in reserved tomato juice mixture. Season with salt and pepper to taste, then nestle tofu into sauce. Bring to simmer over medium heat, cover, and cook until tofu is warmed through and sauce thickens slightly, about 2 minutes.

6. Whisk remaining 1 tablespoon oil and remaining 1 teaspoon lime juice together in large bowl. Add cilantro, scallions, and avocado and toss to coat. Season with salt and pepper to taste. Serve rancheros with warm tortillas and lime wedges, topped with herb and avocado salad.

VARIATION

Huevos Rancheros with Avocado

Omit tofu, salt, pepper. Reduce oil to 3 tablespoons and chili powder to 2 tablespoons. After stirring reserved tomato juice mixture into roasted tomatoes in skillet in step 5, sprinkle evenly with 1 cup shredded pepper Jack cheese. Make 4 shallow indentations (about 2 inches wide) in surface of tomato mixture using back of spoon. Crack 2 eggs into each indentation and sprinkle eggs with ¼ teaspoon table salt and ⅛ teaspoon pepper. Cover and cook over medium-low heat until egg whites are just set and yolks are still runny, 5 to 10 minutes.

1. Adjust oven rack to middle position and heat oven to 500 degrees. Line rimmed baking sheet with parchment paper. Drain tomatoes in fine-mesh strainer set over bowl, pressing to extract as much juice as possible. Reserve 1¼ cups tomato juice and discard remainder. Whisk 1 tablespoon lime juice and sugar into tomato juice.

2. Combine onion, chiles, 2 tablespoons oil, 2 tablespoons chili powder, garlic, and drained tomatoes in second bowl. Transfer tomato mixture to prepared baking sheet and spread in even layer to edges of sheet. Roast until charred in spots, 35 to 40 minutes, stirring and redistributing into even layer halfway through baking.

3. Meanwhile, spread tofu on paper towel–lined baking sheet and let drain for 20 minutes. Gently press dry with paper towels, sprinkle with salt and pepper, and sprinkle both sides with remaining ½ teaspoon chili powder.

4. Heat 1 tablespoon oil in 12-inch nonstick skillet over medium-high heat until just smoking. Add tofu and cook until golden and crisp on both sides, 5 to 7 minutes; transfer to paper towel–lined plate.

Tofu Scramble with Bell Pepper, Shallot, and Basil

Serves 4 `FAST`

Why This Recipe Works This satisfying, creamy scramble is quick enough to make on any day of the week and simple enough to manage before you've even had your morning coffee. It's just as great alongside toast and jam as it is tucked into a portable breakfast burrito or soft taco. To achieve a rich, egg-like texture and a subtle but satisfying flavor, we tried silken, soft, medium, and firm tofu. The soft tofu proved the best choice for scrambling, yielding pieces that, when crumbled, were smooth and creamy. (Silken tofu produced a looser scramble, and firmer tofu varieties developed into hard curds.) We kept the vegetable additions simple with bell pepper and shallot, and basil stirred in at the end added a fresh touch. A small amount of turmeric contributed subtle depth of flavor and a nice touch of golden color. We also found that the tofu could be crumbled into smaller or larger pieces to resemble egg curds of different sizes. If you cannot find soft tofu, you can use silken tofu, but your scramble will be significantly wetter. Do not use firm tofu in this recipe.

14 ounces soft tofu, drained and patted dry
1½ teaspoons vegetable oil
1 small red bell pepper, stemmed, seeded, and chopped fine
1 shallot, minced
¾ teaspoon table salt
⅛ teaspoon ground turmeric
⅛ teaspoon pepper
2 tablespoons finely chopped fresh basil

1. Crumble tofu into ¼- to ½-inch pieces. Spread tofu on paper towel–lined baking sheet and let drain for 20 minutes, then gently press dry with paper towels. Heat oil in 10-inch nonstick skillet over medium heat until shimmering. Add bell pepper and shallot and cook until softened, about 5 minutes.

2. Stir in tofu, salt, turmeric, and pepper and cook until tofu is hot, about 2 minutes. Off heat, stir in basil and serve.

VARIATION

Tofu Scramble with Tomato and Scallions
Omit red bell pepper. Add 1 seeded and finely chopped tomato and 1 minced garlic clove to pan with shallot in step 1; cook until tomato is no longer wet, 3 to 5 minutes. Substitute 2 tablespoons minced scallions for basil.

Tofu Scramble with Bell Pepper, Shallot, and Basil

Sweet Potato Red Flannel Hash with Tempeh

Sweet Potato Red Flannel Hash with Tempeh

Serves 4 **FAST**

Why This Recipe Works Red flannel hash gets its name from the deep red beets scattered throughout, reminiscent of the check on a flannel plaid. Our vegan version features tempeh instead of eggs and sweet potato in addition to the classic combination of beets and russet potatoes for a dish that is true weekend comfort food. The seasoned and browned tempeh cubes provided a satisfyingly hearty bite and a savory flavor that made tasters go back for seconds and even thirds. To make the process speedy, we parcooked the vegetables in the microwave until tender and then moved them to the skillet to brown and crisp, rounding out the flavors with onion, garlic, and thyme and stirring in some plant-based creamer (or heavy cream) for richness and binding. As for the tempeh, we first tried cooking it along with the vegetables, but it kept the hash from cohering. Instead, we seared the tempeh separately, built the hash, and then scattered the cubes over the top along with a handful of scallions. The hash stayed together, and the salty richness of the tempeh perfectly balanced the sweet vegetables underneath for a hearty, colorful breakfast.

- 1 russet potato (8 ounces), peeled and cut into ½-inch pieces
- 1 small sweet potato (8 ounces), peeled and cut into ½-inch pieces
- 8 ounces beets, peeled and cut into ½-inch pieces
- ¼ cup vegetable oil, divided
- ¾ teaspoon table salt, divided
- ¾ teaspoon pepper, divided
- 8 ounces tempeh, cut into ½-inch pieces
- 1 tablespoon soy sauce
- 1 onion, chopped fine
- 2 garlic cloves, minced
- ½ teaspoon minced fresh thyme or ¼ teaspoon dried
- ⅓ cup plant-based creamer or dairy heavy cream
- 2 scallions, sliced thin

1. Combine russet potato, sweet potato, beets, 1 tablespoon oil, ½ teaspoon salt, and ½ teaspoon pepper in bowl. Microwave, covered, stirring occasionally, until russet potato is translucent around edges and sweet potato and beets are fork-tender, 8 to 10 minutes.

2. Meanwhile, heat 1 tablespoon oil in 12-inch nonstick skillet over medium-high heat until just smoking. Add tempeh, soy sauce, remaining ¼ teaspoon salt, and remaining ¼ teaspoon pepper and cook, stirring occasionally, until well browned, 4 to 6 minutes. Transfer to bowl and cover with foil.

3. Heat remaining 2 tablespoons oil in now-empty skillet over medium-high heat until shimmering. Add onion and cook until softened, about 5 minutes. Stir in garlic and thyme and cook until fragrant, about 30 seconds.

4. Stir in microwaved vegetables and any accumulated juices and creamer. Using back of spatula, firmly pack vegetables into skillet and cook undisturbed for 2 minutes. Flip hash, 1 portion at a time, and repack into pan. Repeat flipping process every few minutes until vegetables are nicely browned, 6 to 8 minutes. Top with reserved tempeh, sprinkle with scallions, and serve.

Brussels Sprouts Hash
Serves 4 `FAST`

Why This Recipe Works Earthy brussels sprouts and sweet carrots combine with potatoes in this fast and hearty hash. But hashing together different vegetables presented a challenge: The potatoes and carrots took longer than the brussels sprouts to soften. Starting the potatoes and carrots in the microwave with a little oil solved the problem, turning them tender in only 5 minutes. Meanwhile, we cooked the brussels sprouts in the skillet to get good browning. We first tried slicing or shredding the sprouts, but the small pieces tended to steam rather than brown. Cutting the sprouts into wedges provided nice flat surfaces that picked up flavorful browning. Next, we added the microwaved carrots and potatoes along with onion, garlic, thyme, and a little water to help the brussels sprouts finish cooking through. This hash is plenty substantial as is, but if you would like to top it with eggs, see the variation. Look for small brussels sprouts no bigger than a golf ball, as they're likely to be sweeter and more tender than large sprouts. If you can find only large sprouts, halve them and cut each half into thirds.

- 1 pound red potatoes, unpeeled, cut into ½-inch pieces
- 2 carrots, peeled and cut into ½-inch pieces
- 3 tablespoons extra-virgin olive oil, divided
- 1¼ teaspoons table salt, divided
- ½ teaspoon pepper, divided
- 1 pound brussels sprouts, trimmed and quartered lengthwise
- 1 onion, chopped fine
- 2 tablespoons water
- 1 tablespoon minced fresh thyme
- 1 garlic clove, minced
- 1 tablespoon refined coconut oil or unsalted butter
- 2 scallions, sliced thin

1. Combine potatoes, carrots, 1 tablespoon extra-virgin olive oil, ½ teaspoon salt, and ¼ teaspoon pepper in large bowl. Microwave, covered, stirring occasionally, until vegetables are tender, 5 to 7 minutes.

2. Meanwhile, heat 1 tablespoon extra-virgin olive oil in 12-inch nonstick skillet over medium-high heat until shimmering. Add brussels sprouts and cook until browned, 6 to 8 minutes, stirring occasionally. Add microwaved vegetables and any accumulated juices, onion, water, thyme, garlic, remaining 1 tablespoon extra-virgin olive oil, remaining ¾ teaspoon salt, and remaining ¼ teaspoon pepper. Reduce heat to medium, cover, and cook until brussels sprouts are just tender, 5 to 7 minutes longer, stirring halfway through cooking.

3. Off heat, stir in coconut oil and season with salt and pepper to taste. Sprinkle with scallions and serve.

VARIATION
Brussels Sprouts Hash with Poached Eggs
In step 3, after seasoning with salt and pepper, make 4 shallow indentations (about 2 inches wide) in surface of hash using back of spoon. Crack 2 eggs into each indentation and sprinkle eggs with ¼ teaspoon table salt and ⅛ teaspoon pepper. Cover and cook over medium-low heat until egg whites are just set and yolks are still runny, 5 to 10 minutes. Sprinkle with scallions and serve.

Hash Brown Omelet with Kimchi

Serves 2 to 4 `FAST`

Why This Recipe Works Hash browns seem to be becoming more rare these days, but this simple recipe, where we turn hash browns into an "omelet" with a vegetable filling and a creamy topping, will bring these thin, crisply sautéed potato cakes back to the table. High-starch russet potatoes worked best; they held together well, browned beautifully, and had the most pronounced potato flavor. And there was no need to precook them—raw grated potatoes (squeezed of moisture) developed a tender interior and a deeply browned crust. We cooked the potato cake in a sizzling skillet until browned on the bottom, then flipped it, added kimchi and scallions on top, and let the potatoes finish cooking and browning before folding them over the filling. While we love the combination of hash browns and kimchi, you can use a variety of fillings, including sautéed mushrooms, peppers and onions, or greens. We like the unadorned variation alongside either of our tofu scrambles (page 31). Use the large holes of a box grater or the shredding disk of a food processor to shred the potatoes. To prevent the potatoes from turning brown, shred them just before cooking. Read the label to be sure your kimchi is vegan.

2 tablespoons plant-based mayonnaise or
  egg-based mayonnaise
¼ teaspoon toasted sesame oil
⅛ teaspoon grated lime zest
1 pound russet potatoes, peeled and shredded
¼ teaspoon table salt
  Pinch pepper
2 tablespoons vegetable oil, divided
⅔ cup kimchi, drained and chopped
1 scallion, white and green parts separated and
  sliced thin
1 tablespoon chopped fresh cilantro

1. Whisk mayonnaise, sesame oil, and lime zest together in bowl; set aside until ready to serve.

2. Wrap potatoes in clean dish towel and squeeze thoroughly of excess moisture. Toss potatoes with salt and pepper in bowl.

3. Heat 1 tablespoon vegetable oil in 12-inch nonstick skillet over medium-high heat until shimmering. Spread potatoes in even layer in skillet and press firmly to flatten. Reduce heat to medium and cook until dark golden and crisp, 8 to 10 minutes.

4. Slide hash browns onto large plate. Add remaining 1 tablespoon vegetable oil to now-empty skillet. Invert hash browns onto second plate and slide, browned side up, back into skillet; press firmly to flatten. Sprinkle kimchi and scallion whites over half of hash brown, then cook over medium heat until bottom is dark golden and crisp, 6 to 8 minutes.

Hash Brown Omelet with Kimchi

5. Fold hash brown in half over filling and slide onto cutting board. Cut in half, then sprinkle with cilantro and scallion greens and serve immediately with sesame-lime mayonnaise.

VARIATION
Classic Hash Browns
Omit mayonnaise, sesame oil, lime zest, kimchi, scallion, and cilantro. Substitute refined coconut oil or unsalted butter for vegetable oil.

Avocado Toast

Serves 4 `FAST`

Why This Recipe Works We can never decide whether we like savory or sweet versions of loaded toast better, but then we remind ourselves that there's no need to choose. Avocado toast—the original loaded toast—is healthy, delicious, satisfying, and here to stay. Though it's one of the simplest things to make for brunch or lunch, it's still definitely worth a discussion of how to make it even better. We took ours up a notch by whisking together a lemony vinaigrette and mixing it in as we mashed one of the avocados, giving our dish a distinct citrusy punch while preserving its bright color. Smeared on toasted rustic country bread, topped with sliced avocado for a multitextured avocado experience, and then sprinkled with a little coarse sea salt and red pepper flakes, our version of this zeitgeist definer is spectacularly tasty. See the variation if you would like to top it with fried eggs.

- 2 tablespoons extra-virgin olive oil
- 1 teaspoon grated lemon zest plus 1 tablespoon juice
- ⅛ teaspoon plus ¼ teaspoon coarse sea salt or kosher salt, divided
- ⅛ teaspoon pepper
- 2 ripe avocados
- 4 (½-inch-thick) slices crusty bread
- ¼ teaspoon red pepper flakes (optional)

1. Adjust oven rack 4 inches from broiler element and heat broiler. Whisk oil, lemon zest and juice, ⅛ teaspoon salt, and pepper together in small bowl. Halve and pit 1 avocado. Carefully make ½-inch crosshatch incisions in flesh with butter knife, cutting down to but not through skin. Insert spoon between skin and flesh, gently scoop out avocado cubes, and add to bowl with oil mixture. Mash avocado into vinaigrette with potato masher or fork. Halve remaining avocado, remove pit and peel, and slice thin; set aside.

2. Meanwhile, arrange bread in single layer on rimmed baking sheet and broil until bread is deep golden and toasted on both sides, 1 to 2 minutes per side.

3. Spread mashed avocado mixture evenly on toasts and arrange avocado slices evenly over top. Sprinkle with remaining ¼ teaspoon salt and pepper flakes, if using. Serve.

VARIATION
Avocado Toast with Fried Eggs
Crack 4 eggs into 2 small bowls (2 eggs per bowl) and sprinkle with pinch salt and pinch pepper. Heat 2 teaspoons extra-virgin olive oil in 12-inch nonstick skillet over medium-high heat until shimmering. Pour 1 bowl of eggs into 1 side of pan and second bowl into other side. Cover and cook for 1 minute. Remove skillet from heat and let sit, covered, for 15 to 45 seconds for runny yolks (white around edge of yolk will be barely opaque), 45 to 60 seconds for soft but set yolks, or about 2 minutes for medium-set yolks. Top avocado toasts with fried eggs before serving.

Black Beans on Toast with Tomato and Avocado
Serves 4 FAST

Why This Recipe Works "Beans on toast" sounds vaguely British, but this bean-topped toast has a bold Southwestern flavor profile that will liven up your morning in all-American style. Once you take a bite, the hearty rusticity of mashed black beans on toasted crusty bread elevated with a bit of spice, fresh cherry tomatoes, some creamy avocado slices, and a good squeeze of lime will be hard to argue with. And you don't even have to get any pans dirty. By simply mashing our beans in a bowl with a little hot water, olive oil, and lime zest and juice, we were able to get a flavorsome and well-textured base. For a splash of color, heat, and acidity, we loved the addition of spicy quick-pickled onions, which can be made up to a week ahead. (If you don't have them on hand, a pinch of red pepper flakes will give you some heat.) A liberal garnish of cilantro leaves freshened all the flavors. With just 10 minutes of work, we had a fantastic upgrade to loaded toast. For an accurate measure of boiling water, bring a full kettle of water to boil and then measure out the desired amount.

- 4 ounces cherry tomatoes, quartered
- 4 teaspoons extra-virgin olive oil, divided
  Pinch plus ½ teaspoon table salt, divided
- ⅛ teaspoon pepper, divided
- 1 (15-ounce) can black beans, rinsed
- ¼ cup boiling water
- ½ teaspoon grated lime zest plus 1 tablespoon juice
- 4 (½-inch-thick) slices crusty bread
- 1 ripe avocado, halved, pitted, and sliced thin
- ¼ cup Quick Sweet-and-Spicy Pickled Red Onions (page 99) (optional)
- ¼ cup fresh cilantro leaves

1. Adjust oven rack 4 inches from broiler element and heat broiler. Combine tomatoes, 1 teaspoon oil, pinch salt, and pinch pepper in bowl. Mash beans, boiling water, lime zest and juice, remaining ½ teaspoon salt, remaining pinch pepper, and remaining 1 tablespoon oil with potato masher to coarse puree in second bowl, leaving some whole beans intact.

2. Meanwhile, arrange bread in single layer on rimmed baking sheet. Broil until bread is deep golden and toasted on both sides, 1 to 2 minutes per side.

3. Spread mashed bean mixture evenly on toasts and divide avocado evenly over top. Sprinkle with tomatoes; pickled onions, if using; and cilantro. Serve.

Sautéed Grape and Almond Butter Toast

1 tablespoon refined coconut oil or unsalted butter
1 pound seedless red grapes, halved (2⅔ cups)
1 tablespoon sugar
1½ teaspoons minced fresh thyme, divided
⅛ teaspoon table salt
½ teaspoon grated lemon zest plus 1 teaspoon juice
4 (½-inch-thick) slices crusty bread
½ cup almond butter
¼ cup sliced almonds, toasted

1. Adjust oven rack 4 inches from broiler element and heat broiler. Melt oil in 12-inch nonstick skillet over medium-high heat. Add grapes, sugar, 1 teaspoon thyme, and salt, and cook, stirring occasionally, until grapes begin to soften and juices thicken, about 7 minutes; transfer to bowl, stir in lemon zest and juice, and set aside to cool slightly.

2. Meanwhile, arrange bread in single layer on rimmed baking sheet. Broil until bread is deep golden and toasted on both sides, 1 to 2 minutes per side.

3. Spread almond butter evenly over toasts and, using slotted spoon, top with grapes. Drizzle with grape juice to taste and sprinkle with almonds and remaining ½ teaspoon thyme. Serve.

Sautéed Grape and Almond Butter Toast

Serves 4 FAST

Why This Recipe Works You'll never look at PB&J the same way again after you try this sweet loaded toast, which takes America's most popular sandwich to whole new heights. Rather than load up on sugary jam, we went for a different, playful presentation: sautéed grapes. Not only did we get away with using much less sugar, but we were also able to give the grapes a creative new flavor makeover. We loved using thyme with the grapes for its warm and slightly peppery notes, and lemon zest and juice were just the thing to wake up the whole mixture. Using a 12-inch skillet was essential, as the wide surface area allowed the mixture to reduce and thicken in a much shorter time (we didn't want to wait too long to dive in). In order to make this fantastic topping really shine, we chose almond butter, as the flavor of the peanut butter we initially tried was a little too overwhelming. Finally, we topped the toast with sliced almonds for added crunch. We prefer our homemade Almond Butter (page 24) here, but you can use store-bought.

Banana-Hazelnut Toast

Serves 4 FAST

Why This Recipe Works Toast covered with chocolate-hazelnut spread and bananas is a kid-friendly favorite, but here we've given it a sophisticated, grown-up reboot. First, the chocolate-hazelnut spread: Yes, you could use the famous jarred stuff, but we created a homemade version as easy to make as it was superior in flavor and texture (like the texture of organic nut butter). Not to mention it's make-ahead friendly, vegan, and less sweet than store-bought. Next, the bananas: We wanted to caramelize them without turning them into a dessert and were able to achieve this with just a little brown sugar and water, plus a touch of cinnamon. We loved the way the cinnamon enhanced the browning of the bananas and added a fantastic warmth to the overall flavor of the toast. Finally, for added crunch: a sprinkling of toasted hazelnuts. We encourage a gentle dusting of confectioners' sugar for a pop of visual contrast. Look for yellow bananas with very few spots; overly ripe bananas will fall apart during cooking. We prefer our homemade Chocolate-Hazelnut Spread here, but you can use store-bought.

1 tablespoon refined coconut oil or unsalted butter
3 ripe bananas, peeled and sliced ½ inch thick on bias
2 tablespoons water
1 tablespoon packed brown sugar
¾ teaspoon ground cinnamon
⅛ teaspoon table salt
1 teaspoon lemon juice
4 (½-inch-thick) slices crusty bread
½ cup Chocolate-Hazelnut Spread
¼ cup skinned, chopped, and toasted hazelnuts
Confectioners' sugar (optional)

1. Adjust oven rack 4 inches from broiler element and heat broiler. Melt oil in 12-inch nonstick skillet over medium heat. Add bananas, water, sugar, cinnamon, and salt and cook, stirring frequently, until bananas have just softened at edges, 2 to 3 minutes; transfer to bowl, stir in lemon juice, and set aside to cool slightly.

2. Meanwhile, arrange bread in single layer on rimmed baking sheet. Broil until bread is deep golden and toasted on both sides, 1 to 2 minutes per side.

3. Spread chocolate-hazelnut spread evenly over toasts and top with banana mixture. Sprinkle with hazelnuts and confectioners' sugar, if using. Serve.

Almond Granola with Dried Fruit

Serves 18 (**Makes** about 9 cups)

Why This Recipe Works Store-bought granola suffers from many shortcomings. It's often gravelly and dry, overly sweet, and infuriatingly expensive. Our homemade granola boasts large clusters; a crisp, rich texture; and just a touch of toasty sweetness. We found that the secret to getting this perfect texture was to firmly pack the granola mixture into a rimmed baking sheet before baking. Once it was baked, we could break it into crunchy clumps of any size of our choosing. Chopping the almonds by hand was best for superior texture and crunch; we tried the food processor but it did a lousy job of chopping the nuts evenly. To complement the nuts, we also liked plenty of chewy, wholesome raisins. For sweetness and to bind the granola together, we added modest amounts of light brown sugar and maple syrup. A little salt and vanilla were the only other flavorings we needed. You can substitute an equal quantity of slivered or sliced almonds for the whole almonds and an equal amount of your favorite dried fruit for the raisins. Do not use quick oats in this recipe.

REMOVING SKINS FROM BLANCHED NUTS

1. Place blanched and cooled nuts in dish towel and rub to remove skins.

2. Remove nuts from towel, leaving skins behind.

Chocolate-Hazelnut Spread
Makes 1½ cups
Hazelnut oil is the best choice here, but walnut oil also works; even with vegetable oil, your spread will still be superior to store-bought. Blanching the raw hazelnuts is the easiest way to remove their skins.

2 cups hazelnuts
6 tablespoons baking soda
1 cup (4 ounces) confectioners' sugar
⅓ cup (1 ounce) unsweetened cocoa powder
2 tablespoons hazelnut oil
1 teaspoon vanilla extract
⅛ teaspoon table salt

1. Fill large bowl halfway with ice and water. Bring 4 cups water to boil. Add hazelnuts and baking soda and boil for 3 minutes. Transfer nuts to ice bath with slotted spoon, drain, and rub skins off with dish towel.

2. Adjust oven rack to middle position and heat oven to 375 degrees. Place hazelnuts in single layer on rimmed baking sheet and roast until fragrant and golden brown, 12 to 15 minutes, rotating sheet halfway through roasting.

3. Process hazelnuts in food processor until oil is released and smooth, loose paste forms, about 5 minutes, scraping down sides of bowl often.

4. Add sugar, cocoa, oil, vanilla, and salt and process until fully incorporated and mixture begins to loosen slightly and becomes glossy, about 2 minutes, scraping down sides of bowl as needed.

5. Transfer spread to jar with tight-fitting lid. (Chocolate-hazelnut spread can be stored at room temperature or refrigerated for up to 1 month.)

⅓ cup maple syrup
⅓ cup packed (2⅓ ounces) light brown sugar
4 teaspoons vanilla extract
½ teaspoon table salt
½ cup vegetable oil
5 cups old-fashioned rolled oats
2 cups raw almonds, chopped coarse
2 cups raisins, chopped

1. Adjust oven rack to upper-middle position and heat oven to 325 degrees. Line rimmed baking sheet with parchment paper. Whisk maple syrup, sugar, vanilla, and salt together in large bowl. Whisk in oil. Fold in oats and almonds until thoroughly coated.

2. Transfer oat mixture to prepared sheet and spread into thin, even layer. Using stiff metal spatula, compress oat mixture until very compact. Bake until lightly browned, 40 to 45 minutes, rotating pan halfway through baking.

3. Remove granola from oven and let sheet cool on wire rack, about 1 hour. Break cooled granola into pieces of desired size and stir in raisins. Serve. (Granola can be stored at room temperature for up to 2 weeks.)

Quinoa Granola with Sunflower Seeds and Almonds

Quinoa Granola with Sunflower Seeds and Almonds

Serves 18 (**Makes** about 9 cups)

Why This Recipe Works Once we mastered our classic oat-based granola, we wanted to branch out and experiment with an oat-free version. We loved the crunch that toasted quinoa brought to a granola mixture, and we balanced the whole grains with quinoa flakes, which mimicked the texture of rolled oats and added a more delicate crunch that tasters found appealing. Almonds and sunflower seeds were mild enough to pair well with the quinoa, while unsweetened flaked coconut contributed flavor without making our granola too sweet. To complement the earthy flavor of the quinoa, we used extra-virgin olive oil. Maple syrup and a hefty amount of vanilla rounded things out with rich, warm sweetness, and the syrup held everything together in granola's signature clumps. Stirring in dried cherries gave the finished quinoa granola a pop of bright fruitiness. We like the convenience of prewashed quinoa; rinsing removes the quinoa's bitter protective coating (called saponin). If you buy unwashed quinoa, rinse it and then spread it out on a clean dish towel to dry for 15 minutes.

½ cup maple syrup
4 teaspoons vanilla extract
½ teaspoon table salt
¼ cup extra-virgin olive oil
2 cups whole almonds, chopped coarse
2 cups unsweetened flaked coconut
1 cup quinoa flakes
1 cup prewashed white quinoa
1 cup raw sunflower seeds
2 cups dried cherries, chopped

1. Adjust oven rack to upper-middle position and heat oven to 325 degrees. Line rimmed baking sheet with parchment paper. Whisk maple syrup, vanilla, and salt together in large bowl. Whisk in oil. Fold in almonds, coconut, quinoa flakes, quinoa, and sunflower seeds until thoroughly coated.

2. Transfer quinoa mixture to prepared sheet and spread into thin, even layer. Using stiff metal spatula, compress quinoa mixture until very compact. Bake until deep golden, 45 to 55 minutes.

3. Remove granola from oven and let sheet cool on wire rack, about 1 hour. Break cooled granola into pieces of desired size and stir in dried cherries. Serve. (Granola can be stored at room temperature for up to 2 weeks.)

Three-Grain Breakfast Bowl

Serves 4

Why This Recipe Works This hearty porridge presents an ideal opportunity to enjoy several kinds of whole grains in one bowl. Millet's mellow corn-like flavor and fine, starchy texture balanced the quinoa's nutty, earthy flavor, while a smaller amount of amaranth added bold anise flavor and an intriguing, almost caviar-like texture. Cooking the grains in plenty of liquid encouraged them to swell and some to burst and release their starches, creating a creamy porridge. However, the 30-minute simmering time took longer than we wanted to wait for this hot cereal. So we hydrated the grains in hot water the night before. In the morning, we cooked the soaked grains in plant-based (or dairy) milk along with warm spices for just 8 minutes. Stirring in blueberries and a bit of maple syrup at the end accentuated the millet's sweetness, balanced the sometimes-bitter quinoa, and tamed the robust flavor of the amaranth. We like the convenience of prewashed quinoa; rinsing removes the quinoa's bitter protective coating (called saponin). If you buy unwashed quinoa, rinse it and then spread it out on a clean dish towel to dry for 15 minutes.

Carrot Spice Steel-Cut Oatmeal

    4 cups water
    ½ cup millet, rinsed
    ½ cup prewashed white quinoa
    ¼ cup amaranth, rinsed
    ½ teaspoon table salt
    1 cup plant-based milk or dairy milk, plus
       extra as needed
    ½ teaspoon ground cinnamon
    ⅛ teaspoon ground nutmeg
  7½ ounces (1½ cups) blueberries, raspberries,
       and/or blackberries
    2 tablespoons maple syrup

1. Bring water to boil in large saucepan over high heat. Remove pan from heat; stir in millet, quinoa, amaranth, and salt. Cover saucepan and let sit overnight.

2. Stir milk, cinnamon, and nutmeg into grains and bring to simmer over medium-high heat. Reduce heat to medium-low and cook, stirring occasionally, until grains are tender and mixture is thickened, 8 to 10 minutes.

3. Stir in berries and syrup and adjust consistency with additional hot milk as needed; porridge will thicken as it sits. Serve.

Carrot Spice Steel-Cut Oatmeal

Serves 4

Why This Recipe Works While mixing fruit into oatmeal is certainly welcome, carrots are a more unexpected—yet equally pleasing—addition. Here we adapted the warm flavors of carrot cake, with grated carrot, currants, toasted pecans, dark brown sugar, and cinnamon. We enhanced the carroty flavor by using a combination of carrot juice and plant-based (or dairy) milk as the cooking liquid. Most oatmeal fans agree that the steel-cut version of the grain offers superior flavor and texture, but many understandably balk at the 40-minute cooking time typically required for steel-cut oats. We were able to decrease the cooking time to only 10 minutes by stirring steel-cut oats into boiling water the night before. As with our Three-Grain Breakfast Bowl, this enabled the grains to hydrate and soften overnight. In the morning, we added our juice and milk and then simmered the mixture for just a few minutes, until thick and creamy. A brief resting period off the heat ensured the perfect consistency. The oatmeal will continue to thicken as it cools. If you prefer a looser consistency, thin the oatmeal with boiling water.

3 cups water
1 cup steel-cut oats
¾ teaspoon table salt
½ cup carrot juice
½ cup plant-based milk or dairy milk
½ cup finely grated carrot
¼ cup packed dark brown sugar
⅓ cup dried currants
½ teaspoon ground cinnamon
2 tablespoons coarsely chopped toasted pecans

1. Bring water to boil in large saucepan over high heat. Remove pan from heat; stir in oats and salt. Cover saucepan and let sit overnight.

2. Stir carrot juice, milk, carrot, sugar, currants, and cinnamon into oats and bring to boil over medium-high heat. Reduce heat to medium and cook, stirring occasionally, until oats are softened but still retain some chew and mixture thickens and resembles warm pudding, 4 to 6 minutes. Remove saucepan from heat and let sit for 5 minutes. Stir, top with pecans, and serve.

NOTES FROM THE TEST KITCHEN

DRIED FRUIT

The concentrated sweet-tart flavor of dried fruits is a delicious complement to sweet or savory dishes. Here's a quick rundown of our favorites.

Apricots Apricots treated with sulfur dioxide keep longer and have a sunny orange color; untreated apricots are much darker. They taste the same, however.

Blueberries The dried variety are typically wild blueberries, which are small and fleshy, with a highly concentrated blueberry flavor.

Cherries Ninety percent of dried cherries are made from sour cherries. Often the dried sour cherries are sweetened, but sometimes not.

Cranberries Fresh cranberries are usually infused with sweetened cranberry juice in the process of being dried.

Currants Currants are made from black Corinth grapes (not currant berries). Often called Zante currants, these fruits are smaller than raisins.

Figs Dried figs are relatively low in sugar compared to other dried fruits. Our favorite varieties are Calimyrna and Smyrna.

Goji Berries Intensely tart-sweet dried goji berries were once exotic but are now more readily available. Fresh and frozen goji berries are far more difficult to find.

Millet Porridge with Maple Syrup
Serves 4

Why This Recipe Works The fine texture and mild corny flavor of tiny millet grains make them extremely versatile in both sweet and savory applications (see our Curried Millet Cakes with Peach-Ginger Chutney on page 107 for a savory example). Sweet versions of simple millet porridge have been traditional hearty staples in eastern Europe and western Russia for centuries. For our modern take, we started by cooking the seeds in plenty of water, covered, until they turned tender; we then added plant-based (or dairy) milk for richness and continued to cook the millet, uncovered, to encourage the swollen seeds to burst and release their starch, thickening the porridge. Simple flavorings of maple syrup and cinnamon, plus a little salt, were all our porridge needed to turn it into a comforting, satisfying morning meal.

3 cups water
1 cup millet, rinsed
⅛ teaspoon ground cinnamon
⅛ teaspoon table salt
1 cup plant-based milk or dairy milk
3 tablespoons maple syrup

1. Bring water, millet, cinnamon, and salt to boil in medium saucepan over high heat. Reduce heat to low, cover, and cook until millet has absorbed all water and is almost tender, about 20 minutes.

2. Uncover and increase heat to medium, add milk, and simmer, stirring frequently, until millet is fully tender and mixture is thickened, about 10 minutes. Stir in maple syrup and serve.

Hot Quinoa Cereal with Blueberries and Almonds

Serves 6   FAST

Why This Recipe Works Toasting quinoa, as we do for Quinoa Granola with Sunflower Seeds and Almonds (page 38), brings out its deeply nutty qualities. But leaving it untoasted, as we do here, keeps its preparation quicker and its flavor profile on the more neutral side of the fence so that it can work with a variety of stir-ins. We started by cooking the grain with water until it was almost done and then we added plant-based (or dairy) milk for richness and a flavor boost and continued to cook until the milk was mostly absorbed and the quinoa had the consistency of porridge. With the technique nailed down, we looked at flavorings. Blueberries, almonds, and maple syrup were a great trio, and we particularly liked almond milk in this combo. Sweet-tart raspberries were delicious with mildly nutty sunflower seeds in a more unexpected pairing, while golden raisins, pistachios, cardamom, and brown sugar instead of maple syrup gave us an appealing version with an Indian-inspired profile. We like the convenience of prewashed quinoa; rinsing removes the quinoa's bitter protective coating (called saponin). If you buy unwashed quinoa, rinse it and then spread it out on a clean dish towel to dry for 15 minutes.

- 1 cup prewashed white quinoa
- 1 cup water
- ⅛ teaspoon table salt
- 1 cup plant-based milk or dairy milk, plus extra as needed
- 5 ounces (1 cup) fresh blueberries
- ½ cup whole almonds, toasted and chopped
- 1 tablespoon maple syrup or honey

1. Bring quinoa, water, and salt to simmer in medium saucepan over medium-high heat. Reduce heat to low, cover, and continue to simmer until quinoa is just tender, 15 to 17 minutes.

2. Uncover, stir in milk, and cook, stirring often, until milk is mostly absorbed and mixture has thickened and has consistency of porridge, about 10 minutes. Stir in blueberries, almonds, and maple syrup and adjust consistency with additional hot milk as needed; mixture will thicken as it sits. Serve.

VARIATIONS
Hot Quinoa Cereal with Raspberries and Sunflower Seeds
Substitute raspberries for blueberries and toasted sunflower seeds for almonds.

Hot Quinoa Cereal with Golden Raisins and Pistachios
Substitute ½ cup golden raisins for blueberries, shelled pistachios for almonds, and 2 tablespoons packed brown sugar for maple syrup. Add pinch ground cardamom along with raisins in step 2.

Pepita, Almond, and Goji Berry Muesli

Serves 4

Why This Recipe Works Muesli was created more than 100 years ago as a combination of rolled oats, nuts, seeds, and dried fruit soaked overnight in milk or water for improved texture and digestibility. Modern mueslis can include multitudes of ingredients, but we didn't want to get fussy. A mixture of 3 parts oats to 2 parts add-ins offered an ideal balance of tastes and textures. While traditionally everything is raw, we found that toasting the nuts and seeds brought greater complexity to this simple cereal. For the nuts, we chose almonds. Picking a seed proved trickier. Soaked flaxseeds and chia seeds were overpowering in flavor and texture, but we

Pepita, Almond, and Goji Berry Muesli

loved the richness of toasted pepitas. We then added raisins and antioxidant-packed goji berries, which benefited from the soaking, as it softened their chewy texture. We finished with a handful of fresh fruit for serving. To make a single serving, combine ½ cup muesli with ⅓ cup plant-based (or dairy) milk in bowl, cover, and refrigerate overnight. Muesli can also be served like regular cold cereal (with no overnight soaking).

1½ cups old-fashioned rolled oats
¼ cup raisins
¼ cup goji berries
¼ cup sliced almonds, toasted and chopped
¼ cup pepitas, toasted
1⅔ cups plant-based milk or dairy milk
5 ounces (1 cup) blueberries, raspberries, and/or blackberries

1. Combine oats, raisins, goji berries, almonds, and pepitas in bowl. (Muesli can be stored at room temperature for up to 2 weeks.)

2. Stir milk into muesli until combined. Cover bowl with plastic wrap and refrigerate overnight.

3. Sprinkle with berries and serve.

VARIATION
Sunflower Seed, Hazelnut, and Cherry Muesli
Substitute dried cherries for goji berries; toasted, skinned, and chopped hazelnuts for almonds; and sunflower seeds for pepitas.

Chia Pudding with Fresh Fruit and Coconut
Serves 4

Why This Recipe Works When chia seeds are combined with liquid and soaked overnight, they create a seemingly magic gel, which thickens to produce a no-cook tapioca-like pudding. Thanks to that apparent alchemy and chia's neutral flavor, the pudding makes a spectacular canvas for fruity toppings. We initially tried to cut back on the overnight soak by scalding the milk to speed up the thickening process. And it worked, sort of: After just 15 minutes, the hot pudding had thickened as much as it had after a cold overnight soak. But that speed came with downsides: a decidedly grassier, "seedier" flavor and the loss of the fresh notes we enjoyed in the cold-soaked pudding. So we stuck with the hands-off overnight method. Before we put it to bed for the night, we

gave the pudding a quick second whisk 15 minutes after its initial mixing to make sure all the chia hydrated and to prevent clumping. To flavor the base pudding, we kept things simple with vanilla extract and maple syrup—all the better to let our imagination run wild when it came to toppings.

2 cups plant-based milk or dairy milk, plus extra for serving
½ cup chia seeds
2 tablespoons maple syrup, plus extra for serving
1½ teaspoons vanilla extract
¼ teaspoon table salt
10 ounces (2 cups) blueberries, raspberries, blackberries, or sliced strawberries, and/or sliced bananas
¼ cup unsweetened flaked coconut, toasted

1. Whisk milk, chia seeds, maple syrup, vanilla, and salt together in bowl. Let mixture sit for 15 minutes, then whisk again to break up any clumps. Cover bowl with plastic wrap and refrigerate for at least 8 hours or up to 1 week.

2. Adjust consistency of pudding with additional milk as needed. Top individual portions of pudding with ½ cup fruit and 1 tablespoon coconut, and drizzle with maple syrup to taste before serving.

TOASTING COCONUT

Spread coconut in even layer on large plate and microwave on high power until golden brown, stirring at 30-second intervals. Time will vary depending on amount of coconut.

Blueberry Muffins
Serves 12 (**Makes** 12 muffins)

Why This Recipe Works The classic blueberry muffin never goes out of style, and plant-based eating doesn't mean you have to give up this comforting favorite morning treat. We tested versions with plant-based yogurt, plant-based milk, and vegetable oil, and while these swaps were fairly straightforward and interchangeable with dairy products, replacing the eggs was not as easy. As we learned, most egg substitutes do not result in a tender muffin with an open crumb. But aquafaba, the liquid in canned chickpeas that is so versatile in vegan baking, came to our rescue; when whipped with cream of tartar in a stand mixer, the aquafaba transformed into a stiff foam that trapped tiny air bubbles just like whipped eggs would do, and this translated into a fluffy muffin crumb structure identical to that of our favorite nonvegan blueberry muffin. A sprinkling of turbinado sugar over the tops sealed the deal, creating golden brown, crisp, and shimmering muffin tops that made these muffins look as appealing as those in a bakery case. You can substitute frozen (unthawed) blueberries for fresh in this recipe.

2⅔ cups (13⅓ ounces) all-purpose flour
1 cup (7 ounces) granulated sugar
1 tablespoon baking powder
½ teaspoon baking soda
¾ teaspoon table salt
5 ounces (1 cup) blueberries
1 cup plain plant-based yogurt or dairy yogurt
⅔ cup plant-based milk or dairy milk
7 tablespoons vegetable oil
1½ ounces (3 tablespoons) aquafaba (page 16)
½ teaspoon cream of tartar
2 tablespoons turbinado sugar

Chia Pudding with Fresh Fruit and Coconut

1. Adjust oven rack to upper-middle position and heat oven to 425 degrees. Thoroughly grease 12-cup muffin tin. Whisk flour, sugar, baking powder, baking soda, and salt together in large bowl. Add blueberries and gently toss to combine. Whisk yogurt, milk, and oil in second bowl until smooth; set aside.

2. Using stand mixer fitted with whisk attachment, whip aquafaba and cream of tartar on high speed until stiff foam that clings to whisk forms, 3 to 9 minutes. Using rubber spatula, fold yogurt mixture into flour mixture until no dry flour remains; do not overmix (batter will be thick). Stir one-third of whipped aquafaba into batter to lighten, then add remaining aquafaba and gently fold batter with rubber spatula until no white streaks remain.

3. Divide batter evenly among prepared muffin cups. Sprinkle turbinado sugar evenly over top. Bake until golden and toothpick inserted in center comes out clean, 18 to 22 minutes, rotating muffin tin halfway through baking. Let muffins cool in muffin tin for 20 minutes, then transfer to wire rack and let cool for at least 10 minutes. Serve warm or at room temperature.

Blueberry Muffins

Cherry, Orange, and Rosemary Muffins

Serves 12 (Makes 12 muffins)

Why This Recipe Works For this delicate, cakey muffin, we used a simple mixture of plant-based yogurt and plant-based milk to replace the usual dairy ingredients (although you can use dairy, if you like). As with our Blueberry Muffins, most of the common egg substitutes we tried gave us heavy, dense muffins, but aquafaba, the liquid found in canned chickpeas, acted as the perfect stand-in for eggs when whipped to stiff peaks and folded into the batter. While we love fresh fruit in our muffins, we also love dried fruit and wanted to incorporate that in this recipe. We first tried figs, but they absorbed too much moisture from the batter, resulting in dry muffins; plus, the crunch from the seeds was a little off-putting for some tasters. Dried cherries were the resounding winner. Lots of orange zest brightened up the muffins, while the subtle piney notes from the rosemary made them feel sophisticated.

2⅔ cups (13⅓ ounces) all-purpose flour
  1 cup (7 ounces) granulated sugar
  1 tablespoon baking powder
  ½ teaspoon baking soda
1½ teaspoons minced fresh rosemary
  ¾ teaspoon table salt
  2 cups dried cherries
  1 cup plain plant-based yogurt or dairy yogurt
  ⅔ cup plant-based milk or dairy milk
  7 tablespoons vegetable oil
  1 tablespoon grated orange zest
1½ ounces (3 tablespoons) aquafaba (page 16)
  ½ teaspoon cream of tartar
  2 tablespoons turbinado sugar

1. Adjust oven rack to upper-middle position and heat oven to 425 degrees. Thoroughly grease 12-cup muffin tin. Whisk flour, granulated sugar, baking powder, baking soda, rosemary, and salt together in large bowl. Add dried cherries and gently toss to combine. Whisk yogurt, milk, oil, and orange zest in second bowl until smooth; set aside.

2. Using stand mixer fitted with whisk attachment, whip aquafaba and cream of tartar on high speed until stiff foam that clings to whisk forms, 3 to 9 minutes. Using rubber spatula, fold yogurt mixture into flour mixture until no dry flour remains; do not overmix (batter will be thick). Stir one-third of whipped aquafaba into batter to lighten, then add remaining aquafaba and gently fold batter with rubber spatula until no white streaks remain.

3. Divide batter evenly among prepared muffin cups. Sprinkle turbinado sugar evenly over top. Bake until golden and toothpick inserted in center comes out clean, 18 to 22 minutes, rotating muffin tin halfway through baking. Let muffins cool in muffin tin for 20 minutes, then transfer to wire rack and let cool for at least 10 minutes. Serve warm or at room temperature.

Currant Scones

Serves 8 (Makes 8 scones) `FAST`

Why This Recipe Works Light, fluffy, and barely sweet, traditional British-style cream scones are made by cutting cubes of chilled butter into the dry ingredients for the greatest flakiness. As the scones bake, the butter melts, creating little air pockets. To try to replicate this, we turned to coconut oil, our preferred fat for vegan baking. Since it is solid at room temperature, it behaved similar to butter in terms of distribution throughout the dough. Because coconut oil doesn't have the water content that butter does, we found that we could skip the step of chilling the coconut oil to keep it solid while working with it. Instead, we simply pinched room-temperature coconut oil into pieces and pulsed them into the dry ingredients in the food processor for even distribution of the fat. You need room-temperature (solid) coconut oil for this recipe; it does not need to be melted. The dough will be quite soft and wet; dust the counter and your hands with flour. Make sure not to overwork the dough and to bake the scones on two stacked baking sheets so the bottoms don't scorch. Do not use dairy products in this recipe; the dough will not come together.

  2 cups (10 ounces) all-purpose flour
  3 tablespoons sugar
  1 tablespoon baking powder
  ½ teaspoon table salt
  5 tablespoons refined coconut oil
  ½ cup dried currants
  ¾ cup plus 2 tablespoons plant-based
     creamer, divided

1. Adjust oven rack to middle position and heat oven to 450 degrees. Set rimmed baking sheet in second rimmed baking sheet and line with parchment paper.

2. Pulse flour, sugar, baking powder, and salt in food processor until combined, about 3 pulses. Pinch off ¼-inch pieces of oil into flour mixture and pulse until mixture resembles coarse cornmeal with some pea-size pieces of oil remaining, about 10 pulses. Transfer mixture to large bowl and stir in currants. Stir in creamer until dough begins to form, about 30 seconds.

3. Turn dough and any floury bits out onto lightly floured counter and knead until rough, slightly sticky ball forms, 5 to 10 seconds. Pat dough into 8-inch round and cut into 8 wedges. Evenly space wedges on prepared sheet and brush tops with remaining 2 tablespoons creamer. Bake until tops are light golden brown, 12 to 15 minutes, rotating sheet halfway through baking. Transfer scones to wire rack and let cool for at least 10 minutes. Serve warm or at room temperature.

VARIATION
Lemon-Glazed Ginger Scones
Omit 2 tablespoons creamer for brushing. Substitute ½ cup chopped crystallized ginger for currants and add ginger to food processor with oil. Whisk 1¾ cups confectioners' sugar, 1 teaspoon grated lemon zest, and 3 tablespoons lemon juice in bowl until smooth. Pour glaze over cooled scones and let sit for 10 minutes before serving.

Spiced Sweet Potato Scones with Chocolate and Pepitas
Serves 8 (**Makes** 8 scones)

Why This Recipe Works The unexpected flavors in these scones will make them a highly anticipated treat on any morning table. There are plenty of pumpkin-flavored baked goods out there, so we thought sweet potato would make a fun twist on that theme. Initially we tried grating it (a no-go: it looked weirdly like shredded cheese), so then we tried microwaving a whole sweet potato and scooping out the flesh, which made for a better texture. A trio of warm spices (ginger, cinnamon, and nutmeg) enhanced the sweet potato flavor. We added a handful of pepitas for color and crunch and a generous dose of mini chocolate chips. A brush with plant-based creamer before baking gave our scones a subtle sheen worthy of the brunch table. You need room-temperature (solid) coconut oil for this recipe; it does not need to be melted. The dough will be quite soft and wet; dust the counter and your hands with flour. Make sure not to overwork the dough and to bake the scones on two stacked baking sheets so the bottoms don't scorch. Do not use dairy products in this recipe; the dough will not come together. Not all chocolate chips are vegan; read the package carefully.

Currant Scones

Spiced Sweet Potato Scones with Chocolate and Pepitas

NUTS AND SEEDS

Tiny but mighty, nuts and seeds are indispensable ingredients in any plant-based pantry. They are high in protein, with abundant healthy fats, vitamins and minerals, great texture, and rich flavor. Plus, their convenience and versatility make them a supersimple way to add all these nutrients to virtually any dish, from breakfast to main courses or sides to desserts. Here's what you need to know to make the most of these powerhouses.

Storing Nuts and Seeds All nuts and seeds are high in oil and will become rancid fairly quickly if left at room temperature. In the test kitchen, we store all nuts and seeds in the freezer in freezer-safe zipper-lock bags. They will keep for months stored this way, and there's no need to defrost before using or toasting them.

Toasting Nuts Toasting nuts deepens their flavors and gives them a satisfying crunchy texture. To toast a small amount (less than 1 cup), put the nuts in a dry small skillet over medium heat. Shake the skillet occasionally to prevent scorching and toast until they are lightly browned and fragrant, 3 to 8 minutes. To toast more than 1 cup, spread the nuts in a single layer on a rimmed baking sheet and toast in a 350-degree oven. To promote even toasting, shake the baking sheet every few minutes, and toast until the nuts are lightly browned and fragrant, 5 to 10 minutes. To avoid burning them, remove them from the skillet or baking sheet immediately after toasting.

Toasting Seeds Toast seeds in a dry 12-inch nonstick skillet over medium heat until the seeds turn golden and fragrant, about 5 minutes. To prevent burning, remove them from the skillet after toasting.

Skinning Toasted Nuts The skins from some nuts, such as hazelnuts and walnuts, can impart a bitter flavor and an undesirable texture in some dishes. To remove the skins from toasted nuts, simply rub the hot toasted nuts inside a clean dish towel.

1 small sweet potato (8 ounces), unpeeled, pricked with fork several times
1½ cups (7½ ounces) all-purpose flour
½ cup (2¾ ounces) whole-wheat flour
3 tablespoons sugar
1 tablespoon baking powder
½ teaspoon table salt
½ teaspoon ground cinnamon
½ teaspoon ground ginger
⅛ teaspoon ground nutmeg
5 tablespoons refined coconut oil
⅓ cup (2 ounces) mini bittersweet chocolate chips
¼ cup raw pepitas
¾ cup plus 2 tablespoons unsweetened plant-based creamer, divided

1. Adjust oven rack to middle position and heat oven to 400 degrees. Set rimmed baking sheet in second rimmed baking sheet and line with parchment paper. Microwave sweet potato on plate until very soft, 6 to 9 minutes, flipping potato over halfway through microwaving. Immediately slice potato in half lengthwise to release steam and set aside to cool.

2. Pulse all-purpose flour, whole-wheat flour, sugar, baking powder, salt, cinnamon, ginger, and nutmeg in food processor until combined, about 3 pulses. Pinch off ¼-inch pieces of oil into flour mixture and pulse until mixture resembles coarse cornmeal, about 10 pulses. Transfer mixture to large bowl and stir in chocolate chips and pepitas.

3. Scoop sweet potato flesh from skins into now-empty processor bowl (you should have ½ cup sweet potato); discard skins. Add ¾ cup creamer to sweet potato and process until smooth puree forms, about 10 seconds. Stir sweet potato–creamer mixture into dry ingredients until dough begins to form, about 30 seconds.

4. Turn dough and any floury bits out onto lightly floured counter and knead until rough, slightly sticky ball forms, 5 to 10 seconds. Pat dough into 8-inch round and cut into 8 wedges. Evenly space wedges on prepared sheet, and brush tops with remaining 2 tablespoons creamer. Bake until light golden brown, 16 to 18 minutes, rotating sheet halfway through baking. Transfer scones to wire rack and let cool for at least 10 minutes. Serve warm or at room temperature.

VARIATION

Maple-Glazed Spiced Sweet Potato Scones

Omit 2 tablespoons creamer for brushing. Substitute dried cranberries for mini chocolate chips. Whisk ¾ cup confectioners' sugar, 3 tablespoons maple syrup, and 1 teaspoon water in bowl until smooth. Pour glaze over cooled scones and let sit for 10 minutes before serving.

Savory Drop Biscuits

Serves 8 (Makes 8 biscuits) `FAST`

Why This Recipe Works Served for brunch alongside a scramble or our tofu frittata (page 30), simply smeared with jam, or even paired with a warm bowl of soup for lunch or dinner, drop biscuits are delicious and supereasy. These tender little breads get their name from their signature method of simply stirring the liquid ingredients (typically melted fat and buttermilk) into the dry ingredients and then "dropping" the clumpy, wet batter onto the baking sheet and popping it into the oven. The method can turn out disappointingly gummy results because of the melted fat, and we faced the same challenge while developing our vegan-optional rendition. We overcame it by melting and slightly cooling the fat before adding it to cold liquid; the melted fat then solidified into tiny clumps. These little lumps of fat worked to our advantage when stirred throughout the batter, making for consistently tender biscuits. Adding lemon juice to the batter gave our biscuits a welcome buttermilk-like tang while allowing us to use either plant-based or dairy milk, and the juice boosted the leavening power of the baking powder and baking soda to create light and fluffy biscuits. Be sure to bake the biscuits on two stacked baking sheets so the bottoms don't scorch.

- 2 cups (10 ounces) all-purpose flour
- 2 teaspoons baking powder
- ½ teaspoon baking soda
- 1 teaspoon sugar
- ¾ teaspoon table salt
- 1 cup plant-based milk or dairy milk, chilled
- ½ cup refined coconut oil or 8 tablespoons unsalted butter, melted and cooled slightly
- 1 tablespoon lemon juice

1. Adjust oven rack to middle position and heat oven to 475 degrees. Set rimmed baking sheet in second baking sheet and line with parchment paper.

2. Whisk flour, baking powder, baking soda, sugar, and salt together in large bowl. Whisk milk, melted oil, and lemon juice together in second bowl (oil will clump). Stir milk mixture into flour mixture until just incorporated.

3. Using greased ⅓-cup dry measuring cup, drop level scoops of batter 1½ inches apart on prepared sheet. Bake until tops are golden, 12 to 14 minutes, rotating sheet halfway through baking.

4. Transfer biscuits to wire rack and let cool for at least 5 minutes. Serve warm or at room temperature.

Classic Pancakes

Serves 4 to 6 `FAST`

Why This Recipe Works These buttermilk-style pancakes are fluffy, tender, and full of toasty, buttery, rise-and-shine flavor. To develop a vegan-optional version, we needed to find successful substitutes for the buttermilk and eggs—without compromising on flavor or texture. Acidic buttermilk, when combined with alkaline baking soda, yields a fluffy crumb and a rich, complex flavor in pancakes. We were able to achieve this effect using a combination of plant-based (or dairy) milk and lemon juice, plus baking soda. When we simply omitted eggs from the recipe, the pancakes were pasty and mushy. We tested our way through substitutes, and we liked the way ground flaxseeds provided structure and just the right amount of chew. We simply added the flax to the dry ingredients; the milk hydrated it and unleashed its binding properties. We prefer ground golden flaxseeds for their mild flavor and more golden color, and the marginally fluffier texture they give our pancakes, but ground brown flaxseeds can be used. The pancakes can be cooked on an electric griddle. Set the griddle temperature to 350 degrees and cook as directed.

Classic Pancakes

- 2 cups (10 ounces) all-purpose flour
- 2 tablespoons sugar
- 1 tablespoon baking powder
- ½ teaspoon baking soda
- 1 teaspoon ground golden flaxseeds
- ¾ teaspoon table salt
- 2 cups plant-based milk or dairy milk, room temperature
- 3 tablespoons refined coconut oil or unsalted butter, melted and cooled slightly, plus 2 teaspoons refined coconut oil or unsalted butter, divided
- 2 tablespoons lemon juice

1. Adjust oven rack to middle position and heat oven to 200 degrees. Set wire rack in rimmed baking sheet and place in oven. Whisk flour, sugar, baking powder, baking soda, ground flaxseeds, and salt together in large bowl. Whisk milk, 3 tablespoons melted oil, and lemon juice together in second bowl. Make well in center of flour mixture, add milk mixture to well, and gently whisk until just incorporated with few lumps remaining (do not overmix).

2. Melt 1 teaspoon oil in 12-inch nonstick skillet over medium heat. Using paper towels, carefully wipe out oil, leaving thin film of oil on bottom and sides of pan. Using ¼-cup measure, portion batter into pan in 3 places. Cook until edges are set, first side is golden, and bubbles on surface are just beginning to break, 2 to 3 minutes.

3. Flip pancakes and continue to cook until second side is golden, 1 to 2 minutes. Serve immediately or transfer to wire rack in oven and tent with aluminum foil. Repeat with remaining batter, using remaining 1 teaspoon oil as needed.

100-Percent Whole-Wheat Pancakes

Serves 4 to 6 `FAST`

Why This Recipe Works Think a whole-wheat pancake that's delicious and superlatively light and fluffy—and that can also be made vegan—is impossible? Think again, because here it is. Many whole-wheat pancakes call for a mix of whole-wheat and all-purpose flours, but we found that we got an even better result using only whole-wheat flour. That's because whole-wheat flour doesn't contribute to gluten development to the degree that white flour does, so these pancakes were ultratender. To replace the eggs, we tried multiple substitutes, but they all weighed down our pancakes. In fact, we found that, unlike with our Classic Pancakes, which became pasty and mushy without any egg substitutes,

100-Percent Whole-Wheat Pancakes

we liked these whole-wheat pancakes best with no egg replacers at all. The whole-wheat flour is higher in protein than white flour, so it's hefty enough to support a crumb that's made fluffy by just the right combination of baking soda and lemon juice. The pancakes can be cooked on an electric griddle. Set the griddle temperature to 350 degrees and cook as directed.

- 2 cups (11 ounces) whole-wheat flour
- 2 tablespoons packed brown sugar
- 2 teaspoons baking powder
- ½ teaspoon baking soda
- ¾ teaspoon table salt
- 2½ cups plant-based milk or dairy milk, room temperature
- ¼ cup refined coconut oil or 4 tablespoons unsalted butter, melted and cooled slightly, plus 2 teaspoons refined coconut oil or unsalted butter, divided
- 2 tablespoons lemon juice
- 2 teaspoons vanilla extract

1. Adjust oven rack to middle position and heat oven to 200 degrees. Set wire rack in rimmed baking sheet and place in oven.

2. Whisk flour, sugar, baking powder, baking soda, and salt together in large bowl. Whisk milk, ¼ cup melted oil, lemon juice, and vanilla together in second bowl. Make well in center of flour mixture, add milk mixture to well, and whisk until smooth.

3. Melt 1 teaspoon oil in 12-inch nonstick skillet over medium heat. Using paper towels, carefully wipe out oil, leaving thin film of oil on bottom and sides of pan. Using ¼-cup measure, portion batter into pan in 3 places. Cook until edges are set, first side is golden, and bubbles on surface are just beginning to break, 2 to 3 minutes.

4. Flip pancakes and continue to cook until second side is golden, 1 to 2 minutes. Serve immediately or transfer to wire rack in oven and tent with aluminum foil. Repeat with remaining batter, using remaining 1 teaspoon oil as needed.

Carrot Cake Pancakes
Serves 4 to 6   **FAST**

Why This Recipe Works These pancakes are carrot cake in acceptable brunch form: tangy, packed with shredded carrots and toasted walnuts, and redolent of cinnamon. We followed a similar template to our Classic Pancakes (page 47), using all-purpose flour, plant-based (or dairy) milk, lemon juice, baking soda, and ground flaxseeds to replace eggs. As a crowning touch, we made a sweetened, vanilla-scented yogurt sauce for serving—an irresistible and vegan-optional take on cream cheese frosting that makes these pancakes worthy of a leisurely weekend morning. We prefer ground golden flaxseeds for their mild flavor and more golden color, and the marginally fluffier texture they give our pancakes, but ground brown flaxseeds can be used. The pancakes can be cooked on an electric griddle. Set the griddle temperature to 350 degrees and cook as directed.

1¼	cups plain plant-based yogurt or dairy yogurt
6	tablespoons (2⅔ ounces) sugar, divided
2½	teaspoons vanilla extract, divided
2	cups (10 ounces) all-purpose flour
1	tablespoon baking powder
½	teaspoon baking soda
1½	teaspoons ground cinnamon
1	teaspoon ground golden flaxseeds
¾	teaspoon table salt
⅛	teaspoon ground nutmeg
2	cups plant-based milk or dairy milk, room temperature

3	tablespoons refined coconut oil or unsalted butter, melted and cooled slightly, plus 2 teaspoons refined coconut oil or unsalted butter, divided
2	tablespoons lemon juice
2	cups shredded carrots
¾	cup toasted chopped walnuts

1. Adjust oven rack to middle position and heat oven to 200 degrees. Set wire rack in rimmed baking sheet and place in oven. Whisk yogurt, 3 tablespoons sugar, and ½ teaspoon vanilla together in small bowl; set aside.

2. Whisk flour, baking powder, baking soda, cinnamon, ground flaxseeds, salt, nutmeg, and remaining 3 tablespoons sugar together in large bowl. Whisk milk, 3 tablespoons melted oil, lemon juice, and remaining 2 teaspoons vanilla together in second bowl. Make well in center of flour mixture, add milk mixture to well, and gently whisk until just incorporated with few lumps remaining (do not overmix). Stir in carrots until just combined.

3. Melt 1 teaspoon oil in 12-inch nonstick skillet over medium heat. Using paper towels, carefully wipe out oil, leaving thin film of oil on bottom and sides of pan. Using ¼-cup measure, portion batter into pan in 3 places. Cook until edges are set, first side is golden, and bubbles on surface are just beginning to break, 2 to 3 minutes. Sprinkle 2 teaspoons walnuts over each pancake.

4. Flip pancakes and continue to cook until second side is golden, 1 to 2 minutes. Serve immediately with yogurt sauce or transfer to wire rack in oven and tent with aluminum foil. Repeat with remaining batter, using remaining 1 teaspoon oil as needed.

Belgian Waffles
Serves 4 (**Makes** four 7-inch waffles)   **FAST**

Why This Recipe Works Belgian is our favorite style of waffle—thick, with deep pockets, plus a crispy, browned crust and a rich, custardy interior that holds up to liberal pours of maple syrup. We were delighted when we were able to create a version that met this ideal without eggs. Our waffles owe their custardy interior in large part to a key ingredient: cornstarch. Without any cornstarch, the waffles had an airy, hollow interior, while too much cornstarch yielded dense, doughy insides. A moderate amount, however, produced a delicate yet pleasantly chewy, nearly soufflé-like texture. To achieve a crisp, golden, slightly lacy exterior, we opted for coconut oil; vegetable oil yielded a tougher, chewier crust. We also found that a small amount of baking soda helped our waffles brown like

Belgian Waffles

1. Heat waffle iron according to manufacturer's instructions. Adjust oven rack to middle position and heat oven to 200 degrees. Set wire rack in rimmed baking sheet and place in oven.

2. Whisk flour, cornstarch, sugar, baking powder, baking soda, and salt together in large bowl. Whisk milk, melted oil, lemon juice, and vanilla together in second bowl. Make well in center of flour mixture, add milk mixture to well, and gently whisk until just incorporated with few lumps remaining (do not overmix).

3. Spray preheated waffle iron with vegetable oil spray. Add scant 1 cup batter to waffle iron and cook according to manufacturer's instructions until crisp, firm, and golden, 5 to 6 minutes. Serve immediately or transfer to wire rack in oven. Repeat with remaining batter.

Crunchy Cinnamon French Toast
Serves 4 **FAST**

Why This Recipe Works Since French toast is basically bread dipped into a mixture of milk and eggs, we knew it would be challenging to create a vegan-optional version. We experimented with many batters, all using plant-based milk mixed with various combinations of flour, cornstarch, aquafaba, chia seeds, and/or flaxseeds in an attempt to replace the eggs. In the end, we found that simple cornstarch created the cleanest and crispest covering for our delicate slices of bread (and it works with dairy milk, too). A persistent problem with all of our batters was gooey insides in the finished French toast. Adapting the soaking method to just barely saturate the bread before baking the slices on a sheet pan in the oven did the trick and created a pleasant contrast between a crunchy outside and a tender, custardy inside. And even better, the entire batch cooked at the same time, so no one has to wait. We developed this recipe with presliced sandwich bread of standard thickness (½ to ¾ inch thick) and roughly 4 by 6 inches in size; do not use thin-sliced sandwich bread or rustic artisan loaves. Different breads will absorb varying amounts of batter; use the lower end of the time range for soaking softer, more delicate slices. Be sure to use vegetable oil spray; it contains lecithin, which ensures that the oil stays well distributed, preventing the toast from sticking to the pan. This recipe can easily be halved; just be sure to use a smaller rimmed baking sheet.

conventional versions. The final step in getting a golden, crisp crust was nailing the cooking time; we needed to cook the waffles for 5 to 6 minutes, significantly longer than for many other waffle recipes. While many waffle makers have an indicator light and an audible alert to tell you when your waffle is done, we always suggest following the visual cues to determine doneness. Do not use dairy products in this recipe; the batter will be too liquidy and will run out the sides of the waffle iron.

- 2 cups (10 ounces) all-purpose flour
- 3 tablespoons cornstarch
- 2 tablespoons sugar
- 1 tablespoon baking powder
- ¼ teaspoon baking soda
- ½ teaspoon table salt
- 2 cups plant-based milk, room temperature
- ¼ cup refined coconut oil, melted and cooled slightly
- 1 tablespoon lemon juice
- 1 teaspoon vanilla extract

6 tablespoons (1½ ounces) cornstarch
2 tablespoons sugar
1 teaspoon ground cinnamon
¼ teaspoon ground nutmeg
¼ teaspoon table salt
1½ cups plant-based milk or dairy milk
2 tablespoons vegetable oil
2 teaspoons vanilla extract
8 slices hearty sandwich bread

1. Adjust 1 oven rack to lowest position and second rack 5 to 6 inches from broiler element. Heat oven to 425 degrees. Generously spray bottom and sides of 18 by 13-inch rimmed baking sheet with vegetable oil spray.

2. Whisk cornstarch, sugar, cinnamon, nutmeg, and salt together in large bowl. Add milk, oil, and vanilla and whisk until combined; transfer to shallow dish. Working with 1 slice of bread at a time, soak bread in milk mixture until just saturated, 3 to 5 seconds per side. Using your hands and spatula for extra support, lift bread out of batter, allowing excess batter to drip back into dish, then place on prepared sheet. Repeat with remaining bread and batter, arranging soaked bread in single layer on sheet and whisking batter between each slice to recombine.

3. Bake on lower rack until bottoms of slices are golden brown, 12 to 18 minutes, rotating sheet halfway through baking. Transfer sheet to upper rack, heat broiler, and broil until tops of slices are golden brown, watching carefully and rotating sheet as needed to prevent burning, 1 to 4 minutes.

4. Carefully flip each slice broiled side down. Serve.

Banana Bread
Serves 8 to 10 (**Makes** 1 loaf)

Why This Recipe Works Banana bread is cherished for its moist, buttery texture and deep banana flavor. Most of the starches in bananas turn to sugar as they ripen, which is why most recipes call for overripe bananas. However, while working on this stellar vegan-optional version of the beloved treat, we found ourselves turning out loaf after loaf of dense, wet, and sticky breads. That's how we discovered something surprising: Ripe but firm bananas—those that still look good enough to eat—are the best for vegan banana bread. Because just-ripe bananas are starchier, they contributed to a banana bread with a more open crumb and a structure so sturdy on its own that it didn't require the addition of any egg substitute at all. And these just-ripe bananas work great with either plant-based or dairy yogurt in the batter. If you use a 9 by 5-inch loaf pan, start checking for doneness 5 minutes earlier.

Banana Bread

2 cups (10 ounces) all-purpose flour
¾ cup (5¼ ounces) sugar
¾ teaspoon baking soda
½ teaspoon table salt
½ cup walnuts, toasted and chopped coarse (optional)
3 ripe large bananas (1¼ pounds), peeled
6 tablespoons vegetable oil
⅓ cup plain plant-based yogurt or dairy yogurt
1 tablespoon lemon juice
2 teaspoons vanilla extract

1. Adjust oven rack to lower-middle position and heat oven to 350 degrees. Grease 8½ by 4½-inch loaf pan. Whisk flour, sugar, baking soda, and salt together in large bowl. Stir in walnuts, if using; set aside.

2. Pulse bananas in food processor until mostly smooth, with some ½-inch lumps remaining, about 10 pulses. Add oil, yogurt, lemon juice, and vanilla and continue to pulse until well combined and only pea-size lumps of banana remain, about 4 pulses.

3. Gently fold banana mixture into flour mixture until just combined. Transfer batter to prepared pan and smooth top. Bake until top is firm and deep golden, about 1 hour, rotating pan halfway through baking.

4. Let bread cool in pan for 10 minutes. Remove bread from pan and let cool completely on wire rack, about 3 hours, before serving.

Zucchini Bread
Serves 8 to 10 (**Makes** 1 loaf)

Why This Recipe Works Zucchini bread, vegan or not, doesn't get enough love. Baked goods are a great way to use up a bounty of zucchini, and this quick bread, with walnuts, cinnamon, and nutmeg, is worthy of adoration. Because of its high moisture content, zucchini produces a moist crumb, but if not used correctly, it can leave baked goods extremely wet and gummy. By removing a majority of the juice from the zucchini, along with most other sources of moisture, and lowering the fat, we were able to use a whopping 1½ pounds of squash without sacrificing a moist and tender crumb. Because of the amount of moisture still given to us from the zucchini, we were even able to omit dairy altogether and use vegetable oil in lieu of eggs. If you use a 9 by 5-inch loaf pan, start checking for doneness 5 minutes earlier than advised. The zucchini mixture will at first look dry, but as it starts to shed moisture it will quickly gain a batter-like consistency. Use the large holes of a box grater to shred the zucchini.

1½ pounds zucchini, shredded
1¼ cups packed (8¾ ounces) brown sugar
6 tablespoons vegetable oil
1 teaspoon vanilla extract
1½ cups (7½ ounces) all-purpose flour
½ cup (2¾ ounces) whole-wheat flour
1 tablespoon ground cinnamon
1½ teaspoons table salt
1 teaspoon baking powder
1 teaspoon baking soda
½ teaspoon ground nutmeg
¾ cup walnuts, toasted and chopped (optional)
1 tablespoon granulated sugar

1. Adjust oven rack to middle position and heat oven to 325 degrees. Grease 8½ by 4½-inch loaf pan. Wrap zucchini in clean dish towel and squeeze thoroughly of excess moisture, discarding liquid (you should have ½ to ⅔ cup liquid). Whisk brown sugar, oil, and vanilla together in medium bowl. Fold in zucchini until combined (mixture will look dry).

Zucchini Bread

2. Whisk all-purpose flour, whole-wheat flour, cinnamon, salt, baking powder, baking soda, and nutmeg together in large bowl. Gently fold zucchini mixture and walnuts, if using, into flour mixture until just combined. Transfer batter to prepared pan, smooth top, and sprinkle with granulated sugar.

3. Bake until top is firm and toothpick inserted in center comes out with few moist crumbs attached, 1 hour 5 minutes to 1¼ hours, rotating pan halfway through baking. Let bread cool in pan on wire rack for 30 minutes. Remove bread from pan and let cool completely on wire rack, about 3 hours, before serving.

Coffee Cake
Serves 8 to 10

Why This Recipe Works A perfect, indulgent coffee cake consists of two simple elements: a rich cake and a lightly spiced crumb topping. But most dairy-free and egg-free versions we encountered were either dry and cottony or dense and sticky. We set out to make the ultimate vegan-optional coffee cake—flavorful and tender yet with enough structure to support a nutty topping. For simplicity and less cleanup, we used our food processor from start to finish to make both the topping and the batter. Substituting vegan products for the dairy elements turned out to be easy (and the two are interchangeable in this recipe), and after testing through a roster of egg substitutes, we realized that the best replacement was none at all. Our eggless coffee cake was plenty tender, but it did need more lift, so we increased the amount of leavener and liquid. We also found that using both all-purpose flour and whole-wheat flour gave our cake better structure. A final trick: Letting the cake batter rest in the pan for 15 minutes before sprinkling on the topping ensured that the cake rose properly under its weight. A bit of melted coconut oil and water were the perfect binder for a topping that formed into sturdy crumb nuggets on top of our cake.

Streusel

- ½ cup pecans, toasted
- ¼ cup packed (1¾ ounces) brown sugar
- ⅓ cup (1⅔ ounces) all-purpose flour
- ½ teaspoon ground cinnamon
- ⅛ teaspoon table salt
- 2 tablespoons refined coconut oil or unsalted butter, melted and cooled slightly
- 2 teaspoons water

Cake

- 1¼ cups (6¼ ounces) all-purpose flour
- 1¼ cups (8¾ ounces) granulated sugar
- ¾ cup (4⅛ ounces) whole-wheat flour
- 1¼ teaspoons ground cinnamon
- 1¼ teaspoons baking powder
- ½ teaspoon baking soda
- ¾ teaspoon table salt
- 6 tablespoons refined coconut oil or unsalted butter, cut into 6 pieces and softened
- 1¼ cups plant-based milk or dairy milk
- 4 teaspoons lemon juice
- 1¼ teaspoons vanilla extract

1. For the streusel Adjust oven rack to lower-middle position and heat oven to 350 degrees. Grease 9-inch spring-form pan. Place pan on rimmed baking sheet. Process pecans and sugar in food processor until finely ground, about 10 seconds. Add flour, cinnamon, and salt and pulse to combine, about 5 pulses. Add melted oil and water and pulse until oil is fully incorporated and mixture begins to form clumps, 8 to 10 pulses. Transfer streusel to bowl. Using your fingers, break apart any large clumps (streusel should have fine, sandy texture); set aside.

2. For the cake Process all-purpose flour, sugar, whole-wheat flour, cinnamon, baking powder, baking soda, and salt in clean, dry food processor until combined, about 10 seconds. Add oil and pulse until mixture resembles fine meal, five to eight 5-second pulses. Add milk, lemon juice, and vanilla; pulse until dry ingredients are moistened, 4 to 5 pulses. Scrape down sides of bowl. Continue to pulse until mixture is well combined, 4 or 5 pulses. Transfer batter to prepared pan and smooth top. Let batter rest for 15 minutes.

3. Starting at edges of pan, sprinkle streusel in even layer over batter, breaking apart any large clumps that may have formed. Bake on baking sheet until center is firm and skewer inserted into center comes out clean, 55 minutes to 1 hour. Transfer cake to wire rack and let cool in pan for 20 minutes. Remove sides of pan and let cake cool completely, about 3 hours. Slide offset spatula between cake and pan bottom and carefully slide cake onto platter. Cut into wedges with serrated knife and serve.

Coffee Cake

CHAPTER 2

SOUPS, STEWS, AND CHILIS

For more soups, stews, and chilis, see Chapter 9.

■ FAST (45 minutes or less total time)
Photos: Moroccan Lentil and Chickpea Soup; Chickpea Curry; French Onion Soup; Butternut
Squash Chili with Quinoa and Peanuts

Creamy Curried Cauliflower Soup

Serves 4 to 6

Why This Recipe Works Pureed cauliflower soups tend to be loaded with cream and thickened with flour, rendering them leaden. But thanks to cauliflower's unique qualities, we were able to create a smooth and creamy soup without the addition of dairy or other ingredients to dull the nutty, sweet flavor of this vegetable. We added the cauliflower to simmering water in two stages to bring out both the grassy flavor of lightly cooked cauliflower and the sweeter flavor of longer-cooked cauliflower in our soup. A modest amount of curry powder, sautéed onion, and leek gave the soup a delicious flavor profile. To complement the curry, we stirred in ½ cup of canned coconut milk—just enough to add some creamy flair—and a touch of lime juice. Finally, we browned some cauliflower florets to use as a flavorful garnish. Be sure to thoroughly trim the cauliflower's core of green leaves and leaf stems, which can be fibrous and can contribute to a grainy texture in the soup.

- 1 head cauliflower (2 pounds)
- ¼ cup extra-virgin olive oil, divided, plus extra for serving
- 1 leek, white and light green part only, halved lengthwise, sliced thin, and washed thoroughly
- 1 small onion, halved and sliced thin
- 1½ teaspoons table salt
- 1½ tablespoons grated fresh ginger
- 1 tablespoon curry powder
- 4½ cups water
- ½ cup canned coconut milk
- 1 tablespoon lime juice
- 2 scallions, sliced thin on bias

1. Pull off outer leaves of cauliflower and trim stem. Using paring knife, cut around core to remove; slice core thin and reserve. Cut heaping 1 cup of ½-inch florets from head of cauliflower; set aside. Cut remaining cauliflower crosswise into ½-inch-thick slices.

2. Heat 3 tablespoons oil in large saucepan over medium-low heat until shimmering. Add leek, onion, and salt and cook, stirring often, until leek and onion are softened but not browned, about 7 minutes. Stir in ginger and curry powder and cook until fragrant, about 30 seconds. Stir in water, sliced core, and half of sliced cauliflower. Increase heat to medium-high and bring to simmer. Reduce heat to medium-low and simmer gently for 15 minutes. Add remaining sliced cauliflower and simmer until cauliflower is tender and crumbles easily, 15 to 20 minutes.

3. Meanwhile, heat remaining 1 tablespoon oil in 8-inch skillet over medium heat until shimmering. Add reserved florets and cook, stirring often, until golden brown, 6 to 8 minutes; transfer to bowl and season with salt to taste.

4. Working in batches, process soup in blender until smooth, about 45 seconds. Return pureed soup to clean pot and bring to brief simmer over medium heat. Off heat, stir in coconut milk and lime juice and season with salt to taste. Serve, sprinkling individual bowls with browned florets and scallions and drizzling with extra oil.

PLANT POWER

CAULIFLOWER

Cauliflower contains a unique fiber composition that makes for a silky puree. All vegetables have both insoluble and soluble fiber. Insoluble fiber remains intact even after cooking, but the soluble kind fully breaks down during cooking, which contributes viscosity to a dish. Cauliflower has a leg up on other vegetables in that it has very little fiber overall, and half of it is soluble. This means that cauliflower is easily pureed into a velvety soup with no cream at all.

Creamy White Bean Soup

Serves 4 to 6

Why This Recipe Works This recipe delivers a creamy, smooth bean soup in less than an hour. Using canned beans (rather than dried) gave us a great head start, since they are already uniformly soft. We briefly simmered canned great Northern beans and their seasoned canning liquid with softened aromatic vegetables and herbs. Heating the beans caused their moderate level of starches to hydrate, which made the soup creamy but not stodgy. Blending the beans with some of the vegetable broth helped their skins break down so that the puree was completely smooth. Herb oil and crispy capers were quick-to-make but impressive garnishes that complemented the relatively neutral soup base with vibrant color, flavor, and texture. Use a conventional blender here; an immersion blender will not produce as smooth a soup. Do not drain or rinse the beans; their liquid contributes to the soup's flavor and body. Because the salt content of canned beans varies from brand to brand, season to taste at the end of cooking.

Herb Oil and Crispy Capers

- ⅓ cup extra-virgin olive oil
- ¼ cup capers, rinsed and patted dry
- 2 tablespoons minced fresh parsley
- 1 tablespoon chopped fresh basil

Soup

- ¼ cup refined coconut oil or 4 tablespoons unsalted butter, divided
- ½ cup chopped onion
- 1 small celery rib, chopped fine
- 3 sprigs fresh thyme
- 2 garlic cloves, sliced
  Pinch cayenne pepper
- 2 (15-ounce) cans great Northern beans
- 2 cups vegetable broth, divided
- ½ teaspoon lemon juice, plus extra for seasoning

1. For the herb oil and crispy capers Combine oil and capers in medium bowl (capers should be mostly submerged). Microwave until capers are darkened in color and have shrunk, about 5 minutes, stirring halfway through microwaving. Using slotted spoon, transfer capers to paper towel–lined plate (they will continue to crisp as they cool); set aside. Reserve caper oil.

2. For the soup Heat 2 tablespoons oil in large saucepan over medium heat until shimmering. Add onion and celery and cook, stirring frequently, until softened but not browned, 6 to 8 minutes. Add thyme sprigs, garlic, and cayenne and cook, stirring constantly, until fragrant, about 1 minute. Add beans and their liquid and stir to combine. Reduce heat to medium-low, cover, and cook, stirring occasionally, until beans are heated through and just starting to break down, 6 to 8 minutes. Remove saucepan from heat and discard thyme sprigs.

3. Process bean mixture in blender on low speed until thick, smooth puree forms, about 2 minutes. With blender running, add 1 cup broth and remaining 2 tablespoons oil. Increase speed to high and continue to process until oil is incorporated and mixture is pourable, about 1 minute.

4. Return soup to clean saucepan and whisk in remaining 1 cup broth. Cover and bring to simmer over medium heat, adjusting consistency with up to 1 cup hot water as needed. Off heat, stir in lemon juice. Season with salt and extra lemon juice to taste.

5. Stir parsley and basil into reserved caper oil. Drizzle each portion of soup with herb oil, sprinkle with capers, and serve.

Creamy Curried Cauliflower Soup

Creamy White Bean Soup

Carrot-Ginger Soup

Serves 6

Why This Recipe Works Sometimes the simplest recipes get overcomplicated as more and more versions appear. Case in point: carrot-ginger soup, whose namesake flavors often get elbowed out with the addition of other vegetables, dairy, or even fruits. For a fresh, clean-tasting soup, we decided to go back to the basics. With a combination of cooked carrots and carrot juice, we were able to achieve well-rounded, fresh carrot flavor. Using a mixture of grated fresh ginger and crystallized ginger gave us bright, punchy ginger flavor with a moderate kick of heat. Finally, for a silky-smooth texture, we added a touch of baking soda to help break down the carrots and ginger, producing a perfectly creamy soup. We finished with some simple garnishes of chopped chives and plant-based (or dairy) sour cream to provide texture and tang. In addition to these accompaniments, serve the soup with Classic Croutons (page 142), if you like.

- 2 tablespoons vegetable oil
- 2 onions, chopped fine
- ¼ cup minced crystallized ginger
- 1 tablespoon grated fresh ginger
- 2 garlic cloves, peeled and smashed
- 2 teaspoons table salt
- 1 teaspoon sugar
- 2 pounds carrots, peeled and sliced ¼ inch thick
- 4 cups water
- 1½ cups carrot juice, divided
- 2 sprigs fresh thyme
- ½ teaspoon baking soda
- 1 tablespoon cider vinegar
  Chopped chives
  Plant-based sour cream or dairy sour cream

1. Heat oil in large saucepan over medium heat. Stir in onions, crystallized ginger, fresh ginger, garlic, salt, and sugar. Cook, stirring often, until onions are softened but not browned, 5 to 7 minutes.

2. Stir in carrots, water, ¾ cup carrot juice, thyme sprigs, and baking soda. Increase heat to high and bring to simmer. Reduce heat to medium-low, cover, and simmer gently until carrots are very tender, 20 to 25 minutes.

3. Discard thyme sprigs. Working in batches, process soup in blender until smooth, 1 to 2 minutes. Return pureed soup to clean pot and stir in vinegar and remaining ¾ cup carrot juice.

4. Return soup to brief simmer over medium heat. Season with salt and pepper to taste. Serve, garnishing individual bowls with chives and sour cream.

Carrot-Ginger Soup

Sweet Potato Soup

Serves 4 to 6

Why This Recipe Works What's the secret to our creamy sweet potato soup's deep, earthy-sweet flavor? Keeping the skins in play: Making good use of the vegetable trimmings rather than simply throwing them out adds greater flavor and minimizes food waste. We peeled the potatoes and reserved one-quarter of the skins. Before simmering and pureeing the peeled potatoes, we coaxed out more natural sweetness by soaking them in hot water, which allowed their starches to turn into pure sugar. Pureeing the reserved potato peels right along with the softened potatoes added earthy depth to the natural sweetness of the potato flesh—a contrast we reinforced with a little brown sugar and a touch of cider vinegar. A sprinkling of minced chives to finish added a pop of green color and a delicate oniony flavor.

- ¼ cup refined coconut oil or 4 tablespoons unsalted butter
- 1 shallot, sliced thin
- 4 sprigs fresh thyme
- 4¼ cups water

2 pounds sweet potatoes, peeled, halved lengthwise, and sliced ¼ inch thick, ¼ of peels reserved
1 tablespoon packed brown sugar
1½ teaspoons table salt
½ teaspoon cider vinegar
¼ teaspoon pepper
Minced fresh chives

1. Melt oil in large saucepan over medium-low heat. Add shallot and thyme and cook until shallot is softened but not browned, about 5 minutes. Add water, increase heat to high, and bring to simmer. Remove pot from heat, add sweet potatoes and reserved peels, and let stand uncovered for 20 minutes.

2. Add sugar, salt, vinegar, and pepper. Bring to simmer over high heat. Reduce heat to medium-low, cover, and cook until potatoes are very soft, about 10 minutes.

3. Discard thyme sprigs. Working in batches, process soup in blender until smooth, 45 to 60 seconds. Return soup to clean pot. Bring to simmer over medium heat, adjusting consistency if desired. Season with salt and pepper to taste. Serve, topping each portion with sprinkle of chives.

Creamy Kohlrabi Soup
Serves 4 to 6

Why This Recipe Works This simple, deeply satisfying soup uses nearly every part of the vegetable—root-to-leaf cooking, so to speak. Similar to cauliflower, kohlrabi is particularly low in overall fiber, so it tends to blend up beautifully into velvety soups and purees. We started by cooking the mild-flavored kohlrabi in an aromatic base of coconut oil or butter, onions, and vegetable stock and then blending it all up. Tasters loved the smooth texture but wanted even more kohlrabi flavor. Switching from broth to water helped to highlight the delicate flavor of the vegetable, but to really amplify the brassica flavor, we added a bit of dry mustard. (Brassicas like kohlrabi belong to the mustard family and share the same aromatic compounds that give mustard its characteristic zing.) To give more richness and body to the soup, we added a bit of plant-based milk to this base. For textural variation, we even cooked the kohlrabi greens in the soup at the end, which added a welcome element of contrast. Macadamia nuts and chives sprinkled on top made a crunchy garnish. If your kohlrabi comes without its leaves, you can substitute 4 ounces kale, stemmed and cut into 1-inch pieces.

¼ cup refined coconut oil or 4 tablespoons unsalted butter
1 onion, chopped
1¼ teaspoons table salt
4 pounds kohlrabi with leaves, kohlrabi trimmed, peeled, and cut into ½-inch pieces (6 cups), leaves stemmed and cut into 1-inch pieces (2 cups)
2 cups water, plus extra as needed
1 cup plant-based milk or dairy whole milk
1½ teaspoons dry mustard
⅓ cup salted dry-roasted macadamia nuts, chopped coarse
1 tablespoon minced fresh chives

1. Melt oil in Dutch oven over medium heat. Add onion and salt and cook, stirring occasionally, until softened, about 5 minutes. Stir in kohlrabi pieces, water, and milk and bring to simmer. Cover, reduce heat to medium-low, and cook, stirring occasionally, until kohlrabi is tender (paring knife should slip easily in and out of pieces), 10 to 12 minutes.

2. Using slotted spoon, transfer 1½ cups kohlrabi to bowl. Continue to cook soup, covered, until remaining kohlrabi is very tender and easily breaks apart when poked with paring knife, 6 to 8 minutes. Stir in mustard.

3. Working in batches, process soup in blender until smooth, about 1 minute. Return soup to now-empty pot and bring to simmer over medium-low heat. Add kohlrabi leaves and cook, stirring occasionally, until tender and vibrant green, about 5 minutes. Off heat, stir in reserved cooked kohlrabi. Adjust consistency with extra hot water as needed. Season with salt to taste. Sprinkle individual portions with macadamia nuts and chives before serving.

Chickpea Noodle Soup
Serves 6

Why This Recipe Works Chicken noodle soup is often thought of as the ultimate comfort food, so we took it as a personal challenge to create a robust plant-based version that anyone would be excited to make. Veganizing this deeply savory classic seemed daunting, but we actually found it totally achievable with a pantry-friendly combination of broth and noodles. To replace the chicken, we chose chickpeas; we liked the creamy texture, neutral flavor, and heartiness they added to the soup—and the fun phonetic similarity between the two ingredients wasn't lost on us. We sautéed onion, carrots, and celery to infuse our soup with flavor, but this broth still lacked the soul-satisfying comfort of chicken noodle. We tested various go-to plant-based flavor enhancers ranging from miso paste to porcini powder before settling on a unanimous favorite: Umami-packed nutritional yeast turned our soup from ordinary to one that reminded us of Grandma's. Simmering the chickpeas, sautéed aromatics, and broth together before adding the noodles fully developed the soup's flavor while also creating a creamy texture in the beans.

- 2 tablespoons vegetable oil
- 1 onion, chopped fine
- 3 carrots, peeled and sliced ¼ inch thick
- 2 celery ribs, sliced ¼ inch thick
- ¼ teaspoon pepper
- 3 tablespoons nutritional yeast
- 2 teaspoons minced fresh thyme or ¾ teaspoon dried
- 2 bay leaves
- 6 cups vegetable broth
- 2 (15-ounce) cans chickpeas, rinsed
- 2 ounces (½ cup) ditalini pasta
- 2 tablespoons minced fresh parsley

1. Heat oil in Dutch oven over medium heat until shimmering. Add onion, carrots, celery, and pepper and cook, stirring occasionally, until softened, 5 to 7 minutes. Stir in nutritional yeast, thyme, and bay leaves and cook until fragrant, about 30 seconds.

2. Stir in broth and chickpeas and bring to boil. Reduce heat to medium-low and simmer, partially covered, until flavors meld, about 10 minutes.

3. Stir in pasta, increase heat to medium-high, and boil until just tender, about 10 minutes. Off heat, discard bay leaves and stir in parsley. Season with salt and pepper to taste, and serve.

Black Bean Soup
Serves 6

Why This Recipe Works Sweet, spicy, and smoky flavors are all carefully balanced in this luscious black bean soup. Because the beans are so prominent here, we used dried beans, which released flavor and texture into the broth as they cooked. Usually we soak dried beans overnight to soften their skins and promote even cooking, but since getting some blown-out beans actually contributed to the thick texture we wanted, we skipped this step. To enhance the savory elements, we added dried porcini mushrooms and bay leaves to the simmering liquid. Aromatic onions, celery, and carrot, plus cumin and red pepper flakes, rounded out the flavors. Dried beans tend to cook unevenly without soaking, so be sure to taste several beans to determine their doneness in step 1. You can prepare the soup ingredients while the beans simmer. Garnishes are essential for this soup, as they add not only flavor but also texture and color. Serve with lime wedges, minced fresh cilantro, diced red onion, and diced avocado.

Beans
- 1 pound (2½ cups) dried black beans, picked over and rinsed
- 5 cups water, plus extra as needed
- 1 ounce dried porcini mushrooms, rinsed and minced
- 2 bay leaves
- 1 teaspoon table salt
- ⅛ teaspoon baking soda

Soup
- 3 tablespoons extra-virgin olive oil
- 2 large onions, chopped fine
- 3 celery ribs, chopped fine
- 1 large carrot, peeled and chopped fine
- 6 garlic cloves, minced
- 1½ tablespoons ground cumin
- ½ teaspoon red pepper flakes
- 6 cups vegetable broth
- 2 tablespoons cornstarch
- 2 tablespoons water
- 2 tablespoons lime juice

1. For the beans Combine all ingredients in large saucepan. Bring to boil, skimming any impurities that rise to surface. Cover, reduce heat to low, and simmer gently until beans are tender, 1¼ to 1½ hours. (If after 1½ hours beans are not tender, add 1 cup more water and continue to simmer until beans are tender.) Discard bay leaves; do not drain beans.

2. For the soup Heat oil in Dutch oven over medium heat until shimmering. Add onions, celery, and carrot and cook until vegetables are softened and lightly browned, 12 to 15 minutes.

3. Stir in garlic, cumin, and pepper flakes and cook until fragrant, about 1 minute. Stir in broth and cooked beans with their cooking liquid and bring to boil. Reduce heat to medium-low and cook, uncovered and stirring occasionally, until flavors have blended, about 30 minutes.

4. Puree 1½ cups beans and 2 cups liquid in blender until smooth, about 1 minute, then return to pot. Whisk cornstarch and water together in bowl, then gradually stir half of cornstarch mixture into simmering soup. Continue to simmer soup, stirring occasionally, until slightly thickened, 3 to 5 minutes. (If at this point soup is thinner than desired, repeat with remaining cornstarch mixture.) Off heat, stir in lime juice and season with salt and pepper to taste. Serve.

Classic Tuscan White Bean Soup with Egg

Soup

1 large onion, chopped
2 celery ribs, chopped
4 garlic cloves, peeled
1 (28-ounce) can whole peeled tomatoes
½ cup extra-virgin olive oil
¾ teaspoon table salt
⅛ teaspoon red pepper flakes
8 cups vegetable broth
1 fennel bulb, 2 tablespoons fronds minced, stalks discarded, bulb halved, cored, and cut into ½-inch pieces
2 (15-ounce) cans cannellini beans, drained with liquid reserved, beans rinsed
1 small head escarole (10 ounces), trimmed and cut into ½-inch pieces
½ cup chopped fresh parsley
1 tablespoon minced fresh oregano
Grated Pecorino Romano cheese (optional)
Lemon wedges

Toast

10 (½-inch-thick) slices thick-crusted country bread
¼ cup extra-virgin olive oil
⅛ teaspoon table salt
Pinch pepper

Classic Tuscan White Bean Soup

Serves 8 to 10

Why This Recipe Works Acquacotta is one of Italy's great traditional soups, originating in Tuscany but now found in various renditions around that country. Our version features creamy cannellini beans (canned for convenience), faintly bitter escarole, tender fennel, and chopped tomatoes. Though "acquacotta" translates as "cooked water," a name that reflects its humble peasant origins, we amped up the flavor by using vegetable broth and a soffritto, a mixture of sautéed onion, celery, and garlic. We thickened the broth with the bean canning liquid and served our finished soup in the traditional Tuscan way: ladled over toasted and seasoned country bread, turning a humble vegetable soup into a hearty one-bowl meal. If you would like to use cheese, we prefer the robust flavor of Pecorino Romano here. And if you would like to try another traditional version of acquacotta that incorporates egg yolks to further thicken and enrich the soup, see the variation.

1. For the soup Pulse onion, celery, and garlic in food processor until very finely chopped, 15 to 20 pulses, scraping down sides of bowl as needed. Transfer onion mixture to Dutch oven. Add tomatoes and their juice to now-empty processor and pulse until tomatoes are finely chopped, 10 to 12 pulses; set aside.

2. Stir oil, salt, and pepper flakes into onion mixture. Cook over medium-high heat, stirring occasionally, until light brown fond begins to form on bottom of pot, 12 to 15 minutes. Stir in tomatoes, increase heat to high, and cook, stirring frequently, until mixture is very thick and rubber spatula leaves distinct trail when dragged across bottom of pot, 9 to 12 minutes.

3. Add broth and fennel bulb to pot and bring to simmer. Reduce heat to medium-low and simmer until fennel begins to soften, 5 to 7 minutes. Stir in beans and escarole and cook until fennel is tender, about 10 minutes.

4. Stir reserved bean liquid into soup. Stir in parsley, oregano, and fennel fronds. Season with salt and pepper to taste.

5. For the toast Adjust oven rack 5 inches from broiler element and heat broiler. Place bread on aluminum foil–lined rimmed baking sheet, drizzle with oil, and sprinkle with salt and pepper. Broil until bread is deep golden brown.

6. Place 1 slice bread in bottom of each individual serving bowl. Ladle soup over toasted bread. Serve, passing Pecorino, if using, and lemon wedges separately.

VARIATION
Classic Tuscan White Bean Soup with Egg
In step 4, whisk 2 large egg yolks with reserved bean liquid before stirring into soup.

Butternut Squash and White Bean Soup with Parsley-Sage Pesto

Serves 6 to 8

Why This Recipe Works This rustic version of butternut squash soup more than holds its own as a meal. Instead of the usual creamy pureed style of butternut squash soup, we opted for something a little different, featuring chunks of squash paired with creamy cannellini beans to give our soup some heft and plenty of varying textures. Since we were wrangling the squash, we chose canned cannellini beans for greater convenience. Because the bulb portion of the squash is difficult to cut into cubes that will cook evenly, and because it naturally cooks faster than the denser neck portion, we cut the bulb into wedges, cooked them in the broth until they were soft, and then mashed them to make a "squash stock" that gave our soup base body and flavor. We then cooked the neck portion, cut into chunks, in this stock. A swirl of parsley-sage pesto, which we quickly made in the food processor, lent just the right bright, fresh herbal finish. You can substitute our Vegan Pesto (page 23) for the pesto in this recipe.

Parsley-Sage Pesto
½ cup walnuts, toasted
2 garlic cloves, minced
1 cup fresh parsley leaves
½ cup fresh sage leaves
¾ cup extra-virgin olive oil
⅛ teaspoon salt

Butternut Squash and White Bean Soup with Parsley-Sage Pesto

Soup
1 (2- to 2½-pound) butternut squash, peeled
4 cups vegetable broth
3 cups water
5 tablespoons refined coconut oil or unsalted butter, divided
1 tablespoon soy sauce
1 pound leeks, white and light green parts only, halved lengthwise, sliced thin, and washed thoroughly
1 tablespoon tomato paste
2 garlic cloves, minced
¾ teaspoon table salt
¼ teaspoon pepper
3 (15-ounce) cans cannellini beans
1 teaspoon white wine vinegar

1. For the pesto Pulse walnuts and garlic in food processor until coarsely chopped, about 5 pulses. Add parsley and sage. With processor running, slowly add oil until incorporated. Transfer to bowl, stir in salt, and season with pepper to taste; set aside.

2. For the soup Cut round bulb section off squash and cut in half lengthwise. Discard seeds, then cut each half into 4 wedges.

3. Bring squash wedges, broth, water, ¼ cup oil, and soy sauce to boil in medium saucepan over high heat. Reduce heat to medium, partially cover, and simmer vigorously until squash is very tender and starting to fall apart, about 20 minutes. Remove pot from heat and use potato masher to mash squash, still in broth, until completely broken down. Cover to keep warm; set aside.

4. While broth cooks, cut neck of squash into ½-inch pieces. Heat remaining 1 tablespoon oil in Dutch oven over medium heat until shimmering. Add leeks and tomato paste and cook, stirring occasionally, until leeks are softened and tomato paste is darkened, about 5 minutes. Add garlic and cook until fragrant, about 30 seconds. Add squash pieces, salt, and pepper and cook, stirring occasionally, for 5 minutes. Add squash broth and bring to simmer. Partially cover and cook for 10 minutes.

5. Add beans and their liquid, partially cover, and cook, stirring occasionally, until squash is just tender, 15 to 20 minutes. Stir in vinegar and season with salt and pepper to taste. Serve, passing pesto separately.

Lentil and Escarole Soup
Serves 6

Why This Recipe Works When cooked properly in soup, lentils should have a delicate, firm-tender bite and deep, earthy flavor. We achieved that goal here, but the real revelation is their partner, the escarole. While escarole is common enough as a soup ingredient, recipes typically call for a long simmering time after it's added. Here we stirred it in toward the end of cooking so that the leaves retained much of their sturdy chicory character and flavor. The optional Parmesan rind adds some umami, but of course you may omit it. We prefer lentilles du Puy (French green lentils) or brown lentils for this soup; black will also work, but don't use red or yellow (note that cooking times may vary depending on the type of lentils you use).

¼ cup extra-virgin olive oil, plus extra for serving
1 onion, chopped fine
1 carrot, peeled and chopped fine
1 celery rib, chopped fine
½ teaspoon table salt
6 garlic cloves, sliced thin
2 tablespoons minced fresh parsley

4 cups vegetable broth, plus extra as needed
3 cups water
8 ounces (1¼ cups) lentilles du Puy or brown lentils, picked over and rinsed
1 (14.5-ounce) can diced tomatoes
1 Parmesan cheese rind (optional)
2 bay leaves
½ head escarole (8 ounces), trimmed and cut into ½-inch pieces
Vegan Parmesan Substitute (page 27) or grated dairy Parmesan

1. Heat oil in Dutch oven over medium heat until shimmering. Add onion, carrot, celery, and salt and cook until softened and lightly browned, 8 to 10 minutes. Stir in garlic and parsley and cook until fragrant, about 30 seconds. Stir in broth; water; lentils; tomatoes and their juice; Parmesan rind, if using; and bay leaves and bring to simmer. Cover, leaving lid slightly ajar, reduce heat to medium-low, and simmer until lentils are tender, 25 to 30 minutes.

2. Discard Parmesan rind, if using, and bay leaves. Stir in escarole, 1 handful at a time, and cook until wilted, about 5 minutes. Adjust consistency with extra hot broth as needed. Season with salt and pepper to taste. Drizzle individual portions with extra oil and serve, passing grated vegan Parmesan substitute separately.

Red Lentil Soup with North African Spices
Serves 6

Why This Recipe Works Green or brown lentils are the more conventional choice when making lentil soup, but this version of lentil soup uses colorful, quick-cooking red lentils, which are mashed into a rustic, textural puree after cooking. To start, a spice mix of coriander, cumin, ginger, cinnamon, black pepper, and cayenne brought warm complexity in minutes as we bloomed them in our pot after sautéing an onion. Tomato paste and garlic completed the base before the addition of the lentils, and a mix of vegetable broth and water gave the soup a full, rounded character. After only 15 minutes of cooking, the lentils were soft enough to be pureed simply with a whisk. A generous dose of lemon juice brought all the flavors into focus, and a drizzle of spice-infused oil and a sprinkle of fresh cilantro completed the transformation of commonplace ingredients into a richly flavored yet wholly comforting soup.

¼ cup extra-virgin olive oil, divided
1 large onion, chopped fine
½ teaspoon table salt
¾ teaspoon ground coriander
½ teaspoon ground cumin
¼ teaspoon ground ginger
¼ teaspoon pepper
⅛ teaspoon ground cinnamon
   Pinch cayenne pepper
1 tablespoon tomato paste
1 garlic clove, minced
4 cups vegetable broth, plus extra as needed
2 cups water
10½ ounces (1½ cups) red lentils, picked over and rinsed
2 tablespoons lemon juice
1½ teaspoons dried mint, crumbled
1 teaspoon paprika
¼ cup chopped fresh cilantro

1. Heat 2 tablespoons oil in large saucepan over medium heat until shimmering. Add onion and salt and cook, stirring occasionally, until softened, about 5 minutes. Stir in coriander, cumin, ginger, pepper, cinnamon, and cayenne and cook until fragrant, about 2 minutes. Stir in tomato paste and garlic and cook for 1 minute.

2. Stir in broth, water, and lentils and bring to vigorous simmer. Cook, stirring occasionally, until lentils are soft and about half are broken down, about 15 minutes.

3. Whisk soup vigorously until broken down to coarse puree, about 30 seconds. Adjust consistency with extra hot broth as needed. Stir in lemon juice and season with salt to taste. Cover and keep warm.

4. Heat remaining 2 tablespoons oil in 8-inch skillet over medium heat until shimmering. Off heat, stir in mint and paprika. Serve soup, drizzling individual portions with 1 teaspoon spiced oil and sprinkling with cilantro.

Mushroom Barley Soup
Serves 6 to 8

Why This Recipe Works Both mushrooms and barley pack unique, robust flavors that can shine on their own or bring out the best in others. In this case, make that "each other." A richly flavored soup punctuated with pieces of meaty mushroom and nuggets of chewy barley, this combo is just the thing to take the bite out of a cold winter's night. The trick here was getting the earthy savoriness of the mushrooms to peacefully coexist with the sweet nuttiness of the barley. We found that although

vegetable broth worked well, our deeply flavored Umami Broth was the perfect bridge to join these ingredients together harmoniously. Carrots complemented the sweetness of the barley, garlic enhanced the mushrooms, and thyme was another flavor bridge. If cremini or portobello mushrooms are unavailable, use white button mushrooms, though the soup won't be as flavorful. You can also use a combination of white button mushrooms and cremini or portobello mushrooms.

3 tablespoons extra-virgin olive oil
1 onion, chopped fine
1 pound cremini mushrooms, stemmed and quartered
1 pound portobello mushrooms, stemmed and cut into ¼-inch pieces
¾ teaspoon table salt, divided
2 carrots, peeled and chopped
3 garlic cloves, minced
9 cups Umami Broth (page 22) or vegetable broth
½ cup pearl barley
2 teaspoons minced fresh thyme or ½ teaspoon dried

1. Heat oil in large Dutch oven over medium-high heat until shimmering. Add onion and cook until softened, about 5 minutes. Stir in cremini mushrooms, portobello mushrooms, and ¼ teaspoon salt and cook until mushrooms have softened and browned, 10 to 15 minutes.

2. Stir in carrots and garlic and cook for 1 minute. Stir in broth, barley, thyme, and remaining ½ teaspoon salt. Bring to simmer and cook until barley is tender, about 50 minutes. Season with salt and pepper to taste, and serve.

Turkish Tomato, Bulgur, and Red Pepper Soup
Serves 6 to 8

Why This Recipe Works Many soups hailing from the Mediterranean and Middle East are intriguing because they are often enriched with good-for-you grains that fill you up— perfect for a plant-based dinner. A case in point is this Turkish tomato and red bell pepper soup that incorporates bulgur. We started by softening the red peppers and onion before creating a solid flavor backbone with garlic, tomato paste, white wine, dried mint, smoked paprika, and red pepper flakes. For additional smokiness and umami flavor, canned fire-roasted tomatoes did the trick. When stirred into the soup, the bulgur absorbed the surrounding flavors and gave off some of its starch, which created a silky texture. Since bulgur is so

Turkish Tomato, Bulgur, and Red Pepper Soup

1. Heat oil in Dutch oven over medium heat until shimmering. Add bell peppers, onion, salt, and pepper and cook until vegetables are softened and lightly browned, 6 to 8 minutes. Stir in garlic, dried mint, paprika, and pepper flakes and cook until fragrant, about 30 seconds. Stir in tomato paste and cook for 1 minute.

2. Stir in wine, scraping up any browned bits, and simmer until reduced by half, about 1 minute. Add tomatoes and their juice and cook, stirring occasionally, until tomatoes soften and begin to break apart, about 10 minutes.

3. Stir in broth, water, and bulgur and bring to simmer. Reduce heat to low, cover, and simmer gently until bulgur is tender, about 20 minutes. Season with salt and pepper to taste. Serve, sprinkling individual bowls with mint.

Tortilla Soup
Serves 6 to 8 **FAST**

Why This Recipe Works Chicken may seem integral to classic tortilla soup (known in Mexico as sopa Azteca), but this deeply flavorful version made us change our outlook. By breaking down tortilla soup into its three main components—the flavor base (tomatoes, garlic, onion, and chiles), the stock, and the garnishes (including fried tortilla strips)—we found that we could make a compelling plant-based version. Typically, the vegetables are charred on a comal (griddle) and then pureed and fried. We made a puree from smoky chipotles in adobo sauce, tomatoes, onion, garlic, and jalapeño and then fried the puree in a small amount of oil. We then added vegetable broth along with cilantro and oregano (a substitute for the Mexican herb epazote). For hearty protein, we used black beans. To garnish, we oven-toasted lightly oiled tortilla strips. For a spicier soup, reserve, mince, and add the jalapeño ribs and seeds. Serve with diced avocado, chopped fresh cilantro, and lime wedges, if desired.

quick-cooking, we stirred it in toward the end of cooking, giving it just enough time to become tender. A sprinkle of fresh mint gave the soup a final punch of flavor. When shopping, don't confuse bulgur with cracked wheat, which has a much longer cooking time and will not work in this recipe.

- 2 tablespoons extra-virgin olive oil
- 2 red bell peppers, stemmed, seeded, and chopped
- 1 onion, chopped
- ¾ teaspoon table salt
- ¼ teaspoon pepper
- 3 garlic cloves, minced
- 1 teaspoon dried mint, crumbled
- ½ teaspoon smoked paprika
- ⅛ teaspoon red pepper flakes
- 1 tablespoon tomato paste
- ½ cup dry white wine
- 1 (28-ounce) can diced fire-roasted tomatoes
- 4 cups vegetable broth
- 2 cups water
- ¾ cup medium-grind bulgur, rinsed
- ⅓ cup chopped fresh mint

- 8 (6-inch) corn tortillas, cut into ½-inch-wide strips
- 3 tablespoons vegetable oil, divided
  Pinch plus ⅛ teaspoon table salt, divided
- 2 tomatoes, cored and quartered
- 1 large white onion, quartered
- ½ jalapeño chile, stemmed, seeded, and quartered
- 4 garlic cloves, peeled
- 1 tablespoon minced canned chipotle chile in adobo sauce
- 8 cups vegetable broth
- 2 (15-ounce) cans black beans, rinsed
- 8 sprigs fresh cilantro
- 1 sprig fresh oregano

1. Adjust oven rack to middle position and heat oven to 425 degrees. Toss tortilla strips with 1 tablespoon oil, spread on rimmed baking sheet, and bake, stirring occasionally, until deep golden brown and crisp, 8 to 12 minutes. Sprinkle with pinch salt and transfer to paper towel–lined plate.

2. Meanwhile, process tomatoes, onion, jalapeño, garlic, and chipotle in food processor until smooth, about 30 seconds, scraping down sides of bowl as needed. Heat remaining 2 tablespoons oil in Dutch oven over medium heat until shimmering. Add pureed tomato mixture and remaining ⅛ teaspoon salt and cook, stirring frequently, until mixture has darkened in color and liquid has evaporated, about 10 minutes.

3. Stir in broth, beans, cilantro sprigs, and oregano sprig, scraping up any browned bits, and bring to simmer. Cook until flavors meld, about 20 minutes.

4. Off heat, remove herb sprigs and season with salt and pepper to taste. Place some tortilla strips in bottom of individual bowls and ladle soup over top. Serve, passing remaining tortilla strips separately.

French Onion Soup
Serves 6

Why This Recipe Works It's hard to imagine this bistro classic without molten cheesy toast floating on a rich and savory beef broth. But imagine we did, and we guarantee our vegan version is every bit as satisfying. Like the beefy version, this is a bit of a project, but we broke it down into parts. First, the broth: We turned to our Umami Broth, full of glutamate-packed ingredients that gave us deeper flavor than regular vegetable broth. Next, the croutons: We knew melted plant-based cheese would be a disappointing sub for the traditional Gruyère. Instead, we tossed cubes of baguette in a mixture of oil, nutritional yeast, miso, mustard, and vinegar and then baked them, giving us crisp-on-the-outside and chewy-on-the-inside bits of bread with the rich, nutty, tangy flavors of aged cheese. (The croutons were so delicious on their own we were afraid we might not have any left for the soup!) Finally, we turned to our favorite, almost hands-free method of caramelizing onions: baking them in the oven, thus minimizing the time needed to tend to them on the stove. No longer just in our imagination, our dream was realized—no cheese or beef needed. That being said, if you would like to use Gruyère, see the variation. We prefer yellow onions in this recipe; do not use sweet onions (Vidalia or Walla Walla). The Dutch oven will be completely full when you add the onions, but they will shrink in volume significantly.

Soup
- 4 pounds onions, halved and sliced ¼ inch thick through root end
- 3 tablespoons extra-virgin olive oil
- 1½ teaspoons table salt, divided
- 2½ cups water, divided
- ½ cup dry sherry
- 6 cups Umami Broth (page 22)
- 6 sprigs fresh thyme, tied with kitchen twine
- 1 bay leaf
- ½ teaspoon pepper
- ½ teaspoon sugar

Umami Croutons
- ¼ cup extra-virgin olive oil
- 3 tablespoons nutritional yeast
- 1 teaspoon white miso
- 1 teaspoon Dijon mustard
- ¼ teaspoon distilled white vinegar
- ⅛ teaspoon table salt
- 6 ounces baguette, cut into 1-inch pieces (5 cups)

1. For the soup Adjust oven rack to lower-middle position and heat oven to 400 degrees. Combine onions, oil, and 1 teaspoon salt in Dutch oven. Cover, transfer pot to oven, and cook for 1 hour (onions will be moist and slightly reduced in volume). Remove pot from oven and use wooden spoon to stir onions, scraping any browned onions from sides of pot. Return pot to oven with lid slightly ajar and continue to cook until onions are very soft and golden brown, 1¼ to 1½ hours longer, stirring onions and scraping up any browned bits from bottom and sides of pot after 1 hour. (Onions, prepared through step 1, can be cooled in pot and refrigerated for up to 3 days before proceeding.)

2. Carefully remove pot from oven and place over medium heat. Reduce oven temperature to 350 degrees. Cook onions, stirring frequently and scraping up any browned bits on bottom and sides of pot until onions are well browned, 10 to 15 minutes (reduce heat to medium-low if onions brown too quickly). Stir in ½ cup water, scraping up any browned bits, and cook until water mostly evaporates, about 2 minutes. Stir in sherry and cook, scraping up any browned bits, until sherry mostly evaporates, about 3 minutes.

3. Stir in broth, thyme sprigs, bay leaf, pepper, sugar, remaining ½ teaspoon salt, and remaining 2 cups water. Bring to simmer, then cover and simmer over low heat for 30 minutes. Discard thyme sprigs and bay leaf and season with salt and pepper to taste.

French Onion Soup

4. For the croutons While soup simmers, whisk oil, nutritional yeast, miso, mustard, vinegar, and salt together in large bowl. Add baguette and, using your hands, massage oil mixture into bread. Transfer to rimmed baking sheet and bake until golden brown and crisp, 13 to 15 minutes. (Croutons may be stored in airtight container for up to 1 day.)

5. Divide soup evenly among individual serving bowls and top with croutons. Serve.

VARIATION

French Onion Soup with Gruyère Croutons

For croutons, omit nutritional yeast, miso, mustard, and vinegar; increase salt to ¼ teaspoon and add ¼ teaspoon pepper. After baking croutons in step 4, remove croutons from oven and increase oven temperature to 500 degrees. Arrange six 12-ounce ovensafe crocks on second rimmed baking sheet, then divide soup evenly among crocks and top with croutons. Sprinkle 2 cups shredded Gruyère cheese evenly over croutons and bake until Gruyère is melted and soup is bubbly around edges, 5 to 7 minutes. Let cool for 5 minutes before serving.

Vegetable Tagine with Chickpeas and Olives
Serves 4 **FAST**

Why This Recipe Works Traditional North African tagines—fragrant, spiced stews of vegetables, beans, dried fruits, and slowly braised meats—are long-simmered affairs with myriad ingredients. But emphasizing the vegetables and skipping the meat makes this tagine fast enough for any weeknight without sacrificing flavor. We used canned chickpeas for speed, and microwaving the potatoes and carrots before adding them to the pot streamlined the process even further. Some tagines call for a laundry list of individual spices; we used garam masala, plus paprika. Green olives, golden raisins, and lemon emphasized Moroccan flavors. We prefer our homemade Garam Masala (page 330), but you may use store-bought. Serve with couscous or rice.

- 1 pound red potatoes, cut into ½-inch chunks
- 1 pound carrots, peeled and cut into ½-inch pieces
- ¼ cup extra-virgin olive oil, divided
- 1 teaspoon table salt
- ½ teaspoon pepper
- 1 onion, halved and sliced thin
- 4 (3-inch) strips lemon zest, sliced into matchsticks, plus 2 tablespoons juice
- 5 garlic cloves, minced
- 4 teaspoons paprika
- 2 teaspoons garam masala
- 3 cups vegetable broth
- 2 (15-ounce) cans chickpeas, rinsed
- ½ cup pitted green olives, halved
- ½ cup golden raisins
- ¼ cup minced fresh cilantro

1. Combine potatoes, carrots, 2 tablespoons oil, salt, and pepper in bowl, cover, and microwave until vegetables begin to soften, about 10 minutes.

2. Meanwhile, heat remaining 2 tablespoons oil in Dutch oven over medium-high heat until shimmering. Add onion and lemon zest and cook until onion begins to brown, about 8 minutes. Stir in garlic, paprika, and garam masala and cook until fragrant, about 30 seconds.

3. Add microwaved potatoes and carrots to Dutch oven and stir to coat with spices. Stir in broth, chickpeas, olives, and raisins. Cover and simmer gently until flavors blend, about 10 minutes. Uncover and simmer until vegetables are tender and sauce is slightly thickened, about 7 minutes. Stir in lemon juice and cilantro and season with salt and pepper to taste. Serve.

Eggplant and Kale Soup

Roasted Eggplant and Tomato Soup

Rustic Leek and Potato Soup
Serves 6 to 8

Why This Recipe Works We love leek and potato soup whether it's smooth and elegant or it's chunky and hearty, as it is here. In a rustic version, we want big bites of tender potatoes, but too often the soup ends up more like a chowder, with potatoes that are flaking and falling apart. To prevent that, we found that low-starch red potatoes were the best option, because they held their shape and didn't become waterlogged during cooking. Removing the pot from the heat toward the end of cooking allowed the potatoes to finish cooking through in the hot broth without becoming overcooked or mushy. To infuse our soup with the delicate flavor of the leeks, we sautéed a hefty 5 pounds of leeks to deepen their flavor, cooking them until they were tender but not falling apart so that there would still be bites of leeks in our rustic soup. Garlic, thyme, and a couple of bay leaves were all we needed to round out the flavors of this simple, country-style soup. Leeks can vary in size. If yours have large white and light green sections, use fewer leeks.

6	tablespoons refined coconut oil or unsalted butter
4–5	pounds leeks, white and light green parts only, halved lengthwise, sliced 1 inch thick, and washed thoroughly (11 cups)
½	teaspoon table salt
4	garlic cloves, minced
1	teaspoon minced fresh thyme
1	tablespoon all-purpose flour
3	cups vegetable broth
2¼	cups water
2	bay leaves
1¾	pounds red potatoes, peeled and cut into ¾-inch pieces

1. Melt oil in Dutch oven over medium heat. Stir in leeks and salt, cover, and cook, stirring occasionally, until leeks are tender but not mushy, 15 to 20 minutes (do not brown). Stir in garlic and thyme and cook until fragrant, about 30 seconds. Stir in flour and cook for 2 minutes.

2. Increase heat to high and gradually stir in broth and water. Stir in bay leaves and potatoes, cover, and bring to boil. Reduce heat to medium-low and simmer until potatoes are almost tender, 5 to 7 minutes.

3. Remove pot from heat and let sit, covered, until potatoes are tender and flavors meld, 10 to 15 minutes. Discard bay leaves and season with salt and pepper to taste. Serve.

PREPARING LEEKS

1. Trim and discard root and dark green leaves.

2. Cut trimmed leek in half lengthwise, then slice into pieces sized according to recipe.

3. Rinse cut leeks thoroughly using salad spinner or bowl of water to remove dirt and sand.

Eggplant and Kale Soup

Serves 4   FAST

Why This Recipe Works The meaty taste and texture of eggplant combined with a potent combination of spices (cumin, coriander, ginger, garlic, and Aleppo pepper) makes for a satisfying vegetable soup that comes together quickly on any weeknight. We diced the eggplant and browned it before setting it aside. Adding more olive oil to the Dutch oven, we bloomed the spices, garlic, and ginger in it. Then we cooked the broth and spices together until the flavors melded. We added the eggplant back in off the heat and also stirred in a generous amount of baby kale to bring pleasant chewiness, peppery flavor, and bright color. Sliced almonds added a delicate crunch, cilantro lent freshness, and the tang of Greek yogurt made for a rich, nuanced topping. A finishing sprinkle of Aleppo pepper gave us a pop of bright red color. If you can't find Aleppo pepper, you can substitute ½ teaspoon paprika mixed with ¼ teaspoon minced red pepper flakes.

  6 tablespoons extra-virgin olive oil, divided
1¼ pounds eggplant, cut into ½-inch pieces
  2 garlic cloves, minced
1½ teaspoons ground coriander
1½ teaspoons ground cumin
  1 teaspoon grated fresh ginger
  ¾ teaspoon ground dried Aleppo pepper, divided
  ¼ teaspoon ground cinnamon
  ½ teaspoon table salt
  ¼ teaspoon pepper
  3 cups vegetable broth
1½ cups water
  2 ounces (2 cups) baby kale, chopped coarse
  ½ cup plant-based Greek yogurt or dairy whole Greek yogurt
  2 tablespoons sliced almonds, toasted
  2 tablespoons minced fresh cilantro

1. Heat ¼ cup oil in Dutch oven over medium-high heat until just smoking. Add eggplant and cook, stirring occasionally, until tender and deeply browned, 6 to 8 minutes; transfer to bowl.

2. Combine garlic, coriander, cumin, ginger, ½ teaspoon Aleppo pepper, cinnamon, salt, and pepper in small bowl. Add remaining 2 tablespoons oil and garlic mixture to now-empty pot and cook over medium heat until fragrant, about 30 seconds. Stir in broth and water, scraping up any browned bits, and bring to simmer. Reduce heat to medium-low, cover partially, and cook until flavors meld, about 15 minutes.

3. Off heat, stir in kale and eggplant along with any accumulated juices. Let sit until wilted, about 2 minutes. Season with salt and pepper to taste. Dollop each portion with 2 tablespoons yogurt and sprinkle evenly with almonds, cilantro, and remaining ¼ teaspoon Aleppo pepper before serving.

Roasted Eggplant and Tomato Soup

Serves 4 to 6

Why This Recipe Works Taking our inspiration from the many eastern Mediterranean dishes that pair eggplant with tomato, we developed this supersatisfying soup in which we pureed the two for a wonderfully creamy result. We found we could skip the common prep task of salting, rinsing, and drying the eggplant before cooking since we would be pureeing it. We left the skin on for deeper eggplant flavor, diced the eggplant, and broiled it to develop some smoky char. To build our soup, we started with the usual aromatics (onion and garlic) and added the flavorful North African warm spice blend ras el hanout (plus some extra cumin), which gave the soup a complexly spiced base. Looking to obtain a subtle sweetness without sugar, we added ¼ cup of raisins, which, once pureed, also gave our soup body. And we reserved some broiled eggplant pieces to add to the pureed soup for a pleasantly chunky texture. Lemon juice provided brightness, a sprinkling of almonds contributed a pleasant crunch, and cilantro added freshness. We prefer our homemade Ras el Hanout (page 174), but you may use store-bought.

- 2 pounds eggplant, cut into ½-inch pieces
- 6 tablespoons extra-virgin olive oil, divided, plus extra for serving
- 1 onion, chopped
- ¾ teaspoon table salt
- ¼ teaspoon pepper
- 2 garlic cloves, minced
- 1½ teaspoons ras el hanout
- ½ teaspoon ground cumin
- 4 cups vegetable broth, plus extra as needed
- 1 (14.5-ounce) can diced tomatoes, drained
- ¼ cup raisins
- 1 bay leaf
- 2 teaspoons lemon juice
- 2 tablespoons slivered almonds, toasted
- 2 tablespoons minced fresh cilantro

1. Adjust oven rack 4 inches from broiler element and heat broiler. Toss eggplant with 5 tablespoons oil, then spread on aluminum foil–lined rimmed baking sheet. Broil eggplant for 10 minutes. Stir eggplant and continue to broil until mahogany brown, 5 to 7 minutes; let cool on baking sheet. Set aside 2 cups eggplant.

2. Heat remaining 1 tablespoon oil in large saucepan over medium heat until shimmering. Add onion, salt, and pepper and cook until onion is softened and lightly browned, 5 to 7 minutes. Stir in garlic, ras el hanout, and cumin and cook until fragrant, about 30 seconds. Stir in broth, tomatoes, raisins, bay leaf, and remaining eggplant and bring to simmer. Reduce heat to low, cover, and simmer gently until eggplant is softened, about 20 minutes.

3. Discard bay leaf. Working in batches, process soup in blender until smooth, about 2 minutes. Return soup to clean saucepan and stir in reserved 2 cups eggplant. Heat soup gently over low heat until hot and adjust consistency with extra hot broth as needed. Stir in lemon juice and season with salt and pepper to taste. Serve, sprinkling individual bowls with almonds and cilantro and drizzling with extra oil.

Moroccan Lentil and Chickpea Soup
Serves 6 to 8

Why This Recipe Works Different versions of this classic Moroccan lentil soup, known as harira, can be found all over North Africa. It's always full of warm spices and fresh herbs, and it may be bulked up with chickpeas or fava beans, pasta or rice, tomatoes, hearty greens, or sometimes even lamb, beef, or chicken. Our recipe carefully streamlines the ingredient list and technique to deliver all the bold North African flavors you'd want from a legume-based harira in just a fraction of the time. Lentils are quick-cooking to begin with, and using canned chickpeas instead of dried saved about 2 hours of cooking time. Paring down the number of spices to just the must-have additions made it a dish most people can prepare without a special trip to the market. Using large amounts of just two herbs made for quicker prep and a more efficient use of fresh ingredients. Finishing the dish with fresh lemon juice helped focus all the flavors. We like to garnish this soup with a small amount of our homemade Harissa (page 292), a fiery North African chili paste. Alternatively, look for harissa at large supermarkets.

- ⅓ cup extra-virgin olive oil
- 1 large onion, chopped fine
- 2 celery ribs, chopped fine
- 5 garlic cloves, minced
- 1 tablespoon grated fresh ginger
- 2 teaspoons ground coriander
- 2 teaspoons smoked paprika
- 1 teaspoon ground cumin
- ½ teaspoon ground cinnamon
- ⅛ teaspoon red pepper flakes
- ¾ cup minced fresh cilantro, divided
- ½ cup minced fresh parsley, divided
- 8 cups vegetable broth
- 1 (15-ounce) can chickpeas, rinsed
- 1 cup brown lentils, picked over and rinsed
- 1 (28-ounce) can crushed tomatoes
- ½ cup orzo
- 4 ounces Swiss chard, stemmed and cut into ½-inch pieces
- 2 tablespoons lemon juice, plus lemon wedges for serving

Moroccan Lentil and Chickpea Soup

1. Heat oil in Dutch oven over medium-high heat until shimmering. Add onion and celery and cook, stirring frequently, until translucent and starting to brown, 7 to 8 minutes. Reduce heat to medium, add garlic and ginger, and cook until fragrant, 1 minute. Stir in coriander, paprika, cumin, cinnamon, and pepper flakes and cook for 1 minute. Stir in ½ cup cilantro and ¼ cup parsley and cook for 1 minute.

2. Stir in broth, chickpeas, and lentils; increase heat to high and bring to simmer. Reduce heat to medium-low, partially cover, and gently simmer until lentils are just tender, about 20 minutes.

3. Stir in tomatoes and pasta and simmer, partially covered, for 7 minutes, stirring occasionally. Stir in chard and continue to cook, partially covered, until pasta is tender, about 5 minutes. Off heat, stir in lemon juice, remaining ¼ cup cilantro, and remaining ¼ cup parsley. Season with salt and pepper to taste. Serve, passing lemon wedges separately.

Spring Vegetable Soup
Serves 6

Why This Recipe Works Light and fresh yet substantial enough to serve for dinner with some crusty whole-grain bread, this soup makes delicious use of tender green vegetables of the new season, including asparagus, baby spinach, and peas. Since these vegetables by their very nature are delicate in flavor and texture, we realized that we would need to build a rich, flavorful broth using sturdier vegetables; namely, the classic trio of onion, carrot, and celery, with a little extra help from leek and fennel. Chopping all of these into small pieces and sweating them in the Dutch oven to soften them caused them to release their flavors more quickly into simmering vegetable broth (which we also boosted with aromatics including garlic and herbs). Then we strained this liquid and essentially poached our spring vegetables in the full-flavored broth. If you can find new red potatoes, use those; regular red potatoes also work fine. A sprinkle of chopped tarragon brought even more fresh spring flavor to our soup.

Broth
- 2 onions, chopped fine
- 1 carrot, peeled and chopped fine
- 1 celery rib, minced
- 1 leek, white and light green part only, chopped fine, and washed thoroughly
- 1 bulb fennel, chopped fine
- 3 garlic cloves
- 1 teaspoon vegetable oil
- ½ teaspoon table salt
- 7 cups vegetable broth
- 2 black peppercorns, crushed
- 5 sprigs fresh parsley
- 1 sprig fresh thyme

Soup
- 12 ounces red potatoes, unpeeled, cut into ¾-inch pieces
- 1 pound leeks, white and light green parts only, halved lengthwise, cut into 1-inch pieces, and washed thoroughly
- 8 ounces asparagus, trimmed and cut on bias into 1-inch lengths
- 3 ounces (3 cups) baby spinach
- 1 cup frozen peas
- 2 tablespoons minced fresh tarragon

1. For the broth Combine onions, carrot, celery, leek, fennel, garlic, oil, and salt in Dutch oven. Cover and cook over low heat, stirring often, until vegetables have softened, 8 to 10 minutes. Stir in broth, peppercorns, parsley, and thyme. Bring to boil over medium-high heat; reduce heat to medium-low and simmer until flavors meld, about 15 minutes. Strain broth through fine-mesh strainer; discard solids. (Broth can be refrigerated for up to 3 days or frozen for up to 2 months.)

2. For the soup Bring broth to simmer in large saucepan over medium heat. Add potatoes and leeks and simmer for about 5 minutes. Add asparagus and cook until all vegetables are just tender, about 5 minutes. Off heat, stir in spinach, peas, and tarragon, cover, and let sit until heated through, about 4 minutes. Season with salt and pepper to taste. Serve immediately.

Tuscan Tomato and Bread Soup
Serves 6

Why This Recipe Works Tuscany's signature salt-free bread is a ubiquitous staple, eaten more frequently than pasta or rice. Leftover or stale bread is never thrown away, and so throughout history, this desire not to waste food has inspired the creation of many Tuscan recipes using leftover bread—including soup. On paper, pappa al pomodoro is a tomato-bread soup finished with basil; in the pot, the ingredients meld to form a fragrant porridge-like stew that feels downright luxurious. We knew that picking the right type of tomato and processing it properly would be key. We tested every manner of canned tomatoes and pureed them, but this resulted in an acidic slurry that was just too tomatoey. However, fresh tomatoes were wan if not perfectly ripe. For an all-season soup, we returned to canned; as it turned out, it wasn't the tomatoes but our handling of them that was giving us inferior results. Chopping canned whole tomatoes (which we liked for their sweetness), rather than pureeing them, worked much better, giving us a soup with a balanced profile and texture. To mimic stale bread, we simply put it in the oven at a low temperature until it dried out and crisped up.

6 ounces rustic Italian bread, crusts removed, cut into 1-inch pieces (about 3 cups)
¼ cup extra-virgin olive oil, plus extra for serving
1 red onion, chopped fine
½ teaspoon table salt
3 garlic cloves, minced
¼ teaspoon red pepper flakes

6 cups vegetable broth
2 (28-ounce) cans whole peeled tomatoes, drained and chopped coarse
½ cup chopped fresh basil
Vegan Parmesan Substitute (page 27) or grated dairy Parmesan

1. Adjust oven rack to middle position and heat oven to 225 degrees. Arrange bread in single layer on rimmed baking sheet and bake, stirring occasionally, until dry and crisp, about 40 minutes.

2. Meanwhile, heat oil in Dutch oven over medium heat until shimmering. Add onion and salt and cook until softened, about 5 minutes. Stir in garlic and pepper flakes and cook until fragrant, about 30 seconds. Stir in broth and tomatoes and bring to simmer. Reduce heat to medium-low, cover, and cook until tomatoes are softened, about 20 minutes.

3. Stir in bread, pressing on cubes to submerge in liquid. Cover and cook until bread is softened, about 15 minutes. Off heat, whisk soup vigorously until bread is completely broken down and soup is thickened. Stir in basil. Season with salt and pepper to taste. Drizzle individual portions with extra oil and serve, passing vegan Parmesan substitute separately.

Thai Coconut Soup with Tofu
Serves 8

Why This Recipe Works Thai coconut soup is velvety and rich with a coconut flavor that's balanced by aromatic heat and fresh-tasting add-ins. As in many Southeast Asian dishes, a lively contrast of ingredients and flavors is essential: Fragrant lemongrass, pungent fish sauce (in this case, fish sauce substitute), fiery chiles, tart citrus juice, peppery ginger, sharp garlic, and aromatic herbs combine to create a tantalizing dish. While chicken is traditionally used to bulk up this soup, we opted for tofu, along with meaty shiitake mushrooms and crunchy snow peas. Thai red curry paste packs a spicy punch along with floral, fruity flavors, and it's a convenient way to incorporate ingredients such as Thai chiles, galangal, and makrut lime leaves. We sautéed the shiitake mushrooms at the start along with the aromatics to deeply infuse the soup with their flavor, and we waited until the last 5 minutes of cooking to heat the tofu and snow peas through, which preserved their delicate texture. With a final garnish of cilantro leaves, sliced scallion greens, and lime wedges, this soup was ready to enjoy. Not all brands of red curry paste are vegan, so read labels carefully.

1 tablespoon vegetable oil

4 ounces shiitake mushrooms, stemmed and cut into ½-inch pieces

2 stalks lemongrass, trimmed to bottom 6 inches and minced (3 tablespoons)

2 tablespoons minced fresh ginger

1 garlic clove, minced

4 teaspoons Thai red curry paste

6 cups vegetable broth, divided

3 tablespoons Fish Sauce Substitute (page 22)

1 tablespoon sugar

2 (14-ounce) cans coconut milk

14 ounces extra-firm tofu, cut into ½-inch pieces

6 ounces snow peas, strings removed, cut into ½-inch pieces

3 tablespoons lime juice (2 limes), plus lime wedges for serving

½ cup fresh cilantro leaves

3 scallions, green parts only, sliced thin on bias

1. Heat oil in Dutch oven over medium heat until shimmering. Add mushrooms, lemongrass, ginger, and garlic and cook, stirring constantly, until fragrant, about 30 seconds. Add curry paste and cook, stirring constantly, until fragrant, about 30 seconds. Whisk ½ cup broth into pot, scraping up any browned bits.

2. Stir in remaining 5½ cups broth, fish sauce substitute, and sugar and bring to boil. Reduce heat to low and simmer, partially covered, for 20 minutes.

3. Stir in coconut milk, tofu, snow peas, and lime juice and bring to simmer. Cook until tofu is warmed through and snow peas are just tender, about 5 minutes. Season with salt and pepper to taste, and serve with cilantro, scallions, and lime wedges.

FLAVOR BOOSTER

THAI CURRY PASTE

Store-bought curry paste conveniently provides a wallop of authentic Thai flavor—rich herbal notes, complexity, and heat—in one little jar. Red curry paste combines a number of hard-to-find authentic Thai aromatics—including galangal (Thai ginger), red bird's eye chiles, lemongrass, and makrut lime leaves. Green curry paste is made from fresh green Thai chiles, lemongrass, galangal, garlic, and other spices. Be sure to read labels, since not all brands are vegan.

Tuscan Tomato and Bread Soup

Thai Coconut Soup with Tofu

Chickpea Curry

Serves 4 `FAST`

Why This Recipe Works This simple, speedy weeknight curry using pantry ingredients plus a few fresh ones punches far above its weight in terms of flavor payoff. It can be made with any number of different vegetables, but we wanted to keep it easy, so we cut up a generous amount of green bell peppers and added a minced jalapeño to bring a little spiciness to the green pepper vibe. We sautéed the bell peppers first until they were starting to brown and then added the jalapeño, garlic, ginger, and curry powder to bloom briefly in the hot oil. In went the chickpeas, tomatoes, and coconut milk, and after a quick simmer, dinner was served. To make this curry spicier, add the seeds from the chile. Serve with rice.

- 2 tablespoons vegetable oil
- 2 green bell peppers, stemmed, seeded, and cut into 1-inch pieces
- 1½ teaspoons table salt
- ½ teaspoon pepper
- 1 jalapeño chile, stemmed, seeded, and minced
- 4 garlic cloves, minced
- 1 tablespoon grated fresh ginger
- 1 tablespoon curry powder
- 2 (15-ounce) cans chickpeas, rinsed
- 1 (14.5-ounce) can diced tomatoes
- 1 (14-ounce) can coconut milk

1. Heat oil in Dutch oven over medium-high heat until shimmering. Add bell peppers, salt, and pepper and cook until bell peppers are beginning to brown, 5 to 7 minutes. Add jalapeño, garlic, ginger, and curry powder and cook until fragrant, about 30 seconds.

2. Add chickpeas, tomatoes and their juice, and coconut milk and bring to boil. Cover, reduce heat to medium-low, and simmer until bell peppers are tender and flavors meld, about 20 minutes, stirring occasionally. Serve.

Watercress and Shiitake Mushroom Soup with Tofu

Serves 4 to 6 `FAST`

Why This Recipe Works This simple and quick Chinese-inspired soup starts with our deeply flavored Umami Broth, but amps up its flavor even more by simmering it with fresh shiitake and dried porcini mushrooms, rice wine, and aromatics including scallions and ginger. We added pieces of firm tofu at the end of cooking, just long enough to warm them through. Generous handfuls of bright green watercress, also stirred in at the end, add a fresh, peppery finish.

- 14 ounces firm tofu, cut into ¾-inch pieces
- 1 tablespoon vegetable oil
- 6 scallions, white and green parts separated, whites minced and greens sliced thin
- 4 teaspoons grated fresh ginger
- 3 garlic cloves, minced
- 8 ounces shiitake mushrooms, stemmed, and sliced ¼ inch thick
- ¼ ounce dried porcini mushrooms, rinsed and minced
- ¼ cup Shaoxing wine or dry sherry
- 4 cups Umami Broth (page 22) or vegetable broth
- 3 ounces watercress (3 cups), large stems removed
- 2 tablespoons soy sauce, plus extra for seasoning

1. Spread tofu on paper towel–lined baking sheet and let drain for 20 minutes. Heat oil in large Dutch oven over medium heat until shimmering. Add scallion whites, ginger, and garlic and cook until softened, about 1 minute. Stir in shiitake and porcini mushrooms, cover, and cook until mushrooms have softened, 3 to 5 minutes.

2. Stir in wine, scraping up any browned bits, and simmer until nearly evaporated, about 1 minute. Stir in broth and continue to simmer, uncovered, until flavors meld, about 10 minutes. (Broth can be refrigerated for up to 3 days. Reheat broth before continuing with recipe.)

3. Stir in watercress, soy sauce, and tofu and simmer until tofu is hot, about 5 minutes. Sprinkle with scallion greens, season with soy sauce and pepper to taste, and serve.

Shiitake Ramen

Serves 4 to 6

Why This Recipe Works Our ideal ramen involves a big hearty bowl of steaming noodles in a powerful, complex broth; we were thrilled to discover that we could achieve this in a vegan ramen just as effectively as we have done with pork versions. We added kombu, a Japanese seaweed, to aromatics, water, and vegetable broth; supplementing the kombu with shiitake mushroom stems and soy sauce provided a triple hit of umami. Mirin, a sweet Japanese rice wine, rounded out the savory profile. Finally, red miso lent smoky complexity and body. Instant ramen noodles are handily vegan and maintained good chew. (We threw away the seasoning packet.) We stirred in delicate shiitake caps until they were just cooked. Bean sprouts provided crispness, and sliced scallions and toasty

Shiitake Ramen

1. Combine bean sprouts, 1 teaspoon soy sauce, 1 teaspoon oil, and vinegar in small bowl; set aside. Heat remaining 1 tablespoon oil in large saucepan over medium-high heat until shimmering. Stir in onion and cook until softened and lightly browned, 5 to 7 minutes. Add ginger and garlic and cook until lightly browned, about 2 minutes.

2. Stir in broth, 4 cups water, mushroom stems, mirin, kombu, and remaining soy sauce and bring to boil. Reduce heat to low, cover, and simmer until flavors meld, about 1 hour.

3. Strain broth through fine-mesh strainer into large bowl, pressing on solids to extract as much broth as possible; discard solids. Wipe saucepan clean with paper towels and return strained broth to now-empty saucepan. Whisk miso into broth and bring to gentle simmer over medium heat, whisking to dissolve miso completely. Stir in sliced mushroom caps and cook until warmed through, about 1 minute; season with salt to taste. Remove from heat and cover to keep warm.

4. Meanwhile, bring 4 quarts water to boil in large pot. Add ramen and 1 tablespoon salt and cook, stirring often, until al dente. Drain noodles and divide evenly among individual bowls. Ladle soup over noodles, garnish with bean sprouts, scallions, and sesame seeds, and serve.

Ultimate Vegan Chili
Serves 6 to 8

Why This Recipe Works We harvested from many branches of the plant world to develop this incredibly satisfying chili. Since meat adds depth in different ways, we sought multiple ways to replace it. For bulk, we used a mix of beans along with bulgur. Dried beans developed great flavor with the long simmer; we brined them first to prevent blowouts. A combination of umami-rich ingredients—tomatoes, dried shiitake mushrooms, and soy sauce—added savoriness. Walnuts are high in flavor-boosting glutamates; when we ground some and stirred them in, they contributed richness and body. For the dried chiles, we chose ancho and New Mexican, toasted them until fragrant, and then ground them. We also incorporated fresh jalapeño into the tomato mixture. You can substitute chili powder for the dried chiles; grind the shiitakes and oregano and add them to the pot with ¼ cup chili powder in step 4. We recommend a mix of at least two types of beans, one creamy (such as cannellini or navy) and one earthy (such as pinto, black, or red kidney). When shopping, don't confuse bulgur with cracked wheat, which has a longer cooking time and will not work here. For a spicier chili, use both jalapeños. Serve with your favorite toppings.

sesame seeds topped things off. A sprinkling of shichimi togarashi (a common Japanese spice mix) is lovely on the ramen; look for it in the international aisle of the supermarket.

- 4 ounces (2 cups) bean sprouts
- 3 tablespoons soy sauce, divided
- 4 teaspoons toasted sesame oil, divided
- 1 tablespoon seasoned rice vinegar
- 1 onion, chopped
- 1 (2-inch) piece ginger, peeled and sliced ¼ inch thick
- 5 garlic cloves, smashed and peeled
- 4 cups Umami Broth (page 22) or vegetable broth
- 8 ounces shiitake mushrooms, stems removed and reserved, caps sliced thin
- ¼ cup mirin
- ½ ounce kombu
- 2 tablespoons red miso
- 12 ounces dried ramen noodles, seasoning packets discarded
    Table salt for cooking ramen
- 2 scallions, sliced thin on bias
- 1 tablespoon toasted black sesame seeds

Table salt for brining beans

1 pound (2½ cups) assorted dried beans, picked over and rinsed

2 dried ancho chiles

2 dried New Mexican chiles

½ ounce dried shiitake mushrooms, chopped coarse

4 teaspoons dried oregano

½ cup walnuts, toasted

1 (28-ounce) can diced tomatoes, drained with juice reserved

3 tablespoons tomato paste

1-2 jalapeño chiles, stemmed and chopped coarse

3 tablespoons soy sauce

6 garlic cloves, minced

¼ cup vegetable oil

2 pounds onions, chopped fine

1¼ teaspoons table salt

1 tablespoon ground cumin

⅔ cup medium-grind bulgur

¼ cup minced fresh cilantro

1. Dissolve 3 tablespoons salt in 4 quarts cold water in large container. Add beans and soak at room temperature for at least 8 hours or up to 24 hours. Drain and rinse well.

2. Adjust oven rack to middle position and heat oven to 300 degrees. Spread anchos and New Mexican chiles on rimmed baking sheet and toast until fragrant and puffed, about 8 minutes. Transfer to plate, let cool for 5 minutes, then remove stems and seeds. Working in batches, grind toasted chiles, mushrooms, and oregano in spice grinder until finely ground.

3. Process walnuts in food processor until finely ground, about 30 seconds; transfer to bowl. Process tomatoes, tomato paste, jalapeño(s), soy sauce, and garlic in food processor until tomatoes are finely chopped, about 45 seconds.

4. Heat oil in Dutch oven over medium-high heat until shimmering. Add onions and salt and cook, stirring occasionally, until onions begin to brown, 8 to 10 minutes. Reduce heat to medium, stir in ground chile mixture and cumin, and cook, stirring constantly, until fragrant, about 1 minute. Stir in beans and 7 cups water and bring to boil. Cover pot, transfer to oven, and cook for 45 minutes.

5. Stir in bulgur, walnuts, tomato mixture, and reserved tomato juice. Continue to cook, covered, until beans are fully tender, about 2 hours. Remove pot from oven, stir well, and let sit, uncovered, for 20 minutes. Stir in cilantro before serving.

STARCHES

Both beans and bulgur contain a lot of natural starches, so we capitalized on that to create great body in our Ultimate Vegan Chili. After we took the chili out of the oven, we gave it a vigorous stir and then let it rest for 20 minutes. This stirring helped to release the plant starches from the beans and the bulgur. This starch then clustered around the fat droplets in the chili, preventing them from coalescing and helping to create a thick, velvety emulsion that never left an unappealing slick of oil on top of the chili.

Weeknight Meaty Chili

Serves 6 to 8 **FAST**

Why This Recipe Works This speedy, family-friendly weeknight chili is a win-win for everyone, especially for those who are trying to reduce their meat intake but who still appreciate the flavor and texture of meat. To create a chili that feels familiar (nostalgic, even) using plant-based meat, we built aromatic flavors from onion, garlic and red bell peppers (which we chopped coarse for a heartier texture) before cooking the plant-based beef just until no longer pink (cooked beyond medium, it started to toughen up and turn chewy). Chili powder, cumin, and oregano brought intense earthy fragrance, while chipotle chile brought smoky heat. Canned kidney beans were a reliable shortcut—saving time with no sacrifice in flavor or texture—and added plenty of heartiness. Tomato sauce brought just the right amount of sauciness, and chopped canned whole peeled tomatoes added tomato texture without tasting raw or being overly chunky. Use the lesser amount of chipotle chile if you prefer a milder level of spiciness. We prefer Impossible Burger in this recipe; see page 9 for more information. Load this up with all your favorite chili toppings.

2 tablespoons vegetable oil

2 onions, chopped fine

2 red bell peppers, stemmed, seeded, and chopped

4 garlic cloves, minced

1 tablespoon chili powder

2 teaspoons ground cumin

1-2 teaspoons minced canned chipotle chile in adobo sauce

Weeknight Meaty Chili

½   teaspoon dried oregano
½   teaspoon table salt
¼   teaspoon pepper
12 ounces plant-based beef (page 9)
2   (15-ounce) cans kidney beans, rinsed
1   (28-ounce) can whole peeled tomatoes, drained, juice reserved, and chopped fine
1   (15-ounce) can tomato sauce
1   cup water

1. Heat oil in Dutch oven over medium heat until shimmering. Add onions, bell peppers, garlic, chili powder, cumin, chipotle, oregano, salt, and pepper and cook, stirring frequently, until vegetables are softened, 8 to 10 minutes. Stir in plant-based beef and cook, breaking up meat with wooden spoon, until no longer pink, about 3 minutes.

2. Stir in beans, tomatoes and reserved juice, tomato sauce, and water, and bring to simmer. Reduce heat to low and simmer until chili thickens slightly, 15 to 20 minutes. Season with salt and pepper to taste, and serve.

Roasted Poblano and White Bean Chili
Serves 4 to 6

Why This Recipe Works Fresh chiles take center stage in this white bean chili, with a trio of poblanos, Anaheims, and jalapeños providing the complexity we were looking for. We broiled the poblanos and Anaheims to develop depth and smokiness and kept the jalapeño flavor bright by simply sautéeing them. Processing some of the roasted peppers with a portion of the beans and broth thickened the chili. We broiled fresh corn kernels to add a toasty, caramelized element to them and then simmered the cobs in the chili to extract even more flavor, removing the cobs and adding the broiled kernels at the end of cooking. To make this chili spicier, add the seeds from the chiles. If you can't find Anaheim chiles, add two extra poblanos and one extra jalapeño. Serve with plant-based or dairy sour cream, tortilla chips, and lime wedges, if desired.

5   poblano chiles, halved lengthwise, stemmed, and seeded
3   Anaheim chiles, halved lengthwise, stemmed, and seeded
3   tablespoons vegetable oil, divided
3   ears corn, kernels cut from cobs and cobs reserved
2   onions, cut into large pieces
2   jalapeño chiles, stemmed, seeded, and chopped
2   (15-ounce) cans cannellini beans, rinsed, divided
4   cups vegetable broth, divided
6   garlic cloves, minced
1   tablespoon tomato paste
1   tablespoon ground cumin
1½ teaspoons ground coriander
½   teaspoon table salt
1   (15-ounce) can pinto beans, rinsed
4   scallions, green parts only, sliced thin
¼   cup minced fresh cilantro
1   tablespoon lime juice

1. Adjust oven rack 6 inches from broiler element and heat broiler. Toss poblanos and Anaheims with 1 tablespoon oil and spread, skin side up, on aluminum foil–lined rimmed baking sheet. Broil until chiles begin to blacken and soften, about 10 minutes, rotating sheet halfway through broiling. Transfer broiled chiles to bowl, cover with plastic wrap, and let steam until skins peel off easily, 10 to 15 minutes. Peel poblanos and Anaheims, then cut into ½-inch pieces, reserving any accumulated juice.

Roasted Poblano and White Bean Chili

2. Meanwhile, toss corn kernels with 1 tablespoon oil, spread evenly on foil-lined baking sheet, and broil, stirring occasionally, until beginning to brown, 5 to 10 minutes; let cool on baking sheet.

3. Pulse onions and jalapeños in food processor to consistency of chunky salsa, 6 to 8 pulses; transfer to bowl. In now-empty food processor, process 1 cup cannellini beans, 1 cup broth, and ½ cup chopped roasted chiles and any accumulated juice until smooth, about 45 seconds.

4. Heat remaining 1 tablespoon oil in Dutch oven over medium heat until shimmering. Add onion-jalapeño mixture and cook until softened, 5 to 7 minutes. Stir in garlic, tomato paste, cumin, coriander, and salt and cook until tomato paste begins to darken, about 2 minutes. Stir in remaining 3 cups broth, scraping up any browned bits. Stir in pureed chile-bean mixture, remaining roasted chiles, remaining cannellini beans, pinto beans, and corn cobs. Bring to simmer, then reduce heat to low and simmer gently until thickened and flavorful, about 40 minutes.

5. Discard corn cobs. Stir in broiled corn kernels and let heat through, about 1 minute. Off heat, stir in scallions, cilantro, and lime juice and season with salt and pepper to taste. Serve.

Butternut Squash Chili with Quinoa and Peanuts
Serves 6

Why This Recipe Works This stick-to-your-ribs African-style butternut squash chili features bold spices, a hefty amount of garlic and ginger, and aromatic coconut milk. It gets its silky body from a combination of blended peanuts and squash, which we roasted with chopped onions until both the squash and the onions started to char around the edges, giving the chili incredible flavor. We pureed a portion of the roasted vegetables with the dry-roasted peanuts to create a rich, smooth base. We sautéed sweet bell pepper and spicy jalapeño and briefly bloomed the warm spices before adding in the liquid. A combination of diced tomatoes and coconut milk made a creamy but bright broth, and nutty quinoa added heartiness and a subtle pop of texture. We like the convenience of prewashed quinoa; rinsing removes the quinoa's bitter protective coating (called saponin). If you buy unwashed quinoa, rinse it and then spread it out on a clean dish towel to dry for 15 minutes. To make this chili spicier, add the seeds from the chile. Serve with hot sauce.

Butternut Squash Chili with Quinoa and Peanuts

3 pounds butternut squash, peeled, seeded, and cut into ½-inch pieces (9 cups)
2 onions, cut into ½-inch pieces
6 tablespoons vegetable oil, divided
1 tablespoon table salt, divided
1¼ teaspoons pepper, divided
5 cups water, divided, plus extra as needed
¾ cup salted dry-roasted peanuts, chopped, divided
1 large red bell pepper, stemmed, seeded, and cut into ½-inch pieces
1 jalapeño chile, stemmed, seeded, and minced
2 tablespoons grated fresh ginger
3 garlic cloves, minced
¾ teaspoon ground cinnamon
¾ teaspoon ground coriander
½ teaspoon cayenne pepper
1 (14.5-ounce) can diced tomatoes
1 (14-ounce) can coconut milk
1 cup prewashed white quinoa
¼ cup minced fresh cilantro or parsley

1. Adjust oven racks to upper-middle and lower-middle positions and heat oven to 450 degrees. Toss squash, onions, ¼ cup oil, 1 teaspoon salt, and ½ teaspoon pepper together in bowl. Spread vegetables in even layer over 2 rimmed baking sheets. Roast vegetables, stirring occasionally, until tender, 45 to 50 minutes, switching and rotating sheets halfway through roasting.

2. Process ½ cup roasted vegetables, 2 cups water, and ¼ cup peanuts in food processor until smooth, about 1 minute.

3. Heat remaining 2 tablespoons oil in Dutch oven over medium-high heat until shimmering. Add bell pepper, jalapeño, and remaining 2 teaspoons salt and cook until peppers start to soften, about 5 minutes. Stir in ginger, garlic, cinnamon, coriander, cayenne, and remaining ¾ teaspoon pepper and cook until fragrant, about 30 seconds.

4. Stir in tomatoes and their juice, coconut milk, quinoa, and remaining 3 cups water and bring to boil. Reduce heat to low and simmer, stirring occasionally, until quinoa is tender, about 15 minutes.

5. Stir in pureed vegetable mixture and remaining roasted vegetables and let heat through, about 3 minutes. Season with salt and pepper to taste. Adjust consistency with additional hot water as needed. Serve, sprinkling individual bowls with cilantro and remaining ½ cup peanuts.

Black Bean Chili
Serves 6 to 8

Why This Recipe Works Since black beans are the focal point of this chili, we decided to start with dried beans. Often we brine dried beans in salted water before cooking to avoid having some of the beans burst open during cooking. For this chili, however, we thought that some exploded beans would actually add a textural dimension that we wanted, so we skipped the brining. After blooming spices and sautéing chopped white mushrooms and aromatics in oil (which gave the chili meaty texture and flavor), we added the beans along with broth and water and cooked them in the oven until tender and well seasoned. Whole cumin seeds and chipotle added depth and smokiness, and, surprisingly, toasted mustard seeds added a pungency and complexity that tasters loved. A sprinkle of minced cilantro brightened the dish. We strongly prefer the texture and flavor of mustard seeds and cumin seeds in this chili, but you can substitute ½ teaspoon dry mustard and/or ½ teaspoon ground cumin, added to the pot with the chili powder in step 3. We also prefer our Everyday Chili Powder (recipe follows), though you may use store-bought. Serve with lime wedges, plant-based sour cream, chopped tomatoes, and/or finely chopped onion.

1 pound white mushrooms, trimmed and broken into rough pieces
1 tablespoon mustard seeds
2 teaspoons cumin seeds
3 tablespoons vegetable oil
1 onion, chopped fine
9 garlic cloves, minced
1 tablespoon minced canned chipotle chile in adobo sauce
3 tablespoons chili powder
2½ cups vegetable broth
2½ cups water, plus extra as needed
1 pound (2½ cups) dried black beans, picked over and rinsed
1 tablespoon packed light brown sugar
⅛ teaspoon baking soda
2 bay leaves
1 (28-ounce) can crushed tomatoes
2 red bell peppers, stemmed, seeded, and cut into ½-inch pieces
½ cup minced fresh cilantro

1. Adjust oven rack to lower-middle position and heat oven to 325 degrees. Pulse mushrooms in food processor until coarsely chopped and uniform in size, about 10 pulses.

2. Toast mustard seeds and cumin seeds in Dutch oven over medium heat, stirring constantly, until fragrant, about 1 minute. Stir in oil, onion, and processed mushrooms, cover, and cook until vegetables have released their liquid, about 5 minutes. Uncover and continue to cook until vegetables are browned, 5 to 10 minutes.

3. Stir in garlic and chipotle and cook until fragrant, about 30 seconds. Stir in chili powder and cook, stirring constantly, until fragrant, about 1 minute. Stir in broth, water, beans, sugar, baking soda, and bay leaves and bring to simmer, skimming as needed. Cover, transfer to oven, and cook for 1 hour.

4. Stir in crushed tomatoes and bell peppers and continue to cook in oven, covered, until beans are fully tender, about 1 hour. (If chili begins to stick to bottom of pot or is too thick, add water as needed.)

5. Remove pot from oven and discard bay leaves. Stir in cilantro and season with salt and pepper to taste. Serve.

Everyday Chili Powder
Makes ½ cup
This balanced all-purpose powder is mild but has perceptible smoke and heat. We prefer the robust flavor of Mexican oregano, but you can substitute any dried oregano.

- 2 ounces (7 to 8) dried New Mexican chiles, stemmed, seeded, and torn into ½-inch pieces (1½ cups)
- 1 teaspoon cumin seeds
- ½ teaspoon dried Mexican oregano
- 1 tablespoon paprika
- ½ teaspoon garlic powder
- ¼ teaspoon cayenne pepper

Working in batches, process New Mexican chiles, cumin seeds, and oregano in spice grinder until finely ground, about 30 seconds. Stir in paprika, garlic powder, and cayenne. (Chili powder can be stored in airtight container for up to 1 month.)

Italian Vegetable Stew
Serves 6 to 8

Why This Recipe Works Italy's ciambotta is a ratatouille-like stew chock-full of vegetables that makes for a hearty and comforting one-bowl meal. We wanted to avoid the sorry fate of most recipes, which end in mushy vegetables drowning in a weak broth. In order to optimize the texture of the zucchini and peppers, we employed a skillet to cook off their excess water. To create a flavorful, umami-enhanced broth, we embraced eggplant's natural tendency to fall apart and cooked it until it completely assimilated into a thickened, tomato-enriched sauce. Finally, we found that a potent (and cheese-free) version of pesto, with both basil and oregano, olive oil, plenty of garlic, and red pepper flakes, provided the biggest flavor punch when added near the end of cooking. We love this with crusty bread for sopping up all the saucy broth.

Pesto
- ⅓ cup chopped fresh basil
- ⅓ cup fresh oregano leaves
- 6 garlic cloves, minced
- 2 tablespoons extra-virgin olive oil
- ¼ teaspoon red pepper flakes

Stew
- 12 ounces eggplant, peeled and cut into ½-inch pieces
- 2 teaspoons table salt, divided
- ¼ cup extra-virgin olive oil, divided
- 1 large onion, chopped
- 1 pound russet potatoes, peeled and cut into ½-inch pieces
- 2 tablespoons tomato paste
- 2¼ cups water, divided
- 1 (28-ounce) can whole peeled tomatoes, drained with juice reserved, chopped coarse
- 2 zucchini, halved lengthwise, seeded, and cut into ½-inch pieces
- 2 red or yellow bell peppers, stemmed, seeded, and cut into ½-inch pieces
- 1 cup shredded fresh basil

1. **For the pesto** Process all ingredients in food processor until finely ground, about 1 minute, scraping down sides of bowl as necessary.

Italian Vegetable Stew

5. Meanwhile, heat remaining 1 tablespoon oil in 12-inch skillet over high heat until just smoking. Add zucchini, bell peppers, and remaining ½ teaspoon salt and cook, stirring occasionally, until vegetables are browned and tender, 10 to 12 minutes. Push vegetables to sides of skillet. Add pesto to clearing and cook until fragrant, about 1 minute. Stir pesto into vegetables and transfer to bowl. Off heat, add remaining ¼ cup water to skillet and scrape up browned bits.

6. Remove Dutch oven from heat and stir in vegetable mixture and water from skillet. Cover and let stew sit for 20 minutes to let flavors meld. Stir in basil, season with salt to taste, and serve.

2. For the stew Toss eggplant with 1½ teaspoons salt in bowl. Line surface of large plate with double layer of coffee filters and lightly spray with vegetable oil spray. Spread eggplant evenly over coffee filters and microwave until dry to touch and slightly shriveled, 8 to 12 minutes, tossing halfway through cooking.

3. Heat 2 tablespoons oil in Dutch oven over high heat until shimmering. Add eggplant, onion, and potatoes and cook, stirring frequently, until eggplant browns, about 2 minutes.

4. Push vegetables to sides of pot. Add 1 tablespoon oil and tomato paste to clearing and cook, stirring often, until brown fond develops on bottom of pot, about 2 minutes. Stir in 2 cups water and tomatoes and their juice, scraping up any browned bits. Bring to boil. Reduce heat to medium, cover, and gently simmer until eggplant is completely broken down and potatoes are tender, 20 to 25 minutes.

NOTES FROM THE TEST KITCHEN

FREEZING AND REHEATING SOUPS, STEWS, AND CHILIS

Soups, stews, and chilis make a generous number of servings, making it convenient to stock your freezer with leftovers so you can reheat them whenever you like. To freeze them correctly, first you'll need to cool the pot. As tempting as it might seem, don't transfer the hot contents straight to the freezer or refrigerator. This can increase the fridge's internal temperature to unsafe levels for all the other food. Letting the pot cool on the countertop for an hour helps the temperature drop to about 75 degrees, at which point you can transfer it safely to the freezer. For faster cooling, you can divide the contents of the pot into a number of storage containers to allow the heat to dissipate more quickly, or you can cool it rapidly by using a frozen bottle of water to stir the contents of the pot.

To reheat soups, stews, and chilis, we prefer to simmer them gently on the stovetop in a sturdy, heavy-bottomed pot. And note that while most soups, stews, and chilis store just fine, those that contain pasta or dairy (plant-based or traditional) do not—the pasta turns bloated and mushy, and the dairy curdles as it freezes. Instead, make and freeze the dish without including the pasta or dairy component. After you have thawed the soup, stew, or chili and it has been heated through, you can stir in the uncooked pasta and simmer until just tender, or stir in the dairy and continue to heat gently until hot (do not boil).

Caribbean-Style Swiss Chard and Butternut Squash Stew

Serves 4

Why This Recipe Works Inspired by an earthy, spicy Caribbean stew that pairs the local callaloo leaves with squash in a rich, coconut-infused broth, we set out to create a plant-based version (it traditionally includes pork). We found that Swiss chard was a good alternative to replicate the earthy, slightly citrusy notes of the callaloo leaves. A combination of fresh chile and cayenne pepper gave the stew a robust heat that balanced the sweetness of the butternut squash. A handful of recipes called for a few dashes of Angostura bitters, an aromatic alcohol infused with herbs and citrus. While not a must, the bitters gave the stew a uniquely authentic flavor. We pureed a small portion of the stew to give it a thick consistency and bright green color, while leaving most of the greens and squash in large bites. You can substitute delicata or carnival squash for the butternut squash if you prefer. To make this stew spicier, add the seeds from the chile.

- 2 tablespoons vegetable oil
- 2 onions, chopped fine
- 4 scallions, minced
- ½ teaspoon table salt
- 4 garlic cloves, minced
- 1 habanero or Scotch bonnet chile, stemmed, seeded, and minced
- 1 teaspoon minced fresh thyme or ¼ teaspoon dried
  Pinch cayenne pepper
- 3½ cups vegetable broth
- 2 pounds butternut squash, peeled, seeded, and cut into ½-inch pieces (6 cups)
- 1 pound Swiss chard, stemmed and cut into 1-inch pieces
- 1 cup canned coconut milk
  Angostura bitters (optional)

1. Heat oil in Dutch oven over medium heat until shimmering. Stir in onions, scallions, and salt and cook until vegetables are softened, 5 to 7 minutes. Stir in garlic, habanero, thyme, and cayenne and cook until fragrant, about 30 seconds.

2. Stir in broth and squash, scraping up any browned bits, and bring to boil. Reduce to gentle simmer and cook for 15 minutes. Stir in chard and continue to simmer until squash and chard are tender, 10 to 15 minutes. Stir in coconut milk and bring to brief simmer.

3. Process 2 cups stew in blender until smooth, about 45 seconds; return to pot. Season with salt and bitters, if using, to taste, and serve.

Celeriac, Fennel, and Apple Chowder

Serves 6

Why This Recipe Works Homely-looking celeriac (known more commonly as celery root) is a year-round staple in supermarkets, but most cooks walk right by it. That's a shame, because this knobby tuber boasts refreshing herbal flavors with notes of anise, mint, mild radish, and celery. Its creamy (rather than starchy) texture makes it the perfect choice for a hearty vegetable chowder. To further enhance its anise flavor, we sautéed a chopped fennel bulb along with big pieces of onion. For a sweet, fruity counterpoint, we added some grated apple. Chunks of tender red potatoes bulked up the chowder. For a bright citrus note, we simmered a strip of orange zest in the broth. To get the perfect amount of body, we pureed 2 cups of the chowder with a modest amount of plant-based creamer (or dairy heavy cream) and then stirred the puree back into the pot. Finally, we stirred in minced fresh fennel fronds to brighten the finished chowder.

- 2 tablespoons refined coconut oil or unsalted butter
- 1 onion, cut into ½-inch pieces
- 1 fennel bulb, 1 tablespoon fronds minced, stalks discarded, bulb halved, cored, and cut into ½-inch pieces
- 1½ teaspoons table salt
- 6 garlic cloves, minced
- 2 teaspoons minced fresh thyme or ¾ teaspoon dried
- 2 tablespoons all-purpose flour
- ½ cup dry white wine
- 4 cups vegetable broth
- 1½ cups water
- 1 celery root (14 ounces), peeled and cut into ½-inch pieces
- 12 ounces red potatoes, unpeeled, cut into ½-inch pieces
- 1 Golden Delicious apple, peeled and shredded
- 1 bay leaf
- 1 (3-inch) strip orange zest
- ¼ cup plant-based creamer or dairy heavy cream

1. Melt oil in Dutch oven over medium heat. Add onion, fennel pieces, and salt and cook until vegetables are softened, 5 to 7 minutes. Stir in garlic and thyme and cook until fragrant, about 30 seconds. Stir in flour and cook for 1 minute. Stir in wine, scraping up any browned bits and smoothing out any lumps, and cook until nearly evaporated, about 1 minute.

2. Stir in broth, water, celery root, potatoes, apple, bay leaf, and orange zest and bring to boil. Reduce heat to low, partially cover, and simmer gently until stew is thickened and vegetables are tender, 35 to 40 minutes.

3. Off heat, discard bay leaf and orange zest. Puree 2 cups chowder and creamer in blender until smooth, about 1 minute, then return to pot. Stir in fennel fronds, season with salt and pepper to taste, and serve.

PEELING CELERY ROOT

1. Trim slice from top and bottom of celery root, then stand root on flat bottom.

2. Starting from top, carefully cut away tough outer skin in strips.

Green Gumbo
Serves 6 to 8

Why This Recipe Works Originally a Lenten dish served throughout Louisiana, green gumbo, or gumbo z'herbes, starts similarly to other gumbo, with a dark oil-flour roux providing thickening power and toasty, nutty richness. But what's added next sets this stewy dish apart from its seafood- and meat-filled Creole and Cajun cousins: greens, and lots of them. In developing our own version, we found recipes with up to 13 different greens, from turnip tops to parsley and carrot greens to more familiar standbys like collards and kale. To streamline an already-long ingredient list, we found that we could trim down our greens to just two types: a mix of heartier greens (collards, mustard greens, or kale) and softer greens (spinach or Swiss chard) for a nice balance of chew and silkiness (but feel free to experiment with the greens you have on hand). To balance the earthiness of the abundant greens, we amped up the spice and smoke with cayenne and smoked paprika, echoing the smokiness of gumbos that include smoked meats. While it's not traditional, we loved the texture and heartiness that additional vegetables—okra, green beans, and black-eyed peas—brought, and a finishing splash of vinegar added just the right brightness. While we prefer frozen

Caribbean-Style Swiss Chard and Butternut Squash Stew

Celeriac, Fennel, and Apple Chowder

okra in this recipe, you can use fresh okra; choose pods that are 3 inches or shorter, and salt them to reduce sliminess (see variation). You can use frozen spinach instead of fresh; if your package is less than 12 ounces, you can make up the difference with the heartier greens. Serve over rice.

½ cup vegetable oil
½ cup all-purpose flour
1 large onion, chopped fine
2 celery ribs, chopped fine
1 green bell pepper, stemmed, seeded, and chopped fine
3 garlic cloves, minced
1 tablespoon minced fresh thyme or 1 teaspoon dried
2¼ teaspoons table salt, divided
2 teaspoons smoked paprika
1 teaspoon cayenne pepper
5 cups water
12 ounces collard greens, mustard greens, or kale, stemmed, and cut into 1-inch pieces
1 cup frozen cut okra
1 (15-ounce) can black-eyed peas, rinsed
12 ounces curly-leaf spinach or Swiss chard, stemmed, and cut into 1-inch pieces
6 ounces green beans, trimmed and cut into 1-inch lengths
1 tablespoon cider vinegar, plus extra for seasoning
2 scallions, sliced thin (optional)

1. Heat oil in Dutch oven over medium-high heat until just smoking. Using rubber spatula, stir in flour and cook, stirring constantly, until mixture is color of peanut butter, 2 to 5 minutes. Reduce heat to medium-low and continue to cook, stirring constantly, until roux has darkened to color of milk chocolate, 5 to 10 minutes longer.

2. Stir in onion, celery, bell pepper, garlic, thyme, 1 teaspoon salt, paprika, and cayenne. Cover, and cook, stirring frequently until vegetables have softened, 8 to 10 minutes.

3. Stir in water, scraping up any browned bits, and bring to boil. Stir in collards 1 handful at a time, okra, and remaining 1¼ teaspoons salt. Cover, reduce heat to low, and simmer until greens are just tender, 5 to 7 minutes. Stir in black-eyed peas; spinach, 1 handful at a time; and green beans and simmer until green beans and spinach are tender, about 5 minutes. Stir in vinegar and season with salt, pepper, and additional vinegar to taste. Sprinkle with scallions, if using. Serve.

VARIATION
Green Gumbo with Fresh Okra
Substitute 4 ounces trimmed fresh okra for frozen okra. Before starting step 1, toss trimmed okra with ¼ teaspoon salt. Let sit for 1 hour, stirring halfway through. Rinse well, then cut into 1-inch pieces; set aside until ready to use in step 3.

Vegan Mapo Tofu
Serves 4 to 6

Why This Recipe Works Mapo tofu is a spicy Sichuan classic and popular menu choice in Chinese restaurants, traditionally containing minced or ground pork or beef. Our vegan rendition is equally bold in flavor, with a balanced spiciness and a complex sauce. We started with cubed soft tofu, poached gently in salted water to firm up the cubes and help them stay intact in the braise. For the sauce base, we used plenty of ginger and garlic along with four Sichuan pantry powerhouses: Asian broad bean chili paste, fermented black beans, Sichuan chili powder, and Sichuan peppercorns. A small amount of finely chopped mushrooms brought umami depth. In place of the chili oil often called for, we used a generous amount of vegetable oil, extra Sichuan chili powder, and toasted sesame oil. We finished the dish with just the right amount of cornstarch to create a velvety texture. If you can't find Sichuan chili powder, an equal amount of Korean red pepper flakes (gochugaru) is a good substitute. In a pinch, use 2½ teaspoons ancho chile powder and ½ teaspoon cayenne pepper. If you can't find fermented black beans, you can use an equal amount of fermented black bean paste or sauce or 2 additional teaspoons of Asian broad bean chili paste. Serve with white rice.

2 cups water
½ teaspoon table salt
½ ounce dried shiitake mushrooms
1 tablespoon Sichuan peppercorns
12 scallions
28 ounces soft tofu, cut into ½-inch pieces
9 garlic cloves, peeled
1 (3-inch) piece ginger, peeled and cut into ¼-inch rounds
⅓ cup Asian broad bean chili paste
1 tablespoon fermented black beans
½ cup vegetable oil, divided
1 tablespoon Sichuan chili powder

Vegan Mapo Tofu

4. Process garlic, ginger, chili paste, and black beans in food processor until coarse paste forms, 1 to 2 minutes, scraping down sides of bowl as needed. Add ¼ cup vegetable oil, chili powder, and 1 teaspoon peppercorns and continue to process until smooth paste forms, 1 to 2 minutes. Transfer spice paste to bowl.

5. Place reserved soaked mushrooms and fresh shiitake mushrooms in now-empty processor and pulse until finely chopped, 15 to 20 pulses (do not overprocess). Heat 2 tablespoons vegetable oil and mushroom mixture in large saucepan over medium heat, breaking up mushrooms with wooden spoon, until mushrooms begin to brown and stick to bottom of saucepan, 5 to 7 minutes. Transfer mushroom mixture to bowl.

6. Add remaining 2 tablespoons vegetable oil and spice paste to now-empty saucepan and cook, stirring frequently, until paste darkens and oil begins to separate from paste, 2 to 3 minutes. Gently pour tofu with mushroom liquid into saucepan, followed by hoisin, sesame oil, and mushroom mixture. Cook, gently stirring frequently, until dish comes to simmer, 2 to 3 minutes. Whisk soy sauce and cornstarch together in small bowl. Add cornstarch mixture to saucepan and continue to cook, stirring frequently, until thickened, 2 to 3 minutes. Transfer to serving dish, sprinkle with remaining peppercorns, and serve. (Mapo tofu can be refrigerated for up to 24 hours.)

FLAVOR BOOSTER

SICHUAN PEPPERCORNS
These reddish-brown husks are neither peppercorns nor are they related to chiles. They're the dried fruit rinds of the Chinese prickly ash tree. Sichuan peppercorns have a lemony tartness and a piney aroma, but they are best known for the unique tingling sensation they produce on the lips and tongue, thanks to a compound called hydroxy-alpha-sanshool, which acts on receptors that usually respond to touch. The peppercorns don't actually cause our skin to vibrate, but they send signals to the brain that we interpret as vibration or numbing; some people also perceive these signals as heat.

---

4 ounces fresh shiitake mushrooms, stemmed, or oyster mushrooms, trimmed
2 tablespoons hoisin sauce
2 teaspoons toasted sesame oil
2 tablespoons soy sauce
1 tablespoon cornstarch

1. Microwave water, salt, and dried mushrooms in covered large bowl until steaming, about 1 minute. Let sit until softened, about 5 minutes. Drain mushrooms in fine-mesh strainer, reserving liquid; set aside soaked mushrooms and return liquid to large bowl.

2. Place peppercorns in small bowl and microwave until fragrant, 15 to 30 seconds. Let cool completely. Once cool, grind in spice grinder or mortar and pestle (you should have 1½ teaspoons).

3. Using side of chef's knife, lightly crush white parts of scallions, then cut scallions into 1-inch pieces. Place tofu and scallions in bowl with reserved mushroom liquid and microwave until steaming, 5 to 7 minutes. Let sit while preparing remaining ingredients.

CHAPTER 3
SANDWICHES, BURGERS, PIZZA, AND MORE

■ FAST (45 minutes or less total time)

Photos: Spiced Cauliflower Burgers; Thin-Crust Pesto Pizza with Fennel and Cauliflower; Black Bean and Sweet Potato Tacos

Philly-Style Broccoli Rabe, Portobello, and Cheez Sandwiches

Serves 4

Why This Recipe Works A sub roll stuffed with spicy, juicy, garlicky goodness is uber-satisfying, and nobody does these sandwiches like Philadelphia. The lesser-known underdog rival to the Philly cheesesteak loads up a hoagie (aka Italian sub) roll with roasted pork, garlicky broccoli rabe, provolone, and vinegary hot peppers. We decided to make the broccoli rabe the star of our reimagined feast in a bun and use meaty portobellos to stand in for the pork. Cooking 2 pounds of the mushrooms in one batch initially crowded the pan, but placing a lid over the heaping mound trapped enough steam to let them quickly shed excess moisture so that flavorful browning could begin after we removed the lid. Fennel, rosemary, and a little soy brought heaps of savory flavor. Broiling the broccoli rabe let us cook a whole pound in just a few minutes while taming its bitterness and providing a little crispness. We piled the veggies into rolls, topped them with hot cherry peppers, and finished with our rich plant-based Cheez Sauce. This is a sandwich all eaters can get behind. To crack fennel, use a mortar and pestle or place the seeds on a cutting board and rock the bottom edge of a skillet over them until they crack. You will need a 12-inch nonstick skillet with a tight-fitting lid.

- 5 tablespoons extra-virgin oil, divided
- 2 pounds portobello mushroom caps, sliced ¼ inch thick
- ¾ teaspoon table salt, divided
- ¾ teaspoon fennel seeds, cracked
- ¾ teaspoon minced fresh rosemary
- 1 teaspoon soy sauce
- 2 garlic cloves, minced
- ¼ teaspoon red pepper flakes
- 1 pound broccoli rabe, trimmed, stems cut into 1-inch pieces, leaves and florets left whole
- 4 (8-inch) Italian sub rolls, split lengthwise and toasted
- 2 tablespoons sliced jarred hot cherry peppers (optional)
- 1 cup Cheez Sauce (page 26)

1. Adjust oven rack 4 inches from broiler element and heat broiler. Heat 2 tablespoons oil in 12-inch nonstick skillet over medium-high heat until shimmering. Add mushrooms and ¼ teaspoon salt; cover; and cook, stirring occasionally, until mushrooms have released their liquid, 5 to 7 minutes (skillet will be very full and lid may not close completely at first but will as mushrooms shrink). Uncover and continue to cook, stirring occasionally, until well browned, 10 to 12 minutes longer. Off heat, clear center of skillet; add 1 tablespoon oil, fennel seeds, and rosemary; and stir to combine. Stir in soy sauce and cover to keep warm.

2. Meanwhile, combine garlic, pepper flakes, remaining 2 tablespoons oil, and remaining ½ teaspoon salt in bowl. Pour oil mixture over broccoli rabe on aluminum foil–lined rimmed baking sheet and toss to coat. Broil until half of leaves are well browned, 2 to 2½ minutes. Using tongs, toss to expose unbrowned leaves. Return sheet to oven and continue to broil until most leaves are lightly charred and stems are crisp-tender, 2 to 2½ minutes longer.

3. Divide cooked mushrooms and broccoli rabe among rolls; top with cherry peppers, if using; and drizzle with cheez sauce. Serve immediately.

MLTs

Serves 4

Why This Recipe Works A classic BLT sandwich appeals because it balances a few simple ingredients—salty-crisp bacon, sweet-juicy tomatoes, and refreshing lettuce tied together with a slick of mayonnaise—so well. To create a flavor-packed plant-based version that's just as appealing as the porky variety, we used strips of portobello mushrooms, which made an excellent stand-in for bacon. When sautéed and seasoned with smoked paprika and a little salt, they brought meaty texture, umami character, and even some smokiness. Using a full 1½ pounds of mushrooms provided plenty of substance without causing the sandwich to fall apart. We kept the juicy tomatoes but swapped the usual romaine for arugula, enjoying how its peppery bite perked up the other flavors. Finally, for a rich, tangy, creamy spread, we mixed avocado and yogurt and happily slathered it on toasted rustic bread to complete the sandwich.

- 1 tablespoon extra-virgin olive oil
- 1 shallot, minced
- 1½ pounds portobello mushroom caps, gills removed, sliced ½ inch thick
- ½ teaspoon plus ⅛ teaspoon table salt, divided
- 1 garlic clove, minced
- ½ teaspoon smoked paprika
- 1 ripe avocado, halved and pitted

MLTs

2 tablespoons plain plant-based yogurt or dairy yogurt

8 slices rustic bread, toasted

2 tomatoes, cored and sliced thin

2 ounces (2 cups) baby arugula

1. Heat oil in 12-inch nonstick skillet over medium heat. Add shallot and cook until softened, about 2 minutes. Add mushrooms and ½ teaspoon salt, cover, and cook, stirring occasionally, until mushrooms have released their moisture, 10 to 12 minutes.

2. Uncover, increase heat to medium-high, and cook until mushrooms are lightly browned, about 10 minutes. Stir in garlic and smoked paprika and cook until fragrant, about 30 seconds. Remove pan from heat and let mushrooms cool slightly, about 10 minutes.

3. Just before serving, combine avocado, yogurt, and remaining ⅛ teaspoon salt in small bowl and mash until smooth. Spread avocado mixture evenly over 4 toast slices. Assemble 4 sandwiches by evenly layering mushrooms, tomatoes, then arugula. Top with remaining 4 toast slices. Serve.

Chickpea Salad Sandwiches
Serves 6 `FAST`

Why This Recipe Works Sandwiches made with chicken or tuna salads are old standbys, but we wanted to put a modern spin on this category by using protein-packed chickpeas as our salad base—but still with all the richness and saucy texture of a traditional deli salad. Mayonnaise (plant-based or egg-based) helped the cause, but too much of it masked the savory chickpea flavor, so we decided to use some of the chickpeas to make a hummus-style puree. We buzzed a portion of the chickpeas with mayo, water, and lemon juice in the food processor for the perfect creamy binder. Then we added the remaining chickpeas to the mixture and briefly pulsed them to give us good textural contrast. To round things out, we turned to classic flavors: Chopped celery provided crunch, dill pickle brought salty brininess, and scallions and herbs finished the salad with bright, fresh flavor. It makes a creamy, luscious sandwich sure to satisfy any lunchtime craving. Serve on toasted bread with lettuce, tomato, and/or sliced avocado if desired. This salad is also delicious served in lettuce wraps.

2 (15-ounce) cans chickpeas, rinsed, divided

½ cup plant-based mayonnaise or egg-based mayonnaise

¼ cup water

1 tablespoon lemon juice

½ teaspoon table salt

2 celery ribs, finely chopped

⅓ cup dill pickles, finely chopped

2 scallions, sliced thin

2 tablespoons minced fresh parsley, dill, or tarragon

12 slices hearty sandwich bread, toasted

1. Process ¾ cup chickpeas, mayonnaise, water, lemon juice, and salt in food processor until smooth, about 30 seconds, scraping down sides of bowl as needed.

2. Add remaining chickpeas to food processor and pulse until coarsely chopped with some larger pieces remaining, about 4 pulses.

3. Combine chickpea mixture, celery, pickles, scallions, and parsley in large bowl and season with salt and pepper to taste. Spread chickpea salad evenly over 6 bread slices. Top with remaining bread slices and serve.

VARIATION

Curried Chickpea Salad Sandwiches
Add 1 tablespoon curry powder to chickpea mixture in food processor in step 1 and substitute ½ cup golden raisins for pickles.

SAUCES FOR YOUR SANDWICH

A good sauce can elevate the simplest sandwich into a memorable meal. All of these sauces are superversatile beyond sandwiches as well. The yogurt-based sauces enliven rice dishes or serve as a dip for flatbread. The Tomato-Chile Sauce is great on scrambled tofu or eggs or stirred into noodles. Use the Romesco Sauce for a dip for crudités (page 352). Drizzle the Cilantro Sauce or Avocado Crema on nachos or enchiladas.

Cilantro-Mint Chutney
Makes about 1 cup
This herb-based chutney comes together in a flash in the food processor, with no need to chop the herbs in advance. If using dairy yogurt, we prefer whole-milk yogurt.

- 2 cups fresh cilantro leaves
- 1 cup fresh mint leaves
- ⅓ cup plain plant-based yogurt or dairy yogurt
- ¼ cup finely chopped onion
- 1 tablespoon lime juice
- 1½ teaspoons sugar
- ½ teaspoon ground cumin
- ¼ teaspoon table salt

Process all ingredients in food processor until smooth, about 20 seconds, scraping down sides of bowl as needed. (Chutney can be refrigerated for up to 2 days.)

Cilantro Sauce
Makes about ¾ cup
You can use plain plant-based yogurt in place of the plant-based sour cream, if you prefer.

- ¼ cup plant-based mayonnaise or egg-based mayonnaise
- ¼ cup plant-based sour cream or dairy sour cream
- 3 tablespoons water
- 3 tablespoons minced fresh cilantro
- ¼ teaspoon table salt

Whisk all ingredients together in bowl. (Sauce can be refrigerated for up to 2 days.)

Tomato-Chile Sauce
Makes about 1½ cups
This zingy sauce is a classic accompaniment to Falafel (page 94).

- 1 (15-ounce) can diced tomatoes, drained
- ½ cup fresh cilantro leaves and stems
- 3 garlic cloves, minced
- 1 tablespoon red pepper flakes
- 1 tablespoon red wine vinegar, plus extra for seasoning
- 1 teaspoon ground cumin
- 1 teaspoon ground coriander
- ¾ teaspoon table salt
- ½ teaspoon smoked paprika
- ⅛ teaspoon sugar
- 2 tablespoons extra-virgin olive oil

Process tomatoes, cilantro, garlic, pepper flakes, vinegar, cumin, coriander, salt, paprika, and sugar in food processor until smooth paste forms, 20 to 30 seconds. With processor running, slowly add oil until fully incorporated, about 5 seconds. Transfer to bowl and season with salt and extra vinegar to taste. (Sauce can be refrigerated for up to 2 days.)

Herbed Yogurt Sauce
Makes about 1 cup

- 1 cup plain plant-based yogurt or dairy yogurt
- 2 tablespoons minced fresh cilantro
- 2 tablespoons minced fresh mint
- 1 garlic clove, minced

Whisk all ingredients in bowl until combined. Season with salt and pepper to taste. Let sit until flavors meld, about 30 minutes. (Sauce can be refrigerated for up to 2 days.)

Herbed Yogurt Sauce

Romesco Sauce

Makes about ¾ cup

Pungent and rich, this classic Spanish sauce comes together quickly with jarred roasted red peppers.

- ⅔ cup jarred roasted red peppers, patted dry
- ¼ cup slivered almonds, toasted
- ¼ cup fresh parsley leaves
- 3 tablespoons extra-virgin olive oil
- 1 tablespoon sherry vinegar
- 1 garlic clove, minced
- ¼ teaspoon table salt

Process all ingredients in food processor until smooth, about 1 minute, scraping down sides of bowl as needed. Season with salt and pepper to taste. (Sauce can be refrigerated for up to 2 days.)

Avocado Crema

Makes about ½ cup

- ½ avocado, pitted and chopped coarse
- ¼ cup chopped fresh cilantro
- 3 tablespoons water
- 1 tablespoon lime juice
- 1 tablespoon plain plant-based yogurt or dairy yogurt

Process all ingredients in food processor until completely smooth, about 1 minute, scraping down sides of bowl as needed. Season with salt and pepper to taste. Serve. (Crema can be refrigerated with plastic wrap pressed flush to surface for up to 2 days.)

Summer Rolls with Tofu and Spicy Almond Butter Sauce

Serves 4

Why This Recipe Works Despite their evocative name, many summer rolls contain mostly rice noodles, leaving fresh vegetables as an afterthought. For our version, we skipped the noodles altogether and gathered up a rainbow of healthful veggies to fill the rice paper wrappers. A mix of red cabbage, red bell pepper, cucumber, and carrots delivered color and crunch. Fresh basil added herbal notes, and strips of marinated tofu made the rolls hearty enough for lunch. Instead of the typical thin soy dipping sauce, we whisked up a sriracha-spiked almond butter sauce. Thick and rich, it clung to our rolls, taking this dish to a new level. Be sure to make one roll at a time to keep the wrappers moist and pliable. Brands of rice paper wrappers vary in the time they take to soak and become pliable. You can use smooth or chunky almond or peanut butter.

Sauce
- 3 tablespoons almond or peanut butter
- 3 tablespoons water
- 1 tablespoon rice vinegar
- 1 tablespoon soy sauce
- 2 teaspoons grated fresh ginger
- 1 teaspoon sriracha
- 1 garlic clove, minced

Rolls
- 6 tablespoons rice wine vinegar, divided
- 1 tablespoon soy sauce
- 2 teaspoons sriracha
- 2 scallions, sliced thin on bias
- 7 ounces extra-firm tofu, cut into 3-inch-long by ½-inch-thick strips
- 3½ cups shredded red cabbage
- 12 (8-inch) round rice paper wrappers
- 1 cup fresh basil leaves
- 1 red bell pepper, stemmed, seeded, and cut into 2-inch-long matchsticks
- ½ seedless English cucumber, cut into 3-inch-long matchsticks
- 2 carrots, peeled and shredded

1. For the sauce Whisk all ingredients until well combined; set aside.

2. For the rolls Whisk 2 tablespoons vinegar, soy sauce, sriracha, and scallions in small bowl until well combined. Place tofu in shallow dish, then pour soy sauce mixture over top and let sit for 1 hour. Toss cabbage with remaining ¼ cup

Summer Rolls with Tofu and Spicy Almond Butter Sauce

vinegar and let sit for 1 hour. Drain cabbage in fine mesh strainer, pressing gently with back of spatula to remove as much liquid as possible. Transfer to large plate and pat dry with paper towels.

3. Spread clean, damp dish towel on work surface. Fill 9-inch pie plate with 1 inch room-temperature water. Working with 1 wrapper at a time, submerge each in water until just pliable, 10 seconds to 2 minutes; lay softened wrapper on towel. Scatter 3 basil leaves over wrapper. Arrange 5 matchsticks each of bell pepper and cucumber horizontally on wrapper, leaving 2-inch border at bottom. Top with 1 tablespoon carrots, then arrange 2 tablespoons cabbage on top of carrots. Place 1 strip tofu horizontally on top of vegetables, being sure to shake off excess marinade.

4. Fold bottom of wrapper over filling, pulling back on it firmly to tighten it around filling, then fold sides of wrapper in and continue to roll tightly into spring roll. Transfer to platter and cover with second damp dish towel.

5. Repeat with remaining wrappers and filling. Serve with almond butter sauce. (Spring rolls are best eaten immediately but can be covered with a clean, damp dish towel and refrigerated for up to 4 hours.)

Korean Barbecue Tempeh Wraps

Serves 4

Why This Recipe Works Boldly flavored, sweet-and-sticky Korean barbecue is always a hit, and this tempeh wrap includes all those winning flavors, proving that you don't need meat to enjoy it. Tempeh has a great firm, chewy texture that stood out once wrapped, and its slight bitterness worked beautifully with the flavor-packed barbecue sauce. To give the tempeh a deeply browned crust, we seared it in a skillet before tossing it with the quick sauce made from soy sauce, garlic, sugar, sriracha, and rice vinegar, which balanced the tempeh with sweetness, tang, and a little heat. Including some cornstarch and simmering the sauce for 5 minutes gave it a thick, velvety consistency, and it clung nicely to the tempeh. For vegetables and herbs, we chose thinly sliced baby bok choy, radishes, and scallions for cool crunch, plus whole cilantro leaves for freshness. We tossed half of the barbecue sauce with the tempeh and then drizzled the other half over the vegetables so the wrap would have great flavors in every bite.

- ¾ cup sugar
- 6 tablespoons soy sauce
- 6 tablespoons water
- 5 garlic cloves, minced
- 1½ tablespoons rice vinegar
- 1½ teaspoons sriracha
- 1½ teaspoons cornstarch
- ¼ cup vegetable oil, divided
- 1 pound tempeh, cut crosswise into ½-inch-thick strips, divided
- 4 (10-inch) flour tortillas
- 2 large heads baby bok choy (4 ounces each), sliced thin crosswise
- 1 cup fresh cilantro leaves
- 3 radishes, trimmed, halved, and sliced thin
- 2 scallions, sliced thin

1. Whisk sugar, soy sauce, water, garlic, vinegar, sriracha, and cornstarch together in bowl.

2. Heat 2 tablespoons oil in 12-inch nonstick skillet over medium heat until shimmering. Add half of tempeh and cook until golden brown, 2 to 4 minutes per side; transfer to paper towel–lined plate. Repeat with remaining 2 tablespoons oil and remaining tempeh.

3. Add sugar-soy mixture to now-empty skillet and simmer over medium-low heat until thickened and measures 1 cup, about 5 minutes; transfer to bowl. Toss tempeh with half of sauce in separate bowl.

4. Lay tortillas on counter; arrange tempeh, bok choy, cilantro, radishes, and scallions in center of each tortilla; then drizzle each with 1 tablespoon sauce. Fold short sides then bottom of each tortilla over filling, pulling back firmly to tighten tortilla around filling, then continue to roll tightly. Serve with remaining sauce.

Tofu Banh Mi

Serves 4

Why This Recipe Works Vietnamese street food is arguably some of the best in the world, and the banh mi is one stellar example. In Vietnam, "banh mi" is simply a term for all kinds of bread, but Americans recognize the phrase as a terrific sandwich featuring chicken, pork, or tofu on a mayo-slathered roll, with crunchy pickled vegetables and fresh herbs to offset the protein and mayo's richness. For our plant-forward version, we obviously chose tofu, but of course, simply stuffing a sandwich with slabs of tofu wouldn't do the dish justice. Instead, we sliced the tofu into planks and drained them on paper towels to sop up the excess water, which can inhibit browning and crisping during cooking. Then we dredged the planks in cornstarch and seared them in a hot skillet until they were nicely browned. The cornstarch coating created a pleasingly delicate crispy-fried crust without using too much oil. For the vegetables, we quick-pickled cucumber slices and shredded carrot in lime juice and fish sauce substitute. The cucumber was cooling and the carrots added sweet crunch. The mayo sauce brings all the components of a banh mi together. We spiked our mayo with sriracha for a spicy kick, and we sprinkled fresh cilantro on our sandwich for an authentic garnish.

- 14 ounces firm tofu, sliced crosswise into ½-inch-thick planks
- ¼ teaspoon table salt
- ⅛ teaspoon pepper
- 2 carrots, peeled and shredded
- ½ cucumber, peeled, halved lengthwise, seeded, and sliced thin
- 1 teaspoon grated lime zest plus 1 tablespoon juice
- 1 tablespoon Fish Sauce Substitute (see page 22)
- ¼ cup plant-based mayonnaise or egg-based mayonnaise
- 1 tablespoon sriracha
- ⅓ cup cornstarch
- 3 tablespoons vegetable oil
- 4 (8-inch) sub rolls, split and toasted
- ⅓ cup fresh cilantro leaves

1. Spread tofu on paper towel–lined baking sheet and let drain for 20 minutes. Gently press dry with paper towels and sprinkle with salt and pepper.

2. Meanwhile, combine carrots, cucumber, lime juice, and fish sauce substitute in bowl and let sit for 15 minutes. Whisk mayonnaise, sriracha, and lime zest together in second bowl.

3. Spread cornstarch in shallow dish. Dredge seasoned tofu in cornstarch and transfer to plate. Heat oil in 12-inch non-stick skillet over medium-high heat until just smoking. Add tofu and cook until crisp and browned, about 4 minutes per side; transfer to paper towel–lined plate.

4. Spread mayonnaise mixture evenly over cut sides of each roll. Layer tofu, pickled vegetables (leave liquid in bowl), and cilantro evenly in rolls. Press gently on sandwiches to set. Serve.

Falafel

Serves 6 (**Makes** 24 falafel)

Why This Recipe Works For moist, tender falafel packed with flavorful seasonings, we started by soaking dried chickpeas overnight to soften them slightly before grinding them into coarse bits along with onion, herbs, garlic, and spices. Instead of binding the dough with uncooked flour, which yields bready fritters, we mixed in a cooked flour paste that added moisture without making the dough too fragile to form and fry. Cooking the fritters at a relatively low 325 degrees allowed their particularly moist interiors to fully cook by the time their exteriors were brown and crisp. Use a Dutch oven that holds 6 quarts or more. An equal amount of chickpea flour can be substituted for the all-purpose flour; if using, increase the water in step 3 to ½ cup. Do not substitute canned or quick-soaked chickpeas; they will make leaden falafel. Stuff the sandwiches with any combo of shredded lettuce, chopped tomatoes, chopped cucumbers, fresh cilantro, Quick Pickled Turnips and Carrots with Lemon and Coriander, and Tomato-Chile Sauce (page 90). Serve the first batch of falafel immediately or hold it in a 200-degree oven while the second batch cooks.

- 8 ounces dried chickpeas, picked over and rinsed
- ¾ cup fresh cilantro leaves and stems
- ¾ cup fresh parsley leaves
- ½ onion, chopped fine
- 2 garlic cloves, minced
- 1½ teaspoons ground coriander
- 1 teaspoon ground cumin
- 1 teaspoon table salt
- ¼ teaspoon cayenne pepper

Sizzling Saigon Crepes

- ¼ cup all-purpose flour
- 2 teaspoons baking powder
- 2 quarts vegetable oil
- 4 to 6 (8-inch) pita breads
- 1 recipe Tahini-Yogurt Sauce (page 249)

1. Place chickpeas in large container and cover with water by 2 to 3 inches. Soak at room temperature for at least 8 hours or up to 24 hours. Drain well.

2. Process cilantro, parsley, onion, garlic, coriander, cumin, salt, and cayenne in food processor for 5 seconds. Scrape down sides of bowl. Continue to process until mixture resembles pesto, about 5 seconds longer. Add chickpeas and pulse 6 times. Scrape down sides of bowl. Continue to pulse until chickpeas are coarsely chopped and resemble sesame seeds, about 6 more pulses. Transfer mixture to large bowl and set aside.

3. Whisk flour and ⅓ cup water in bowl until no lumps remain. Microwave, whisking every 10 seconds, until mixture thickens to stiff, smooth, pudding-like consistency that forms mound when dropped from end of whisk into bowl, 40 to 80 seconds. Stir baking powder into flour paste.

4. Add flour paste to chickpea mixture and, using rubber spatula, mix until fully incorporated. Divide mixture into 24 pieces and gently roll into golf ball–size spheres, transferring spheres to parchment paper–lined rimmed baking sheet once formed. (Formed falafel can be refrigerated for up to 2 hours.)

5. Heat oil in large Dutch oven over medium-high heat to 325 degrees. Add half of falafel and fry, stirring occasionally, until deep brown, about 5 minutes. Adjust burner, if necessary, to maintain oil temperature of 325 degrees. Using slotted spoon or wire skimmer, transfer falafel to paper towel–lined baking sheet. Return oil to 325 degrees and repeat with remaining falafel. Stuff each pita with 4 falafel balls, and serve immediately with tahini sauce.

Quick Pickled Turnips and Carrots with Lemon and Coriander
Makes about 4 cups
To ensure that the turnips are tender, peel them thoroughly to remove not only the tough outer skin but also the fibrous layer of flesh just beneath.

    1 teaspoon coriander seeds
    1 teaspoon mustard seeds
 1½ cups cider vinegar
    ¾ cup water
    1 tablespoon sugar
    ½ teaspoon red pepper flakes
    ½ teaspoon table salt
    1 pound turnips, peeled and cut into ½ by
       ½ by 2-inch batons
    1 red onion, halved and sliced thin
    2 carrots, peeled and sliced thin on bias
    4 (3-inch) strips lemon zest

Toast coriander seeds and mustard seeds in medium saucepan over medium heat, stirring frequently, until fragrant, about 2 minutes. Add vinegar, water, sugar, pepper flakes, and salt and bring to boil, stirring to dissolve sugar and salt. Remove saucepan from heat and add turnips, onion, carrots, and lemon zest, pressing to submerge vegetables. Cover and let cool completely, 30 minutes. (Cooled vegetables can be refrigerated for up to 1 week.)

Sizzling Saigon Crepes
Serves 8 (Makes 9 crepes)

Why This Recipe Works Named banh xeo for the sizzling sound the batter makes when it hits the hot pan, these crispy, paper-thin, yellow Vietnamese crepes are stuffed with fillings, wrapped with lettuce and fresh herbs, and dipped into a tart-sweet sauce. The crepes are naturally vegan; though pork and shrimp are often used in the stuffing, we created a vegetable-based version with a simple combo of bean sprouts, shredded carrots, and sliced onions. The crepe batter is also simple, made with water, rice flour, and coconut milk. To make the flipping and folding of the delicate crepes easy, we used a 10-inch nonstick skillet. For the dipping sauce, we combined fish sauce substitute with lime juice, sugar, fresh chiles, and garlic. Do not substitute regular flour or cornstarch for the rice flour. If you can't find Thai basil, you can use regular basil. To allow for trial and error, the recipe yields 9 crepes.

Dipping Sauce and Garnish
 ⅓ cup Fish Sauce Substitute (page 22)
 ¼ cup warm water
    3 tablespoons lime juice (2 limes)
    2 tablespoons sugar
    2 Thai, serrano, or jalapeño chiles, stemmed, seeded, and minced
    1 garlic clove, minced
    2 heads red or green leaf lettuce, leaves separated
    1 cup fresh Thai basil leaves
    1 cup fresh cilantro leaves

Crepes
 2¾ cups water
 1¾ cups rice flour
 ½ cup coconut milk
    4 scallions, sliced thin
 1½ teaspoons table salt, divided
    1 teaspoon ground turmeric
 ¼ cup vegetable oil, divided
    1 onion, halved and sliced thin
    1 pound carrots, peeled and shredded
    6 ounces (3 cups) bean sprouts

1. For the dipping sauce and garnish Whisk fish sauce substitute, warm water, lime juice, sugar, chiles, and garlic in bowl until sugar dissolves. Divide sauce among 8 small bowls. Arrange lettuce, basil, and cilantro on serving platter.

2. For the crepes Adjust oven rack to middle position and heat oven to 200 degrees. Set wire rack in rimmed baking sheet. Whisk water, flour, coconut milk, scallions, 1 teaspoon salt, and turmeric in bowl until combined.

3. Heat 1 tablespoon oil in 10-inch nonstick skillet over medium-high heat until shimmering. Add onion and remaining ½ teaspoon salt and cook until onion is softened, 5 to 7 minutes. Transfer to bowl. Add carrots to skillet and cook until tender, about 2 minutes. Transfer to bowl with onions and let cool slightly. Stir in bean sprouts and set vegetable mixture aside.

4. Wipe out skillet with paper towels. Heat 1 teaspoon oil in now-empty skillet over medium-high heat until just smoking. Whisk batter to recombine, then pour ½ cup batter into skillet while swirling pan gently to distribute it evenly over pan bottom. Reduce heat to medium and cook crepe until edges pull away from sides and are deep golden, 3 to 5 minutes.

5. Gently slide spatula underneath edge of crepe, grasp edge with your fingertips, and flip crepe. Cook until spotty brown on second side, 2 to 3 minutes. Slide crepe out of skillet and onto prepared wire rack and transfer to oven to keep warm. Repeat with remaining oil and remaining batter.

6. Divide vegetable mixture evenly among crepes and fold crepes in half. Serve crepes with dipping sauce, passing garnish platter separately. (To eat, slice off wedge of crepe, nestle basil and cilantro in lettuce leaf, wrap wedge in lettuce, and dip into sauce.)

COOKING SAIGON CREPES

1. Quickly whisk batter to recombine, then pour ½ cup batter into skillet while swirling pan gently to distribute evenly over pan bottom.

2. Reduce heat to medium and cook crepe until edges pull away from sides and are deep golden, 3 to 5 minutes. Slide spatula underneath edge, grasp edge with your fingertips, and flip.

3. Slide crepe out of skillet and onto wire rack set in rimmed baking sheet; transfer to 200-degree oven to keep warm.

Mumbai Frankie Wraps
Serves 4

Why This Recipe Works In Mumbai, India's largest city, easy-to-eat street foods such as these wraps are hugely popular. Frankies take many forms but tend to share a few key characteristics. A warm, tender, whole-wheat flatbread (chapati or roti) is filled with a delectably spiced mixture of potatoes, along with proteins or vegetables, and topped with condiments such as chutneys, sauces, and pickles before being rolled up. For our take on the frankie, we wanted to develop a wrap where each element on its own was simple and delicious but together formed a veritable cornucopia of well-balanced flavors and textures. We started with Yukon Gold potatoes, which we mashed with an aromatic mixture of shallot, ginger, garlic, turmeric, and coriander and enriched with creamy coconut milk. We spread the mixture over our wrap, sprinkled it with a combo of mildly spiced roasted cauliflower and chickpeas, and topped it with sweet-spicy onion pickles and a bright herbal chutney before rolling it into a cone shape. We prefer to make our own homemade Whole-Wheat Wraps, but you can substitute store-bought chapati or roti. We do not recommend naan or other (thicker) flatbreads. For easiest assembly, we recommend making the pickled onions, chutney, and wraps ahead.

12 ounces cauliflower florets, cut into 1-inch pieces
1 (15-ounce) can chickpeas, rinsed
2 tablespoons vegetable oil, divided
¾ teaspoon garam masala
¾ teaspoon table salt, divided
1 pound Yukon Gold potatoes, peeled and cut into 1-inch pieces
1 shallot, minced
3 garlic cloves, minced
1 tablespoon grated fresh ginger
1 teaspoon ground turmeric
⅛ teaspoon ground coriander
 Pinch cayenne pepper
½ cup canned coconut milk
1 recipe Whole-Wheat Wraps (Chapati) (page 97), warmed
¼ cup Cilantro-Mint Chutney (page 90)
¼ cup Quick Sweet-and-Spicy Pickled Red Onions (page 99)

1. Adjust oven rack to lowest position and heat oven to 500 degrees. Line rimmed baking sheet with aluminum foil. Toss cauliflower, chickpeas, 1 tablespoon oil, garam masala, and ¼ teaspoon salt together in bowl. Spread cauliflower mixture in even layer on prepared sheet and roast, stirring

Mumbai Frankie Wraps

halfway through roasting, until cauliflower is spotty brown and tender, about 10 minutes; set aside. (Cauliflower mixture can be refrigerated up to 24 hours; let come to room temperature before serving.)

2. Place potatoes and remaining ½ teaspoon salt in large saucepan, add cold water to cover by 1 inch, and bring to boil over high heat. Reduce heat to medium and simmer until potatoes are tender, about 12 minutes; drain well.

3. Heat remaining 1 tablespoon oil in now-empty saucepan over medium heat until shimmering. Add shallot and cook until softened and lightly browned, 3 to 5 minutes. Stir in garlic, ginger, turmeric, coriander, and cayenne and cook until fragrant, about 30 seconds. Stir in coconut milk, scraping up any browned bits, and bring to simmer. Stir in potatoes, then remove from heat and mash with potato masher until mostly smooth, about 2 minutes. Season with salt to taste; set aside. (Potato mixture can be refrigerated up to 24 hours; heat in microwave, covered, before serving.)

4. Divide potato mixture evenly among whole-wheat wraps, then spread in even layer over half of each wrap. Divide cauliflower mixture evenly over top, then top each with 2 tablespoons chutney and 2 tablespoons pickled onions. Roll into cone shape and serve.

Whole-Wheat Wraps (Chapati)
Serves 4 (Makes 4 wraps)

- ¾ cup (4⅛ ounces) whole-wheat flour
- ¾ cup (3¾ ounces) all-purpose flour
- 1 teaspoon table salt
- ½ cup warm water (110 degrees)
- 3 tablespoons plus 2 teaspoons vegetable oil, divided

1. Whisk flours and salt together in bowl. Stir in water and 3 tablespoons oil until cohesive dough forms. Transfer dough to lightly floured counter and knead by hand to form smooth ball, 1 minute.

2. Divide dough into 4 pieces and cover with plastic wrap. Working with 1 piece at a time (keep remaining pieces covered), form into ball by stretching dough around your thumbs and pinching edges together so that top is smooth. Place ball seam side down on clean counter and shape into smooth, taut ball. Place on plate seam side down, cover with plastic wrap, and let sit for 30 minutes. (Dough balls can be refrigerated for up to 3 days.)

3. Line rimmed baking sheet with parchment paper. Roll 1 dough ball into 9-inch round on lightly floured counter (keep remaining pieces covered). Transfer to prepared sheet and top with additional sheet of parchment. Repeat with remaining dough balls.

4. Heat 12-inch cast-iron or nonstick skillet over medium heat for 3 minutes. Add ½ teaspoon oil to skillet, then use paper towels to carefully wipe out skillet, leaving thin film of oil on bottom; skillet should be just smoking. (If using 12-inch nonstick skillet, heat ½ teaspoon oil over medium heat in skillet until shimmering, then wipe out skillet.)

5. Place 1 dough round in hot skillet and cook until dough is bubbly and bottom is browned in spots, about 2 minutes. Flip dough and cook until puffed and second side is spotty brown, 1 to 2 minutes. Transfer to clean plate and cover with dish towel to keep warm. Repeat with remaining dough rounds and oil. Serve. (Cooked wraps can be refrigerated for up to 3 days or frozen for up to 3 months. To freeze, layer wraps between parchment and store in zipper-lock bag. To serve, stack wraps on plate, cover with damp dish towel, and microwave until warm, 60 to 90 seconds.)

Baja-Style Cauliflower Tacos

Black Bean and Sweet Potato Tacos

Baja-Style Cauliflower Tacos
Serves 6

Why This Recipe Works Baja California evokes images of tacos (typically, with seafood) and margaritas on sunny, breezy patios. Here we re-create that feeling at home, bringing veggies to the forefront. Battered cauliflower bites were the perfect stand-in for mild white fish. To achieve a crisp exterior without deep-frying, we cut the cauliflower into florets, dunked them in seasoned coconut milk and rolled them in a mix of panko and shredded coconut, and roasted them. The coconut milk stood in for eggs while also boosting richness and adding the flavors of a cabana-shaded getaway. A bed of slaw with juicy mango and spicy jalapeño brought crunch, sweetness, and heat. For a cool, creamy sauce, we whipped up equal parts mayonnaise and sour cream (plant-based or dairy), plus cilantro and a bit of lime zest. Garnish with Spicy Pickled Radishes (page 328) and lime wedges if you like.

3	cups (7½ ounces) coleslaw mix
½	mango, peeled and cut into ¼-inch pieces (¾ cup)
2	tablespoons lime juice
1	tablespoon chopped fresh cilantro
1	tablespoon minced jalapeño chile
1¼	teaspoons table salt, divided
1	cup unsweetened shredded coconut
1	cup panko bread crumbs
1	cup canned coconut milk
1	teaspoon garlic powder
1	teaspoon ground cumin
¼	teaspoon cayenne
½	head cauliflower (1 pound), trimmed and cut into 1-inch pieces
12	(6-inch) corn tortillas, warmed
1	recipe Cilantro Sauce (page 90)

1. Adjust oven rack to middle position and heat oven to 450 degrees. Combine coleslaw mix, mango, lime juice, cilantro, jalapeño, and ¼ teaspoon salt in bowl; cover; and refrigerate until ready to serve.

2. Spray rimmed baking sheet with vegetable oil spray. Combine coconut and panko in shallow dish. Whisk coconut milk, garlic powder, cumin, cayenne, and remaining 1 teaspoon salt together in bowl. Add cauliflower to coconut milk mixture; toss to coat well. Working with 1 piece cauliflower at a time, remove from coconut milk, letting excess drip back into bowl, then coat well with coconut-panko mixture, pressing gently to adhere; transfer to prepared sheet.

3. Bake until cauliflower is tender, golden, and crisp, 20 to 25 minutes, flipping cauliflower and rotating sheet halfway through baking.

4. Divide slaw evenly among warm tortillas and top with cauliflower. Drizzle with cilantro sauce and serve.

Black Bean and Sweet Potato Tacos
Serves 6

Why This Recipe Works One great thing about the proliferation of taco restaurants is the varied plant-based fillings that are featured, from cauliflower to mushrooms and more. It inspired us to create this delicious combo of sweet potatoes and poblano chiles, which we seasoned with fragrant garlic, cumin, coriander, and oregano. Roasting the vegetables produced caramelized exteriors and tender interiors. Adding black beans ramped up the protein for a satiating meal. Instead of topping the tacos with queso fresco or sour cream (which you could do, if you prefer), we made an avocado crema. For a tangy, spicy finish, we sprinkled the tacos with our Quick Sweet-and-Spicy Pickled Red Onions.

- 3 tablespoons extra-virgin olive oil
- 3 garlic cloves, minced
- 1½ teaspoons ground cumin
- 1½ teaspoons ground coriander
- 1 teaspoon minced fresh oregano or ¼ teaspoon dried
- 1 teaspoon table salt
- ½ teaspoon pepper
- 1 pound sweet potatoes, peeled and cut into ½-inch pieces
- 4 poblano chiles, stemmed, seeded, and cut into ½-inch-wide strips
- 1 large onion, halved and sliced ½ inch thick
- 1 (15-ounce) can black beans, rinsed
- ¼ cup chopped fresh cilantro
- 12 (6-inch) corn tortillas, warmed
- 1 recipe Avocado Crema (page 91)
- 1 recipe Quick Sweet-and-Spicy Pickled Red Onions (optional)

1. Adjust oven racks to upper-middle and lower-middle positions and heat oven to 450 degrees. Whisk oil, garlic, cumin, coriander, oregano, salt, and pepper together in large bowl. Add potatoes, poblanos, and onion to oil mixture and toss to coat.

2. Spread vegetable mixture in even layer over 2 foil-lined rimmed baking sheets. Roast vegetables until tender and golden brown, about 30 minutes, stirring vegetables and switching and rotating sheets halfway through baking.

3. Return vegetables to now-empty bowl, add black beans and cilantro, and gently toss to combine. Divide vegetables evenly among warm tortillas and top with avocado crema and pickled onions. Serve.

Quick Sweet-and-Spicy Pickled Red Onions
Makes about 1 cup

Use these versatile pickles on anything from the Mumbai Frankie Wraps (page 96) to Black Bean Chilaquiles Verdes (page 278) to Double Smashie Burgers (page 101).

- 1 red onion, halved and sliced thin through root end
- 1 cup red wine vinegar
- ⅓ cup sugar
- 2 jalapeño chiles, stemmed, seeded, and cut into thin rings
- ¼ teaspoon table salt

Place onion in bowl. Bring vinegar, sugar, jalapeños, and salt to simmer over medium-high heat in saucepan, stirring occasionally, until sugar dissolves. Pour hot vinegar mixture over onion, cover, and let cool completely, about 1 hour. Drain cooled vegetables in colander. Serve. (Drained pickled onions can be refrigerated for up to 1 week.)

Jackfruit Tinga Tacos
Serves 6

Why This Recipe Works Although it's related to the tiny fig, the jackfruit is the largest tree fruit in the world, weighing up to 80 pounds! In its mature (that is, ripe) form, jackfruit tastes like a combination of papaya, pineapple, and mango. However, green, immature jackfruit is altogether different: vegetal, dense, and very fibrous. When canned in water or brine, green jackfruit tastes more like an artichoke heart than a fruit, and it is widely used in many Asian cuisines as a meat substitute. Once cooked, it shreds beautifully into tender morsels reminiscent of pulled pork or chicken. We tried jackfruit as a substitute for shredded meat in a range of recipes (shawarmas, gyros, barbecue-style sandwiches), and our favorite was this Mexican-style tinga taco. We started by crisping the jackfruit in the skillet and then set it aside and built a savory sauce using tomato sauce enriched with aromatic onion, garlic, and oregano, plus some chipotle chiles in adobo sauce for smoky depth. After a few minutes simmering in the sauce, the jackfruit was tender enough to mash into a rich, flavorful taco filling, which we served in corn tortillas, topped with a bright, aromatic slaw and creamy avocado pieces. You can find canned jackfruit in most well-stocked supermarkets. Purchase young green (rather than ripe or mature) jackfruit in large pieces (rather than shredded) packed in water, not syrup. You will need a 12-inch nonstick skillet with a tight-fitting lid for this recipe.

3 tablespoons plus 1 teaspoon vegetable oil, divided
1 tablespoon cider vinegar
2 cups shredded green or red cabbage
1 carrot, peeled and shredded
2 tablespoons minced fresh cilantro
2 scallions, sliced thin
2 (14.5-ounce) cans young green jackfruit packed in water, rinsed and patted dry
1 small onion, chopped fine
3 garlic cloves, minced
1 teaspoon dried oregano
1 teaspoon minced canned chipotle chile in adobo sauce
1 (8-ounce) can tomato sauce
¼ cup water
¼ teaspoon table salt
12 (6-inch) corn tortillas, warmed
1 avocado, halved, pitted, and cut into ½-inch pieces

1. Whisk 2 tablespoons oil and vinegar together in bowl. Add cabbage, carrot, cilantro, and scallions and toss to combine. Season with salt and pepper to taste, cover, and refrigerate until ready to serve.

2. Heat 1 tablespoon oil in 12-inch nonstick skillet over medium-high heat until shimmering. Add jackfruit in single layer and cook until well browned on all sides, flipping occasionally, about 8 minutes. Transfer jackfruit to plate; set aside.

3. Add onion and remaining 1 teaspoon oil to now-empty skillet and cook over medium heat until softened and lightly browned, 5 to 7 minutes. Stir in garlic, oregano, and chipotle and cook until fragrant, about 30 seconds. Stir in tomato sauce, water, and salt and bring to simmer. Add jackfruit to sauce, cover, and cook until jackfruit is very tender, about 8 minutes, flipping jackfruit once halfway through cooking.

4. Remove skillet from heat and, using potato masher, mash jackfruit until thoroughly shredded and well coated in sauce. Divide jackfruit evenly among warm tortillas and top with slaw and avocado. Serve.

Plant-Based Beef Tacos
Serves 6 FAST

Why This Recipe Works Crispy corn tortillas cradling a simmered meaty filling and loaded with favorite toppings always disappear in a flash. Quick weeknight versions normally rely on ground beef, which seemed like a great template for a plant-based beef version. Initially we were mightily disappointed: Plant-based beef cooked beyond medium tends to turn unappealingly tough. So, altering the template, we added it to the skillet last. First we softened aromatics—onion, garlic, and green bell peppers—before blooming spices and tomato paste in the oil for a deeply flavorful base. Then we browned the plant-based meat lightly so that it wouldn't overcook and finished it off with a 1-minute simmer with a little water to turn our plant-based meat mixture into a delicious taco filling that you'd be hard-pressed to distinguish from beef. The spice level of chili powder varies greatly by brand; we like a little heat in our tacos but if you don't or you're unsure of how spicy your chili powder is, feel free to omit the cayenne. We prefer Impossible Burger in this recipe.

1 tablespoon vegetable oil
1 onion, chopped fine
1 green bell pepper, stemmed, seeded, and chopped fine
½ teaspoon table salt, divided
4 garlic cloves, minced
1 tablespoon chili powder
1 teaspoon ground cumin
¼ teaspoon cayenne pepper (optional)
2 tablespoons tomato paste
12 ounces plant-based beef (page 9)
½ teaspoon pepper
¼ cup water
12 taco shells, warmed
    Shredded iceberg lettuce
    Salsa
    Plant-based yogurt or dairy sour cream

1. Heat oil in 12-inch nonstick skillet over medium heat until shimmering. Add onion, bell pepper, and ¼ teaspoon salt and cook until softened and just beginning to brown,

Double Smashie Burgers

---

plant-based meat has made in recent years, we were excited to turn our efforts to the ultimate fast-food-style burger, complete with our "special sauce" and "cheez." Making regular quarter-pound patties yielded decent results, but what impressed tasters most was the exterior of the burgers, which achieved the complex flavors of the Maillard reaction that make up browning in protein. In order to make double the impression, we doubled the number of burgers by making them thinner. We found that plant-based meat does not fare as well as beef when cooked to well done, and so our little patties had a tendency to overcook before they browned. Using a Dutch oven to smash down the burgers on their first side allowed them to get the browning we wanted in less time. Then it was just a matter of layering them with our savory, creamy plant-based Cheez Sauce and adding the requisite toppings. We prefer Impossible Burger in this recipe. Plant-based beef is easier to handle and shape if it is chilled. You can use any pie plate or baking dish to press the patties, but we prefer glass so you can see the size of the patty as you're pressing.

12 ounces plant-based beef (page 9)
½ teaspoon table salt
¼ teaspoon pepper
1 recipe Classic Burger Sauce (page 102), divided
4 hamburger buns, toasted if desired
1½ cups shredded iceberg lettuce
1 tablespoon vegetable oil
½ cup Cheez Sauce (page 26), warmed, divided
¼ cup finely chopped onion
¼ cup dill pickle chips

1. Wrap bottom of Dutch oven with aluminum foil. Cut sides of 1-quart zipper-lock bag, leaving bottom seam intact.

2. Divide meat into eight 1½-ounce portions, then roll each portion into balls. Enclose 1 ball in split bag. Using clear pie plate or baking dish, press ball into even 3½-inch-wide patty. Remove patty from bag and transfer to platter. Repeat with remaining meat balls. Sprinkle patties on 1 side with salt and pepper.

3. Spread 1 tablespoon burger sauce over each bun bottom, then top with lettuce; set aside. Heat oil in 12-inch nonstick skillet over high heat until just smoking. Place 4 patties in skillet and weight with prepared pot. Cook until well browned on first side, about 1 minute. Remove pot, flip patties, and cook until just cooked through on second side, about 15 seconds. Transfer burgers to prepared bun bottoms, then top each burger with 1 tablespoon cheez sauce. Add remaining 4 patties to fat left in skillet and repeat cooking process.

4. Divide patties among burgers and top with remaining cheez sauce, onion, pickle chips, and bun tops. Serve, passing remaining burger sauce separately.

---

5 to 7 minutes. Stir in garlic; chili powder; cumin; and cayenne, if using, and cook until fragrant, about 30 seconds. Stir in tomato paste and cook until rust-colored, 1 to 2 minutes.

2. Stir in plant-based beef, pepper, and remaining ¼ teaspoon salt and cook until meat is lightly browned, 3 to 5 minutes, breaking up meat with wooden spoon. Stir in water and simmer until sauce is thickened, about 1 minute. Divide filling evenly among taco shells and serve with lettuce, salsa, and yogurt.

Double Smashie Burgers
Serves 4

Why This Recipe Works There's a reason beyond convenience why fast-food burgers are so beloved—it's that particular combination of salty, crispy, sweet, sour, pickled, savory, and meaty that fast-food chains do so well. Bean-based or vegetable-based burgers, while delicious in their own right, tend to be higher in moisture, and so achieving an exterior crust is harder and the end result doesn't evoke that familiar flavor and texture. With the huge steps forward that

BURGER TOPPINGS

Sure, there are many condiments and toppings available at the grocery store, but these homemade versions take only a minor effort and guarantee you'll always have plant-based condiments on hand. These toppings will take your lineup beyond the standard ketchup, mustard, and mayo, and not only can they enhance your burgers—they can steal the show.

Classic Burger Sauce

Makes about 1 cup
Sometimes called "special sauce," this simple burger topping combines a few familiar ingredients to create a supercharged sauce.

½ cup plant-based mayonnaise or egg-based mayonnaise
¼ cup ketchup
2 teaspoons sweet pickle relish
2 teaspoons sugar
2 teaspoons distilled white vinegar
1 teaspoon pepper

Whisk all ingredients together in bowl. (Sauce can be refrigerated for up to 4 days.)

Pub Burger Sauce

Makes about 1 cup
For a pub-worthy burger sauce with intense salty, sweet, and umami flavors, we swapped out the usual ketchup and relish for flavor-packed soy sauce and vegan Worcestershire.

¾ cup plant-based mayonnaise or egg-based mayonnaise
2 tablespoons soy sauce
1 tablespoon packed dark brown sugar
1 tablespoon vegan Worcestershire sauce
1 tablespoon minced fresh chives
1 garlic clove, minced
¾ teaspoon pepper

Whisk all ingredients together in bowl. (Sauce can be refrigerated for up to 4 days.)

Barbecue Sauce

Makes about 2 cups
Ketchup makes an ideal base ingredient for this tangy barbecue sauce, which can also serve as a dipping sauce.

1 tablespoon vegetable oil
1 onion, chopped fine
Pinch table salt
1 garlic clove, minced
1 teaspoon chili powder
1¼ cups ketchup
6 tablespoons molasses
3 tablespoons cider vinegar
2 tablespoons vegan Worcestershire sauce
2 tablespoons Dijon mustard

1. Heat oil in medium saucepan over medium heat until shimmering. Add onion and salt and cook until onion is softened, about 5 minutes. Stir in garlic and chili powder and cook until fragrant, about 30 seconds.

2. Whisk in ketchup, molasses, vinegar, Worcestershire, and mustard. Bring sauce to simmer and cook, stirring occasionally, until thickened and reduced to about 2 cups, about 25 minutes.

3. Let barbecue sauce cool slightly, then transfer to airtight container and let cool to room temperature. (Barbecue sauce can be refrigerated for up to 4 days.)

Caramelized Onion Jam

Makes about 1 cup
The savory sweetness, rich color, and thick texture of this jam belie its simplicity.

3 tablespoons extra-virgin olive oil
1¼ pounds onions, halved and sliced thin
1 bay leaf
½ teaspoon minced fresh rosemary
½ teaspoon table salt

¼ teaspoon pepper
2 garlic cloves, peeled and smashed
¼ cup balsamic vinegar
¼ cup water
2 tablespoons sugar

1. Heat oil in Dutch oven over medium-high heat until shimmering. Add onions, bay leaf, rosemary, salt, and pepper. Cover and cook, stirring occasionally, until onions have softened, about 10 minutes.

2. Stir in garlic. Reduce heat to medium-low and cook, uncovered, scraping up any browned bits, until onions are golden brown, about 15 minutes.

3. Stir in vinegar, water, and sugar, scraping up any browned bits. Increase heat to medium-high and simmer until mixture is thickened and rubber spatula or wooden spoon leaves distinct trail when dragged across bottom of pot, about 2 minutes.

4. Discard bay leaf. Transfer onion mixture to food processor and pulse to jam-like consistency, about 5 pulses. Transfer onion jam to airtight container and let cool to room temperature. (Onion jam can be refrigerated for up to 4 days.)

Quick Pickle Chips

Quick Pickle Chips
Makes about 2 cups
No canning is required for these quick bread-and-butter pickle slices, which can be made in an afternoon.

¾ cup seasoned rice vinegar
1 garlic clove, peeled and halved
¼ teaspoon ground turmeric
⅛ teaspoon black peppercorns
⅛ teaspoon yellow mustard seeds
8 ounces pickling cucumbers, trimmed, sliced ¼ inch thick crosswise
2 sprigs fresh dill

1. Bring vinegar, ¼ cup water, garlic, turmeric, peppercorns, and mustard seeds to boil in medium saucepan over medium-high heat.

2. Fill one 1-pint jar with hot tap water to warm. Drain jar, then pack with cucumbers and dill sprigs. Using funnel and ladle, pour hot brine over cucumbers to cover. Let cool to room temperature, about 30 minutes. Cover and refrigerate until chilled and flavors meld, about 3 hours. Serve. (Pickles can be refrigerated for up to 6 weeks.)

Shoestring Onion Rings
Makes about 3 cups
These shatteringly crisp shoestring onion rings are a guaranteed game-changer. We prefer a yellow onion here, but a white onion will also work.

1 onion, sliced into thin rings
½ cup distilled white vinegar
½ cup all-purpose flour
½ teaspoon table salt
¼ teaspoon pepper
¼ teaspoon cream of tartar
2 cups peanut or vegetable oil

1. Separate onion rings and combine with vinegar in bowl. Combine flour, salt, pepper, and cream of tartar in large bowl.

2. Heat oil in 12-inch nonstick skillet over medium-high heat to 350 degrees. Drain onion rings; toss with flour mixture until evenly coated. Working in batches, fry onions, stirring occasionally, until golden brown and crisp, about 5 minutes. Transfer to paper towel–lined plate and season with salt and pepper to taste.

Spiced Cauliflower Burgers
Serves 4

Why This Recipe Works These burgers are bursting with flavors inspired by North Africa. We love the contrast between their creamy, nutty interiors and crunchy, golden exteriors. The trick to achieving this was to first roast the cauliflower, which took less than 30 minutes; this intensified its flavor and made it easy to mash the florets. Before roasting, we tossed the florets with oil and ras el hanout, a spice blend that contains cumin, coriander, cinnamon, and other warm spices. After roasting and mashing the cauliflower, we added panko (which worked far better than flour) and some aquafaba (the liquid from a can of chickpeas) for binding (instead of an egg), along with shredded carrots and golden raisins. Peppery baby arugula and herbed yogurt sauce provided a fresh burst of flavor, and toasted sliced almonds sprinkled over the top added textural interest. Use the large holes of a box grater to shred the carrot. We prefer our homemade Ras el Hanout (page 174), but you can use a store-bought blend.

1½ pounds cauliflower florets, cut into 1-inch pieces
3 tablespoons extra-virgin olive oil, divided
1 teaspoon ras el hanout
½ teaspoon table salt
⅛ teaspoon pepper
½ cup panko bread crumbs
1 small carrot, peeled and shredded
¼ cup golden raisins
2 ounces (¼ cup) aquafaba (page 16)
4 hamburger buns, toasted if desired
¼ cup Herbed Yogurt Sauce (page 90)
3 tablespoons sliced almonds, toasted
1 cup baby arugula

1. Adjust oven rack to middle position and heat oven to 450 degrees. Line rimmed baking sheet with aluminum foil. Toss cauliflower with 1 tablespoon oil, ras el hanout, salt, and pepper, and spread cauliflower in even layer over prepared sheet. Roast until well browned and tender, about 20 minutes. Let cool slightly and transfer to bowl of food processor.

2. Line clean rimmed baking sheet with parchment paper. Add panko, carrot, raisins, and aquafaba to cauliflower mixture and pulse until coarsely ground and mixture comes together, about 6 pulses. Divide cauliflower mixture into 4 equal portions. Using your lightly moistened hands, firmly pack each portion into ¾-inch-thick patty and place on prepared sheet. Cover with plastic wrap and refrigerate until patties are firm, at least 30 minutes or up to 24 hours.

3. Heat remaining 2 tablespoons oil in 12-inch nonstick skillet over medium heat until shimmering. Place patties in skillet and cook until deep golden brown and crisp on first side, 3 to 5 minutes. Using 2 spatulas, gently flip patties and cook until browned and crisp on second side, 3 to 5 minutes. Serve burgers on buns, topped with yogurt sauce, almonds, and arugula.

Grilled Portobello Burgers
Serves 4

Why This Recipe Works Too often the portobello burger menu option is a thin, limp mushroom cap that's swallowed up by its bun. Our version, layered with a vibrant sun-dried tomato and roasted red pepper topping and spread with fragrant basil mayo, is rich and juicy. We started by marinating the portobellos in a simple vinaigrette, which considerably boosted their complexity. Cutting a shallow crosshatch pattern into the caps not only allowed the mushrooms to soak up more marinade, but also prevented the skin from turning chewy while it cooked—a common pitfall. We grilled the mushrooms alongside sliced red onions, which we brushed with the remaining marinade to unify the flavors. Once the mushrooms had taken on rich char, we topped them with our mixture of roasted red peppers and sun-dried tomatoes; the briny topping brightened the rich, meaty star. Then we stacked the stuffed mushrooms on buns along with the onions, peppery arugula, and a slather of the mayo.

4 portobello mushroom caps (4 to 5 inches in diameter), gills removed
½ cup extra-virgin olive oil
3 tablespoons red wine vinegar
1 garlic clove, minced
1 teaspoon table salt
½ teaspoon pepper
½ cup jarred roasted red peppers, patted dry and chopped
½ cup oil-packed sun-dried tomatoes, patted dry and chopped
¼ cup plant-based mayonnaise or egg-based mayonnaise
¼ cup chopped fresh basil
4 (½-inch-thick) slices red onion
4 burger buns, toasted if desired
1 cup baby arugula

1. Cut 1/16-inch-deep slits on top side of mushroom caps, spaced 1/2 inch apart, in crosshatch pattern. Combine oil, vinegar, garlic, salt, and pepper in 1-gallon zipper-lock bag. Add mushroom caps, press out air, seal, turn to coat, and let sit for at least 30 minutes or up to 1 hour.

2. Combine red peppers and sun-dried tomatoes in bowl. Combine mayonnaise and basil in second bowl. Push 1 toothpick horizontally through each onion slice to keep rings intact. Remove mushroom caps from bag, then brush onions all over with any remaining marinade in bag.

3A. For a charcoal grill Open bottom vent completely. Light large chimney starter filled with charcoal briquettes (6 quarts). When top coals are partially covered with ash, pour evenly over grill. Set cooking grate in place, cover, and open lid vent completely. Heat grill until hot, about 5 minutes.

3B. For a gas grill Turn all burners to high, cover, and heat grill until hot, about 15 minutes. Turn all burners to medium-high.

4. Clean and oil cooking grate. Place mushrooms, gill side up, and onions on grill. Cook (covered if using gas) until mushrooms have released their liquid and are charred on first side, 4 to 6 minutes. Flip mushrooms and onions and continue to cook (covered if using gas) until mushrooms are charred on second side, 3 to 5 minutes.

5. Transfer onions to platter and discard toothpicks. Transfer mushrooms to platter, gill side up, and divide pepper-tomato mixture evenly among caps, packing down mixture.

6. Grill buns cut sides down until lightly charred, about 1 minute. Spread basil mayonnaise evenly over bun bottoms. Assemble 4 burgers by layering mushrooms, onions, then arugula on bun bottoms. Top with bun tops and serve.

SCORING MUSHROOMS FOR GRILLING

Using tip of sharp knife, lightly score top of each mushroom cap in crosshatch pattern 1/16 inch deep.

Spiced Cauliflower Burgers

Grilled Portobello Burgers

Lentil and Mushroom Burgers
Serves 12

Why This Recipe Works Sturdy brown lentils give these burgers great earthy flavor. We combined the lentils with bulgur, which bulked them up and absorbed any excess moisture that the lentils retained after cooking. Some well-browned mushrooms added meatiness to our patties, but tasters craved an even bigger umami boost, so we incorporated buttery cashews, which added savory richness. To bind the ingredients into a cohesive patty, we first tried ground flaxseed, but it imparted a muddy flavor. Instead, using a decent amount—⅓ cup—of aquafaba, plus panko bread crumbs, gave us excellent cohesion. Don't confuse bulgur with cracked wheat, which has a much longer cooking time and will not work in this recipe. This recipe yields a lot of burgers, but they freeze very well for up to a month, making this a great make-ahead recipe.

Curried Millet Cakes with Peach-Ginger Chutney

¾	cup dried brown lentils, picked over and rinsed
1	teaspoon table salt, plus salt for cooking lentils and bulgur
½	cup vegetable oil, divided, plus extra as needed
1	pound cremini mushrooms, trimmed and sliced thin
2	onions, chopped fine
1	celery rib, minced
1	small leek, white and light green parts only, chopped fine and washed thoroughly (½ cup)
2	garlic cloves, minced
¾	cup medium-grind bulgur, rinsed
1	cup raw cashews
2⅔	ounces (⅓ cup) aquafaba (page 16)
2	cups panko bread crumbs
12	burger buns, toasted if desired

1. Bring 3 cups water, lentils, and 1 teaspoon salt to boil in medium saucepan. Reduce heat to medium-low and simmer until lentils just begin to fall apart, about 25 minutes. Drain lentils, transfer to paper towel–lined baking sheet, and pat dry.

2. Meanwhile, heat 2 tablespoons oil in 12-inch nonstick skillet over medium heat until shimmering. Add mushrooms and cook until golden, about 12 minutes. Stir in onions, celery, leek, and garlic and cook until browned, 10 to 15 minutes. Transfer to sheet with lentils and let cool, about 30 minutes.

3. Combine 2 cups water, bulgur, and ¼ teaspoon salt in large bowl and microwave, covered, until softened, about 5 minutes. Drain in fine-mesh strainer and press with rubber spatula to remove excess moisture; let cool slightly. Pulse cashews in food processor until finely ground, about 25 pulses.

4. Combine lentil mixture, bulgur, ground cashews, and aquafaba in bowl. Pulse half of bulgur mixture in now-empty

food processor until coarsely ground but cohesive, about 15 pulses. Transfer mixture to large bowl. Repeat with remaining bulgur mixture and transfer to bowl. Stir in panko and salt.

5. Adjust oven rack to middle position and heat oven to 200 degrees. Divide mixture into 12 equal portions; using your lightly moistened hands, firmly pack each portion into ½-inch-thick patty. (Burgers can be refrigerated for up to 3 days or frozen for up to 1 month. To freeze, transfer patties to 2 parchment paper–lined rimmed baking sheets and freeze until firm, about 1 hour. Stack patties, separated by parchment paper, wrap in plastic wrap, and place in zipper-lock freezer bag. Do not thaw patties before cooking.)

6. Heat 2 tablespoons oil in now-empty skillet over medium heat until shimmering. Gently lay 4 patties in skillet and cook until crisp and well browned on first side, about 4 minutes. Gently flip patties and cook until crisp and well browned on second side, about 4 minutes, adding extra oil if skillet looks dry.

7. Transfer burgers to wire rack set in rimmed baking sheet and place in oven to keep warm. Wipe out skillet with paper towels and repeat in 2 batches with remaining oil and remaining patties. Transfer to buns and serve.

Curried Millet Cakes with Peach-Ginger Chutney

Serves 4

Why This Recipe Works Millet's nutty, corn-like flavor is the perfect foil for a variety of seasonings, and since it releases a sticky starch as it cooks, it makes for perfectly cohesive plant-based burger patties. Here we combined millet with colorful baby spinach and shredded carrots for patties with bright vegetable flavor, while some minced shallot provided aromatic balance. Creamy yogurt (plant-based or dairy) added moisture and richness and also served as a binder. Curry powder gave our burgers an Indian-inspired flavor profile, which perfectly complemented the topping of sweet-savory peach chutney; using readily available frozen peaches made the chutney a snap to assemble. Pan-frying the patties created a flavorful crust on the exterior while maintaining a moist interior. A dollop of cooling plain yogurt tempered the chutney's heat. Tasters found burger buns to be a bit much with these dense burgers, so we decided to ditch the bread; we suggest serving these wrapped in iceberg or Bibb lettuce leaves or alongside a salad.

Peach-Ginger Chutney
- 1 shallot, minced
- 1 tablespoon vegetable oil
- 1 teaspoon grated fresh ginger
- ⅛ teaspoon table salt
- Pinch red pepper flakes
- 1½ cups ripe fresh or thawed frozen peaches, cut into ½-inch pieces
- 2 tablespoons packed light brown sugar
- 2 tablespoons cider vinegar

Cakes
- 1 cup millet, rinsed
- 2 cups water
- 1 teaspoon table salt, divided
- 3 tablespoons vegetable oil, divided
- 1 shallot, minced
- 6 ounces (6 cups) baby spinach, chopped
- 2 carrots, peeled and shredded
- 2 teaspoons curry powder
- ¼ teaspoon pepper
- ⅔ cup plain plant-based or dairy yogurt, divided
- 2 tablespoons minced fresh cilantro

1. For the peach-ginger chutney Microwave shallot, oil, ginger, salt, and pepper flakes in small bowl, stirring occasionally, until shallot has softened, about 1 minute. Stir in peaches, sugar, and vinegar and microwave until peaches have softened and mixture has thickened, 6 to 8 minutes, stirring once halfway through microwaving. Set aside to cool to room temperature. (Chutney can be refrigerated for up to 3 days; let come to room temperature before serving.)

2. For the cakes Line rimmed baking sheet with parchment paper. Combine millet, water, and ½ teaspoon salt in medium saucepan and bring to simmer over medium-high heat. Reduce heat to low, cover, and simmer gently until millet is tender and most of water has been absorbed, 15 to 20 minutes. Off heat, let millet sit, covered, until liquid is fully absorbed, about 10 minutes. Transfer millet to large bowl and let cool for 15 minutes.

3. Heat 1 tablespoon oil in 12-inch nonstick skillet over medium heat until shimmering. Add shallot and cook until softened, about 3 minutes. Stir in spinach, carrots, and remaining ½ teaspoon salt and cook until spinach is wilted, about 2 minutes. Stir in curry powder and pepper and cook until fragrant, about 30 seconds; transfer to bowl with millet. Wipe skillet clean with paper towels.

4. Stir ⅓ cup yogurt and cilantro into millet mixture until well combined. Divide millet mixture into 4 equal portions. Using your lightly moistened hands, firmly pack each portion into ¾-inch-thick patty and place on prepared sheet. Cover with plastic wrap and refrigerate until patties are firm, at least 30 minutes or up to 24 hours.

5. Heat remaining 2 tablespoons oil in now-empty skillet over medium-low heat until shimmering. Place patties in skillet and cook until deep golden brown and crisp on first side, 5 to 7 minutes. Using 2 spatulas, gently flip patties and cook until browned and crisp on second side, 5 to 7 minutes. Serve with remaining ⅓ cup yogurt and chutney.

Black Bean Burgers

Serves 6

Why This Recipe Works These hearty burgers have a Southwestern flair, thanks to the ground tortilla chips that we used as a binder and the flavor enhancements of scallions, cilantro, garlic, ground cumin and coriander, and hot sauce. We pulsed the black beans in the food processor with the tortilla chips, adding the beans near the end of processing so that they maintained some texture. When looking for something other than an egg to help pull everything together, we discovered that using some of the liquid from the canned beans provided the necessary cohesion to make the burgers hold together. The black bean liquid also boosted the overall flavor of the burgers. To ensure that we retained control over the moisture content of our burgers, we dried the rinsed beans well to remove excess water. When forming the patties, it's important to pack them together firmly.

2 (15-ounce) cans black beans, rinsed, with
   6 tablespoons bean liquid reserved
2 tablespoons all-purpose flour
4 scallions, minced
3 tablespoons minced fresh cilantro
2 garlic cloves, minced
1 teaspoon ground cumin
1 teaspoon hot sauce (optional)
½ teaspoon ground coriander
¼ teaspoon table salt
¼ teaspoon pepper
1 ounce tortilla chips, crushed (½ cup)
¼ cup vegetable oil, divided
6 burger buns, toasted if desired

1. Line rimmed baking sheet with triple layer of paper towels, spread beans over towels, and let sit for 15 minutes.

2. Whisk reserved bean liquid and flour in large bowl until well combined and smooth. Stir in scallions; cilantro; garlic; cumin; hot sauce, if using; coriander; salt; and pepper until well combined. Process tortilla chips in food processor until finely ground, about 30 seconds. Add black beans and pulse until beans are coarsely ground, about 5 pulses. Transfer bean mixture to bowl with flour mixture and mix until well combined. (Mixture can be refrigerated for up to 24 hours.)

3. Adjust oven rack to middle position and heat oven to 200 degrees. Divide mixture into 6 equal portions. Using your lightly moistened hands, firmly pack each portion into ¾-inch-thick patty. (Patties can be frozen for up to 1 month. Transfer patties to 2 parchment paper–lined rimmed baking sheets and freeze until firm, about 1 hour. Stack patties, separated by parchment paper, wrap in plastic wrap, and place in zipper-lock freezer bag. Thaw completely before cooking.)

4. Heat 1 tablespoon oil in 10-inch nonstick skillet over medium heat until shimmering. Gently lay 3 patties in skillet and cook until crisp and well browned on first side, about 5 minutes. Gently flip patties, add 1 tablespoon oil, and cook until crisp and well browned on second side, 3 to 5 minutes.

5. Transfer burgers to wire rack set in rimmed baking sheet and place in oven to keep warm. Wipe out skillet with paper towels and repeat with remaining 2 tablespoons oil and remaining patties. Transfer to buns and serve.

Chickpea Cakes
Serves 6   FAST

Why This Recipe Works Convenient canned chickpeas, blended with plenty of seasonings and aromatics and pan-fried until crisp and deep golden brown, make flavorful patties in a flash that can be served as an appealing main course alongside (or on top of) a big salad. Pureeing the chickpeas completely resulted in mushy, homogeneous cakes; instead, we pulsed them in the food processor until they were coarsely ground but still retained some texture. To bind the patties, aquafaba liquid from the can along with panko bread crumbs did the trick, and for richness we added olive oil. A combination of coriander, cayenne pepper, scallions, and cilantro ensured that these patties were ultraflavorful. If you like, serve these cakes with Herbed Yogurt Sauce (page 90) or Tahini-Yogurt Sauce (page 249). Avoid overmixing the chickpea mixture in step 1 or the cakes will have a mealy texture.

   2 (15-ounce) cans chickpeas, drained with 6 ounces
      (¾ cup) aquafaba reserved (page 16)
   6 tablespoons extra-virgin olive oil, divided
   1 teaspoon ground coriander
   ⅛ teaspoon cayenne pepper
   ⅛ teaspoon table salt
   1 cup panko bread crumbs
   2 scallions, sliced thin
   3 tablespoons minced fresh cilantro
   1 shallot, minced
      Lemon wedges

1. Pulse chickpeas in food processor until coarsely ground, about 8 pulses. Whisk reserved aquafaba, 2 tablespoons oil, coriander, cayenne, and salt together in medium bowl. Gently stir in chickpeas, panko, scallions, cilantro, and shallot until combined. Divide chickpea mixture into 6 equal portions. Using your lightly moistened hands, firmly pack each portion into ¾-inch-thick cake. (Cakes can be refrigerated, wrapped in plastic wrap, for up to 24 hours.)

2. Adjust oven rack to middle position and heat oven to 200 degrees. Heat 2 tablespoons oil in 12-inch nonstick skillet over medium heat until shimmering. Place 3 cakes in skillet and cook until deep golden brown and crisp on first side, 4 to 5 minutes. Using 2 spatulas, gently flip cakes and cook until browned and crisp on second side, 4 to 5 minutes.

3. Transfer cakes to wire rack set in rimmed baking sheet and place in oven to keep warm. Wipe out skillet with paper towels and repeat with remaining 2 tablespoons oil and remaining 3 patties. Serve with lemon wedges.

Pinto Bean–Beet Burgers

Pinto Bean–Beet Burgers

Serves 8

Why This Recipe Works You may be surprised to learn that beet juice is sometimes used in plant-based beef, for its color. But in this modern bean-based burger, we used shredded beets to bring a lighter texture and sweet-earthy flavor. We added substance and heft with bulgur and used ground nuts to provide meaty richness. Plenty of garlic and mustard deepened and united all the savory flavors. While the bulgur cooked, we pulsed the other ingredients in the food processor. To bind the burgers, we hit upon a surprising ingredient: carrot baby food. The pureed carrots added the necessary tackiness to make the patties cohesive, and their subtle sweetness heightened that of the shredded beets. Panko bread crumbs further bound the mixture and helped the patties sear up with a nicely crisp crust. When shopping, don't confuse bulgur with cracked wheat, which has a much longer cooking time and will not work here. Use the large holes of a box grater or a food processor fitted with a shredding disk to shred the beets. This recipe makes a lot of burgers, but they freeze very well.

1½ teaspoons table salt, plus salt for cooking bulgur
⅔ cup medium-grind bulgur, rinsed
1 large beet (9 ounces), peeled and shredded
¾ cup walnuts
½ cup fresh basil leaves
2 garlic cloves, minced
1 (15-ounce) can pinto beans, rinsed
1 (4-ounce) jar carrot baby food
1 tablespoon whole-grain mustard
½ teaspoon pepper
1½ cups panko bread crumbs
6 tablespoons vegetable oil, divided, plus extra as needed
8 hamburger buns, toasted if desired

1. Bring 1½ cups water and ½ teaspoon salt to boil in small saucepan. Off heat, stir in bulgur, cover, and let sit until tender, 15 to 20 minutes. Drain bulgur, spread onto rimmed baking sheet, and let cool slightly.

2. Pulse beet, walnuts, basil, and garlic in food processor until finely chopped, about 12 pulses, scraping down sides of bowl as needed. Add beans, carrot baby food, 2 tablespoons water, mustard, pepper, and salt and pulse until well combined, about 8 pulses. Transfer mixture to large bowl and stir in panko and cooled bulgur.

3. Divide beet-bulgur mixture into 8 equal portions. Using your lightly moistened hands, firmly pack each portion into ¾-inch-thick patty. (Patties can be refrigerated for up to 3 days or frozen for up to 1 month. To freeze, transfer patties to 2 parchment paper–lined rimmed baking sheets and freeze until firm, about 1 hour. Stack patties, separated by parchment paper, wrap in plastic wrap, and place in zipper-lock freezer bag. Do not thaw patties before cooking.)

4. Adjust oven rack to middle position and heat oven to 200 degrees. Set wire rack in rimmed baking sheet. Heat 3 tablespoons oil in 12-inch nonstick skillet over medium-high heat until shimmering. Place 4 patties in skillet and cook until well browned and crisp on first side, about 4 minutes. Using 2 spatulas, gently flip patties and continue to cook until well browned and crisp on second side, about 4 minutes, adding extra oil as needed if skillet looks dry. Transfer burgers to prepared rack and keep warm in oven. Wipe skillet clean with paper towels and repeat with remaining 3 tablespoons oil and remaining 4 patties. Serve burgers on buns.

Thin-Crust Pizza with Broccoli and Sun-Dried Tomatoes

Serves 4 to 6 (**Makes** two 13-inch pizzas)

Why This Recipe Works Homemade pizza is a blank canvas just waiting to be painted with creative toppings. We love this combo of garlicky sautéed broccoli and umami-packed sun-dried tomatoes, and our easy method results in a thin-crust pizza pie as good as any you can get at a gourmet pizzeria. Leaving the edge of the pizza slightly thicker than the center ensured a chewy yet crisp outer crust. For the crispiest bottom crust, we used a baking stone. If you do not have one, you can use a preheated rimless (or inverted) baking sheet. You can shape the second dough ball while the first pizza bakes, but don't top the pizza until right before you bake it. We prefer to use one of our homemade doughs for this pizza, but you may use store-bought if you prefer.

- 1 (28-ounce) can whole peeled tomatoes, drained with juice reserved
- 5 teaspoons extra-virgin olive oil, divided
- 5 garlic cloves, minced, divided
- 1 teaspoon red wine vinegar
- 1 teaspoon dried oregano
- ½ teaspoon table salt
- ¼ teaspoon pepper
- 1 recipe Thin-Crust Pizza Dough or Whole-Wheat Pizza Dough (page 113)
- 8 ounces broccoli florets, cut into 1-inch pieces
- ¼ cup water
- ½ cup oil-packed sun-dried tomatoes, patted dry and sliced thin
- 6 ounces mozzarella cheese, shredded (1½ cups) (optional)
- 2 tablespoons grated Parmesan cheese (optional)

1. Process tomatoes, 1 tablespoon oil, 2 garlic cloves, vinegar, oregano, salt, and pepper in food processor until smooth, about 30 seconds. Transfer mixture to liquid measuring cup and add reserved tomato juice until sauce measures 2 cups. (Sauce can be refrigerated for up to 1 week or frozen for up to 1 month.)

2. One hour before baking, adjust oven rack to upper-middle position, set baking stone on rack, and heat oven to 500 degrees. Remove dough from refrigerator and divide in half. Shape each half into smooth, tight ball. Space dough balls 3 inches apart on lightly oiled rimmed baking sheet, cover loosely with greased plastic wrap, and let rest for 1 hour.

3. Meanwhile, heat remaining 2 teaspoons oil in 12-inch nonstick skillet over medium heat until shimmering. Add broccoli and cook until lightly browned, about 5 minutes. Stir in remaining garlic and cook until fragrant, about 30 seconds. Add water, cover, and cook for 3 minutes. Uncover, add sun-dried tomatoes, and cook until broccoli is tender and water is evaporated, about 2 minutes. Season with salt and pepper to taste.

4. Heat broiler for 10 minutes. Meanwhile, coat 1 dough ball generously with flour and place on well-floured counter (keep second dough ball covered). Using your fingertips, gently flatten dough into 8-inch round, leaving 1 inch of outer edge slightly thicker than center. Using your hands, gently stretch dough into 12-inch round, working along edges and giving dough quarter turns as you stretch. Transfer dough to well-floured peel and stretch into 13-inch round.

5. Spread 1 cup sauce evenly over dough, leaving ½-inch border. Sprinkle ¾ cup mozzarella and 1 tablespoon Parmesan over sauce, if using, then top with half of broccoli mixture. Slide pizza carefully onto stone and return oven to 500 degrees. Bake until crust is well browned and cheese is golden in spots, 10 to 12 minutes, rotating pizza halfway through baking. Transfer pizza to wire rack and let cool for 5 minutes. Heat broiler for 10 minutes. Repeat shaping, topping, and baking for second pizza. Slice and serve.

Thin-Crust Pesto Pizza with Fennel and Cauliflower

Serves 4 to 6 (**Makes** two 13-inch pizzas)

Why This Recipe Works Tomato sauce pies are great, but there are also countless pizza offerings now that don't include tomatoes. To freshen things up, we often like to use garlicky pesto as a base for our other toppings. When we simply omitted the Parmesan from the pesto to make it vegan, we didn't even miss it: We got all the rich, savory flavor we desired from the olive oil, pine nuts, and garlic. For a vegetable topper, we thought some sweet, caramelized cauliflower and fragrant fennel would serve as delicious opposing forces to the bold sauce. A sprinkle of more pine nuts and fresh basil was a nice call-out to the pesto underneath. For the crispiest bottom crust, we used a baking stone. If you do not have one, you can use a preheated rimless (or inverted) baking sheet. You can shape the second dough ball while the first pizza bakes, but don't top the pizza until right before you bake it. We prefer to use one of our homemade doughs for this pizza, but you may use store-bought if you prefer.

Thin-Crust Pesto Pizza with Fennel and Cauliflower

3. Meanwhile, heat remaining 2 tablespoons oil in 12-inch nonstick skillet over medium heat until shimmering. Add cauliflower, fennel, water, and remaining ¼ teaspoon salt; cover and cook until vegetables begin to soften, about 5 minutes. Uncover, increase heat to medium-high, and cook until tender and browned around edges, 10 to 12 minutes; transfer to bowl.

4. Heat broiler for 10 minutes. Meanwhile, coat 1 dough ball generously with flour and place on well-floured counter (keep second dough ball covered). Using your fingertips, gently flatten dough into 8-inch round, leaving 1 inch of outer edge slightly thicker than center. Using your hands, gently stretch dough into 12-inch round, working along edges and giving dough quarter turns. Transfer dough to well-floured peel and stretch into 13-inch round.

5. Spread half of pesto over dough, leaving ¼-inch border around edge, then sprinkle with half of cauliflower mixture. Slide pizza carefully onto stone and return oven to 500 degrees. Bake until crust is well browned, 10 to 12 minutes, rotating pizza halfway through baking. Transfer pizza to wire rack, let cool for 5 minutes, then sprinkle with 1 tablespoon shredded basil and 1 tablespoon pine nuts. Heat broiler for 10 minutes. Repeat shaping, topping, and baking for second pizza. Slice and serve.

---

2 cups fresh basil leaves plus 2 tablespoons shredded
½ cup extra-virgin olive oil, divided
6 tablespoons pine nuts, toasted, divided
2 garlic cloves, minced
¾ teaspoon table salt, divided
1 recipe Thin-Crust Pizza Dough or Whole-Wheat Pizza Dough (page 113)
2 cups chopped cauliflower
1 fennel bulb, stalks discarded, bulb halved, cored, and cut into ½-inch pieces
3 tablespoons water

1. One hour before baking, adjust oven rack to upper-middle position, set baking stone on rack, and heat oven to 500 degrees. Process 2 cups basil leaves, 6 tablespoons oil, ¼ cup pine nuts, garlic, and ½ teaspoon salt in food processor until smooth, scraping down sides of bowl as needed, about 1 minute; transfer to bowl. (Pesto can be refrigerated for up to 4 days.)

2. Remove dough from refrigerator and divide in half. Shape each half into smooth, tight ball. Space dough balls 3 inches apart on lightly oiled rimmed baking sheet, cover loosely with greased plastic wrap, and let rest for 1 hour.

Thin-Crust Pizza Dough
Makes enough for two 13-inch pizzas

3 cups (16½ ounces) bread flour
2 tablespoons sugar
½ teaspoon instant or rapid-rise yeast
1⅓ cups ice water
1 tablespoon vegetable oil
1½ teaspoons table salt

1. Process flour, sugar, and yeast in food processor until combined, about 2 seconds. With processor running, slowly add ice water and process until dough is just combined and no dry flour remains, about 10 seconds. Let dough rest for 10 minutes.

2. Add oil and salt to dough and process until dough forms satiny, sticky ball that clears sides of bowl, 30 to 60 seconds. Transfer dough to lightly oiled counter and knead by hand to form smooth, round ball, about 1 minute. Place dough seam side down in lightly greased large bowl, cover tightly with plastic wrap, and refrigerate for at least 24 hours or up to 3 days.

Thin-Crust Pizza with Mushrooms and Cashew Ricotta

Serves 4 to 6 (**Makes** two 13-inch pizzas)

Why This Recipe Works Tangy, cooling dollops of homemade seasoned cashew ricotta top layers of umami-rich mushrooms for a beautiful lesson in texture and flavor contrasts. We fortified workhorse creminis with meaty shiitakes, garlic, and soy sauce and mixed oil, lemon, and salt, plus a little water, into our multipurpose Cashew Ricotta. A sprinkling of parsley before serving added bright green color and fresh herbal flavor. For the crispiest bottom crust, we used a baking stone. If you do not have one, you can use a preheated rimless (or inverted) baking sheet. You can shape the second dough ball while the first pizza bakes, but don't top the pizza until right before you bake it. You may use store-bought dough if you prefer.

Thin-Crust Pizza with Mushrooms and Cashew Ricotta

- 1 recipe Thin-Crust Pizza Dough (page 111) or Whole-Wheat Pizza Dough
- ⅔ cup Cashew Ricotta (page 26) or dairy ricotta cheese
- 7 tablespoons extra-virgin olive oil, divided, plus extra for serving
- 3 tablespoons water
- ½ teaspoon grated lemon zest plus ¾ teaspoon juice
- ⅛ teaspoon plus ½ teaspoon table salt, divided
- 12 ounces cremini mushrooms, trimmed and sliced thin
- 12 ounces shiitake mushrooms, stemmed and sliced thin
- 3 garlic cloves, minced
- 2 tablespoons soy sauce
- ¼ cup chopped fresh parsley

1. One hour before baking, adjust oven rack to upper-middle position, set baking stone on rack, and heat oven to 500 degrees. Remove dough from refrigerator and divide in half. Shape each half into smooth, tight ball. Space dough balls 3 inches apart on lightly oiled rimmed baking sheet, cover loosely with greased plastic wrap, and let rest for 1 hour.

2. Combine cashew ricotta, 1 tablespoon oil, water, lemon zest and juice, and ⅛ teaspoon salt in bowl and refrigerate until ready to use. (Cashew ricotta mixture can be refrigerated for up to 1 week.)

3. Meanwhile, heat 2 tablespoons oil in 12-inch nonstick skillet over medium heat until shimmering. Add cremini mushrooms, shiitake mushrooms, and remaining ½ teaspoon salt, cover, and cook until mushrooms have released their liquid, about 8 minutes. Uncover and cook until mushrooms are dry and starting to brown, about 15 minutes. Stir in garlic and

cook until fragrant, about 30 seconds. Stir in soy sauce, scraping up browned bits, and cook until mushrooms are coated and pan is nearly dry, about 30 seconds. Transfer mushrooms to bowl; set aside.

4. Heat broiler for 10 minutes. Meanwhile, coat 1 dough ball generously with flour and place on well-floured counter (keep second dough ball covered). Using your fingertips, gently flatten dough into 8-inch round, leaving 1 inch of outer edge slightly thicker than center. Using your hands, gently stretch dough into 12-inch round, working along edges and giving dough quarter turns. Transfer dough to well-floured peel and stretch into 13-inch round.

5. Spread 2 tablespoons oil over dough, leaving ¼-inch border around edge, then sprinkle with half of cooked mushrooms. Slide pizza carefully onto stone and return oven to 500 degrees. Bake until crust is well browned, 10 to 12 minutes, rotating pizza halfway through baking. Transfer pizza to wire rack, dollop half of cashew ricotta mixture over pizza in small spoonfuls, then let cool for 5 minutes. Sprinkle with parsley and drizzle with extra oil. Heat broiler for 10 minutes. Repeat shaping, topping, and baking for second pizza. Slice and serve.

Whole-Wheat Pizza Dough
Makes enough for two 13-inch pizzas

1½ cups (8¼ ounces) whole-wheat flour
1 cup (5½ ounces) bread flour
2 teaspoons sugar
¾ teaspoon instant or rapid-rise yeast
1¼ cups ice water
2 tablespoons extra-virgin olive oil
1¾ teaspoons table salt

1. Process whole-wheat flour, bread flour, sugar, and yeast in food processor until combined, about 2 seconds. With processor running, slowly add ice water and process until dough is just combined and no dry flour remains, about 10 seconds. Let dough rest for 10 minutes.

2. Add oil and salt to dough and process until dough forms satiny, sticky ball that clears sides of bowl, 45 to 60 seconds. Transfer dough to lightly oiled counter and knead by hand to form smooth, round ball, about 1 minute. Place dough seam side down in lightly greased large bowl, cover tightly with plastic wrap, and refrigerate for at least 18 hours or up to 2 days.

Lavash with Romesco, Tomatoes, and Spinach
Serves 4 (Makes 2 flatbreads) `FAST`

Why This Recipe Works Lavash, a thin round or rectangular flatbread popular throughout the Middle East, makes a great sandwich wrap, but we discovered that it also bakes up beautifully with a crisp, cracker-like crust, making it a sophisticated stand-in for traditional pizza crust. To get the lavash crisp enough to hold toppings, we brushed the breads with oil and toasted them quickly in the oven. Then we spread them with a base of romesco sauce and topped them with a flavorful mixture of thawed frozen spinach, fresh cherry tomatoes, and fruity green olives before returning them to the oven to finish baking. To garnish them in style, we grated almonds over the top, which looked like cheese while adding their own unique flavor and texture.

10 ounces frozen spinach, thawed, squeezed dry, and chopped
5 ounces cherry or grape tomatoes, halved
½ cup pitted green olives, chopped
¼ cup extra-virgin olive oil, divided
1 garlic clove, minced
¼ teaspoon red pepper flakes
¼ teaspoon table salt
¼ teaspoon pepper
2 (12 by 9-inch) lavash breads
1 recipe Romesco Sauce (page 91)
2 tablespoons whole blanched almonds (optional)

1. Adjust oven racks to upper-middle and lower-middle positions and heat oven to 475 degrees. Combine spinach, tomatoes, olives, 2 tablespoons oil, garlic, pepper flakes, salt, and pepper in bowl. Brush both sides of lavash with remaining 2 tablespoons oil, lay on 2 baking sheets, and bake until crisp and golden brown, about 4 minutes, switching and rotating sheets and flipping lavash halfway through baking.

2. Spread romesco evenly over each lavash, then top with spinach mixture. Bake until warmed through, about 4 minutes, switching and rotating sheets halfway through baking. Using rasp-style grater, finely grate almonds over top, if using. Slice and serve.

VARIATION
Lavash with Tahini Sauce, Cauliflower, and Fennel
You will need a 12-inch nonstick skillet with a tight-fitting lid.

¼ cup extra-virgin olive oil, divided
½ head cauliflower (1 pound), cored and cut into ½-inch pieces (3 cups)
1 fennel bulb, stalks discarded, bulb halved, cored, and cut into ½-inch pieces
3 tablespoons water
1 teaspoon ground coriander
1 garlic clove, minced
½ teaspoon table salt
¼ teaspoon red pepper flakes
1 tablespoon capers, rinsed and chopped
2 (12 by 9-inch) lavash breads
½ cup Tahini Sauce (page 249)
2 scallions, sliced thin on bias
½ teaspoon smoked paprika

1. Adjust oven racks to upper-middle and lower-middle positions and heat oven to 475 degrees. Heat 2 tablespoons oil in 12-inch nonstick skillet over medium-high heat until shimmering. Add cauliflower, fennel, water, coriander, garlic, salt, and pepper flakes, cover, and cook until vegetables begin to soften, about 5 minutes. Uncover and cook until lightly browned, 5 to 7 minutes. Off heat, stir in capers.

2. Brush both sides of lavash with remaining 2 tablespoons oil, lay on 2 baking sheets, and bake until crisp and golden brown, about 4 minutes, flipping lavash halfway through baking.

3. Spread fennel mixture evenly over each lavash. Drizzle with tahini sauce and sprinkle with scallions and paprika. Slice and serve.

GRATING ALMONDS

Finely grate whole, blanched, untoasted almonds using a rasp-style grater to get cheese-like shreds.

Pide with Eggplant and Tomatoes

Serves 6 to 8 (**Makes** 6 pide)

Why This Recipe Works The hallmark of this Turkish flatbread is its signature canoe shape. Since pide varies from region to region, we tested a few traditional dough recipes. Tasters preferred the dough fermented overnight in the refrigerator because it baked up with a crisp outer crust and chewy, irregular interior. For toppings, tasters loved the classic Turkish combination of eggplant, red bell pepper, and tomatoes. Sautéing the eggplant eliminated any excess moisture, and pulsing canned whole tomatoes in the food processor gave our topping the best texture. We accented the vegetables with smoky paprika, spicy red pepper flakes, and a healthy amount of mint. If you would like to add cheese, sprinkle ¼ cup crumbled feta over each dough oval after you top it with the eggplant mixture. If you don't have a baking stone, you can use a preheated rimless (or inverted) baking sheet. Press and roll the remaining three dough balls into ovals while the first set of pide bake, but don't top and shape the pide until right before baking.

Dough

- 3 cups (16½ ounces) bread flour
- 2 teaspoons sugar
- ½ teaspoon instant or rapid-rise yeast
- 1⅓ cups ice water
- 1 tablespoon extra-virgin olive oil
- 1½ teaspoons table salt

Toppings

- 1 (28-ounce) can whole peeled tomatoes
- 6 tablespoons extra-virgin olive oil, divided
- 1 pound eggplant, cut into ½-inch pieces
- ½ red bell pepper, chopped
- ½ teaspoon salt
- 3 garlic cloves, minced
- ¼ teaspoon red pepper flakes
- ½ teaspoon smoked paprika
- 6 tablespoons minced fresh mint, divided
- ¼ cup pine nuts, toasted

1. For the dough Pulse flour, sugar, and yeast in food processor until combined, about 5 pulses. With processor running, slowly add ice water and process until dough is just combined and no dry flour remains, about 10 seconds. Let dough rest for 10 minutes.

2. Add oil and salt to dough and process until dough forms satiny, sticky ball that clears sides of bowl, 30 to 60 seconds. Transfer to lightly oiled counter and knead by hand to form smooth, round ball, about 30 seconds. Place dough seam side down in lightly greased large bowl, cover tightly with plastic wrap, and refrigerate for at least 24 hours or up to 3 days.

3. For the toppings Pulse tomatoes and their juice in now-empty food processor until coarsely ground, about 12 pulses. Heat 2 tablespoons oil in 12-inch nonstick skillet over medium-high heat until shimmering. Add eggplant, bell pepper, and salt and cook, stirring occasionally, until softened and beginning to brown, 5 to 7 minutes. Stir in garlic, pepper flakes, and paprika and cook until fragrant, about 30 seconds.

4. Add tomatoes, bring to simmer, and cook, stirring occasionally, until mixture is very thick and measures 3½ cups, about 10 minutes. Off heat, stir in ¼ cup mint and season with salt and pepper to taste; let cool completely before using.

5. One hour before baking, adjust oven rack to upper-middle position, set baking stone on rack, and heat oven to 500 degrees. Press down on dough to deflate. Transfer to clean counter and divide in half, then cut each half into thirds; cover with greased plastic. Working with 1 piece of dough at a time (keeping remaining pieces covered), shape dough into smooth, taut balls. Space balls at least 3 inches apart on counter, cover loosely with greased plastic, and let rest for 1 hour.

Pide with Eggplant and Tomatoes

Mushroom Musakhan
Serves 4 (Makes 2 flatbreads)

Why This Recipe Works Musakhan is a popular Palestinian dish featuring a flatbread traditionally topped with roasted chicken, caramelized onions, pine nuts, and lemony sumac, a signature spice of the region. For our plant-forward version, we swapped chicken for robust, juicy sautéed portobello mushrooms. To amp up the onion flavor, we made a warm-spiced caramelized onion jam with sumac, allspice, and cardamom. The traditional base for musakhan is taboon bread, a thick, crisp flatbread that is cooked in a clay oven. In translating this to a home oven, we found that our Whole-Wheat Pizza Dough worked very well. To ensure crisp edges, we heated a baking stone in the oven at 500 degrees for an hour, and we superheated the oven by briefly turning on the broiler before sliding the musakhan onto the pizza stone to bake. If you do not have a baking stone, you can use a preheated rimless (or inverted) baking sheet.

1 recipe Whole-Wheat Pizza Dough (page 113)
½ cup extra-virgin olive oil, divided
2 tablespoons minced fresh oregano or 2 teaspoons dried
4 garlic cloves, minced
1½ tablespoons ground sumac
¼ teaspoon ground allspice
⅛ teaspoon ground cardamom
2 pounds onions, halved and sliced ¼ inch thick
2 teaspoons packed light brown sugar
1½ teaspoons table salt, divided
¼ cup pine nuts
2 pounds portobello mushroom caps, gills removed, caps halved and sliced ½ inch thick
2 tablespoons minced fresh chives

6. Cut six 16 by 6-inch pieces of parchment paper. Generously coat 1 dough ball with flour and place on well-floured counter. Press and roll into 14 by 5½-inch oval. Arrange oval on parchment rectangle and reshape as needed. (If dough resists stretching, let it relax for 10 to 20 minutes before trying to stretch it again.) Repeat with 2 more dough balls and parchment rectangles.

7. Brush each dough oval with 1 teaspoon oil, then top each with ½ cup eggplant mixture, leaving ¾-inch border around edges. Fold long edges of dough over filling to form canoe shape and pinch ends together to seal. Brush outer edges of each pide with 1 teaspoon oil and transfer shaped pides (still on parchment rectangles) to pizza peel.

8. Slide each parchment rectangle with pide onto baking stone, spacing pides at least 1 inch apart. Bake until crust is golden brown and edges are crisp, 10 to 15 minutes. Transfer pides to wire rack, discard parchment, and let cool for 5 minutes. Sprinkle cooled pides with 1 tablespoon mint and 2 tablespoons pine nuts, slice, and serve. Repeat with remaining 3 dough balls, 3 parchment rectangles, 2 tablespoons oil, 1½ cups eggplant mixture, 1 tablespoon mint, and 2 tablespoons pine nuts.

1. One hour before baking, adjust oven rack to upper-middle position, set baking stone on rack, and heat oven to 500 degrees. Remove dough from refrigerator. Press down on dough to deflate. Transfer dough to clean counter, divide in half, and shape each half into smooth, taut ball. Space dough balls 3 inches apart, cover loosely with greased plastic wrap, and let rest for 1 hour.

2. Combine 1 tablespoon oil, oregano, garlic, sumac, allspice, and cardamom in bowl. Heat 2 tablespoons oil in 12-inch nonstick skillet over high heat until shimmering. Add onions, sugar, and ½ teaspoon salt and stir to coat. Cook, stirring occasionally, until onions begin to soften and release some moisture, about 5 minutes. Reduce heat to medium and continue to cook, stirring often, until onions are well caramelized, 35 to 40 minutes. (If onions are sizzling or scorching, reduce heat. If onions are not browning after 15 to 20 minutes, increase heat.) Push onions to sides of skillet. Add oregano-garlic mixture to center and cook, mashing mixture into skillet, until fragrant, about 30 seconds. Stir oregano-garlic mixture into onions.

3. Transfer onion mixture to food processor and pulse to jamlike consistency, about 5 pulses. Transfer to bowl, stir in pine nuts, and season with salt and pepper to taste; let cool completely before using.

4. Wipe skillet clean with paper towels. Heat 2 tablespoons oil in now-empty skillet over medium-high heat until shimmering. Add half of mushrooms and ½ teaspoon salt and cook, stirring occasionally, until evenly browned, 8 to 10 minutes; transfer to separate bowl. Repeat with 2 tablespoons oil, remaining mushrooms, and remaining ½ teaspoon salt; transfer to bowl and let cool completely before using.

5. Heat broiler for 10 minutes. Meanwhile, working with 1 piece of dough at a time (keep other pieces covered), coat dough ball generously with flour and place on well-floured counter. Press and roll into 12 by 8-inch oval. Transfer oval to well-floured pizza peel and stretch into 15 by 8-inch oval. (If dough resists stretching, let it relax for 10 to 20 minutes before trying to stretch it again.) Using fork, poke entire surface of oval 10 to 15 times.

6. Spread half of onion mixture evenly on dough, edge to edge, and arrange half of mushrooms on top. Slide flatbread carefully onto baking stone and return oven to 500 degrees. Bake until bottom crust is evenly browned and edges are crisp, about 10 minutes, rotating flatbread halfway through baking. Transfer flatbread to wire rack and let cool for 5 minutes. Drizzle with 1½ teaspoons oil and sprinkle with 1 tablespoon chives. Heat broiler for 10 minutes. Repeat shaping, topping, and baking for second flatbread. Slice and serve.

Red Pepper Coques
Serves 4 to 6 (**Makes** 4 flatbreads)

Why This Recipe Works Coques are the Catalan version of the thin and crunchy topped flatbreads that can be found in any Spanish tapas bar. We set our sights on an intensely savory version topped with bold Spanish flavors. To get the perfect crust, we started with our thin-crust pizza dough. But to set our coque crust apart from regular pizza and get an extra-crisp base, we increased the amount of oil in the dough and brushed each dough oval with oil before baking. This helped both the bottom and the top crisp up and imparted an earthy

Red Pepper Coques

flavor to the dough. We found that parbaking the dough before topping reinforced crispness and created the sturdy base we were looking for. To top the coques, we turned to sweet onions and rich roasted red peppers, along with garlic, red pepper flakes, and sherry vinegar. Cooking the topping before spreading it over the parbaked dough intensified the flavors while cutting the baking time in half. If you cannot fit two coques on a single baking sheet, bake them in 2 batches.

Dough
- 3 cups (16½ ounces) bread flour
- 2 teaspoons sugar
- ½ teaspoon instant or rapid-rise yeast
- 1⅓ cups ice water
- 3 tablespoons extra-virgin olive oil
- 1½ teaspoons table salt

Topping
- ½ cup extra-virgin olive oil, divided
- 2 large onions, halved and sliced thin
- 2 cups jarred roasted red peppers, patted dry and sliced thin
- 3 tablespoons sugar
- 3 garlic cloves, minced
- 1½ teaspoons table salt
- ¼ teaspoon red pepper flakes
- 2 bay leaves
- 3 tablespoons sherry vinegar
- ¼ cup pine nuts (optional)
- 1 tablespoon minced fresh parsley

1. For the dough Pulse flour, sugar, and yeast in food processor until combined, about 5 pulses. With processor running, slowly add ice water and process until dough is just combined and no dry flour remains, about 10 seconds. Let dough rest for 10 minutes.

2. Add oil and salt to dough and process until dough forms satiny, sticky ball that clears sides of bowl, 30 to 60 seconds. Transfer dough to lightly floured counter and knead by hand to form smooth, round ball, about 30 seconds. Place dough seam side down in lightly greased large bowl or container, cover tightly with plastic wrap, and refrigerate for at least 24 hours or up to 3 days.

3. Remove dough from refrigerator. Press down on dough to deflate. Transfer dough to clean counter, divide into 4 pieces, and cover loosely with greased plastic. Working with 1 piece of dough at a time (keep remaining pieces covered), form into smooth, taut balls. Space dough balls 3 inches apart, cover loosely with greased plastic, and let rest for 1 hour.

4. For the topping Heat 3 tablespoons oil in 12-inch nonstick skillet over medium heat until shimmering. Stir in onions, red peppers, sugar, garlic, salt, pepper flakes, and bay leaves. Cover and cook, stirring occasionally, until onions are softened and have released their juice, about 10 minutes. Remove lid and continue to cook, stirring often, until onions are golden brown, 10 to 15 minutes. Off heat, discard bay leaves. Transfer onion mixture to bowl, stir in vinegar, and let cool completely before using.

5. Adjust oven racks to upper-middle and lower-middle positions and heat oven to 500 degrees. Coat 2 rimmed baking sheets with 2 tablespoons oil each. Generously coat 1 dough ball with flour and place on well-floured counter. Press and roll into 14 by 5-inch oval. Arrange oval on prepared sheet, with long edge fit snugly against 1 long side of sheet, and reshape as needed. (If dough resists stretching, let it relax for 10 to 20 minutes before trying to stretch it again.) Repeat with remaining dough balls, arranging 2 ovals on each sheet, spaced ½ inch apart. Using fork, poke surface of dough 10 to 15 times.

6. Brush dough ovals with remaining 1 tablespoon oil and bake until puffed, 6 to 8 minutes, switching and rotating sheets halfway through baking.

7. Scatter onion mixture evenly over flatbreads, from edge to edge, then sprinkle with pine nuts, if using. Bake until topping is heated through and edges of flatbreads are deep golden brown and crisp, about 15 minutes, switching and rotating sheets halfway through baking. Let flatbreads cool on sheets for 10 minutes, then transfer to cutting board using metal spatula. Sprinkle with parsley, slice, and serve.

Scallion Pancakes with Dipping Sauce
Serves 4 to 6

Why This Recipe Works Scallion pancakes may be Chinese favorites, but they're a revelation when cooked from scratch. They're made from just flour, water, oil, scallions, and salt, and the secret to their hidden depths of rich flavor and flaky golden-brown layers lies in the method. We used boiling water, which helped keep the pancake dough firmer and less sticky. This made it easier to complete the rolling, coiling, and rerolling process required to shape the pancakes. Then we cooked the pancakes one at a time in a hot skillet, first covered to cook the pancake through and then uncovered to crisp up the exterior. A simple slit cut in the center of each pancake allowed steam to escape, which resulted in more even browning and better crisping. The finishing touch was a quick sweet-salty dipping sauce. We strongly recommend weighing the flour for the pancakes. For this recipe we prefer the steady, consistent heat of a cast-iron skillet. For an accurate measurement of boiling water, bring a full kettle of water to a boil and then measure out the desired amount.

Dipping Sauce
- 1 scallion, sliced thin
- 2 tablespoons soy sauce
- 1 tablespoon water
- 2 teaspoons rice vinegar
- 1 teaspoon light agave syrup or honey
- 1 teaspoon toasted sesame oil
- Pinch red pepper flakes

Pancakes

- 1½ cups (7½ ounces) plus 1 tablespoon all-purpose flour, divided
- ¾ cup boiling water
- 7 tablespoons vegetable oil, divided
- 1 tablespoon toasted sesame oil
- 1 teaspoon kosher salt
- 4 scallions, sliced thin

1. For the dipping sauce Whisk all ingredients together in small bowl.

2. For the pancakes Using wooden spoon, mix 1½ cups flour and boiling water in bowl to form rough dough. When cool enough to handle, transfer dough to lightly floured counter and knead until it forms ball that is tacky but no longer sticky, about 4 minutes (dough will not be perfectly smooth). Cover loosely with plastic wrap and let rest for 30 minutes.

3. While dough is resting, stir together 1 tablespoon vegetable oil, sesame oil, and remaining 1 tablespoon flour.

4. Divide dough in half. Cover 1 half of dough with plastic wrap and set aside. Roll remaining dough into 12-inch round. Drizzle 1 tablespoon oil-flour mixture over surface and then use pastry brush to spread evenly over entire surface. Sprinkle with ½ teaspoon salt and half of scallions. Roll dough into cylinder. Coil cylinder into spiral, tuck end underneath, and flatten spiral with your palm. Cover with plastic wrap and repeat with remaining dough, oil-flour mixture, salt, and scallions.

5. Place 10-inch cast-iron skillet over low heat for 10 minutes. Place 2 tablespoons oil in skillet and increase heat to medium-low. Roll first pancake into 9-inch round. Cut ½-inch slit in center of pancake. Place pancake in pan (oil should sizzle). Cover and cook until pancake is slightly puffy and deep golden brown on underside, 1 to 1½ minutes. (If underside is not browned after 1 minute, turn heat up slightly. If it is browning too quickly, turn heat down slightly.)

6. Drizzle 1 tablespoon oil over pancake. Use pastry brush to distribute oil over entire surface. Carefully flip pancake. Cover and cook until second side is deep golden brown, 1 to 1½ minutes. Uncover skillet and flip pancake. Cook uncovered until very deep golden brown and crispy on underside, 30 to 60 seconds. Flip and cook second side until very deep golden brown and crispy, 30 to 60 seconds. Transfer to wire rack. Repeat with remaining oil and pancake. Cut each pancake into 8 wedges and serve with dipping sauce.

Savory Fennel-Apple Tarte Tatin

Serves 4

Why This Recipe Works Yes, tarte Tatin is traditionally a dessert, made by caramelizing apples in a little butter and lots of sugar and then baking them with a pie dough top. After cooking, it's inverted and the juices seep deliciously into the crust. Here's our savory version (still with apples, but paired with fresh fennel), and we simplified the recipe while we were at it. The fennel was a revelation—it quickly picked up beautiful caramelization on the outside while the center turned meltingly dense and silky. We started with olive oil and just a little sugar in a cold skillet. This allowed us to carefully arrange fennel wedges in an attractive pinwheel; we then filled in the gaps with sliced fennel and set the pan over high heat to jump-start browning on the underside of the fennel (the sugar helped with this). Then we placed some sliced apple and sage on top, covered it with convenient store-bought puff pastry, and finished it in the oven. The apples gently steamed over the fennel and turned into a sage-infused apple sauce, a perfect base for the fennel once the tart was inverted. To cut through the richness of the dish, we served it with a mustardy watercress salad. Look for fennel bulbs that are about 4 inches tall after trimming. Do not core the fennel bulb that is cut into wedges. Many store-bought puff pastry brands are vegan, but check ingredient lists carefully to make sure.

- 1 (9½ by 9-inch) sheet puff pastry, thawed
- 3 tablespoons extra-virgin olive oil, divided
- 1 tablespoon sugar
- ½ teaspoon plus pinch table salt, divided
- 2 fennel bulbs, stalks discarded (1 bulb cut into 6 wedges, 1 bulb halved, cored, and cut lengthwise into ½-inch-thick slices)
- 2 Granny Smith apples, peeled, cored, halved, and sliced ½ inch thick
- 4 teaspoons chopped fresh sage
- 2 teaspoons sherry vinegar
- ¼ teaspoon Dijon mustard
- 6 ounces (6 cups) watercress, torn into bite-size pieces
- 2 tablespoons chopped toasted and skinned hazelnuts
- 2 ounces (½ cup) goat cheese, crumbled (optional)

Savory Fennel-Apple Tarte Tatin

Transfer skillet to oven and bake until crust is deep golden brown, about 45 minutes. Transfer skillet to wire rack and let cool for 10 minutes.

4. Meanwhile, whisk vinegar, mustard, remaining 1 tablespoon oil, and remaining pinch salt together in large bowl. Add watercress and hazelnuts and toss to coat. Season with salt and pepper to taste.

5. Run paring knife around edge of crust to loosen. Using dish towels or potholders, carefully place serving platter on top of skillet, and, holding platter and skillet firmly together, invert tart onto serving platter. Transfer any fennel slices that stick to skillet to tart. Sprinkle with goat cheese, if using, and serve with salad.

ASSEMBLING SAVORY FENNEL-APPLE TARTE TATIN

1. Arrange fennel wedges in pinwheel shape in skillet.

2. Fill in remaining gaps with sliced fennel.

3. Slide prepared puff pastry on top of filling in skillet and press any excess dough up sides of skillet.

1. Adjust oven rack to middle position and heat oven to 375 degrees. Unfold pastry onto lightly floured counter and roll into 11-inch square. Using pizza cutter or sharp knife, cut pastry into 11-inch circle. Transfer to parchment paper–lined rimmed baking sheet, cover loosely with plastic wrap, and refrigerate while preparing filling.

2. Swirl 2 tablespoons oil over bottom of 10-inch ovensafe nonstick skillet, then sprinkle with sugar and ¼ teaspoon salt. Arrange fennel wedges in pinwheel shape, fanning out from center of circle. Fill in gaps with sliced fennel. Cook, without stirring, over high heat until fennel turns deep golden brown, 7 to 9 minutes (if pan is not sizzling after 2 minutes, adjust cook time accordingly).

3. Off heat, sprinkle with apple, sage, and ¼ teaspoon salt. Carefully transfer chilled dough to skillet, centering over filling. Being careful of hot skillet, gently fold excess dough up against skillet wall (dough should be flush with skillet edge). Using paring knife, pierce dough evenly over surface 10 times.

Tomato Tart with Cashew Ricotta

Socca with Swiss Chard, Pistachios, and Apricots

Tomato Tart with Cashew Ricotta
Serves 4

Why This Recipe Works Fresh tomato tarts conjure up delightful images of al fresco lunches, but many recipes don't live up to that promise, with their watery fillings and soggy bottoms. So we developed a flavorful, sturdy, foolproof tart shell—which happens to use coconut oil rather than butter. To prevent cracking and puffing, we took a multitiered approach: We rolled rather than crumbled the dough into the tart pan, chilled the dough in the pan, and used pie weights during the first 30 minutes of baking. For our filling, we made a rich base that can be either vegan or vegetarian using your choice of Cashew Ricotta plus Vegan Parmesan Substitute or dairy ricotta plus Parmesan cheese, along with tangy chopped jarred artichoke hearts and fragrant lemon zest. For an elegant topping, we salted slices of plum tomatoes and let them drain before shingling them over the creamy base. Drizzling the tomatoes with a mixture of olive oil and minced garlic before baking infused them with flavor. We finished the baked tart with a flourish of fresh basil.

1¾ cups (8¾ ounces) all-purpose flour
1 tablespoon sugar
¾ teaspoon table salt, divided
½ cup coconut oil, melted and cooled slightly
¼ cup water
3 plum tomatoes, cored and sliced ¼ inch thick
3 tablespoons extra-virgin olive oil, divided
1 garlic clove, minced
1 cup jarred whole baby artichoke hearts packed in water, rinsed, patted dry, and chopped
½ cup Cashew Ricotta (page 26) or dairy ricotta cheese
⅓ cup Vegan Parmesan Substitute (page 27) or grated dairy Parmesan cheese
1 teaspoon grated lemon zest
2 tablespoons chopped fresh basil

1. Whisk flour, sugar, and ¼ teaspoon salt together in bowl. Add melted oil and water and stir with rubber spatula until dough forms. Roll dough into 12-inch circle between 2 large sheets of parchment paper. Remove top sheet parchment, and, working quickly, gently invert dough (still on bottom sheet) onto 9-inch tart pan with removable bottom. Center dough over pan, letting excess dough hang over edge, and peel away remaining parchment. Ease dough into pan by gently lifting edge of dough with your hand while pressing into corners and fluted sides of pan with your other hand. Run rolling pin over top of pan to remove any excess dough. Prick dough all over with fork, then wrap pan loosely in plastic wrap and refrigerate for at least 30 minutes. (Dough-lined tart pan can be refrigerated for up to 24 hours or frozen for up to 1 month.) Adjust oven rack to middle position and heat oven to 350 degrees.

2. Line chilled tart shell with double layer of aluminum foil and fill with pie weights. Place pan on rimmed baking sheet and bake until tart shell is pale and mostly dry, 30 to 35 minutes, rotating sheet halfway through baking.

3. Remove foil and weights and continue to bake tart shell until light golden brown and firm to touch, 15 to 25 minutes, rotating pan halfway through baking. Transfer sheet to wire rack and let cool slightly.

4. Meanwhile, spread tomatoes over triple layer of paper towels, sprinkle with remaining ½ teaspoon salt, and let sit for 30 minutes. Combine 2 tablespoons oil and garlic in small bowl. In separate bowl, combine artichoke hearts, cashew ricotta, vegan Parmesan substitute, lemon zest, and remaining 1 tablespoon oil, and season with salt and pepper to taste.

5. Increase oven temperature to 425 degrees. Spread ricotta mixture evenly over bottom of cooled tart shell. Blot tomatoes dry with paper towels and shingle attractively on top of filling in concentric circles. Drizzle with garlic-oil mixture.

6. Bake tart on sheet until tomatoes are slightly wilted and tart shell is deep golden brown, 20 to 25 minutes, rotating sheet halfway through baking.

7. Let tart cool on sheet for at least 10 minutes or up to 2 hours. To serve, remove outer metal ring of tart pan, slide thin metal spatula between tart and tart pan bottom, and carefully slide tart onto serving platter or cutting board. Sprinkle with basil before serving.

Socca with Swiss Chard, Pistachios, and Apricots

Serves 4 (**Makes** 5 socca)

Why This Recipe Works Made with chickpea flour, socca is a satisfying, savory flatbread that is popular in southern France. The loose, pancake-like batter comes together in a minute: Simply whisk together chickpea flour, water, olive oil, turmeric, salt, and pepper. Traditionally the batter is poured into a cast-iron skillet and baked in a wood-burning oven to make a large socca with a blistered top and a smoky flavor. In a home oven, however, this technique produced socca that was dry and limp. So to achieve crispy, golden-brown flatbreads, we ditched the oven for the higher heat of the stovetop.

Because flipping one large socca turned out to be not as easy as we'd hoped, we made several smaller flatbreads in an 8-inch skillet instead. As an added bonus, these elegant flatbreads had a higher ratio of crunchy crust to tender interior. To complement our savory flatbreads, we came up with a topping of Swiss chard, dried apricots, and toasted pistachios, along with cumin and allspice, that was earthy, sweet, and delicious.

Batter
1½ cups (6¾ ounces) chickpea flour
½ teaspoon table salt
½ teaspoon pepper
½ teaspoon turmeric
1½ cups water
6 tablespoons plus 1 teaspoon extra-virgin olive oil, divided

Topping
1 tablespoon extra-virgin olive oil
1 onion, chopped fine
2 garlic cloves, minced
¾ teaspoon ground cumin
¼ teaspoon table salt
⅛ teaspoon allspice
12 ounces Swiss chard, stemmed and chopped
3 tablespoons finely chopped dried apricots
2 tablespoons finely chopped toasted pistachios
1 teaspoon white wine vinegar

1. For the batter Adjust oven rack to middle position and heat oven to 200 degrees. Set wire rack in rimmed baking sheet and place in oven. Whisk chickpea flour, salt, pepper, and turmeric together in bowl. Slowly whisk in water and 3 tablespoons oil until combined and smooth.

2. Heat 2 teaspoons oil in 8-inch nonstick skillet over medium-high heat until shimmering. Add ½ cup batter to skillet, tilting pan to coat bottom evenly. Reduce heat to medium and cook until crisp at edges and golden brown on bottom, 3 to 5 minutes. Flip socca and continue to cook until second side is browned, about 2 minutes. Transfer to wire rack in warm oven and repeat to make 4 more socca, working with 2 teaspoons oil and ½ cup batter at a time.

3. For the topping Heat oil in 12-inch nonstick skillet over medium heat until shimmering. Add onion and cook until softened, about 5 minutes. Stir in garlic, cumin, salt, and allspice and cook until fragrant, about 30 seconds. Stir in Swiss chard and apricots and cook until chard is wilted, 4 to 6 minutes. Off heat, stir in pistachios and vinegar and season with salt and pepper to taste. Top each cooked socca with ⅓ cup chard mixture, slice, and serve.

CHAPTER 4
VEGETABLE SALADS

For grain salads, see Chapter 7. For bean salads, see Chapter 8.

■ FAST (45 minutes or less total time)
Photos: Raw Beet and Carrot Noodle Salad with Almond-Sesame Dressing; Spinach Salad with Carrots, Oranges, and Sesame; Potato, Green Bean, and Tomato Salad; Mediterranean Chopped Salad

SALAD GREENS

With such a wide array of salad greens to choose from nowadays, it's helpful to know how to mix and match them to build interesting salads beyond the recipes in this chapter. Many greens are great on their own, while others are better used as part of a mixed salad. No matter what type of greens you buy, make sure to select the freshest ones possible.

TYPE/DESCRIPTION	YIELD	SERVING SUGGESTIONS
Arugula (also called Rocket or Roquette) Delicate dark green leaves with a peppery bite; sold in bunches, usually with roots attached, or prewashed in cellophane bags; bruises easily and can be very sandy, so wash thoroughly in several changes of water before using.	5-ounce bag (5 cups) 6-ounce bunch (3 cups)	Serve alone for a full-flavored salad or add to romaine, Bibb, or Boston lettuce to give a spicy punch; for a classic salad, combine with Belgian endive, radicchio, and Quick Pickled Grapes (page 143).
Belgian Endive Small, compact head of firm white or pale yellow leaves; should be completely smooth and blemish-free; slightly bitter flavor and crisp texture; one of the few salad greens we routinely cut rather than tear; remove whole leaves from the head and slice crosswise into bite-size pieces.	4-ounce head (1 cup sliced)	Add to watercress or to Bibb, Boston, or loose-leaf lettuce; combine with diced apples and walnuts; use whole leaves in place of crackers with dips.
Bibb Lettuce Small, compact heads; pale- to medium-green leaves; soft, buttery outer leaves; inner leaves have a surprising crunch and a sweet, mild flavor.	8-ounce head (8 cups)	Combine with watercress or endive or with Boston, loose-leaf, or romaine lettuce; great tossed with fresh herbs (whole parsley leaves, chives, or dill).
Boston Lettuce Loose, fluffy head, ranging in color from pale green to red-tipped; similar in texture and flavor to Bibb lettuce, but with softer leaves.	8-ounce head (8 cups)	Combine with baby spinach, watercress, or endive or with Bibb or romaine lettuce; terrific as a bed for Red Lentil Kibbeh (page 291) or Chickpea Cakes (page 108).
Chicory (also called Curly Endive) Loose, feathery head of bright green, bitter leaves; texture is somewhat chewy.	10-ounce head (10 cups)	Add to bitter greens salads or use sparingly to add punch to mild mixed greens; great with Balsamic Mustard Vinaigrette (page 127) or Walnut Vinaigrette (page 127).
Escarole A kind of chicory with tough, dark green leaves and a mildly bitter flavor; inner leaves are slightly milder.	15-ounce head (15 cups)	Use as an accent to romaine; serve on its own with Balsamic Mustard Vinaigrette (page 127) or Orange-Ginger Vinaigrette (page 126).
Frisée A kind of chicory; milder in flavor than other chicories, but with similar feathery leaves; pale green to white in color.	10-ounce head (4 cups)	Combine with arugula or watercress or with Boston or Bibb lettuce; serve on its own with warm balsamic vinaigrette; great paired with Roasted Garlic Vinaigrette (page 126) and toasted almonds.

TYPE/DESCRIPTION	YIELD	SERVING SUGGESTIONS
Iceberg A large, round, tightly packed head of pale green leaves; very crisp and crunchy, with minimal flavor.	1-pound head (12 cups)	Tear into chunks and toss with Bibb, Boston, or loose-leaf lettuce; stands up well to our creamless creamy dressings (page 128).
Loose-Leaf Lettuces (specifically Red Leaf and Green Leaf) Ruffled dark red or green leaves that grow in big, loose heads; versatile, with a soft yet crunchy texture; green leaf is crisp and mild; red leaf is earthier.	12-ounce head (12 cups)	Pair red leaf with romaine lettuce or watercress; pair green leaf with arugula, radicchio, or watercress; great on sandwiches or as a bed for grain or bean salads.
Mâche (also called Lamb's Tongue or Lamb's Lettuce) Small heads of three or four stems of small, sweet, deep green leaves; very delicate; usually sold prewashed in bags; if buying heads, wash thoroughly, can be sandy.	4-ounce bag (4 cups)	Combine with arugula or watercress; perfect on its own with Spiced Pepitas or Pumpkin Seeds and Tahini-Lemon Vinaigrette (page 127).
Mesclun (also called Mesclune, Spring Mix, Field Greens) A mix of up to 14 different baby greens, including spinach, red leaf, oak leaf, frisée, radicchio, green leaf; delicate leaves; flavors range from mild to slightly bitter depending on the blend.	4 ounces bagged or loose (4 cups)	Great as a delicate salad; terrific paired with Quick Pickled Grapes (page 143) and Pomegranate Vinaigrette (page 126).
Radicchio Tight heads of red or deep purple leaves streaked with white ribs; bitter flavor.	10-ounce head (3 cups)	Cut into ribbons and mix with arugula, endive, or watercress, or with red or green leaf, Boston, or Bibb lettuce; adds color to any salad.
Romaine Long, full heads with stiff and deep green leaves; crisp, crunchy leaves with a mild, earthy flavor; also sold in bags of three romaine hearts; tough outer leaves should be discarded from full heads.	6-ounce heart (4 cups) 14-ounce head (9 cups)	A great all-purpose lettuce; mix with spinach, watercress, arugula, endive, or radicchio or with Boston, Bibb, or red leaf lettuce; good on sandwiches and plant-based burgers.
Spinach (Flat-Leaf, Curly-Leaf, and Baby) All varieties are vibrant green with an earthy flavor; choose tender flat-leaf or baby spinach for raw salads; tough curly-leaf spinach is better steamed and sautéed; rinse loose spinach well to remove dirt; varieties available prewashed in bags.	5-ounce bag (5 cups) 11-ounce bunch (5 cups)	Delicious mixed with arugula, watercress, or napa cabbage or with romaine, Bibb, Boston, or loose-leaf lettuce; classic as a wilted salad with a warm vinaigrette and Crispy Shallots (page 142).
Watercress Delicate dark green leaves with tough, bitter stems; refreshing mustard-like flavor similar to arugula; usually sold in bunches, sometimes available prewashed in bags; if buying watercress in bunches, take care to wash thoroughly.	2-ounce bunch (2 cups)	Adds flavorful punch and texture to mildly flavored or tender greens such as Bibb or Boston lettuce; delicious on its own with tart green apples, smoked almonds, and a mustard-based dressing.

SALAD DRESSINGS

Once you learn some tips about how to mix and match salad greens (page 124), you'll also want some creative yet easy dressings to accompany them. Here are several of our favorite vegan recipes, including simple fruit-based and mustard-based vinaigrettes as well as plant-based creamy recipes. You will also find other dressings within the recipes in this chapter.

Pomegranate Vinaigrette

Makes about 1 cup

This versatile dressing perfectly pairs sweet and tart flavors for a bolder take on an ordinary vinaigrette. The variations mix up the flavor profiles with herbs, spices, and different fruits. To avoid off-flavors, make sure to reduce the fruit juice in a nonreactive stainless-steel saucepan.

- 2 cups pomegranate juice
- 3 tablespoons red wine vinegar
- 2 tablespoons extra-virgin olive oil
- 1 tablespoon minced shallot
- ½ teaspoon table salt
- ½ teaspoon pepper

Bring pomegranate juice to boil in small saucepan over medium-high heat. Reduce to simmer and cook until thickened and juice measures about ⅔ cup, 15 to 20 minutes. Transfer syrup to medium bowl and refrigerate until cool, about 15 minutes. Whisk in vinegar, oil, shallot, salt, and pepper until combined. (Vinaigrette can be refrigerated for up to 1 week; whisk to recombine.)

VARIATIONS

Apple Cider–Sage Vinaigrette

Substitute apple cider for pomegranate juice, and cider vinegar for red wine vinegar. Add ½ teaspoon minced fresh sage to syrup with vinegar.

Orange-Ginger Vinaigrette

Substitute orange juice for pomegranate juice, and lime juice for red wine vinegar. Add 1 teaspoon grated fresh ginger to syrup with lime juice.

Roasted Garlic Dressing

Makes about 1 cup

Two whole heads of roasted garlic pureed in the blender with olive oil, cider vinegar, mustard, and thyme give this flavorful dressing a mellow sweet-savory flavor and a thick and creamy consistency without any need for a dairy component.

- 2 large garlic heads
- 2 tablespoons water, divided
- 2 pinches plus ½ teaspoon table salt, divided
- 2 tablespoons extra-virgin olive oil
- 4 teaspoons cider vinegar
- 1 tablespoon Dijon mustard
- ½ teaspoon minced fresh thyme
- ¼ teaspoon pepper

1. Adjust oven rack to upper-middle position and heat oven to 400 degrees. Cut ½ inch off top of each garlic head to expose tops of cloves. Set each garlic head, cut side up, on small sheet of aluminum foil and sprinkle with 1 tablespoon water and pinch salt. Gather foil up around garlic tightly to form packet, place directly on oven rack, and roast for 45 minutes.

2. Carefully open just top of each foil packet to expose garlic and continue to roast until garlic is soft and golden brown, about 20 minutes. Let roasted garlic cool for 20 minutes, reserving any juice in foil packets.

3. Squeeze garlic cloves from skins. Process roasted garlic, reserved garlic juice, oil, vinegar, mustard, thyme, pepper, and remaining ½ teaspoon salt in blender until thick and smooth, about 1 minute. (Dressing can be refrigerated for up to 1 week; whisk to recombine.)

Balsamic Mustard Vinaigrette

Makes ¼ cup

Balsamic vinegar is assertive enough to stand up to a larger amount of Dijon mustard. Fresh thyme adds an earthy herbal note to the sweetness of the vinegar. This vinaigrette is best for dressing strongly flavored greens such as escarole, watercress, arugula, and radicchio.

- 1 tablespoon balsamic vinegar
- 2 teaspoons Dijon mustard
- 1½ teaspoons minced shallot
- ½ teaspoon plant-based mayonnaise or egg-based mayonnaise
- ½ teaspoon minced fresh thyme
- ⅛ teaspoon table salt
- Pinch pepper
- 3 tablespoons extra-virgin olive oil

Whisk vinegar, mustard, shallot, mayonnaise, thyme, salt, and pepper together in bowl. While whisking constantly, drizzle in oil until completely emulsified. (Vinaigrette can be refrigerated for up to 1 week; whisk to recombine.)

Roasted Garlic Dressing

Walnut Vinaigrette

Makes ¼ cup

Using roasted walnut oil in combination with olive oil brings a toasty, buttery depth of flavor to this elegant vinaigrette. Used on mild greens, the dressing really shines; its buttery quality also tempers the bite of bitter greens.

- 1 tablespoon white wine vinegar
- 1½ teaspoons minced shallot
- ½ teaspoon plant-based mayonnaise or egg-based mayonnaise
- ½ teaspoon Dijon mustard
- ⅛ teaspoon table salt
- Pinch pepper
- 1½ tablespoons roasted walnut oil
- 1½ tablespoons extra-virgin olive oil

Whisk vinegar, shallot, mayonnaise, mustard, salt, and pepper together in bowl. While whisking constantly, drizzle in oils until completely emulsified. (Vinaigrette can be refrigerated for up to 1 week; whisk to recombine.)

Tahini-Lemon Vinaigrette

Makes ½ cup

Tahini's subtle, nutty flavor pairs with bright lemon juice and pungent garlic for a Mediterranean flavor profile. This dressing is best for dressing sturdy but mild-tasting greens such as romaine and Bibb lettuce.

- 2½ tablespoons lemon juice
- 2 tablespoons tahini
- 1 tablespoon water
- 1 garlic clove, minced
- ½ teaspoon table salt
- ⅛ teaspoon pepper
- ¼ cup extra-virgin olive oil

Whisk lemon juice, tahini, water, garlic, salt, and pepper together in bowl. While whisking constantly, drizzle in oil until completely emulsified. (Vinaigrette can be refrigerated for up to 1 week; whisk to recombine.)

Creamless Creamy Dressing

Makes 2 cups

For an all-purpose yet luscious dairy-free creamy dressing, we turned to cashews to achieve the perfect consistency. You'll need a conventional blender for this recipe; an immersion blender or food processor will produce a grainy, thin dressing. Use unsalted raw cashews, not roasted, to ensure the proper flavor balance. Our variations turn this into an herbal green goddess dressing, a Mediterranean dressing with tahini and red peppers, and an Asian dressing with miso and ginger.

    1 cup raw cashews
    ¾ cup water, plus extra as needed
    3 tablespoons cider vinegar
  1¼ teaspoons table salt
    1 teaspoon onion powder
    ½ teaspoon sugar
    ¼ teaspoon garlic powder
    2 tablespoons minced fresh chives
    1 tablespoon minced fresh parsley
    ½ teaspoon pepper

1. Process cashews in blender on low speed to consistency of fine gravel mixed with sand, 10 to 15 seconds. Add water, vinegar, salt, onion powder, sugar, and garlic powder and process on low speed until combined, about 5 seconds. Let mixture sit for 15 minutes.

2. Process on low speed until all ingredients are well blended, about 1 minute. Scrape down blender jar. Process on high speed until dressing is smooth and creamy, 3 to 4 minutes. Transfer dressing to bowl. Cover and refrigerate until cold, about 45 minutes. Stir in chives, parsley, and pepper. Thin with extra water, adding 1 tablespoon at a time, to desired consistency. Season with salt and pepper to taste. (Dressing can be refrigerated for up to 1 week.)

VARIATIONS

Creamless Creamy Green Goddess Dressing

Omit onion powder. Decrease cashews to ¾ cup, salt to ¾ teaspoon, and pepper to ¼ teaspoon. Substitute lemon juice for cider vinegar. Increase parsley to ⅓ cup and chives to ⅓ cup. Add 1 tablespoon chopped fresh tarragon to water mixture in step 1.

Creamless Creamy Green Goddess Dressing

Creamless Creamy Roasted Red Pepper and Tahini Dressing

Decrease cashews to ½ cup and increase garlic powder to ½ teaspoon. Substitute 1 (12-ounce) jar roasted red peppers, drained and chopped coarse, for water. Substitute sherry vinegar for cider vinegar and 3 tablespoons tahini for onion powder. Substitute 2 teaspoons toasted sesame oil for sugar and ½ teaspoon smoked paprika for pepper. Increase salt to 1½ teaspoons and add pinch cayenne pepper to bell pepper mixture in step 1. Omit chives and parsley.

Creamless Creamy Ginger-Miso Dressing

Omit salt, garlic powder, chives, and parsley. Decrease water to ⅔ cup. Substitute ¼ cup rice vinegar for cider vinegar, 2 tablespoons white miso for onion powder, 2 tablespoons soy sauce for sugar, and 2 tablespoons grated fresh ginger for pepper. Add 1 teaspoon toasted sesame oil with water in step 1.

Avocado-Grapefruit Salad

Serves 4 to 6   `FAST`

Why This Recipe Works Avocado's rich buttery, nutty flavors combined with grapefruit's invigoratingly bright acidity and tartness makes for a satisfyingly complex and fresh-flavored salad. Layering the components simply on a platter instead of tossing them together in a bowl highlighted the natural beauty and color contrast of the fruits. We dressed the salad with a simple vinaigrette made from the juices left behind from cutting the grapefruit, along with vinegar and mustard; because grapefruit can be quite tart, adding a small amount of sugar to the dressing created the right level of sweet counterpoint. In lieu of a bed of salad greens, which we found detracted from the beautiful colors of the avocado and grapefruit, we sprinkled the composed salad with a healthy handful of fresh herbs and some chopped toasted hazelnuts for a bit of crunchy texture. For more information about segmenting citrus fruits, see page 138.

  3 red grapefruits
  2 ripe avocados, halved, pitted, and sliced ¼ inch
     thick
  ¼ cup fresh mint leaves, torn
  ¼ cup fresh cilantro leaves
  ¼ cup hazelnuts, toasted, skinned, and chopped
  3 tablespoons extra-virgin olive oil
  1 tablespoon minced shallot
  1 teaspoon white wine vinegar
  1 teaspoon Dijon mustard
  1 teaspoon sugar
  ½ teaspoon table salt

1. Cut off both ends of grapefruits, then cut away peel and pith. Holding fruit over bowl, use paring knife to slice between membranes to release segments. Reserve 2 tablespoons grapefruit juice.

2. Arrange avocado slices in single layer on large platter. Distribute grapefruit evenly over top. Sprinkle mint, cilantro, and hazelnuts over top.

3. Whisk oil, shallot, vinegar, mustard, sugar, salt, and reserved grapefruit juice together in bowl. Drizzle dressing over salad. Serve immediately.

Raw Beet and Carrot Noodle Salad with Almond-Sesame Dressing

Serves 6   `FAST`

Why This Recipe Works Spiralizing is an easy way to fill your plate with vegetables, and this mix of beets and carrots looks particularly stunning. Cutting the raw vegetables into noodles gave them an appealing crisp-tender texture, a perfect foil for the creamy dressing, which we made by whisking together almond butter, tahini, lime juice, soy sauce, hefty doses of ginger and garlic, and toasted sesame oil. We tossed our veggie noodles with the dressing, scallions, and cilantro and sprinkled them with toasted sesame seeds. Tasters loved the contrast of bright and aromatic ginger and herbs with the nutty dressing and earthy-sweet vegetables. For the best noodles, use beets that are at least 1½ inches in diameter and carrots that are at least ¾ inch across at the thinnest end and 1½ inches across at the thickest end. We prefer to spiralize our own vegetables, but you can substitute store-bought spiralized raw beets and carrots, though they tend to be drier and less flavorful. You can use smooth or chunky almond or peanut butter in this recipe. To make this recipe gluten-free, you must use gluten-free soy sauce or tamari.

Almond-Sesame Dressing
  ¼ cup almond or peanut butter
  3 tablespoons tahini
  3 tablespoons lime juice (2 limes), plus lime wedges
     for serving
  1 tablespoon soy sauce
  1 tablespoon agave syrup or honey
  1 tablespoon grated fresh ginger
  2 garlic cloves, minced
  ½ teaspoon toasted sesame oil
  ½ cup hot water

Noodles
  1 pound beets, trimmed and peeled
  1 pound carrots, trimmed and peeled
  5 scallions, sliced thin on bias
  ¼ cup fresh cilantro leaves
  1 tablespoon sesame seeds, toasted

1. For the dressing Whisk almond butter, tahini, lime juice, soy sauce, agave syrup, ginger, garlic, and sesame oil in large bowl until well combined. Whisking constantly, add hot water, 1 tablespoon at a time, until dressing has consistency of heavy cream (you may not need all of water).

2. For the noodles Using spiralizer, cut beets and carrots into ⅛-inch-thick noodles; then cut beet and carrot noodles into 6-inch lengths.

3. Add beet and carrot noodles and scallions to dressing and toss well to combine. Sprinkle with cilantro and sesame seeds. Serve with lime wedges.

Roasted Beet and Carrot Salad with Cumin and Pistachios

Serves 4 to 6

Why This Recipe Works Though beets and carrots are served raw in the spiralized noodle salad on page 129, they also make a winning combination when roasted, since roasting enhances all their earthy sweetness. To turn roasted beets and carrots into a salad, we tossed them with an equally earthy vinaigrette while they were still hot, which allowed them to absorb maximum flavor. Cumin added warmth to the dressing, and shallot gave it a subtle oniony bite. Pistachios lent color and nutty crunch. Adding lemon zest and chopped parsley just before serving resulted in a bright, well-balanced salad. Wrapping the beets in foil allowed them to cook gently and still attain a distinct, concentrated roasted flavor. Steaming them individually in foil before slicing them also minimized "bleeding" of any liquid. You can use golden or red beets (or a mix of both) in this recipe. To ensure even cooking, use beets that are of similar size—2 to 3 inches in diameter. If your beets are larger, the cooking time will be longer.

- 1 **pound beets, trimmed**
- 1 **pound carrots, peeled and sliced on bias**
  - ¼ **inch thick**
- 2½ **tablespoons extra-virgin olive oil, divided**
- ¾ **teaspoon table salt, divided**
- ½ **teaspoon plus ⅛ teaspoon pepper, divided**
- 1 **tablespoon grated lemon zest plus 3 tablespoons juice, divided**
- 1 **small shallot, minced**
- 1 **teaspoon agave syrup or honey**
- ½ **teaspoon ground cumin**
- ½ **cup shelled pistachios, toasted and chopped**
- 2 **tablespoons minced fresh parsley**

1. Adjust oven racks to middle and lowest positions. Place rimmed baking sheet on lower rack and heat oven to 450 degrees.

Rainbow Salad with Crispy Tempeh

2. Wrap beets individually in aluminum foil and place on second rimmed baking sheet. Toss carrots with 1 tablespoon oil, ½ teaspoon salt, and ½ teaspoon pepper.

3. Working quickly, arrange carrots in single layer in hot baking sheet and place baking sheet with beets on middle rack. Roast until carrots are tender and well browned on 1 side, 20 to 25 minutes, and skewer inserted into center of beets meets little resistance (you will need to unwrap beets to test them), 35 to 45 minutes.

4. Open foil packets to allow steam to escape and let cool slightly. Once beets are cool enough to handle, rub off skins using paper towels. Slice beets into ½-inch-thick wedges, and, if large, cut in half crosswise.

5. Whisk lemon juice, shallot, agave syrup, cumin, remaining ¼ teaspoon salt, and remaining ⅛ teaspoon pepper together in large bowl. Whisking constantly, slowly drizzle in remaining 1½ tablespoons oil. Add beets and carrots, toss to coat, and let cool to room temperature, about 20 minutes.

6. Add pistachios, parsley, and lemon zest to bowl with beets and carrots and toss to coat. Season with salt and pepper to taste. Serve.

CARROTS

We've found that it's usually important not to skip peeling carrots. Carrot skin contains high levels of two compounds, falcarindiol and dicaffeic acid, which protect the carrot from oxidation and fungi invasions but which taste bitter. Carrot flesh tastes sweeter than the skin because it contains only very small amounts of these compounds.

Rainbow Salad with Crispy Tempeh

Serves 4

Why This Recipe Works Arranging a rainbow of fruits and vegetables on a bed of greens makes a stunning presentation—and a healthful plant-based meal—but we also wanted a salad bowl that tasted as good as it looked. Cherry tomatoes and a segmented orange offered bright acidity, which we balanced with buttery avocado and crisp radishes for their peppery snap and cheerful pink hue. To contrast with all the raw vegetables, we roasted purply-red beets to bring out their natural sweetness. A refreshing dressing with orange juice and ginger complemented our salad, but we still wanted protein. A generous amount of our Crispy Tempeh was just the crunchy umami bomb this salad needed. If you would like to add cheese, we suggest a small amount of tangy blue cheese.

- 1 pound beets, trimmed
- 2 oranges
- 10 ounces (10 cups) baby arugula
- ½ cup Orange-Ginger Vinaigrette (page 126), divided
- 8 ounces cherry tomatoes, halved
- 1 ripe avocado, cut into ½-inch pieces
- 8 radishes, trimmed, halved, and sliced thin
- 1 recipe Crispy Tempeh (page 23)

1. Adjust oven rack to middle position and heat oven to 400 degrees. Wrap beets individually in aluminum foil and place on rimmed baking sheet. Roast until beets can be easily pierced with paring knife, 45 minutes to 1 hour, removing beets individually from oven as they finish cooking.

2. Open foil packets to allow steam to escape and let cool slightly. Once beets are cool enough to handle, rub off skins using paper towels. Cut beets into ¾-inch pieces and set aside to cool.

3. Cut away peel and pith from oranges. Holding fruit over bowl, use paring knife to slice between membranes to release segments. Toss arugula with half of vinaigrette to coat, then season with salt and pepper to taste. Divide among individual serving bowls, then top with orange segments, tomatoes, avocado, radishes, and beets. Drizzle with remaining vinaigrette and sprinkle with Crispy Tempeh. Serve.

Broccoli Salad with Creamy Avocado Dressing

Serves 4 to 6 **FAST**

Why This Recipe Works A combination of crisp broccoli, dried fruit, nuts, and creamy dressing makes for a classic picnic salad. For a modern, plant-based version of this old-school favorite, we ditched the heavy, often overly sweet mayo-based dressing in favor of a citrusy, garlicky avocado version. We got the best texture and flavor by quickly steaming the broccoli and then shocking it in ice water. Steaming also allowed us to cook the tougher broccoli stalks, leaving nothing to waste. By placing the chopped stalks in the boiling water and perching the florets on top to steam, we ensured that both became tender at the same time. Toasted almonds added crunch and dried cranberries provided a pop of tart brightness. Fresh tarragon brought everything together.

Creamy Avocado Dressing

- 1 avocado, halved, pitted, and cut into ½-inch pieces
- 2 tablespoons extra-virgin olive oil
- 1 teaspoon grated lemon zest plus 3 tablespoons juice
- 1 garlic clove, minced
- ¾ teaspoon table salt
- ¼ teaspoon pepper

Broccoli Salad

- Table salt for cooking broccoli
- 1½ pounds broccoli, florets cut into 1-inch pieces, stalks peeled, halved lengthwise, and sliced ¼ inch thick
- ½ cup dried cranberries
- ½ cup sliced almonds, toasted
- 1 shallot, sliced thin
- 1 tablespoon minced fresh tarragon

1. For the dressing Process all ingredients in food processor until smooth, about 30 seconds, scraping down sides of bowl as needed. Season with salt and pepper to taste.

2. For the broccoli salad Bring 1 cup water and ½ teaspoon salt to boil in large saucepan over high heat. Add broccoli stalks, then place florets on top of stalks so that they sit just above water. Cover and cook until broccoli is bright green and crisp-tender, about 3 minutes. Meanwhile, fill large bowl halfway with ice and water. Drain broccoli well, transfer to ice bath, and let sit until just cool, about 2 minutes. Transfer broccoli to triple layer of paper towels and dry well.

3. Gently toss broccoli with dressing, cranberries, almonds, shallot, and tarragon in separate large bowl until evenly coated. Season with salt and pepper to taste. Serve.

Brussels Sprout and Kale Slaw with Herbs and Peanuts
Serves 4

Why This Recipe Works Raw brussels sprouts and kale leaves may sound like an odd (and chewy) combination for a salad, but these two cabbage-like vegetables pair perfectly together, and their chewiness is easily tempered. As a bonus, since the uncooked leaves hold up well for hours, this Southeast Asian–inspired slaw is ideal for making ahead. We created a simple cider vinegar and coriander vinaigrette and marinated the thinly sliced brussels sprouts in the dressing to soften them slightly. A vigorous massage tenderized the sliced kale leaves in just a minute. We then showered the dressed vegetables with chopped peanuts and fresh cilantro and mint. A squeeze of lime juice gave this slaw a bright finish. Lacinato kale (also known as dinosaur or Tuscan kale) is more tender than curly-leaf and red kale; if using curly-leaf or red kale, increase the massaging time to 5 minutes. Do not use baby kale.

- ⅓ cup cider vinegar
- 3 tablespoons sugar
- ½ teaspoon ground coriander
- ½ teaspoon table salt
- ¼ teaspoon pepper
- 2 tablespoons extra-virgin olive oil
- 1 pound brussels sprouts, trimmed, halved, and sliced very thin
- 8 ounces Lacinato kale, stemmed and sliced into ¼-inch strips (4½ cups)
- ¼ cup dry-roasted, salted peanuts, roughly chopped
- 1 tablespoon chopped fresh cilantro
- 1 tablespoon chopped fresh mint
  Lime juice

1. Whisk vinegar, sugar, coriander, salt, and pepper together in large bowl. Whisking constantly, drizzle in oil. Add brussels sprouts and toss to combine. Cover and let sit at room temperature for at least 30 minutes or up to 2 hours.

2. Vigorously squeeze and massage kale with your hands until leaves are uniformly darkened and slightly wilted, about 1 minute. Add kale, peanuts, cilantro, and mint to bowl with brussels sprouts and toss to combine. Season with salt and lime juice to taste, and serve.

CHOPPING AND MINCING FRESH HERBS

To chop: Gather leaves into tight pile and hold with your nonknife hand. Use rocking motion to slice thin. Turn sliced leaves 90 degrees and repeat.

To mince: Chop, then go over pile again by placing fingertips of your nonknife hand flat on top of knife spine and moving blade up and down with your knife hand while using knife tip as pivot.

Tangy Apple-Cabbage Slaw
Serves 10

Why This Recipe Works Piquant, vinegary slaw is a favorite Southern picnic salad. This version features tender cabbage, crunchy tart apples, and a sweet-and-spicy vinegar-based dressing. Because cabbage is relatively watery, we salted the cut cabbage to draw out excess moisture before dressing it, which prevented moisture from diluting the dressing later and leaving us with a watery slaw. Granny Smith apples worked best in this recipe—tasters loved their tartness and sturdy crunch. We cut the apples into matchsticks so they could be easily mixed with the cabbage while retaining their crispness. Cider vinegar gave the dressing a fruity flavor that complemented the apples, while red pepper flakes, scallions, and mustard added some punch. To help the dressing integrate, we heated it—chopped cabbage absorbs a hot dressing especially well. Look for yellowish or light green Granny Smith apples—they are riper than dark green Grannies, which will be more sour.

- 1 head green cabbage (2 pounds), cored and chopped fine
- 1½ teaspoons table salt, for salting cabbage
- 2 Granny Smith apples, cored and sliced into thin matchsticks
- 2 scallions, sliced thin
- ½ cup cider vinegar
- ½ cup sugar
- 6 tablespoons vegetable oil
- 1 tablespoon Dijon mustard
- ¼ teaspoon red pepper flakes

1. Toss cabbage with salt in colander set over large bowl and let sit until wilted, at least 1 hour or up to 4 hours. Rinse cabbage under cold running water. Press, but do not squeeze, to drain, and pat dry with paper towels. Combine wilted cabbage, apples, and scallions in large bowl.

2. Bring vinegar, sugar, oil, mustard, and pepper flakes to boil in medium saucepan, then pour over cabbage mixture and toss to coat. Refrigerate until chilled, about 1 hour. Season with salt and pepper to taste. Serve. (Slaw can be refrigerated for up to 1 day.)

Warm Cabbage Salad with Crispy Tofu

Serves 4 to 6

Why This Recipe Works Paired with crispy pan-fried tofu and a zesty dressing, convenient bagged coleslaw mix transforms into an impressive yet quick main-dish salad. For the dressing, we combined oil, vinegar, soy sauce, sugar, and Asian chili-garlic sauce and heated the mixture in the microwave. Then we tossed it with the coleslaw mix, crunchy chopped peanuts, scallions, cilantro, and mint. Draining the soft tofu to remove excess moisture, dredging it in a simple mixture of cornmeal and cornstarch, and quickly pan-frying it created the perfect light, crispy crust to contrast with its creamy interior. We prefer the texture of soft or medium-firm tofu here. Firm or extra-firm tofu will also work, but the pan-fried pieces will taste drier. Bags of coleslaw mix can vary in size, but a few ounces more or less won't make a difference here. To make the dish spicier, use the higher amount of Asian chili-garlic sauce. To make this recipe gluten-free, you must use gluten-free soy sauce or tamari.

Brussels Sprout and Kale Slaw with Herbs and Peanuts

Warm Cabbage Salad with Crispy Tofu

Roasted Cauliflower Salad with Golden Raisins and Almonds

Cucumber Salad with Chile, Mint, and Basil

28 ounces soft tofu, halved lengthwise and sliced crosswise into 3-inch-long by ½-inch-thick fingers
½ teaspoon table salt
¼ teaspoon pepper
3 tablespoons vegetable oil
5 tablespoons rice vinegar
2 tablespoons soy sauce
2 tablespoons sugar
1–2 teaspoons Asian chili-garlic sauce
1 (14-ounce) bag green coleslaw mix
¾ cup dry-roasted peanuts, chopped
4 scallions, sliced thin
½ cup fresh cilantro leaves
½ cup chopped fresh mint
¾ cup cornstarch
¼ cup cornmeal
¾ cup vegetable oil for frying

1. Spread tofu over paper towel–lined baking sheet, let drain for 20 minutes, then gently press dry with paper towels. Sprinkle with salt and pepper.

2. Meanwhile, whisk 3 tablespoons oil, vinegar, soy sauce, sugar, and chili-garlic sauce together in bowl, cover, and microwave until simmering, 1 to 2 minutes. Measure out and reserve 2 tablespoons dressing separately for drizzling over tofu. Toss remaining dressing with coleslaw mix, peanuts, scallions, cilantro, and mint.

3. Combine cornstarch and cornmeal in shallow dish. Working with several tofu pieces at a time, coat thoroughly with cornstarch mixture, pressing gently to adhere; transfer to wire rack set in rimmed baking sheet.

4. Heat ¾ cup oil in 12-inch nonstick skillet over medium-high heat until shimmering. Working in 2 batches, cook tofu until crisp and golden on all sides, about 4 minutes. Gently lift tofu from oil, letting excess oil drip back into skillet, and transfer to paper towel–lined plate. Drizzle tofu with reserved dressing and serve with cabbage salad.

Roasted Cauliflower Salad with Golden Raisins and Almonds
Serves 4

Why This Recipe Works We used ever-adaptable cauliflower two ways in this vibrant salad. We roasted the florets from the head of cauliflower until tender and caramelized and then blitzed the chopped raw core in the food processor to add to the salad for a pleasantly crunchy grain-like texture and stronger, more vegetal flavor that contrasted with the more mellow softened cauliflower florets. A lemon-coriander vinaigrette, parsley, and mint added brightness. We stirred in a sweet-and-savory mix of minced shallot and golden raisins, and toasted almonds provided crunch and richness. Our two variations change up the dried fruits and nuts for different but equally delicious flavor profiles.

1 head cauliflower (2 pounds)
5 tablespoons extra-virgin olive oil, divided
1¼ teaspoons table salt, divided
1 teaspoon pepper, divided
⅓ cup golden raisins
1 shallot, minced
1 teaspoon grated lemon zest plus 1 tablespoon juice
1 teaspoon ground coriander
1 cup fresh parsley leaves
½ cup fresh mint leaves
¼ cup sliced almonds, toasted

1. Adjust oven rack to lowest position and heat oven to 475 degrees. Trim outer leaves from cauliflower and cut stem flush with bottom of head. Flip cauliflower stem side up. Using kitchen shears, cut around stem and core to remove large florets. Chop core and set aside. Cut florets through stems into 1-inch pieces (you should have about 6 cups florets).

2. Toss florets, 1 tablespoon oil, 1 teaspoon salt, and ½ teaspoon pepper together in bowl. Transfer to rimmed baking sheet and roast until florets are tender and browned on bottoms, 12 to 15 minutes. Let cool for 15 minutes.

3. While florets are roasting, combine raisins, shallot, lemon zest and juice, coriander, remaining ¼ cup oil, remaining ¼ teaspoon salt, and remaining ½ teaspoon pepper in large bowl; set aside.

4. Transfer core to food processor and process until finely chopped, 10 to 20 seconds, scraping down sides of bowl as needed; transfer to bowl with dressing. Add parsley and mint to now-empty processor and pulse until coarsely chopped, 5 to 7 pulses, scraping down sides of bowl as needed; transfer to bowl with dressing.

5. Add florets and almonds to bowl with dressing mixture and toss to combine. Season with salt and pepper to taste. Serve.

VARIATIONS

Roasted Cauliflower Salad with Apricots and Hazelnuts
Substitute chopped dried apricots for golden raisins, ½ teaspoon smoked paprika for coriander, and hazelnuts, toasted, skinned, and chopped, for almonds.

Roasted Cauliflower Salad with Cranberries and Pistachios
Substitute dried cranberries for golden raisins, ground fennel for coriander, and shelled pistachios, toasted and chopped, for almonds.

TOASTING NUTS

For amounts less than 1 cup: Place nuts in single layer in dry skillet set over medium heat and toast, stirring frequently, until they are fragrant and slightly darkened, 3 to 5 minutes. Transfer toasted nuts to plate and let them cool completely.

For amounts greater than 1 cup: Spread nuts in single layer on rimmed baking sheet and toast in 350-degree oven until they are fragrant and slightly darkened, 8 to 12 minutes, shaking sheet halfway through toasting (for smaller nuts, such as pine nuts, check them earlier).

Cucumber Salad with Chile, Mint, and Basil

Serves 4 to 6   FAST

Why This Recipe Works Cucumbers make a light, crisp, and refreshing salad—provided they're not soggy from their own liquid and swimming in a watery dressing. For a cucumber salad with good crunch, we drained the sliced cucumbers on paper towels to remove some of their moisture while we prepared the dressing. To prevent the dressing from getting watered down, we made a concentrated version with ⅓ cup vinegar (which we reduced to 2 tablespoons) and just 2 teaspoons oil. When tossed with the cucumbers, this potent mixture retained its bright flavor as the vegetable continued to release moisture. Spicy Thai chiles, fresh basil and mint, and crunchy chopped peanuts nicely complemented the cool cucumber. Be sure to slice the cucumbers ⅛ to 3/16 inch thick. This salad is best served within an hour of being dressed. To make this recipe gluten-free, you must use gluten-free soy sauce or tamari in the Fish Sauce Substitute.

4 cucumbers, peeled, halved lengthwise, seeded, and sliced very thin

⅓ cup white wine vinegar

2 Thai chiles, stemmed, seeded, and minced

1 tablespoon lime juice

1 tablespoon Fish Sauce Substitute (page 22)

2 teaspoons vegetable oil

2 teaspoons sugar

1 teaspoon table salt

¼ cup chopped fresh mint

¼ cup chopped fresh basil

¼ cup dry-roasted peanuts, toasted and chopped coarse

1. Spread cucumber slices evenly on paper towel–lined baking sheet. Refrigerate while preparing dressing.

2. Bring vinegar to simmer in small saucepan over medium-low heat and cook until reduced to 2 tablespoons, 4 to 6 minutes. Transfer to large bowl and let cool to room temperature, about 10 minutes. Whisk in chiles, lime juice, fish sauce substitute, oil, sugar, and salt.

3. Just before serving, add cucumbers, mint, and basil to dressing and gently toss to combine. Let salad sit for at least 5 minutes, then toss again. Sprinkle with peanuts and serve.

Fattoush
Serves 4 to 6 `FAST`

Why This Recipe Works Combining summery vegetables and herbs, toasted pita, and tangy sumac, fattoush hails from Lebanon and is found across the eastern Mediterranean. Sumac is a commonly used spice in the region, both in cooked preparations and as a finishing spice, and we used an ample amount of this citrusy spice, in the dressing to intensify the flavor and also as a garnish for the finished salad. To prevent the bread from becoming soggy, many recipes call for eliminating excess moisture by seeding and salting the cucumbers and tomatoes. We skipped these steps in order to preserve the crisp texture of the cucumber and the flavorful seeds and juice of the tomatoes. Instead, we made the pita pieces moisture-repellent by brushing their craggy sides with plenty of olive oil before baking them. The oil prevented the pita from absorbing moisture from the salad while allowing the pieces to pick up flavor from the lemony dressing. The success of this recipe depends on ripe, in-season tomatoes.

2 (8-inch) pita breads

7 tablespoons extra-virgin olive oil, divided

⅛ teaspoon plus ¼ teaspoon table salt, divided

⅛ teaspoon pepper

3 tablespoons lemon juice

4 teaspoons ground sumac, plus extra for sprinkling

¼ teaspoon minced garlic

1 pound ripe tomatoes, cored and cut into ¾-inch pieces

1 English cucumber, peeled and sliced ⅛ inch thick

1 cup arugula, chopped coarse

½ cup chopped fresh cilantro

½ cup chopped fresh mint

4 scallions, sliced thin

1. Adjust oven rack to middle position and heat oven to 375 degrees. Using kitchen shears, cut around perimeter of each pita and separate into 2 thin rounds. Cut each round in half. Place pitas smooth side down on wire rack set in rimmed baking sheet. Brush 3 tablespoons oil on surface of pitas and sprinkle with ⅛ teaspoon salt and pepper. (Pitas do not need to be uniformly coated; oil will spread during baking.) Bake until pitas are crisp and light golden brown, 10 to 14 minutes. Let cool completely.

2. Whisk lemon juice, sumac, garlic, and remaining ¼ teaspoon salt together in large bowl and let sit for 10 minutes. Whisking constantly, slowly drizzle in remaining ¼ cup oil. Add tomatoes, cucumber, arugula, cilantro, mint, and scallions. Break pitas into ½-inch pieces and add to bowl; gently toss to coat. Season with salt and pepper to taste. Serve, sprinkling individual portions with extra sumac.

Endive, Beet, and Pear Slaw
Serves 4 to 6 `FAST`

Why This Recipe Works This colorful, unexpected slaw uses no cabbage. Instead, we combined the natural mild bitterness and light texture of endive with the dense, earthy sweetness of beets and the floral fruitiness of pears. Tossing the shredded beets with a combination of sugar and salt and then spinning them in a salad spinner extracted some of their water, which otherwise would make for a watery slaw. We let them sit in the sugar and salt mixture while we got to work prepping the remaining ingredients and mixing up an elegant sherry vinegar–Dijon vinaigrette. To make this efficient to prepare, we recommend shredding and treating the beets before prepping the remaining ingredients. Shred the beets on the large holes of a box grater or with the shredding disk of a food processor.

1½ pounds beets, trimmed, peeled, and shredded

¼ cup sugar, plus extra for seasoning

1½ teaspoons table salt, divided

Endive, Beet, and Pear Slaw

Bitter Greens, Carrot, and Chickpea Salad
Serves 4 **FAST**

Why This Recipe Works Spinach is typically the green of choice for tossing with a warm vinaigrette, but we wanted to create a lightly wilted salad with a warm vinaigrette featuring greens that don't get as much attention: curly frisée, ruffled escarole, and frilly chicory. Alone or in combination, these bitter greens make a robust canvas for equally bold, flavorful ingredients. But it turned out that just drizzling a hot vinaigrette over these leaves wasn't quite enough to wilt them. So instead, we warmed up a Dutch oven by sautéing the salad mix-ins (carrots, raisins, and almonds), let it cool, and then added the greens and a lemony vinaigrette off the heat. A few turns of the tongs and the greens developed just the right slightly softened texture we were after. Convenient canned chickpeas added protein and savory substance to the salad. Feta will add a creamy, salty note, if you choose to include it. The volume measurement of the greens may vary depending on the variety or combination used.

Vinaigrette
- 2 tablespoons extra-virgin olive oil
- 1 tablespoon grated lemon zest plus 6 tablespoons juice (2 lemons)
- 1 tablespoon Dijon mustard
- 1 tablespoon minced shallot
- ½ teaspoon ground cumin
- ½ teaspoon ground coriander
- ¼ teaspoon smoked paprika
- ¼ teaspoon cayenne pepper
- ¼ teaspoon table salt
- ¼ teaspoon pepper

Salad
- 1 (15-ounce) can chickpeas, rinsed
  Pinch table salt
- 1 tablespoon extra-virgin olive oil
- 3 carrots, peeled and shredded
- ¾ cup raisins, chopped
- ½ cup slivered almonds
- 12 ounces (10–12 cups) bitter greens, such as escarole, chicory, and/or frisée, torn into bite-size pieces
- ⅓ cup mint leaves, chopped
- 1½ ounces feta cheese, crumbled (⅓ cup) (optional)

- 3 tablespoons sherry vinegar, plus extra for seasoning
- 2 tablespoons Dijon mustard
- ½ teaspoon pepper
- ½ cup extra-virgin olive oil
- 2 heads Belgian endive (4 ounces each), halved, cored, and sliced thin on bias
- 2 pears, peeled, halved, cored, and cut into ⅛-inch matchsticks
- 1 cup fresh cilantro leaves

1. Toss beets with sugar and 1 teaspoon salt in large bowl and let sit until partially wilted and reduced in volume by one-third, about 15 minutes.

2. Meanwhile, whisk vinegar, mustard, pepper, and remaining ½ teaspoon salt together in large serving bowl. Whisking constantly, slowly drizzle in oil until combined.

3. Transfer beets to salad spinner and spin until excess water is removed, 10 to 20 seconds. Transfer beets to bowl with dressing. Add endive, pears, and cilantro to bowl with beets and toss to combine. Season with salt, pepper, extra sugar, and extra vinegar to taste. Serve immediately.

1. For the vinaigrette Whisk all ingredients in bowl until emulsified.

2. For the salad Toss chickpeas with 1 tablespoon vinaigrette and salt in bowl; set aside. Heat oil in Dutch oven over medium heat until shimmering. Add carrots, raisins, and almonds and cook, stirring frequently, until carrots are wilted, 4 to 5 minutes. Remove pot from heat and let cool for 5 minutes.

3. Add half of remaining vinaigrette to pot, then add half of greens and toss for 1 minute to warm and wilt. Add remaining greens and mint followed by remaining vinaigrette and continue to toss until greens are evenly coated and warmed through, about 2 minutes. Season with salt and pepper to taste. Transfer greens to serving platter, top with chickpeas and feta, if using, and serve.

Escarole and Orange Salad with Green Olive Vinaigrette

Serves 4 to 6 `FAST`

Why This Recipe Works Escarole is a flavorful tender green that's in season all through the winter and is as delicious raw in a salad as it is quickly sautéed. While this Sicilian-inspired salad especially brightens up a wintertime table, it's delicious any time of year. Citrus fruits have a natural affinity for olive oil, salt, and pepper, and so we combined oranges treated this way with our escarole. Green olives added a briny umami element. To underscore the citrusy flavor, we used orange zest to boost the vinaigrette, and we cut the oranges into sections instead of larger rounds, so they were more evenly and abundantly distributed throughout the salad. That said, when arranging the orange segments on the escarole, leave behind any juice that is released, or it will dilute the dressing.

  2 oranges
  ½ cup brine-cured green olives, chopped
  ⅓ cup extra-virgin olive oil
  3 shallots, minced
  2 tablespoons sherry vinegar
  1 garlic clove, minced
  1 head escarole (1 pound), trimmed and chopped
  ½ cup slivered almonds, toasted

1. Grate 1 teaspoon orange zest from 1 orange. Whisk olives, oil, shallots, vinegar, garlic, and orange zest in large bowl until combined. Add escarole and toss to coat. Season with salt and pepper to taste.

Bitter Greens, Carrot, and Chickpea Salad

2. Cut off both ends of oranges, then cut away peel and pith. Holding fruit over separate bowl, use paring knife to slice between membranes to release segments. Divide dressed greens among individual serving plates, top with orange segments, and sprinkle with almonds. Serve.

SEGMENTING CITRUS

1. Slice off top and bottom of citrus, then cut away peel and pith using paring knife.

2. Holding fruit over bowl, slice between membranes to release individual segments.

Roasted Fennel and Mushroom Salad with Radishes

Serves 4

Why This Recipe Works Fennel and mushrooms both develop a tender yet still firm consistency and retain their structure rather than collapsing when roasted, making for a roasted salad with plenty of substance. First we tossed the vegetables with a little olive oil and seasoned them with salt and pepper, plus a pinch of sugar to aid in caramelization. To guarantee maximum browning, we arranged them in an even layer on a preheated baking sheet in a 500-degree oven. Tossing the roasted fennel and mushrooms with a simple vinaigrette while they were still hot allowed for better flavor absorption. To freshen up our roasted vegetables, we added crisp, raw radishes and some of the minced fennel fronds to the mix. If your fennel bulbs come without the fronds (the delicate greenery attached to the stems), substitute 1 tablespoon chopped fresh tarragon.

2 fennel bulbs, fronds minced, stalks discarded, bulbs halved, cored, and cut crosswise into ½-inch-thick slices
20 ounces cremini mushrooms, trimmed, quartered if large or halved if medium
3 tablespoons extra-virgin olive oil, divided
¾ teaspoon table salt, divided
¼ teaspoon plus ⅛ teaspoon pepper, divided
¼ teaspoon sugar
2 tablespoons lemon juice
1 teaspoon Dijon mustard
6 radishes, trimmed, halved, and sliced thin

1. Adjust oven rack to lowest position, place large rimmed baking sheet on rack, and heat oven to 500 degrees. Toss fennel and mushrooms with 2 tablespoons oil, ½ teaspoon salt, ¼ teaspoon pepper, and sugar in bowl. Working quickly, carefully spread fennel and mushrooms over hot baking sheet in even layer. Roast until vegetables are tender and well browned on 1 side, 20 to 25 minutes (do not stir during roasting).

2. Meanwhile, whisk lemon juice, mustard, remaining ¼ teaspoon salt, and remaining ⅛ teaspoon pepper together in now-empty bowl. Whisking constantly, drizzle in remaining 1 tablespoon oil.

3. Add hot vegetables to bowl with vinaigrette, toss, and let cool to room temperature, about 30 minutes. Stir in radishes and transfer to serving platter. Sprinkle with fronds and serve.

Crisp and Creamy Kale Salad

Serves 2 to 4

Why This Recipe Works One of the many reasons we love kale is for its versatility: It's just as good as a hearty base for a salad as it is when crisped up into crunchy, salty kale chips. So here we decided to combine these two different treatments for a leafy salad with crispy elements: kale on kale. Since raw kale can be a bit chewy, we let it soak and soften in its warm rinsing water for 10 minutes. Then we baked a portion into crispy kale chips and used the other portion as our leafy salad base. We also used almonds in two ways: We blended some into a bright herb-and-lemon dressing to provide creamy richness, and we used sliced almonds for crunch in the salad. The result was a simple and hearty but texturally diverse salad. We prefer Lacinato kale (also known as dinosaur or Tuscan kale) to curly-leaf kale in this recipe, but either will work. Do not use baby kale. If you would like to include cheese, we like the robust flavor of Pecorino Romano.

Crispy Kale Topping
3½ ounces kale, stemmed and cut into 2-inch pieces
2 tablespoons vegetable oil
4 teaspoons sesame seeds, toasted
½ teaspoon kosher salt
¼ teaspoon sugar
¼ teaspoon cayenne pepper

Salad
5 ounces kale, stemmed and cut into 2-inch pieces
1 cup sliced almonds, toasted, divided
1½ cups fresh parsley leaves
6 tablespoons water
¼ cup vegetable oil
¼ cup grated Pecorino Romano cheese (optional)
3 tablespoons lemon juice
2 teaspoons fresh thyme leaves
½ teaspoon kosher salt
¼ teaspoon sugar

1. For the topping Adjust oven rack to middle position and heat oven to 275 degrees. Line rimmed baking sheet with parchment paper. Place kale in large bowl, cover with warm tap water, and swish to remove grit. Let kale sit for 10 minutes, then remove from water and dry thoroughly. Toss kale and oil in medium bowl until kale is well coated, about 30 seconds. Spread kale evenly on prepared sheet. Wipe bowl clean with paper towels. Bake kale until dry, crispy, and translucent, 30 to 40 minutes, turning leaves halfway through baking. Carefully return kale to bowl, leaving excess oil on sheet.

2. Thoroughly combine sesame seeds, salt, sugar, and cayenne in small bowl. Gently toss crispy kale and sesame seed mixture until evenly coated and kale is broken into ½- to 1-inch pieces.

3. For the salad Place kale in large bowl, cover with warm tap water, and swish to remove grit. Let kale sit for 10 minutes, then remove from water and dry thoroughly. Combine kale and ¾ cup almonds in large bowl.

4. Process parsley; water; oil; Pecorino, if using; lemon juice; thyme; salt; sugar; and remaining ¼ cup almonds in blender on high speed until smooth and creamy, about 2 minutes, scraping down sides of blender jar halfway through processing. Transfer ¾ cup dressing to bowl with kale mixture; toss until kale is well coated. Season with salt and pepper to taste. Divide salad among shallow bowls or plates, sprinkle with crispy kale topping, and drizzle with remaining dressing. Serve.

Kale Caesar Salad
Serves 4 to 6

Why This Recipe Works The success of any Caesar salad rests on its dressing. And given that Caesar dressing traditionally contains Parmesan and anchovies and gets its richness from egg yolks, a stellar plant-based version may seem unthinkable. For our reimagined dressing, we used creamy vegan mayo. To mimic the flavors that anchovies and Parmesan provide, we incorporated briny capers and umami-boosting nutritional yeast. The result was luxurious, even thicker and creamier than classic versions and a perfect match for sturdy kale. Soaking the kale in a warm water bath for just 10 minutes tenderized the sturdy vegetable. Our next step: chilling the dressed salad to cool it down and let the flavors meld. Tasters felt that the nutritional yeast provided the requisite cheesy flavor, but you can serve the salad with a sprinkling of our Vegan Parmesan Substitute (page 27) or dairy Parmesan, if desired. Or try sprinkling it with crumbled Cheese Frico (recipe follows).

Salad
- 1 pound curly kale, stemmed and cut into 1-inch pieces
- 5 ounces baguette, cut into ¾-inch cubes (4 cups)
- 2 tablespoons extra-virgin olive oil
- ¼ teaspoon pepper
- ⅛ teaspoon table salt

Kale Caesar Salad

Caesar Dressing
- 6 tablespoons plant-based mayonnaise or egg-based mayonnaise
- 1½ tablespoons nutritional yeast
- 1½ tablespoons lemon juice
- 1½ tablespoons capers, rinsed
- 2 teaspoons white wine vinegar
- 2 teaspoons vegan Worcestershire sauce
- 1 garlic clove, minced
- ¾ teaspoon Dijon mustard
- ½ teaspoon table salt
- ½ teaspoon pepper
- 3 tablespoons extra-virgin olive oil

1. For the salad Place kale in large bowl, cover with warm tap water, and swish to remove grit. Let kale sit for 10 minutes, then remove from water and dry thoroughly.

2. Adjust oven rack to middle position and heat oven to 350 degrees. Toss baguette with oil, pepper, and salt in bowl. Spread on rimmed baking sheet and bake until golden and crisp, about 15 minutes; set aside and let cool completely, about 15 minutes. (Croutons can be stored at room temperature for up to 24 hours.)

3. For the dressing Process mayonnaise, nutritional yeast, lemon juice, capers, vinegar, Worcestershire, garlic, mustard, salt, and pepper in blender until smooth, about 30 seconds. With blender running, slowly add oil until emulsified. Toss kale with dressing in large bowl and refrigerate for at least 20 minutes or up to 6 hours to chill. Toss salad with croutons and serve.

Cheese Frico
Makes 1½ cups

A thin, crispy, crumbly topping lets individual diners customize their salad with cheese, if desired. We prefer aged Asiago, but aged Manchego is also a good option. Use a rasp-style grater to grate the cheese.

4 ounces aged Asiago cheese, finely grated (2 cups), divided

1. Sprinkle half of cheese evenly over bottom of cold 10-inch nonstick skillet. Cook over medium heat until edges are lacy and light golden, 2 to 3 minutes. Remove skillet from heat and let sit for 1 minute.

2. Using 2 spatulas, carefully flip frico. Return to medium heat and cook until second side is golden, about 1 minute. Carefully slide frico to plate and set aside until cooled, about 10 minutes.

3. Wipe skillet clean with paper towels and repeat with remaining cheese. Let cool to room temperature, then crumble into bite-size pieces. (Frico can be stored in airtight container at room temperature for up to 5 days.)

Orange-Jícama Salad with Sweet and Spicy Peppers
Serves 8   **FAST**

Why This Recipe Works For this Mexican-inspired salad, we began by setting orange wedges in a strainer to drain. For a zesty dressing assertive enough to stand up to the sweet oranges, we flavored lime juice and olive oil with cumin and mustard. Jícama and red bell pepper added vegetable crunch, while jalapeños lent a hint of heat. Cilantro and scallion greens contributed herbal freshness. Fresh parsley can be substituted for the cilantro. Toast the ground cumin in a dry skillet over medium heat until fragrant (about 30 seconds) and then remove from the heat so the cumin won't scorch.

6 oranges
6 tablespoons lime juice (3 limes)
1 teaspoon ground cumin, toasted
¾ teaspoon table salt, divided
½ teaspoon Dijon mustard
½ cup vegetable oil
2 pounds jícama, peeled and cut into 2-inch-long matchsticks
2 red bell peppers, stemmed, seeded, and cut into ⅛-inch-wide strips
4 jalapeño chiles, stemmed, seeded, quartered lengthwise, and quarters cut crosswise into ⅛-inch-thick slices
1 cup chopped fresh cilantro
6 scallions, green parts only, sliced thin on bias

1. Cut away peel and pith from oranges. Halve oranges from end to end. Cut each half lengthwise into 3 wedges, then cut crosswise into ¼-inch pieces. Place orange pieces in fine-mesh strainer set over bowl; let drain to remove excess juice.

2. Whisk lime juice, cumin, ½ teaspoon salt, and mustard together in large bowl. Whisking constantly, gradually add oil.

3. Toss jícama and bell peppers with remaining ¼ teaspoon salt in large bowl until combined. Add jícama mixture, jalapeños, cilantro, scallions, and oranges to bowl with dressing and toss well to combine. Divide salad among individual plates, drizzle with any remaining dressing in bowl, and serve immediately.

SALAD TOPPERS

Crispy, crunchy, packing umami or a boost of protein, these toppers offer an easy way to turn a head of greens, a mix of vegetables, or even a soup or sandwich into something exciting. All can be made ahead and will add texture, flavor, and seasonings to your next salads. Other great salad toppers include Vegan Parmesan Substitute (page 27), Crispy Tempeh (page 23), Spiced Roasted Chickpeas (page 355), Orange-Fennel Spiced Almonds (page 356), Cheese Frico (page 141), and Hard-Cooked Eggs (page 145).

Classic Croutons
Makes 3 cups
Choose your favorite hearty sandwich bread (either fresh or stale) to make these all-purpose croutons. To make herbed croutons, add ¾ teaspoon of your favorite dried herbs along with the salt and pepper.

- 6 slices hearty sandwich bread, crusts removed, cut into ½-inch cubes (3 cups)
- 3 tablespoons extra-virgin olive oil
- ⅛ teaspoon table salt
  Pinch pepper

Adjust oven rack to middle position and heat oven to 350 degrees. Toss bread with oil, sprinkle with salt and pepper, and spread on rimmed baking sheet. Bake until golden brown and crisp, 20 to 25 minutes, stirring halfway through baking. Let cool and serve. (Croutons can be stored at room temperature for up to 3 days.)

Crispy Tortilla Strips
Makes 2 cups
Crunchy corn tortilla strips are a fun and flavorful alternative to croutons. For ease of preparation, instead of frying them, we turned to the oven.

- 8 (6-inch) corn tortillas, cut into ½-inch-wide strips
- 1 tablespoon extra-virgin olive oil or vegetable oil

Adjust oven rack to middle position and heat oven to 425 degrees. Toss tortilla strips with oil, spread on rimmed baking sheet, and bake, stirring frequently, until deep golden brown and crisp, 8 to 12 minutes. Transfer to paper towel–lined plate and season with salt to taste. (Tortilla strips can be stored at room temperature for up to 1 week.)

Crispy Shallots
Makes ½ cup
Crispy shallots add an oniony flavor boost to any salad. To make the preparation as simple as possible, we used the microwave to create shallots with a fried exterior with minimal mess.

- 3 shallots, sliced thin
- ½ cup vegetable oil, for frying

Microwave shallots and oil in medium bowl for 5 minutes. Stir shallots, then microwave for 2 more minutes. Repeat stirring and microwaving in 2-minute increments until beginning to brown, then repeat stirring and microwaving in 30-second increments until deep golden brown. Using slotted spoon, transfer shallots to paper towel–lined plate and season with salt to taste. Let drain and crisp for about 5 minutes. (Shallots can be stored in airtight container at room temperature for up to 1 month.)

Spiced Pepitas or Sunflower Seeds
Makes ½ cup
Salty, spicy toasted seeds are an easy topping that brings crunch and elevates a basic salad in a snap.

- 2 teaspoons extra-virgin olive oil or vegetable oil
- ½ cup pepitas or sunflower seeds
- ½ teaspoon paprika
- ½ teaspoon coriander
- ¼ teaspoon table salt

Heat oil in 12-inch skillet over medium heat until shimmering. Add pepitas, paprika, coriander, and salt. Cook, stirring constantly, until seeds are toasted, about 2 minutes; transfer to bowl and let cool. (Seeds can be stored in airtight container at room temperature for up to 5 days.)

Pistachio Dukkah

Makes ½ cup

This Middle Eastern spice blend adds a powerful boost of flavor when sprinkled over salads, beans, or grains. If you don't own a spice grinder, you can process the spices in a mini food processor.

1½ teaspoons coriander seeds, toasted
¾ teaspoon cumin seeds, toasted
½ teaspoon fennel seeds, toasted
2 tablespoons sesame seeds, toasted
3 tablespoons shelled pistachios, toasted and chopped fine
½ teaspoon flake sea salt, such as Maldon
½ teaspoon pepper

Process coriander seeds, cumin seeds, and fennel seeds in spice grinder until finely ground, about 30 seconds. Add sesame seeds and pulse until coarsely ground, about 4 pulses; transfer to small bowl. Stir in pistachios, salt, and pepper. (Dukkah can be refrigerated for up to 3 months.)

Quick Pickled Grapes

Umami Croutons

Makes 5 cups

With a trifecta of nutritional yeast, miso, and mustard, these flavor-packed croutons are so delicious that you can simply snack on them as is. Of course, they would also be at home on any salad or soup.

¼ cup extra-virgin olive oil
3 tablespoons nutritional yeast
1 teaspoon white miso
1 teaspoon Dijon mustard
¼ teaspoon distilled white vinegar
⅛ teaspoon table salt
6 ounces baguette, cut into 1-inch pieces (5 cups)

Adjust oven rack to middle position and heat oven to 400 degrees. Whisk oil, nutritional yeast, miso, mustard, vinegar, and salt together in large bowl. Add baguette and, using your hands, massage oil mixture into bread. Transfer to rimmed baking sheet and bake until golden brown and crisp, 13 to 15 minutes. Let cool and serve. (Croutons can be stored at room temperature for up to 3 days.)

Quick Pickled Grapes

Makes 1⅓ cups

Pickling adds a vibrantly acidic pop and subtly savory quality to grapes, bringing a tart and sweet element to a salad.

⅓ cup white wine vinegar
1 tablespoon sugar
½ teaspoon table salt
8 ounces seedless grapes, halved

Microwave vinegar, sugar, and salt in medium bowl until simmering, 1 to 2 minutes. Stir in grapes and let sit, stirring occasionally, for 45 minutes. Drain. (Drained pickled grapes can be refrigerated for up to 1 week.)

Pea Green Salad with Warm Apricot-Pistachio Vinaigrette

Serves 4 to 6　`FAST`

Why This Recipe Works Pea greens (also known as pea shoots or pea tendrils) are the young and tender leafy tips of the pea plant. Initially a farmers' market find in the spring and summer, they are increasingly appearing in the produce aisle of large supermarkets. Both the stems and the leaves of the pea plant are edible, making these delicate greens a lovely choice for a light salad. We complemented the grassy pea greens by adding fresh peas, endive, and a warm, fruity vinaigrette that both offset the faintly bitter quality of the pea greens and lightly wilted them. We steamed the fresh peas in a skillet until just tender. In the same skillet, we toasted pistachios in oil and then took the skillet off the heat to add the rest of the dressing, as the hot oil would sizzle otherwise. The last step was simply tossing the warmed vinaigrette with the pea greens, cooked peas, and a bit of Belgian endive for crunch. You can substitute thawed frozen peas for the fresh peas; if using frozen peas, skip step 1.

- 1 pound fresh peas, shelled (1¼ cups)
- 3 tablespoons white wine vinegar
- 2 teaspoons whole-grain mustard
- ½ teaspoon sugar
- ¼ teaspoon table salt
- ½ cup dried apricots, chopped
- 1 small shallot, halved and sliced thin
- 3 tablespoons vegetable oil
- ⅓ cup shelled pistachios, chopped
- 8 ounces (8 cups) pea greens
- 2 heads Belgian endive (8 ounces), trimmed, halved lengthwise, and sliced ¼ inch thick

1. Bring peas and ¼ cup water to simmer in 10-inch skillet over medium-high heat. Cover, reduce heat to medium-low, and cook, stirring occasionally, until peas are tender, 5 to 7 minutes. Drain peas and set aside. Wipe skillet clean with paper towels.

2. Whisk vinegar, mustard, sugar, and salt together in medium bowl. Add apricots and shallot, cover, and microwave until steaming, 30 seconds to 1 minute. Stir to submerge shallot, then let cool to room temperature, about 15 minutes.

3. Heat oil in now-empty skillet over medium heat until shimmering. Add pistachios and cook, stirring frequently, until toasted and fragrant, 1 to 2 minutes. Off heat, stir in shallot mixture and let sit until heated through, about 30 seconds.

4. Gently toss pea greens, endive, and peas with warm vinaigrette in large bowl until evenly coated and wilted slightly. Season with salt and pepper to taste. Serve.

French Potato Salad with Dijon Mustard and Fines Herbes

Serves 4 to 6　`FAST`

Why This Recipe Works French-style potato salad shuns the typical mayo-heavy dressing in favor of a bold wine vinaigrette. Visually appealing small skin-on red potatoes are the traditional choice. The cooked potatoes should be tender but not mushy, and the bright vinaigrette should thoroughly permeate them. To eliminate the common problem of torn skins and broken slices, we sliced the potatoes before boiling rather than after. To evenly infuse the warm tubers with the garlicky vinaigrette, we spread them on a baking sheet and poured the dressing over the top. Gently folding in the fresh herbs just before serving helped keep the potatoes intact. We stayed in France for our variation with fennel and black olives. If you would like to add Hard-Cooked Eggs (recipe follows), gently fold sliced cooked eggs into the salad along with the shallots and herbs. If fresh chervil isn't available, substitute an additional ½ tablespoon of minced parsley and an additional ½ teaspoon of tarragon. Use small red potatoes measuring 1 to 2 inches in diameter.

- 2 pounds small red potatoes, unpeeled, sliced ¼ inch thick
  Table salt for cooking potatoes
- 1 garlic clove, peeled and threaded on skewer
- ¼ cup extra-virgin olive oil
- 1½ tablespoons champagne vinegar or white wine vinegar
- 2 teaspoons Dijon mustard
- ½ teaspoon pepper
- 1 small shallot, minced
- 1 tablespoon minced fresh chervil
- 1 tablespoon minced fresh parsley
- 1 tablespoon minced fresh chives
- 1 teaspoon minced fresh tarragon

1. Place potatoes and 2 tablespoons salt in large saucepan and add water to cover by 1 inch. Bring to boil over high heat, reduce heat to medium-low, and simmer until potatoes are just tender and paring knife can be slipped in and out of potatoes with little resistance, 5 to 6 minutes.

2. While potatoes are cooking, lower skewered garlic into simmering water and blanch for 45 seconds. Run garlic under cold running water, then remove from skewer and mince.

3. Drain potatoes, reserving ¼ cup cooking water. Arrange hot potatoes close together in single layer on rimmed baking sheet. Whisk oil, minced garlic, vinegar, mustard, pepper, and reserved potato cooking water together in bowl, then drizzle evenly over potatoes. Let potatoes sit at room temperature until flavors meld, about 10 minutes. (Potatoes can be refrigerated for up to 8 hours; return to room temperature before serving.)

4. Transfer potatoes to large bowl. Combine shallot, chervil, parsley, chives, and tarragon in small bowl, then sprinkle over potatoes and combine gently using rubber spatula. Serve.

VARIATION
French Potato Salad with Fennel, Tomato, and Olives

If desired, chop 1 tablespoon of the fennel fronds and add it to the salad with the parsley.

Omit chervil, chives, and tarragon. Increase parsley to 3 tablespoons. Add ½ bulb thinly sliced fennel, 1 cored and chopped tomato, and ¼ cup pitted oil-cured black olives, quartered, to salad with shallots and parsley.

Hard-Cooked Eggs

Be sure to use eggs that have no cracks and are cold from the refrigerator. You can cook the eggs up to three days ahead.

4–6 large eggs

1. Bring 1 inch water to rolling boil in medium saucepan over high heat. Place eggs in steamer basket and transfer basket to saucepan. Cover, reduce heat to medium-low, and cook eggs for 13 minutes.

2. Using tongs or slotted spoon, transfer eggs to ice bath and let sit for 15 minutes. Remove from ice bath and peel or store.

Pea Green Salad with Warm Apricot-Pistachio Vinaigrette

French Potato Salad with Dijon Mustard and Fines Herbes

Green Goodness Salad with Tofu

Serves 4 `FAST`

Why This Recipe Works To qualify as a green goddess salad, one thing is required: creamy green goddess dressing, which gets its herbaceous flavor and appealing pale green hue from a wallop of fresh herbs—and which typically contains sour cream or buttermilk. Once we had our creamless version of green goddess nailed, we took the concept further by creating a "goodness" bowl with an abundance of green foods, including baby spinach, broccoli, edamame, and chopped pistachios. Raw broccoli proved a bit too crunchy and strong tasting, so we quickly sautéed it to give it some nice char, which softened its texture and mellowed its flavor. To give our salad a finishing creamy touch to complement the dressing, we added buttery sliced avocado.

- 14 ounces extra-firm tofu, cut into ¾-inch pieces
- ¼ teaspoon plus ⅛ teaspoon table salt, divided
- ⅛ teaspoon pepper
- 2 tablespoons extra-virgin olive oil, divided
- 8 ounces broccoli florets, cut into 1-inch pieces
- 1½ tablespoons water
- 1 garlic clove, minced
- ¼ teaspoon minced fresh thyme or pinch dried
- 8 ounces (8 cups) baby spinach
- 1 cup Creamless Creamy Green Goddess Dressing (page 128), divided
- 1 ripe avocado, sliced thin
- ½ cup frozen shelled edamame beans, thawed and patted dry
- ¼ cup shelled pistachios, toasted and chopped

1. Spread tofu over paper towel–lined baking sheet, let drain for 20 minutes, then gently press dry with paper towels. Sprinkle with ¼ teaspoon salt and pepper.

2. Heat 2 teaspoons oil in 12-inch nonstick skillet over medium-high heat until shimmering. Add tofu and cook until lightly browned, 6 to 8 minutes; transfer to bowl.

3. Heat 1 tablespoon oil in now-empty skillet over medium-high heat until just smoking. Add broccoli and remaining ⅛ teaspoon salt and cook, without stirring, until beginning to brown, about 2 minutes. Add water, cover, and cook until broccoli is bright green but still crisp, about 2 minutes. Uncover and continue to cook until water has evaporated and broccoli is crisp-tender, about 2 minutes.

4. Clear center of pan, add remaining 1 teaspoon oil, garlic, and thyme and cook, mashing garlic into skillet until fragrant, about 30 seconds. Stir garlic mixture into broccoli. Off heat, season with salt and pepper to taste, and let cool slightly.

5. Toss spinach with half of dressing to coat, then season with salt and pepper to taste. Divide among individual serving bowls then top with tofu, broccoli, avocado, and edamame. Drizzle with remaining dressing and sprinkle with pistachios. Serve.

Spinach Salad with Carrots, Oranges, and Sesame

Serves 6 `FAST`

Why This Recipe Works When you hear "spinach salad," you may think that bacon or cheese needs to be involved, since those are typical additions. But spinach salad can go in a number of more plant-forward directions, from a simple classic salad with red onion and mushrooms to one enlivened with mixed berries and nuts to our variation that includes another salad green, an herb, and strawberries. This rendition is boldly flavored with toasted sesame oil and seeds. Since spinach and oranges make a great pairing—both visually and on the palate—we decided to add orange segments to the salad and then used the juice and zest in our dressing. We combined them with rice vinegar and a small amount of toasted sesame oil, using neutral-tasting canola oil as the base. A bit of mustard and mayonnaise kept our dressing emulsified. Shaved carrots and sliced scallions further complemented the earthy spinach, and a sprinkling of toasted sesame seeds added a finishing crunch. For more information on segmenting citrus fruits, see page 138.

- 2 oranges
- 2 carrots, peeled
- 2 tablespoons rice vinegar
- 1 small shallot, minced
- 1 teaspoon Dijon mustard
- ¾ teaspoon plant-based mayonnaise or egg-based mayonnaise
- ⅛ teaspoon table salt
- 2½ tablespoons vegetable oil
- ¾ teaspoon toasted sesame oil
- 6 ounces (6 cups) baby spinach
- 2 scallions, sliced thin
- 1½ teaspoons toasted sesame seeds

1. Grate ½ teaspoon zest from 1 orange; set zest aside. Cut off both ends of oranges, then cut away peel and pith. Holding fruit over fine-mesh strainer set in bowl, use paring knife to slice between membranes to release segments. Measure out and reserve 2 tablespoons juice; discard remaining juice. Using vegetable peeler, shave carrots lengthwise into ribbons.

Green Goodness Salad with Tofu

Whisk basil, vinegar, shallot, mustard, mayonnaise, orange zest and juice, pepper, and salt together in large bowl. While whisking constantly, drizzle in oil until completely emulsified. Add spinach, frisée, and strawberries and gently toss to coat. Serve.

2. Whisk orange zest and reserved juice, vinegar, shallot, mustard, mayonnaise, and salt together in large bowl. While whisking constantly, drizzle in both oils until completely emulsified. Add orange segments, carrots, spinach, and scallions and gently toss to coat. Sprinkle with sesame seeds. Serve.

Potato, Green Bean, and Tomato Salad
Serves 4

Why This Recipe Works Whereas our French Potato Salad (page 144) is all about the potatoes, this rendition includes a variety of colorful vegetables. Here we added green beans, grape tomatoes, shallot, and plenty of fresh herbs to Yukon Gold potatoes. The secret to getting tender spuds and vibrant green beans was to stagger their cooking. We cooked the potatoes in boiling water until just tender and then added the beans so both vegetables finished cooking at the same time. We marinated the tomatoes in a pungent dressing while the other vegetables cooked and then tossed everything together before serving. A handful of parsley leaves and chopped dill provided a refreshing herbal pop. Since you're not peeling the potatoes, be sure to scrub them well. High-quality extra-virgin olive oil makes a big difference here. You can substitute cherry tomatoes for the grape tomatoes. For the best results, use a rubber spatula to combine the ingredients in steps 3 and 4.

VARIATION
Spinach Salad with Frisée and Strawberries

- 2 tablespoons chopped fresh basil
- 5 teaspoons balsamic vinegar
- 1 small shallot, minced
- 1 teaspoon Dijon mustard
- ¾ teaspoon plant-based mayonnaise or egg-based mayonnaise
- ½ teaspoon grated orange zest plus 2 tablespoons juice
- ½ teaspoon pepper
- ⅛ teaspoon table salt
- 3 tablespoons extra-virgin olive oil
- 6 ounces (6 cups) baby spinach
- 1 head frisée (6 ounces), chopped
- 5 ounces strawberries, hulled and quartered (1 cup)

- 1½ pounds Yukon Gold potatoes, unpeeled, cut into ¾-inch pieces
- ¾ teaspoon table salt, plus salt for cooking vegetables
- 1 pound green beans, trimmed and cut into 1-inch pieces
- ½ cup extra-virgin olive oil
- ¼ cup white wine vinegar
- ¾ teaspoon pepper
- 6 ounces grape tomatoes, halved
- ¼ cup capers
- 1 shallot, sliced thin
- 2 teaspoons Anchovy Substitute (page 23)
- ½ cup fresh parsley leaves
- ¼ cup chopped fresh dill

1. Place potatoes and 2 teaspoons salt in large saucepan and cover with water by 1 inch. Bring to boil over high heat. Reduce heat to medium-low and simmer until potatoes are almost tender, about 7 minutes. Add green beans and continue to cook until both vegetables are tender, about 7 minutes.

2. Meanwhile, whisk oil, vinegar, pepper, and salt together in large bowl; measure out ¼ cup dressing and set aside. Add tomatoes, capers, shallot, and anchovy substitute to bowl with remaining dressing and toss to coat; set aside.

3. Drain potatoes and green beans thoroughly in colander, then spread out on rimmed baking sheet. Drizzle reserved dressing over potatoes and green beans and, using rubber spatula, gently toss to combine. Let cool slightly, about 15 minutes.

4. Add parsley, dill, and potato mixture to bowl with tomato mixture and toss to combine. Season with salt and pepper to taste. Serve.

Roasted Butternut Squash Salad with Za'tar and Parsley

Serves 4 to 6

Why This Recipe Works Pairing roasted squash with bold flavors and textural contrasts results in a hearty salad that's delicious warm or at room temperature. We found that roasting in a hot oven on the lowest rack produced perfectly browned squash pieces with a firm center in about 30 minutes. The traditional Middle Eastern spice blend za'atar (a pungent combination of toasted sesame seeds, thyme, marjoram, and sumac) balanced the natural sweetness of the squash. Dusting the za'atar over the hot squash worked similarly to toasting the spice, enhancing its flavor. For a foil to the tender squash, we landed on toasted pumpkin seeds for a textural accent and to reinforce the squash's nutty flavor. Pomegranate seeds added a burst of tartness and color. You can substitute chopped red grapes or small blueberries for the pomegranate seeds.

3–3½	pounds butternut squash, peeled, seeded, and cut into ½-inch pieces (8–10 cups)
¼	cup extra-virgin olive oil, divided
1¼	teaspoons table salt, divided
½	teaspoon pepper
1	teaspoon za'atar
1	small shallot, minced
2	tablespoons lemon juice
2	tablespoons pomegranate molasses
¾	cup fresh parsley leaves
⅓	cup unsalted pepitas, toasted
½	cup pomegranate seeds

1. Adjust oven rack to lowest position and heat oven to 450 degrees. Toss squash with 1 tablespoon oil in bowl and sprinkle with 1 teaspoon salt and pepper. Lay squash in single layer on rimmed baking sheet and roast until well browned and tender, 30 to 35 minutes, stirring halfway through roasting time. Remove squash from oven, sprinkle with za'atar, and let cool for 15 minutes.

2. Whisk shallot, lemon juice, pomegranate molasses, and remaining ¼ teaspoon salt together in large bowl. Whisking constantly, drizzle in remaining 3 tablespoons oil. Add squash, parsley, and pepitas and toss gently to combine. Arrange on platter, sprinkle with pomegranate seeds, and serve.

Peach and Tomato Salad

Serves 4 to 6   `FAST`

Why This Recipe Works This gorgeous, unexpected salad takes advantage of beautiful summertime fruits and vegetables (although technically, the tomato is a fruit). We combined ripe, sweet, in-season peaches and tomatoes. Salting and draining the tomatoes helped concentrate their flavors by removing excess liquid that would water down the salad. We balanced the natural sweetness of the fruits with acidic cider vinegar, lemon juice, and lemon zest in the dressing. Thinly sliced shallot kept the salad on the savory side, and torn mint leaves added a fresh herbal note. Perfectly ripe peaches and tomatoes are essential to this recipe, as they are to the variation, which is a riff on a classic Caprese salad.

1	pound ripe tomatoes, cored, cut into ½-inch-thick wedges, and wedges halved crosswise
1	teaspoon table salt, divided
3	tablespoons extra-virgin olive oil, plus extra for drizzling
2	tablespoons cider vinegar
½	teaspoon grated lemon zest plus 1 tablespoon juice
½	teaspoon pepper
1	pound ripe peaches, halved, pitted, cut into ½-inch-thick wedges, and wedges halved crosswise
1	shallot, sliced thin
⅓	cup fresh mint leaves, torn

1. Combine tomatoes and ½ teaspoon salt in bowl and toss to coat; transfer to colander and let drain in sink for 30 minutes.

2. Whisk oil, vinegar, lemon zest and juice, pepper, and remaining ½ teaspoon salt together in large bowl. Add peaches, shallot, and drained tomatoes to dressing and gently toss to coat. Season with salt and pepper to taste. Transfer to platter and sprinkle with mint. Drizzle with extra oil. Serve.

Peach and Tomato Salad

VARIATION
Peach, Tomato, and Mozzarella Caprese
Toss 12 ounces fresh mozzarella cheese, halved and sliced ¼ inch thick, in with the peaches.

Cherry Tomato Salad with Mango and Lime-Curry Vinaigrette

Serves 4 to 6

Why This Recipe Works For this Indian-inspired salad, we tossed quartered cherry tomatoes with a little salt and sugar to help extract some of the liquid and prevent a soggy salad. We then used a salad spinner to separate the tomato liquid from the flesh, reserving the liquid so that we could reduce it to an umami-rich concentrate. Adding shallot, lime juice, and curry powder and drizzling in olive oil turned the concentrate into a dressing, ready to be reunited with the tomatoes. Juicy mango and chopped cilantro filled out this brightly flavored and colored salad. If you don't have a salad spinner, wrap the

bowl tightly with plastic wrap after the salted tomatoes have sat for 30 minutes and gently shake to remove seeds and excess liquid. Strain the liquid and proceed. If you have less than ½ cup of juice after spinning, proceed with the recipe using the entire amount of juice you do have and reduce it to 3 tablespoons as directed (the cooking time will be shorter).

1½ pounds cherry tomatoes, quartered
½ teaspoon sugar
¼ teaspoon table salt
1 mango, pitted, peeled, and cut into ½-inch pieces
½ cup toasted slivered almonds
3 tablespoons chopped fresh cilantro
1 shallot, minced
4 teaspoons lime juice
¼ teaspoon curry powder
2 tablespoons extra-virgin olive oil

1. Toss tomatoes with sugar and salt in bowl and let sit for 30 minutes. Transfer tomatoes to salad spinner and spin until seeds and excess liquid have been removed, 45 to 60 seconds, stopping to redistribute tomatoes several times during spinning. Add tomatoes, mango, almonds, and cilantro to large bowl; set aside.

2. Strain ½ cup tomato liquid through fine-mesh strainer into liquid measuring cup; discard remaining liquid. Bring tomato liquid, shallot, lime juice, and curry powder to simmer in small saucepan over medium heat and cook until reduced to 3 tablespoons, 6 to 8 minutes. Transfer to small bowl and let cool to room temperature, about 5 minutes. Whisking constantly, slowly drizzle in oil. Drizzle dressing over salad and gently toss to coat. Season with salt and pepper to taste. Serve.

Panzanella

Serves 4   FAST

Why This Recipe Works When this rustic, hearty Italian bread and tomato salad is done well, the sweet juice of the tomatoes mixes with a bright-tasting vinaigrette, moistening chunks of thick-crusted bread until they're softened and just a little chewy—but the line between lightly moistened and unpleasantly soggy is thin. We found that toasting fresh bread in the oven worked better than using the traditional day-old bread. The bread lost enough moisture in the oven to absorb the flavorful dressing without getting mushy. A 10-minute soak yielded perfectly moistened bread ready to be tossed with the tomatoes, which we salted first to remove excess liquid and intensify their flavor. A thinly sliced cucumber and shallot for crunch plus a handful of chopped fresh basil perfected our salad. The variations are a little bolder: One adds garlic and capers, while the other replaces the cucumber and basil with red bell pepper and arugula. The success of this recipe depends on high-quality ingredients, including ripe, in-season tomatoes, fruity olive oil, and fresh basil. Your bread may vary in density, so you may not need the entire loaf. Be ready to serve this dish immediately after it is assembled.

- 1 (1-pound) loaf rustic Italian or French bread, cut or torn into 1-inch pieces (6 cups)
- ½ cup extra-virgin olive oil, divided
- ¾ teaspoon table salt, divided
- 1½ pounds ripe tomatoes, cored, seeded, and cut into 1-inch pieces
- 3 tablespoons red wine vinegar
- ¼ teaspoon pepper
- 1 cucumber, peeled, halved lengthwise, seeded, and sliced thin
- 1 shallot, sliced thin
- ¼ cup chopped fresh basil

1. Adjust oven rack to middle position and heat oven to 400 degrees. Toss bread pieces with 2 tablespoons oil and ¼ teaspoon salt in bowl and spread in single layer on rimmed baking sheet. Toast bread until just starting to turn light golden, 15 to 20 minutes, stirring halfway through baking. Let cool to room temperature.

2. Meanwhile, gently toss tomatoes with remaining ½ teaspoon salt in large bowl. Transfer to colander set over now-empty bowl and let drain for 15 minutes, tossing occasionally.

3. Whisk vinegar, pepper, and remaining 6 tablespoons oil into drained tomato juices. Add toasted bread, toss to coat, and let sit for 10 minutes, tossing occasionally. Add drained tomatoes, cucumber, shallot, and basil, and toss to coat. Season with salt and pepper to taste, and serve immediately.

VARIATIONS
Panzanella with Garlic and Capers
Whisk 2 tablespoons rinsed capers and 1 minced garlic clove into dressing before adding toasted bread.

Panzanella with Peppers and Arugula
Substitute 1 thinly sliced stemmed and seeded red bell pepper for cucumber and 1 cup coarsely chopped baby arugula for basil.

Grilled Vegetable Salad

Grilled Vegetable Salad
Serves 4 to 6

Why This Recipe Works Grilling vegetables gives them a smoky, flavorful char that elevates a summery vegetable salad. Strategically cutting the vegetables into large pieces resulted in just the right amount of charring and helped ensure that the vegetables didn't slip through the grill grate—no grill basket needed. Scoring crosshatch marks on the cut sides of the eggplant and zucchini allowed some of their moisture to evaporate on the grill. Chopping the veggies into bite-size pieces meant we got a bit of everything in every bite. Dressing the vegetables while they were still warm helped them absorb the garlicky, citrusy vinaigrette more effectively.

Vinaigrette
- 1 tablespoon lemon juice
- 2 teaspoons Dijon mustard
- 1 garlic clove, minced
- ¼ teaspoon table salt
- ⅛ teaspoon pepper
- 3 tablespoons extra-virgin olive oil
- 2 tablespoons chopped fresh basil, chives, or parsley

Vegetables

- 2 red bell peppers
- 1 eggplant, halved lengthwise
- 1 zucchini (8 to 10 ounces), halved lengthwise
- 1 red onion, cut into ½-inch-thick rounds
- 4 plum tomatoes, cored and halved lengthwise
- 3 tablespoons extra-virgin olive oil
- 1 teaspoon table salt
- ½ teaspoon pepper

1. For the vinaigrette Whisk lemon juice, mustard, garlic, salt, and pepper together in large bowl. Whisking constantly, slowly drizzle in oil. Stir in basil and set aside.

2. For the vegetables Slice ¼ inch off tops and bottoms of bell peppers and remove cores. Make slit down 1 side of each bell pepper, then press flat into 1 long strip, removing ribs and remaining seeds with knife as needed. Cut strips in half crosswise (you should have 4 bell pepper pieces).

3. Using sharp paring knife, cut ½-inch crosshatch pattern in flesh of eggplant and zucchini, being careful to cut down to but not through skin. Push toothpick horizontally through each onion round to keep rings intact while grilling. Brush tomatoes, bell peppers, zucchini, and onion all over with oil, then brush eggplant with remaining oil (it will absorb more oil than other vegetables). Sprinkle vegetables with salt and pepper.

4A. For a charcoal grill Open bottom vent completely. Light large chimney starter filled with charcoal briquettes (6 quarts). When top coals are partially covered with ash, pour evenly over grill. Set cooking grate in place, cover, and open lid vent completely. Heat grill until hot, about 5 minutes.

4B. For a gas grill Turn all burners to high, cover, and heat grill until hot, about 15 minutes. Turn all burners to medium-high.

5. Clean and oil cooking grate. Place vegetables on cooking grate, cut sides down, and cook until skins of bell peppers, eggplant, and tomatoes are well browned and interiors of eggplant and zucchini are tender, 10 to 16 minutes, flipping and moving vegetables as necessary to ensure even cooking and transferring vegetables to baking sheet as they finish cooking. Place bell peppers in bowl, cover with plastic wrap, and let steam to loosen skins, about 5 minutes.

6. When cool enough to handle, peel bell peppers and tomatoes, discarding skins. Using spoon, scoop eggplant flesh out of skin; discard skin. Chop all vegetables into 1-inch pieces, transfer to bowl with vinaigrette, and toss to coat. Serve warm or at room temperature.

SLICING BELL PEPPERS FOR GRILLING

 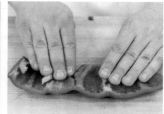

1. Slice off tops and bottoms of bell peppers and remove cores.

2. Cut down 1 side of each pepper, then press flat into 1 long strip.

Moroccan Tempeh Salad

Serves 4 FAST

Why This Recipe Works This multitextured salad is redolent with favorite Moroccan flavors of sweet apricot, tart lemon, and warm spices. Two salad greens, plus parsley and shallot, formed the salad bed. And two plant-based protein sources—chickpeas and our umami-rich Crispy Tempeh— ensured this salad was satisfyingly hearty. To give the dressing complex flavor, we reached for garam masala, a spice blend of coriander, cumin, ginger, cinnamon, and black pepper. We also added a little more coriander and some agave syrup for depth. Blooming the spices in the microwave deepened their flavors for an even bolder dressing. Tossing half the dressing with our greens and drizzling the remaining dressing on just before serving made the flavors pop. We prefer our Homemade Garam Masala (page 330), but you can use a store-bought blend.

- 6 tablespoons plus 2 teaspoons extra-virgin olive oil, divided
- 1 teaspoon garam masala
- ½ teaspoon ground coriander
- ¼ cup lemon juice (2 lemons)
- 2 teaspoons light agave syrup or honey
- ½ teaspoon table salt
- ½ teaspoon pepper
- 2 romaine lettuce hearts (12 ounces), cut into 1-inch pieces
- 4 ounces (4 cups) watercress
- 2 tablespoons minced fresh parsley
- 1 shallot, sliced thin
- 1 recipe Crispy Tempeh (page 23)
- 1 cup canned chickpeas, rinsed
- ½ cup dried apricots, chopped coarse

1. Microwave 2 teaspoons oil, garam masala, and coriander in medium bowl until fragrant, about 30 seconds. Whisk lemon juice, agave, salt, and pepper into spice mixture until combined. While whisking constantly, drizzle in remaining 6 tablespoons oil until combined.

2. Toss romaine, watercress, parsley, and shallot with half of vinaigrette to coat, then season with salt and pepper to taste. Divide among individual serving bowls, then top with crispy tempeh, chickpeas, and apricots. Drizzle with remaining vinaigrette. Serve.

Tofu Salad with Vegetables
Serves 6

Why This Recipe Works Creamy, custard-like soft tofu makes a great foil for crisp sliced raw vegetables in this Asian main-dish salad. To drain the tofu of excess moisture, we cut it into cubes and placed them on multiple layers of paper towels to drain. Broiling the drained tofu gave it some light charring and additional flavor. For the vegetables, we chose carrots, snow peas, and bell peppers for both their crisp textures and their bright colors. Bean sprouts added more nice crunch and a clean flavor. For the dressing, tasters favored a blend of peanut butter, hoisin sauce, lime juice, toasted sesame oil, and garlic, a combination that created the right balance of salty, acidic, and savory. A little chili-garlic sauce added a touch of heat. Thinly sliced scallions, minced cilantro, and toasted sesame seeds gave our salad just the right finishing touches. We prefer the texture of soft tofu in this recipe; however, firm tofu may be substituted.

Peanut Dressing
- 3 tablespoons creamy peanut butter
- 3 tablespoons hot water
- ¼ cup hoisin sauce
- 4 teaspoons lime juice
- 2 teaspoons toasted sesame oil
- 1 garlic clove, minced
- ¾ teaspoon Asian chili-garlic sauce
- ½ teaspoon table salt

Salad
- 28 ounces soft tofu, cut into ¾-inch pieces
- ½ teaspoon table salt
- ¼ teaspoon pepper
- 8 ounces snow peas, strings removed, cut into ½-inch pieces
- 1 red or yellow bell pepper, stemmed, seeded, and cut into ½-inch pieces

- 4 ounces (2 cups) bean sprouts
- 2 carrots, peeled and shredded
- 2 scallions, sliced thin on bias
- 3 tablespoons minced fresh cilantro
- 1 tablespoon toasted sesame seeds

1. For the dressing Whisk peanut butter and water in large bowl until smooth, then whisk in hoisin, lime juice, sesame oil, garlic, chili-garlic sauce, and salt until combined; set aside.

2. For the salad Position oven rack 6 inches from broiler element and heat broiler. Line rimmed baking sheet with aluminum foil. Spread tofu on paper towel–lined baking sheet and let drain for 20 minutes. Gently press dry with paper towels. Sprinkle with salt and pepper.

3. Gently toss tofu with half of dressing in separate bowl and spread in even layer on prepared sheet. Broil tofu until spotty brown, 5 to 6 minutes.

4. Add snow peas, bell pepper, bean sprouts, carrots, and scallions to bowl with remaining dressing and gently toss to coat. Gently fold in tofu, cilantro, and sesame seeds. Season with pepper to taste, and let sit until flavors meld, about 15 minutes. Serve.

Mediterranean Chopped Salad
Serves 6 `FAST`

Why This Recipe Works A major appeal of a chopped salad is that all the ingredients are cut to a uniform size and tossed together, allowing for a taste of everything in each bite. But old-style chopped salads tend to be laden down with deli meats and cheeses and drowned in a heavy dairy-based dressing. With a world of plant-forward options at our disposal, we decided to steer our salad in a lighter, fresher Mediterranean direction, starting with escarole as the base leafy green. To that we added chopped cucumbers and grape tomatoes, salting and draining them first to remove excess moisture, and red onion. To make our salad substantial enough for a main course, we incorporated hearty chickpeas, briny kalamata olives, and rich, crunchy walnuts. A small amount of (optional) feta is a creamy, tangy addition. A simple red wine vinaigrette let the salad's many flavors shine through. Cherry tomatoes can be substituted for the grape tomatoes.

- 1 cucumber, halved lengthwise, seeded, and cut into ½-inch pieces
- 10 ounces grape tomatoes, quartered
- 1 teaspoon table salt

Chopped Winter Salad with Butternut Squash

3 tablespoons red wine vinegar
1 garlic clove, minced
3 tablespoons extra-virgin olive oil
1 (15-ounce) can chickpeas, rinsed
½ cup pitted kalamata olives, chopped
½ small red onion, chopped fine
½ cup chopped fresh parsley
1 head escarole (1 pound), trimmed and cut into ½-inch pieces
2 ounces feta cheese, crumbled (½ cup) (optional)
½ cup walnuts, toasted and chopped

1. Toss cucumber and tomatoes with salt and let drain in colander for 15 minutes.

2. Whisk vinegar and garlic together in large bowl. Whisking constantly, drizzle in oil. Add drained cucumber-tomato mixture, chickpeas, olives, onion, and parsley and toss to coat. Let sit for at least 5 minutes or up to 20 minutes.

3. Add escarole; feta, if using; and walnuts and toss gently to combine. Season with salt and pepper to taste. Serve.

Chopped Winter Salad with Butternut Squash
Serves 4 FAST

Why This Recipe Works In the butternut squash salad on page 148, squash is the star, whereas in this recipe it's part of an ensemble cast. We introduced more elements for lots of different textures and flavors: an assertive salad green, a milder salad green, sweet apple, and toasted hazelnuts. To accentuate the flavor of the squash, we cut it into small pieces and tossed them with balsamic vinegar and olive oil before roasting them. The vinegar caramelized in the oven and complemented the earthy sweetness of the squash. Chopped, toasted hazelnuts and raw cubed apple added crunchy contrast to the riot of leafy greens and creamy squash. Feta cheese, if you choose to include it, adds a tangy note. There's no need to peel the apple. We prefer Fuji, but any sweet apple will work here.

1 small (1½- to 2-pound) butternut squash, peeled, seeded, and cut into ½-inch cubes (about 4½ cups)
¼ cup extra-virgin olive oil, divided
3 tablespoons balsamic vinegar, divided
¼ teaspoon plus ⅛ teaspoon table salt, divided
¼ teaspoon plus ⅛ teaspoon pepper, divided
1 tablespoon Dijon mustard
1 head radicchio (6 ounces), trimmed, cored, and sliced into ½-inch-thick pieces
1 romaine lettuce heart (6 ounces), cored and cut into 1-inch pieces
1 Fuji apple, halved, cored, and cut into 1-inch cubes
½ cup hazelnuts, toasted, skinned, and chopped
2 ounces feta cheese, crumbled (½ cup) (optional)

1. Adjust oven rack to lowest position and heat oven to 450 degrees. Toss squash with 1 tablespoon oil, 1½ teaspoons vinegar, ¼ teaspoon salt, and ¼ teaspoon pepper.

2. Spread squash in single layer on aluminum foil–lined rimmed baking sheet and roast until well browned and tender, 20 to 25 minutes, stirring halfway through roasting. Remove squash from oven and let cool for 5 to 10 minutes.

3. Whisk mustard, remaining 2½ tablespoons vinegar, remaining ⅛ teaspoon salt, and remaining ⅛ teaspoon pepper together in large bowl. Whisking constantly, slowly drizzle in remaining 3 tablespoons oil until incorporated.

4. Add radicchio, romaine, and apple to bowl with dressing and toss to combine. Divide salad among individual serving dishes. Top with squash and sprinkle with hazelnuts. Crumble feta over top, if using. Season with salt and pepper to taste. Serve.

CHAPTER 5

THE PASTA AND NOODLE BOWL

■ FAST (45 minutes or less total time)
Photos: Spicy Basil Rice Noodles with Crispy Tofu, Snap Peas, and Bell Peppers; Spiced Vegetable Couscous; Spaghetti with Spring Vegetables

Penne with Roasted
Cherry Tomato Sauce

Pasta alla Norma

Penne with Roasted Cherry Tomato Sauce

Serves 4 to 6

Why This Recipe Works Pasta with fresh tomatoes and herbs represents Italian cuisine at its finest—basic ingredients combined with a deft hand to create an elevated final dish that is far more delicious and satisfying than the sum of its parts. And it's naturally vegan, though you may never have thought of it that way: With fresh sauces such as this one, Italians often forgo grated cheese. For our version, we started with cherry tomatoes since they are reliably sweet, high-quality, and available year-round and enhanced their flavor by tossing them with olive oil, a little sugar (to balance their acidity), salt, pepper, red pepper flakes, and slivered garlic. A splash of balsamic vinegar added some color and tang to the mixture. We then sprinkled shallot on top and roasted them in a single layer on a baking sheet, which allowed their excess liquid to cook off and concentrated the tomatoes' sweetness. Chopped fresh basil was the perfect and classic finishing touch.

 1 shallot, sliced thin
 ¼ cup extra-virgin olive oil, divided
 2 pounds cherry or grape tomatoes, halved
 3 large garlic cloves, sliced thin
 1 tablespoon balsamic vinegar
 1½ teaspoons sugar
 ½ teaspoon table salt, plus salt for cooking pasta
 ¼ teaspoon pepper
 ¼ teaspoon red pepper flakes
 1 pound penne
 ¼ cup coarsely chopped fresh basil

1. Adjust oven rack to middle position and heat oven to 350 degrees. Toss shallot with 1 teaspoon oil in bowl. In separate bowl, gently toss tomatoes with remaining oil, garlic, vinegar, sugar, salt, pepper, and pepper flakes. Spread tomato mixture in even layer in rimmed baking sheet, scatter shallot over tomatoes, and roast until edges of shallot begin to brown and tomato skins are slightly shriveled, 35 to 40 minutes. (Do not stir tomatoes during roasting.) Let cool for 5 to 10 minutes.

2. Meanwhile, bring 4 quarts water to boil in large pot. Add pasta and 1 tablespoon salt and cook, stirring often, until al dente. Reserve ½ cup cooking water, then drain pasta and return it to pot. Using rubber spatula, scrape tomato mixture into pot with pasta. Add basil and toss to combine. Before serving, adjust consistency with reserved cooking water as needed and season with salt and pepper to taste.

Pasta alla Norma

Serves 4 to 6 `FAST`

Why This Recipe Works Pasta alla Norma gets its name from the epic opera *Norma*, composed by Vincenzo Bellini, a native of Catania. Eggplant is the star of this Sicilian dish, which also features a robust tomato sauce with garlic and red pepper flakes. Anchovies are traditionally included, but we found that our Anchovy Substitute worked quite well as a replacement. Shreds of ricotta salata cheese (an aged version of ricotta) are also traditional. Here, they're optional—since we incorporated salty, briny olives and capers into our sauce, this dish packs plenty of punch without the dairy. We salted and microwaved the eggplant to quickly draw out its moisture so that it wouldn't absorb too much oil. Then we sautéed it in just a tablespoon of oil until it was perfectly browned and built our pungent tomato sauce in the same skillet. We waited until the last minute to combine the eggplant and sauce; this prevented the eggplant from soaking up too much tomato and becoming soggy. If coffee filters are not available, food-safe, undyed paper towels can be substituted when microwaving the eggplant. Be sure to remove the eggplant from the microwave immediately so that the steam can escape. To prevent the eggplant from breaking up into small pieces, do not peel the skin and do not stir it frequently when sautéing in step 2.

- 1½ pounds eggplant, cut into ½-inch pieces
- ½ teaspoon table salt, plus salt for cooking pasta
- ¼ cup extra-virgin olive oil, divided, plus extra for serving
- 4 garlic cloves, minced
- ¼ teaspoon red pepper flakes
- 1 (28-ounce) can crushed tomatoes
- 2 teaspoons Anchovy Substitute (page 23)
- ½ cup pitted kalamata olives, chopped coarse
- 6 tablespoons minced fresh parsley
- 2 tablespoons capers, rinsed
- 1 pound rigatoni
  Shredded ricotta salata cheese (optional)

1. Line large plate with double layer of coffee filters and coat lightly with vegetable oil spray. Toss eggplant with salt in bowl, then spread evenly over prepared plate. Microwave, uncovered, until eggplant is dry to touch and slightly shriveled, about 10 minutes, tossing halfway through cooking. Let eggplant cool slightly, then return to bowl and toss gently with 1 tablespoon oil.

2. Heat 1 tablespoon oil in 12-inch nonstick skillet over medium-high heat until shimmering. Add eggplant and cook, stirring occasionally, until well browned and fully tender, about 10 minutes; transfer to clean plate.

3. Let now-empty skillet cool slightly, about 3 minutes. Add 1 tablespoon oil, garlic, and pepper flakes to cooled skillet and cook over medium heat until fragrant, about 1 minute. Stir in tomatoes and anchovy substitute, increase heat to medium-high, and simmer, stirring occasionally, until slightly thickened, 8 to 10 minutes.

4. Stir in eggplant and cook until eggplant is warmed through and flavors meld, 3 to 5 minutes. Stir in olives, parsley, capers, and remaining 1 tablespoon oil and season with salt to taste.

5. Meanwhile, bring 4 quarts water to boil in large pot. Add pasta and 1 tablespoon salt and cook, stirring often, until al dente. Reserve ½ cup cooking water, then drain pasta and return it to pot. Add sauce and toss to combine. Adjust consistency with reserved cooking water as needed and season with salt and pepper to taste. Serve with extra oil and ricotta salata, if using.

Fiery Macaroni

Serves 4 `FAST`

Why This Recipe Works The heart of this gutsy Southern Italian dish known as maccheroni di fuoco is a potent chile-garlic oil that dresses bucatini pasta inside and out, allowing the long tubular strands to fully absorb the flavor-packed spicy oil. We gently cooked whole cloves of garlic in extra-virgin olive oil to turn their flavor sweeter, rounder, and mellower before mincing them and returning them to the oil. Calabrian peperoncini flakes are quite spicy and they have smoky notes that became even more complex when bloomed in the oil. Allowing the seasoned oil to steep while we toasted panko bread crumbs and cooked our pasta bolstered its intensity. The topping of rustic toasted bread crumbs is traditional for this pasta—a holdover from times when Southern Italians were too poor to afford cheese. You may top it with Parmesan in addition to the bread crumbs, if you like. Calabrian peperoncini flakes are available at most Italian markets; if you can't find them, 1½ teaspoons of ground dried arbol chiles are the next best substitute in this dish. This pasta is intended to be fiery hot, but you can make it milder by using the lesser amount of peperoncini flakes.

- ½ cup plus 1 tablespoon extra-virgin olive oil
- 4 garlic cloves, peeled
- 2–4 teaspoons Calabrian peperoncini flakes
- ½ cup panko bread crumbs
- ⅛ plus ½ teaspoon table salt, divided, plus salt for cooking pasta
- 1 pound bucatini
- 2 tablespoons chopped fresh parsley

1. Cook ¼ cup oil and garlic in 8-inch skillet over medium-low heat, turning occasionally, until garlic begins to brown, 5 to 7 minutes. Stir in peperoncini flakes and cook until slightly darkened in color, about 45 seconds. Immediately transfer oil mixture to bowl and let cool for 5 minutes. Transfer garlic to cutting board, mince to paste, then return to oil mixture. Let sit until flavors meld, about 20 minutes.

2. Wipe skillet clean with paper towels. Cook panko, 1 tablespoon oil, and ⅛ teaspoon salt in now-empty skillet over medium heat, stirring often, until lightly toasted, 3 to 5 minutes. Transfer to clean bowl and set aside for serving.

3. Meanwhile, bring 4 quarts water to boil in large pot. Add pasta and 1 tablespoon salt and cook, stirring often, until al dente. Reserve ½ cup cooking water, then drain pasta and return it to pot. Add parsley, oil mixture, ¼ cup reserved cooking water, remaining ¼ cup oil, and remaining ½ teaspoon salt and toss to combine. Adjust consistency with remaining reserved cooking water as needed. Season with salt and pepper to taste. Sprinkle individual portions with bread crumbs before serving.

Penne with Red Pepper Pesto
Serves 4 to 6　FAST

Why This Recipe Works From the toe of the Italian boot, pesto alla calabrese trades the familiar basil–pine nut base of Genovese pesto for a combination of sweet and hot red peppers. For layered flavor, we sautéed some red bell peppers—first covered to soften and then uncovered to develop browning—and then added some raw red bell pepper for fresh, fruity bite. For the heat, we used smoky Calabrian peperoncini flakes. Fresh tomato, onion, garlic, and basil added further complexity to the mixture. A modest amount of cheese is usually added to pesto alla calabrese. We found that a combination of our Cashew Ricotta and Vegan Parmesan Substitute worked equally as well as dairy versions, contributing rich creaminess and salty tang without dulling the vegetables' flavor. Calabrian peperoncini flakes are available at most Italian markets; if you can't find them, you can substitute red pepper flakes in this dish, though they do not have the same smoky flavor.

3　red bell peppers, stemmed, seeded, and cut into ¼-inch-wide strips (5 cups)
3　tablespoons extra-virgin olive oil, divided
1　teaspoon table salt, divided, plus salt for cooking pasta
¼　teaspoon pepper
1　small onion, chopped
1　plum tomato, cored, seeded, and chopped
⅓　cup chopped fresh basil
½–1　teaspoon Calabrian peperoncini flakes
1　teaspoon garlic, minced, divided
⅓　cup Cashew Ricotta (page 26) or dairy ricotta cheese
¼　cup Vegan Parmesan Substitute (page 27) or grated dairy Parmesan cheese
1　teaspoon white wine vinegar, plus extra for seasoning
1　pound penne

1. Combine two-thirds of bell peppers, 1 tablespoon oil, ¼ teaspoon salt, and pepper in 12-inch nonstick skillet. Cover and cook over medium-low heat, stirring occasionally, until bell peppers are softened and just beginning to brown, about 15 minutes.

2. Add onion, tomato, basil, peperoncini flakes, and ½ teaspoon garlic and cook, uncovered, stirring occasionally, until onion is softened and bell peppers are browned in spots, 6 to 7 minutes. Remove skillet from heat and let cool for 5 minutes.

3. Process cashew ricotta, vegan Parmesan substitute, cooked bell pepper mixture, remaining one-third bell peppers, and remaining ¾ teaspoon salt in food processor until coarsely ground, about 20 seconds, scraping down sides of bowl as needed. With processor running, add vinegar and remaining 2 tablespoons oil and process until smooth, about 1 minute, scraping down sides of bowl as needed.

4. Meanwhile, bring 4 quarts water to boil in large pot. Add pasta and 1 tablespoon salt and cook, stirring often, until al dente. Reserve ½ cup cooking water, then drain pasta and return it to pot. Add pesto and toss to combine. Before serving, adjust consistency with reserved cooking water as needed and season with salt, pepper, and vinegar to taste.

Gemelli with Pesto, Potatoes, and Green Beans
Serves 4 to 6　FAST

Why This Recipe Works Serving two starches together may seem unusual, but in the northwestern Italian region of Liguria, it's a classic way to serve green pesto. Pasta is the base of the dish, while the potatoes' starch lends body to the sauce and tender green beans add flavor. We tested various potatoes and found that waxy red ones made the creamiest sauce. Some recipes call for cooking the potatoes, green beans, and pasta together in the same pot, but this consistently resulted in one or more elements being overcooked. Cooking them separately ensured that each maintained the best texture and flavor. Our Vegan Pesto, with its bright basil and mellow garlic flavors, brought all the elements together seamlessly. You will need a

10-inch skillet with a tight-fitting lid. We like gemelli here to trap the thick, chunky sauce, but penne or rigatoni also works. Use red potatoes measuring 3 inches or more in diameter.

Table salt for cooking pasta and vegetables
12 ounces green beans, trimmed and cut into 1½-inch lengths
1 pound large red potatoes, peeled and cut into ½-inch pieces
1 pound gemelli
1 recipe Vegan Pesto (page 23)
1 tablespoon lemon juice
½ teaspoon pepper

1. Bring ½ cup water and ¼ teaspoon salt to boil in 10-inch skillet over medium heat. Add green beans, cover, and cook until tender, 5 to 8 minutes. Drain green beans and transfer to rimmed baking sheet.

2. Meanwhile, bring 4 quarts water to boil in large pot. Add potatoes and 1 tablespoon salt and cook until potatoes are tender but still hold their shape, 9 to 12 minutes. Using slotted spoon, transfer potatoes to sheet with beans.

3. Add pasta to boiling water and cook, stirring often, until al dente. Reserve 1 cup cooking water, then drain pasta and return it to pot. Add pesto, lemon juice, ¼ cup reserved cooking water, pepper, and potatoes and beans and stir vigorously with rubber spatula until sauce has creamy appearance. Adjust consistency with remaining reserved cooking water as needed, season with salt and pepper to taste, and serve.

Whole-Wheat Spaghetti with Greens, Beans, and Tomatoes
Serves 4 to 6   FAST

Why This Recipe Works This rustic trio of pasta, greens, and beans is another fine example of the knack Italians have for transforming humble ingredients into elevated meals. We combined whole-wheat spaghetti with curly-leaf spinach, creamy cannellini beans, and sweet diced tomatoes. To create a strong savory presence that wasn't dependent on cheese, we employed a one-two umami punch of white miso and cheesy-tasting nutritional yeast. To ensure that everything would fit in one pan, we wilted half of the spinach before adding the rest with the tomatoes and broth. Then we braised the spinach in the broth and followed by adding the beans and some olives for a briny pop of flavor. This mixture had to simmer with the pasta for just a couple minutes to create a harmonious dish. The skillet will be very full once you add all the spinach in step 2, but the greens will become manageable as they wilt.

Whole-Wheat Spaghetti with Greens, Beans, and Tomatoes

¼ cup extra-virgin olive oil, divided, plus extra for serving
8 garlic cloves, peeled (5 sliced thin, 3 minced)
Pinch plus ¾ teaspoon table salt, divided, plus salt for cooking pasta
1 onion, chopped fine
½ teaspoon red pepper flakes
1¼ pounds curly-leaf spinach, stemmed and cut into 1-inch pieces, divided
¾ cup vegetable broth
2 tablespoons white miso
2 tablespoons nutritional yeast
1 (14.5-ounce) can diced tomatoes, drained
1 (15-ounce) can cannellini beans, rinsed
¾ cup pitted kalamata olives, chopped coarse
1 pound whole-wheat spaghetti
Vegan Parmesan Substitute (page 27) or grated dairy Parmesan cheese (optional)

1. Cook 3 tablespoons oil and sliced garlic in 12-inch skillet over medium heat, stirring often, until garlic turns golden but not brown, about 3 minutes. Using slotted spoon, transfer garlic to paper towel–lined plate; sprinkle with pinch salt.

2. Add onion to oil left in skillet and cook over medium heat until softened and just beginning to brown, 5 to 7 minutes. Stir in minced garlic and pepper flakes and cook until fragrant, about 30 seconds. Add half of spinach and cook, tossing occasionally, until beginning to wilt, about 2 minutes. Whisk broth, miso, and nutritional yeast together in bowl, then add to skillet with tomatoes, remaining spinach, and remaining ¾ teaspoon salt. Bring to simmer, then cover and cook, tossing occasionally, until spinach is completely wilted, about 10 minutes (mixture will be somewhat loose and watery at this point). Stir in beans and olives, then remove skillet from heat and cover to keep warm.

3. Meanwhile, bring 4 quarts water to boil in large pot. Add pasta and 1 tablespoon salt and cook, stirring often, until nearly al dente. Reserve ½ cup cooking water, then drain pasta and return it to pot. Stir in spinach mixture and cook over medium heat, tossing to combine, until pasta is al dente and most of liquid is absorbed, about 2 minutes.

4. Off heat, stir in remaining 1 tablespoon oil. Adjust consistency with reserved cooking water as needed and season with salt and pepper to taste. Serve, sprinkling individual portions with garlic chips and vegan Parmesan substitute and drizzling with extra oil.

Farfalle and Summer Squash with Tomatoes, Basil, and Pine Nuts

Serves 4 to 6

Why This Recipe Works This summery pasta dish is light and flavorful. We kept the skin on the squash to keep the pieces intact (and add color), then salted the squash to release excess liquid and concentrate the vegetable's flavor. This step was essential to keep the sauce from ending up too watery. It also allowed us to get good browning; it took just 5 minutes in a hot skillet to lightly char each batch. To accompany the squash, we chose halved grape tomatoes, fresh basil, and crunchy pine nuts. We finished the sauce with balsamic vinegar to give it a kick and paired it with farfalle to best trap the flavor-packed ingredients. We loved the lightness of this dish without any Parmesan—vegan or dairy. A combination of zucchini and summer squash makes for a nice mix of colors, but either may be used exclusively, if desired. We prefer kosher salt in this recipe because residual grains are easily wiped away from the squash. If using table salt, be sure to reduce all of the salt amounts in the recipe by half.

2 pounds zucchini and/or summer squash, halved lengthwise and sliced ½ inch thick
  Kosher salt for salting squash and cooking pasta
5 tablespoons extra-virgin olive oil, divided
3 garlic cloves, minced
½ teaspoon red pepper flakes
1 pound farfalle
12 ounces grape tomatoes, halved
½ cup chopped fresh basil
¼ cup pine nuts, toasted
2 tablespoons balsamic vinegar

1. Toss zucchini with 1 tablespoon salt in colander and let drain for 30 minutes. Pat zucchini dry with paper towels and carefully wipe away any residual salt.

2. Heat 1 tablespoon oil in 12-inch nonstick skillet over high heat until just smoking. Add half of zucchini and cook, stirring occasionally, until golden brown and slightly charred, 5 to 7 minutes, reducing heat if skillet begins to scorch; transfer to large plate. Repeat with 1 tablespoon oil and remaining zucchini.

3. Heat 1 tablespoon oil in now-empty skillet over medium heat until shimmering. Add garlic and pepper flakes and cook until fragrant, about 30 seconds. Stir in squash and cook until warmed through, about 30 seconds.

4. Meanwhile, bring 4 quarts water to boil in large pot. Add pasta and 2 tablespoons salt and cook, stirring often, until al dente. Reserve ½ cup cooking water, then drain pasta and return it to pot. Add squash mixture, tomatoes, basil, pine nuts, vinegar, and remaining 2 tablespoons oil and toss to combine. Before serving, adjust consistency with reserved cooking water as needed and season with salt and pepper to taste.

Campanelle with Roasted Cauliflower, Garlic, and Walnuts

Serves 4 to 6

Why This Recipe Works Bold, rustic flavors and hearty textures make this an exceptionally satisfying pasta meal. High-heat roasting transformed the mild-mannered cauliflower into an intensely flavored, sweetly nutty foil for the campanelle, a ruffled cone-shaped pasta that looks a little like a flower. For golden cauliflower, we sliced the head into wedges to create maximum surface area while leaving the core and florets intact. Tossing the wedges with a little sugar jump-started browning; preheating the baking sheet (accomplished while roasting the garlic) before arranging the cauliflower on it also helped to develop lots of color. For the sauce, we roasted two

Campanelle with Roasted Cauliflower, Garlic, and Walnuts

PREPARING GARLIC FOR ROASTING

1. Rinse garlic head and remove outer papery skin. Cut top quarter off of garlic head so that tops of cloves are exposed.

2. Place garlic head cut side up in center of 12-inch square of aluminum foil, drizzle with oil, and wrap securely.

3. After roasted garlic head has cooled, remove from foil. Using your hand or flat edge of chef's knife, squeeze garlic cloves from skins, starting from root end and working up.

whole heads of garlic and tempered its bold assertiveness with Parmesan (vegan or dairy). We stirred in parsley and topped each serving with a handful of crunchy toasted walnuts.

- 2 garlic heads
- 1 teaspoon plus 6 tablespoons extra-virgin olive oil, divided
- 1 head cauliflower (2 pounds), cut into 8 equal wedges
- 1 teaspoon table salt, plus salt for cooking pasta
- ¼ teaspoon pepper
- ¼ teaspoon sugar
- 2 tablespoons lemon juice, plus extra for seasoning
- ¼ teaspoon red pepper flakes
- 1 pound campanelle
- ½ cup Vegan Parmesan Substitute (page 27) or grated dairy Parmesan cheese
- 1 tablespoon chopped fresh parsley
- ¼ cup walnuts, toasted and chopped coarse

1. Adjust oven rack to middle position, place large rimmed baking sheet on rack, and heat oven to 500 degrees. Remove outer papery skins from garlic; cut top quarters of heads and discard. Place garlic heads, cut side up, in center of 12-inch square of aluminum foil and drizzle each with ½ teaspoon oil. Wrap garlic heads tightly in foil. Place packet on oven rack next to baking sheet and roast until garlic is very tender, about 40 minutes.

2. While garlic roasts, combine cauliflower wedges, 2 tablespoons oil, salt, pepper, and sugar in bowl; rub gently to distribute oil and seasonings. Remove baking sheet from oven and carefully lay cauliflower wedges cut side down on hot baking sheet. Roast cauliflower until well browned and tender, 20 to 25 minutes.

3. Transfer cauliflower and garlic packet to cutting board and let cool slightly, about 10 minutes. Once cool enough to handle, cut cauliflower into ½-inch pieces and unwrap garlic. Gently squeeze garlic cloves from skin into medium bowl, and mash smooth with fork. Stir in lemon juice and pepper flakes, then slowly whisk in remaining ¼ cup oil.

4. Meanwhile, bring 4 quarts water to boil in large pot. Add pasta and 1 tablespoon salt and cook, stirring often, until al dente. Reserve 1 cup cooking water, then drain pasta and return it to pot. Add chopped cauliflower, garlic sauce, vegan Parmesan substitute, parsley, and ¼ cup reserved cooking water and toss to combine. Adjust consistency with remaining reserved ¾ cup cooking water as needed and season with salt, pepper, and extra lemon juice to taste. Sprinkle individual portions with walnuts and serve.

Orecchiette with Broccoli Rabe and White Beans

Serves 4 to 6 `FAST`

Why This Recipe Works Orecchiette is the quintessential pasta shape of Puglia, the heel of the Italian boot. It is often served with greens, traditionally turnip tops, though broccoli rabe is also frequently used. Sometimes the dish includes sausage to add richness and offset the slight bitterness of the greens. For our plant-based rendition, we swapped in buttery, creamy white beans, which achieved the same effect in conjunction with our Vegan Parmesan Substitute (or dairy Parmesan). To boost the beans' flavor, we cooked a shallot with garlic, oregano, and fennel seeds before adding the beans. To ensure that the thick stalks, tender leaves, and small florets of the broccoli rabe all cooked evenly, we boiled them briefly, pulling them from the pot just as they turned crisp-tender. You can substitute 2 pounds of broccoli, cut into 1-inch florets, for the broccoli rabe.

¼ cup extra-virgin olive oil
1 shallot, minced
6 garlic cloves, minced
1 teaspoon minced fresh oregano or ¼ teaspoon dried
½ teaspoon fennel seeds, crushed
¼ teaspoon red pepper flakes
1 (15-ounce) can cannellini beans, rinsed
1 pound broccoli rabe, trimmed and cut into 1½-inch pieces
   Table salt for cooking vegetables and pasta
1 pound orecchiette
1 cup Vegan Parmesan Substitute (page 27) or grated dairy Parmesan cheese

1. Heat oil in 12-inch nonstick skillet over medium heat until shimmering. Add shallot and cook until softened, about 2 minutes. Stir in garlic, oregano, fennel seeds, and pepper flakes and cook until fragrant, about 30 seconds. Stir in beans and cook until warmed through, about 2 minutes; set aside.

2. Meanwhile, bring 4 quarts water to boil in large pot. Add broccoli rabe and 1 tablespoon salt and cook, stirring often, until crisp-tender, about 2 minutes. Using slotted spoon, transfer broccoli rabe to skillet with bean mixture.

3. Return water to boil, add pasta, and cook, stirring often, until al dente. Reserve 1 cup cooking water, then drain pasta and return it to pot. Add bean–broccoli rabe mixture, vegan Parmesan substitute, and ⅓ cup reserved cooking water and toss to combine. Before serving, adjust consistency with remaining reserved ⅔ cup cooking water as needed and season with salt and pepper to taste.

Spaghetti with Spring Vegetables

Serves 4 to 6 `FAST`

Why This Recipe Works For this spin on the Italian American favorite pasta primavera, we made inventive use of zucchini by overcooking it with olive oil and aromatics to break it down and create a silky, creamy-feeling, but cream-free sauce that nicely coated our favorite spring vegetables (asparagus and peas) and spaghetti. Thanks to a tip we picked up from a legendary old-school New York City chef, we briefly marinated cherry tomatoes with oil and garlic and spooned them over the top of the pasta, along with some fresh mint, to finish off our dish with contrasting color and a lively lilt. The zucchini slices will break down as they cook to create a base for the sauce; do not be alarmed when the slices turn soft and creamy and lose their shape. If you use dairy cheese for garnish, we prefer Pecorino Romano in this dish.

6 ounces cherry tomatoes, halved
6 tablespoons extra-virgin olive oil, divided, plus extra for serving
5 garlic cloves (1 small, minced; 4 sliced thin)
¾ teaspoon table salt, divided, plus salt for cooking pasta
¼ teaspoon pepper
1 pound spaghetti
1 zucchini, halved lengthwise and sliced ¼ inch thick
⅛ teaspoon red pepper flakes
1 pound asparagus, trimmed and cut on bias into 1-inch lengths
1 cup frozen peas, thawed
¼ cup minced fresh chives
1 tablespoon lemon juice
¼ cup Vegan Parmesan Substitute (page 27) or grated dairy Pecorino Romano cheese
2 tablespoons torn fresh mint leaves

1. Toss tomatoes, 1 tablespoon oil, minced garlic, ¼ teaspoon salt, and pepper together in bowl; set aside.

2. Bring 4 quarts water to boil in large Dutch oven. Add pasta and 1 tablespoon salt and cook, stirring often, until al dente. Drain pasta and return it to pot.

3. Meanwhile, heat 3 tablespoons oil in 12-inch nonstick skillet over medium-low heat until shimmering. Add zucchini, pepper flakes, sliced garlic, and remaining ½ teaspoon salt and cook, covered, until zucchini softens and breaks down, 10 to 15 minutes, stirring occasionally. Add asparagus, peas, and ¾ cup water and bring to simmer over medium-high heat. Cover and cook until asparagus is crisp-tender, about 2 minutes.

4. Add vegetable mixture, chives, lemon juice, and remaining 2 tablespoons oil to pasta and toss to combine; season with salt and pepper to taste. Transfer to serving bowl, sprinkle with vegan Parmesan substitute, and drizzle with extra oil. Spoon tomatoes and their juices over top and sprinkle with mint. Serve.

Pasta e Ceci
Serves 4 to 6 `FAST`

Why This Recipe Works The comforting Italian stew known as pasta e ceci is prepared in different ways in different households, but it always combines a small pasta shape with chickpeas. We began ours by pulsing carrots, celery, and garlic into a soffritto and then cooking the soffritto in a Dutch oven to build a flavorful fond. A little Anchovy Substitute added an umami boost. Red pepper flakes introduced some heat and minced fresh rosemary added a woodsy quality. We decided that chopped tomatoes were essential, but for speed we turned to canned peeled tomatoes and chopped them in the food processor. They went into the pot with canned chickpeas (including their starchy liquid for added body) to simmer. The chickpeas began to soften after just 10 minutes, at which point we added ditalini and cooked the stew a little longer. The chickpeas took on a creamy softness that complemented the tender pasta and thick, silky broth. Another short pasta can be used, but substitute by weight and not by volume.

- 1 small carrot, peeled and chopped
- 1 small celery rib, chopped
- 4 garlic cloves, peeled
- 1 onion, halved and cut into 1-inch pieces
- 1 (14-ounce) can whole peeled tomatoes, drained
- ¼ cup extra-virgin olive oil, plus extra for serving
- ½ teaspoon Anchovy Substitute (page 23)
- ¼ teaspoon red pepper flakes
- 2 teaspoons minced fresh rosemary
- 2 (15-ounce) cans chickpeas (do not drain)
- 2 cups water
- 1 teaspoon table salt
- 8 ounces (1½ cups) ditalini
- 1 tablespoon lemon juice
- 1 tablespoon minced fresh parsley
- ½ cup Vegan Parmesan Substitute (page 27) or grated dairy Parmesan cheese

1. Pulse carrot, celery, and garlic in food processor until finely chopped, 8 to 10 pulses. Add onion and pulse until onion is cut into ⅛- to ¼-inch pieces, 8 to 10 pulses; transfer carrot mixture to Dutch oven. Pulse tomatoes in now-empty food processor until coarsely chopped, 8 to 10 pulses; set aside.

Spaghetti with Spring Vegetables

Pasta e Ceci

2. Add oil to carrot mixture in Dutch oven and cook over medium heat, stirring frequently, until fond begins to form on bottom of pot, about 5 minutes. Add anchovy substitute, pepper flakes, and rosemary and cook until fragrant, about 1 minute. Stir in tomatoes, chickpeas and their liquid, water, and salt and bring to boil, scraping up any browned bits. Reduce heat to medium-low and simmer for 10 minutes. Add pasta and cook, stirring frequently, until tender, 10 to 12 minutes. Stir in lemon juice and parsley and season with salt and pepper to taste. Sprinkle with vegan Parmesan substitute, drizzle with extra oil, and serve.

Fideos with Chickpeas
Serves 4

Why This Recipe Works One of the biggest stars of traditional Spanish cooking is fideos, a richly flavored relative of paella that calls for breaking noodles into small lengths and toasting them until nut-brown before cooking them in a garlicky, tomatoey stock with seafood and chorizo. We thought the bold tomato stock and toasted noodles would work well with chickpeas, another common Spanish ingredient, so we developed our plant-foward version using those. For the sofrito, we finely chopped the onion (so it browned more

Fideos with Chickpeas

quickly) and used chopped canned tomatoes. White wine and the juice from our canned tomatoes, along with smoked paprika, made a stock with complex depth of flavor. If your skillet is not broiler-safe, once the pasta is tender, transfer the mixture to a broiler-safe 13 by 9-inch baking dish lightly coated with extra-virgin olive oil. Broil and serve as directed.

- 8 ounces spaghettini or thin spaghetti, broken into 1- to 2-inch lengths
- 2 teaspoons plus 2 tablespoons extra-virgin olive oil, divided
- 1 onion, chopped fine
- ½ teaspoon table salt, divided
- 1 (14.5-ounce) can diced tomatoes, drained and chopped fine, juice reserved
- 3 garlic cloves, minced
- 1½ teaspoons smoked paprika
- 2¾ cups water
- 1 (15-ounce) can chickpeas, rinsed
- ½ cup dry white wine
- ½ teaspoon pepper
- 1 tablespoon chopped fresh parsley
  Lemon wedges

1. Toss pasta and 2 teaspoons oil in broiler-safe 12-inch skillet until pasta is evenly coated. Toast pasta over medium-high heat, stirring frequently, until browned and releases nutty aroma (pasta should be color of peanut butter), 6 to 10 minutes; transfer to bowl.

2. Wipe out now-empty skillet, add remaining 2 tablespoons oil, and heat over medium-high heat until shimmering. Add onion and ¼ teaspoon salt and cook until onion is softened, about 5 minutes. Stir in tomatoes and cook until mixture is thick, dry, and slightly darkened in color, 4 to 6 minutes.

BREAKING PASTA FOR FIDEOS

 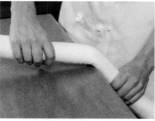

1. Loosely fold 4 ounces of spaghettini in dish towel, keeping pasta flat, not bunched.

2. Press pasta bundle repeatedly against edge of counter to break pasta into 1- to 2-inch lengths. Repeat with remaining 4 ounces spaghettini.

3. Reduce heat to medium, stir in garlic and smoked paprika, and cook until fragrant, about 30 seconds. Stir in toasted pasta until thoroughly combined. Stir in water, chickpeas, wine, pepper, reserved tomato juice, and remaining ¼ teaspoon salt. Increase heat to medium-high and bring to simmer. Cook uncovered, stirring occasionally, until liquid is slightly thickened and pasta is just tender, 8 to 10 minutes. Meanwhile, adjust oven rack 5 to 6 inches from broiler element and heat broiler.

4. Transfer skillet to oven and broil until surface of pasta is dry with crisped, browned spots, 5 to 7 minutes. Let cool for 5 minutes, then sprinkle with parsley; serve with lemon wedges.

Fettuccine with Walnut Sauce

Serves 4 to 6   FAST

Why This Recipe Works The creamy walnut sauce that cloaks the fettuccine in this dish comes together quickly in the food processor while the pasta cooks but is a powerhouse of rich, nutty flavor. Equal parts plant-based (or dairy) creamer and Vegan Parmesan Substitute (or Parmesan) add thickness and saltiness to the sauce, while lemon juice brightens and lightens the mixture. A touch of nutmeg adds a warm spice element that heightens the nutty flavor of the toasted walnuts. We held back ¼ cup of walnuts from the sauce, chopping them and sprinkling on top of the finished pasta (along with some parsley) for crunchy contrast.

  1 **pound fettuccine**
  1 **teaspoon table salt, plus salt for cooking pasta**
2¼ **cups (9 ounces) walnuts, toasted**
 ¼ **cup plant-based creamer or dairy heavy cream**
 ¼ **cup Vegan Parmesan Substitute (page 27) or grated dairy Parmesan cheese**
  1 **tablespoon lemon juice**
  1 **garlic clove, minced**
 ⅛ **teaspoon nutmeg**
 ½ **teaspoon pepper**
  2 **tablespoons chopped fresh parsley**

  1. Bring 4 quarts water to boil in large pot. Add pasta and 1 tablespoon salt and cook, stirring often, until al dente. Reserve 1 cup cooking water, then drain pasta and return it to pot.

  2. Chop ¼ cup walnuts; set aside. Process remaining 2 cups walnuts, plant-based creamer, vegan Parmesan substitute, lemon juice, garlic, nutmeg, pepper, and salt in food processor to coarse paste, about 30 seconds.

  3. Add walnut sauce and reserved cooking water to pasta and toss to combine. Season with salt and pepper to taste. Sprinkle with parsley and reserved chopped walnuts. Serve.

Cashew e Pepe e Funghi

Serves 4 to 6   FAST

Why This Recipe Works We had hoped to develop a vegan version of either pasta carbonara or pasta cacio e pepe, but as it turned out, tasters loved this oh-so-creamy dish that includes the best hallmarks of both of these Italian favorites. Having done lots of work with cashews in the test kitchen, we knew that this nut would be able to provide a richly thick and creamy (but not heavy) sauce base because of its uniquely low fiber and high starch content. We discovered that by breaking the cashews up in a blender (to increase their surface area), we could soak them for just 15 minutes in the flavorful sauce ingredients. We usually use raw cashews for their more neutral flavor, but since we only used ½ cup here, we tried roasting them; this added nuanced warmth without imparting a nutty taste. Miso and nutritional yeast each contributed different aspects of umami to the sauce. Plenty of coarsely ground pepper added subtle warmth. And oyster mushrooms were a revelation. Because they contain very little moisture (relative to other mushrooms), they quickly cooked into chewy, golden, almost bacon-y nuggets. Some parsley and a splash of lemon juice provided freshness and acidity. You can substitute portobello mushrooms for the oyster mushrooms, but the mushroom "bacon" won't be nearly as crisp.

 ½ **cup roasted cashews**
 ¼ **cup nutritional yeast**
  2 **tablespoons white miso**
 ½ **teaspoon table salt, plus salt for cooking pasta**
 ¼ **cup extra-virgin olive oil**
  6 **ounces oyster mushrooms, trimmed and chopped**
  5 **garlic cloves, sliced thin**
  1 **teaspoon coarsely ground pepper**
  1 **pound spaghetti**
  2 **tablespoons chopped fresh parsley**
  1 **teaspoon lemon juice**

  1. Process cashews in blender on low speed to consistency of fine gravel mixed with sand, 10 to 15 seconds. Add 1½ cups water, nutritional yeast, miso, and salt and process on low speed until combined, about 5 seconds. Scrape down sides of blender jar and let mixture sit for 15 minutes.

2. Process on low speed until all ingredients are well blended, about 1 minute. Scrape down sides of blender jar, then process on high speed until sauce is completely smooth, 3 to 4 minutes.

3. Heat oil in 12-inch skillet over medium-high heat until shimmering. Add mushrooms and cook until deep golden brown and crisp, 7 to 10 minutes. Off heat, stir in garlic and pepper and cook using residual heat of skillet until fragrant, about 1 minute.

4. Meanwhile, bring 4 quarts water to boil in large pot. Add pasta and 1 tablespoon salt and cook, stirring often, until al dente. Reserve ½ cup cooking water, then drain pasta and return it to pot.

5. Add sauce, mushroom mixture, parsley, and lemon juice to pasta and toss until sauce is thickened slightly and pasta is well coated, about 1 minute. Before serving, adjust consistency with reserved cooking water as needed and season with salt and pepper to taste.

Creamy Cashew Mac and Cheese
Serves 4 to 6

Why This Recipe Works Homestyle stovetop mac and cheese is a comfort-food favorite for all ages, and we were determined to craft an irresistible version that didn't require cheese. Many recipes we consulted called for pureeing ingredients ranging from squash or potatoes to sunflower seeds and even cannellini beans for the sauce, but those approaches didn't get us to our goal. Our winning formula turned out to be a mixture of cashews, cauliflower, and plant-based milk, simmered together and then blended until smooth. The rich fat from the cashews and the light, silken texture of the cauliflower (plus the low fiber content of both ingredients) made for a decadent-tasting, pasta-coating sauce. Funky nutritional yeast, when combined with mustard powder for bite, tomato paste for sweetness, and vinegar for tang, gave the dish a remarkable cheesy flavor, while turmeric provided the expected color. The sauce will be loose as you add the macaroni, but it will thicken as it finishes cooking and is served.

⅓ cup refined coconut oil
¼ cup nutritional yeast
4 teaspoons dry mustard
1 tablespoon tomato paste
2 garlic cloves, minced
2 teaspoons table salt, plus salt for cooking pasta
½ teaspoon ground turmeric

Creamy Cashew Mac and Cheese

4½ cups plant-based milk or dairy milk
10 ounces cauliflower florets, cut into ½-inch pieces (3 cups)
1¼ cups raw cashews, chopped
1 pound elbow macaroni
1 tablespoon distilled white vinegar

1. Heat oil in large saucepan over medium heat until melted and shimmering. Stir in nutritional yeast, mustard, tomato paste, garlic, salt, and turmeric and cook until fragrant, about 30 seconds. Stir in milk, scraping up any browned bits, and bring to simmer over medium-high heat. Stir in cauliflower florets and cashews, reduce heat to medium-low, and cook, partially covered, until cauliflower is very soft and falls apart easily when poked with fork, about 20 minutes.

2. Working in 2 batches, process cauliflower mixture in blender until smooth, about 2 minutes, scraping down sides of blender jar as needed.

3. Meanwhile, bring 4 quarts water to boil in large pot. Add macaroni and 1 tablespoon salt and cook, stirring often, until nearly al dente. Reserve ½ cup cooking water, then drain macaroni.

4. Transfer pureed cauliflower mixture to now-empty pot and bring to gentle simmer over medium-low heat. Add drained macaroni and vinegar and cook, stirring constantly, until warmed through and sauce is slightly thickened, about 3 minutes. Adjust consistency with reserved cooking water as needed, season with salt and pepper to taste, and serve immediately.

Fettuccine Alfredo
Serves 4 to 6

Why This Recipe Works Classic fettuccine Alfredo is, of course, loaded with cream, Parmesan cheese, and butter, so beyond the dietary decadence, veganizing this luxurious Roman dish came with definite challenges. To replicate the creaminess of the original version, we started with the silky base of pureed cauliflower and cashews that we used in our Creamy Cashew Mac and Cheese (page 166). Here, though, we were looking for a more subtly flavored, silkier sauce, with the slightly sweet notes of traditional Alfredo. So instead of nutritional yeast, we used miso paste, combining it with coconut oil for the richness of a cream sauce and a savory-sweet balance. Just as with traditional fettuccine Alfredo, the texture of this sauce changes dramatically as the dish stands for a few minutes; serving in warmed bowls helps ensure that it retains its creamy texture while it's being eaten.

2½ cups plant-based milk or dairy milk
⅓ cup refined coconut oil
3 tablespoons white miso
1 teaspoon table salt, plus salt for cooking pasta
10 ounces cauliflower florets, cut into ½-inch pieces (3 cups)
¾ cup raw cashews, chopped
1 pound fettuccine
 Pinch ground nutmeg
2 tablespoons chopped fresh parsley

1. Combine milk, oil, miso, and salt in large saucepan and bring to simmer over medium-high heat, whisking to dissolve miso. Stir in cauliflower florets and cashews, reduce heat to medium-low, and cook, partially covered, until cauliflower is very soft and falls apart easily when poked with fork, about 20 minutes.

2. Process cauliflower mixture and ½ cup water in blender until smooth, about 2 minutes, scraping down sides of blender jar as needed.

3. Meanwhile, bring 4 quarts water to boil in large pot. Add pasta and 1 tablespoon salt and cook, stirring often, until nearly al dente. Reserve ½ cup cooking water, then drain pasta.

4. Transfer pureed cauliflower mixture to now-empty pot. Whisk in nutmeg and bring to gentle simmer over medium-low heat. Add drained pasta and cook, stirring constantly, until warmed through and sauce is slightly thickened, about 3 minutes. Adjust consistency with reserved cooking water as needed, season with salt and pepper to taste, sprinkle with parsley, and serve immediately.

Mushroom Bolognese
Serves 4 to 6

Why This Recipe Works Traditional Bolognese sauce gets its rich flavor from a combination of several types of meat, but we were confident we could create a savory, lush, and decadent Bolognese without it. To mimic the meat sauce's long-cooked richness, we turned to one of the original plant-based meat substitutes: the mighty mushroom. Two types of mushrooms helped us re-create that complexity. Using 2 pounds of fresh cremini mushrooms gave the sauce a satisfyingly chunky, substantial texture, and minced dried porcini delivered concentrated umami flavor. To further boost the savory umami profile, we added tomato paste and soy sauce. Red wine lent richness and depth, and a little sugar balanced the dish. Bolognese often includes a pour of cream; we found that plant-based creamer—just 3 tablespoons—stirred in at the end worked just as well as dairy cream to round out the sauce and make for a silky finish.

2 pounds cremini mushrooms, trimmed and quartered
1 carrot, peeled and chopped
1 small onion, chopped
1 (28-ounce) can whole peeled tomatoes
3 tablespoons extra-virgin olive oil
½ ounce dried porcini mushrooms, rinsed and minced
3 garlic cloves, minced
1 teaspoon sugar
2 tablespoons tomato paste
1 cup dry red wine
½ cup vegetable broth
1 tablespoon soy sauce
½ teaspoon table salt, plus salt for cooking pasta
¼ teaspoon pepper
3 tablespoons plant-based creamer or dairy heavy cream
1 pound fettuccine

1. Working in batches, pulse cremini mushrooms in food processor until pieces are no larger than ½ inch, 5 to 7 pulses, scraping down sides of bowl as needed; transfer to large bowl.

Pulse carrot and onion in now-empty processor until finely chopped, 5 to 7 pulses; transfer to bowl with processed mushrooms. Pulse tomatoes and their juice in now-empty processor until finely chopped, 6 to 8 pulses; set aside separately.

2. Heat oil in Dutch oven over medium heat until shimmering. Add processed mushroom mixture and porcini mushrooms, cover, and cook, stirring occasionally, until vegetables release their liquid, about 5 minutes. Uncover, increase heat to medium-high, and cook until vegetables begin to brown, 12 to 15 minutes.

3. Stir in garlic and sugar and cook until fragrant, about 30 seconds. Stir in tomato paste and cook for 1 minute. Stir in wine and simmer until nearly evaporated, about 5 minutes.

4. Stir in reserved processed tomatoes, broth, soy sauce, salt, and pepper and bring to simmer. Reduce heat to medium-low and simmer until sauce has thickened but is still moist, 8 to 10 minutes. Off heat, stir in creamer.

5. Meanwhile, bring 4 quarts water to boil in large pot. Add pasta and 1 tablespoon salt and cook, stirring often, until al dente. Reserve ½ cup cooking water, then drain pasta and return it to pot. Add sauce and toss to combine. Before serving, adjust consistency with reserved cooking water as needed and season with salt and pepper to taste.

Spaghetti and Meatless Meatballs

Serves 4 to 6

Why This Recipe Works This recipe is proof positive that a good plant-based meatball is not an oxymoron. To develop a vegan meatball that had the savory flavor and heft of a classic meat-based version, we turned to vegan protein crumbles—one of the original meat substitutes—which provided great structure and chew. Also known as TVP (texturized vegetable protein), vegan protein crumbles are a neutral-flavor soy protein product that is sold dehydrated in bags. A full pound of meaty cremini mushrooms, pulsed fine in a food processor and deeply browned in a skillet, boosted the savory flavor and meaty texture of our meatball mixture. Since both of these ingredients were crumbly, we needed a strong binder. Stirring panko bread crumbs and aquafaba (the liquid from canned chickpeas) into the mix helped. We also found that 4 ounces of chopped eggplant, sautéed with the mushrooms, was a lovely silky additional binder without too strong a flavor. To make the porcini powder, grind the dried porcini mushrooms in a spice grinder until they are reduced to fine dust.

Sauce
- 2 (28-ounce) cans crushed tomatoes
- 2 tablespoons extra-virgin olive oil
- 1 onion, chopped fine
- 1 teaspoon table salt
- ¼ teaspoon pepper
- 4 garlic cloves, minced
- 1 tablespoon tomato paste
- ¼ cup dry red wine
- ½ cup chopped fresh basil, divided
- ½ teaspoon sugar

Meatless Meatballs
- 1 pound cremini mushrooms, trimmed and quartered
- 4 ounces eggplant, cut into 1-inch pieces (1¾ cups)
- 1 onion, chopped
- 4 garlic cloves, minced
- 2 tablespoons extra-virgin olive oil
- ⅛ ounce dried porcini mushrooms, finely ground (1 tablespoon)
- 1 teaspoon table salt
- ¼ teaspoon pepper
- 12 ounces vegan protein crumbles, broken into small pieces
- 1 cup panko bread crumbs
- ¼ cup chopped fresh parsley
- 3 tablespoons aquafaba (page 16)

- 1 pound spaghetti
  Table salt for cooking pasta

1. For the sauce Process tomatoes in food processor until smooth, about 30 seconds. Heat oil in large pot over medium heat until shimmering. Add onion, salt, and pepper and cook until onion is softened and just beginning to brown, 5 to 7 minutes.

2. Stir in garlic and tomato paste and cook until fragrant, about 30 seconds. Stir in wine and cook, scraping up any browned bits, until evaporated, about 1 minute. Stir in processed tomatoes and bring to boil. Reduce heat to low and simmer gently until sauce is slightly thickened, 10 to 15 minutes. Off heat, stir in ¼ cup basil and sugar. Season with salt and pepper to taste; cover to keep warm. (Sauce can be refrigerated for up to 1 day.)

3. For the meatballs Meanwhile, adjust oven rack to upper-middle position and heat oven to 400 degrees. Line rimmed baking sheet with parchment paper and spray with vegetable oil spray. Pulse cremini mushrooms in clean, dry food processor until pieces are no larger than ¼ inch, 5 to 7 pulses; transfer to bowl. Pulse eggplant, onion, and garlic in now-empty processor until chopped fine, 6 to 8 pulses; transfer to bowl with mushrooms.

Spaghetti and
Meatless Meatballs

Hearty Vegetable Lasagna

Serves 8 to 10

Why This Recipe Works This stick-to-your-ribs plant-forward rendition of lasagna is so hearty and loaded with a variety of vegetables that we promise everyone will leave the table feeling satisfied. For a cheesy but not heavy filling element to stand in for ricotta cheese, we wanted something a bit lighter and fluffier than our regular Vegan Ricotta. After testing our way (unsuccessfully) through plant-based béchamel sauces, tofu-based fillings, and vegan soft cheeses, we found success in a winning combination of cooked cashews and cauliflower. Since both are relatively low in fiber and cashews are high in starch, they combined perfectly in a food processor with water and olive oil to mimic the texture of a soft ricotta-like cheese. We liked it so much that we even dolloped some on top after baking. Be sure to let the lasagna cool for the full 25 minutes to set up before cutting it.

Tomato Sauce

- 1 (28-ounce) can crushed tomatoes
- 1 (14.5-ounce) can diced tomatoes, drained
- ¼ cup chopped fresh basil
- 3 tablespoons extra-virgin olive oil
- 2 garlic cloves, minced
- 1 teaspoon sugar
- ½ teaspoon table salt
- ¼ teaspoon red pepper flakes

Filling

- 8 ounces cauliflower florets, cut into ½-inch pieces (2¼ cups)
- 1½ cups raw cashews, chopped
- 2 teaspoons table salt
- ¼ cup extra-virgin olive oil, divided
- 1 tablespoon chopped fresh basil

Vegetables

- 1 pound eggplant, peeled and cut into ½-inch pieces
- 1 pound white mushrooms, trimmed and sliced thin
- 3 tablespoons extra-virgin olive oil, divided
- 1 garlic clove, minced
- ¾ teaspoon table salt, divided
- 1 pound zucchini, cut into ½-inch pieces

Lasagna

- 12 no-boil lasagna noodles
- 1 tablespoon extra-virgin olive oil
- 1 tablespoon chopped fresh basil

4. Heat oil in 12-inch nonstick skillet over medium heat until shimmering. Add processed vegetables, ground porcini mushrooms, salt, and pepper, cover, and cook, stirring occasionally, until vegetables have released their liquid, about 5 minutes. Uncover, increase heat to medium-high, and cook until vegetables are well browned, about 15 minutes; transfer to large bowl.

5. Add protein crumbles, panko, parsley, and aquafaba to bowl with browned vegetables and toss to combine. Using your hands, knead mixture well until cohesive and sticky, about 1 minute.

6. Shape vegetable mixture into 24 meatballs (about 2 tablespoons each) and space evenly on prepared sheet. Bake until browned and firm, 25 to 30 minutes, gently turning meatballs and rotating sheet halfway through baking.

7. Meanwhile, bring 4 quarts water to boil in large pot. Add pasta and 1 tablespoon salt and cook, stirring often, until al dente. Reserve ½ cup cooking water, then drain pasta and return it to pot. Measure out 4 cups sauce and toss with pasta to combine. Adjust consistency with reserved cooking water as needed and season with salt and pepper to taste. Top individual portions of spaghetti with meatballs and sprinkle with remaining ¼ cup basil. Serve, passing remaining sauce separately.

Big-Batch Meatless Meat Sauce with Chickpeas and Mushrooms

Makes 6 cups; enough for 2 pounds pasta

Having a big batch of red sauce portioned out in the freezer can be a lifesaver on busy nights. For a crowd-pleasing vegan version of a classic tomato-meat sauce, we started with cremini mushrooms and tomato paste—both rich sources of savory umami. Extra-virgin olive oil did double duty, both enriching the sauce and helping to toast the aromatics: garlic, dried oregano, and red pepper flakes. We bulked up the sauce with chopped chickpeas. To thin the sauce without diluting its flavor, we added vegetable broth. Make sure to rinse the chickpeas after pulsing them in the food processor or the sauce will be too thick.

- 10 ounces cremini mushrooms, trimmed
- 1 onion, chopped
- 1 (15-ounce) can chickpeas, rinsed
- 6 tablespoons extra-virgin olive oil, divided
- 1 teaspoon table salt
- ¼ cup tomato paste
- 5 garlic cloves, minced
- 1¼ teaspoons dried oregano
- ¼ teaspoon red pepper flakes
- 1 (28-ounce) can crushed tomatoes
- 2 cups vegetable broth
- 2 tablespoons chopped fresh basil

1. Working in batches, pulse mushrooms in food processor until pieces are no larger than ⅛ to ¼ inch, 7 to 10 pulses, scraping down sides of bowl as needed; transfer to bowl. Pulse onion in now-empty food processor until finely chopped, 7 to 10 pulses, scraping down sides of bowl as needed; set aside separately. Pulse chickpeas in again-empty food processor until chopped into ¼-inch pieces, 7 to 10 pulses. Transfer chickpeas to fine-mesh strainer and rinse under cold running water until water runs clear; drain well.

2. Heat 5 tablespoons oil in Dutch oven over medium-high heat until shimmering. Add mushrooms and salt and cook, stirring occasionally, until mushrooms are browned and fond has formed on bottom of pot, about 8 minutes.

3. Stir in onion and cook until softened, about 5 minutes. Add tomato paste and cook, stirring constantly, until mixture is rust-colored, 1 to 2 minutes. Reduce heat to medium and push vegetables to sides of pot. Add remaining 1 tablespoon oil, garlic, oregano, and pepper flakes to center and cook, stirring constantly, until fragrant, about 30 seconds. Stir in tomatoes and broth; bring to simmer over high heat. Reduce heat to low and simmer sauce for 5 minutes, stirring occasionally.

4. Stir drained chickpeas into sauce in pot and simmer until sauce is slightly thickened, about 15 minutes. Stir in basil and season with salt and pepper to taste. (Sauce can be refrigerated for up to 2 days or frozen for up to 1 month.)

1. For the tomato sauce Process all ingredients in food processor until smooth, scraping down sides of bowl as needed, about 30 seconds. Transfer sauce to bowl and set aside. (Sauce can be refrigerated for up to 1 day.)

2. For the filling Bring 3 quarts water to boil in large saucepan. Add cauliflower florets, cashews, and salt and cook until cauliflower is very soft and falls apart easily when poked with fork, about 20 minutes. Drain cauliflower mixture and let cool slightly, about 5 minutes.

3. Process cauliflower mixture, 3 tablespoons oil, and ¼ cup water in clean, dry food processor until smooth, scraping down sides of bowl as needed, about 2 minutes (mixture will be slightly grainy). Season with salt and pepper to taste. Transfer ¼ cup mixture to bowl and stir in remaining 1 tablespoon oil and basil; set aside for topping. (Mixtures can be refrigerated for up to 3 days.)

4. For the vegetables Adjust oven rack to upper-middle position and heat oven to 450 degrees. Toss eggplant and mushrooms with 2 tablespoons oil, garlic, and ½ teaspoon salt in bowl, then spread in even layer on rimmed baking sheet. Toss zucchini with remaining 1 tablespoon oil and remaining ¼ teaspoon salt in now-empty bowl. Roast eggplant-mushroom mixture until beginning to wilt, about 15 minutes. Remove sheet from oven, stir zucchini into vegetables, and continue to roast, stirring occasionally, until mushrooms are lightly browned, eggplant and zucchini are tender, and most of juices have evaporated, 15 to 20 minutes. Set aside. (Cooked vegetables can be refrigerated for up to 1 day.)

5. For the lasagna Adjust oven rack to middle position and heat oven to 375 degrees. Grease 13 by 9-inch baking dish. Spread 1⅓ cups tomato sauce over bottom of dish. Arrange 4 noodles on top. Spread half of cauliflower filling over

Hearty Vegetable Lasagna

noodles, followed by half of vegetables. Spread 1⅓ cups tomato sauce over vegetables. Repeat layering with 4 noodles, remaining cauliflower filling, and remaining vegetables. Arrange remaining 4 noodles on top, and cover completely with remaining tomato sauce.

6. Cover dish with aluminum foil and bake until edges are bubbling, 45 to 50 minutes, rotating dish halfway through baking. Dollop lasagna evenly with 8 to 10 spoonfuls of reserved cauliflower topping, and let cool for 25 minutes. Drizzle with oil, sprinkle with basil, and serve.

Baked Ziti with Creamy Leeks, Kale, and Sun-Dried Tomatoes
Serves 4 to 6

Why This Recipe Works This fresh take on baked ziti is substantial and gratifyingly vegetable-forward. Taking a cue from our Spaghetti with Spring Vegetables (page 162), we wondered if we could create a creamy, aromatic sauce for baked pasta with a vegetable foundation, and it turned out

that the often underestimated leek emerged as the winner. We sautéed 2 pounds of sliced leeks until they began to caramelize, added some thyme, deglazed with a splash of dry white wine, and then simmered the mixture in vegetable broth until the leeks were meltingly soft and ready to be blended into a smooth, velvety sauce. Meanwhile, in the pot we used to parcook our pasta, we sautéed baby kale and sun-dried tomatoes with a generous dose of garlic plus red pepper flakes, mixed in our sauce and cooked pasta, and then baked it all tightly covered in a baking dish so the pasta could finish cooking while absorbing some of the flavorful leek sauce. For a savory, crispy topping, we combined panko bread crumbs with our Vegan Parmesan Substitute (or dairy Parmesan), plus a bit of fragrant lemon zest, and broiled it all to crispy, golden baked-pasta perfection. If you can't find baby kale, substitute 8 ounces kale, stemmed and chopped.

½ cup panko bread crumbs
¼ cup Vegan Parmesan Substitute (page 27) or grated dairy Parmesan
¼ cup extra-virgin olive oil, divided
½ teaspoon grated lemon zest, plus lemon wedges for serving
2 pounds leeks, white and light green parts only, halved lengthwise, sliced thin, and washed thoroughly
¾ teaspoon table salt, divided, plus salt for cooking pasta
⅛ teaspoon pepper
2 teaspoons minced fresh thyme or ¾ teaspoon dried
½ cup dry white wine
2 cups vegetable broth
1 pound ziti
6 garlic cloves, minced
¼ teaspoon red pepper flakes
6 cups (6 ounces) baby kale
¼ cup oil-packed sun-dried tomatoes, chopped coarse
2 tablespoons chopped fresh parsley

1. Adjust oven rack to upper-middle position and heat oven to 450 degrees. Combine panko, vegan Parmesan substitute, 1 tablespoon oil, and lemon zest in bowl; set aside.

2. Heat 2 tablespoons oil in Dutch oven over medium heat until shimmering. Stir in leeks, ½ teaspoon salt, and pepper and cook until softened and lightly browned, 8 to 12 minutes. Stir in thyme and cook until fragrant, about 30 seconds. Stir in wine, scraping up any browned bits, and cook until evaporated, about 2 minutes. Stir in broth and bring to boil. Reduce heat to low, cover, and simmer until leeks are very tender, about 8 minutes. Process leek mixture in blender on high speed until very smooth, about 2 minutes. Season with salt and pepper to taste.

3. Meanwhile, bring 4 quarts water to boil in Dutch oven. Add pasta and 1 tablespoon salt and cook, stirring often, until nearly al dente. Reserve 1½ cups cooking water, then drain pasta. Cook remaining 1 tablespoon oil, garlic, and pepper flakes in now-empty pot over medium heat until fragrant, about 1 minute. Stir in kale, sun-dried tomatoes, and remaining ¼ teaspoon salt and cook, stirring occasionally, until kale is wilted and tomatoes are softened, about 3 minutes. Off heat, stir in cooked pasta, leek mixture, and 1 cup reserved cooking water; season with salt and pepper to taste. Adjust consistency with remaining ½ cup cooking water as needed (sauce should be thick but still creamy).

4. Transfer pasta mixture to broiler-safe 13 by 9-inch baking dish, smoothing top with rubber spatula. Cover tightly with aluminum foil and bake until sauce is bubbling, 10 to 12 minutes. Remove baking dish from oven and heat broiler. Remove aluminum foil and sprinkle panko mixture evenly over pasta. Broil until panko mixture is golden brown, about 2 minutes. Sprinkle with parsley and serve with lemon wedges.

Pasta Salad with Asparagus and Red Peppers

Serves 6 to 8

Why This Recipe Works A great homemade pasta salad is cohesive and thought-out rather than just thrown together with odds and ends from the refrigerator. Store-bought versions often seem either to involve a heavy creamy dressing that masks the colors and flavors of the other ingredients or to be laden with a thick, acidic vinaigrette and sometimes, oddly, chunks of salami. We wanted something lighter, more refreshing, and vegan-optional, so we elevated our pasta salad with roasted asparagus and red bell peppers and a garlic-infused dressing made with bright lemon juice (rather than vinegar, which made it too acidic and leached color from our vegetables). Better than any sad assembly from the deli case, this pasta salad looks just as good as it tastes.

1½ pounds asparagus, trimmed and cut into 2-inch lengths
3 large red bell peppers, stemmed, seeded, and cut into 1½-inch pieces
2 tablespoons plus ½ cup extra-virgin olive oil, divided
1¼ teaspoons table salt, divided, plus salt for cooking pasta
¼ teaspoon pepper

Pasta Salad with Asparagus and Red Peppers

1 pound fusilli
1 garlic clove, minced
½ teaspoon grated lemon zest plus ¼ cup juice (2 lemons)
⅓ cup Vegan Parmesan Substitute (page 27) or grated dairy Parmesan
3 tablespoons chopped fresh chives

1. Adjust oven rack to middle position and heat oven to 425 degrees. Toss asparagus and bell peppers with 2 tablespoons oil, ½ teaspoon salt, and pepper in bowl. Transfer vegetables to baking sheet and roast until tender and lightly browned, 15 to 17 minutes. Let cool completely.

2. Meanwhile, bring 4 quarts water to boil in large pot. Add pasta and 1 tablespoon salt and cook, stirring often, until al dente. Drain pasta.

3. Whisk garlic, lemon zest and juice, remaining ½ cup oil, and remaining ¾ teaspoon salt together in large bowl. Add vegan Parmesan substitute, chives, roasted vegetables, and pasta and toss to combine; let salad cool completely. Season with salt and pepper to taste, and serve. (Pasta salad can be refrigerated for up to 24 hours.)

Orzo Salad with Arugula and Sun-Dried Tomatoes

Serves 4

Why This Recipe Works Orzo serves as a perfect vehicle for warm or chilled pasta salads. Its small rice-like shape provides just enough bulk to make a satisfying salad that can act as a partner for any number of other dishes, from Chickpea Cakes (page 108) to Roasted Artichokes with Lemon and Basil (page 188). We decided that our orzo salad would burst with flavors that made us feel like we were visiting the sunny Mediterranean. After cooking and draining the pasta, we transferred the still-warm orzo to a rimmed baking sheet to cool and tossed it with some olive oil to prevent clumping. We then dressed the orzo with a simple vinaigrette made with balsamic vinegar and a bit of garlic; the subtle dressing added tangy flavor but still allowed the rest of the ingredients to shine through. We chose plenty of bold mix-in ingredients: our Vegan Parmesan Substitute (or dairy Parmesan), peppery fresh arugula, sweet sun-dried tomatoes, briny olives, aromatic basil, and toasted pine nuts for a slight nutty crunch.

1¼ cups orzo
½ teaspoon table salt, plus salt for cooking pasta
¼ cup extra-virgin olive oil, divided, plus extra for serving
3 tablespoons balsamic vinegar
2 garlic cloves, minced
½ teaspoon pepper
2 ounces (2 cups) baby arugula, chopped
½ cup Vegan Parmesan Substitute (page 27) or grated dairy Parmesan cheese
½ cup oil-packed sun-dried tomatoes, minced
½ cup pitted kalamata olives, halved
½ cup chopped fresh basil
¼ cup pine nuts, toasted

1. Bring 2 quarts water to boil in large pot. Add orzo and 1½ teaspoons salt and cook, stirring often, until al dente. Drain orzo and transfer to rimmed baking sheet. Toss with 1 tablespoon oil and let cool completely, about 15 minutes.

2. Whisk vinegar, garlic, pepper, salt, and remaining 3 tablespoons oil together in large bowl. Add arugula, vegan Parmesan substitute, tomatoes, olives, basil, pine nuts, and cooled orzo and toss to coat. Season with salt and pepper to taste.

3. Let salad sit at room temperature for 30 minutes to allow flavors to meld. Serve, drizzling with extra oil.

Toasted Orzo Pilaf with Fennel, Orange, and Olives

Serves 6 to 8

Why This Recipe Works This unusual pilaf is super-flavorful thanks to the fact that we toasted the orzo until golden brown before adding liquid. We turned to creative Greek-inspired flavors for this sophisticated dish, first sautéing fennel and onion in olive oil and then adding aromatics including garlic, orange zest, and fennel seeds. We browned the orzo in the skillet before adding the cooking liquid; a combination of vegetable broth, white wine, and water provided the most balanced flavor. Kalamata olives gave our pilaf an umami quality while adding contrasting texture and briny flavor. Finally, we stirred in some chopped toasted walnuts; their nutty richness enhanced the toasted qualities of the orzo. A pinch of nutmeg finished our pilaf with a complementary yet subtle warmth.

2 tablespoons extra-virgin olive oil
1 fennel bulb, stalks discarded, bulb halved, cored, and chopped fine
1 onion, chopped fine
¾ teaspoon table salt
2 garlic cloves, minced
1 teaspoon grated orange zest
¾ teaspoon fennel seeds
  Pinch red pepper flakes
2⅔ cups orzo
2 cups vegetable broth
1½ cups water
¾ cup dry white wine
½ cup pitted kalamata olives, chopped
½ cup toasted walnuts, chopped
  Pinch ground nutmeg

1. Heat oil in 12-inch nonstick skillet over medium heat until shimmering. Add fennel, onion, and salt and cook until softened and lightly browned, 5 to 7 minutes. Stir in garlic, orange zest, fennel seeds, and pepper flakes and cook until fragrant, about 30 seconds. Add orzo and cook, stirring frequently, until orzo is lightly browned, about 5 minutes.

2. Stir in broth, water, and wine and bring to boil. Cook, stirring occasionally, until all liquid has been absorbed and orzo is al dente, 10 to 15 minutes. Stir in olives, walnuts, and nutmeg, and season with salt and pepper to taste. Serve.

Spiced Vegetable Couscous

Serves 4 to 6

Why This Recipe Works This easy vegetable couscous dish was inspired by culinary traditions of North Africa, where couscous is frequently used in all manner of dishes. We chose a colorful combination of cauliflower, zucchini, and red bell pepper. To encourage deep caramelization on the cauliflower, we cut it into small, even pieces and started it in a cold pan, ensuring that it cooked through before developing a golden exterior. We then quickly sautéed zucchini and bell pepper with garlic, lemon zest, and ras el hanout—a flavorful North African spice blend. Marjoram, added at the end, gave a hit of freshness. We prefer our homemade Ras el Hanout; you can use store-bought, but flavor and spice level vary by brand.

- 1 head cauliflower (2 pounds), cored and cut into 1-inch florets
- 6 tablespoons extra-virgin olive oil, divided, plus extra for serving
- 1¼ teaspoons table salt, divided
- ½ teaspoon pepper
- 1½ cups couscous
- 1 zucchini, cut into ½-inch pieces
- 1 red bell pepper, stemmed, seeded, and cut into ½-inch pieces
- 4 garlic cloves, minced
- 2 teaspoons Ras el Hanout
- 1 teaspoon grated lemon zest, plus lemon wedges for serving
- 1¾ cups vegetable broth
- 1 tablespoon minced fresh marjoram

1. Toss cauliflower florets with 2 tablespoons oil, ¾ teaspoon salt, and pepper in 12-inch nonstick skillet. Cover and cook over medium-high heat until florets start to brown and edges just start to become translucent, about 5 minutes.

2. Continue to cook, uncovered, stirring every 2 minutes, until florets turn golden brown in several spots, about 10 minutes. Transfer to bowl and wipe skillet clean with paper towels.

3. Heat 2 tablespoons oil in now-empty skillet over medium-high heat until shimmering. Add couscous and cook, stirring frequently, until grains begin to brown, 3 to 5 minutes. Transfer to separate bowl and wipe skillet clean with paper towels.

4. Heat remaining 2 tablespoons oil in again-empty skillet over medium-high heat until just smoking. Add zucchini, bell pepper, and remaining ½ teaspoon salt and cook until tender, 6 to 8 minutes. Stir in garlic, ras el hanout, and lemon zest and cook until fragrant, about 30 seconds. Stir in broth and bring to simmer.

Ras el Hanout

Makes about ½ cup

A mix of warm spices delivers big flavor. If you can't find Aleppo pepper, substitute ½ teaspoon paprika plus ½ teaspoon red pepper flakes.

- 16 cardamom pods
- 4 teaspoons coriander seeds
- 4 teaspoons cumin seeds
- 2 teaspoons anise seeds
- 2 teaspoons ground dried Aleppo pepper
- ½ teaspoon allspice berries
- ¼ teaspoon black peppercorns
- 4 teaspoons ground ginger
- 2 teaspoons ground nutmeg
- 2 teaspoons ground cinnamon

Process cardamom pods, coriander, cumin, anise, Aleppo pepper, allspice, and peppercorns in spice grinder until finely ground, about 30 seconds. Stir in ginger, nutmeg, and cinnamon.

5. Remove skillet from heat and stir in couscous. Cover and let sit until liquid is absorbed and couscous is tender, about 7 minutes. Add cauliflower and marjoram and fluff with fork to combine. Season with salt and pepper to taste and drizzle with extra oil. Serve with lemon wedges.

Moroccan-Style Couscous with Chickpeas

Serves 6 **FAST**

Why This Recipe Works Couscous with chickpeas and vegetables is a popular Moroccan dish, and we tried a few different approaches for our variation before settling on a game plan: Toast the couscous for nuttiness, sauté the vegetables, toast the spices, add chickpeas, simmer, and finally add the couscous, which we needed only to hydrate with boiling water. We tasted our way through many vegetables and ultimately limited our selection to carrots, onions, and peas, each of which brought a distinctive flavor, texture, and color. Classic Moroccan spices (coriander, ground ginger, and ground anise) supported the vegetables' flavor. Three cloves of garlic jazzed up the vegetable broth, and a hefty amount of parsley stirred in at the end rounded out all the flavors.

Moroccan-Style Couscous with Chickpeas

7 minutes. Stir in garlic, coriander, ginger, and anise and cook until fragrant, about 30 seconds. Stir in broth and chickpeas and bring to simmer.

3. Remove skillet from heat and stir in peas and couscous. Cover and let sit until liquid is absorbed and couscous is tender, about 7 minutes. Add parsley and fluff with fork to combine. Season with salt and pepper to taste and drizzle with extra oil. Serve with lemon wedges.

Hearty Pearl Couscous with Eggplant, Spinach, and White Beans
Serves 6

Why This Recipe Works Pearl couscous serves as the base for this hearty meal with great visual appeal. Also known as Israeli couscous, pearl couscous has larger grains than regular couscous—about the size of a caper. A superflavorful spice blend made with citrusy sumac, nutty-sweet fenugreek, and floral cardamom further gave the dish an Israeli-inspired identity. We tossed eggplant with a teaspoon of the blend before microwaving, which bloomed the spices' flavors and quickly cooked off the eggplant's excess moisture, bypassing the need to salt and drain the eggplant. We then seared the eggplant to develop savory browning before building an aromatic broth base in which to cook our couscous. Adding convenient canned beans and baby spinach made it a meal. Do not substitute regular couscous in this dish, as it requires a different cooking method and will not work in this recipe.

- ¼ cup extra-virgin olive oil, divided, plus extra for serving
- 1½ cups couscous
- 2 carrots, peeled and chopped fine
- 1 onion, chopped fine
- 1 teaspoon table salt
- 3 garlic cloves, minced
- 1 teaspoon ground coriander
- 1 teaspoon ground ginger
- ¼ teaspoon ground anise seed
- 1¾ cups vegetable broth
- 1 (15-ounce) can chickpeas, rinsed
- 1½ cups frozen peas
- ½ cup chopped fresh parsley
  Lemon wedges

- 1 teaspoon ground sumac
- 1 teaspoon ground fenugreek
- ½ teaspoon table salt
- ½ teaspoon pepper
- ¼ teaspoon ground cardamom
- 1 pound eggplant, cut into ½-inch pieces
- 1½ cups pearl couscous
- 5 tablespoons extra-virgin olive oil, divided, plus extra for serving
- 1 onion, chopped
- 3 garlic cloves, minced
- 1 tablespoon tomato paste
- 2 cups vegetable broth
- 1 (15-ounce) can great Northern beans, rinsed
- 3 ounces (3 cups) baby spinach

1. Heat 2 tablespoons oil in 12-inch skillet over medium-high heat until shimmering. Add couscous and cook, stirring frequently, until grains begin to brown, 3 to 5 minutes. Transfer to bowl and wipe skillet clean with paper towels.

2. Heat remaining 2 tablespoons oil in now-empty skillet over medium heat until shimmering. Add carrots, onion, and salt and cook until softened and lightly browned, 5 to

1. Combine sumac, fenugreek, salt, pepper, and cardamom in small bowl. Line large plate with double layer of coffee filters and spray with vegetable oil spray. Toss eggplant with ½ teaspoon spice mixture and spread evenly on coffee filters. Microwave eggplant, uncovered, until dry to touch and slightly shriveled, 7 to 10 minutes, tossing halfway through microwaving.

2. Heat couscous and 2 tablespoons oil in 12-inch nonstick skillet over medium heat, stirring frequently, until about half of grains are golden brown, about 5 minutes. Transfer to bowl and wipe skillet clean with paper towels.

3. Toss eggplant with 1 teaspoon spice mixture. Heat 1 tablespoon oil in now-empty skillet over medium-high heat until shimmering. Add eggplant and cook, stirring occasionally, until well browned, 5 to 7 minutes. Transfer to separate bowl.

4. Heat remaining 2 tablespoons oil in again-empty skillet over medium heat until shimmering. Add onion and cook until softened and lightly browned, 5 to 7 minutes. Stir in garlic, tomato paste, and remaining spice mixture and cook until fragrant, about 1 minute.

5. Stir in broth, beans, and couscous and bring to simmer. Reduce heat to medium-low, cover, and simmer, stirring occasionally, until broth is absorbed and couscous is tender, 9 to 12 minutes. Off heat, stir in spinach and eggplant, cover, and let sit until warmed through and spinach is wilted, about 3 minutes. Season with salt and pepper to taste and drizzle with extra oil. Serve.

Spicy Peanut
Rice Noodle Bowl

Spicy Peanut Rice Noodle Bowl

Serves 4 to 6   FAST

Why This Recipe Works This sweet, savory, and spicy noodle bowl is a real stunner, boasting a colorful medley of texturally interesting toppings. We combined tender rice noodles with savory edamame, tangy lightly pickled carrots, and crunchy cabbage, and we draped it all with a rich peanut sauce that's a little zingy, a little sweet, and enlivened with a hint of curry powder for aromatic appeal. Instead of taking the time to pickle our carrots in advance of making the dish, we simply added seasoned rice vinegar to shredded carrots and let them sit while the rice noodles softened in hot water. After the soaking period, we started the cooking process by first quickly sautéing the edamame just until it was speckled brown but still maintained a tender-crisp texture and fresh flavor. After removing the beans from the skillet, we finished cooking the noodles in the same pan with half of our sauce and some water until the noodles were perfectly tender. Cooking the noodles in the sauce lightly glazed and flavored them. After topping our noodle bowls with the veggies, we added plenty of garnishes—fragrant Thai basil, chopped peanuts, lime wedges, and a light pour of additional sauce were the perfect finish. To make this sauce spicier, add the seeds from the chiles. You can use serrano or jalapeño chiles in place of Thai chiles. If you can't find Thai basil you can substitute regular basil. We prefer the flavor of seasoned rice vinegar to pickle the carrots in this recipe.

1 cup shredded carrots
5 tablespoons seasoned rice vinegar, divided
12 ounces (¼-inch wide) rice noodles
¼ cup vegetable oil, divided
2 Thai chiles, stemmed, seeded, and minced
3 garlic cloves, minced
1 tablespoon grated fresh ginger
1½ teaspoons curry powder
⅓ cup creamy peanut butter
2 tablespoons soy sauce
1 tablespoon sugar
1 cup frozen edamame
1 cup shredded red cabbage
⅓ cup dry-roasted peanuts, chopped
2 tablespoons torn fresh Thai basil
Lime wedges

1. Combine carrots and 2 tablespoons vinegar in small bowl; set aside. Bring 4 quarts water to boil in large pot. Remove from heat, add noodles, and let sit, stirring occasionally, until soft and pliable but not fully tender. Drain noodles.

2. Meanwhile, heat 1 tablespoon oil in medium saucepan over medium heat until shimmering. Stir in Thai chiles, garlic, ginger, and curry powder and cook until fragrant, about 30 seconds. Stir in ½ cup water, peanut butter, soy sauce, sugar, and remaining 3 tablespoons vinegar and bring to simmer. Cook, stirring occasionally, until slightly thickened and flavors meld, about 2 minutes. Adjust consistency as needed with additional water. Transfer sauce to bowl.

3. Heat 1 tablespoon oil in 12-inch nonstick skillet over medium-high heat until just smoking. Add edamame and cook until spotty brown but still bright green, about 2 minutes; transfer to bowl. In now-empty skillet, heat remaining 2 tablespoons oil over medium heat until shimmering. Add drained noodles, 1¼ cups water, and ½ cup peanut sauce and cook until sauce has thickened slightly and noodles are well coated and tender, about 1 minute.

4. Divide noodles among individual serving bowls, then top with carrots, edamame, and cabbage. Drizzle with remaining peanut sauce, sprinkle with peanuts and basil, and serve with lime wedges.

Tofu Pad Thai
Serves 4

Why This Recipe Works With its sweet-sour-salty-spicy sauce, tender rice noodles, bean sprout topping, and bits of scrambled egg or shrimp, pad thai is Thailand's most well-known noodle dish. We wanted an equally craveable vegan version that featured crispy tofu as its protein. But no matter the protein, getting the noodles right is paramount to pad thai: We soaked rice noodles in hot water to soften them before stir-frying for tender but not sticky noodles. To create the punchy but balanced flavor profile, we combined our Fish Sauce Substitute, sugar, cayenne, and vinegar, adding tamarind paste for the bright, fruity, pleasantly sour taste essential to this dish. For the crispy tofu, we cut extra-firm tofu into bite-size pieces, dredged them in cornstarch, and quickly pan-fried them until golden. Chopped peanuts, bean sprouts, thinly sliced scallions, and lime wedges completed our authentic-tasting pad thai. For an accurate measurement of boiling water, bring a full kettle of water to a boil and then measure out the desired amount. This dish comes together very quickly, so make sure to prep all your ingredients before you start cooking.

TAMARIND PASTE
Sweet-tart, dark brownish-red tamarind is frequently used in Thai cuisine and is a necessary ingredient for an authentic-looking and -tasting pad thai. It's commonly sold in paste (also called pulp) as well as in concentrate form. The paste is firm, sticky, and filled with seeds and fibers, which is why we strain it. We favor tamarind paste because it has a fresher, brighter flavor than the concentrate.

Sauce
- 3 tablespoons tamarind paste
- ¾ cup boiling water
- ¼ cup Fish Sauce Substitute (page 22)
- 3 tablespoons sugar
- 2 tablespoons rice vinegar
- 1 tablespoon vegetable oil
- ⅛ teaspoon cayenne pepper

Noodles, Tofu, and Garnish
- 8 ounces (¼-inch-wide) rice noodles
- 14 ounces extra-firm tofu, cut into ¾-inch pieces
- ⅓ cup cornstarch
- ¼ cup vegetable oil, divided
- 1 shallot, minced
- 3 garlic cloves, minced
- 6 ounces (3 cups) bean sprouts
- 4 scallions, sliced thin on bias
- ¼ cup minced fresh cilantro
- 2 tablespoons chopped dry-roasted peanuts
  Lime wedges

1. **For the sauce** Soak tamarind paste in boiling water until softened, about 10 minutes. Strain mixture through fine-mesh strainer, pressing on solids to extract as much pulp as possible; discard solids. Whisk fish sauce substitute, sugar, vinegar, oil, and cayenne into tamarind liquid in bowl.

2. **For the noodles, tofu, and garnish** Bring 4 quarts water to boil in large pot. Remove from heat, add noodles, and let sit, stirring occasionally, until soft and pliable but not fully tender. Drain noodles. Meanwhile, spread tofu on paper towel–lined baking sheet and let drain for 20 minutes. Gently pat dry with paper towels.

3. Toss drained tofu with cornstarch in bowl. Heat 3 tablespoons oil in 12-inch nonstick skillet over medium-high heat until just smoking. Add tofu and cook, turning as needed, until crisp and browned on all sides, 8 to 10 minutes; transfer to paper towel–lined plate to drain.

4. Heat remaining 1 tablespoon oil in now-empty skillet over medium heat until shimmering. Add shallot and garlic and cook until lightly browned, about 2 minutes.

5. Whisk sauce to recombine. Add noodles and sauce to skillet, increase heat to high, and cook, tossing gently, until noodles are evenly coated, about 1 minute. Add browned tofu, bean sprouts, and scallions and cook, tossing gently, until tofu is warmed through and noodles are tender, about 2 minutes. Season with salt to taste, sprinkle with cilantro and peanuts, and serve with lime wedges.

Spicy Basil Rice Noodles with Crispy Tofu, Snap Peas, and Bell Peppers

Serves 4 to 6

Why This Recipe Works These brightly flavored Thai noodles are fragrant with fresh basil and infused with heat thanks to a paste of chiles, garlic, and shallots. Cooking the mixture briefly deepened and mellowed the flavor of the aromatics. Fish Sauce Substitute, brown sugar, lime juice, and broth added sweet and savory flavors. A whopping 2 cups of basil gives this dish its trademark freshness; we stirred it in at the end to keep its flavor prominent. Pan-fried tofu, coated with a light layer of cornstarch, offered contrasting creamy and crispy textures, and snap peas and red bell pepper strips added crunch. To make this dish spicier, add the chile seeds. If you can't find ⅜-inch-wide rice noodles, substitute ¼-inch-wide rice noodles. If you can't find Thai chiles, substitute serranos or jalapeños. If you can't find Thai basil, you can use Italian basil.

12	ounces (⅜-inch-wide) rice noodles
14	ounces extra-firm tofu, cut into 1-inch pieces
8	Thai chiles, stemmed and seeded
6	garlic cloves, peeled
4	shallots, peeled
2	cups vegetable broth
¼	cup Fish Sauce Substitute (page 22)
¼	cup packed brown sugar
3	tablespoons lime juice (2 limes)
¼	teaspoon table salt
⅛	teaspoon pepper
½	cup cornstarch
7	tablespoons vegetable oil, divided
6	ounces sugar snap peas, strings removed
1	red bell pepper, stemmed, seeded, sliced into ¼-inch-wide strips, and halved crosswise
2	cups fresh Thai basil leaves

SOAKING RICE NOODLES

Undersoaked These noodles are undersoaked and are still too hard. They will take too long to stir-fry.

Oversoaked These noodles are oversoaked and are too soft and gummy. They will overcook when stir-fried and stay tangled.

Properly soaked These noodles are perfectly soaked and just softened. They will turn tender when stir-fried and remain separated.

1. Bring 4 quarts water to boil in large pot. Remove from heat, add noodles, and let sit, stirring occasionally, until soft and pliable but not fully tender. Drain noodles. While noodles soak, spread tofu on paper towel–lined baking sheet and let drain for 20 minutes. Gently pat dry with paper towels.

2. Meanwhile, pulse chiles, garlic, and shallots in food processor into smooth paste, about 20 pulses, scraping down bowl as needed. Whisk broth, fish sauce substitute, sugar, and lime juice together in bowl.

3. Sprinkle tofu with salt and pepper, then toss with cornstarch in bowl. Heat 3 tablespoons oil in 12-inch nonstick skillet over medium-high heat until just smoking. Add tofu and cook, turning as needed, until crisp and browned on all sides, 8 to 10 minutes; transfer to paper towel–lined plate to drain.

4. Wipe out now-empty skillet with paper towels, add 1 tablespoon oil, and heat over high heat until just smoking. Add snap peas and bell pepper and cook, stirring often, until vegetables are crisp-tender and beginning to brown, 3 to 5 minutes; transfer to bowl.

5. Add remaining 3 tablespoons oil to now-empty skillet and heat over medium-high heat until shimmering. Add processed chile mixture and cook until moisture evaporates and color deepens, 3 to 5 minutes. Add drained noodles and broth mixture and cook, tossing gently, until sauce has thickened and noodles are well coated and tender, 5 to 10 minutes.

6. Stir in cooked vegetables and basil and cook until basil wilts slightly, about 1 minute. Top individual portions with crispy tofu and serve.

Thai Curry Rice Noodles with Crispy Tofu and Broccoli

Serves 4

Why This Recipe Works Morsels of crispy tofu, tender vegetables (broccoli, red bell pepper, and scallions), and hearty rice noodles mingle with a coconut-curry sauce in a dish that tastes so complex you won't believe it's a cinch to prepare. The tofu, vegetables, and noodles and sauce are cooked in stages and then combined in the same skillet. While the noodles hydrated in a bowl of hot water, we crisped our tofu cubes after dusting them with a light coating of cornstarch. Then we wiped out the skillet, sautéed our vegetables, stirred in deeply aromatic curry paste, and built the sauce with coconut milk, some water, and just a teaspoon of brown sugar for a hint of sweetness. We added the softened noodles to the skillet with the vegetables and sauce and simmered everything together until the noodles were cooked through and the sauce was thickened. To finish, we topped the noodles with the crispy tofu, followed by a generous helping of fresh Thai basil. Fresh lime wedges offered a welcome splash of brightness. If you can't find Thai basil, you can substitute Italian basil.

8 ounces (¼-inch-wide) rice noodles

14 ounces firm tofu, cut into ¾-inch pieces

¾ teaspoon table salt, divided

⅛ teaspoon pepper

3 tablespoons cornstarch

3 tablespoons vegetable oil, divided

6 ounces broccoli, florets cut into 1-inch pieces, stalks peeled and cut into ½-inch pieces

1 red bell pepper, stemmed, seeded, and cut into ½-inch pieces

4 scallions, white parts cut into 1-inch lengths, green parts sliced thin

¼ cup Thai red curry paste

½ cup canned coconut milk

½ cup water

1 teaspoon packed brown sugar

¼ cup chopped fresh Thai basil
    Lime wedges

1. Bring 4 quarts water to boil in large pot. Remove from heat, add noodles, and let sit, stirring occasionally, until soft and pliable but not fully tender. Drain noodles and rinse with cold water until water runs clear. Drain noodles again and set aside. While noodles soak, spread tofu over paper towel–lined baking sheet and let drain for 20 minutes. Gently pat tofu dry with paper towels.

2. Sprinkle tofu with ¼ teaspoon salt and pepper, then toss with cornstarch in bowl. Heat 2 tablespoons oil in 12-inch nonstick skillet over medium-high heat until just smoking. Add tofu and cook, turning as needed, until crisp and browned on all sides, 8 to 10 minutes; transfer to paper towel–lined plate to drain.

3. Wipe out now-empty skillet with paper towels, add remaining 1 tablespoon oil, and heat over medium heat until shimmering. Add broccoli florets and stalks, bell pepper, scallion whites, and remaining ½ teaspoon salt and cook until softened and lightly browned, 3 to 5 minutes. Push vegetables to sides of skillet. Add curry paste to center and cook, mashing paste into skillet, until fragrant, about 30 seconds. Stir curry paste into vegetables, then stir in coconut milk, water, and sugar, scraping up any browned bits, and bring to simmer.

4. Add drained rice noodles, tossing to combine, and cook, tossing gently, until sauce has thickened slightly and noodles are well coated and tender, about 3 minutes. Season with salt and pepper to taste and top with crispy tofu, scallion greens, and basil. Serve with lime wedges.

Sweet Potato Noodles with Shiitakes and Spinach

Serves 4 to 6   `FAST`

Why This Recipe Works One of Korea's most beloved celebratory dishes is made using sweet potato starch noodles and vegetables for a result that is both stunning and delicious. The flavorful, balanced sauce made from sesame oil, soy sauce, sugar, sesame seeds, and garlic makes it clear why throughout much of history, Korean royalty kept this dish to themselves. Going with a variety of vegetables, we needed to stagger their cooking times to ensure that they were properly cooked. After cooking the noodles, we stir-fried earthy shiitake mushrooms and an onion. We then added carrots and scallions, which needed less time to cook. Last, the addition of stir-fried spinach helped bulk up the vegetable ratio in our simple but luxurious noodle dish. This dish often includes a thin egg omelet, and we have included a variation if you would like to try it. If you can't find sweet potato noodles (sometimes sold as sweet potato starch noodles or sweet potato glass noodles),

Sweet Potato Noodles
with Shiitakes, Spinach,
and Eggs

1. Bring 4 quarts water to boil in large pot. Remove from heat, add noodles, and let sit, stirring occasionally, until noodles are soft and pliable but not fully tender. Drain noodles and rinse under cold running water until chilled. Drain noodles again and toss with 2 teaspoons sesame oil; set aside.

2. Combine two-thirds garlic and 2 teaspoons vegetable oil in small bowl; set aside. Whisk soy sauce, sugar, sesame seeds, remaining 2 tablespoons sesame oil, and remaining garlic in second small bowl until sugar has dissolved; set aside.

3. Heat remaining 1 tablespoon vegetable oil in 12-inch skillet over high heat until just smoking. Add mushrooms, carrots, and onion and cook, stirring constantly, until onion and carrots are crisp-tender, 4 to 6 minutes. Add scallions and spinach and cook until wilted, about 2 minutes.

4. Push vegetables to 1 side of skillet. Add garlic mixture to clearing and cook, mashing mixture into skillet, until fragrant, about 30 seconds. Stir garlic mixture into vegetables. Add noodles and sauce and cook, stirring constantly, until mixture is thoroughly combined and noodles are well coated and tender, 2 to 4 minutes. Serve.

VARIATION

Sweet Potato Noodles with Shiitakes, Spinach, and Eggs

Lightly beat 2 large eggs in bowl. After step 2, heat 1 teaspoon vegetable oil in 12-inch nonstick skillet over medium heat until shimmering. Using paper towel, wipe out skillet, leaving thin film of oil on bottom and sides. Add beaten egg and gently tilt and shake skillet until mixture forms even 10-inch round omelet. Cover and cook until bottom of omelet is spotty brown and top is just set, about 30 seconds. Loosen edges of omelet with rubber spatula and slide onto cutting board. Cut omelet into 2-inch-wide strips. Slice each strip crosswise ¼ inch thick. Sprinkle omelet strips over finished dish before serving.

substitute cellophane noodles. Toast the sesame seeds in a dry skillet over medium heat until fragrant (about 1 minute), and then quickly remove the seeds from the pan to prevent the seeds from scorching. You will need a 12-inch nonstick skillet with a tight-fitting lid for this recipe.

- 8 ounces (⅛-inch-wide) dried sweet potato noodles, broken into 12-inch lengths
- 2 tablespoons plus 2 teaspoons toasted sesame oil, divided
- 3 garlic cloves, minced
- 1 tablespoon plus 2 teaspoons vegetable oil, divided
- ¼ cup soy sauce
- 3 tablespoons sugar
- 1 tablespoon sesame seeds, toasted
- 8 ounces shiitake mushrooms, stemmed and sliced thin
- 2 carrots, peeled and cut into 2-inch-long matchsticks
- 1 small onion, halved and sliced ½ inch thick
- 2 scallions, sliced thin
- 8 ounces (8 cups) baby spinach

PLANT POWER

CELLOPHANE NOODLES

Korean sweet potato noodles belong to the cellophane noodle family, also called glass noodles because of their translucence. These types of noodles, which can vary in thickness and be round or flat, are made from the extracted starch of sweet or white potatoes, yams, beans (such as mung beans), tapioca (from the cassava plant), or even the flowering canna lily. Cellophane noodles have a softer yet chewier texture (sometimes described as "bouncy") as compared to wheat noodles.

Vegetable Lo Mein

Serves 4 to 6 `FAST`

Why This Recipe Works Most takeout lo mein ends up being a disappointment, with mushy noodles, a greasy sauce, and barely any vegetables. We were after a crowd-pleasing, fresh-tasting lo mein with properly chewy noodles in a salty-sweet sauce with loads of veggies—and we wanted it in less time than it would take for takeout to arrive. A combination of classic Chinese ingredients made for a simple, balanced sweet-and-savory sauce. A full pound of meaty shiitake mushrooms paired with napa cabbage and sweet red bell peppers provided the vegetable substance we were looking for; we stir-fried the vegetables in batches so that each would get cooked to perfection. A hit of Asian chili-garlic sauce at the end brightened this dish and gave it a nice kick of heat. Fresh Chinese noodles may or may not contain egg; check the label if this is a concern. If Chinese noodles are unavailable, you may use spaghetti or linguine.

Sauce
- ½ cup vegetable broth
- 3 tablespoons soy sauce
- 2 tablespoons mushroom oyster sauce
- 2 tablespoons hoisin sauce
- 1 tablespoon toasted sesame oil
- 1 teaspoon cornstarch
- ¼ teaspoon five-spice powder

Noodles and Vegetables
- 3 tablespoons vegetable oil, divided
- 4 teaspoons grated fresh ginger
- 3 garlic cloves, minced
- 1 pound shiitake mushrooms, stemmed and halved if small or quartered if large
- 10 scallions, white parts sliced thin and green parts cut into 1-inch pieces
- 2 red bell peppers, stemmed, seeded, and sliced into ¼-inch-wide strips
- ½ small head napa cabbage, cored and cut into ½-inch-thick pieces (4 cups)
- ¼ cup Shaoxing wine or dry sherry
- 1 pound fresh Chinese noodles or spaghetti or linguine
- 1 tablespoon Asian chili-garlic sauce

1. For the sauce Whisk all ingredients together in bowl.

2. For the noodles and vegetables Combine 1 tablespoon oil, ginger, and garlic in bowl. Heat 1 tablespoon oil in 12-inch nonstick skillet over medium heat until just smoking. Add mushrooms and cook, tossing slowly but constantly, until lightly browned, 6 to 8 minutes. Stir in scallions and cook until wilted, 2 to 3 minutes; transfer to separate bowl.

3. Add remaining 1 tablespoon oil, bell peppers, and cabbage to now-empty skillet, and cook, stirring constantly, until spotty brown, about 8 minutes. Push vegetables to one side of skillet. Add garlic mixture to clearing and cook, mashing mixture into skillet, until fragrant, about 30 seconds. Stir garlic mixture into vegetables.

4. Stir in wine and cook until liquid is nearly evaporated, 30 to 60 seconds. Stir in mushroom mixture and sauce and simmer until thickened, 1 to 2 minutes; cover and set aside.

5. Meanwhile, bring 4 quarts water to boil in large pot. Add noodles and cook, stirring often, until tender. Drain noodles and return them to pot. Add cabbage mixture and chili-garlic sauce and toss to combine. Serve.

Mee Goreng

Serves 4 to 6

Why This Recipe Works This one-dish Indonesian favorite features spicy pan-fried noodles with vegetables, a special sweet soy sauce, and a garnish of crispy shallots. Meat or shrimp is often included, but for our meatless version, we featured tofu, tossed with cornstarch and quickly pan-fried until crispy on the

Mee Goreng

outside and creamy on the inside. To keep the vegetables simple, we chose bok choy as the star—along with the traditional fried shallots, of course. To give the dish plenty of spice, we added a hefty amount of sambal oelek (a sauce made from ground chiles without added flavorings). Typically, this dish is made with a sweet soy sauce, but since this can be difficult to find, we experimented with alternatives and found that a mixture of dark brown sugar, molasses, and regular soy sauce was a perfect substitute. Don't skip the lime wedges; squeezing them over the finished dish is important for balancing the flavors. Fresh Chinese noodles may or may not contain egg; check the label if this is a concern. If Chinese noodles are unavailable, you may use spaghetti or linguine.

- 1 pound fresh Chinese noodles or spaghetti or linguine
- 14 ounces extra-firm tofu, cut into 1-inch pieces
- ¼ cup packed dark brown sugar
- ¼ cup molasses
- ¼ cup soy sauce
- 4 large shallots (2 minced, 2 sliced thin)
- 3 garlic cloves, minced
- 2 teaspoons sambal oelek
- ¼ teaspoon table salt
- ⅛ teaspoon pepper
- 2 tablespoons cornstarch
- 5 tablespoons vegetable oil, divided
- 1 pound bok choy, stalks and greens separated and sliced ½ inch thick
- 4 scallions, sliced thin on bias
  Lime wedges

1. Bring 4 quarts water to boil in large pot. Add noodles and cook, stirring often, until tender. Drain noodles. While the noodles cook, spread tofu over paper towel–lined baking sheet and let drain for 20 minutes.

2. Whisk sugar, molasses, and soy sauce together in bowl. In separate bowl, combine minced shallots, garlic, and sambal oelek.

3. Gently pat tofu dry with paper towels, sprinkle with salt and pepper, then toss with cornstarch in bowl. Heat 3 tablespoons oil in 12-inch nonstick skillet over medium heat until just smoking. Add tofu and cook, turning as needed, until crisp and browned on all sides, 8 to 10 minutes; transfer to paper towel–lined plate to drain.

4. Heat 1 tablespoon oil in now-empty skillet over medium heat until shimmering. Add sliced shallots and cook, stirring constantly, until golden, about 5 minutes; transfer to second paper towel–lined plate.

5. Add remaining 1 tablespoon oil to now-empty skillet and heat until shimmering. Add bok choy stalks and cook, stirring constantly, until crisp-tender, about 3 minutes. Push vegetables to one side of skillet. Add garlic mixture to clearing and cook, mashing mixture into skillet, until fragrant, about 30 seconds. Stir garlic mixture into vegetables.

6. Stir in noodles, crisped tofu, bok choy leaves, and scallions. Whisk sauce to recombine, add to skillet and cook, stirring constantly, until sauce is thickened, 1 to 2 minutes. Sprinkle with shallots and serve with lime wedges.

Sesame Noodles with Sweet Peppers and Cucumbers
Serves 4 to 6 **FAST**

Why This Recipe Works Chilled sesame noodles are quick and easy to make and wonderful to serve on a hot summer night. To avoid the pitfalls of most sesame noodle recipes— gummy noodles and bland, pasty sauce—we rinsed the cooked noodles to rid them of excess starch. This also cooled them down quickly. Tossing the noodles with sesame oil separately, before adding the sauce, also helped keep them from absorbing too much sauce and becoming gummy. Chunky peanut butter processed with toasted sesame seeds worked surprisingly well for the sauce's base. Garlic, ginger, soy sauce, rice vinegar, hot sauce, and brown sugar rounded out the flavors, and thinning the sauce with hot water created the best texture to coat the noodles without being gloppy. Takeout sesame noodles often have little or no vegetables, but we added red bell pepper, cucumber, scallion, and carrot. We prefer the flavor and texture of chunky peanut butter in the sauce, and we like conventional peanut butter here, as it tends to be sweeter than natural versions. Fresh Chinese noodles may or may not contain egg; check the label if this is a concern. If Chinese noodles are unavailable, you may use spaghetti or linguine.

Sauce
- 5 tablespoons soy sauce
- ¼ cup sesame seeds, toasted, divided
- ¼ cup chunky peanut butter
- 2 tablespoons rice vinegar
- 2 tablespoons packed light brown sugar
- 1 tablespoon grated fresh ginger
- 2 garlic cloves, minced
- 1 teaspoon hot sauce
- 5 tablespoons hot water

Noodles and Vegetables

- 1 pound fresh Chinese noodles or spaghetti or linguine
  Table salt for cooking noodles
- 2 tablespoons toasted sesame oil
- 1 red bell pepper, sliced into ¼-inch-wide strips
- 1 cucumber, peeled, halved lengthwise, seeded, and cut crosswise into ⅛-inch-thick slices
- 4 scallions, sliced thin on bias
- 1 carrot, shredded
- 1 tablespoon chopped fresh cilantro

1. For the sauce Process soy sauce, 3 tablespoons sesame seeds, peanut butter, vinegar, sugar, ginger, garlic, and hot sauce in blender or food processor until smooth, about 30 seconds. With blender running, add hot water, 1 tablespoon at a time, until sauce has consistency of heavy cream.

2. For the noodles and vegetables Bring 6 quarts water to boil in large pot. Add noodles and 1 tablespoon salt and cook, stirring often, until tender. Drain noodles and rinse under cold running water until chilled. Drain noodles again and toss with oil. Add bell pepper, cucumber, scallions, carrot, and sauce and toss to combine. Divide evenly among bowls, sprinkle with remaining 1 tablespoon sesame seeds and cilantro, and serve.

Udon Noodles with Mustard Greens and Shiitake-Ginger Sauce

Serves 4 to 6

Why This Recipe Works Noodles and greens are a common pairing throughout Asia. Here, the spicy bite of mustard greens and the rustic chew of udon noodles make a great partnership that's delicate yet filling. Udon are fat noodles made of wheat flour that are sold dried or semi-dried. Since they're starchy and a bit sweet, they stand up well to savory sauces, so we made a highly aromatic and flavorful broth from Asian pantry staples, first browning meaty shiitake mushrooms for flavor and then adding water and mirin along with rice vinegar, soy sauce, cloves of garlic, and a chunk of fresh ginger. Dried shiitake mushrooms, sesame oil, and chili-garlic sauce rounded out the flavors. After this mixture simmered and reduced, we had a sauce that was light and brothy but supersavory—perfect for pairing with our cooked noodles and greens. Because fresh noodles cook so quickly, make sure to add the greens to the pot before the noodles. Do not substitute other types of noodles for the udon noodles here.

- 1 tablespoon vegetable oil
- 8 ounces shiitake mushrooms, stemmed and sliced thin
- ¼ cup mirin
- 3 tablespoons rice vinegar
- 3 tablespoons soy sauce
- 2 garlic cloves, smashed and peeled
- 1 (1-inch) piece ginger, peeled, halved, and smashed
- ½ ounce dried shiitake mushrooms, rinsed and minced
- 1 teaspoon toasted sesame oil
- 1 teaspoon Asian chili-garlic sauce
- 1 pound mustard greens, stemmed and cut into 2-inch pieces
  Table salt for cooking noodles and greens
- 1 pound fresh udon noodles

1. Heat vegetable oil in Dutch oven over medium-high heat until shimmering. Add fresh mushrooms and cook, stirring occasionally, until softened and lightly browned, about 5 minutes. Stir in 2 cups water, mirin, vinegar, soy sauce, garlic, ginger, dried mushrooms, sesame oil, and chili-garlic sauce and bring to simmer. Reduce heat to medium-low and simmer until liquid has reduced by half, 8 to 10 minutes. Off heat, discard garlic and ginger and cover pot to keep warm.

Udon Noodles with Mustard Greens and Shiitake-Ginger Sauce

2. Meanwhile, bring 4 quarts water to boil in large pot. Add mustard greens and 1 tablespoon salt and cook until greens are nearly tender, about 5 minutes. Add noodles and cook until greens and noodles are tender, about 2 minutes. Reserve ⅓ cup cooking water, drain noodles and greens, and return them to pot. Add sauce and reserved cooking water and toss to combine. Cook over medium-low heat, tossing constantly, until sauce clings to noodles, about 1 minute. Season with salt and pepper to taste, and serve.

Soba Noodles with Roasted Eggplant and Sesame

Serves 4 `FAST`

Why This Recipe Works Hearty eggplant has a satisfyingly meaty texture that stands up quite well to rich, nutty, pleasantly chewy soba noodles in this recipe. To keep preparation straightforward and speedy, we decided that eggplant would be the only vegetable we included, so we used a generous amount. Roasting proved an easy, hands-off way to cook the eggplant; tossing it with vegetable oil and soy sauce beforehand helped to amp up its mild flavor and also draw out its moisture, resulting in pieces that were crisped on the outside and creamy on the inside. For the sauce, we started with more soy sauce for savory richness. Vegan oyster sauce, Asian chili-garlic sauce, toasted sesame oil, and some sugar provided a nice balance of spicy and sweet flavors, while a little sake contributed clean, acidic notes that bolstered the complexity of the sauce. A sprinkling of fresh cilantro and sesame seeds brightened up our earthy dish. You may substitute dry vermouth for the sake.

- 3 pounds eggplant, cut into 1-inch pieces
- ¼ cup vegetable oil
- ⅓ cup soy sauce, divided
- ⅓ cup sugar
- 3 tablespoons vegan oyster sauce
- 3 tablespoons toasted sesame oil
- 5 teaspoons sake or dry vermouth
- 1½ tablespoons Asian chili-garlic sauce
- 12 ounces dried soba noodles
- ¾ cup fresh cilantro leaves
- 2 teaspoons sesame seeds, toasted

1. Adjust oven racks to upper-middle and lower-middle positions and heat oven to 450 degrees. Line 2 rimmed baking sheets with aluminum foil and spray with vegetable oil spray. Toss eggplant with vegetable oil and 1 tablespoon soy sauce, then spread evenly on prepared baking sheets. Roast until eggplant is well browned and tender, 25 to 30 minutes, stirring and switching sheets halfway through roasting.

2. Combine sugar, oyster sauce, sesame oil, sake, chili-garlic sauce, and remaining soy sauce in small saucepan. Cook over medium heat, whisking often, until sugar has dissolved, about 1 minute; cover and set aside.

3. Meanwhile, bring 4 quarts water to boil in large pot. Add noodles and cook, stirring often, until tender. Reserve ½ cup cooking water, then drain noodles and return them to pot. Add sauce and roasted eggplant and toss to combine. Add reserved cooking water as needed to adjust consistency. Sprinkle individual portions with cilantro and sesame seeds and serve.

Chilled Soba Noodles with Cucumbers, Snow Peas, and Radishes

Serves 4 to 6 `FAST`

Why This Recipe Works Soba noodles, made from buckwheat flour or a buckwheat-wheat flour blend, have a chewy texture and nutty flavor and are often enjoyed chilled. For a refreshing cold noodle dish, we cooked soba noodles in unsalted boiling water until tender but still resilient and rinsed them under cold running water to remove excess starch and prevent sticking. We then tossed the soba with a miso-based dressing, which clung to and flavored the noodles without overpowering their distinct taste. We also cut a mix of vegetables into varying sizes so they'd incorporate nicely into the noodles while adding crunch and color. Sprinkling strips of toasted nori over the top added umami, a touch of brininess, and crisp textural interest. Plain pretoasted seaweed snacks can be substituted for the toasted nori, and yellow, red, or brown miso can be substituted for the white miso, if desired. This dish isn't meant to be overtly spicy, but if you prefer more heat, use the full ½ teaspoon of red pepper flakes. These chilled noodles pair nicely with tofu for lunch or a light dinner.

- 8 ounces dried soba noodles
- 1 (8-inch square) sheet nori (optional)
- 3 tablespoons white miso
- 3 tablespoons mirin
- 2 tablespoons toasted sesame oil
- 1 tablespoon sesame seeds
- 1 teaspoon grated fresh ginger
- ¼–½ teaspoon red pepper flakes
- ⅓ English cucumber, quartered lengthwise, seeded, and sliced thin on bias
- 4 ounces snow peas, strings removed, cut lengthwise into matchsticks
- 4 radishes, trimmed, halved, and sliced thin
- 3 scallions, sliced thin on bias

1. Bring 4 quarts water to boil in large pot. Add noodles and cook, stirring often, until tender. Drain noodles and rinse under cold running water until chilled. Drain noodles again.

2. Grip nori sheet, if using, with tongs and hold about 2 inches above low flame on gas burner. Toast nori, flipping every 3 to 5 seconds, until nori is aromatic and shrinks slightly, about 20 seconds. If you do not have a gas stove, toast nori on rimmed baking sheet in 275-degree oven until it is aromatic and shrinks slightly, 20 to 25 minutes, flipping nori halfway through toasting. Using scissors, cut nori into four 2-inch strips. Stack strips and cut crosswise into thin strips.

3. Whisk miso, mirin, oil, 1 tablespoon water, sesame seeds, ginger, and pepper flakes together in large bowl. Add noodles and toss to combine. Add cucumber; snow peas; radishes; scallions; and nori, if using, and toss well to evenly distribute. Season with salt to taste, and serve.

FLAVOR BOOSTER

NORI
All dried sea vegetables are loaded with umami and subtle briny flavors, and nori is a great introduction if you aren't familiar with them. It's probably the most well-known sea vegetable in the U.S. because it is what's used to wrap sushi rolls. Sheets of dried nori can be found in packets at Asian markets or in the Asian section of the supermarket. For a snacking chip made from nori, see page 354.

Soba Noodles with
Roasted Eggplant and
Sesame

Chilled Soba Noodles
with Cucumbers, Snow
Peas, and Radishes

CHAPTER 6

VEGETABLE DISHES BIG AND SMALL

■ FAST (45 minutes or less total time)
Photos: Curry Roasted Cabbage Wedges with Tomatoes and Chickpeas; Horta

Roasted Artichokes
with Lemon and Basil

Roasted Artichokes with Lemon and Basil

Serves 4 **FAST**

Why This Recipe Works In most dishes using fresh artichokes, 90 percent of the work involves cleaning them. For that reason, we found frozen artichokes to be a great starting point for this flavorful dish, which can be served with Chickpea Cakes (page 108), on pizza, or tossed with pasta. Roasting the artichokes coaxed out their delicate vegetal notes. Since frozen artichokes contain a considerable amount of water, which can prevent browning and dilute flavor, we preheated a baking sheet in a very hot oven; tossed the artichokes and a couple of garlic cloves with olive oil, salt, and pepper; and then spread everything out on the sizzling sheet. The excess water quickly evaporated during roasting, giving us golden-brown, deeply flavored artichokes. Lining the baking sheet with foil made cleanup a snap. After the garlic cooled slightly, we minced it and tossed it in a simple lemon-basil dressing, which beautifully highlighted the artichokes. To thaw frozen artichokes quickly, microwave them in a covered bowl for 3 to 5 minutes; drain them and pat dry before using.

18 ounces frozen artichokes, thawed and patted dry
2 garlic cloves, peeled
3 tablespoons extra-virgin olive oil, divided
½ teaspoon table salt
⅛ teaspoon pepper
1 tablespoon lemon juice
1 tablespoon chopped fresh basil

1. Adjust oven rack to middle position, place aluminum foil–lined rimmed baking sheet on rack, and heat oven to 450 degrees. Toss artichokes and garlic with 2 tablespoons oil, salt, and pepper in bowl. Spread vegetables evenly over hot baking sheet and roast until browned around edges, 15 to 20 minutes.

2. Remove vegetables from oven and let cool slightly. Mince roasted garlic, then combine with lemon juice, basil, and remaining 1 tablespoon oil in large bowl. Add roasted artichokes and toss to coat. Season with salt and pepper to taste. Serve.

VARIATIONS
Roasted Artichokes with Fennel, Mustard, and Tarragon

Roast 1 small fennel bulb, trimmed and sliced thin, along with artichokes and garlic. Reduce lemon juice to 1 teaspoon, substitute 1 tablespoon minced fresh tarragon for basil, and add 1 tablespoon whole-grain mustard to dressing.

Stir-Fried Asparagus with
Shiitake Mushrooms

Roasted Artichokes with Olives, Bell Pepper, and Lemon

Roast ½ cup coarsely chopped pitted kalamata olives and 1 coarsely chopped red bell pepper along with artichokes and garlic. Substitute 1 tablespoon minced fresh parsley for basil.

Stir-Fried Asparagus with Shiitake Mushrooms

Serves 4 `FAST`

Why This Recipe Works Asparagus is a natural candidate for stir-frying because it cooks in a flash, making this dish great for serving over rice or as a quick side for Stir-Fried Tempeh with Orange Sauce (page 300). The intense heat beautifully caramelizes it, while the short cooking time ensures that it emerges crisp-tender. Starting with a hot skillet and then stirring the asparagus only occasionally during cooking allowed the asparagus to char before it overcooked and brought out a natural sweetness that paired perfectly with a potent sauce inspired by Chinese flavors. Thinly sliced shiitake mushrooms complemented the fresh asparagus and added some meaty heft. To ensure that the asparagus and mushrooms cooked evenly, we added a bit of water, which created a small amount of steam that cooked the vegetables through before evaporating and leaving behind a flavorful, clingy glaze. Look for asparagus spears no thicker than ½ inch.

- 2 tablespoons water
- 1 tablespoon soy sauce
- 1 tablespoon Shaoxing wine or dry sherry
- 2 teaspoons packed brown sugar
- 2 teaspoons grated fresh ginger
- 1 teaspoon toasted sesame oil
- 1 tablespoon vegetable oil
- 1 pound thin asparagus, trimmed and cut on bias into 2-inch lengths
- 4 ounces shiitake mushrooms, stemmed and sliced thin
- 2 scallions, green parts only, sliced thin on bias

1. Combine water, soy sauce, Shaoxing wine, sugar, ginger, and sesame oil in bowl.

2. Heat vegetable oil in 12-inch nonstick skillet over high heat until smoking. Add asparagus and mushrooms and cook, stirring occasionally, until asparagus is spotty brown, 3 to 4 minutes. Add soy sauce mixture and cook, stirring twice, until asparagus is crisp-tender, 1 to 2 minutes. Transfer to platter, sprinkle with scallion greens, and serve.

Roasted Asparagus with Mint-Orange Gremolata

Serves 4 to 6 `FAST`

Why This Recipe Works These meaty thick asparagus spears become a delicious meal when dolloped with Cashew Ricotta (page 26) or dairy ricotta and a sprinkling of toasted panko. We needed to tailor our oven roasting for the delicate asparagus, since simply tossing the spears with oil, salt, and pepper and spreading them on a baking sheet didn't always produce reliably crisp-tender spears. After a few tests, we discovered that thicker asparagus held up better to roasting. To ensure a hard sear on our spears, we preheated the baking sheet and resisted the urge to give it a shake during roasting, as we often do with other vegetables. The result was intense, flavorful browning on one side of the asparagus and vibrant green on the other. For seasoning, we took our cue from Italian cuisine and prepared a bright gremolata of minced fresh herbs; our two variations change up the herbs. You can use white or green asparagus in this recipe; if using white, peel just the outermost layer of the bottom halves of the spears. Look for asparagus spears ½ to ¾ inch in diameter.

- 2 tablespoons minced fresh mint
- 2 tablespoons minced fresh parsley
- 2 teaspoons grated orange zest
- 1 garlic clove, minced
  Pinch cayenne pepper
- 2 pounds thick asparagus
- 2 tablespoons plus 2 teaspoons extra-virgin olive oil, divided
- ½ teaspoon table salt
- ¼ teaspoon pepper

1. Adjust oven rack to lowest position, place rimmed baking sheet on rack, and heat oven to 500 degrees. Combine mint, parsley, orange zest, garlic, and cayenne in bowl; set aside.

2. Trim bottom inch of asparagus spears and discard. Peel bottom halves of spears until white flesh is exposed. Place asparagus in large baking pan and toss with 2 tablespoons oil, salt, and pepper.

3. Transfer asparagus to preheated sheet and spread into even layer. Roast, without moving asparagus, until undersides of spears are browned, tops are vibrant green, and tip of paring knife inserted at base of largest spear meets little resistance, 8 to 10 minutes. Transfer asparagus to serving platter, drizzle with remaining 2 teaspoons oil, sprinkle with gremolata, and serve immediately.

VARIATIONS

Roasted Asparagus with Cilantro-Lime Gremolata
Omit mint and cayenne. Substitute ¼ cup minced fresh cilantro for parsley and lime zest for orange zest.

Roasted Asparagus with Tarragon-Lemon Gremolata
Omit cayenne. Substitute tarragon for mint and lemon zest for orange zest.

Braised Asparagus, Peas, and Radishes with Tarragon

Serves 4 to 6   FAST

Why This Recipe Works Braising asparagus is a delightful way to capitalize on its tender springtime freshness. We started by softening shallot and other aromatics in olive oil; then we poured in water and lemon and orange zest and dropped in a bay leaf to build a flavorful braising liquid. Adding the vegetables in stages ensured that each cooked at its own rate and maintained a crisp texture. Peppery radishes, which turned soft and mellow with cooking, nicely complemented the greener notes of asparagus and peas (frozen peas were reliably sweet, and adding them off the heat prevented overcooking). In no time at all, we had a simple, warm dish of radiant vegetables in an invigorating, complex broth, proof positive that braising can bring out the best in even delicate ingredients. Chopped tarragon added a final fresh note. To make this delicate dish a main course, serve with white beans or top with a soft-cooked egg. Either way, crusty bread is a must. Look for asparagus spears no thicker than ½ inch.

- ¼ cup extra-virgin olive oil
- 1 shallot, sliced into thin rounds
- 2 garlic cloves, sliced thin
- 3 fresh thyme sprigs
  Pinch red pepper flakes
- 10 radishes, trimmed and quartered
- 1¼ cups water
- 2 teaspoons grated lemon zest
- 2 teaspoons grated orange zest
- 1 bay leaf
- 1 teaspoon table salt
- 1 pound thin asparagus, trimmed and cut into 2-inch lengths
- 2 cups frozen peas
- 4 teaspoons chopped fresh tarragon

1. Cook oil, shallot, garlic, thyme sprigs, and pepper flakes in Dutch oven over medium heat until shallot is just softened, about 2 minutes. Stir in radishes, water, lemon zest, orange zest, bay leaf, and salt and bring to simmer. Reduce heat to medium-low, cover, and cook until radishes can be easily pierced with tip of paring knife, 3 to 5 minutes. Stir in asparagus, cover, and cook until tender, 3 to 5 minutes.

2. Off heat, stir in peas, cover, and let sit until heated through, about 5 minutes. Discard thyme sprigs and bay leaf. Stir in tarragon and season with salt and pepper to taste. Serve.

Braised Beets with Lemon and Almonds

Serves 4 to 6

Why This Recipe Works This streamlined stovetop recipe for beets maximized their sweet, earthy flavor with minimal mess. We didn't cover the beets entirely with water to braise them; using just 1¼ cups of water meant they partially simmered and partially steamed. Halving the beets cut down our cooking time. In just 45 minutes, the beets were tender and their skins slipped off easily. We reduced the braising liquid and added brown sugar and vinegar to make a glossy glaze. Shallot, toasted almonds, fresh mint and thyme, and a little lemon zest finished the dish. Look for beets that are 2 to 3 inches in diameter. You can use an 11-inch straight-sided sauté pan in place of the Dutch oven in this recipe. The beets can be served warm or at room temperature. If serving at room temperature, add the nuts (or seeds, if making the variation with lime and pepitas) and fresh herbs right before serving. While they will tint your dinner a lovely shade of pink, these beets make a great addition to Almost Hands-Free Fennel Risotto (page 251). Or serve them alongside Moroccan-Style Couscous with Chickpeas (page 174).

- 1½ pounds beets, trimmed and halved horizontally
- 1¼ cups water
- ¾ teaspoon table salt, divided
- 3 tablespoons distilled white vinegar
- 1 tablespoon packed light brown sugar
- 1 shallot, sliced thin
- 1 teaspoon grated lemon zest
- ¼ teaspoon pepper
- ½ cup whole almonds, toasted and chopped
- 2 tablespoons chopped fresh mint
- 1 teaspoon chopped fresh thyme

Braised Beets with
Lemon and Almonds

Braised Beets with Orange and Walnuts

Substitute orange zest for lemon zest, walnuts for almonds, and parsley for mint.

NOTES FROM THE TEST KITCHEN

REMOVING BEET STAINS

No matter how hard you scrub your hands, simple soap and water do little to remove red beet stains. Rubbing a dab of whitening toothpaste with peroxide over the area helps erase the stains.

Steamed Broccoli with Lime-Cumin Dressing

Serves 4 to 6   FAST

Why This Recipe Works Steamed broccoli doesn't have to be boring. To add bold flavor without fuss to simply cooked florets and stalks, we experimented with tossing uncooked dressings with steamed broccoli and found that potent flavorings such as citrus juices, onion or garlic, chiles, and spices, all of which are assertive enough to stand up to the strong flavor of broccoli, worked best. You will need a collapsible steamer basket for this recipe. We like to serve this with Cuban-Style Black Beans and Rice (page 279).

Dressing
- ¼ cup finely chopped red onion
- 3 tablespoons extra-virgin olive oil
- 1 teaspoon grated lime zest plus 1 tablespoon juice
- ½ teaspoon ground cumin
- ⅛ teaspoon hot sauce, plus extra for serving

Broccoli
- 1½ pounds broccoli, florets cut into 1-inch pieces, stalks peeled and sliced ¼ inch thick

1. For the dressing Whisk all ingredients together in large bowl; set aside for serving.

2. For the broccoli Bring 1 inch water to boil in Dutch oven. Place broccoli in collapsible steamer basket, then transfer basket to pot. Cover and cook until broccoli is tender and bright green, about 5 minutes.

3. Transfer broccoli to bowl with dressing and gently toss to combine. Season with salt and extra hot sauce to taste. Serve warm or at room temperature.

1. Place beets, cut side down, in single layer in Dutch oven. Add water and ¼ teaspoon salt and bring to simmer over high heat. Reduce heat to low, cover, and simmer until beets are tender and can be easily pierced with paring knife, 45 to 50 minutes.

2. Transfer beets to cutting board to cool slightly. Meanwhile, increase heat to medium-high and reduce cooking liquid, stirring occasionally, until pan is almost dry, 5 to 6 minutes. Add vinegar and sugar, return to boil, and cook, stirring constantly with heat-resistant spatula, until spatula leaves wide trail when dragged through glaze, 1 to 2 minutes. Remove pan from heat.

3. Once beets are cool enough to handle, rub off skins with paper towels and cut into ½-inch wedges. Add beets, shallot, lemon zest, pepper, and remaining ½ teaspoon salt to glaze and toss to coat. Transfer to serving platter; sprinkle with almonds, mint, and thyme; and serve.

VARIATIONS
Braised Beets with Lime and Pepitas
Omit thyme. Substitute lime zest for lemon zest, toasted pepitas for almonds, and cilantro for mint.

Roasted Broccoli with Garlic

Serves 4 to 6 `FAST`

Why This Recipe Works These roasted broccoli wedges have sweet, full flavor and dappled browning that make them worthy of prime placement on your plate. Given its awkwardly shaped configuration of sturdy, dense stalks and more delicate shrubby florets, broccoli can be tricky to oven-roast. Our technique gave us evenly cooked broccoli—both florets and stalks. The way we prepped the broccoli was the key. We sliced the crown in half and then cut each half into uniform wedges. We cut the stalks into rectangular pieces slightly smaller than the more delicate wedges. This promoted even cooking and great browning by maximizing contact with the hot baking sheet. Preheating the baking sheet on the lowest rack of the oven gave us even better browning. Tossing a scant ½ teaspoon of sugar over the broccoli along with salt, pepper, and a splash of olive oil produced crisp-tipped florets and blistered and browned stalks.

1¾ pounds broccoli
3 tablespoons extra-virgin olive oil
3 garlic cloves, minced
½ teaspoon sugar
½ teaspoon table salt
   Pinch pepper
   Lemon wedges

1. Adjust oven rack to lowest position, place rimmed baking sheet on rack, and heat oven to 500 degrees. Cut broccoli horizontally at juncture of crowns and stalks. Cut crowns into 4 wedges if 3 to 4 inches in diameter or 6 wedges if 4 to 5 inches in diameter. Trim tough outer peel from stalks, then cut into ½-inch-thick planks 2 to 3 inches long.

2. Toss broccoli with oil, garlic, sugar, salt, and pepper in bowl. Working quickly, lay broccoli in single layer, flat sides down, on hot sheet. Roast until stalks are well browned and tender and florets are lightly browned, 9 to 11 minutes. Transfer to serving platter and serve with lemon wedges.

VARIATION

Roasted Broccoli with Shallots and Fennel Seeds
Omit garlic. While broccoli roasts, heat 1 tablespoon extra-virgin olive oil in 8-inch skillet over medium heat until shimmering. Add 3 thinly sliced shallots and cook until softened and lightly browned, 5 to 6 minutes. Stir in 1 teaspoon cracked fennel seeds and cook until shallots are golden brown, 1 to 2 minutes; remove from heat. Toss roasted broccoli with shallot mixture before serving.

CUTTING A BROCCOLI CROWN INTO WEDGES

1. Cut broccoli horizontally at juncture of crown and stalk, then cut crown in half through central stalk.

2. Cut crowns that measure 4 inches in diameter into 4 wedges.

Broccoli Rabe and Spicy Tomato Sauce

Serves 4 to 6

Why This Recipe Works Whether you serve this on its own with crusty bread, as a pasta sauce, or as a topping for Creamy Polenta (page 270), this arrabbiata-inspired broccoli rabe will steal the show at the dinner table. The assertively bitter flavor of broccoli rabe, or rapini, is often tamed by blanching it first in salted water, and we did that here. Then we gently braised it in a zesty tomato sauce, which we started by sautéing onions—finely diced for more surface area—in extra-virgin olive oil. Dried herbs and garlic completed the base flavors, while a generous amount of red pepper flakes brought some heat. Canned crushed tomatoes, which require no chopping or pureeing, made up the bulk of the sauce. Our Vegan Parmesan Substitute lent nutty richness, and chopped parsley gave this a bright, fresh finish. Be sure to set up the ice water bath before cooking the broccoli rabe, as plunging it into the cold water immediately after blanching retains its bright green color and ensures that it doesn't overcook.

2 pounds broccoli rabe, trimmed
½ teaspoon table salt, plus salt for cooking broccoli rabe
1 tablespoon extra-virgin olive oil, plus extra for serving
1 small onion, chopped fine
4 garlic cloves, minced
¾ teaspoon red pepper flakes
¼ teaspoon dried oregano
1 (28-ounce) can crushed tomatoes
¼ teaspoon sugar

½ cup Vegan Parmesan Substitute (page 27) or grated dairy Parmesan cheese

2 tablespoons chopped fresh basil or parsley

1. Bring 4 quarts water to boil in Dutch oven. Fill large bowl halfway with ice and water. Cut tops (leaves and florets) of broccoli rabe from stalks and separate. Add broccoli rabe stalks and 1 tablespoon salt to boiling water and cook for 1 minute. Add broccoli rabe tops and cook until tops are just tender and wilted, about 1 minute. Drain broccoli rabe, then transfer to bowl of ice water and let sit until chilled. Drain again and thoroughly pat dry.

2. Heat oil in now-empty pot over medium heat until shimmering. Add onion and salt and cook until softened, about 5 minutes. Stir in garlic, pepper flakes, and oregano and cook until fragrant, about 30 seconds.

3. Stir in tomatoes and sugar and bring to simmer. Stir in broccoli rabe and cook until sauce is thickened slightly and broccoli rabe is tender, about 10 minutes. Season with salt and pepper to taste. Transfer to serving platter, drizzle with extra oil, and sprinkle with vegan Parmesan substitute and basil. Serve.

Broiled Broccoli Rabe

Broiled Broccoli Rabe

Serves 4 FAST

Why This Recipe Works This favorite Italian broccoli variant is actually closely related to the turnip. Broiling broccoli rabe creates deep caramelization, which adds a touch of contrasting sweetness to the bitter notes of this vegetable. And it takes mere minutes, requiring nothing more than a rimmed baking sheet. Thanks to our broiling method, we were able to skip the usual step of blanching. We simply tossed the pieces with the garlicky oil and they were ready for the oven. For some true Italian comfort food, toss this with white beans. It also makes a bracing foil as a side dish for our creamy Fettuccine Alfredo (page 167).

3 tablespoons extra-virgin olive oil, divided

1 pound broccoli rabe, trimmed

1 garlic clove, minced

¾ teaspoon kosher salt

¼ teaspoon red pepper flakes

Lemon wedges

1. Adjust oven rack 4 inches from broiler element and heat broiler. Brush rimmed baking sheet with 1 tablespoon oil.

2. Cut tops (leaves and florets) of broccoli rabe from stalks, keeping tops whole, then cut stalks into 1-inch pieces. Transfer to prepared sheet.

3. Combine remaining 2 tablespoons oil, garlic, salt, and pepper flakes in small bowl. Pour oil mixture over broccoli rabe and toss to combine.

4. Broil until exposed half of leaves are well browned, 2 to 2½ minutes. Using tongs, toss to expose unbrowned leaves. Return sheet to oven and continue to broil until most leaves are lightly charred and stalks are crisp-tender, 2 to 2½ minutes. Serve with lemon wedges.

TRIMMING BROCCOLI RABE

Trim off tough ends of broccoli rabe.

**Skillet-Roasted Brussels Sprouts
with Pomegranate and Pistachios**

1 pound brussels sprouts, trimmed and halved
5 tablespoons extra-virgin olive oil
1 tablespoon pomegranate molasses
½ teaspoon ground cumin
¼ teaspoon table salt
¼ cup shelled pistachios, toasted and chopped fine
2 tablespoons pomegranate seeds

1. Arrange brussels sprouts in single layer, cut sides down, in 12-inch nonstick skillet. Drizzle oil evenly over brussels sprouts. Cover skillet, place over medium-high heat, and cook until brussels sprouts are bright green and cut sides have started to brown, about 5 minutes.

2. Uncover and continue to cook until cut sides of brussels sprouts are deeply and evenly browned and paring knife meets little to no resistance, 2 to 3 minutes, adjusting heat and moving sprouts as needed to prevent them from overbrowning. While sprouts cook, combine pomegranate molasses, cumin, and salt in small bowl.

3. Off heat, add pomegranate molasses mixture to skillet and stir to evenly coat brussels sprouts. Season with salt and pepper to taste. Transfer to serving platter, sprinkle with pistachios and pomegranate seeds, and serve.

VARIATIONS
**Skillet-Roasted Brussels Sprouts with Mustard
and Brown Sugar**
Omit pistachios and pomegranate seeds. Substitute 1 tablespoon Dijon mustard, 1 tablespoon packed brown sugar, 2 teaspoons white wine vinegar, and ⅛ teaspoon cayenne pepper for pomegranate molasses and cumin.

**Skillet-Roasted Brussels Sprouts with Gochujang
and Sesame Seeds**
Gochujang is a savory Korean red chili paste that can be found in Asian markets or large supermarkets. Substitute 1 tablespoon gochujang and 1 tablespoon rice vinegar for pomegranate molasses and cumin and 2 teaspoons toasted sesame seeds for pistachios and pomegranate seeds.

Skillet-Roasted Brussels
Sprouts with Pomegranate
and Pistachios

Serves 4 to 6 `FAST`

Why This Recipe Works These delicious brussels sprouts are great on their own or spooned over a bed of pureed butternut squash. For speedy stovetop sprouts that were deeply browned on the cut sides while still bright green on the uncut sides and crisp-tender within, we started them in a cold skillet with plenty of oil and cooked them covered. This gently heated the brussels sprouts and created a steamy environment that cooked them through without any extra moisture needed. We then removed the lid and continued to cook the sprouts cut sides down so they could develop a substantial, caramelized exterior. Using enough oil to completely coat the skillet ensured that all the sprouts made full contact with the fat to brown evenly. To elevate the flavor of the roasted sprouts, we added pomegranate molasses and cumin; pistachios and pomegranate seeds gave them a colorful and flavorful finish. You will need a 12-inch nonstick skillet with a tight-fitting lid for this recipe.

Stir-Fried Bok Choy with
Soy Sauce and Ginger

Serves 4 to 6 `FAST`

Why This Recipe Works Bok choy—a type of Chinese cabbage that has stalks and leaves attached to a base, without any core—has a mildly peppery flavor and a light, crisp texture. The speed of stir-frying nicely preserves the delicate nature of

Caption: Skillet-Roasted Brussels Sprouts with Pomegranate and Pistachios

this vegetable. We sliced the bok choy heads and started the stalks first in the skillet and then added the greens later. This way, both stalks and greens ended up perfectly cooked. Be sure to add the ginger, and then the soy sauce mixture, just as the edges of the stalks turn translucent; otherwise, the stalks will soften too much and won't retain their bite. Try this with Sweet Chili Glazed Tofu (page 303) or crispy pan-fried tofu and rice.

- 2 tablespoons soy sauce
- 1 teaspoon sugar
- 2 tablespoons vegetable oil
- 1½ pounds bok choy, stalks halved lengthwise then cut crosswise into ½-inch pieces, greens sliced into ½-inch-thick pieces
- 1 tablespoon grated fresh ginger

1. Whisk soy sauce and sugar in small bowl until sugar has dissolved.

2. Heat oil in 12-inch nonstick skillet over high heat until just smoking. Add bok choy stalks and cook, stirring constantly, until edges begin to turn translucent, about 5 minutes. Stir in ginger and cook until fragrant, about 30 seconds. Add bok choy greens and soy sauce mixture and cook, stirring frequently, until greens are wilted and tender, about 1 minute. Serve.

Curry Roasted Cabbage Wedges with Tomatoes and Chickpeas

Caption: Curry Roasted Cabbage Wedges with Tomatoes and Chickpeas

Curry Roasted Cabbage Wedges with Tomatoes and Chickpeas

Serves 4 **FAST**

Why This Recipe Works Cabbage may lack the dramatic appearance of other cruciferous vegetables—the bumpy reptilian leaves of Lacinato kale or striking hue of purple cauliflower. But cut it into wedges and roast it, creating charred, crispy edges with tender, sweet layers underneath, and we guarantee this humble vegetable will be the center of your plate. We first brushed the wedges with a curry-infused oil, with a little sugar to help with browning. Then we covered the cabbage with aluminum foil before putting the baking sheet on the lower rack of a hot oven to steam the wedges and jump-start browning on the undersides. Instead of flipping them, we found that simply uncovering them for the last part of cooking, and adding another drizzle of oil, crisped and browned the upper sides while maximizing browning underneath. To complete our meal, we simmered an aromatic chickpea-tomato curry in a skillet on the stovetop while the cabbage roasted. When slicing the cabbage into wedges, be sure to slice through the core, leaving it intact so the wedges don't fall apart. Smaller 2-pound cabbages work best here; if you have a larger cabbage, you can remove the outer leaves until it weighs about 2 pounds, though it may not brown as well. Serve with Herbed Yogurt Sauce (page 90), if you like.

- 7 tablespoons vegetable oil, divided
- 1 tablespoon curry powder, divided
- 1½ teaspoons sugar
- 1 teaspoon table salt
- ¼ teaspoon pepper
- 1 head green cabbage (2 pounds)
- 2 garlic cloves, minced
- 2 teaspoons grated fresh ginger
- 2 (15-ounce) cans chickpeas, undrained
- 10 ounces grape tomatoes, halved
- ¼ cup chopped fresh cilantro

1. Adjust oven rack to lowest position and heat oven to 500 degrees. Combine ¼ cup oil, 2 teaspoons curry powder, sugar, salt, and pepper in small bowl. Halve cabbage through core and cut each half into 4 approximately 2-inch-wide wedges, leaving core intact (you will have 8 wedges).

2. Arrange cabbage wedges in even layer on rimmed baking sheet, then brush cabbage all over with oil mixture. Cover tightly with aluminum foil and roast for 10 minutes. Remove foil and drizzle 2 tablespoons oil evenly over wedges. Return cabbage to oven and roast uncovered, until cabbage is tender and sides touching sheet are well browned, 12 to 15 minutes.

3. Meanwhile, heat remaining 1 tablespoon oil in 12-inch skillet over medium-high heat until shimmering. Add garlic, ginger, and remaining 1 teaspoon curry powder and cook, mashing mixture into skillet, until fragrant, about 30 seconds. Add chickpeas and their liquid and tomatoes and bring to simmer. Cook, stirring frequently, until tomatoes begin to break down and mixture has thickened slightly, 7 to 9 minutes.

4. Divide cabbage among individual plates and spoon chickpea mixture over top. Sprinkle with cilantro and serve.

Roasted Carrots and Shallots with Chermoula

Serves 4 to 6   `FAST`

Why This Recipe Works Roasted carrots with a garlicky herb sauce make a hearty side that can be turned into a meal by serving them over a full-flavored grain like farro. We discovered that there are two keys to good browning when roasting carrots: evenly coating them with fat and correctly positioning the baking sheet in the oven. Melting the coconut oil (or butter) first helps coat the carrots evenly before they go onto the baking sheet. The fat itself helps brown the vegetables while also keeping them from sticking. And the closer the heat source is to the baking sheet, the better the browning, so we roasted the halved carrots on the lowest oven rack. The result was tender, sweet, and almost caramel-like on the roasted sides. To spice up this simple preparation, we introduced an intense, spicy green chermoula and plenty of toasted pine nuts. Choose carrots that are about 1½ inches in diameter at the thicker end. If your carrots are smaller, leave them whole; if they're larger, extend the roasting time slightly.

Carrots

- 1½ pounds carrots, peeled and halved lengthwise
- 4 large shallots, peeled and halved through root end
- 2 tablespoons refined coconut oil or unsalted butter, melted
- ½ teaspoon table salt
- ¼ teaspoon pepper
- 2 tablespoons coarsely chopped toasted pine nuts

Roasted Carrots and Shallots with Chermoula

Chermoula

- ¾ cup fresh cilantro leaves
- 2 tablespoons lemon juice
- 4 garlic cloves, minced
- 1 serrano chile, stemmed, seeded, and minced
- ½ teaspoon ground cumin
- ½ teaspoon table salt
- ⅛ teaspoon cayenne pepper
- ¼ cup extra-virgin olive oil

1. For the carrots Adjust oven rack to lowest position and heat oven to 450 degrees. Toss carrots, shallots, melted oil, salt, and pepper together in bowl to coat. Spread carrot-shallot mixture in even layer on rimmed baking sheet, cut sides down. Roast until tender and cut sides are well browned, 15 to 25 minutes.

2. For the chermoula Process cilantro, lemon juice, garlic, serrano, cumin, salt, and cayenne in food processor until finely chopped, about 1 minute, scraping down sides of bowl as needed. With processor running, slowly add oil until incorporated. Transfer to small bowl.

3. Transfer carrots and shallots to serving platter and season with salt to taste. Drizzle with chermoula and sprinkle with pine nuts. Serve.

Pan-Roasted Cauliflower with Capers and Pine Nuts

Serves 4 to 6 `FAST`

Why This Recipe Works Roasting cauliflower is a fabulous way to caramelize its sugars and transform this mild vegetable into something nutty and sweet. We wanted to create a stovetop roasting method that would deliver oven results, but in a faster time frame. Heating olive oil and then adding florets resulted in the craggy exteriors browning before the interiors softened. On the other hand, adding water to the pan to soften the florets resulted in anemic, bland cauliflower. But, similarly to our stovetop roasted brussels sprouts on page 194, starting the oil and cauliflower together in a cold pan, first covered, then uncovered, resulted in caramelized, tender florets. A combination of capers, lemon zest, pine nuts, and chives put a Mediterranean flavor spin on the cauliflower, making it just as appropriate for serving over pasta as serving as a side (try it with Easy Baked Quinoa with Lemon, Garlic, and Parsley on page 271). You will need a 12-inch nonstick skillet with a tight-fitting lid for this recipe.

- ¼ cup extra-virgin olive oil, divided
- 1 head cauliflower (2 pounds), cut into 1½-inch florets
- ¾ teaspoon table salt
- ½ teaspoon pepper
- 2 tablespoons capers, rinsed and minced
- 1 teaspoon grated lemon zest, plus lemon wedges for serving
- ¼ cup pine nuts, toasted
- 2 tablespoons minced fresh chives

1. Combine 2 tablespoons oil and cauliflower florets in 12-inch nonstick skillet and sprinkle with salt and pepper. Cover skillet and cook over medium-high heat until florets start to brown and edges just start to become translucent (do not lift lid during this time), about 5 minutes.

2. Uncover and continue to cook, stirring occasionally, until golden, about 12 minutes.

3. Push florets to edges of skillet. Add remaining 2 tablespoons oil, capers, and lemon zest to center and cook, stirring with rubber spatula, until fragrant, about 30 seconds. Stir caper mixture into florets and continue to cook, stirring occasionally, until florets are tender but still firm, about 3 minutes.

4. Remove skillet from heat and stir in pine nuts and chives. Transfer florets to serving platter. Serve with lemon wedges.

VARIATION

Pan-Roasted Cauliflower with Cumin and Pistachios
Heat 1 teaspoon cumin seeds and 1 teaspoon coriander seeds in 12-inch nonstick skillet over medium heat, stirring frequently, until lightly toasted and fragrant, 2 to 3 minutes. Transfer to spice grinder or mortar and pestle and grind coarse. Wipe out skillet. Substitute ground cumin-coriander mixture, ½ teaspoon paprika, and pinch cayenne pepper for capers; lime zest for lemon zest; and 3 tablespoons chopped fresh mint for chives. Substitute ¼ cup pistachios, toasted and chopped, for pine nuts. Serve with lime wedges.

Grilled Cauliflower

Serves 4 to 6

Why This Recipe Works Grilling is another fantastic way to develop the sweet, nutty flavors of cauliflower. An added benefit of the grill is a kiss of smoky char. To ensure that the florets wouldn't fall through the grate, though, we needed to cut the cauliflower head into larger pieces. To make sure the wedges cooked through evenly on the grill, we first microwaved the wedges until they were just tender and then briefly grilled them to pick up that color and flavor that only the grill can provide. Dunking the cauliflower in a saltwater solution before microwaving seasoned it all over, even in the nooks and crannies; adding some sugar to this liquid encouraged more browning once the wedges hit the grill. Using tongs or a thin metal spatula to gently flip the wedges helps keep them intact. This dish stands well on its own, but to dress it up, serve it sprinkled with 1 tablespoon of Pistachio Dukkah (page 143).

- 1 head cauliflower (2 pounds)
- ¼ cup table salt, for dunking
- 2 tablespoons sugar, for dunking
- 2 tablespoons extra-virgin olive oil, divided
- 1 tablespoon minced fresh chives
  Lemon wedges

1. Trim outer leaves of cauliflower and cut stem flush with bottom. Cut head through core into 6 equal wedges so that core and florets remain intact.

2. Whisk 2 cups water, salt, and sugar in medium bowl until salt and sugar dissolve. Holding wedges by core, gently dunk in salt-sugar mixture until evenly moistened (do not dry—residual water will help cauliflower steam). Transfer wedges, rounded side down, to large plate and cover with inverted large bowl. Microwave until cauliflower is translucent and tender and paring knife inserted in thickest stem of florets (not into core) meets no resistance, 14 to 16 minutes.

3. Carefully (bowl and cauliflower will be very hot) transfer cauliflower to paper towel–lined plate and pat dry. (Microwaved cauliflower can be held at room temperature for up to 2 hours.)

4A. For a charcoal grill Open bottom vent completely. Light large chimney starter three-quarters filled with charcoal briquettes (4½ quarts). When top coals are partially covered with ash, pour evenly over grill. Set cooking grate in place, cover, and open lid vent completely. Heat grill until hot, about 5 minutes.

4B. For a gas grill Turn all burners to high, cover, and heat grill until hot, about 15 minutes. Turn all burners to medium-high.

5. Clean and oil cooking grate. Brush cut sides of wedges with 1 tablespoon oil. Place cauliflower, cut side down, on grill and cook, covered, until well browned with spots of charring, 3 to 4 minutes. Using tongs or thin metal spatula, flip cauliflower and cook second cut side until well browned with spots of charring, 3 to 4 minutes. Flip again so cauliflower is sitting on rounded edge and cook until browned, 1 to 2 minutes.

6. Transfer cauliflower to large platter. Drizzle with remaining 1 tablespoon oil and sprinkle with chives. Serve with lemon wedges.

CUTTING CAULIFLOWER FOR GRILLING

After trimming away any leaves and cutting stem flush with bottom of head, carefully slice into 6 equal wedges, keeping core and florets intact.

Cauliflower Rice
Serves 4 to 6 `FAST`

Why This Recipe Works Cauliflower is a true shape-shifter of a vegetable. This method of preparing it results in a lighter, neutral-flavored but nutrient-dense side that works in literally any dish where you would use white rice. The key was to blitz the florets in a food processor until transformed into perfect rice-size granules. To make our cauliflower rice foolproof, we worked in batches, making sure all the florets broke down evenly. Next, shallot and a small amount of vegetable broth boosted the flavor. To ensure that the cauliflower was tender

but still maintained a rice-like chew, we first steamed it in a covered pot, then finished cooking it uncovered to evaporate any remaining moisture, for beautifully fluffy cauliflower rice.

> 1 head cauliflower (2 pounds), cut into 1-inch florets (6 cups)
> 1 tablespoon extra-virgin olive oil
> 1 shallot, minced
> ½ cup vegetable broth
> ¾ teaspoon table salt
> 2 tablespoons minced fresh parsley

1. Working in 2 batches, pulse cauliflower florets in food processor until finely ground into ¼- to ⅛-inch pieces, 6 to 8 pulses, scraping down sides of bowl as needed; transfer to bowl.

2. Heat oil in large saucepan over medium-low heat until shimmering. Add shallot and cook until softened, about 3 minutes. Stir in cauliflower, broth, and salt. Cover and cook, stirring occasionally, until cauliflower is tender, 12 to 15 minutes.

3. Uncover and continue to cook, stirring occasionally, until cauliflower rice is almost completely dry, about 3 minutes. Off heat, stir in parsley and season with salt and pepper to taste. Serve.

VARIATION
Curried Cauliflower Rice
Add ¼ teaspoon ground cardamom, ¼ teaspoon ground cinnamon, and ¼ teaspoon ground turmeric to saucepan with shallot. Substitute 1 tablespoon minced fresh mint for parsley and stir ¼ cup toasted sliced almonds into cauliflower rice with mint.

Buddha Bowl with Cauliflower, Sweet Potatoes, and Avocados
Serves 4

Why This Recipe Works There are no strict guidelines defining a Buddha bowl, so we forged our own path toward enlightenment: this nourishing vegan bowl that emphasizes vegetables. Instead of a grain base, we chose cauliflower rice, cooking it with red pepper flakes and turmeric to impart both spice and bright color. Roasted sweet potatoes, spinach, and avocado added the perfect balance of flavor and texture. For a sauce, our creamless roasted red pepper and tahini dressing, made with soaked cashews, tricked our taste buds with its

Buddha Bowl with Cauliflower, Sweet Potatoes, and Avocados

1. Adjust oven rack to middle position and heat oven to 400 degrees. Toss potatoes, 1 tablespoon oil, and ¼ teaspoon salt together in bowl, then spread in even layer on rimmed baking sheet. Roast until potatoes are beginning to brown, 15 to 20 minutes, flipping slices halfway through roasting. Season with salt and pepper to taste, and set aside.

2. Meanwhile, working in 2 batches, pulse cauliflower in food processor until finely ground into ¼- to ⅛-inch pieces, 6 to 8 pulses, scraping down sides of bowl as needed. Heat remaining 2 teaspoons oil in large saucepan over medium-low heat until shimmering. Add garlic, pepper flakes, and turmeric and cook until fragrant, about 30 seconds. Stir in cauliflower, water, and remaining ¼ teaspoon salt, cover, and cook, stirring occasionally, until cauliflower is tender, 12 to 15 minutes.

3. Uncover and continue to cook, stirring occasionally, until cauliflower rice is nearly dry, about 3 minutes. Stir in spinach and cook until spinach just begins to wilt, about 30 seconds. Season with salt and pepper to taste.

4. Divide cauliflower rice among individual serving bowls then top with reserved sweet potatoes and avocado. Drizzle with tahini dressing and sprinkle with chickpeas. Serve.

Whipped Cauliflower
Serves 4 to 6   **FAST**

Why This Recipe Works Cauliflower takes another chameleon-like turn here, transforming into a lighter but still comforting take on mashed potatoes. This recipe is a great way to introduce picky eaters to the wonders of this versatile vegetable. Cauliflower has a low fiber content and half of its fiber is soluble, meaning it breaks down during cooking and processes into a silky-smooth puree. We first tried simply mashing steamed cauliflower but ended up with a wet, sloppy mess. When we ditched the potato masher and pureed cauliflower in the food processor instead, we got a smooth, velvety dish that makes a delightful bed for Sautéed Mushrooms with Shallots and Thyme (page 209). This recipe can easily be doubled using a Dutch oven in place of the saucepan.

  1 head cauliflower (2 pounds), cored and cut into
     1-inch pieces
  3 tablespoons refined coconut oil or unsalted butter
  ½ teaspoon table salt

1. Bring 1 cup water to boil in large saucepan over high heat, then add cauliflower. Cover, reduce heat to medium, and cook until very tender, 16 to 20 minutes, stirring once halfway through cooking.

creamy texture and roasted, smoky flavor. Finally, a generous handful of crispy spiced chickpeas added bursts of texture. To kick this up a notch, add some store-bought sauerkraut. We prefer to make our own cauliflower rice, but you can use store-bought refrigerated or frozen cauliflower rice; reduce the covered cooking time in step 2 to 10 minutes.

    1 pound sweet potatoes, unpeeled, halved
      lengthwise and sliced crosswise ¼ inch thick
    5 teaspoons extra-virgin olive oil, divided
    ½ teaspoon table salt, divided
    1 head cauliflower (2 pounds), cored and cut into
      1-inch florets (6 cups)
    2 garlic cloves, minced
¼–½ teaspoon red pepper flakes
    ½ teaspoon ground turmeric
    1 cup water
    2 cups baby spinach
    2 ripe avocados, sliced thin
    ½ cup Creamless Creamy Roasted Red Pepper and
      Tahini Dressing (page 128)
    1 cup Spiced Roasted Chickpeas (page 355)

Cauliflower Steaks with Salsa Verde

Thai Red Curry with Cauliflower

2. Drain cauliflower and transfer to food processor. Add oil and salt and process until completely smooth, about 4 minutes, scraping down sides of bowl as needed. Adjust consistency with hot water as needed. Season with salt and pepper to taste. Serve.

VARIATION
Whipped Cauliflower with Fennel, Garlic, and Lemon
Melt oil in 8-inch nonstick skillet over medium heat until shimmering. Add 3 minced garlic cloves, 1 teaspoon ground fennel, and ⅛ teaspoon red pepper flakes and cook until fragrant, about 30 seconds; set aside. Add spiced oil and 1½ teaspoons grated lemon zest to food processor with cauliflower in step 2.

Cauliflower Steaks with Salsa Verde
Serves 4 **FAST**

Why This Recipe Works Plant-based cooking allows us to reimagine what we put at the center of our plates, and here is a case in point. When you cook thick planks of cauliflower, they develop a meaty texture and become deeply flavorful and caramelized. Recipes for cauliflower steaks abound, but many of them involve fussy transitions between stovetop and oven. We sought a simple way to produce four perfectly cooked steaks simultaneously, so we opted for a rimmed baking sheet and a scorching oven. Steaming the cauliflower briefly by covering the baking sheet with foil, followed by high-heat uncovered roasting on the lowest oven rack, produced dramatic-looking seared steaks with tender interiors. To elevate them to centerpiece status, we brushed the hot steaks with a vibrant Italian-style salsa verde. If you like, serve with our Vegan Parmesan Substitute (page 27) or grated dairy Parmesan cheese.

1½ cups fresh parsley leaves
½ cup fresh mint leaves
½ cup extra-virgin olive oil, divided
2 tablespoons water
1½ tablespoons white wine vinegar
1 tablespoon capers, rinsed
1 garlic clove, minced
⅛ teaspoon plus ½ teaspoon table salt, divided
2 heads cauliflower (2 pounds each)
¼ teaspoon pepper
Lemon wedges

CUTTING CAULIFLOWER INTO STEAKS

1. After trimming leaves and cutting stem flush with bottom florets, halve head lengthwise through core.

2. Cut one 1½-inch-thick slab from each cauliflower half. Reserve remaining cauliflower for another use.

1. Pulse parsley, mint, ¼ cup oil, water, vinegar, capers, garlic, and ⅛ teaspoon salt in food processor until mixture is finely chopped but not smooth, about 10 pulses, scraping down sides of bowl as needed. Transfer sauce to small bowl and set aside. (Sauce can be refrigerated for up to 2 days.)

2. Adjust oven rack to lowest position and heat oven to 500 degrees. Working with 1 head cauliflower at a time, discard outer leaves of cauliflower and trim stem flush with bottom florets. Halve cauliflower lengthwise through core. Cut one 1½-inch-thick slab lengthwise from each half, trimming any florets not connected to core. Repeat with remaining cauliflower. (You should have 4 steaks; reserve remaining cauliflower for another use.)

3. Place steaks on rimmed baking sheet and drizzle with 2 tablespoons oil. Sprinkle with ¼ teaspoon salt and ⅛ teaspoon pepper and rub to distribute. Flip steaks and repeat with remaining 2 tablespoons oil, remaining ¼ teaspoon salt, and remaining ⅛ teaspoon pepper.

4. Cover baking sheet tightly with foil and roast for 5 minutes. Remove foil and roast until bottoms of steaks are well browned, 8 to 10 minutes. Gently flip and continue to roast until tender and second sides are well browned, 6 to 8 more minutes.

5. Transfer steaks to platter and brush evenly with ¼ cup salsa verde. Serve with lemon wedges and remaining salsa verde.

Thai Red Curry with Cauliflower
Serves 4 `FAST`

Why This Recipe Works For this curry—streamlined but still featuring rich, warm flavors—we whisked up a potent sauce with canned coconut milk, Thai red curry paste, our fish sauce substitute, brown sugar, and lime. Roasting the cauliflower on the stovetop was easy: We steamed it in a covered skillet for 5 minutes and then we uncovered it to drive off any remaining

water, tenderizing the cauliflower further and browning it. We bloomed garlic and ginger and then stirred in the curry sauce to meld with the other ingredients. You can use regular basil if you can't find Thai basil. You will need a 12-inch nonstick skillet with a tight-fitting lid for this recipe. Read the label to make sure your red curry paste is vegan. Serve over rice.

- 1 (13.5-ounce) can coconut milk
- 3 tablespoons Fish Sauce Substitute (page 22)
- 1 tablespoon packed light brown sugar
- 2 teaspoons Thai red curry paste
- 1 teaspoon grated lime zest plus 1 tablespoon juice
- ⅛ teaspoon red pepper flakes
- 1 teaspoon plus 2 tablespoons vegetable oil, divided
- 2 garlic cloves, minced
- 1 teaspoon grated fresh ginger
- 1 large head cauliflower (3 pounds), cut into ¾-inch florets
- ¼ cup water
- ⅛ teaspoon table salt
- ¼ cup fresh Thai basil leaves, torn

1. Whisk coconut milk, fish sauce substitute, sugar, curry paste, lime zest and juice, and pepper flakes together in bowl. Combine 1 teaspoon oil, garlic, and ginger in second bowl.

2. Combine remaining 2 tablespoons oil, cauliflower florets, water, and salt in 12-inch nonstick skillet. Cover skillet and cook over high heat until florets start to brown and edges just start to become translucent (do not lift lid), about 5 minutes. Uncover and continue to cook, stirring occasionally, until florets are tender and well browned, 8 to 10 minutes.

3. Push florets to sides of skillet. Add garlic mixture to center and cook, mashing mixture into pan, until fragrant, about 30 seconds. Stir garlic mixture into florets and reduce heat to medium-high. Whisk coconut milk mixture to recombine, then add to skillet and simmer until slightly thickened, about 4 minutes. Off heat, stir in basil and serve.

VARIATION

Thai Red Curry with Bell Peppers and Tofu
Omit cauliflower, water, and salt. Spread 14 ounces tofu, cut into ¾-inch pieces, on paper towel–lined baking sheet and let drain for 20 minutes. Gently press dry with paper towels. Toss tofu with ⅓ cup cornstarch; transfer to fine-mesh strainer and shake gently to remove excess cornstarch. Add coated tofu to heated oil in step 2 and cook until crisp and well browned on all sides, 12 to 15 minutes; transfer to bowl. Add 2 red bell peppers, cut into 2-inch-long matchsticks, to oil left in skillet and cook until crisp-tender, about 2 minutes, before adding garlic mixture. Return tofu to skillet with sauce.

Whole Pot-Roasted Cauliflower
with Tomatoes and Olives

Quick Collard Greens

Whole Pot-Roasted Cauliflower with Tomatoes and Olives
Serves 4

Why This Recipe Works A pot-roasted whole head of cauliflower makes an impressive main course, hearty and comforting yet visually striking, especially when cloaked in a Sicilian-inspired tomato sauce, as we do here. The recipes we came across for pot-roasted cauliflower all started by searing the cumbersome whole head first in an attempt to brown the exterior. But we found this task unwieldy, with the cauliflower slipping from our tongs and the hot oil spitting at our forearms. And browning was spotty at best. Furthermore, once it was coated in our piquant sauce of chunky tomatoes, golden raisins, and salty anchovy substitute, capers, and olives, we couldn't taste or see the difference between browned and unbrowned cauliflower. So we skipped the hassle. To ensure that all of the rich flavors penetrated the dense vegetable, we started by cooking it upside down and spooned some of the sauce into the crevices between the stalk and florets. Then we flipped it right side up, spooned more sauce over the top, and left the pot uncovered to finish cooking. The sauce thickened but remained plentiful and the flavors intensified as the cauliflower became fork-tender.

 2 (28-ounce) cans whole peeled tomatoes
 2 tablespoons extra-virgin olive oil, plus extra for serving
 6 teaspoons Anchovy Substitute (page 23)
 6 garlic cloves, minced
 ¼ teaspoon red pepper flakes
 ¼ teaspoon table salt
 1 head cauliflower (2 pounds)
 ¼ cup golden raisins
 ¼ cup pitted kalamata olives, chopped coarse
 3 tablespoons capers, rinsed
 ½ cup Vegan Parmesan Substitute (page 27) or grated dairy Parmesan cheese
 ¼ cup minced fresh parsley

1. Adjust oven rack to middle position and heat oven to 450 degrees. Pulse tomatoes and their juice in food processor until coarsely chopped, 6 to 8 pulses.

2. Cook oil, anchovy substitute, garlic, and pepper flakes in Dutch oven over medium heat, stirring constantly, until fragrant, about 2 minutes. Stir in tomatoes and salt, bring to simmer, and cook until slightly thickened, about 10 minutes.

3. Meanwhile, trim outer leaves of cauliflower and cut stem flush with bottom florets. Stir raisins, olives, and capers into tomatoes in pot, then nestle cauliflower, stem side up, into sauce. Spoon some of sauce over top, cover, transfer pot to oven, and roast until cauliflower is just tender (paring knife slips in and out of core with some resistance), 30 to 35 minutes.

4. Uncover pot and using tongs, flip cauliflower stem side down. Spoon some of sauce over cauliflower, then scrape down sides of pot. Continue to roast, uncovered, until cauliflower is tender, 10 to 15 minutes.

5. Remove pot from oven. Sprinkle cauliflower with vegan Parmesan substitute and parsley and drizzle with extra oil. Cut cauliflower into wedges and serve, spooning sauce over individual portions.

Quick Collard Greens

Serves 4 to 6 `FAST`

Why This Recipe Works Our quick blanch-and-sauté recipe for tough collard greens will give you the same tender results as long braising, making this recipe accessible for a quick weeknight dinner. Stemming the greens was a necessary first step, and blanching the leaves in salt water tenderized them quickly and neutralized their bitter qualities. To remove excess water left from blanching, we used a spatula to press on the drained greens and then rolled them up in a dish towel to dry them further. We chopped the compressed collards into thin slices perfect for quickly sautéing with pungent, aromatic garlic and spicy red pepper flakes, which provided immediate potent seasoning. You can substitute mustard or turnip greens for the collards; reduce their boiling time to 2 minutes. For a classic Southern meal, add cooked black-eyed peas.

    Table salt for cooking greens
2½ pounds collard greens, stemmed and halved
    lengthwise
 3 tablespoons extra-virgin olive oil
 2 garlic cloves, minced
 ¼ teaspoon red pepper flakes

1. Bring 4 quarts water to boil in large pot over high heat. Stir in 1 tablespoon salt, then add collard greens, 1 handful at a time. Cook until tender, 4 to 5 minutes. Drain and rinse with cold water until greens are cool, about 1 minute. Press greens with rubber spatula to release excess liquid. Place greens on dish towel and compress into 10-inch log. Roll up towel tightly, then remove greens from towel. Cut greens crosswise into ¼-inch slices.

2. Heat oil in 12-inch nonstick skillet over medium-high heat until just smoking. Scatter greens in skillet and cook, stirring frequently, until just beginning to brown, 3 to 4 minutes. Stir in garlic and pepper flakes and cook until greens are spotty brown, 1 to 2 minutes. Season with salt and pepper to taste, and serve.

STEMMING HEARTY GREENS

1A. To stem greens with thick stems, such as collards and kale, hold leaf at base of stem and use knife to slash leafy portion from either side of tough stem.

1B. Alternatively, fold each leaf in half and cut along edge of rib to remove the thickest part of rib and stem.

Sesame-Hoisin Braised Escarole

Serves 4 to 6 `FAST`

Why This Recipe Works A Chinese flavor profile enlivens this easy take on braised greens. Our starting foundation was chopped onion, browned to bring out its sweetness, to which we added garlic, red pepper flakes, and lots of leafy, slightly bitter escarole. Sautéing half of the greens briefly before adding the rest allowed us to fit everything in the pot. We then removed the lid so most of the remaining liquid could evaporate as the escarole finished cooking. Adding the savory sauce during the last few minutes ensured the sauce would have enough time to season the greens without over-reducing and becoming too thick. To boost the sesame flavor and add textural contrast, we sprinkled toasted sesame seeds over the top. For a light meal, serve this over rice or with Sweet Chili Glazed Tofu (page 303).

 2 tablespoons extra-virgin olive oil
 1 onion, chopped fine
 1 garlic clove, minced
 ¼ teaspoon red pepper flakes
 2 heads escarole (2 pounds), trimmed and
    sliced ½ inch thick
 ¼ teaspoon table salt
 1 tablespoon hoisin sauce
 1 tablespoon rice vinegar
 1 tablespoon toasted sesame oil
 2 teaspoons soy sauce
 2 tablespoons sesame seeds, toasted

1. Heat olive oil in Dutch oven over medium heat until shimmering. Add onion and cook until softened and lightly browned, 5 to 7 minutes. Stir in garlic and pepper flakes and cook until fragrant, about 30 seconds. Stir in half of escarole and cook until beginning to wilt, about 2 minutes. Stir in remaining escarole and salt. Cover, reduce heat to medium-low, and cook, stirring occasionally, until greens are tender, about 10 minutes.

2. Uncover and increase heat to medium. Stir in hoisin, rice vinegar, sesame oil, and soy sauce. Cook until most of liquid has evaporated, about 3 minutes. Season with salt and pepper to taste. Sprinkle with sesame seeds and serve.

Grilled Eggplant with Cherry Tomatoes and Cilantro Vinaigrette

Serves 4 to 6

Why This Recipe Works When grilled, the skin of the eggplant turns beautifully brown and becomes crisp in spots. And the great advantage of grilling is that there is no need to salt the eggplant in advance because the moisture vaporizes or drips harmlessly through the cooking grate into the hot fire. In our tests, we found that thinner slices can fall apart on the cooking grate. Thicker pieces, ideally ¾-inch-thick rounds, better withstand the rigors of grilling. To impart flavor to the eggplant while we grilled it, we whisked together a mixture of olive oil and minced garlic, brushing it on liberally. Our pungent vinaigrette for serving included shallot, lime juice, and a little cayenne pepper, with quartered cherry tomatoes added for their bright flavor. We spooned this over the grilled eggplant slices for a simple but superflavorful result. To turn this into a meal, serve with pasta or crusty bread.

½ cup plus 1 tablespoon extra-virgin olive oil, divided
1 shallot, minced
2 tablespoons minced fresh cilantro
2 tablespoons lime juice
¼ teaspoon table salt
  Pinch cayenne pepper
6 ounces cherry tomatoes, quartered
2 garlic cloves, minced
1½ pounds eggplant, sliced into ¾-inch-thick rounds

1. Whisk 6 tablespoons oil, shallot, cilantro, lime juice, salt, and cayenne together in medium bowl. Add tomatoes and toss to coat; set aside.

2. Whisk garlic and remaining 3 tablespoons oil together in small bowl and season with salt and pepper to taste. Brush eggplant with oil mixture.

3A. For a charcoal grill Open bottom vent completely. Light large chimney starter filled with charcoal briquettes (6 quarts). When top coals are partially covered with ash, pour evenly over grill. Set cooking grate in place, cover, and open lid vent completely. Heat grill until hot, about 5 minutes.

3B. For a gas grill Turn all burners to high, cover, and heat grill until hot, about 15 minutes. Leave all burners on high.

4. Clean and oil cooking grate. Grill eggplant (covered if using gas) until browned and tender, 4 to 5 minutes per side. Transfer to serving platter. Spoon vinaigrette over eggplant. Serve immediately.

Walkaway Ratatouille

Serves 6 to 8

Why This Recipe Works This Provençal specialty transforms late-summer produce into a richly flavorful and aromatic stew. But most ratatouille recipes call for labor- and time-intensive treatments like salting and/or pressing to remove excess moisture from the vegetables. While we didn't want a watery ratatouille, we also wanted a streamlined recipe. So we sautéed onions and aromatics and then added chunks of eggplant and tomatoes before transferring the pot to the oven, where the dry, ambient heat would thoroughly evaporate excess moisture, concentrate and intensify flavors, and caramelize some of the vegetables. After 45 hands-off minutes, the tomatoes and eggplant became meltingly soft and could be mashed into a thick, silky sauce. Zucchini and bell peppers went into the pot at that point, so that they retained some texture. Finishing the dish with fresh herbs, sherry vinegar, and extra-virgin olive oil tied everything together. This dish is best prepared using ripe, in-season tomatoes. If they are not available, substitute one 28-ounce can of whole peeled tomatoes, drained and chopped. We love this with crusty bread or over couscous—sometimes with an egg on top.

⅓ cup plus 1 tablespoon extra-virgin olive oil, divided
2 large onions, cut into 1-inch pieces
8 large garlic cloves, peeled and smashed
1¾ teaspoons table salt, divided
¾ teaspoon pepper, divided
1½ teaspoons herbes de Provence
¼ teaspoon red pepper flakes
1 bay leaf
2 pounds plum tomatoes, peeled, cored, and chopped coarse

Walkaway Ratatouille

peppers, remaining ¼ teaspoon salt, and remaining ¼ teaspoon pepper and return to oven. Cook, uncovered, until zucchini and bell peppers are just tender, 20 to 25 minutes.

4. Remove pot from oven, cover, and let sit until zucchini is translucent and easily pierced with tip of paring knife, 10 to 15 minutes. Using wooden spoon, scrape any browned bits from sides of pot and stir back into ratatouille. Discard bay leaf.

5. Stir in 1 tablespoon basil, parsley, and vinegar. Season with salt and pepper to taste. Transfer to large platter, drizzle with remaining 1 tablespoon oil, and sprinkle with remaining 1 tablespoon basil. Serve warm or at room temperature.

Stir-Fried Japanese Eggplant

Serves 4 to 6 **FAST**

Why This Recipe Works Eggplant is neutral in flavor, but it sucks up whatever flavors you cook it with. That quality makes it ideal for stir-fries with deeply savory sauces that cling to each piece of vegetable. We particularly liked Japanese eggplant here for its very creamy flesh and relative lack of seeds. Cooking the eggplant over high heat in a shallow skillet allowed its excess moisture to evaporate quickly without presalting, leaving the eggplant browned and tender. For our sauce, we opted for soy sauce, Shaoxing wine, and, for umami depth, hoisin sauce. Just a teaspoon of cornstarch thickened the sauce to the glossy consistency characteristic of restaurant-style stir-fries. Scallions and fresh cilantro lent the dish some herbaceous notes that played nicely off the savory sauce. We prefer Japanese eggplant here, but this recipe works with Italian or globe eggplant. You can substitute dry sherry for the Shaoxing wine. Serve over udon noodles or rice.

Sauce
- ½ cup vegetable broth
- ¼ cup Shaoxing wine or dry sherry
- 3 tablespoons hoisin sauce
- 1 tablespoon soy sauce
- 1 teaspoon cornstarch
- 1 teaspoon toasted sesame oil

Eggplant
- 1 teaspoon plus 2 tablespoons vegetable oil, divided
- 6 garlic cloves, minced
- 1 tablespoon grated fresh ginger
- 1½ pounds Japanese eggplant, cut into ¾-inch pieces
- 2 scallions, sliced thin on bias
- ½ cup fresh cilantro sprigs, cut into 2-inch pieces
- 1 tablespoon sesame seeds, toasted

1½ pounds eggplant, peeled and cut into 1-inch pieces
2 small zucchini, halved lengthwise and cut into 1-inch pieces
1 red bell pepper, stemmed, seeded, and cut into 1-inch pieces
1 yellow bell pepper, stemmed, seeded, and cut into 1-inch pieces
2 tablespoons chopped fresh basil, divided
1 tablespoon minced fresh parsley
1 tablespoon sherry vinegar

1. Adjust oven rack to middle position and heat oven to 400 degrees. Heat ⅓ cup oil in Dutch oven over medium-high heat until shimmering. Add onions, garlic, 1 teaspoon salt, and ¼ teaspoon pepper and cook, stirring occasionally, until onions are translucent and starting to soften, about 10 minutes. Stir in herbes de Provence, pepper flakes, and bay leaf and cook until fragrant, about 1 minute. Stir in tomatoes, eggplant, ½ teaspoon salt, and ¼ teaspoon pepper.

2. Transfer pot to oven and cook, uncovered, until vegetables are very tender and spotty brown, 40 to 45 minutes.

3. Remove pot from oven and, using potato masher, mash eggplant mixture to coarse puree. Stir in zucchini, bell

1. For the sauce Whisk all ingredients together in bowl; set aside.

2. For the eggplant Combine 1 teaspoon oil, garlic, and ginger in small bowl. Heat 1 tablespoon oil in 12-inch nonstick skillet over high heat until just smoking. Add half of eggplant and cook, stirring frequently, until browned and tender, 4 to 5 minutes; transfer to bowl. Repeat with remaining 1 tablespoon oil and eggplant.

3. Return first batch of eggplant and any accumulated juices to skillet and push to sides. Add garlic-ginger mixture to center and cook, mashing mixture into skillet, until fragrant, about 30 seconds. Stir garlic-ginger mixture into eggplant. Whisk sauce to recombine, then add to skillet and cook until eggplant is well coated and sauce is thickened, about 30 seconds. Off heat, stir in scallions and cilantro and sprinkle with sesame seeds. Serve.

Fennel Confit
Serves 6 to 8

Why This Recipe Works The confit technique is most often used with duck, but it's also a versatile way of transforming vegetables ("confit" simply means to preserve something, with either fat or sugar). Fennel is an excellent candidate, since long cooking times coax out its hidden flavors and turn it luxuriously creamy. We love to serve this with grain, bean, or pasta salads or as a topping for our Potato Galette (page 219). Most recipes we found called for up to a whopping 2 quarts of olive oil, but we discovered that arranging two layers of fennel slabs in the bottom of a large Dutch oven allowed us to use just 3 cups of oil. The oil didn't fully cover the fennel, but the fennel shrank and released liquid during cooking, causing it to sink. We flavored the oil with lemon zest, garlic, and complementary fennel seeds and caraway seeds. The oven provided even heat for the 2-hour cooking time and was completely hands-off. The fennel emerged buttery and aromatic, and pieces that remained above the oil became golden and caramelized, which tasters loved. We finished with a scattering of fennel fronds. Don't core the fennel before cutting it into slabs; the core will help hold the slabs together during cooking. This recipe will yield extra oil that can be strained, cooled, and stored for up to 2 weeks for use in salad dressings or for dipping bread.

- 3 fennel bulbs, 2 tablespoons fronds minced, stalks discarded, bulbs cut lengthwise into ½-inch-thick slabs
- ¼ teaspoon table salt

Fennel Confit

- 3 garlic cloves, lightly crushed and peeled
- 3 (2-inch) strips lemon zest, plus lemon wedges for serving
- 1 teaspoon caraway seeds
- 1 teaspoon fennel seeds
- 3 cups extra-virgin olive oil
  Flake sea salt

1. Adjust oven rack to middle position and heat oven to 300 degrees. Arrange half of fennel, cut side down, in single layer in Dutch oven. Sprinkle with ⅛ teaspoon salt. Repeat with remaining fennel and remaining ⅛ teaspoon salt. Scatter garlic, lemon zest, caraway seeds, and fennel seeds over top, then add oil (fennel may not be completely submerged).

2. Cover pot, transfer to oven, and cook until fennel is very tender and is easily pierced with tip of paring knife, about 2 hours.

3. Remove pot from oven. Using slotted spoon, transfer fennel to serving platter, brushing off any garlic, lemon zest, caraway seeds, or fennel seeds that stick to fennel. Drizzle ¼ cup cooking oil over fennel, sprinkle with fennel fronds, and sprinkle with sea salt to taste. Serve with lemon wedges.

Horta

Serves 4 to 6 `FAST`

Why This Recipe Works In Greece, where this recipe hails from, "horta" simply means any wild greens, prepared simply: either boiled or steamed and then drizzled with plenty of good olive oil, sprinkled with salt, and served with lemon wedges for generous squeezing. Unabashedly bitter dandelion greens are especially popular prepared in this manner. Tasters preferred the boiled version to the steamed version, noting that the former was brighter green in color and less muddy-tasting. We looked at possible additions: olives, tomatoes, herbs, and even feta cheese, but, in the end, tradition prevailed. Tasters wanted their horta free of distracting adjunct flavors. Olive oil, salt, and lemon were all they desired to get the best flavor from these greens. This dish can be served warm, at room temperature, or chilled. Use mature dandelion greens for this recipe; do not use baby dandelion greens. To transform this into a main course, add chickpeas, toasted bread crumbs, and a yogurt sauce.

    2   pounds dandelion greens, trimmed and
        cut into 2-inch lengths
        Table salt for cooking greens
    ¼   cup extra-virgin olive oil
        Lemon wedges

1. Bring 4 quarts water to boil in large pot over high heat. Add dandelion greens and 1 tablespoon salt and cook until thickest stems are just tender, 4 to 7 minutes. Drain greens in colander and, using rubber spatula, gently press greens to release excess liquid.

2. Transfer greens to serving platter, drizzle with oil, and season with flake sea salt to taste. Serve with lemon wedges.

Mediterranean Braised Green Beans

Serves 4 to 6

Why This Recipe Works In the crisp-tender craze of recent years, a lesser-known but time-honored approach to cooking green beans has become overlooked and underappreciated. A slow braise turns green beans into something silky-smooth and altogether different. This Mediterranean version calls for sautéing the aromatics on the stovetop in a Dutch oven, then adding the green beans and tomatoes and transferring the pot to the oven for hands-off simmering until the sauce is thickened and the beans become infused with the tomato and

garlic. The small amount of baking soda helps break down the pectin in the beans more quickly. The best part is the velvety texture of the beans: The slow cooking renders them so meltingly tender that they're almost creamy. This is great with crusty bread for soaking up every drop of the luscious sauce.

    5   tablespoons extra-virgin olive oil, divided
    1   onion, chopped fine
    4   garlic cloves, minced
        Pinch cayenne pepper
    1½ cups water
    ½   teaspoon baking soda
    1½ pounds green beans, trimmed and cut into
        2- to 3-inch lengths
    1   (14.5-ounce) can diced tomatoes, drained with
        juice reserved, chopped coarse
    1   tablespoon tomato paste
    1   teaspoon table salt
    ¼   teaspoon pepper
    ¼   cup chopped fresh parsley
        Red wine vinegar

1. Adjust oven rack to lower-middle position and heat oven to 275 degrees. Heat 3 tablespoons oil in Dutch oven over medium heat until shimmering. Add onion and cook, stirring occasionally, until softened, 3 to 5 minutes. Add garlic and cayenne and cook until fragrant, about 30 seconds. Add water, baking soda, and green beans and bring to simmer. Reduce heat to medium-low and cook, stirring occasionally, for 10 minutes. Stir in tomatoes and their juice, tomato paste, salt, and pepper.

2. Cover pot, transfer to oven, and cook until sauce is slightly thickened and green beans can be easily cut with side of fork, 40 to 50 minutes. Stir in parsley and season with vinegar to taste. Drizzle with remaining 2 tablespoons oil and serve warm or at room temperature.

Quick Roasted Green Beans

Serves 4 `FAST`

Why This Recipe Works Mature supermarket green beans are often tough and dull, needing special treatment to become tender and flavorful. Roasting is a great option, giving older green beans a flavor comparable to sweet, fresh-picked beans. Our remarkably simple test produced outstanding results: Beans roasted in a 450-degree oven with only olive oil, salt, and pepper transformed from starchy specimens into deeply caramelized, full-flavored beans. Just 20 minutes of roasting reversed the aging process (converting starch back to sugar) and encouraged flavorful browning. One tablespoon of oil was enough to lend flavor and moisture without making the beans greasy. Lining the pan with aluminum foil prevented scorching and made for easy cleanup of this superfast side.

1 pound green beans, trimmed
1 tablespoon extra-virgin olive oil
½ teaspoon table salt

1. Adjust oven rack to middle position and heat oven to 450 degrees. Line rimmed baking sheet with aluminum foil. Spread green beans on sheet and drizzle with oil. Using your hands, toss to coat evenly. Sprinkle with salt, toss to coat, and distribute in even layer. Roast for 10 minutes.

2. Remove sheet from oven. Using tongs, redistribute green beans. Continue roasting until green beans are dark golden brown in spots and have started to shrivel, 10 to 12 minutes. Season with salt and pepper to taste and serve.

Braised Leeks
Serves 4 to 6

Why This Recipe Works Gently aromatic and meltingly tender, braised leeks are an irresistible side dish for a tofu frittata or scramble or alongside Roasted Smashed Potatoes (page 218). Browning the leeks before adding the braising liquid to the skillet yielded deep flavor, and a simple dressing of white wine vinegar, Dijon mustard, garlic, and olive oil enhanced this depth of flavor. We also found that adding some of the leek braising liquid gave the dressing even more complexity. A sprinkling of tarragon at the end brightened the dish. We prefer to use leeks measuring 1 inch or less in diameter here, because they're more tender than fatter leeks. If you have larger leeks, discard their first two outer layers because they tend to be fibrous. Orienting the leeks in one direction makes them easier to transfer in and out of the skillet. When trimming the leeks, be careful to leave the root ends intact so that the layers stay together when the leeks are halved.

3 pounds small leeks, white and light green parts only
  Pinch plus ¼ teaspoon table salt, divided
  Pinch plus ¼ teaspoon pepper, divided
6 tablespoons extra-virgin olive oil, divided
1 cup vegetable broth
1 tablespoon white wine vinegar
1 teaspoon Dijon mustard
1 small garlic clove, minced
1 tablespoon chopped fresh tarragon

1. Trim roots from leeks, leaving ends intact so layers stay together when halved. Halve leeks lengthwise, wash thoroughly between layers to remove any dirt, and pat dry with paper towels. Sprinkle cut sides with pinch salt and pinch pepper.

2. Heat 1 tablespoon oil in 12-inch nonstick skillet over medium-high heat until shimmering. Add half of leeks to skillet, with root ends pointed in same direction, and cook until browned, about 2 minutes per side. Transfer to plate. Repeat with 1 tablespoon oil and remaining leeks.

3. Return all leeks to skillet, facing same direction. Add broth and bring to boil. Cover, reduce heat to medium-low, and simmer until leeks are tender when poked with tip of paring knife, 10 to 12 minutes. Using slotted spatula, transfer leeks to shallow serving platter, leaving braising liquid in skillet.

4. Increase heat to medium-high and bring braising liquid to boil; cook until reduced to about 2 tablespoons, 2 to 4 minutes. Transfer braising liquid to small jar (or bowl) and add vinegar, mustard, garlic, remaining ¼ cup oil, remaining ¼ teaspoon salt, and remaining ¼ teaspoon pepper. Affix lid and shake jar vigorously until vinaigrette is emulsified, about 15 seconds (or whisk in bowl). Spoon vinaigrette over leeks. Sprinkle with tarragon and serve.

Grilled Onions with Balsamic Vinaigrette
Serves 4 to 6

Why This Recipe Works While they more than stand on their own as a side dish, grilled onions also make a great veggie burger or risotto topping. Grilling halved onions cut side down directly over the flame until very dark ensured that they developed sufficient chargrilled flavor; we then transferred them to a covered disposable pan to finish cut side up so they would cook through evenly, turning buttery soft. Leaving the skins on kept the bottoms of the onions from burning but still allowed for plenty of caramelization. The simple balsamic vinaigrette complemented their sweetness while lending a burst of acidity. In step 3, be sure to err on the side of achieving darker charring, as the steaming step that follows will soften the charred appearance and flavor.

½ cup extra-virgin olive oil, divided
3 tablespoons balsamic vinegar
1½ teaspoons table salt, divided
¼ teaspoon pepper
4 onions (8 ounces each)
1 (13 by 9-inch) disposable aluminum pan
1 tablespoon minced fresh chives

1. Whisk 6 tablespoons oil, vinegar, ½ teaspoon salt, and pepper together in bowl; set aside. Trim stem end of onions and halve onions from root end to stem end, leaving skin intact. (Root end can be trimmed, but don't remove it or onions will fall apart.) Brush cut sides of onions with remaining 2 tablespoons oil and sprinkle each half with ⅛ teaspoon salt.

2A. For a charcoal grill Open bottom vent completely. Light large chimney starter three-quarters filled with charcoal briquettes (4½ quarts). When top coals are partially covered with ash, pour evenly over grill. Set cooking grate in place, cover, and open lid vent completely. Heat grill until hot, about 5 minutes.

2B. For a gas grill Turn all burners to high, cover, and heat grill until hot, about 15 minutes. Turn all burners to medium.

3. Clean and oil cooking grate. Place onions cut side down on grill and cook (covered if using gas) until well charred, 10 to 15 minutes, moving onions as needed to ensure even cooking. Flip onions and cook cut side up until lightly charred on skin side, about 5 minutes.

4. Transfer onions cut side up to disposable pan and cover tightly with aluminum foil. Return disposable pan to grill and cook over medium heat (covered if using gas) until onions are tender and easily pierced with paring knife, 10 to 15 minutes. Set aside to cool slightly, about 10 minutes.

5. Remove and discard charred outer skin; arrange onions cut side up on serving platter. Whisk vinaigrette to recombine and drizzle evenly over onions. Sprinkle with chives, season with salt and pepper to taste, and serve.

Sautéed Mushrooms with Shallots and Thyme

Serves 4 to 6   FAST

Why This Recipe Works Simply sautéed mushrooms make a delicious and versatile side dish or a quick lunch when used to top toasted crusty bread spread with plain plant-based or dairy yogurt. But white mushrooms tend to shrink quite a bit when sautéed, so what looks like plenty when raw seems to shrivel away to nothing when cooked. So we developed this quick sauté method that resulted in a large enough quantity to make an ample amount. We discovered that overloading the skillet and extending the cooking time allowed the mushrooms to give up just enough liquid to eventually fit in a single layer and cook properly without shrinking away to nothing. They browned very nicely after we added a little coconut oil (or butter) to the skillet, and from there it was easy to enhance

Sautéed Mushrooms with Shallots and Thyme

the dish with shallot, thyme, and Marsala—a classic flavor combination for complementing mushrooms. Halve mushrooms that are less than 1 inch across and quarter those that are larger than that.

- 1 tablespoon vegetable oil
- 1½ pounds white mushrooms, trimmed and halved if small or quartered if medium or large
- 1 tablespoon refined coconut oil or unsalted butter
- 1 shallot, minced
- 1 tablespoon minced fresh thyme or 1 teaspoon dried
- ¼ cup dry Marsala

1. Heat vegetable oil in 12-inch nonstick skillet over medium-high heat until shimmering. Add mushrooms and cook, stirring occasionally, until they release their liquid, about 5 minutes. Increase heat to high and cook, stirring occasionally, until liquid has evaporated, about 8 minutes.

2. Stir in coconut oil, reduce heat to medium, and cook, stirring often, until mushrooms are dark brown, about 8 minutes.

Stir-Fried Portobellos with
Soy-Maple Sauce

3. Stir in shallot and thyme and cook until shallot is softened, about 3 minutes. Add Marsala and cook until evaporated, about 2 minutes. Season with salt and pepper to taste, and serve.

Stir-Fried Portobellos with Soy-Maple Sauce

Serves 4 to 6

Why This Recipe Works Hefty, meaty portobello mushrooms in conjunction with snow peas and carrots make for a super-satisfying vegetable stir-fry that's great as is or over udon noodles or rice. Cooking the mushrooms in two batches kept them from steaming in their own juices, guaranteeing even cooking and good browning, and adding a boldly flavored glaze gave the mushrooms a sweet-salty flavor boost. We then stir-fried the snow peas and carrots until crisp-tender, added garlic and ginger and cooked them until they were just fragrant, and stirred in the glazed mushrooms and a simple stir-fry sauce to coat everything with its glossy goodness.

Glaze
- 3 tablespoons maple syrup
- 2 tablespoons mirin
- 1 tablespoon soy sauce

Sauce
- ½ cup vegetable broth
- 2 tablespoons soy sauce
- 1½ tablespoons mirin
- 2 teaspoons rice vinegar
- 2 teaspoons cornstarch
- 2 teaspoons toasted sesame oil

Vegetables
- 3 tablespoons vegetable oil, divided
- 2 garlic cloves, minced
- 2 teaspoons grated fresh ginger
- ¼ teaspoon red pepper flakes
- 2 pounds portobello mushroom caps, gills removed, cut into 2-inch wedges, divided
- 8 ounces snow peas, strings removed and sliced ¼ inch thick on bias
- 2 carrots, peeled and cut into 2-inch-long matchsticks

Mushroom Bourguignon

1. **For the glaze** Whisk all ingredients together in bowl.

2. **For the sauce** Whisk all ingredients together in bowl.

3. **For the vegetables** Combine 1 teaspoon oil, garlic, ginger, and pepper flakes in bowl. Heat 1 tablespoon oil in 12-inch nonstick skillet over high heat until shimmering. Add half of mushrooms and cook, without stirring, until browned on one side, 2 to 3 minutes. Flip mushrooms, reduce heat to medium, and cook until second side is browned and mushrooms are tender, about 5 minutes. Transfer to second bowl. Repeat with 1 tablespoon oil and remaining mushrooms.

4. Return all mushrooms to pan, add glaze, and cook over medium-high heat, stirring frequently, until glaze is thickened and mushrooms are coated, 1 to 2 minutes. Transfer mushrooms to bowl.

5. Wipe now-empty skillet clean with paper towels. Heat remaining 2 teaspoons oil in clean skillet over high heat until shimmering. Add snow peas and carrots and cook, stirring occasionally, until vegetables are crisp-tender, about 5 minutes. Clear center of skillet, add garlic mixture, and cook, mashing mixture into skillet, until fragrant, about 30 seconds. Stir garlic mixture into vegetables.

6. Return mushrooms to skillet. Whisk sauce to recombine, then add to skillet. Cook, stirring constantly, until sauce is thickened, 1 to 2 minutes. Serve.

REMOVING PORTOBELLO GILLS

To remove mushroom gills, simply use spoon to scrape them off before cutting mushroom.

Mushroom Bourguignon
Serves 6 to 8

Why This Recipe Works Chunks of portobello mushrooms napped with a silky, luscious sauce with pearl onions, carrots, garlic, and red wine will have you forgetting that traditional French bourguignon has "boeuf" (beef). Dried porcini mushrooms, tomato paste, and our Anchovy Substitute helped boost the flavor in this stew with their strong umami qualities. We used plenty of fresh herbs while cooking the stew and finished with more before serving. To achieve the body that would normally come from the collagen in the meat breaking down into the sauce, we stirred in some agar-agar flakes (a vegan alternative to gelatin), which gave us a smooth, unctuous sauce and cut the cooking time to boot. Use a good-quality medium-bodied red wine, such as a Burgundy or other Pinot Noir, for this stew. If the pearl onions have a papery outer coating, remove it by rinsing the onions in warm water and gently squeezing individual onions between your fingertips. Serve this over pasta, grains, Whipped Cauliflower (page 199), or Creamy Polenta (page 270).

½ cup extra-virgin olive oil, divided
5 pounds portobello mushroom caps, quartered, divided
1½ cups frozen pearl onions, thawed, divided
½ teaspoon table salt, divided
¼ teaspoon pepper, divided
⅓ cup all-purpose flour
4 cups vegetable broth
1 (750-ml) bottle red wine, divided
2 tablespoons agar-agar flakes
2 tablespoons tomato paste
1 tablespoon Anchovy Substitute (page 23)
2 onions, chopped
2 carrots, peeled and chopped
1 garlic head, cloves separated (unpeeled) and smashed
1 ounce dried porcini mushrooms, rinsed
10 sprigs fresh parsley, plus 3 tablespoons minced
6 sprigs fresh thyme
2 bay leaves
½ teaspoon black peppercorns

1. Heat 3 tablespoons oil in Dutch oven over medium-high heat until shimmering. Add half of portobello mushrooms, half of pearl onions, ¼ teaspoon salt, and ⅛ teaspoon pepper, cover, and cook, stirring occasionally, until mushrooms have released their liquid, 8 to 10 minutes.

2. Uncover and continue to cook, stirring occasionally and scraping bottom of pot, until mushrooms are tender and pan is dry, 12 to 15 minutes. Transfer vegetables to bowl, cover, and set aside. Repeat with 3 tablespoons oil, remaining portobello mushrooms, remaining pearl onions, remaining ¼ teaspoon salt, and remaining ⅛ teaspoon pepper.

3. Add remaining 2 tablespoons oil and flour to now-empty pot and whisk until no dry flour remains. Whisk in broth, 2 cups wine, agar-agar, tomato paste, and anchovy substitute until combined, scraping up any browned bits and smoothing out any lumps. Stir in chopped onions, carrots, garlic, porcini mushrooms, parsley sprigs, thyme sprigs, bay leaves, and peppercorns. Bring to boil and cook, stirring occasionally, until liquid is slightly thickened and onions are translucent and softened, about 15 minutes.

4. Strain liquid through fine-mesh strainer set over large bowl, pressing on solids to extract as much liquid as possible; discard solids. Return liquid to now-empty pot and stir in remaining wine.

5. Bring mixture to boil over medium-high heat. Cook, stirring occasionally, until sauce has thickened to consistency of heavy cream, 5 to 7 minutes. Reduce heat to medium-low, stir in reserved portobello-onion mixture, and cook until just heated through, 3 to 5 minutes. Stir in minced parsley and serve.

PLANT POWER

AGAR-AGAR
Gelatin is made by rendering animal parts, but agar-agar is made from sea vegetables, which are boiled to extract their natural gel and then pressed, dried, and crushed into flakes or ground into a powder. It can be used just like gelatin in recipes as a stabilizing and thickening agent, although agar-agar has more powerful thickening properties, so less of it is needed to achieve the same effect.

Madras Okra Curry

Madras Okra Curry
Serves 4 to 6

Why This Recipe Works Okra has a long and varied history in Indian cuisine. We wanted our Madras-style okra curry to have a plentiful, rich, and pantry-friendly sauce, with okra that retained some of its fresh bite, so we made our sauce with the classic flavors of onion, ginger, garlic, and coconut milk. For convenience, we turned to store-bought Madras curry powder, which is distinguished by its inclusion of red chiles. Searing the okra whole in a skillet and then adding it to the sauce at the end of cooking—rather than letting it stew in the sauce to cook—kept it crisp-tender, with an appealing texture. Fresh cilantro sprigs and bright lime wedges balanced out our rich curry. We prefer the spicier flavor of Madras curry powder here, but you can substitute regular curry powder. Do not use frozen okra here. Serve over rice with a dollop of plant-based or dairy yogurt to tame the heat.

6 tablespoons vegetable oil, divided
1½ pounds okra, stemmed
1 small onion, chopped fine
3 garlic cloves, minced
1 tablespoon grated fresh ginger
1 tablespoon Madras curry powder
2½ cups vegetable broth
1 cup canned coconut milk
2 teaspoons light agave syrup or honey
1 teaspoon cornstarch
¼ teaspoon table salt
10 sprigs fresh cilantro, chopped coarse
Lime wedges

1. Heat 2 tablespoons oil in 12-inch skillet over medium-high heat until just smoking. Add half of okra to skillet and cook, stirring occasionally, until crisp-tender and well browned on most sides, 5 to 7 minutes; transfer to bowl. Repeat with 2 tablespoons oil and remaining okra; transfer to bowl. Let skillet cool slightly.

2. Heat remaining 2 tablespoons oil in now-empty skillet over medium heat until shimmering. Add onion and cook until softened, about 5 minutes. Stir in garlic, ginger, and curry powder and cook until fragrant, about 1 minute. Stir in broth, scraping up any browned bits, and bring to simmer. Cook, stirring occasionally, until reduced to 1¼ cups, 15 to 20 minutes.

3. Whisk coconut milk, agave, and cornstarch in bowl to dissolve cornstarch, then whisk mixture into skillet. Bring to simmer and cook until slightly thickened, about 30 seconds. Stir in okra and any accumulated juices and salt and return to brief simmer to warm through. Season with salt and pepper to taste. Sprinkle with cilantro and serve with lime wedges.

Roasted Okra with Fennel and Oregano

Serves 4 to 6 `FAST`

Why This Recipe Works This easy high-heat roasting technique is a simple, delicious way to bring out the best qualities of whole okra pods. The very hot oven, with its dry environment, prevented the okra from becoming too gelatinous—a common complaint about this vegetable. In fact, the hotter the oven, the better. A 500-degree oven produced okra with pleasant texture inside and a beautifully browned outside. To speed things along, we preheated the baking sheet on the lowest rack. We took our first seasoning combination in a Mediterranean direction, tossing the okra with cracked fennel and dried oregano, along with a fair amount of oil, which gave us a good sear on the okra and helped the spices to toast and bloom. Sesame and cumin proved to be another delicious combination. All that the okra needed was a squeeze of citrus to add brightness, and we had a simple, delicious dish that had okra skeptics asking for seconds. We like to serve this with Warm Farro with Lemon and Herbs (page 265). Do not use frozen okra here.

1½ pounds okra, stemmed
3 tablespoons extra-virgin olive oil
2 teaspoons dried oregano
2 teaspoons fennel seeds, cracked
¼ teaspoon table salt
Lemon wedges

1. Adjust oven rack to lowest position, place rimmed baking sheet on rack, and heat oven to 500 degrees. Toss okra with oil, oregano, fennel, and salt in bowl.

2. Working quickly, carefully transfer okra to hot baking sheet and spread into single layer. Roast until okra is crisp-tender and well browned on most sides, 20 to 25 minutes, stirring occasionally to ensure even browning. Season with salt and pepper to taste. Serve with lemon wedges.

VARIATION

Roasted Okra with Sesame and Cumin

Substitute 1 tablespoon sesame seeds for oregano, 2 teaspoons cracked cumin seeds for fennel seeds, and lime wedges for lemon. Toss cooked okra with 1 teaspoon toasted sesame oil after roasting in step 2.

Greek Stewed Okra with Tomatoes

Serves 6 to 8

Why This Recipe Works The bright-tasting, warmly spiced tomato sauce that envelops whole okra pods in this recipe allows the vegetal green freshness of the okra to shine through. Greek-style tomato sauce is often seasoned with cinnamon, allspice, and other warm baking spices. This version also includes onion, garlic, and lemon juice, for a sweet-savory balance. We found that salting and rinsing the okra pods before stewing them in the liquid minimized their tendency to develop slippery qualities. We prefer the flavor and texture of fresh okra here, but you can substitute frozen whole okra, thawed. Serve over rice or orzo for a flavorful dinner.

2 pounds okra, stemmed
¾ teaspoon table salt, plus salt for salting okra
2 (28-ounce) cans whole peeled tomatoes, drained
½ cup extra-virgin olive oil
1 onion, chopped fine
5 garlic cloves, sliced thin
½ teaspoon ground allspice
¼ teaspoon ground cinnamon
¼ teaspoon pepper
2 tablespoons lemon juice
¼ cup minced fresh parsley

PLANT POWER

OKRA

Okra contains a substance called mucilage, which is a naturally occurring pectin-like substance also found in seaweeds, aloe and other cacti, and flaxseeds. It's made up of chains of sugar molecules secreted outside the okra pod's cells and glycoproteins. Just like other food gels, such as gelatin, agar-agar, and cornstarch slurry, okra's starches need heat and water to fully form a gel. The molecules are loosened by the heat, and they then form a microscopic network that retains the water. Dry heat above 190°F damages the sugar-molecule chains so that they're less able to turn viscous. For recipes that slowly cook fresh okra in a moist environment, as in Greek Stewed Okra with Tomatoes, pretreating the okra with salt draws out the slightly viscous, starchy liquid from the pods, leaving less of it in the finished dish.

1. Toss okra with 2 teaspoons salt in colander and let sit for 1 hour, tossing again halfway through. Rinse well and set aside.

2. Process tomatoes in food processor until smooth, about 1 minute. Heat oil in Dutch oven over medium heat until shimmering. Add onion and cook until softened and lightly browned, 5 to 7 minutes. Stir in garlic, allspice, cinnamon, pepper, and salt and cook until fragrant, about 30 seconds. Stir in tomatoes and lemon juice and bring to simmer. Cook, stirring occasionally, until thickened slightly, about 10 minutes.

3. Stir in okra and return to simmer. Reduce heat to medium-low, cover, and cook, stirring occasionally, until okra is just tender, 20 to 25 minutes. Season with salt and pepper to taste. Sprinkle with parsley and serve.

Sautéed Parsnips with Ginger, Maple, and Fennel Seeds

Sautéed Parsnips with Ginger, Maple, and Fennel Seeds

Serves 4 to 6   FAST

Why This Recipe Works This delicious and dead-easy one-pan dish will definitely linger in your mind. It's simple enough to serve any night of the week but sophisticated enough for company. Cooking the parsnips was a short project: We cut them into uniform sticks and used a smoking-hot pan and minimal stirring so they were charred, caramelized, and cooked through in just minutes. Since parsnips have warm spice and licorice-like notes, we chose glaze ingredients, including fennel seeds and ginger, that would bring out those unique qualities. Maple syrup, soy sauce, and balsamic vinegar gave the glaze the perfect sweet, salty, and tart balance. You can substitute anise seeds for fennel. Look for parsnips with tops no larger than 1 inch in diameter for this recipe. If yours are larger, remove their fibrous cores before cooking. Turn this into an elevated hash by adding sautéed mushrooms and kale.

  2   **tablespoons soy sauce**
  2   **tablespoons balsamic vinegar**
  1   **tablespoon maple syrup**
1½   **teaspoons fennel seeds**
  2   **tablespoons minced fresh ginger**
  1   **teaspoon plus 2 tablespoons vegetable oil, divided**
1½   **pounds parsnips, peeled and cut into 2-inch-long by ½-inch-wide matchsticks**

1. Stir soy sauce, vinegar, maple syrup, and fennel seeds together in bowl; set aside. Combine ginger and 1 teaspoon oil in separate bowl; set aside.

2. Heat remaining 2 tablespoons oil in 12-inch skillet over medium-high heat until just smoking. Add parsnips and cook, stirring occasionally, until well charred and crisp-tender, 5 to 7 minutes.

3. Push parsnips to sides of skillet. Add ginger mixture to center and cook, mashing mixture into pan, until fragrant, about 30 seconds. Stir ginger into parsnips. Add soy mixture and toss to coat parsnips; cook until liquid is reduced to syrupy glaze, about 15 seconds. Serve immediately.

Simple Pureed Parsnips

Serves 4 to 6   FAST

Why This Recipe Works Like cauliflower (page 199), parsnips can be whipped to make a quick and simple puree that ably stands in for mashed potatoes. We steamed the parsnips, rather than boiling them, before processing them in the food processor. This gave us a puree with pure, sweet, and intense parsnip flavor. Parsnips are higher in starch than cauliflower but not as high in starch as potatoes, so you can still puree them in a food processor without turning them into a gummy mess—unlike potatoes. If you don't want to take out your food processor, you can puree the parsnips using any of the tools you might use to mash potatoes, though you will get a more rustic consistency. For a hearty New England–style vegan meal, serve with Baked Navy Beans (page 294).

1½ pounds parsnips, peeled, cut into 2½-inch lengths, and thick ends halved lengthwise
1½ tablespoons refined coconut oil or unsalted butter, softened

1. Bring 1 inch water to boil in covered Dutch oven over medium-high heat (water should not touch bottom of steamer basket).

2. Arrange parsnips in steamer basket. Set steamer basket inside Dutch oven, cover, and cook until they can be easily pierced with paring knife, about 10 minutes. Reserve cooking liquid.

3. Puree parsnips in food processor until smooth, about 1 minute, adding reserved cooking liquid as needed to achieve desired consistency. Return puree to now-empty Dutch oven and reheat over medium-low heat, stirring in oil. Season with salt and pepper to taste. Serve immediately.

Sautéed Snow Peas with Lemon and Parsley

Sautéed Snow Peas with Lemon and Parsley

Serves 4   FAST

Why This Recipe Works Sweet, grassy snow peas are the star component in this superspeedy side. (Or turn it into a main dish by tossing the snow peas with soba noodles and drizzling with toasted sesame oil.) We knew we wanted to caramelize the snow peas a bit to highlight and amplify their delicate flavor. First we tried a traditional stir-fry technique, but the constant stirring left us with greasy, overcooked pods without any browning. Adding a sprinkle of sugar and cooking the peas without stirring for a short time helped to achieve the flavorful sear we were after; we then continued to cook them, stirring constantly, until they were just crisp-tender. To boost flavor, we cleared the center of the pan and quickly sautéed a mixture of minced shallot, oil, and lemon zest before stirring everything together. A squeeze of lemon juice and a sprinkling of parsley just before serving kept this dish fresh and bright. The variations change up the seasonings but keep preparation just as simple.

1 tablespoon vegetable oil, divided
1 small shallot, minced
1 teaspoon finely grated lemon zest plus 1 teaspoon juice, divided
¼ teaspoon table salt
⅛ teaspoon pepper
⅛ teaspoon sugar
12 ounces snow peas, strings removed
1 tablespoon minced fresh parsley

1. Combine 1 teaspoon oil, shallot, and lemon zest in bowl. In separate bowl, combine salt, pepper, and sugar.

2. Heat remaining 2 teaspoons oil in 12-inch nonstick skillet over high heat until just smoking. Add snow peas, sprinkle with salt mixture, and cook, without stirring, for 30 seconds. Stir briefly, then cook, without stirring, for 30 seconds. Continue to cook, stirring constantly, until peas are crisp-tender, 1 to 2 minutes.

3. Push peas to sides of skillet. Add shallot mixture to center and cook, mashing mixture into skillet, until fragrant, about 30 seconds. Stir shallot mixture into peas. Stir in lemon juice and parsley and season with salt and pepper to taste. Serve.

Sautéed Snow Peas with Garlic, Cumin, and Cilantro
Add 2 minced garlic cloves and ½ teaspoon toasted and cracked cumin seeds to shallot mixture in step 1. Substitute ½ teaspoon lime zest for lemon zest, lime juice for lemon juice, and cilantro for parsley.

Sautéed Snow Peas with Lemongrass and Basil
Substitute 2 teaspoons minced fresh lemongrass for lemon zest, lime juice for lemon juice, and basil for parsley.

REMOVING STRINGS FROM SNOW PEAS

To remove fibrous string from snow peas, simply snap off tip of snow pea while pulling down along flat side of pod. The same method also works for snap peas.

Mechouia

Mechouia
Serves 4 to 6

Why This Recipe Works Mechouia is a robustly flavored Tunisian salad of vegetables grilled whole until their skins blacken, then peeled and blended with seasonings. When prepping the vegetables for the grill, we wanted to expose as much surface area to the heat as possible for the most charring, so we halved our eggplant, zucchini, and plum tomatoes lengthwise and stemmed and flattened the bell peppers. We also scored the eggplant and zucchini so they would release their excess moisture as they cooked. A potent combination of coriander, caraway, cumin, paprika, and cayenne infused our vegetables with the dish's characteristic flavor. The heat of the grill worked to bloom the flavor of the spices so they didn't taste raw or harsh, and more of the spices plus garlic, lemon, and a trio of herbs provided a bright, fresh-tasting dressing. Though the vegetables for this dish are traditionally mashed, tasters appreciated the texture of chopped vegetables here. Equal amounts of ground coriander and cumin can be substituted for the whole spices. Serve with grilled pita bread or with hard-cooked eggs and olives.

Dressing
- 2 teaspoons coriander seeds
- 1½ teaspoons caraway seeds
- 1 teaspoon cumin seeds
- 5 tablespoons extra-virgin olive oil
- ½ teaspoon sweet paprika
- ⅛ teaspoon cayenne pepper
- 3 garlic cloves, minced
- ¼ cup chopped fresh parsley
- ¼ cup chopped fresh cilantro
- 2 tablespoons chopped fresh mint
- 1 teaspoon grated lemon zest plus 2 tablespoons juice

Vegetables
- 2 bell peppers (1 red and 1 green), top and bottom trimmed, stemmed and seeded, and peppers flattened
- 1 small eggplant, halved lengthwise and scored on cut side
- 1 zucchini (8 to 10 ounces), halved lengthwise and scored on cut side
- 4 plum tomatoes, cored and halved lengthwise
- ½ teaspoon table salt
- 2 shallots, unpeeled

1. For the dressing Grind coriander seeds, caraway seeds, and cumin seeds in spice grinder until finely ground. Whisk ground spices, oil, paprika, and cayenne together in bowl. Reserve 3 tablespoons oil mixture for brushing vegetables before grilling. Heat remaining oil mixture and garlic in 8-inch skillet over low heat, stirring occasionally, until fragrant and small bubbles appear, 8 to 10 minutes. Transfer to large bowl, let cool for 10 minutes, then whisk in parsley, cilantro, mint, and lemon zest and juice and season with salt to taste.

2. For the vegetables Brush interior of bell peppers and cut sides of eggplant, zucchini, and tomatoes with reserved oil mixture and sprinkle with salt.

3A. For a charcoal grill Open bottom vent completely. Light large chimney starter three-quarters filled with charcoal briquettes (4½ quarts). When top coals are partially covered with ash, pour evenly over grill. Set cooking grate in place, cover, and open lid vent completely. Heat grill until hot, about 5 minutes.

3B. For a gas grill Turn all burners to high, cover, and heat grill until hot, about 15 minutes. Turn all burners to medium-high.

4. Clean and oil cooking grate. Place bell peppers, eggplant, zucchini, tomatoes, and shallots, cut sides down, on grill. Cook (covered if using gas), turning as needed, until tender and slightly charred, 8 to 16 minutes. Transfer eggplant, zucchini, tomatoes, and shallots to baking sheet as they finish cooking; place bell peppers in bowl, cover with plastic wrap, and let steam loosen skins.

5. Let vegetables cool slightly. Peel bell peppers, eggplant, tomatoes, and shallots. Chop all vegetables into ½-inch pieces, then toss gently with dressing in bowl. Season with salt and pepper to taste. Serve warm or at room temperature.

Grilled Peppers with Sherry Vinegar, Green Olives, and Capers

Serves 4 to 6

Why This Recipe Works Grilled red and yellow bell peppers with a simple vinaigrette and topped with green olives, capers, and parsley make a colorful Spanish vegetable dish that would be just as at home next to Tofu Fritatta with Mushrooms (page 30) as on a tapas platter with Spanish Spiced Roasted Chickpeas (page 355) and Stuffed Mushrooms (page 363). The most time-consuming part of this recipe is heating up the grill. We grilled the peppers whole until their skins blackened and then transferred them to a bowl and covered it with plastic wrap so the steam would cause the skins to loosen. We slipped off the skins, cored and seeded the peppers, and sliced them into strips to toss with the other flavorful ingredients.

4 red bell peppers and/or yellow bell peppers (1½ pounds)
2 tablespoons extra-virgin olive oil
1 tablespoon sherry vinegar
6 pitted green olives, chopped (¼ cup)
1 tablespoon capers, drained
1 tablespoon minced fresh parsley

1A. For a charcoal grill Open bottom vent completely. Light large chimney starter three-quarters filled with charcoal briquettes (4½ quarts). When top coals are partially covered with ash, pour evenly over grill. Set cooking grate in place, cover, and open lid vent completely. Heat grill until hot, about 5 minutes.

1B. For a gas grill Turn all burners to high, cover, and heat grill until hot, about 15 minutes. Turn all burners to medium-high.

2. Clean and oil cooking grate. Grill peppers, turning several times with tongs, until skins are blistered and charred on all sides, about 15 minutes.

3. Transfer peppers to medium bowl and cover with plastic wrap; let steam loosen skins. Remove skins; core and seed peppers, then cut into strips 1 inch wide. Return pepper strips with accumulated juices to bowl. Add oil and vinegar and season with salt and pepper to taste; toss gently. Arrange peppers on large platter and scatter with olives, capers, and parsley. Serve warm or at room temperature.

Grilled Potatoes with Garlic and Rosemary

Serves 4 to 6

Why This Recipe Works Grilled potatoes are a summertime classic, and we thought we'd jazz them up a bit by adding earthy, aromatic fresh rosemary and garlic. We initially found it difficult to add sufficient flavor to plain grilled potatoes. Simply coating the raw potatoes with oil, garlic, and rosemary and grilling them produced burnt, bitter garlic and charred rosemary. It turned out that we needed to apply the garlic-oil mixture to the potatoes in layers. Before cooking, we pierced the potatoes, skewered them, seasoned them with salt, brushed on the garlic-rosemary oil, and parcooked them in the microwave. Then, before grilling, we brushed them again with the infused oil. After a shortened grilling time, we tossed them with the oil yet again. We finally had it—tender potatoes infused with smoky, bold grilled flavor. This recipe works best with small potatoes that are about 1½ inches in diameter. If using medium potatoes, 2 to 3 inches in diameter, quarter them.

Grilled Potatoes with Garlic and Rosemary

3. Place potatoes in single layer on large plate and poke each potato several times with skewer. Brush with 1 tablespoon reserved oil and sprinkle with remaining ¼ teaspoon salt. Microwave until potatoes offer slight resistance when pierced with paring knife, about 8 minutes, turning halfway through microwaving. Coat rimmed baking sheet with 1 tablespoon reserved oil. Transfer potatoes to prepared sheet. Brush potatoes with remaining reserved oil and season with salt and pepper.

4A. For a charcoal grill Open bottom vent completely. Light large chimney starter filled with charcoal briquettes (6 quarts). When top coals are partially covered with ash, pour two-thirds evenly over half of grill, then pour remaining coals over other half of grill. Set cooking grate in place, cover, and open lid vent completely. Heat grill until hot, about 5 minutes.

4B. For a gas grill Turn all burners to high, cover, and heat grill until hot, about 15 minutes. Turn all burners to medium-high.

5. Clean and oil cooking grate. Place potatoes on grill (on hotter side if using charcoal) and cook (covered if using gas) until grill marks appear, 3 to 5 minutes, flipping potatoes halfway through cooking. Move potatoes to cooler side of grill (if using charcoal) or turn all burners to medium-low (if using gas). Cover and continue to cook until paring knife slips easily into and out of potatoes, 5 to 8 minutes.

6. Remove potatoes from skewers and transfer to bowl with reserved garlic-oil mixture. Add chives, season with salt and pepper to taste, and toss until thoroughly coated. Serve.

Roasted Smashed Potatoes
Serves 4 to 6

Why This Recipe Works Savor the creamy, smooth texture of mashed potatoes and the satisfying crunch of deep-fried spuds in one foolproof recipe. Success started with choosing the right potato; only small red potatoes, with their moist texture and thin skin, fit the bill. Before we could begin smashing, we needed to soften them, so we parcooked them, covered, on a baking sheet. Unlike boiling, which washed out flavor, this approach kept the potatoes earthy and sweet. After a short rest (very hot potatoes crumbled apart when smashed), we drizzled them with olive oil and smashed them all at once by placing a second baking sheet on top and pushing down. After adding chopped fresh thyme and more olive oil, and another stint in the oven uncovered, we had potatoes that were crisp on the outside and supercreamy inside. Use red potatoes measuring 1 to 2 inches in diameter. Remove them from the baking sheet as soon as they are done browning—they will toughen if left for too long. Add sautéed greens and Garlicky Yogurt Sauce (page 340) to make this a meal.

If the potatoes are larger than 3 inches in diameter, cut each potato into eighths. Since the potatoes are first cooked in the microwave, be sure to use wooden skewers instead of metal. Add all of your favorite loaded baked potato toppings to turn these potatoes into a fun main dish.

- ¼ cup extra-virgin olive oil
- 9 garlic cloves, minced
- 1 teaspoon chopped fresh rosemary
- ¾ teaspoon table salt, divided
- 2 pounds small red potatoes, unpeeled, halved, and threaded onto wooden skewers
- 2 tablespoons chopped fresh chives

1. Heat oil, garlic, rosemary, and ½ teaspoon salt in 8-inch skillet over medium heat until sizzling, about 3 minutes. Reduce heat to medium-low and continue to cook until garlic is just turning golden, about 3 minutes.

2. Strain mixture through fine-mesh strainer into small bowl; press on solids to extract as much liquid as possible. Transfer 1 tablespoon solids and 1 tablespoon oil to large bowl and set aside. Discard remaining solids and reserve remaining oil.

Roasted Smashed Potatoes

1. After rolling parcooked potatoes in oil, space potatoes evenly on baking sheet and place second baking sheet on top; press down firmly on baking sheet until potatoes are ⅓ to ½ inch thick.

2. Sprinkle smashed potatoes with thyme, salt, and pepper; drizzle evenly with remaining oil. Roast as directed until well browned.

2 pounds small red potatoes, unpeeled
¾ cup water
6 tablespoons extra-virgin olive oil
1 teaspoon chopped fresh thyme
¼ teaspoon table salt
⅛ teaspoon pepper

1. Adjust oven racks to top and lowest positions and heat oven to 500 degrees. Arrange potatoes on rimmed baking sheet, pour water into sheet, and wrap tightly with aluminum foil. Cook on lower rack until paring knife can be slipped into and out of center of potatoes with very little resistance (poke through foil to test), 25 to 30 minutes. Remove foil and let cool for 10 minutes. If any water remains on sheet, blot dry with paper towel.

2. Drizzle 3 tablespoons oil over potatoes and roll to coat. Space potatoes evenly on sheet and place second baking sheet on top. Press down firmly on second sheet, flattening potatoes until ⅓ to ½ inch thick. Sprinkle with thyme, salt, and pepper and drizzle evenly with remaining 3 tablespoons oil. Roast potatoes on upper rack for 15 minutes, then transfer potatoes to bottom rack and roast until well browned, 20 to 30 minutes. Serve immediately.

Potato Galette

Serves 6 to 8

Why This Recipe Works With its crispy, golden exterior crust and impressive layered presentation, a potato galette is a simple but sophisticated side or brunch dish. For even cooking and great browning, we began our galette recipe on the stovetop and then slid the pan onto the bottom rack of a hot oven. Using an ovensafe nonstick skillet averted the risk that our potato galette would stick to the pan's bottom and ruin its beautiful appearance. To keep the potatoes from sliding away from one another when we sliced our galette, we included cornstarch in the coconut oil (or butter) that we were using to coat the potatoes and compressed the galette using a cake pan filled with pie weights for the first half of cooking. Slicing the potatoes ⅛ inch thick is crucial for the success of this dish; use a mandoline, a V-slicer, or a food processor fitted with a ⅛-inch-thick slicing blade. You will need a 10-inch ovensafe nonstick skillet for this recipe.

2½ pounds Yukon Gold potatoes, unpeeled, sliced
⅛ inch thick
3 tablespoons refined coconut oil or unsalted butter, melted
1 tablespoon cornstarch
1½ teaspoons chopped fresh rosemary
1 teaspoon table salt
½ teaspoon pepper

1. Adjust oven rack to lowest position and heat oven to 450 degrees. Place potatoes in large bowl and fill with cold water. Swirl to remove excess starch, then drain in colander. Spread potatoes on towels and dry thoroughly.

2. Whisk melted oil, cornstarch, rosemary, salt, and pepper together in large bowl. Add potatoes and toss until thoroughly coated. Place 1 potato slice in center of 10-inch ovensafe non-stick skillet, then overlap slices in circle around center slice, followed by outer circle of overlapping slices. Gently place remaining sliced potatoes on top of first layer, arranging so they form even thickness.

3. Place skillet over medium-high heat and cook until potatoes are sizzling and slices around edge of cake start to turn translucent, about 5 minutes. Spray 12-inch square of aluminum foil with vegetable oil spray. Place foil, sprayed side down, on top of potatoes. Place 9-inch round cake pan on top of foil and fill with 2 cups pie weights. Firmly press down on cake pan to compress potatoes. Transfer skillet to oven and bake for 20 minutes.

4. Remove cake pan and foil from skillet. Continue to bake until paring knife can be inserted in center of cake with no resistance, 15 to 25 minutes. Being careful of hot skillet handle, gently shake pan (skillet handle will be hot) until galette releases from sides of skillet, 2 to 3 minutes. Carefully slide galette onto large plate, place cutting board over galette, and gently invert plate and cutting board together, then remove plate. Using serrated knife, gently cut galette into wedges and serve immediately.

Plant-Based Shepherd's Pie
Serves 4 to 6

Why This Recipe Works With its rich, satisfying filling and playful fluff of mashed potato topping, shepherd's pie has nearly universal appeal. The trouble is, neither the filling nor the topping is vegan-friendly, so we resolved to make a vegan version to please all palates on the coldest of nights. We first looked to the gravy. Sautéing umami-rich mushrooms and tomato paste with onion and garlic created lots of flavor-boosting fond; we then deglazed the pan with Madeira wine before adding the broth. This gravy gave us a backbone of meaty flavor, but the biggest key to success was using vegan protein crumbles. When cooked in our gravy along with the vegetables, they added an appealing ground beef–like chewiness. For the topping, we whipped up some mashed potatoes with chives, adding plant-based milk for creaminess. Using a fork, we created ridges in the potato topping that would brown under the broiler for a traditional presentation.

Plant-Based Shepherd's Pie

2 pounds russet potatoes, peeled and cut into 1-inch pieces
  Table salt for cooking potatoes
⅓ cup plant-based milk or dairy milk
5 tablespoons extra-virgin olive oil, divided
¼ cup minced fresh chives
1 onion, chopped
4 ounces white mushrooms, trimmed and chopped
¼ teaspoon pepper
1 tablespoon tomato paste
2 garlic cloves, minced
2 tablespoons Madeira or ruby port
2 tablespoons all-purpose flour
2½ cups vegetable broth
2 carrots, peeled and chopped
2 teaspoons vegan Worcestershire sauce
2 sprigs fresh thyme
1 bay leaf
12 ounces vegan protein crumbles, broken into small pieces

1. Cover potatoes with water in large saucepan. Add 1 tablespoon salt, bring to simmer over medium-high heat, and cook until potatoes are tender, 8 to 10 minutes.

2. Drain potatoes and return to now-empty saucepan. Using potato masher, mash potatoes until smooth, then stir in milk, ¼ cup oil, and chives. Season with salt and pepper to taste; cover and set aside.

3. Heat remaining 1 tablespoon oil in broiler-safe 10-inch skillet over medium heat until shimmering. Add onion, mushrooms, and pepper and cook until softened, about 5 minutes. Stir in tomato paste and garlic and cook until bottom of skillet is dark brown, about 2 minutes.

4. Stir in Madeira and cook, scraping up any browned bits, until evaporated, about 1 minute. Stir in flour and cook for 1 minute. Stir in broth, carrots, Worcestershire, thyme sprigs, and bay leaf and bring to boil, scraping up any browned bits. Reduce heat to medium-low and simmer gently until carrots and mushrooms are tender, 10 to 15 minutes. Discard thyme sprigs and bay leaf, stir in protein crumbles, and season with salt and pepper to taste.

5. Adjust oven rack 5 inches from broiler element and heat broiler. Transfer mashed potatoes to 1-gallon zipper-lock bag, seal top, and snip off bottom corner to make 1-inch opening. Pipe potatoes evenly over filling to cover. Smooth potatoes with back of spoon, then make ridges over surface with fork. Place skillet on rimmed baking sheet and broil until potatoes are golden and crusty, 5 to 10 minutes. Let cool for 10 minutes before serving.

Spinach with Garlic and Lemon
Serves 4   FAST

Why This Recipe Works The pairing of fresh spinach, savory garlic, and bright lemon is a classic favorite that still deserves attention to prepare it well. We sought tender sautéed leaves seasoned with a perfect balance of garlic and lemon. For the spinach, we found that we greatly preferred the hearty flavor and texture of curly-leaf spinach over baby spinach, which wilted into mush. We cooked the spinach in extra-virgin olive oil and then used tongs to squeeze the cooked spinach in a colander to get rid of all the excess moisture. Lightly toasted minced garlic, cooked after the spinach, added sweet nuttiness. As for seasoning, all the spinach needed was salt and a squeeze of lemon juice. Leave some water clinging to the spinach leaves after rinsing to help encourage steam when cooking. Two pounds of flat-leaf spinach (about three bunches) can be substituted for curly-leaf, but do not use baby spinach because it is much too delicate. Add some sautéed white beans or chickpeas and a sprinkle of Pistachio Dukkah (page 143) or nuts to turn this into a quick meal.

   3 tablespoons extra-virgin olive oil, divided
  20 ounces curly-leaf spinach, stemmed
   2 garlic cloves, minced
     Lemon juice

1. Heat 1 tablespoon oil in Dutch oven over high heat until shimmering. Add spinach 1 handful at a time, stirring and tossing each handful to wilt slightly before adding more. Cook spinach, stirring constantly, until uniformly wilted, about 1 minute. Transfer spinach to colander and squeeze between tongs to release excess liquid. Wipe pot dry with paper towels.

2. Add garlic and remaining 2 tablespoons oil to now-empty pot and cook over medium heat until fragrant, about 30 seconds. Add squeezed spinach and toss to coat. Off heat, season with salt and lemon juice to taste. Serve.

Grilled Radicchio
Serves 4   FAST

Why This Recipe Works Radicchio is extremely popular in Italy, where you're just as likely to find it grilled or roasted as you are to find it raw in a salad. When grilled, the purple leaves become lightly crisp and wonderfully smoky-tasting. To keep the radicchio from falling apart on the grill, we cut it through the core into thick wedges. While we wanted char on our radicchio leaves, we didn't want to burn them; brushing them with a liberal amount of olive oil added flavor and richness and prevented burning. Turning the wedges during cooking ensured that all sides, including the rounded one, spent time facing the fire. A drizzle of good balsamic vinegar was all that was needed to complete this simple side. You can turn this into a main-dish salad (and temper the radicchio's natural bitterness at the same time) by adding roasted cubes of butternut squash, sliced pear, and smoked almonds.

   3 heads radicchio (10 ounces each), quartered
   ¼ cup extra-virgin olive oil
     Balsamic vinegar

1. Place radicchio on rimmed baking sheet, brush with oil, and season with salt and pepper to taste.

2A. For a charcoal grill Open bottom vent completely. Light large chimney starter three-quarters filled with charcoal briquettes (4½ quarts). When top coals are partially covered with ash, pour evenly over grill. Set cooking grate in place, cover, and open lid vent completely. Heat grill until hot, about 5 minutes.

2B. For a gas grill Turn all burners to high, cover, and heat grill until hot, about 15 minutes. Turn all burners to medium-high.

3. Clean and oil cooking grate. Grill radicchio, turning every 1½ minutes, until edges are browned and wilted but centers are still slightly firm, about 5 minutes. Transfer radicchio to serving dish, drizzle with vinegar, and serve.

Saag Tofu
Serves 4 to 6

Why This Recipe Works With a spicy sauce of pureed stewed spinach containing pieces of fresh cheese and often finished with cream or butter, saag paneer is a revered Indian dish and favorite takeout choice. The mild fresh cheese reminded us of firm tofu, so we thought a tofu rendition would make a great vegan version. We built layers of flavor by frying spices and caramelizing onion, jalapeño, garlic, ginger, and tomatoes. Mustard greens, which are often used in this dish in northern India, added texture and pungency. Cashews, pureed into the sauce with some plant-based (or dairy) milk and also sprinkled on top for serving, added buttery richness and body. All we needed to do with the tofu cubes was heat them until they took on a creamy consistency. We prefer firm tofu here, but you can substitute extra-firm tofu; do not use soft tofu, as it will disintegrate. For a spicier dish, include the ribs and seeds from the jalapeño. Serve over rice.

Saag Tofu

14	ounces firm tofu, cut into ½-inch pieces
⅛	teaspoon plus ¾ teaspoon table salt, divided
	Pinch pepper
12	ounces curly-leaf spinach, stemmed
12	ounces mustard greens, stemmed
3	tablespoons vegetable oil
1	teaspoon cumin seeds
1	teaspoon ground coriander
1	teaspoon paprika
½	teaspoon ground cardamom
¼	teaspoon ground cinnamon
1	onion, chopped fine
1	jalapeño chile, stemmed, seeded, and minced
3	garlic cloves, minced
1	tablespoon grated fresh ginger
1	(14.5-ounce) can diced tomatoes, drained and chopped
1½	cups plant-based milk or dairy milk
½	cup roasted cashews, chopped
1	teaspoon sugar
1½	tablespoons lemon juice
3	tablespoons minced fresh cilantro

1. Spread tofu on paper towel–lined baking sheet and let drain for 20 minutes. Gently press dry with paper towels and sprinkle with ⅛ teaspoon salt and pepper.

2. Meanwhile, microwave spinach in bowl, covered, until wilted, about 3 minutes; transfer ½ cup spinach to blender. Chop remaining spinach; set aside. Microwave mustard greens in now-empty bowl, covered, until wilted, about 4 minutes; transfer ½ cup to blender with spinach. Chop remaining mustard greens; set aside.

3. Heat oil in 12-inch skillet over medium-high heat until shimmering. Add cumin seeds, coriander, paprika, cardamom, and cinnamon and cook until fragrant, about 30 seconds. Add onion and remaining ¾ teaspoon salt and cook, stirring frequently, until softened, about 3 minutes. Stir in jalapeño, garlic, and ginger and cook until lightly browned and just beginning to stick to pan, about 3 minutes. Stir in tomatoes, scraping up any browned bits, and cook until pan is dry and tomatoes are beginning to brown, about 4 minutes.

4. Transfer half of onion-tomato mixture, ¾ cup milk, ¼ cup cashews, and sugar to blender with greens and process until smooth, about 1 minute. Add pureed greens, chopped greens, lemon juice, and remaining ¾ cup milk to skillet with remaining onion-tomato mixture and bring to simmer over medium-high heat. Reduce heat to low and season with salt and pepper to taste. Stir in tofu and cook until warmed through, about 2 minutes. Transfer to serving platter, sprinkle with cilantro and remaining ¼ cup cashews, and serve.

Overstuffed Sweet Potatoes with Tofu and Thai Curry
Serves 4

Why This Recipe Works This fresh modern take on stuffed potatoes takes its cue from the tangy and sweet flavors of Thai-style curries. All of the elements—rich, earthy sweet potato halves along with morsels of tofu, broccoli, mushrooms, and bell peppers—are roasted to perfection on a single baking sheet. To create extra-crispy tofu, we dusted pieces of tofu with cornstarch and then we arranged them on one side of an oiled baking sheet and placed the sweet potato halves on the other side. (Halving the sweet potatoes reduced the roasting time from an hour for whole potatoes to a mere 20 minutes.) Once the potatoes were done, we added the other vegetables to the space left on the baking sheet and roasted them until tender in the time it took to finish the crispy tofu. After stuffing the potatoes with the tofu and vegetables, we drizzled them with a curry vinaigrette packed with the bold flavors of lime and curry paste. All this hearty meal needs is a simple green salad. Do not substitute soft tofu here. If you can't find Thai basil, you can substitute Italian basil. Green and red curry paste work equally well; just read the label to ensure that the paste is vegan.

- 14 ounces firm tofu, cut into ¾-inch pieces
- ½ cup plus 1 teaspoon vegetable oil, divided
- 1 teaspoon table salt, divided
- ½ teaspoon pepper, divided
- 6 tablespoons cornstarch
- 2 sweet potatoes (12 ounces each), unpeeled, halved lengthwise
- 8 ounces broccoli florets, cut into ½-inch pieces
- 8 ounces white or cremini mushrooms, trimmed and quartered
- 1 red bell pepper, stemmed, seeded, and cut into ¼-inch-wide strips
- 1 teaspoon grated lime zest plus 2 tablespoons juice
- 2 teaspoons Thai green or red curry paste
- ¼ cup shredded fresh Thai basil

1. Spread tofu over paper towel–lined plate and let drain for 20 minutes.

2. Adjust oven rack to lower-middle position and heat oven to 450 degrees. Brush rimmed baking sheet with 3 tablespoons oil. Gently pat tofu dry with paper towels, sprinkle with ½ teaspoon salt and ¼ teaspoon pepper, then toss with cornstarch in bowl. Arrange tofu in even layer on 1 half of sheet. Arrange potato halves cut side down on empty side of sheet and brush skins with 1 teaspoon oil. Roast until potato halves yield to gentle pressure and centers register 200 degrees, 20 to 25 minutes, flipping tofu with spatula halfway through roasting.

3. Toss broccoli, mushrooms, and bell pepper with 1 tablespoon oil, ¼ teaspoon salt, and ⅛ teaspoon pepper in bowl. Remove sheet from oven, transfer potato halves to plate, and tent with aluminum foil to keep warm. Arrange broccoli mixture in even layer on now-empty side of sheet and roast until vegetables are tender and beginning to brown and tofu is crisp and lightly browned, 10 to 15 minutes, tossing vegetables and flipping tofu halfway through roasting.

4. Whisk lime zest and juice, curry paste, remaining ¼ cup oil, remaining ¼ teaspoon salt, and remaining ⅛ teaspoon pepper together in bowl. Arrange potato halves cut side up on individual serving plates. Using 2 forks, press potato flesh to sides to make room in center for tofu and vegetable mixture. Top potato halves with tofu and vegetable mixture, drizzle with vinaigrette, and sprinkle with basil. Serve.

Vindaloo-Style Sweet Potatoes
Serves 4 to 6

Why This Recipe Works Vindaloo is a complex dish that blends Portuguese and Indian cuisines in a potent braise featuring warm spices, chiles, wine vinegar, tomatoes, onions, garlic, and mustard seeds. It's often made with pork, lamb, or chicken as the main ingredient, but here we translated its comfort-food appeal into a hearty vegan stew. Centering our dish on a combination of sweet potatoes and red potatoes proved just right. To give our stew exceptionally deep flavor, we used a mix of Indian spices, along with bay leaves and mustard seeds, and simmered the spices along with the potatoes. However, after 45 minutes of simmering, the potatoes still weren't fully cooked. A second look at our ingredients showed us why: The acidic environment created by the tomatoes and vinegar was preventing the potatoes from becoming tender. To test our theory, we whipped up another batch, this time leaving out the tomatoes and vinegar until the end, cooking them just enough to mellow their flavors. Sure enough, after just 15 minutes, the potatoes were perfectly tender. If you like, top each serving with a cooling dollop of plant-based or dairy yogurt.

2 tablespoons vegetable oil

2 onions, chopped fine

1 pound sweet potatoes, peeled and
cut into ½-inch pieces

1 pound red potatoes, unpeeled,
cut into ½-inch pieces

1½ teaspoons table salt, divided

10 garlic cloves, minced

4 teaspoons paprika

1 teaspoon ground cumin

¾ teaspoon ground cardamom

½ teaspoon cayenne pepper

¼ teaspoon ground cloves

2½ cups water

2 bay leaves

1 tablespoon mustard seeds

1 (28-ounce) can diced tomatoes

2½ tablespoons red wine vinegar

¼ cup minced fresh cilantro

1. Heat oil in Dutch oven over medium heat until shimmering. Add onions, sweet potatoes, red potatoes, and ½ teaspoon salt and cook, stirring occasionally, until onions are softened and potatoes begin to soften at edges, 10 to 12 minutes.

2. Stir in garlic, paprika, cumin, cardamom, cayenne, and cloves and cook until fragrant and vegetables are well coated, about 2 minutes. Gradually stir in water, scraping up any browned bits. Stir in bay leaves, mustard seeds, and remaining 1 teaspoon salt and bring to simmer. Cover, reduce heat to medium-low, and cook until potatoes are tender, 15 to 20 minutes.

3. Stir in tomatoes and their juice and vinegar and continue to simmer, uncovered, until flavors meld and sauce has thickened slightly, about 15 minutes. Discard bay leaves, stir in cilantro, and season with salt and pepper to taste. Serve.

Sweet Potato Curry with Eggplant, Chickpeas, and Herb Chutney

Serves 4 to 6

Why This Recipe Works Don't let the long ingredient list put you off this ultimate mixed-vegetable curry. For an amazing curry, we started with the sauce. Toasting store-bought curry powder and garam masala increased their flavor dimension substantially and saved us the time of making our own blends. We cooked the spices and aromatics with our vegetables—a texturally diverse combination of creamy sweet potatoes; savory, meaty eggplant; and earthy green beans; plus

a can of chickpeas—so that they would permeate every bite of the dish. Rounding out the sauce was a combination of water, pureed canned tomatoes, and a splash of canned coconut milk for richness. We served the curry with an herb-packed cilantro and mint chutney that can be made with plant-based or dairy yogurt. We prefer the richer flavor of regular coconut milk here; however, light coconut milk can be substituted. To make this curry spicier, add the seeds from the chile. Serve over rice.

Herb Chutney

2 cups fresh cilantro leaves

1 cup fresh mint leaves

⅓ cup plant-based yogurt or dairy yogurt

¼ cup finely chopped onion

1 tablespoon lime juice

1½ teaspoons sugar

½ teaspoon ground cumin

¼ teaspoon table salt

Curry

1 (14.5-ounce) can diced tomatoes

3 tablespoons vegetable oil

4 teaspoons curry powder

1½ teaspoons garam masala

2 onions, chopped fine

12 ounces sweet potatoes, peeled and cut into
1-inch pieces

¼ teaspoon table salt

3 garlic cloves, minced

1 serrano chile, stemmed, seeded, and minced

1 tablespoon grated fresh ginger

1 tablespoon tomato paste

1 pound eggplant, cut into ½-inch pieces

8 ounces green beans, trimmed and cut into
1-inch lengths

1½ cups water

1 (15-ounce) can chickpeas, rinsed

½ cup canned coconut milk

¼ cup minced fresh cilantro

1. For the chutney Process all ingredients in food processor until smooth, about 20 seconds, scraping down sides of bowl as needed. (Chutney can be refrigerated for up to 1 day.)

2. For the curry Pulse diced tomatoes and their juice in clean, dry food processor until nearly smooth, with ¼-inch pieces visible, about 3 pulses. Heat oil in Dutch oven over medium-high heat until shimmering. Add curry powder and garam masala and cook until fragrant, about 10 seconds. Stir in onions, sweet potatoes, and salt and cook, stirring occasionally, until onions are browned and potatoes are golden brown at edges, about 10 minutes.

Sweet Potato Curry with
Eggplant, Chickpeas, and
Herb Chutney

Vegetable Pot Pie
Serves 4 to 6

Why This Recipe Works Pure comfort food, this pot pie features a hearty combination of vegetables napped with a rich, flavorful gravy, all tucked into a flaky, tender crust. When choosing the vegetables, we thought about flavor, appearance, and cooking method. Delicate vegetables like asparagus and leeks turned an unappealing army green in the gravy, and they overcooked by the time the sauce was thickened and the crust was browned. So instead, we chose a combination of longer-cooking vegetables of varying colors, flavors, and textures: mushrooms, sweet potato, turnip, and Swiss chard. So that each vegetable came out tender, we sautéed the mushrooms, sweet potato, and turnip before stirring in the chard. This also helped us to create the delicious gravy—all those vegetables left behind a good amount of fond in the pot. When we whisked in the broth, the fond was incorporated into the sauce, lending it complexity. The sugar in this dough doesn't make it sweet but helps with browning; this dough will be moister than most pie doughs.

Pie Dough

1½ cups (7½ ounces) all-purpose flour
1 tablespoon sugar
½ teaspoon table salt
½ cup plus 1 tablespoon refined coconut oil
¼ cup ice water, plus extra as needed

Filling

¼ cup refined coconut oil, divided
1 onion, chopped fine
8 ounces cremini mushrooms, trimmed and quartered if large or halved if small
1 teaspoon table salt, divided
1 sweet potato (12 ounces), peeled and cut into ½-inch pieces
8 ounces turnips, peeled and cut into ½-inch pieces
3 garlic cloves, minced
½ teaspoon grated lemon zest plus 1 tablespoon juice
8 ounces Swiss chard, stemmed and cut into 1-inch pieces
3 tablespoons all-purpose flour
2 cups vegetable broth
2 tablespoons minced fresh parsley
⅔ cup water
2 teaspoons cornstarch

3. Reduce heat to medium. Stir in garlic, serrano, ginger, and tomato paste and cook until fragrant, about 30 seconds. Add eggplant and green beans and cook, stirring constantly, until vegetables are coated with spices, about 2 minutes.

4. Gradually stir in water, scraping up any browned bits. Stir in chickpeas and tomatoes; bring to simmer. Cover, reduce heat to medium-low, and simmer gently until vegetables are tender, 20 to 25 minutes. Uncover, stir in coconut milk, and cook until warmed through, 1 to 2 minutes. Off heat, stir in cilantro and season with salt and pepper to taste. Serve with chutney.

VARIATION

Potato Curry with Cauliflower, Chickpeas, and Herb Chutney
Substitute 12 ounces red potatoes, unpeeled and cut into ½-inch pieces, for sweet potatoes. Substitute ½ head of cauliflower (1 pound), cored and cut into 1-inch florets, for eggplant and green beans. Stir in 1½ cups of frozen peas with coconut milk in step 4.

1. For the pie dough Process ¾ cup flour, sugar, and salt in food processor until combined, about 5 seconds. Pinch off ½-inch pieces of oil into flour mixture and pulse until sticky and dough begins to come together, 10 to 16 pulses. (If dough clumps around blade, redistribute around workbowl.) Add remaining ¾ cup flour, and pulse until just incorporated, 3 to 6 pulses; transfer to large bowl.

2. Sprinkle ice water over top of dough, then, using rubber spatula, fold and press dough to fully incorporate water and bring dough together, being careful not to overmix. If dough doesn't come together, add up to 1 tablespoon ice water, 1 teaspoon at a time. Form dough into 4-inch disk. (Dough can be wrapped tightly in plastic wrap and refrigerated for up to 2 days or frozen for up to 1 month. Let dough sit at room temperature to soften completely before rolling out, about 2 hours if refrigerated or 4 hours if frozen.)

3. Roll dough between 2 large sheets parchment paper into 10-inch circle. Remove parchment on top of dough. Fold over outer ½-inch edge of dough, then crimp into tidy fluted edge using your fingers. Using paring knife, cut four 2-inch oval-shaped vents in center. Slide parchment paper with crust onto baking sheet and refrigerate until needed.

4. For the filling Meanwhile, adjust oven rack to middle position and heat oven to 400 degrees. Melt 2 tablespoons oil in Dutch oven over medium heat. Stir in onion, mushrooms, and ½ teaspoon salt and cook until mushrooms have released their liquid, about 5 minutes.

5. Stir in sweet potato and turnips. Reduce heat to medium-low, cover, and cook, stirring occasionally, until potato and turnips begin to soften around edges, 7 to 9 minutes. Stir in garlic and lemon zest and cook until fragrant, about 30 seconds. Stir in chard and cook until wilted, about 2 minutes; transfer to bowl.

6. Melt remaining 2 tablespoons oil in now-empty pot over medium-high heat. Stir in flour and cook for 1 minute. Gradually whisk in broth, scraping up any browned bits and smoothing out any lumps. Bring to simmer and cook until sauce thickens slightly, about 1 minute. Off heat, whisk in parsley, lemon juice, and remaining ½ teaspoon salt. Stir in cooked vegetables, along with any accumulated juices, and season with salt and pepper to taste.

7. Transfer filling to 9½-inch deep-dish pie plate set on aluminum foil–lined rimmed baking sheet. Place chilled crust on top. Bake until crust is golden brown and filling is bubbling, about 30 minutes.

8. Whisk water and cornstarch together in small saucepan. Whisking constantly, bring to boil over high heat; remove pot from heat. Transfer pot pie to wire rack and, working quickly, brush surface of pot pie with cornstarch mixture, being careful to avoid pooling. Let cool for 10 minutes before serving.

Green Shakshuka with Eggs

Green Shakshuka
Serves 4 **FAST**

Why This Recipe Works The classic Tunisian dish shakshuka is a humble yet satisfying one-pot preparation, usually consisting of eggs cooked in a long-simmered, spiced tomato and pepper sauce. Our vibrant vegan-optional version makes a few important changes; namely, it goes green and omits the eggs (though we have included a variation with eggs). We tried a variety of vegetable combos and settled on savory Swiss chard and easy-to-prep baby spinach, cooking a cup of the sliced chard stems (any more and their vegetal flavors overwhelmed the dish) with onion to create an aromatic base. We eschewed the traditional strong flavors of cumin and paprika in favor of coriander—its citrusy notes allowed the greens' flavors to hold center stage. The roomy Dutch oven allowed us to wilt the large volume of raw greens easily. We blended a cup of the greens mixture with broth to give the sauce a creamy, cohesive texture, then added frozen peas for contrasting pops of sweetness and texture. The optional feta adds a tangy, creamy element. The Dutch oven will seem crowded when you first add the greens, but they will quickly wilt down. Serve with toasted pita or crusty bread to mop up the sauce. If you make the variation, avoid removing the lid during the first 5 minutes of cooking the eggs, as it will increase their cooking time.

2 pounds Swiss chard, stems removed and reserved, leaves chopped
¼ cup extra-virgin olive oil, divided
1 large onion, chopped fine
¾ teaspoon table salt
4 garlic cloves, minced
2 teaspoons ground coriander
11 ounces (11 cups) baby spinach, chopped
½ cup vegetable broth
1 cup frozen peas
1½ tablespoons lemon juice
2 ounces feta cheese, crumbled (½ cup) (optional)
2 tablespoons chopped fresh dill
2 tablespoons chopped fresh mint

1. Slice chard stems thin to yield 1 cup; discard remaining stems or reserve for another use. Heat 2 tablespoons oil in Dutch oven over medium heat until shimmering. Add chard stems, onion, and salt and cook until vegetables are softened and lightly browned, 5 to 7 minutes. Stir in garlic and coriander and cook until fragrant, about 1 minute.

2. Add chard leaves and spinach. Increase heat to medium-high, cover, and cook, stirring occasionally, until wilted but still bright green, 3 to 5 minutes. Off heat, transfer 1 cup chard mixture to blender. Add broth and process until smooth, about 45 seconds, scraping down sides of blender jar as needed. Stir chard mixture, peas, and lemon juice into pot.

3. Sprinkle with feta, if using; dill; and mint and drizzle with remaining 2 tablespoons oil. Serve immediately.

VARIATION
Green Shakshuka with Eggs
In beginning of step 3, make 4 shallow indentations (about 2 inches wide) in surface of greens using back of spoon. Crack 2 eggs into each indentation, sprinkle with ½ teaspoon dried Aleppo pepper, then sprinkle with ⅛ teaspoon table salt. Cover and cook over medium-low heat until edges of egg whites are just set, 5 to 10 minutes. Off heat, let sit, covered, until whites are fully set and yolks are still runny, 2 to 4 minutes.

Garlicky Swiss Chard
Serves 4 to 6 FAST

Why This Recipe Works A quick one-pot approach to cooking Swiss chard is a fast way to a flavorful and versatile side dish. Chard has a fair amount of moisture, so to avoid watery, overcooked chard, we started cooking the greens in a covered pot just until they wilted down. Then we uncovered the pot and continued to cook the greens until all the liquid evaporated. Cutting the tough stems smaller than the tender leaves meant that we could throw both in the pot at the same time and still get evenly cooked results. Sautéing plenty of garlic in olive oil before adding the chard gave this simple side a big hit of flavor, while a splash of mild white wine vinegar and a pinch of red pepper flakes added brightness and subtle heat. Pair this with French Lentils with Carrots and Parsley (page 287) or White Bean and Mushroom Gratin (page 299) for a comforting meal.

3 tablespoons extra-virgin olive oil, divided
6 garlic cloves, minced
2 pounds Swiss chard, stems chopped fine, leaves sliced into ½-inch-wide strips
¼ teaspoon table salt
⅛ teaspoon red pepper flakes
1 teaspoon white wine vinegar

1. Cook 2 tablespoons oil and garlic in Dutch oven over medium-low heat, stirring occasionally, until garlic is light golden and fragrant, about 3 minutes. Stir in chard, salt, and pepper flakes. Increase heat to high, cover, and cook, stirring occasionally, until chard is wilted but still bright green, 2 to 4 minutes.

2. Uncover and continue to cook, stirring often, until liquid evaporates, 4 to 6 minutes. Stir in vinegar and remaining 1 tablespoon oil. Season with salt and pepper to taste. Serve.

VARIATION
Gingery Swiss Chard
Add 1 tablespoon grated fresh ginger to pot with chard. In step 2, substitute 1 tablespoon toasted sesame oil for olive oil and substitute 4 teaspoons soy sauce for vinegar. Sprinkle chard with 3 tablespoons sliced scallion and ¼ cup chopped salted dry-roasted peanuts before serving.

Roasted Delicata Squash

Chile-Rubbed Butternut Squash
Steaks with Vegan Ranch Dressing

Roasted Delicata Squash
Serves 6 to 8

Why This Recipe Works Delicata is the easiest winter squash to cook because its prettily striated skin is so thin that it doesn't need to be peeled before cooking and eating. Roasting intensifies delicata squash's mild flavors, so we simply sliced the squash into half-moons and roasted the pieces on a baking sheet with coconut oil (or butter) until tender and golden brown, covering them with foil for the first 20 minutes to ensure that each bite cooked up creamy and moist, and flipping the pieces once. A bright sauce made with plenty of fresh herbs, garlic, sherry vinegar, and smoked paprika lent a bold, contrasting flavor punch without overshadowing our lovely star vegetable. To ensure even cooking, choose squashes that are similar in size and shape. To turn this simple side dish into a meal, serve it over a grain such as quinoa or bulgur or even couscous.

Herb Sauce
- ¼ cup minced fresh parsley or chives
- ¼ cup extra-virgin olive oil
- 2 tablespoons sherry vinegar
- 2 garlic cloves, minced
- 1 teaspoon smoked paprika
- ¼ teaspoon table salt

Squash
- 3 delicata squashes (12 to 16 ounces each), ends trimmed, halved lengthwise, seeded, and sliced crosswise ½ inch thick
- 4 teaspoons refined coconut oil or unsalted butter, melted, plus 2 tablespoons refined coconut oil or unsalted butter, cut into 8 pieces
- ½ teaspoon table salt

1. For the sauce Stir all ingredients together in bowl; set aside for serving.

2. For the squash Adjust oven rack to lowest position and heat oven to 425 degrees. Toss squash, melted oil, and salt in bowl to coat. Arrange squash in single layer on rimmed baking sheet. Cover tightly with aluminum foil and bake until squash is tender when pierced with tip of paring knife, 18 to 20 minutes.

3. Uncover and continue to bake until side touching baking sheet is golden brown, 8 to 11 minutes. Remove squash from oven and, using thin metal spatula, flip slices over. Scatter coconut oil pieces over squash. Return to oven and continue to bake until side touching baking sheet is golden brown, 8 to 11 minutes. Transfer squash to serving platter and drizzle with herb sauce. Serve.

Chile-Rubbed Butternut Squash Steaks with Vegan Ranch Dressing

Serves 4 **FAST**

Why This Recipe Works Butternut squash's dense texture gives it a meaty bite, and its mild flavor can handle bold seasonings, making it a great candidate for the steak treatment. To create thick slabs, we used the necks of large butternuts, peeling and slicing them lengthwise. We first tried searing the steaks in a hot skillet before transferring them to the oven, but this made the exteriors soggy. Reversing the process and roasting the steaks before searing ensured the interior was tender, and it dried out the exterior so that it could develop a crust in the skillet. We scored the surface in a crosshatch pattern to create more surface area for absorbing our spice rub, speed up the process of drying out the exterior, and give our steaks the appearance of grill marks. A bold Southwestern rub of smoked paprika, chipotle chile powder, garlic powder, sugar, salt, pepper, and olive oil reminded tasters of blackened steak. Our Vegan Ranch Dressing was a cooling foil to its intensity. Look for butternut squashes with necks at least 5 inches long and 2½ to 3½ inches in diameter.

- ¼ cup extra-virgin olive oil, divided
- 2 teaspoons sugar
- 2 teaspoons smoked paprika
- 1½ teaspoons table salt
- ½ teaspoon chipotle chile powder
- 1 teaspoon garlic powder
- ½ teaspoon pepper
- 2 (3-pound) butternut squashes
- 1 recipe Vegan Ranch Dressing (page 365)

1. Adjust oven rack to middle position and heat oven to 450 degrees. Combine 3 tablespoons oil, sugar, paprika, salt, chile powder, garlic powder, and pepper in bowl; set aside.

2. Working with 1 squash at a time, cut crosswise into 2 pieces at base of neck; reserve bulb for another use. Peel away skin and fibrous threads just below skin (squash should be completely orange, with no white flesh), then carefully cut each piece in half lengthwise. Cut one ¾-inch-thick slab lengthwise from each half. Repeat with remaining squash. (You should have 4 steaks; reserve remaining squash for another use.)

3. Place steaks on wire rack set in rimmed baking sheet. Cut 1/16-inch-deep slits on both sides of steaks, spaced ½ inch apart, in crosshatch pattern, and brush evenly with spice mixture. Flip steaks and brush second side with spice mixture. Roast until nearly tender and knife inserted into steaks meets with some resistance, 15 to 17 minutes; remove from oven.

4. Heat remaining 1 tablespoon oil in 12-inch nonstick skillet over medium-high heat until just smoking. Carefully place steaks in skillet and cook, without moving, until well browned and crisp on first side, about 3 minutes. Flip steaks and continue to cook until well browned and crisp on second side, about 3 minutes. Serve with ranch dressing.

Roasted Butternut Squash with Radicchio

Serves 4 to 6

Why This Recipe Works The popular London-based chef Yotam Ottolenghi introduced us to an alternative squash universe. He roasts thin skin-on half-moons of squash and then tosses them with savory ingredients, from chiles and lime to toasted nuts and spiced yogurt, which serve as a successful foil to the squash's natural sweetness. We decided to adapt this approach in the test kitchen. Our first move was to lose the butternut squash skin and the white layer of flesh underneath, both of which tasters found unappealing. To achieve deeper caramelization on the squash slices, we positioned the baking sheet on the lowest oven rack. We then flipped the squash (and rotated the baking sheet) partway through roasting so that both sides could caramelize. These slices emerged perfectly caramelized, wonderfully sweet, and tender. The crowning touch was a few toppings that provided a mix of contrasting textures and bold flavors. See page 27 for our homemade Vegan Mayonnaise. You can buy prepeeled squash, but the flavor of freshly peeled squash is superior.

Squash
- 1 large (2½- to 3-pound) butternut squash
- 3 tablespoons refined coconut oil or unsalted butter, melted
- ½ teaspoon table salt
- ½ teaspoon pepper

Topping
- 1 tablespoon sherry vinegar
- ½ teaspoon plant-based mayonnaise or egg-based mayonnaise
  Pinch table salt
- 2 tablespoons extra-virgin olive oil
- ½ cup coarsely shredded radicchio
- ½ ounce dairy Parmesan cheese, shaved into thin strips using vegetable peeler (optional)
- 3 tablespoons pine nuts, toasted

1. For the squash Adjust oven rack to lowest position and heat oven to 425 degrees. Using sharp vegetable peeler or chef's knife, remove skin and fibrous threads from squash just below skin (peel until squash is completely orange with no white flesh remaining, roughly ⅛ inch deep). Halve squash lengthwise and scrape out seeds. Place squash, cut side down, on cutting board and slice crosswise ½ inch thick.

2. Toss squash with melted oil, salt, and pepper until evenly coated. Arrange squash on rimmed baking sheet in single layer. Roast squash until side touching sheet toward back of oven is well browned, 25 to 30 minutes. Rotate sheet and continue to bake until side touching sheet toward back of oven is well browned, 6 to 10 minutes. Remove squash from oven and use metal spatula to flip each piece. Continue to roast until squash is very tender and side touching sheet is browned, 10 to 15 minutes.

3. For the topping While squash roasts, whisk vinegar, mayonnaise, and salt together in small bowl. Gradually whisk in oil until smooth.

4. Transfer squash to large serving platter. Drizzle vinaigrette evenly over squash. Sprinkle with radicchio; Parmesan, if using; and pine nuts and serve.

Spaghetti Squash with Garlic
Serves 4 to 6

Why This Recipe Works The delicate flavor and noodle-like appearance of spaghetti squash make it a fun plant-based replacement for pasta, but many recipes bury the squash strands underneath a heavy sauce with too many masking flavors. We kept this recipe simple so that the unique flavor and texture of the squash would shine through. Brushing the squash halves with oil and roasting them cut side down brought out the sweetness of the flesh. Once the squash was cooked, shredding it was as simple as holding the halves over a bowl and scraping them with a fork. After draining the excess liquid, we dressed the squash with fresh basil, lemon juice, and garlic, plus our vegan Parmesan substitute (or dairy Parmesan) for an easy, flavorful dish that tastes like summer. To turn this into an easy meal, toss the squash noodles with cherry tomatoes and chickpeas.

- 1 (2½- to 3-pound) spaghetti squash, halved lengthwise and seeded
- 2 tablespoons extra-virgin olive oil, divided
- ¼ teaspoon table salt
- ⅛ teaspoon pepper
- ¼ cup Vegan Parmesan Substitute (page 27) or grated dairy Parmesan cheese

- 1 tablespoon chopped fresh basil
- 1 teaspoon lemon juice
- 1 garlic clove, minced

1. Adjust oven rack to middle position and heat oven to 450 degrees. Brush cut sides of squash with 1 tablespoon oil and sprinkle with salt and pepper. Place squash, cut side down, on rimmed baking sheet. Roast until squash is tender when pierced with tip of paring knife, 25 to 30 minutes.

2. Flip squash over and let cool slightly. Holding squash with clean dish towel over large bowl, use fork to scrape squash flesh from skin while shredding it into fine pieces, discarding skin.

3. Drain excess liquid from bowl, then gently stir in vegan Parmesan substitute, basil, lemon juice, garlic, and remaining 1 tablespoon oil. Season with salt and pepper to taste, and serve.

Mexican-Style Spaghetti Squash Casserole
Serves 4

Why This Recipe Works Since it's frequently used as a substitute for pasta, spaghetti squash is often paired with Italian ingredients. Here we show off its versatility in two ways: jazzing it up with bright Mexican flavors and using it in a casserole. First we roasted the oblong yellow squash until the delicately sweet strands could be easily shredded from the skins. Minced garlic, smoked paprika, and cumin built an aromatic base for our casserole, and incorporating black beans, corn, tomatoes, and scallions contributed to the Mexican flavors. Minced jalapeño gave just the right amount of gentle heat. We mixed everything together and baked it to meld the flavors. To finish it off, we served our squash with creamy avocado and a squeeze of lime. The queso fresco, if you use it, adds more creamy richness.

- 1 (2½- to 3-pound) spaghetti squash, halved lengthwise and seeded
- 3 tablespoons extra-virgin olive oil, divided
- 1¼ teaspoons table salt, divided
- ¼ teaspoon pepper
- 2 garlic cloves, minced
- ½ teaspoon smoked paprika
- ½ teaspoon ground cumin
- 1 (15-ounce) can black beans, rinsed
- 1 cup frozen corn
- 6 ounces cherry tomatoes, halved
- 6 scallions (4 minced, 2 sliced thin)
- 1 jalapeño chile, stemmed, seeded, and minced

Mexican-Style Spaghetti
Squash Casserole

Grilled Tomatoes
Serves 4 to 6

Why This Recipe Works Grilled tomatoes capture the essence of summer. To ensure that the tomatoes would pick up flavorful charring while still holding their shape on the grill, we cut them crosswise rather than through the stem end. We also used tomatoes that were ripe but firm, since softer tomatoes were more likely to fall apart during grilling. Salting the tomatoes first allowed some of their juice to be drawn out so that they'd be less wet on the grill for better browning. Grilling the tomatoes cut side down first allowed them to caramelize before we flipped them onto their skin sides; the cradle-like skins helped to hold the tomatoes together as they continued to soften. Supermarket vine-ripened tomatoes will also work but won't be as flavorful. Plum tomatoes may be used, but they will be drier in texture. If using plum tomatoes, halve them through the stem end rather than crosswise. Serve these alongside Grilled Portobello Burgers (page 104).

2 pounds ripe tomatoes, cored and halved crosswise
2 tablespoons extra-virgin olive oil, divided
½ teaspoon table salt
¼ teaspoon pepper
2 tablespoons torn basil leaves

1. Toss tomatoes with 1 tablespoon oil, salt, and pepper in large bowl. Let sit for at least 15 minutes or up to 1 hour.

2A. For a charcoal grill Open bottom vent completely. Light large chimney starter filled with charcoal briquettes (6 quarts). When top coals are partially covered with ash, pour evenly over grill. Set cooking grate in place, cover, and open lid vent completely. Heat grill until hot, about 5 minutes.

2B. For a gas grill Turn all burners to high, cover, and heat grill until hot, about 15 minutes. Leave all burners on high.

3. Clean and oil cooking grate. Place tomatoes, cut side down, on grill (reserve any juice left behind in bowl) and cook (covered if using gas) until tomatoes are charred and beginning to soften, 4 to 6 minutes.

4. Using tongs or thin metal spatula, carefully flip tomatoes and continue to cook (covered if using gas) until skins are charred and juice bubbles, 4 to 6 minutes. Transfer tomatoes to large plate. Drizzle with reserved juice and remaining 1 tablespoon oil, sprinkle with basil and flake sea salt, and serve.

1 avocado, halved, pitted, and cut into ½-inch pieces
2 ounces queso fresco, crumbled (½ cup) (optional)
   Lime wedges

1. Adjust oven rack to middle position and heat oven to 375 degrees. Spray 8-inch square baking dish with vegetable oil spray. Brush cut sides of squash with 1 tablespoon oil and sprinkle with ½ teaspoon salt and pepper. Place squash cut side down in prepared dish (squash will not sit flat in dish) and roast until just tender, 40 to 45 minutes. Flip squash cut side up and let sit until cool enough to handle, about 20 minutes.

2. While squash roasts, combine garlic, paprika, cumin, remaining ¾ teaspoon salt, and remaining 2 tablespoons oil in large bowl and microwave until fragrant, about 30 seconds. Stir in beans, corn, tomatoes, minced scallions, and jalapeño until well combined.

3. Using fork, scrape squash into strands over bowl with bean mixture. Stir to combine, then spread mixture evenly in dish and cover tightly with aluminum foil. Bake until warmed through, 20 to 25 minutes.

4. Remove dish from oven. Sprinkle with avocado; queso fresco, if using; and sliced scallions. Serve with lime wedges.

Roasted Tomatoes

Makes about 1½ cups

Why This Recipe Works Roasting tomatoes is a largely hands-off technique that yields the ultimate condiment: bright, concentrated, savory-sweet tomatoes that are soft but retain their shape. There are so many ways to use them, including as a topping for crostini or pizza, in sandwiches, tossed into pasta or grains, or added to a tofu frittata or scramble. The flavorful tomato oil is great in salad dressings or drizzled over roasted vegetables. For intensely flavored tomatoes, we started by cutting the tomatoes into thick slices and arranging them on a foil-lined rimmed baking sheet. Drizzling on plenty of extra-virgin olive oil helped the tomatoes roast faster. Adding smashed garlic cloves lent flavor and fragrance to the tomatoes and oil. Avoid using tomatoes smaller than 3 inches in diameter, which have a smaller ratio of flavorful jelly to skin than larger tomatoes. To double the recipe, use two baking sheets, increase the roasting time in step 2 to 40 minutes, and rotate and switch the sheets halfway through baking. In step 3, increase the roasting time to 1½ to 2½ hours.

- 3 pounds large tomatoes, cored, bottom ⅛ inch trimmed, and sliced ¾ inch thick
- 2 garlic cloves, peeled and smashed
- ¼ teaspoon dried oregano
- ¼ teaspoon kosher salt
- ⅛ teaspoon pepper
- ¾ cup extra-virgin olive oil

1. Adjust oven rack to middle position and heat oven to 425 degrees. Line rimmed baking sheet with aluminum foil. Arrange tomatoes in even layer on prepared sheet, with larger slices around edge and smaller slices in center. Place garlic cloves on tomatoes. Sprinkle with oregano and salt and pepper. Drizzle oil evenly over tomatoes.

2. Roast for 30 minutes, rotating sheet halfway through roasting. Remove sheet from oven. Reduce oven temperature to 300 degrees and prop open door with wooden spoon to cool oven. Using thin spatula, flip tomatoes.

3. Return tomatoes to oven and cook until spotty brown, skins are blistered, and tomatoes have collapsed to ¼ to ½ inch thick, 1 to 2 hours. Remove from oven and let cool completely, about 30 minutes. Discard garlic and serve. (Tomatoes and oil can be refrigerated in airtight container for up to 5 days or frozen for up to 2 months.)

Sautéed Summer Squash

Serves 2 | FAST

Why This Recipe Works This no-fuss dish makes the most of summer squash and zucchini—two vegetables that can overrun your garden if you aren't armed with good recipes for using them. For a unique presentation, we peeled the whole vegetables with a vegetable peeler, discarding the seedy cores. The result was thin, even strips that cooked up quickly. Cooking the squash in a single layer over moderately high heat allowed the translucent ribbons to become crisp-tender without browning, which preserved their fresh flavor and pretty appearance. Pairing the vegetable with herbs and lemon gave the squash a light brightness that tasters liked. Our variation with mint and pistachios made for a cooling summer dish. You should have about 10 ounces of squash after peeling in step 1. Be sure to start checking for doneness at the lower end of the cooking time. For a quick al fresco meal, add roasted red peppers and toss with orzo.

- 1 teaspoon grated lemon zest plus 2 teaspoons juice
- 1 small garlic clove, minced
- 2 yellow squashes and/or zucchini (8 ounces each), ends trimmed
- 2 tablespoons extra-virgin olive oil
- ¼ teaspoon table salt
- ⅛ teaspoon pepper
- 1½ tablespoons chopped fresh parsley

1. Combine lemon juice and garlic in large bowl and set aside for at least 10 minutes. Using vegetable peeler, shave each squash lengthwise into ribbons: Peel off 3 ribbons from 1 side, then turn squash 90 degrees and peel off 3 more ribbons. Continue to turn and peel squash until you reach seeds. Discard core.

2. Whisk 5 teaspoons oil, salt, pepper, and lemon zest into garlic mixture. Heat remaining 1 teaspoon oil in 12-inch non-stick skillet over medium-high heat until just smoking. Add squash and cook, tossing occasionally with tongs, until squash has softened and is translucent, 3 to 4 minutes. Transfer squash to bowl with dressing, add 1 tablespoon parsley, and toss to coat. Season with salt and pepper to taste. Transfer to serving platter and sprinkle with remaining 1½ teaspoons parsley. Serve immediately.

VARIATION

Sautéed Summer Squash with Mint and Pistachios
Omit lemon zest and substitute 1 teaspoon cider vinegar for lemon juice. Substitute 2 tablespoons chopped fresh mint for parsley and sprinkle squash with 1 tablespoon chopped toasted pistachios before serving.

Summer Vegetable Gratin
Serves 4

Why This Recipe Works We loved the idea of a rich bread crumb–topped gratin showcasing our favorite summer vegetables: zucchini, summer squash, and ripe tomatoes. But every version we tried ended up a watery, soggy mess thanks to the large amount of liquid these vegetables released. To fix this problem, we salted the vegetables and let them drain before assembling the casserole. We baked the dish uncovered so that the remaining excess moisture would evaporate in the oven. Layering the tomatoes on top exposed them to more heat so that they ended up roasted and caramelized. To flavor the vegetables, we tossed them with an aromatic garlic-thyme oil and added a layer of caramelized onions. Panko bread crumbs tossed with vegan Parmesan substitute (or dairy Parmesan) and shallots made an elegant topping. We like the combination of the two squashes, but you can also use just zucchini or summer squash; just make sure you buy squash of roughly the same diameter. We prefer kosher salt here because residual grains can easily be wiped away from the vegetables; if using table salt, reduce all of the salt amounts in the recipe by half.

Summer Vegetable Gratin

- 1 pound zucchini, sliced ¼ inch thick
- 1 pound yellow summer squash, sliced ¼ inch thick
- 1 teaspoon kosher salt, plus salt for salting vegetables
- 1½ pounds ripe tomatoes, cored and sliced ¼ inch thick
- 6 tablespoons extra-virgin olive oil
- 2 onions, halved and sliced thin
- 2 garlic cloves, minced
- 1 tablespoon minced fresh thyme
- ½ teaspoon pepper
- ½ cup panko bread crumbs
- ¼ cup Vegan Parmesan Substitute (page 27) or grated dairy Parmesan cheese
- 2 shallots, minced
- ¼ cup chopped fresh basil

1. Toss zucchini and summer squash with 2 teaspoons salt and let drain in colander until vegetables release at least 3 tablespoons liquid, about 45 minutes. Pat zucchini and summer squash dry firmly with paper towels, removing as much liquid as possible.

2. Meanwhile, spread tomatoes out over paper towel–lined baking sheet, sprinkle with 1 teaspoon salt, and let stand for 30 minutes. Thoroughly pat tomatoes dry with paper towels.

3. Heat 1 tablespoon oil in 12-inch nonstick skillet over medium heat until shimmering. Add onions and salt and cook, stirring occasionally, until onions are softened and dark golden brown, 20 to 25 minutes; set aside.

4. Combine garlic, thyme, pepper, and 3 tablespoons oil in bowl; set aside. Meanwhile, combine panko, vegan Parmesan substitute, shallots, and 1 tablespoon oil in separate bowl; set aside.

5. Adjust oven rack to upper-middle position and heat oven to 400 degrees. Grease 3-quart gratin dish (or 13 by 9-inch baking dish) with remaining 1 tablespoon oil. Toss zucchini and summer squash with half of garlic-oil mixture and arrange in greased baking dish. Sprinkle evenly with caramelized onions, then top with tomato slices, overlapping them slightly. Spoon remaining garlic-oil mixture evenly over tomatoes.

6. Bake until vegetables are tender and tomatoes are starting to brown on edges, 40 to 45 minutes. Remove gratin dish from oven and increase heat to 450 degrees. Sprinkle reserved panko mixture evenly over top and continue to bake gratin until bubbling and topping is lightly browned, 5 to 10 minutes. Let cool for 10 minutes, then sprinkle with basil and serve.

Braised Zucchini

Serves 4   `FAST`

Why This Recipe Works Braising is a speedy and convenient stovetop way to prepare a simple but flavorful zucchini dish (which also makes a great topping for pasta or grains). But since the vegetable naturally contains a lot of water, it's easy to end up with waterlogged squash. To avoid this, we brought the zucchini pieces to a boil in a skillet in a mixture of oil, water, basil, garlic, and pepper flakes. We then covered the skillet and let the mixture simmer for 8 minutes, just until the pieces were fork-tender. Stirring it every 2 minutes ensured even tenderness throughout. We added cherry tomatoes and finished cooking the veggies uncovered to drive off excess moisture. Once reduced, the flavorful liquid ably coated the vegetables. If possible, use smaller, in-season zucchini, which have thinner skins and fewer seeds. You will need a 12-inch skillet with a tight-fitting lid for this recipe.

- 4 zucchini (8 ounces each), trimmed, quartered lengthwise, and cut into 2-inch lengths
- ¼ cup extra-virgin olive oil
- ¼ cup water
- 2 sprigs fresh basil
- 2 garlic cloves, sliced thin
- 1 teaspoon table salt
- ¼ teaspoon pepper
- ¼ teaspoon red pepper flakes
- 3 ounces cherry tomatoes, halved
  Lemon wedges

1. Bring zucchini, oil, water, basil sprigs, garlic, salt, pepper, and pepper flakes to boil in 12-inch nonstick skillet over medium-high heat. Cover, reduce heat to medium, and simmer until zucchini is fork-tender, about 8 minutes, stirring with rubber spatula every 2 minutes.

2. Gently stir in tomatoes and cook, uncovered, until tomatoes are just softened, about 2 minutes. Discard basil sprigs. Serve with lemon wedges.

Greek Stewed Zucchini

Serves 4 to 6

Why This Recipe Works Stewed vegetable dishes are popular all over Greece, so we drew inspiration from there in creating this summery stew in which our vegetables retained their individual character while still coming together in a deeply flavored, cohesive dish. After testing a variety of vegetable combinations, we landed on zucchini and tomatoes. We started by browning seeded zucchini on the stovetop (in batches to ensure thorough, even browning), then set it aside while we built our savory tomato sauce. Tasters found canned diced tomatoes mealy, canned crushed tomatoes sludgy and cloying, and fresh tomatoes too inconsistent in quality. Canned whole peeled tomatoes, processed until smooth, gave the dish the right balance of tomato flavor and silky texture. A smattering of kalamata olives complemented the sauce. Once our sauce had simmered and thickened, we stirred in the browned zucchini and transferred the pot to the oven to allow it to gently finish cooking and develop richly concentrated flavor. A traditional garnish of shredded fresh mint, stirred in at the end, added brightness. If possible, use smaller, in-season zucchini, which have thinner skins and fewer seeds. Serve with white beans and crusty bread.

- 1 (28-ounce) can whole peeled tomatoes
- 3 tablespoons extra-virgin olive oil, divided
- 5 zucchini (8 ounces each), trimmed, quartered lengthwise, seeded, and cut into 2-inch lengths
- 1 onion, chopped fine
- ¾ teaspoon table salt
- 3 garlic cloves, minced
- 1 teaspoon minced fresh oregano or ¼ teaspoon dried
- ¼ teaspoon red pepper flakes
- 2 tablespoons chopped pitted kalamata olives
- 2 tablespoons shredded fresh mint

1. Adjust oven rack to lower-middle position and heat oven to 325 degrees. Process tomatoes and their juice in food processor until completely smooth, about 1 minute; set aside.

2. Heat 2 teaspoons oil in Dutch oven over medium-high heat until just smoking. Brown one-third of zucchini, about 3 minutes per side; transfer to bowl. Repeat with 4 teaspoons oil and remaining zucchini in 2 batches; transfer to bowl.

3. Add remaining 1 tablespoon oil, onion, and salt to now-empty pot and cook, stirring occasionally, over medium-low heat until onion is very soft and golden brown, 9 to 11 minutes. Stir in garlic, oregano, and pepper flakes and cook until fragrant, about 30 seconds. Stir in olives and tomatoes, bring to simmer, and cook, stirring occasionally, until sauce has thickened, about 30 minutes.

4. Stir in zucchini and any accumulated juices, cover, and transfer pot to oven. Bake until zucchini is very tender, 30 to 40 minutes. Stir in mint and adjust sauce consistency with hot water as needed. Season with salt and pepper to taste. Serve.

Grilled Zucchini with Red Pepper Sauce

Serves 4 to 6

Why This Recipe Works Scored, charred, and served with a colorful almond-enriched sauce, grilled zucchini halves make a satisfying summer meal alongside bulgur or other simple grains. To get the most charring and to avoid limp, watery grilled pieces, we halved the zucchini lengthwise and scored a crosshatch pattern into the cut sides. After brushing the squash with olive oil, we charred it on the grill right alongside the red bell pepper for our sauce. We then steamed the bell pepper for 5 minutes in a bowl covered with plastic wrap to make the skin easy to remove and blended it with red wine vinegar, garlic, and toasted almonds to create the tangy sauce. For an herbaceous touch, we folded chopped basil into the sauce right before serving. Look for zucchini that are no more than 2 inches in diameter and weigh about 8 ounces each to ensure correct grilling times. Clean and oil the cooking grate thoroughly to prevent the zucchini from sticking. Note that we leave the bell pepper whole (minus the stem and core) and grill only two sides of it.

Grilled Zucchini with
Red Pepper Sauce

- 4 zucchini (8 ounces each), trimmed
- 1 red bell pepper
- 1½ tablespoons plus ⅓ cup extra-virgin olive oil, divided
- 1¼ teaspoons table salt, divided
- ½ teaspoon pepper, divided
- 2 tablespoons sliced almonds, toasted
- 1½ tablespoons red wine vinegar
- 2 small garlic cloves, peeled
- 2 teaspoons chopped fresh basil

1. Cut zucchini in half lengthwise. Using paring knife, cut ½-inch crosshatch pattern, about ¼ inch deep, in flesh of each zucchini half, being careful not to cut through skin. Cut around stem of bell pepper and remove core and seeds. Brush flesh sides of zucchini with 1 tablespoon oil and sprinkle with 1 teaspoon salt and ¼ teaspoon pepper. Brush bell pepper with 1½ teaspoons oil.

2A. For a charcoal grill Open bottom vent completely. Light large chimney starter filled with charcoal briquettes (6 quarts). When top coals are partially covered with ash, pour evenly over grill. Set cooking grate in place, cover, and open lid vent completely. Heat grill until hot, about 5 minutes.

2B. For a gas grill Turn all burners to high, cover, and heat grill until hot, about 15 minutes. Turn all burners to medium-high.

3. Clean and oil cooking grate. Place zucchini, flesh side down, and bell pepper, skin side down, on cooking grate. Cook (covered if using gas) until vegetables are well charred on first side, 7 to 9 minutes, rearranging zucchini as needed to ensure even browning.

4. Flip vegetables and continue to cook (covered if using gas) until fork inserted into zucchini meets little resistance and bell pepper is charred on second side, 8 to 10 minutes. Transfer zucchini to plate, flesh side up, as they finish cooking. Transfer bell pepper to small bowl, cover with plastic wrap, and let sit for 5 minutes.

5. Using spoon, remove skin from bell pepper (it's OK if some small pieces of skin remain; do not rinse bell pepper to remove skin); cut into 1-inch pieces. Process bell pepper, almonds, vinegar, garlic, remaining ⅓ cup oil, remaining ¼ teaspoon salt, and remaining ¼ teaspoon pepper in blender until smooth, 30 to 60 seconds, scraping down sides of blender jar as needed. Transfer sauce to bowl and stir in basil. Season sauce with salt and pepper to taste.

6. Spread half of sauce on serving platter. Arrange zucchini over sauce, flesh side up. Spoon remaining sauce over zucchini, as desired. Serve.

CHAPTER 7
GREAT GRAINS

■ FAST (45 minutes or less total time)
Photos: Spiced Basmati Rice with Cauliflower and Pomegranate; Black Rice Salad with Snap Peas and Ginger-Sesame Vinaigrette

Basmati Rice Pilaf

Serves 4 to 6

Why This Recipe Works White rice makes a great base for a plant-based meal that pleases everyone at the table. But it can be temperamental, foiling the efforts of even the best cooks by turning into a pot of true grit or dissolving into a gummy mess. To prevent these mishaps, we often turn to the pilaf method for cooking long-grain white rice, which relies on using less water and an even, gentle heat to produce distinct grains. Many rice pilaf recipes call for soaking the rice overnight, but we found this unnecessary; simply rinsing the rice before cooking removed excess starch and ensured the fluffy, rather than clumpy, grains that we were after. We sautéed an onion in the saucepan first for an easy flavor boost and then we added the rice. Toasting the rice for a few minutes in the pan deepened its flavor. Instead of following the traditional ratio of 1 cup of rice to 2 cups of water, we found using a little less liquid delivered better results. A dish towel under the lid while the rice finished steaming off the heat absorbed excess moisture in the pan and guaranteed our rice was perfectly fluffy, light, and tender. Long-grain white, jasmine, or Texmati rice can be substituted for the basmati.

- 1 tablespoon extra-virgin olive oil
- 1 small onion, chopped fine
- ¼ teaspoon table salt
- 1½ cups basmati rice, rinsed
- 2¼ cups water

1. Heat oil in large saucepan over medium heat until shimmering. Add onion and salt and cook until onion is softened, about 5 minutes. Stir in rice and cook, stirring often, until grain edges begin to turn translucent, about 3 minutes.

2. Stir in water and bring to simmer. Reduce heat to low, cover, and continue to simmer until rice is tender and water is absorbed, 16 to 18 minutes.

3. Remove pot from heat and lay clean folded dish towel underneath lid. Let sit for 10 minutes. Fluff rice with fork, season with salt and pepper to taste, and serve.

VARIATIONS

Basmati Rice Pilaf with Peas, Scallions, and Lemon
Add 2 minced garlic cloves, 1 teaspoon grated lemon zest, and ⅛ teaspoon red pepper flakes to pot with rice. Before covering rice with dish towel in step 3, sprinkle ½ cup thawed frozen peas over top. When fluffing cooked rice, stir in 2 thinly sliced scallions and 1 tablespoon lemon juice.

Basmati Rice Pilaf with Currants and Toasted Almonds
Add 2 minced garlic cloves, ½ teaspoon ground turmeric, and ¼ teaspoon ground cinnamon to pot with rice. Before covering rice with dish towel in step 3, sprinkle ¼ cup currants over top. When fluffing cooked rice, stir in ¼ cup toasted sliced almonds.

Hands-Off Baked White Rice

Serves 4

Why This Recipe Works Another great method for making foolproof long-grain white rice involves, surprisingly, the oven. For a basic everyday rice that was fast, hands-off, and didn't take up space on the stovetop, we baked it. After a few tests, we uncovered a couple of tricks that ensured perfect rice every time. First, be sure to rinse the rice before combining it with the water for cooking, or the excess starch clinging to the rice will make everything taste gluey. Second, use boiling water, or the rice will take forever to cook through in the oven. This recipe is a blank canvas ready to be paired with anything; the variations add in some seasonings to take the rice in different flavor directions. Basmati, jasmine, or Texmati rice can be substituted for the long-grain white rice. For an accurate measurement of boiling water, bring a full kettle of water to a boil and then measure out the desired amount.

- 2¾ cups boiling water
- 1⅓ cups long-grain white rice, rinsed
- 1 tablespoon extra-virgin olive oil
- ½ teaspoon table salt

1. Adjust oven rack to middle position and heat oven to 450 degrees. Combine all ingredients in 8-inch square baking dish. Cover dish tightly with double layer of aluminum foil. Bake rice until tender and no water remains, about 20 minutes.

2. Remove dish from oven, uncover, and fluff rice with fork, scraping up any rice that has stuck to bottom. Re-cover dish with foil and let sit for 10 minutes. Season with salt and pepper to taste, and serve.

VARIATIONS

Hands-Off Baked Coconut Rice
Substitute 2 cups water, ¾ cup coconut milk, and ⅛ teaspoon ground cardamom for boiling water; microwave in covered bowl until hot, about 2 minutes. When fluffing cooked rice, stir in 1 tablespoon minced fresh cilantro.

Coconut Rice with Bok Choy and Lime

2 teaspoons vegetable oil
2 heads baby bok choy (4 ounces each), stalks sliced ½ inch thick, greens chopped
1 shallot, minced
1½ cups basmati rice, rinsed
1½ cups water
¾ cup canned coconut milk
1 lemongrass stalk, trimmed to bottom 6 inches and smashed
2 teaspoons table salt
2 tablespoons minced fresh cilantro
1 teaspoon grated lime zest plus 2 teaspoons juice

1. Heat oil in large saucepan over medium-high heat until shimmering. Add bok choy stalks and shallot and cook, stirring occasionally, until softened, about 2 minutes.

2. Stir in rice, water, coconut milk, lemongrass, and salt and bring to boil. Reduce heat to low, cover, and simmer gently until liquid is absorbed, 18 to 20 minutes.

3. Fold in cilantro, lime zest and juice, and bok choy greens, cover, and cook until rice is tender, about 3 minutes. Discard lemongrass. Season with salt and pepper to taste, and serve.

Hands-Off Baked Curried Rice
Stir 1 teaspoon curry powder into boiling water before adding to baking dish. When fluffing cooked rice, stir in ¼ cup raisins.

Coconut Rice with Bok Choy and Lime

Serves 4 to 6

Why This Recipe Works Variations on rich, creamy coconut rice are served in diverse countries around the globe as a cooling accompaniment to spicy foods. This dressed-up Thai version features baby bok choy, aromatic lemongrass, lime, and cilantro. We chose basmati rice and followed the traditional method of cooking the rice in coconut milk along with the lemongrass, which steeped in the liquid as the rice simmered. To ensure that the bok choy stalks would turn tender by the time the rice was cooked, we sautéed them in the pan before adding the rice. To finish, we stirred in lime zest and juice and cilantro along with the bok choy greens. Long-grain white, jasmine, or Texmati rice can be substituted for the basmati.

SMASHING LEMONGRASS

1. Trim dry top (this part is usually green) and tough bottom of each stalk.

2. Peel and discard dry outer layer until moist, tender inner stalk is exposed.

3. Smash peeled stalk with back of chef's knife or meat pounder to release maximum flavor.

Jeweled Rice

Serves 4 to 6

Why This Recipe Works Jeweled rice, a staple in Persian cuisine, features basmati rice perfumed with candied carrots, saffron, and cardamom; its name comes from the colorful dried fruit and nuts that traditionally stud its appealingly golden surface. We love the dish's subtle balance between sweet and savory, and we were inspired to re-create it while making it simpler and easier. With ingredients that are soaked, bloomed, parcooked, layered, and steamed, this dish typically uses almost every pot in the kitchen, but we streamlined this version by cooking the rice using an easy pilaf method, adding the spices and some sautéed onion to the water to infuse the rice with rich flavor. While it simmered, we candied the carrots and orange zest. Once the rice was done, we sprinkled our candied mixture and some dried fruit on top and let it plump up while the rice rested off the heat. Finally, we stirred in the almonds and pistachios just before serving so they would retain their crunch. Long-grain white, jasmine, or Texmati rice can be substituted for the basmati.

Jeweled Rice

1	cup sugar
6	(2-inch) strips orange zest, sliced thin lengthwise
2	carrots, peeled and cut into ¼-inch pieces
2	tablespoons extra-virgin olive oil
1	onion, chopped fine
1½	teaspoons table salt
¾	teaspoon saffron threads, crumbled
½	teaspoon ground cardamom
1½	cups basmati rice, rinsed
½	cup currants
½	cup dried cranberries
¼	cup sliced almonds, toasted
¼	cup pistachios, toasted and chopped

1. Bring 2 cups water and sugar to boil in small saucepan over medium-high heat. Stir in orange zest and carrots, reduce heat to medium-low, and simmer until carrots are tender, 10 to 15 minutes. Drain well, transfer to plate, and let cool.

2. Meanwhile, heat oil in large saucepan over medium heat until shimmering. Add onion and salt and cook until onion is softened, about 5 minutes. Stir in saffron and cardamom and cook until fragrant, about 30 seconds. Stir in rice and cook, stirring often, until grain edges begin to turn translucent, about 3 minutes. Stir in 2¼ cups water and bring to simmer. Reduce heat to low, cover, and simmer gently until liquid is absorbed and rice is tender, 16 to 18 minutes.

3. Remove pot from heat and sprinkle candied carrots and orange zest, currants, and cranberries over rice. Cover, laying clean folded dish towel underneath lid, and let sit for 10 minutes. Add almonds and pistachios and fluff gently with fork to combine. Season with salt and pepper to taste, and serve.

SLICING ORANGE ZEST THIN

1. Using vegetable peeler, remove 2-inch-long strip orange zest from orange, avoiding bitter white pith just beneath.

2. Using chef's knife, cut zest strips lengthwise into long, thin pieces.

Spiced Basmati Rice with Cauliflower and Pomegranate

Serves 8 to 10

Why This Recipe Works Rice dishes from North Africa were our inspiration for this fragrant, warmly spiced pilaf-style dish. We paired basmati rice with sweet, earthy roasted cauliflower tossed with a generous amount of black pepper for heat and cumin for a deep, warm flavor. Roasting the cauliflower at a high temperature for a short time caramelized and crisped the florets without rendering them limp and mushy. We added the rice to a flavorful mixture of sautéed onion, garlic, and more spices, simmered it until tender, then added the cauliflower and finished the dish with a burst of sweet, juicy pomegranate seeds and a mix of fresh herbs. Long-grain white, jasmine, or Texmati rice can be substituted for the basmati.

- 1 head cauliflower (2 pounds), cored and cut into ¾-inch florets
- ¼ cup extra-virgin olive oil, divided
- ¾ teaspoons table salt, divided
- ½ teaspoon pepper
- ½ teaspoon ground cumin, divided
- 1 onion, chopped coarse
- 1½ cups basmati rice, rinsed
- 4 garlic cloves, minced
- ½ teaspoon ground cinnamon
- ½ teaspoon ground turmeric
- 2¼ cups water
- ½ cup pomegranate seeds
- 2 tablespoons chopped fresh cilantro
- 2 tablespoons chopped fresh mint

1. Adjust oven rack to lowest position and heat oven to 475 degrees. Toss cauliflower with 2 tablespoons oil, ½ teaspoon salt, pepper, and ¼ teaspoon cumin. Arrange cauliflower in single layer in rimmed baking sheet and roast until just tender, 10 to 15 minutes; set aside.

2. Heat remaining 2 tablespoons oil in large saucepan over medium heat until shimmering. Add onion and remaining ¼ teaspoon salt and cook until softened and lightly browned, 5 to 7 minutes. Add rice, garlic, cinnamon, turmeric, and remaining ¼ teaspoon cumin and cook, stirring frequently, until grain edges begin to turn translucent, about 3 minutes.

3. Stir in water and bring to simmer. Reduce heat to low, cover, and simmer gently until rice is tender and water is absorbed, 16 to 18 minutes.

4. Off heat, lay clean folded dish towel underneath lid and let pilaf sit for 10 minutes. Add roasted cauliflower to pilaf and fluff gently with fork to combine. Season with salt and pepper to taste. Transfer to serving platter and sprinkle with pomegranate seeds, cilantro, and mint. Serve.

Spiced Baked Rice with Roasted Sweet Potatoes and Fennel

Serves 6 to 8

Why This Recipe Works This hearty baked rice dish combines several flavorful elements of North African cuisine—sweet potatoes, green olives, and fennel—along with the distinctive warmth of the spice blend ras el hanout. Roasting yielded sweet potatoes with firm, caramelized exteriors and soft, creamy interiors. We prepared the aromatic base on the stovetop, stirring in the ras el hanout with the rice to ensure that the flavors melded and bloomed. We added enough broth to ensure that our long-grain rice came out tender and not too crunchy and then transferred the pot to the oven. When the rice was cooked, we gently stirred in the potatoes and finished with bright cilantro and lime. Basmati, jasmine, or Texmati rice can be substituted for the long-grain white rice.

- 1½ pounds sweet potatoes, peeled and cut into 1-inch pieces
- ¼ cup extra-virgin olive oil, divided
- ½ teaspoon table salt
- 1 fennel bulb, stalks discarded, bulb halved, cored, and chopped fine
- 1 small onion, chopped fine
- 1½ cups long-grain white rice, rinsed
- 4 garlic cloves, minced
- 2 teaspoons ras el hanout
- 2¾ cups vegetable broth
- ¾ cup large pitted brine-cured green olives, halved
- 2 tablespoons minced fresh cilantro
  Lime wedges

1. Adjust oven rack to middle position and heat oven to 400 degrees. Toss potatoes with 2 tablespoons oil and salt. Arrange potatoes in single layer in rimmed baking sheet and roast until tender and browned, 25 to 30 minutes, stirring potatoes halfway through roasting. Remove potatoes from oven and reduce oven temperature to 350 degrees.

2. Heat remaining 2 tablespoons oil in Dutch oven over medium heat until shimmering. Add fennel and onion and cook until softened, 5 to 7 minutes. Stir in rice, garlic, and ras el hanout and cook, stirring frequently, until grain edges begin to turn translucent, about 3 minutes.

3. Stir in broth and olives and bring to boil. Cover, transfer pot to oven, and bake until rice is tender and liquid is absorbed, 12 to 15 minutes.

4. Remove pot from oven and let sit for 10 minutes. Add potatoes to rice and fluff gently with fork to combine. Season with salt and pepper to taste. Sprinkle with cilantro and serve with lime wedges.

RINSING RICE AND GRAINS

Place rice or grains in fine-mesh strainer and rinse under cool water until water runs clear, occasionally stirring lightly with your hand. Let drain briefly.

Rice Salad with Oranges, Olives, and Almonds

Serves 4 to 6

Why This Recipe Works Briny green olives and sweet oranges are a beloved combination in both Greek and Italian cooking. For a rice salad that could stand up to these bold mix-ins along with a bright vinaigrette, we sought out a method for cooking long-grain rice that would preserve its fresh-from-the-pan tender texture once cooled. Toasting the rice brought out its nutty flavor and helped to keep the grains distinct and separate even when cool. Rather than cooking it pilaf-style, in a small amount of water, we boiled the rice pasta-style, in plenty of water, which washed away excess starch and staved off stickiness. Spreading the cooked rice on a baking sheet allowed it to cool quickly and evenly. We tossed the cooled rice with a simple orange vinaigrette and fresh orange segments, chopped green olives, and crunchy toasted almonds. Our variation takes it in a Mexican direction. We let the salad sit for a short time before serving to give the flavors time to meld. Basmati, jasmine, or Texmati rice can be substituted for the long-grain white rice. Taste the rice as it nears the end of its cooking time; it should be cooked through and still firm, but not crunchy.

1½ cups long-grain white rice
1 teaspoon table salt, plus salt for cooking rice
2 oranges, plus ¼ teaspoon grated orange zest plus 1 tablespoon juice
2 tablespoons extra-virgin olive oil
2 teaspoons sherry vinegar
1 small garlic clove, minced
½ teaspoon pepper
⅓ cup large pitted brine-cured green olives, chopped
⅓ cup slivered almonds, toasted
2 tablespoons minced fresh oregano

1. Bring 4 quarts water to boil in Dutch oven. Meanwhile, toast rice in 12-inch skillet over medium heat until faintly fragrant and some grains turn opaque, 5 to 8 minutes. Add rice and 1½ teaspoons salt to boiling water and cook, stirring occasionally, until rice is tender but not soft, about 9 minutes. Drain rice, spread onto rimmed baking sheet, and let cool completely, about 15 minutes.

2. Cut away peel and pith from oranges. Holding fruit over bowl, use paring knife to slice between membranes to release segments. Whisk oil, vinegar, garlic, orange zest and juice, salt, and pepper together in large bowl. Add rice, orange segments, olives, almonds, and oregano, gently toss to combine, and let sit for 20 minutes. Serve.

VARIATION
Rice Salad with Pineapple, Jícama, and Pepitas

1½ cups long-grain white rice
1 teaspoon table salt, plus salt for cooking rice
2 tablespoons vegetable oil
1 jalapeño chile, stemmed, seeded, and minced
½ teaspoon grated lime zest plus 1 tablespoon juice
1 small garlic clove, minced
½ teaspoon pepper
1 cup finely diced fresh pineapple
1 cup peeled and finely diced jícama
⅓ cup roasted pepitas
2 scallions, sliced thin
3 tablespoons minced fresh cilantro

1. Bring 4 quarts water to boil in Dutch oven. Meanwhile, toast rice in 12-inch skillet over medium heat until faintly fragrant and some grains turn opaque, 5 to 8 minutes. Stir 1½ teaspoons salt and toasted rice into boiling water and cook, stirring occasionally, until rice is tender but not soft, about 9 minutes. Drain rice, spread onto rimmed baking sheet, and let cool completely, about 15 minutes; transfer to large bowl.

Rice Salad with Oranges, Olives, and Almonds

2. Whisk oil, jalapeño, lime zest and juice, garlic, salt, and pepper together in separate bowl, then drizzle over cooled rice. Add pineapple, jícama, pepitas, scallions, and cilantro and toss to combine. Let sit for 20 minutes before serving.

Dolsot Bibimbap with Tempeh
Serves 6

Why This Recipe Works Korean dolsot bibimbap might just be the ultimate rice bowl. It features a crispy rice crust and a variety of lively toppings—some savory, some acidic, some spicy. ("Bibim" means "mixed," "bap" means "rice," and "dolsot" is the heavy stone bowl in which the dish is assembled.) We learned through testing that a Dutch oven held heat well enough to create the desired crust. Some recipes include eggs and meat, but with all of the intriguing, fresh ingredients in this dish, we didn't miss them one bit in our plant-based version. We did, however, want to add some heft, so we incorporated tempeh; the tempeh's nutty and pleasantly bitter notes played nicely with the dish's parade of sweet and sour flavors. The ingredient list is

long, but don't be intimidated. Prepare the pickles, chile sauce, and vegetables a day ahead and warm the vegetables to room temperature in the microwave before adding them to the rice. You can also substitute store-bought kimchi for the pickles. For a true bibimbap experience, bring the pot to the table before stirring the vegetables and tempeh into the rice in step 8.

Pickles
- 1 cup cider vinegar
- 2 tablespoons sugar
- 1½ teaspoons table salt
- 1 cucumber, peeled, quartered lengthwise, seeded, and sliced thin on bias
- 4 ounces (2 cups) bean sprouts

Rice
- 2½ cups short-grain white rice
- 2½ cups water
- ¾ teaspoon table salt

Vegetables and Tempeh
- 2 tablespoons vegetable oil, divided
- 8 ounces tempeh, cut into ½-inch pieces
- ¼ cup soy sauce, divided
- ¼ teaspoon table salt
- ¼ teaspoon pepper
- ½ cup water
- 3 scallions, minced
- 3 garlic cloves, minced
- 1 tablespoon sugar
- 3 carrots, peeled and shredded (2 cups)
- 8 ounces shiitake mushrooms, stemmed and sliced thin
- 10 ounces curly-leaf spinach, stemmed and chopped coarse

Bibimbap
- 2 tablespoons vegetable oil
- 1 tablespoon toasted sesame oil
- 1 recipe Chile Sauce (page 248)

1. For the pickles Whisk vinegar, sugar, and salt together in bowl. Add cucumber and bean sprouts and toss to combine. Press vegetables to submerge, cover, and refrigerate for at least 30 minutes or up to 24 hours.

2. For the rice Bring rice, water, and salt to boil in medium saucepan over high heat. Cover, reduce heat to low, and cook for 7 minutes. Remove saucepan from heat and let sit, covered, until rice is tender, about 15 minutes.

Dolsot Bibimbap with Tempeh

Nasi Goreng with Eggs

3. For the vegetables and tempeh While rice cooks, heat 1 tablespoon oil in 12-inch nonstick skillet over medium-high heat until just smoking. Add tempeh, 1 tablespoon soy sauce, salt, and pepper and cook until well browned, 4 to 6 minutes. Remove from heat and cover to keep warm.

4. Combine water, scallions, garlic, sugar, and remaining 3 tablespoons soy sauce in bowl. Heat 1 teaspoon oil in Dutch oven over high heat until shimmering. Add carrots, stirring to coat. Stir in ⅓ cup scallion mixture and cook until carrots are slightly softened and liquid has evaporated, about 1 minute; transfer to bowl.

5. Heat 1 teaspoon oil in now-empty pot until shimmering. Add mushrooms, stirring to coat. Stir in ⅓ cup scallion mixture and cook until mushrooms are tender and liquid has evaporated, about 3 minutes; transfer to second bowl.

6. Heat remaining 1 teaspoon oil in now-empty Dutch oven until shimmering. Stir in spinach and remaining scallion mixture and cook until spinach is just wilted, about 1 minute. Transfer spinach to third bowl, discard any remaining liquid, and wipe out pot with paper towel.

7. For the bibimbap Heat vegetable oil and sesame oil in now-empty pot over high heat until shimmering. Carefully add cooked rice and press into even layer. Cook, without stirring, until rice begins to form crust on bottom of pot, about 2 minutes. Transfer tempeh, carrots, mushrooms, and spinach to pot and arrange in piles to cover surface of rice. Reduce heat to low and cook until golden brown crust forms on bottom of rice, about 5 minutes.

8. Drizzle 2 tablespoons chile sauce over top. Without disturbing crust, stir rice, vegetables, and tempeh until combined. Scrape large pieces of crust from bottom of pot and stir into rice. Serve in individual bowls, passing pickles and remaining chile sauce separately.

PLANT POWER

AMYLOPECTIN

We prefer sushi rice (sometimes labeled Calrose or japonica rice) in our dolsot bibimbap. Sushi rice has short, squat grains and a distinctive stickiness when cooked, which comes from a relatively high amount of a starch component called amylopectin, which gelatinizes during cooking and results in a creamy, tender texture and subtle chewiness.

Vegan Nasi Goreng
Serves 4 to 6

Why This Recipe Works This Indonesian-style fried rice is typically seasoned with chile paste, shrimp paste, and kecap manis (sweet soy sauce) and garnished with golden fried shallots. The kecap manis can be hard to find, but we discovered that a sauce of molasses, dark brown sugar, soy sauce, and fish sauce substitute was a workable alternative. The fish sauce substitute also helped stand in for the shrimp paste. We created our chile paste by pureeing garlic, shallots, and Thai chiles. To get distinct grains of rice, this dish is traditionally made with day-old rice, but we successfully used our Faux Leftover Rice. We also added broccoli florets, steamed until crisp-tender. If Thai chiles are unavailable, substitute two serranos or two medium jalapeños. This dish is fairly spicy; to reduce the spiciness, remove the ribs and seeds from the chiles or use fewer chiles. You will need a 12-inch nonstick skillet with a tight-fitting lid for this recipe.

7	large shallots, peeled (4 quartered, 3 sliced thin)
5	green or red Thai chiles, stemmed
4	large garlic cloves, peeled
3	packed tablespoons dark brown sugar
3	tablespoons molasses
3	tablespoons soy sauce
3	tablespoons Fish Sauce Substitute (page 22)
1¼	teaspoons table salt
½	cup vegetable oil
1	recipe Faux Leftover Rice (recipe follows)
1	pound broccoli florets, cut into 1-inch pieces
¼	cup water
4	large scallions, sliced thin
	Lime wedges

1. Pulse quartered shallots, Thai chiles, and garlic in food processor until coarse paste forms, about 15 pulses, scraping down sides of bowl as needed; transfer to bowl. In separate bowl, whisk together sugar, molasses, soy sauce, fish sauce substitute, and salt.

2. Cook oil and sliced shallots in 12-inch nonstick skillet over medium heat, stirring constantly, until shallots are golden and crisp, 5 to 10 minutes. Using slotted spoon, transfer shallots to paper towel–lined plate and season with salt to taste. Pour off and reserve oil. Wipe pan with paper towels.

3. Break up any large clumps of rice with your fingers. Combine broccoli and water in now-empty skillet, cover, and cook over medium-high heat until broccoli is crisp-tender and water is absorbed, 4 to 6 minutes; transfer to bowl.

4. Heat 3 tablespoons reserved oil in again-empty skillet over medium heat until just shimmering. Add shallot-chile mixture and cook, mashing mixture into skillet, until golden, 3 to 5 minutes. Whisk molasses mixture to recombine, then add to skillet along with rice and broccoli. Cook, tossing constantly, until mixture is evenly coated and warmed through, and broccoli is tender, about 3 minutes. Off heat, stir in scallions. Transfer to serving platter and garnish with fried shallots. Serve with lime wedges.

VARIATION
Nasi Goreng with Eggs
After wiping out skillet in step 2, heat 1 teaspoon vegetable oil in now-empty skillet over medium heat until shimmering. Add 2 large eggs and ¼ teaspoon table salt and scramble quickly using rubber spatula. Tilt pan to coat bottom of pan, cover, and cook until bottom of omelet is spotty golden brown and top is just set, about 1½ minutes. Slide omelet onto cutting board, roll up into tight log, and cut crosswise into 1-inch-wide segments; leave segments rolled. Repeat with 1 teaspoon vegetable oil and 2 large eggs. Serve with rice.

Faux Leftover Rice
Makes 6 cups
Long-grain white, basmati, or Texmati rice can be substituted for the jasmine rice.

2	cups jasmine rice
2	tablespoons vegetable oil

1. Rinse rice in fine-mesh strainer or colander under cold running water until water runs clear. Place strainer over bowl and set aside.

2. Heat oil in large saucepan over medium heat until shimmering. Add rice and stir to coat grains with oil, about 30 seconds. Add 2⅔ cups water, increase heat to high, and bring to boil. Reduce heat to low, cover, and simmer until all liquid is absorbed, about 18 minutes.

3. Off heat, remove lid and place dish towel folded in half over saucepan; replace lid. Let stand until rice is just tender, about 8 minutes. Spread cooked rice onto rimmed baking sheet and let cool on wire rack for 10 minutes. Transfer sheet to refrigerator and let rice chill for 20 minutes.

Vegetable Fried Rice with Broccoli and Shiitake Mushrooms

Serves 4 to 6 `FAST`

Why This Recipe Works We'll admit it—fried rice is always part of our takeout order from the local Chinese place. But you can make a far more flavorful and healthful plant-based Chinese fried rice at home, with less effort than you think. Just make sure not to use freshly cooked rice, or you'll end up with a gummy mess. Since we don't often have a lot of leftover rice chilling in our fridge, we developed our "faux" leftover rice, which speeds up the process dramatically. Quickly sautéing the vegetables, then the cooked rice, and then combining them with the sauce in the skillet produced such a flavorful dish that it made us rethink our takeout habits. If Chinese broccoli (also called gai lan) is unavailable, you can substitute broccolini. Cut broccolini tops (leaves and florets) from stems, then cut tops into 1-inch pieces. Halve stalks thicker than ½ inch and keep separate from tops. White pepper lends a unique flavor to this dish; black pepper is not a good substitute. Chinese black vinegar is an aged rice-based vinegar. You will need a 12-inch nonstick skillet with a tight-fitting lid for this recipe.

2 tablespoon Chinese black vinegar or sherry vinegar
4 teaspoons soy sauce
1 tablespoon Shaoxing wine or dry sherry
1 tablespoon hoisin sauce
1 tablespoon packed brown sugar
1 teaspoon table salt
¼ teaspoon white pepper
6 scallions, white and green parts separated and sliced thin
¼ cup vegetable oil, divided
2 garlic cloves, minced
12 ounces Chinese broccoli, trimmed
¼ cup water
8 ounces shiitake mushrooms, stemmed and sliced ¼ inch thick
1 recipe Faux Leftover Rice (page 245)
3 tablespoons chopped fresh cilantro

1. Whisk vinegar, soy sauce, Shaoxing wine, hoisin sauce, sugar, salt, and pepper in small bowl until sugar has dissolved; set aside. Combine scallion whites, 2 tablespoons oil, and garlic in second small bowl; set aside.

2. Trim leaves from bottom 3 inches of broccoli stalks and reserve. Cut tops (leaves and florets) from stalks, then cut reserved leaves and tops into 1-inch pieces. Set aside.

Cauliflower Biryani

Quarter stalks lengthwise if more than 1 inch in diameter and halve stalks lengthwise if less than 1 inch in diameter. Keep broccoli stalks separate from leaves and tops.

3. Heat 1 tablespoon oil in 12-inch nonstick skillet over medium heat until just smoking. Add broccoli stalks and water (water will sputter), cover, and cook until broccoli is bright green, about 5 minutes. Uncover, increase heat to high, and continue to cook, tossing slowly but constantly, until all water has evaporated and stalks are crisp-tender, 1 to 3 minutes; transfer to medium bowl.

4. Heat 1 tablespoon oil in now-empty skillet over high heat until just smoking. Add mushrooms and broccoli leaves and tops. Cook, tossing vegetables slowly but constantly, until mushrooms are softened and broccoli tops and leaves are completely wilted, about 5 minutes; transfer to bowl with broccoli stalks.

5. Break up any large clumps of rice with your fingers. Add scallion mixture to again-empty skillet and cook over medium heat, mashing mixture into skillet, until fragrant, about 30 seconds. Add rice, vinegar mixture, vegetable mixture, and scallion greens and increase heat to high. Cook, tossing rice constantly, until mixture is thoroughly combined and heated through, about 3 minutes. Off heat, stir in cilantro. Serve.

Vegetable Fried Rice with Broccoli, Shiitake Mushrooms, and Eggs

After cooking broccoli tops and leaves and mushrooms in step 4, heat 1 tablespoon oil in again-empty skillet over high heat until shimmering. Add 2 large eggs and scramble quickly using rubber spatula. Continue to cook, scraping slowly but constantly along bottom and sides of pan, until eggs just form cohesive mass, 15 to 30 seconds (eggs will not be completely dry). Transfer to bowl with vegetables and break up any large egg curds. Add eggs to scallion mixture with rice, vinegar mixture, vegetable mixture, and scallion greens in step 5.

Cauliflower Biryani

Serves 4 to 6

Why This Recipe Works Biryani places fragrant long-grain basmati center stage, enriching it with saffron and a variety of fresh herbs and pungent spices. However, traditional recipes take a long time to develop deep flavor by steeping whole spices and cooking each component on its own before marrying them. We decided to deconstruct this dish to make it easier and faster, while staying true to its warmth and home-style appeal. We decided to pair our rice with sweet, earthy roasted cauliflower, so we cut the cauliflower into small florets to speed up roasting and tossed it with warm spices to give it deep flavor. While it roasted, we sautéed an onion until golden, then cooked jalapeño, garlic, and more spices until fragrant. We added the rice to this flavorful mixture and simmered it until tender. Once the rice finished cooking, we let the residual heat plump the currants and bloom the saffron while the rice rested. Last, we stirred in lots of bright mint and cilantro and our roasted cauliflower. Biryani is traditionally served with a cooling yogurt sauce; ideally, you should make it before starting the biryani to allow the flavors in the sauce to meld. Long-grain white, jasmine, or Texmati rice can be substituted for the basmati.

- 1 head cauliflower (2 pounds), cored and cut into ½-inch florets
- ¼ cup extra-virgin olive oil, divided
- 1 teaspoon table salt, divided
- ¼ teaspoon pepper
- ¼ teaspoon ground cardamom, divided
- ¼ teaspoon ground cumin, divided
- 1 onion, sliced thin
- 4 garlic cloves, minced
- 1 jalapeño chile, stemmed, seeded, and minced
- ⅛ teaspoon ground cinnamon
- ⅛ teaspoon ground ginger
- 1½ cups basmati rice, rinsed
- 2¼ cups water
- ¼ cup dried currants or raisins
- ½ teaspoon saffron threads, lightly crumbled
- 2 tablespoons chopped fresh cilantro
- 2 tablespoons chopped fresh mint
- 1 recipe Herbed Yogurt Sauce (page 90)

1. Adjust oven rack to middle position and heat oven to 425 degrees. Toss cauliflower, 2 tablespoons oil, ½ teaspoon salt, pepper, ⅛ teaspoon cardamom, and ⅛ teaspoon cumin together in bowl. Spread cauliflower onto rimmed baking sheet and roast until tender, 15 to 20 minutes.

2. Meanwhile, heat remaining 2 tablespoons oil in large saucepan over medium-high heat until shimmering. Add onion and cook, stirring often, until soft and dark brown around edges, 10 to 12 minutes.

3. Stir in garlic, jalapeño, cinnamon, ginger, remaining ⅛ teaspoon cardamom, and remaining ⅛ teaspoon cumin and cook until fragrant, about 1 minute. Stir in rice and cook until well coated, about 1 minute. Add water and remaining ½ teaspoon salt and bring to simmer. Reduce heat to low, cover, and simmer until all liquid is absorbed, 16 to 18 minutes.

4. Remove pot from heat and sprinkle currants and saffron over rice. Cover, laying clean folded dish towel underneath lid, and let sit for 10 minutes. Fold in cilantro, mint, and roasted cauliflower. Season with salt and pepper to taste and serve with yogurt sauce.

FLAVOR BOOSTER

SAFFRON
Sometimes known as "red gold," saffron is the world's most expensive spice. It's made from the dried stigmas of *Crocus sativus* flowers; the stigmas are so delicate they must be painstakingly harvested by hand. (It takes about 200 hours to pick enough stigmas to produce 1 pound of saffron, which typically sells for thousands of dollars.) Luckily, a little saffron goes a long way, adding a distinct reddish-gold color and flavor notes of honey and grass to dishes including this one. You can find it as powder or, more commonly, as threads.

GET SAUCY

These sauces are great with grains, including the Brown Rice Burrito Bowl (page 252) and the Barley Bowl with Roasted Carrots and Snow Peas (page 262), but they are versatile enough to serve as drizzles, dollops, or dips for plenty of other dishes. Drizzle over grilled vegetables, use as salad dressings or dips for crudités, or jazz up a plain bowl of grains.

Soy Dipping Sauce
Makes ⅔ cup

¼ cup soy sauce
2 tablespoons rice vinegar
2 tablespoons mirin
2 tablespoons water
1 scallion, sliced thin
½ teaspoon toasted sesame oil

Combine all ingredients in small bowl. (Sauce can be refrigerated for up to 3 days.)

Za'atar Yogurt Sauce
Makes 1 cup
Different za'atar blends include varying salt amounts, so be sure to adjust seasoning to taste.

1 cup plain plant-based yogurt or dairy yogurt
1 tablespoon za'tar
1 garlic clove, minced
1 teaspoon grated lemon zest plus 1 tablespoon juice

Whisk yogurt, za'atar, garlic, and lemon zest and juice together in bowl and season with salt and pepper to taste. Cover and refrigerate for about 30 minutes before serving. (Sauce can be refrigerated for up to 4 days.)

Chile Sauce
Makes ½ cup
If you can't find the Korean chile paste gochujang, substitute an equal amount of sriracha and omit the water.

¼ cup gochujang
3 tablespoons water
2 tablespoons toasted sesame oil
1 teaspoon sugar

Whisk all ingredients in bowl until well combined. (Sauce can be refrigerated for up to 3 days.)

Creamy Chipotle Sauce
Makes ½ cup
Different plant-based sour creams have varying textures, so you may need to adjust the consistency with water.

¼ cup plant-based mayonnaise or egg-based mayonnaise
¼ cup plant-based sour cream or dairy sour cream
1 tablespoon lime juice
1 tablespoon minced canned chipotle chile in adobo sauce
1 garlic clove, minced

Combine all ingredients in small bowl. (Sauce can be refrigerated for up to 4 days.)

Citrus Sauce
Makes ½ cup

3 tablespoons rice vinegar
2 tablespoons mirin
½ teaspoon sugar
3 tablespoons soy sauce
1 teaspoon grated fresh ginger
½ teaspoon grated orange zest plus 1 tablespoon juice
½ teaspoon grated lime zest plus 1 tablespoon juice

Bring vinegar, mirin, and sugar to boil in small saucepan, then remove from heat. Whisk in soy sauce, ginger, orange zest and juice, and lime zest and juice. Transfer sauce to bowl. (Sauce can be refrigerated for up to 1 day.)

Barley with Lentils, Mushrooms, and Tahini-Yogurt Sauce

Tahini Sauce

Makes 1¼ cup

- ½ cup tahini
- ½ cup water
- ¼ cup lemon juice
- 2 garlic cloves, minced

Whisk all ingredients in bowl until smooth. Season with salt to taste. (Sauce can be refrigerated for up to 4 days.)

Tahini-Yogurt Sauce

Makes 1 cup

- ⅓ cup tahini
- ⅓ cup plain plant-based yogurt or dairy yogurt
- ¼ cup water
- 3 tablespoons lemon juice
- 1 garlic clove, minced
- ¾ teaspoon table salt

Whisk all ingredients in bowl until combined. Season with salt and pepper to taste. Let sit until flavors meld, about 30 minutes. (Sauce can be refrigerated for up to 4 days.)

Classic Mexican Rice

Serves 6 to 8

Why This Recipe Works Traditional Mexican rice is a cornerstone of that country's cuisine. The rice is usually fried until golden, which gives it its signature nutty flavor; tomatoes, onions, garlic, and broth add savory complexity. This versatile side can accompany any number of Mexican dishes, from Pinto Bean and Swiss Chard Enchiladas (page 295) to Baja-Style Cauliflower Tacos (page 98). But many versions we tried turned out soupy, oily, or one-note. We wanted a version with clean, balanced flavor and tender rice that was neither greasy nor watery. Traditionally, the liquid component in this dish is a mix of chicken broth and pureed fresh tomatoes; we swapped in vegetable broth for chicken broth and settled on equal parts of each for the most balanced flavor. For an appealing red color, we added tomato paste, which, although nontraditional, boosted the umami flavor. Sautéing the rice in a small amount of oil before cooking it until golden helped develop the desired toasty notes. Moving the cooking from the stovetop to the oven also ensured that the rice cooked uniformly. A bit of fresh cilantro, fresh minced jalapeños, and a squeeze of lime juice provided brightness and complemented the rich rice. Basmati, jasmine, or Texmati rice can be substituted for the long-grain white rice.

- 2 tomatoes, cored and quartered
- 1 onion, chopped coarse
- 3 jalapeño chiles, stemmed, divided
- ⅓ cup vegetable oil
- 2 cups long-grain white rice, rinsed
- 4 garlic cloves, minced
- 2 cups vegetable broth
- 1 tablespoon tomato paste
- 1½ teaspoons table salt
- ½ cup minced fresh cilantro
  Lime wedges

1. Adjust oven rack to middle position and heat oven to 350 degrees. Process tomatoes and onion in food processor until smooth, about 15 seconds. Transfer mixture to 4-cup liquid measuring cup and spoon off excess as needed until mixture measures 2 cups. Remove ribs and seeds from 2 jalapeños and discard; mince flesh and set aside. Mince remaining 1 jalapeño, including ribs and seeds; set aside.

2. Heat oil in Dutch oven over medium-high heat for 1 to 2 minutes. Drop 3 or 4 grains of rice into oil; if grains sizzle, oil is ready. Add rice and cook, stirring frequently, until light golden and translucent, 6 to 8 minutes.

3. Reduce heat to medium. Add garlic and reserved seeded jalapeños and cook, stirring constantly, until fragrant, about 1½ minutes. Stir in pureed tomato-onion mixture, broth,

tomato paste, and salt and bring to boil. Cover, transfer pot to oven, and bake until liquid is absorbed and rice is tender, 30 to 35 minutes, stirring well after 15 minutes.

4. Remove pot from oven and fold in cilantro and reserved jalapeño with seeds to taste. Serve with lime wedges.

Almost Hands-Free Mushroom Risotto

Serves 6

Why This Recipe Works Risotto is beloved for its plush creaminess—which is derived in no small part from copious amounts of butter and Parmesan. So our challenge was to replicate the test kitchen's classic Almost Hands-Free Risotto without the dairy. Our starting point, cashew cheese, turned the risotto sticky and pasty. Some vegan risotto recipes call for chia seeds, but we found that they speckled the rice with unappealing globules. Simply stirring in olive oil made the risotto too greasy, and store-bought vegan Parm imparted an unpleasant plasticky sheen. We started thinking that creamy vegan risotto wasn't meant to be—until we had an "aha" moment with miso. We like miso for its savory notes, but here it also acted as a thickener, giving the risotto a satiny, creamy gloss. To make our risotto a meal, we added fresh cremini mushrooms and dried porcini. Garnish with Vegan Parmesan Substitute (page 27), if you like. This more hands-off method requires precise timing, so we highly recommend using a timer.

- 4 cups vegetable broth
- 3 cups water
- ⅓ cup white miso
- ¼ cup extra-virgin olive oil, divided
- 1 pound cremini mushrooms, trimmed and sliced ¼ inch thick
- ½ teaspoon table salt, divided
- 1 onion, chopped fine
- 4 garlic cloves, minced
- 1 ounce dried porcini mushrooms, rinsed and minced
- 2 cups Arborio rice
- ½ cup dry white wine
- ¼ cup chopped fresh parsley

1. Bring broth, water, and miso to boil in large saucepan over high heat; reduce heat to medium-low and simmer, whisking occasionally, until miso is dissolved, about 5 minutes. Cover and keep warm over low heat.

Almost Hands-Free Mushroom Risotto

2. Meanwhile, heat 1 tablespoon oil in Dutch oven over medium heat until shimmering. Add cremini mushrooms and ¼ teaspoon salt, cover, and cook until mushrooms have released their liquid, about 5 minutes. Uncover and continue to cook until well browned, 10 to 12 minutes longer; transfer to bowl.

3. Heat 2 tablespoons oil in now-empty pot over medium heat until shimmering. Stir in onion and remaining ¼ teaspoon salt and cook until softened, about 5 minutes. Add garlic and porcini mushrooms and cook until fragrant, about 30 seconds. Add rice and cook, stirring frequently, until grains are translucent around edges, about 3 minutes. Add wine and cook, stirring constantly, until fully absorbed, about 2 minutes. Stir in 5 cups hot broth mixture; reduce heat to medium-low, cover, and simmer until almost all liquid has been absorbed and rice is just al dente, 16 to 19 minutes, stirring twice during cooking.

4. Add ¾ cup hot broth mixture and browned cremini mushrooms, and stir gently and constantly until risotto becomes creamy, about 3 minutes. Remove pot from heat, cover, and let sit for 5 minutes. Stir in parsley and remaining 1 tablespoon oil and season with salt and pepper to taste. Before serving, adjust consistency with additional broth mixture as needed.

VARIATION
Almost Hands-Free Fennel Risotto
Omit porcini mushrooms. Substitute 1 large fennel bulb, stalks discarded, bulb halved, cored, and chopped, for cremini mushrooms. In step 2, reduce uncovered cooking time to 7 to 10 minutes, then add 1 tablespoon Pernod and continue to cook until completely evaporated, about 1 minute, before transferring to bowl.

Baked Brown Rice with Roasted Red Peppers and Onions
Serves 4 to 6

Why This Recipe Works Foolproof and hands-off, baked brown rice is a healthy building-block recipe for plant-based meals. But with just a little extra prep time, you can bulk it up with vegetable add-ins that complement the hearty flavor and texture of the rice. Here, a combination of aromatic browned onions and sweet roasted red peppers made for a simple plant-powered upgrade. To be sure that the aromatics fully penetrated the rice, we sautéed chopped onions until well browned before adding the rice and water to the pot. After bringing the rice to a boil, we transferred the pot to the oven for even cooking. Once the rice was tender, we stirred in chopped roasted red peppers (jarred, for convenience) and let them warm through as the rice rested off the heat. Minced parsley added color and herbal freshness, and we served the dish with a sprinkling of our Vegan Parmesan Substitute and a squeeze of fresh lemon juice. Medium-grain or short-grain brown rice can be substituted for the long-grain rice.

- 4 teaspoons extra-virgin olive oil
- 2 onions, chopped fine
- 1 teaspoon table salt
- 2¼ cups water
- 1 cup vegetable broth
- 1½ cups long-grain brown rice, rinsed
- ¾ cup jarred roasted red peppers, rinsed, patted dry, and chopped
- ½ cup minced fresh parsley
  Vegan Parmesan Substitute (page 27) or grated dairy Parmesan
  Lemon wedges

1. Adjust oven rack to middle position and heat oven to 375 degrees. Heat oil in Dutch oven over medium heat until shimmering. Add onions and salt and cook, stirring occasionally, until softened and well browned, 12 to 14 minutes.

2. Stir in water and broth and bring to boil. Stir in rice, cover, and transfer pot to oven. Bake until rice is tender and liquid is absorbed, 1 hour 5 minutes to 1 hour 10 minutes.

3. Remove pot from oven. Sprinkle red peppers over rice, cover, and let sit for 5 minutes. Add parsley and fluff gently with fork to combine. Season with salt and pepper to taste. Serve with vegan Parmesan substitute and lemon wedges.

VARIATIONS
Baked Brown Rice with Black Beans and Cilantro
Omit 1 onion and Parmesan. Substitute 1 (15-ounce) can black beans, rinsed, for roasted red peppers, ¼ cup minced cilantro for parsley, and lime wedges for lemon wedges. Add 1 stemmed, seeded, and finely chopped green bell pepper to onion in step 1. After softening onion mixture in step 1 add 3 minced garlic cloves to Dutch oven and cook until fragrant, about 30 seconds. Add ¼ teaspoon black pepper to rice mixture with cilantro in step 3.

Baked Brown Rice with Peas, Mint, and Feta
Omit 1 onion and Parmesan. Substitute 1 cup thawed frozen peas for red peppers and ½ cup crumbled feta cheese, ¼ cup minced fresh mint, and ½ teaspoon grated lemon zest for parsley.

Brown Rice Burrito Bowl
Serves 4 to 6

Why This Recipe Works Since a great burrito is really all about the filling—layers of spicy, smoky flavors working together in a cohesive whole—we decided to take the burrito out of its wrapper and put the filling in a bowl so that each of its elements could really shine. We chose brown rice as the base, for its nutty flavor, hearty texture, and nutritional value. While the rice boiled away on the stove, we seared our vegetables in batches in a skillet to get just the right color and char, building flavor in the pan with each batch. Fresh corn provided sweetness and pops of crunch, and poblano peppers offered a subtle background heat. Black beans, cooked with sautéed aromatics, gave our bowl plenty of protein. Seasoning the cooked rice with lime, cumin, and coriander brought classic burrito flavors center stage, and finishing the dish with chipotle sauce lent it creamy, smoky richness. With this warm, hearty bowl, we may never wrap burritos again. Serve with avocado, red onion, pico de gallo, and/or lime wedges.

1½ cups long-grain brown rice, rinsed
¾ teaspoon table salt, divided, plus salt for cooking rice
5 tablespoons extra-virgin olive oil, divided
1 tablespoon lime juice
1½ teaspoons ground cumin, divided
1½ teaspoons ground coriander, divided
½ teaspoon pepper, divided
2 ears corn, kernels cut from cobs
3 garlic cloves, minced, divided
3 poblano chiles, stemmed, seeded, and cut into ½-inch pieces
1 onion, chopped
1 (15-ounce) can black beans, rinsed
1 recipe Creamy Chipotle Sauce (page 248)
¼ cup chopped fresh cilantro

1. Bring 4 quarts water to boil in large pot. Add rice and 1 tablespoon salt, return to boil, and cook, stirring occasionally, until rice is tender, 25 to 30 minutes. Drain rice. Meanwhile, whisk 2 tablespoons oil, lime juice, ½ teaspoon cumin, ½ teaspoon coriander, ¼ teaspoon pepper, and ¼ teaspoon salt together in large bowl. Stir in hot rice and toss to coat. Cover to keep warm.

2. While rice cooks, heat 1 tablespoon oil in 12-inch non-stick skillet over medium-high heat until shimmering. Stir in corn, ¼ teaspoon salt, and remaining ¼ teaspoon pepper and cook until spotty brown, about 3 minutes. Transfer to second bowl and cover to keep warm.

3. Heat 1 tablespoon oil in now-empty skillet over medium-high heat until shimmering. Stir in 2 teaspoons garlic, remaining 1 teaspoon cumin, and remaining 1 teaspoon coriander and cook until fragrant, about 30 seconds. Stir in poblanos and cook until charred and tender, 6 to 8 minutes. Transfer to third bowl and cover to keep warm.

4. Heat remaining 1 tablespoon oil in now-empty skillet over medium heat until shimmering. Add onion and cook until softened and just beginning to brown, 5 to 7 minutes. Stir in remaining garlic and cook until fragrant, about 30 seconds. Stir in beans, ¼ cup water, and remaining ¼ teaspoon salt and bring to simmer. Reduce heat to medium-low and simmer, stirring occasionally, until beans are warmed through and most of liquid has evaporated, about 2 minutes.

5. Divide rice among individual bowls, then top with poblanos, corn, and beans. Drizzle with chipotle sauce, sprinkle with cilantro, and serve.

Brown Sushi Rice Bowl with Tofu and Vegetables

creamier texture of soft tofu here, but firm or extra-firm will work. You can find nori in the international foods aisle of the supermarket. Garnish with pickled ginger, if you like.

3½ cups water
2⅓ cups short-grain brown rice, rinsed
¼ cup mirin
3 tablespoons rice vinegar
28 ounces soft tofu, patted dry and cut into 3-inch-long by ½-inch-thick fingers
½ teaspoon table salt
¼ teaspoon pepper
¾ cup cornstarch
¼ cup cornmeal
2 tablespoons vegetable oil, divided
1 (8 by 7½-inch) sheet nori, crumbled (optional)
6 radishes, sliced thin
1 avocado, halved, pitted, and sliced thin
1 cucumber, peeled, halved lengthwise, seeded, and sliced thin
1 recipe Citrus Sauce (page 248)
4 scallions, sliced thin

1. Bring water and rice to simmer in large saucepan over high heat. Reduce heat to low, cover, and continue to simmer until rice is tender and water is absorbed, 45 to 50 minutes. Remove pot from heat, lay clean folded dish towel underneath lid, and let sit for 10 minutes. Transfer rice to large bowl. Drizzle with mirin and vinegar, then let cool for 20 minutes, gently tossing with wooden paddle or spoon occasionally.

2. While rice cooks, spread tofu over paper towel–lined baking sheet and let drain for 20 minutes. Gently press tofu dry with paper towels and sprinkle with salt and pepper.

3. Adjust oven rack to middle position, place paper towel–lined plate on rack, and heat oven to 200 degrees. Whisk cornstarch and cornmeal together in shallow dish. Working with several pieces of tofu at a time, coat thoroughly with cornstarch mixture, pressing to help coating adhere, and transfer to wire rack set in rimmed baking sheet.

4. Heat 1 tablespoon oil in 12-inch nonstick skillet over medium-high heat until shimmering. Carefully add half of tofu and cook until crisp and lightly golden on all sides, 10 to 12 minutes; transfer to plate in oven. Repeat with remaining 1 tablespoon oil and remaining tofu.

5. Divide rice among individual bowls, then sprinkle with half of nori, if using. Top with browned tofu, radishes, avocado, and cucumber. Drizzle with citrus sauce, sprinkle with scallions, and serve, passing remaining nori separately.

Brown Sushi Rice Bowl with Tofu and Vegetables
Serves 6

Why This Recipe Works Sushi bowls are far easier to prepare than sushi rolls, and—like rolls—they don't have to contain seafood. This healthful bowl overflows with Japanese-inspired vegetable flavors. We started with sticky short-grain brown rice. To infuse the cooked rice with a flavor akin to sushi rice, we tossed it with mirin and rice vinegar. For protein, in place of fish, we dredged soft tofu in a mixture of cornstarch and crunchy cornmeal and cooked it in a skillet. By cutting the tofu into fingers prior to dredging, we were rewarded with four ultracrispy sides that gave way to an appealingly creamy interior. We garnished the bowls with crumbled nori, spicy sliced radishes, rich avocado, cool cucumber, and scallions and dressed the bowls with a potent sauce of soy, ginger, orange, and lime. To save time, prep the tofu and vegetables while the rice cooks. We prefer the

COOKING RICE

Here are three simple methods for basic rice cooking: boiling, pilaf-style, and microwaving. Pilaf-style cooking is our favorite (though boiling rice in ample amounts of water is a great easy method when you want rice to round out a meal or fill a burrito). And after working on it for a while in the test kitchen, we can say that not only does the microwave work for rice, it works really well. Plus you can cook the rice right in the serving bowl. To make rice for a crowd, use the boiling method and double the amount of rice (don't add more water or salt).

Boiling Directions Bring the water to a boil in a large saucepan. Stir in the rice and 2½ teaspoons salt. Return to a boil, then reduce to a simmer and cook until the rice is tender, following the cooking times below. Drain.

Pilaf-Style Directions Rinse the rice. Heat 1 tablespoon oil in a medium saucepan (preferably nonstick) over medium-high heat until shimmering. Stir in the rice and cook until the edges of the grains begin to turn translucent, about 3 minutes. Stir in the water and ¼ teaspoon salt. Bring the mixture to a simmer, then reduce the heat to low, cover, and continue to simmer until the rice is tender and has absorbed all the water, following the cooking times below. Off the heat, place a clean folded dish towel under the lid and let the rice sit for 10 minutes. Fluff the rice with a fork.

Microwave Directions Rinse the rice. Combine the water, the rice, 1 tablespoon oil, and ¼ teaspoon salt in a bowl. Cover and microwave on high (full power) until the water begins to boil, 5 to 10 minutes. Reduce the microwave heat to medium (50 percent power) and continue to cook until the rice is just tender, following the cooking times below. Remove from the microwave and fluff with a fork. Cover the bowl with plastic wrap, poke several vent holes in the plastic with the tip of a knife, and let sit until completely tender, about 5 minutes.

TYPE OF RICE	COOKING METHOD	AMOUNT OF RICE	AMOUNT OF WATER	COOKING TIME
Short- and Medium-Grain White Rice	Boiled	1 cup	4 quarts	10 to 15 minutes
	Pilaf-Style	1 cup	1¾ cups	10 to 15 minutes
	Microwave	X	X	X
Long-Grain White Rice	Boiled	1 cup	4 quarts	12 to 17 minutes
	Pilaf-Style	1 cup	1¾ cups	16 to 18 minutes
	Microwave	1 cup	2 cups	10 to 15 minutes
Short- and Medium-Grain Brown Rice	Boiled	1 cup	4 quarts	22 to 27 minutes
	Pilaf-Style	1 cup	1¾ cups	40 to 50 minutes
	Microwave	1 cup	2 cups	25 to 30 minutes
Long-Grain Brown Rice	Boiled	1 cup	4 quarts	25 to 30 minutes
	Pilaf-Style	1 cup	1¾ cups	40 to 50 minutes
	Microwave	1 cup	2 cups	25 to 30 minutes
Wild Rice	Boiled	1 cup	4 quarts	45 to 40 minutes
	Pilaf-Style	X	X	X
	Microwave	X	X	X
Basmati, Jasmine, or Texmati Rice	Boiled	1 cup	4 quarts	12 to 17 minutes
	Pilaf-Style	1 cup	1¾ cups	16 to 18 minutes
	Microwave	1 cup	2 cups	10 to 15 minutes

X = Not recommended

COOKING GRAINS

Some grains, such as bulgur, cook in minutes, while others, such as barley, take much longer. We have perfected three basic methods for cooking grains. Pilaf-style is our favorite option because it produces grains with a light and fluffy texture and a slightly toasted flavor.

Boiling Directions Bring the water to a boil in a large saucepan. Stir in the grain and ½ teaspoon salt. Return to a boil, then reduce to a simmer and cook until the grain is tender, following the cooking times below. Drain.

Pilaf-Style Directions Rinse and then dry the grains on a towel. Heat 1 tablespoon oil in a medium saucepan (preferably nonstick) over medium-high heat until shimmering. Stir in the grain and toast until lightly golden and fragrant, 2 to 3 minutes. Stir in the water and ¼ teaspoon salt. Bring the mixture to a simmer, then reduce the heat to low, cover, and continue to simmer until the grain is tender and has absorbed all of the water, following the cooking times below. Off the heat, let the grain stand for 10 minutes, then fluff with a fork.

Microwave Directions Rinse the grain. Combine the water, the grain, 1 tablespoon oil, and ¼ teaspoon salt in a bowl. Cover and cook following the times and temperatures below. Remove from the microwave and fluff with a fork. Cover the bowl with plastic wrap, poke several vent holes with the tip of a knife, and let sit until completely tender, about 5 minutes.

TYPE OF GRAIN	COOKING METHOD	AMOUNT OF GRAIN	AMOUNT OF WATER	COOKING TIME
Pearl Barley	Boiled	1 cup	4 quarts	20 to 25 minutes
	Pilaf-Style	X	X	X
	Microwave	X	X	X
Bulgur (medium-to coarse-grind)	Boiled	1 cup	4 quarts	15 to 20 minutes
	Pilaf-Style**	1 cup	1 cup	16 to 18 minutes
	Microwave	1 cup	1 cup	5 to 10 minutes
Farro	Boiled	1 cup	4 quarts	15 to 20 minutes
	Pilaf-Style	X	X	X
	Microwave	X	X	X
Millet	Boiled	X	X	X
	Pilaf-Style***	1 cup	2 cups	15 to 20 minutes
	Microwave	X	X	X
Oat Berries	Boiled	1 cup	4 quarts	30 to 40 minutes
	Pilaf-Style	1 cup	1½ cups	30 to 40 minutes
	Microwave	X	X	X
Quinoa (any color)	Boiled	X	X	X
	Pilaf-Style	1 cup	1 cup + 3 tablespoons	18 to 20 minutes
	Microwave	1 cup	2 cups	5 minutes on medium, then 5 minutes on high
Wheat Berries	Boiled	1 cup	4 quarts	1 hour
	Pilaf-Style	X	X	X
	Microwave	X	X	X

** For pilaf, do not rinse, and skip the toasting step, adding the grain to the pot with the liquid.
*** For pilaf, increase the toasting time until the grains begin to pop, about 12 minutes.   X = Not recommended

Brown Rice Salad with Asparagus and Lemon

Serves 4 to 6

Why This Recipe Works Although we often prefer to bake brown rice, we discovered that it doesn't work in rice salads. Once cooled and drizzled with dressing, the baked rice turned gummy. So instead, we cooked the rice pasta-style, by boiling it in a large pot of water, which washed away its excess starches. Then we spread it out on a baking sheet to cool rapidly, preventing it from overcooking as it sat. To give the rice bright flavor, we drizzled it with lemon juice while it was still warm. While the rice cooled and absorbed the juice, we cooked asparagus pieces in olive oil until browned and tender. For a zesty but simple dressing to highlight the rustic rice and bright asparagus, we whisked together olive oil, minced shallot, and fresh lemon juice and zest. After dressing the rice and asparagus, we let the dressing's flavors permeate the salad. With a sprinkling of toasted almonds and parsley, our salad was loaded with fresh, vibrant flavors and contrasting textures. The optional goat cheese adds a creamy tang. Look for asparagus spears no thicker than ½ inch.

Brown Rice Salad with Jalapeño, Tomatoes, and Avocado

- 1½ cups long-grain brown rice
- ¾ teaspoon table salt, plus salt for cooking rice
- 1 teaspoon grated lemon zest plus 3 tablespoons juice, divided
- 3½ tablespoons extra-virgin olive oil, divided
- 1 pound asparagus, trimmed and cut into 1-inch lengths
- ¾ teaspoon pepper, divided
- 1 shallot, minced
- 2 ounces goat cheese, crumbled (½ cup), divided (optional)
- ¼ cup slivered almonds, toasted, divided
- ¼ cup minced fresh parsley, divided

1. Bring 4 quarts water to boil in large pot. Add rice and 2 teaspoons salt and cook, stirring occasionally, until rice is tender, 22 to 25 minutes. Drain rice, spread onto rimmed baking sheet, and drizzle with 1 tablespoon lemon juice. Let rice cool completely, about 10 minutes; transfer to large bowl.

2. Heat 1 tablespoon oil in 12-inch skillet over high heat until just smoking. Add asparagus, ¼ teaspoon pepper, and ¼ teaspoon salt and cook, stirring occasionally, until asparagus is browned and crisp-tender, about 4 minutes; transfer to plate and let cool slightly.

3. Whisk shallot, remaining ½ teaspoon salt, lemon zest and remaining 2 tablespoons juice, remaining 2½ tablespoons oil, and remaining ½ teaspoon pepper together in large bowl.

Add rice; asparagus; ¼ cup goat cheese, if using; 3 tablespoons almonds; and 3 tablespoons parsley. Gently toss to combine and let sit for 10 minutes. Season with salt and pepper to taste. Transfer to serving platter and sprinkle with remaining ¼ cup goat cheese, if using; remaining 1 tablespoon almonds; and remaining 1 tablespoon parsley. Serve.

VARIATIONS

Brown Rice Salad with Jalapeño, Tomatoes, and Avocado

To make this salad spicier, add the chile seeds.

- 1½ cups long-grain brown rice
- ½ teaspoon table salt, plus salt for cooking rice
- 1 teaspoon grated lime zest plus 3 tablespoons juice (2 limes), divided
- 2½ tablespoons extra-virgin olive oil
- 2 teaspoons agave syrup or honey
- 2 garlic cloves, minced
- ½ teaspoon ground cumin
- ½ teaspoon pepper
- 10 ounces cherry tomatoes, halved

1 avocado, halved, pitted, and cut into ½-inch pieces
1 jalapeño chile, stemmed, seeded, and minced
5 scallions, sliced thin, divided
¼ cup minced fresh cilantro

1. Bring 4 quarts water to boil in large pot. Add rice and 2 teaspoons salt and cook, stirring occasionally, until rice is tender, 22 to 25 minutes. Drain rice, spread onto rimmed baking sheet, and drizzle with 1 tablespoon lime juice. Let rice cool completely, about 10 minutes; transfer to large bowl.

2. Whisk oil, agave, garlic, cumin, pepper, salt, and lime zest and remaining 2 tablespoons juice together in small bowl, then drizzle over cooled rice. Add tomatoes, avocado, and jalapeño and toss to combine. Let sit for 10 minutes.

3. Add ¼ cup scallions and cilantro and toss to combine. Season with salt and pepper to taste. Sprinkle with remaining scallions and serve.

Brown Rice Salad with Fennel, Mushrooms, and Walnuts

Cremini mushrooms can be substituted for the white mushrooms.

1½ cups long-grain brown rice
1¼ teaspoons table salt, divided, plus salt for cooking rice
3 tablespoons white wine vinegar, divided
¼ cup extra-virgin olive oil, divided
1 pound white mushrooms, trimmed and quartered
1 large fennel bulb, stalks discarded, bulb halved, cored, and sliced thin
1 shallot, minced
½ teaspoon pepper
⅔ cup walnuts, toasted and chopped coarse, divided
2 tablespoons minced fresh tarragon
2 tablespoons minced fresh parsley, divided

1. Bring 4 quarts water to boil in large pot. Add rice and 2 teaspoons salt and cook, stirring occasionally, until rice is tender, 22 to 25 minutes. Drain rice, spread onto rimmed baking sheet, and drizzle with 1 tablespoon vinegar. Let rice cool completely, about 10 minutes; transfer to large bowl.

2. Heat 1 tablespoon oil in 12-inch skillet over medium-high heat until shimmering. Add mushrooms and ½ teaspoon salt and cook, stirring occasionally, until pan is dry and mushrooms are browned, 6 to 8 minutes; transfer to plate and let cool.

3. Heat 1 tablespoon oil in now-empty skillet over medium-high heat until shimmering. Add fennel and ¼ teaspoon salt and cook, stirring occasionally, until just browned and crisp-tender, 3 to 4 minutes; transfer to plate with mushrooms and let cool.

4. Whisk shallot, pepper, remaining ½ teaspoon salt, remaining 2 tablespoons vinegar, and remaining 2 tablespoons oil together in small bowl, then drizzle over cooled rice. Add mushroom-fennel mixture and toss to combine. Let sit for 10 minutes.

5. Add ½ cup walnuts, tarragon, and 1 tablespoon parsley and toss to combine. Season with salt and pepper to taste. Sprinkle with remaining walnuts and remaining 1 tablespoon parsley and serve.

COOLING RICE FOR SALAD

After cooking and draining rice, spread onto rimmed baking sheet and drizzle with 1 tablespoon citrus juice or vinegar. Let rice cool completely, about 10 minutes; transfer to large bowl.

Brown Rice Onigiri with Spinach, Edamame, and Sesame

Serves 4 to 6 (Makes 24 onigiri)

Why This Recipe Works Onigiri are a Japanese bento box staple: adorable little bundles of white sushi rice stuffed with morsels of fish, pickled plums, sea vegetables, or other ingredients. To rework them so they'd pack a greater plant-based punch, we first swapped out white rice for short-grain brown rice. But, since brown rice is less sticky than white rice, we skipped the standard rinsing to preserve as much starch as possible. Our next change was more dramatic: Instead of stuffing tidbits of our spinach and edamame filling into balls of rice, we pulsed the filling ingredients along with the rice in the food processor. This enabled us to incorporate far more vegetable "filling" into each onigiri. Plus, slightly processing the rice released more starch, making the mixture easier to shape. We scooped out portions of the rice mixture and, with lightly moistened hands, pressed each into a petite disk, which we found sturdier than the traditional ball shape. Rolling the edges in toasted sesame seeds added a crunchy, nutty contrast, and a simple soy dipping sauce made a tasty accompaniment.

Brown Rice Onigiri with Spinach, Edamame, and Sesame

Vegetable Paella in a Paella Pan

1¾ cups water
1 cup short-grain brown rice
1 cup baby spinach
¾ cup frozen shelled edamame beans, thawed and patted dry
2 (8 by 7½-inch) sheets nori, crumbled
¼ cup sesame seeds, toasted, divided
2 teaspoons grated fresh ginger
½ teaspoon table salt
2 scallions, sliced thin
2 teaspoons toasted sesame oil
Soy Dipping Sauce (page 248)

1. Bring water and rice to simmer in large saucepan over high heat. Reduce heat to low, cover, and simmer gently until rice is tender and water is absorbed, 40 to 45 minutes. Off heat, lay clean dish towel underneath lid, and let sit for 10 minutes. Fluff rice with fork and cover.

2. Pulse spinach, edamame, nori, 2 tablespoons sesame seeds, ginger, salt, scallions, and sesame oil in food processor until mixture is finely ground (it should not be smooth), about 10 pulses. Add rice and pulse until rice is coarsely chopped and mixture is well combined, about 8 pulses.

3. Divide rice mixture into 24 portions (about 1½ tablespoons each) and arrange on parchment-lined baking sheet. Using your lightly moistened hands, roll each portion into ball, then press into disk about 1½ inches wide and ¾ inch thick. Spread remaining 2 tablespoons sesame seeds onto plate. Gently roll sides of disks in sesame seeds, pressing lightly to adhere, and transfer to serving platter. Serve with soy dipping sauce.

Vegetable Paella
Serves 6

Why This Recipe Works Though traditional paella centers on a variety of meat and seafood, our vegetable-focused version highlights an array of hearty vegetables common in Spanish cuisine. We gave the artichokes and peppers deeper flavor by first roasting them and then tossing them with a lemony sauce. We sautéed the fennel with onion to give it a rich caramelized flavor. Kalamata olives brought a briny, umami quality. To give the rice complexity, we bloomed the paprika with garlic and browned diced tomatoes to give them savory depth. We coated the rice with this potent mixture before adding broth, wine, and saffron. For perfectly even cooking, we transferred the paella to the oven. While we prefer the flavor and texture of jarred whole baby artichokes, you can substitute 18 ounces frozen artichoke hearts, thawed and patted dry. Bomba rice is traditional for paella, but you can also use Arborio. Socarrat, a layer of crusty browned rice that forms on the bottom of the pan, is a traditional part of paella. In this version, socarrat does not develop because most of the cooking is done in the oven; if desired, there are directions on how to make a socarrat before serving in step 5.

3 cups jarred whole baby artichokes packed in water, quartered, rinsed, and patted dry
2 red bell peppers, stemmed, seeded, and chopped coarse
½ cup pitted kalamata olives, chopped
9 garlic cloves, peeled (3 whole, 6 minced)
6 tablespoons extra-virgin olive oil, divided
1½ teaspoons table salt, divided
¼ teaspoon pepper
3 tablespoons chopped fresh parsley, divided
2 tablespoons lemon juice
1 onion, chopped fine
1 fennel bulb, stalks discarded, bulb halved, cored, and sliced thin
½ teaspoon smoked paprika
1 (14.5-ounce) can diced tomatoes, drained, minced, and drained again
2 cups Bomba or Arborio rice
3 cups vegetable broth
⅓ cup dry white wine
½ teaspoon saffron threads, crumbled
½ cup frozen peas, thawed

1. Adjust oven rack to lower-middle position, place rimmed baking sheet on rack, and heat oven to 450 degrees. Toss artichokes and peppers with olives, whole garlic cloves, 2 tablespoons oil, ½ teaspoon salt, and pepper in bowl. Spread vegetables in hot sheet and roast until artichokes are browned around edges and peppers are browned, 20 to 25 minutes; let cool slightly.

2. Mince roasted garlic. In large bowl, whisk 2 tablespoons oil, 2 tablespoons parsley, lemon juice, and minced roasted garlic together. Add roasted vegetables and toss to combine. Season with salt and pepper to taste.

3. Reduce oven temperature to 350 degrees. Heat remaining 2 tablespoons oil in Dutch oven over medium heat until shimmering. Add onion and fennel and cook until softened, 8 to 10 minutes.

4. Stir in minced raw garlic and paprika and cook until fragrant, about 30 seconds. Stir in tomatoes and cook until mixture darkens and thickens slightly, about 3 minutes. Stir in rice and cook until grains are well coated with tomato mixture, about 2 minutes. Stir in broth, wine, saffron, and remaining 1 teaspoon salt. Increase heat to medium-high and bring to boil, stirring occasionally. Cover, transfer pot to oven, and bake until liquid is absorbed and rice is tender, 25 to 35 minutes.

5. For optional socarrat, transfer pot to stovetop and remove lid. Cook over medium-high heat for about 5 minutes, rotating pot as needed, until bottom layer of rice is well browned and crisp.

6. Sprinkle roasted vegetables and peas over rice, cover, and let paella sit for 5 minutes. Sprinkle with remaining 1 tablespoon parsley and serve.

VARIATION
Vegetable Paella in a Paella Pan
Substitute 14- to 15-inch paella pan for Dutch oven, increase broth to 3¼ cups, and increase wine to ½ cup. Before placing pan in oven, cover tightly with aluminum foil.

Wild Rice Pilaf with Pecans and Cranberries
Serves 6 to 8

Why This Recipe Works Properly cooked wild rice is tender yet chewy and pleasingly rustic—never crunchy or gluey. Simmering the wild rice in flavorful liquid and then draining off excess proved to be the most foolproof way to produce fluffy wild rice every time. A combination of vegetable broth and water enhanced the rice's nutty earthiness. We also added some white rice to our pilaf to balance the wild rice's assertive flavor and finished our dish with nuts and dried fruit. Cooking times for wild rice vary, so start checking for doneness after 35 minutes. For an accurate measurement of boiling water, bring a full kettle of water to a boil, then measure out the desired amount.

1¾ cups vegetable broth
¼ cup water plus 2¼ cups boiling water
2 bay leaves
8 sprigs fresh thyme, divided into 2 bundles, each tied together with kitchen twine
1 cup wild rice, picked over and rinsed
2 tablespoons extra-virgin olive oil
1 onion, chopped fine
1 large carrot, peeled and chopped fine
1 teaspoon table salt
1½ cups long-grain white rice, rinsed
¾ cup dried cranberries
¾ cup pecans, toasted and chopped coarse
2 tablespoons minced fresh parsley

1. Bring broth, ¼ cup water, bay leaves, and 1 bundle thyme to boil in medium saucepan over medium-high heat. Add wild rice, cover, and reduce heat to low. Simmer until rice is plump and tender and most of liquid has been absorbed, 35 to 45 minutes. Drain rice through fine-mesh strainer, discarding liquid. Discard bay leaves and thyme. Return rice to now-empty saucepan; cover and set aside.

2. Meanwhile, heat oil in medium saucepan over medium-high heat until shimmering. Add onion, carrot, and salt and cook until vegetables are softened, about 4 minutes. Stir in white rice and cook, stirring often, until grain edges begin to turn translucent, about 3 minutes.

3. Stir in 2¼ cups boiling water and second thyme bundle and bring to simmer. Reduce heat to low, cover, and continue to simmer until white rice is tender and water is absorbed, 16 to 18 minutes. Off heat, discard thyme, fluff rice with fork, and stir in cranberries.

4. Gently toss wild rice, white rice mixture, pecans, and parsley together in bowl. Season with salt and pepper to taste, and serve.

VARIATION
Wild Rice Pilaf with Scallions, Cilantro, and Almonds
Omit dried cranberries. Substitute toasted sliced almonds for pecans and cilantro for parsley. Add 2 thinly sliced scallions and 1 teaspoon lime juice to pilaf before serving.

Red Rice and Quinoa Salad
Serves 4 to 6

Why This Recipe Works One rice variety that doesn't get enough play is red rice. Nutty in flavor and highly nutritious, red rice sports—surprise—a husk that is red from the anthocyanins it contains (the same beneficial compounds that make blueberries blue). For a pretty salad, we mixed this rice with nutty white quinoa, cooking them together using the pasta method and giving the rice a head start to ensure that both grains were done at the same time. Then we drained them, drizzled them with lime juice to add bright flavor, and let them cool. Next, to make this salad fresh and a little sweet, we chose dates and orange segments (and used some of the orange juice in our dressing). Cilantro and red pepper flakes added a fresh bite and a bit of spiciness to round it out. We like the convenience of prewashed quinoa; rinsing removes the quinoa's bitter protective coating (called saponin). If you buy unwashed quinoa, rinse it and then spread it out on a clean dish towel to dry for 15 minutes.

¾ cup red rice
   Table salt for cooking rice and quinoa
¾ cup prewashed white quinoa
3 tablespoons lime juice (2 limes), divided
2 oranges
1 small shallot, minced
1 tablespoon minced fresh cilantro plus 1 cup leaves
¼ teaspoon red pepper flakes
¼ cup extra-virgin olive oil
6 ounces pitted dates, chopped (1 cup)

1. Bring 4 quarts water to boil in large pot over high heat. Add rice and 1 tablespoon salt and cook, stirring occasionally, for 15 minutes. Add quinoa to pot and continue to cook until grains are tender, 12 to 14 minutes. Drain rice-quinoa mixture, spread over rimmed baking sheet, drizzle with 2 tablespoons lime juice, and let cool completely, about 15 minutes.

2. Meanwhile, cut away peel and pith from oranges. Holding fruit over bowl, use paring knife to slice between membranes to release segments. Cut segments in half crosswise. If needed, squeeze orange membranes to equal 2 tablespoons juice in bowl.

3. Whisk 2 tablespoons orange juice, shallot, minced cilantro, pepper flakes, and remaining 1 tablespoon lime juice together in large bowl. Whisking constantly, slowly drizzle in oil. Add rice-quinoa mixture, dates, orange segments, and cilantro leaves and toss to combine. Season with salt and pepper to taste, and serve.

Black Rice Salad with Snap Peas and Ginger-Sesame Vinaigrette
Serves 4 to 6

Why This Recipe Works Also known as purple or forbidden rice, black rice is another less common but delicious rice choice. This ancient grain, which once was reserved exclusively for the emperors of China, has a deliciously roasted, nutty taste and can be used in anything from salads to dessert puddings. We stayed true to the rice's geographic roots in creating this colorful rice salad. The emerald green snap peas, red-and-white radishes, and red bell peppers are like jewels against the dramatic-looking black rice. The only drawback of black rice is that it is easy to overcook, so as with other rices, the best approach was to cook it like pasta, in lots of boiling water, giving it space to move around. Then we drained it, drizzled it with a little vinegar for a flavor boost, and let it cool completely on a baking sheet. This ensured perfectly cooked grains that had the expected chew of black rice without any

Red Rice and Quinoa Salad

2. Whisk remaining 3 tablespoons vinegar, olive oil, sesame oil, shallot, chili-garlic sauce, ginger, pepper, and salt in large bowl until combined. Add rice, snap peas, radishes, bell pepper, and cilantro and toss to combine. Season with salt and pepper to taste. Serve.

Herbed Barley Pilaf
Serves 4 to 6

Why This Recipe Works Hearty, nutrient-rich barley has a firm texture that makes it well suited to accompany anything from simple Grilled Onions with Balsamic Vinaigrette (page 208) to robust Sicilian White Beans and Escarole (page 298), so for this dish we chose a fairly simple flavor profile to keep it versatile. Cooking an onion and then toasting the barley before adding a measured amount of water enhanced the barley's inherent nuttiness. But during our testing, we uncovered a major inconsistency: One batch of barley was fully tender in 35 minutes, another in 20, and the next in 40. We realized that the extent to which the barley was pearled, or polished to remove the outer bran, was affecting the cooking time—but since there is often no way to tell by the label, the only way to account for the differences was to put a 20-minute range in the cooking time. After the grains were fully cooked and had absorbed the water, we stirred in a handful of fresh, bold herbs and a bit of lemon juice for a vibrant finish. Do not substitute hulled, hull-less, quick-cooking, or presteamed barley (read the ingredient list on the package to determine this) in this recipe.

3 tablespoons extra-virgin olive oil
1 small onion, chopped fine
½ teaspoon table salt
1½ cups pearl barley, rinsed
2 garlic cloves, minced
1½ teaspoons minced fresh thyme or ½ teaspoon dried
2½ cups water
¼ cup minced fresh parsley
2 tablespoons minced fresh chives
1½ teaspoons lemon juice

1. Heat oil in large saucepan over medium heat until shimmering. Add onion and salt and cook until softened, about 5 minutes. Stir in barley, garlic, and thyme and cook, stirring frequently, until barley is lightly toasted and fragrant, about 3 minutes.
2. Stir in water and bring to simmer. Reduce heat to low, cover, and simmer until barley is tender and water is absorbed, 20 to 40 minutes.

mushiness. We mixed up a vinaigrette with sesame oil, ginger, and chili-garlic sauce, and stirred in some cilantro, and our simple salad was complete.

1½ cups black rice
¼ teaspoon table salt, plus salt for cooking rice
1 teaspoon plus 3 tablespoons rice vinegar, divided
¼ cup extra-virgin olive oil
1 tablespoon toasted sesame oil
2 teaspoons minced shallot
2 teaspoons Asian chili-garlic sauce
1 teaspoon grated fresh ginger
⅛ teaspoon pepper
6 ounces sugar snap peas, strings removed, halved
5 radishes, trimmed, halved, and sliced thin
1 red bell pepper, stemmed, seeded, and chopped fine
¼ cup minced fresh cilantro

1. Bring 4 quarts water to boil in Dutch oven over medium-high heat. Add rice and 1 teaspoon salt and cook until rice is tender, 20 to 25 minutes. Drain rice, spread onto rimmed baking sheet, and drizzle with 1 teaspoon vinegar. Let rice cool completely, about 15 minutes.

3. Off heat, lay clean dish towel underneath lid and let pilaf sit for 10 minutes. Add parsley, chives, and lemon juice to pilaf and fluff gently with fork to combine. Season with salt and pepper to taste. Serve.

Barley Bowl with Roasted Carrots and Snow Peas

Serves 4 to 6

Why This Recipe Works Barley is the star of this hearty bowl that's full of contrasting—and surprising—textures and Middle Eastern flavors, with its warm spices and colorful vegetables. To keep the cooking method easy, we simply boiled the barley and then tossed it with a bright lemon-mint dressing so the warm grains would readily soak it up. While the barley cooked, we pan-roasted coriander-dusted spears of carrots until charred, sweet, and tender. We then threw in crisp snow peas and cooked them until just blistered, so they would retain their green freshness. Toasting sunflower seeds with cumin, cardamom, and a little more coriander gave the dish a warm, aromatic finish. We piled a mound of the dressed barley and vegetables into our bowls, followed by our crunchy seed topping. Finally, a drizzle of our Tahini Sauce pulled all the components of the bowl together. Do not substitute hulled or hull-less barley (read the ingredient list on the package to determine this) in this recipe. If using quick-cooking or presteamed barley, you will need to reduce the cooking time in step 1. We also like this bowl topped with avocado.

- ¼ cup extra-virgin olive oil, divided
- 3 tablespoons minced fresh mint, divided
- 1 teaspoon grated lemon zest plus 2 tablespoons juice
- 1½ cups pearl barley, rinsed
- ¼ teaspoon table salt, plus salt for cooking barley
- 5 carrots, peeled
- ¾ teaspoon ground coriander, divided
- 8 ounces snow peas, strings removed, halved lengthwise
- ⅔ cup raw sunflower seeds
- ½ teaspoon ground cumin
- ⅛ teaspoon ground cardamom
- ½ cup Tahini Sauce (page 249)

Bulgur Salad with Carrots and Almonds

1. Whisk 2½ tablespoons oil, 2 tablespoons mint, and lemon zest and juice together in large bowl, set aside. Bring 4 quarts water to boil in large pot. Add barley and 1 tablespoon salt, return to boil, and cook until tender, 20 to 40 minutes. Drain barley, transfer to bowl with lemon-mint mixture, and toss to combine. Season with salt and pepper to taste, and cover to keep warm.

2. While barley cooks, halve carrots crosswise, then halve or quarter lengthwise to create uniformly sized pieces. Heat 1 tablespoon oil in 12-inch nonstick skillet over medium-high heat until just smoking. Add carrots and ½ teaspoon coriander and cook, stirring occasionally, until lightly charred and just tender, 5 to 7 minutes. Stir in snow peas and cook until spotty brown, 3 to 5 minutes; transfer to second bowl.

3. Heat remaining 1½ teaspoons oil in now-empty skillet over medium heat until shimmering. Add sunflower seeds, cumin, cardamom, remaining ¼ teaspoon coriander, and salt. Cook, stirring constantly, until seeds are toasted, about 2 minutes; transfer to third bowl.

4. Divide barley among individual bowls, then top with carrot–snow pea mixture and sunflower seeds. Drizzle with tahini sauce, sprinkle with remaining 1 tablespoon mint, and serve.

Barley with Lentils, Mushrooms, and Tahini-Yogurt Sauce

Serves 4

Why This Recipe Works Tasters particularly favored black lentils in this hearty dish, for their nutty, robust flavor and ability to hold their shape once cooked. We were happy to find that we could cook the sturdy lentils in the same pot as the barley. Hoping to streamline things even more, we set the cooked barley and lentils aside and attempted to brown the mushrooms in the same saucepan. But the mushrooms were too crowded in the pot, which caused them to steam. Switching to a large nonstick skillet to cook the meaty portobellos and umami-rich porcini resulted in more browning and faster cooking. Our tangy Tahini-Yogurt Sauce balanced all the hearty flavors, and fresh dill and strips of lemon peel brightened the earthy notes. Do not substitute hulled, hull-less, quick-cooking, or presteamed barley (read the package label to determine this) in this recipe. Green or brown lentils can be substituted for the black lentils.

- ½ ounce dried porcini mushrooms, rinsed
- 1 cup pearl barley, rinsed
- ½ cup black lentils, picked over and rinsed
- ½ teaspoon table salt, plus salt for cooking barley and lentils
- 2 tablespoons extra-virgin olive oil
- 1 onion, chopped fine
- 2 large portobello mushroom caps, cut into 1-inch pieces
- 3 (2-inch) strips lemon zest, sliced thin lengthwise
- ¾ teaspoon ground coriander
- ¼ teaspoon pepper
- 2 tablespoons chopped fresh dill
- ½ cup Tahini-Yogurt Sauce (page 249)

1. Microwave 1½ cups water and porcini mushrooms in covered bowl until steaming, about 1 minute. Let sit until softened, about 5 minutes. Drain mushrooms in fine-mesh strainer lined with coffee filter, reserving soaking liquid, and chop mushrooms.

2. Bring 4 quarts water to boil in Dutch oven. Add barley, lentils, and 1 tablespoon salt, return to boil, and cook until tender, 20 to 40 minutes. Drain barley and lentils, return to now-empty pot, and cover to keep warm.

3. Meanwhile, heat oil in 12-inch nonstick skillet over medium heat until shimmering. Add onion and cook until softened, about 5 minutes. Stir in portobello mushrooms, cover, and cook until portobellos have released their liquid and begin to brown, about 4 minutes.

4. Uncover, stir in lemon zest, coriander, salt, and pepper, and cook until fragrant, about 30 seconds. Stir in porcini and porcini soaking liquid, bring to boil, and cook, stirring occasionally, until liquid is thickened slightly and reduced to ½ cup, about 5 minutes. Stir mushroom mixture and dill into barley-lentil mixture and season with salt and pepper to taste. Serve, drizzling individual portions with tahini-yogurt sauce.

Bulgur Salad with Carrots and Almonds

Serves 4 to 6

Why This Recipe Works As versatile as it is nutritious, bulgur is a great medium for delivering big, bold flavor in hearty salads. To bulk up this simple cereal grain into a satisfying no-cook salad, we started by softening the bulgur in a mixture of water, lemon juice, and salt for an hour and a half, until it had the perfect chew and was thoroughly seasoned. Fresh mint, cilantro, and scallions made our salad crisp and bright, and cumin and cayenne added depth of flavor to our simple lemon vinaigrette. Sweet shredded carrots nicely accented the rich, nutty taste of the bulgur, and toasted almonds provided complementary crunch. When shopping, don't confuse bulgur with cracked wheat, which has a much longer cooking time and will not work in this recipe.

- 1½ cups medium-grind bulgur, rinsed
- 1 cup water
- 6 tablespoons lemon juice (2 lemons), divided
- ¾ teaspoon table salt, divided
- ⅓ cup extra-virgin olive oil
- ½ teaspoon ground cumin
- ⅛ teaspoon cayenne pepper
- 4 carrots, peeled and shredded
- 3 scallions, sliced thin
- ½ cup sliced almonds, toasted
- ⅓ cup chopped fresh mint
- ⅓ cup chopped fresh cilantro

1. Combine bulgur, water, ¼ cup lemon juice, and ¼ teaspoon salt in bowl. Cover and let sit at room temperature until grains are softened and liquid is fully absorbed, about 1½ hours.

2. Whisk oil, cumin, cayenne, remaining 2 tablespoons lemon juice, and remaining ½ teaspoon salt together in large bowl. Add bulgur, carrots, scallions, almonds, mint, and cilantro and gently toss to combine. Season with salt and pepper to taste. Serve.

Bulgur with Chickpeas, Spinach, and Za'atar

Serves 4

Why This Recipe Works This robust and very simple main dish combines creamy, nutty chickpeas and hearty bulgur with the clean, vegetal punch of fresh spinach. The aromatic eastern Mediterranean spice blend za'atar, with its fragrant wild herbs, toasted sesame seeds, and tangy sumac, elevates the flavors with little effort. We found that incorporating the za'atar at two points in the cooking process brought out its complexity. First, to release its deep earthiness, we bloomed half of the za'atar in an aromatic base of onion and garlic before adding the bulgur, chickpeas, and cooking liquid. We added the remainder of the za'atar, along with the fresh baby spinach, off the heat; the residual heat in the bulgur was enough to perfectly soften the spinach and to highlight the za'atar's more delicate aromas. When shopping, don't confuse bulgur with cracked wheat, which has a much longer cooking time and will not work in this recipe.

- 3 tablespoons extra-virgin olive oil, divided
- 1 onion, chopped fine
- ½ teaspoon table salt
- 3 garlic cloves, minced
- 2 tablespoons za'atar, divided
- 1 cup medium-grind bulgur, rinsed
- 1 (15-ounce) can chickpeas, rinsed
- ¾ cup vegetable broth
- ¾ cup water
- 3 ounces (3 cups) baby spinach, chopped
- 1 tablespoon lemon juice

1. Heat 2 tablespoons oil in large saucepan over medium heat until shimmering. Add onion and salt and cook until softened, about 5 minutes. Stir in garlic and 1 tablespoon za'atar and cook until fragrant, about 30 seconds.

2. Stir in bulgur, chickpeas, broth, and water and bring to simmer. Reduce heat to low, cover, and simmer gently until bulgur is tender, 16 to 18 minutes.

3. Off heat, lay clean dish towel underneath lid and let bulgur sit for 10 minutes. Add spinach, lemon juice, remaining 1 tablespoon oil, and remaining 1 tablespoon za'atar and fluff gently with fork to combine. Season with salt and pepper to taste. Serve.

Garlicky Tofu Tabbouleh

Tabbouleh

Serves 4 to 6

Why This Recipe Works Tabbouleh, originally from the Middle East, has become a "global salad" found in different iterations around the world. By definition it includes bulgur, parsley, tomato, and onion in a penetrating mint and lemon dressing. In America, we think of it as a grain-based dish, but its original version features parsley first and foremost, so we wanted to be sure to include plenty of that herb. We started by salting and draining the tomatoes to rid them of excess moisture that would make our tabbouleh soggy. Soaking the bulgur in lemon juice and some of the drained tomato liquid, rather than in water, allowed it to absorb loads of flavor as it softened. Tasters felt that chopped raw onion was too strong but that milder scallions added just the right level of flavor. Mint and a bit of cayenne pepper rounded out the dish. Adding the herbs and vegetables to the bulgur while it was still soaking gave all the components time to mingle, resulting in a cohesively flavored dish. Make a meal of this with hummus and pita. Or try the variation with tofu, which is a meal in itself. Don't confuse bulgur with cracked wheat, which has a much longer cooking time and will not work in this recipe.

- 3 tomatoes, cored and cut into ½-inch pieces
- ½ teaspoon table salt, divided
- ½ cup medium-grind bulgur, rinsed
- ¼ cup lemon juice (2 lemons), divided
- 6 tablespoons extra-virgin olive oil
- ⅛ teaspoon cayenne pepper
- 1½ cups minced fresh parsley
- ½ cup minced fresh mint
- 2 scallions, sliced thin

1. Toss tomatoes with ¼ teaspoon salt in fine-mesh strainer set over bowl and let drain, tossing occasionally, for 30 minutes; reserve 2 tablespoons drained tomato juice. Toss bulgur with 2 tablespoons lemon juice and reserved tomato juice in bowl and let sit until grains begin to soften, 30 to 40 minutes.

2. Whisk remaining 2 tablespoons lemon juice, oil, cayenne, and remaining ¼ teaspoon salt together in large bowl. Add tomatoes, bulgur, parsley, mint, and scallions and toss gently to combine. Cover and let sit at room temperature until flavors meld and bulgur is tender, about 1 hour. Before serving, toss salad to recombine and season with salt and pepper to taste.

VARIATION

Garlicky Tofu Tabbouleh

Don't confuse bulgur with cracked wheat, which has a much longer cooking time and will not work in this recipe. You can substitute firm tofu for the extra-firm in this recipe.

- 3 tomatoes, cored and cut into ½-inch pieces
- 1 teaspoon table salt, divided
- ½ cup medium-grind bulgur, rinsed
- ¼ cup lemon juice (2 lemons), divided
- 14 ounces extra-firm tofu, cut into 2-inch pieces
- ⅛ teaspoon pepper
- ¼ cup extra-virgin olive oil, divided
- 3 garlic cloves, minced
- ⅛ teaspoon cayenne pepper
- 1½ cups minced fresh parsley
- ½ cup minced fresh mint
- 2 scallions, sliced thin

1. Toss tomatoes with ¼ teaspoon salt in fine-mesh strainer set over bowl and let drain, tossing occasionally, for 30 minutes; reserve 2 tablespoons drained tomato juice. Toss bulgur with 2 tablespoons lemon juice and reserved tomato juice in bowl and let sit until grains begin to soften, 30 to 40 minutes.

2. Meanwhile, spread tofu on paper towel–lined baking sheet and let drain for 20 minutes. Gently press dry with paper towels and sprinkle with ¼ teaspoon salt and pepper. Pulse tofu in food processor until coarsely chopped, 3 to 4 pulses.

Line baking sheet with clean paper towels. Spread processed tofu over prepared sheet and press gently with paper towels to dry.

3. Heat 2 teaspoons oil in 12-inch nonstick skillet over medium-high heat until shimmering. Add tofu and cook, stirring occasionally, until tofu is lightly browned, 10 to 12 minutes. (Tofu should start to sizzle after about 1½ minutes; adjust heat as needed.) Push tofu to sides of skillet. Add 1 teaspoon oil and garlic to center and cook, mashing garlic into skillet, until fragrant, about 1 minute. Stir mixture into tofu. Transfer to bowl and let cool for 10 minutes.

4. Whisk cayenne, remaining ½ teaspoon salt, remaining 2 tablespoons lemon juice, and remaining 3 tablespoons oil together in large bowl. Add drained tomatoes, soaked bulgur, cooled tofu, parsley, mint, and scallions and toss to combine. Cover and let sit until bulgur is tender, about 1 hour. Toss to recombine and season with salt and pepper to taste before serving.

Warm Farro with Lemon and Herbs
Serves 4 to 6

Why This Recipe Works Nutty, chewy farro is an ancient grain that's been extremely popular in Italian cuisine for centuries. Typically the whole grains are soaked overnight and then cooked gradually for more than an hour, but we wondered if we could streamline this and find a simpler, quicker method. After testing out a few cooking techniques, we learned that boiling the grains in plenty of salted water, pasta-style, and then draining them yielded nicely firm but tender farro—no soaking necessary. For this simple side that showcases the farro, sautéed onion and garlic gave the dish savory backbone, and bright lemon and herbs lent it freshness. Do not substitute quick-cooking or presteamed farro (read the ingredient list on the package to determine this) in this recipe. If using pearled farro, you will need to reduce the cooking time in step 1.

- ½ cup whole farro
- ¼ teaspoon table salt, plus salt for cooking farro
- 3 tablespoons extra-virgin olive oil, divided
- 1 onion, chopped fine
- 1 garlic clove, minced
- ¼ cup chopped fresh parsley
- ¼ cup chopped fresh mint
- 1 tablespoon lemon juice

1. Bring 4 quarts water to boil in Dutch oven. Add farro and 1 tablespoon salt, return to boil, and cook until grains are tender with slight chew, 15 to 30 minutes. Drain farro, return to now-empty pot, and cover to keep warm.

2. Heat 2 tablespoons oil in 12-inch skillet over medium heat until shimmering. Add onion and salt and cook until softened, about 5 minutes. Stir in garlic and cook until fragrant, about 30 seconds.

3. Add remaining 1 tablespoon oil and farro and cook, stirring frequently, until heated through, about 2 minutes. Off heat, stir in parsley, mint, and lemon juice. Season with salt and pepper to taste. Serve.

VARIATION

Warm Farro with Mushrooms and Thyme

Do not substitute quick-cooking or presteamed farro (read the ingredient list on the package to determine this) in this recipe. If using pearled farro, you will need to reduce the cooking time in step 1.

1½ cups whole farro
¼ teaspoon table salt, plus salt for cooking farro
3 tablespoons extra-virgin olive oil, divided
12 ounces cremini mushrooms, trimmed and chopped coarse
1 shallot, minced
1½ teaspoons minced fresh thyme or ½ teaspoon dried
3 tablespoons dry sherry
3 tablespoons minced fresh parsley
1½ teaspoons sherry vinegar, plus extra for serving

1. Bring 4 quarts water to boil in Dutch oven. Add farro and 1 tablespoon salt, return to boil, and cook until grains are tender with slight chew, 15 to 30 minutes. Drain farro, return to now-empty pot, and cover to keep warm.

2. Heat 2 tablespoons oil in 12-inch skillet over medium heat until shimmering. Add mushrooms, shallot, thyme, and ¼ teaspoon salt and cook, stirring occasionally, until moisture has evaporated and vegetables start to brown, 8 to 10 minutes. Stir in sherry and cook, scraping up any browned bits, until skillet is almost dry.

3. Add remaining 1 tablespoon oil and farro and cook, stirring frequently, until heated through, about 2 minutes. Off heat, stir in parsley and vinegar. Season with salt, pepper, and extra vinegar to taste, and serve.

Farro Salad with Asparagus, Snap Peas, and Tomatoes
Serves 4 to 6

Why This Recipe Works This fresh yet hearty salad looks as good as it tastes, with vibrant green and red vegetables against a pale golden grain. Using the pasta method to cook the farro ensured that the grains cooked evenly and quickly. We briefly boiled bite-size pieces of asparagus and snap peas to enhance their color and retain their crisp-tender bite. A lemon-dill dressing served as a citrusy, herbal complement to the earthy farro. Cherry tomatoes and a generous amount of dill offered a fresh finish. The optional feta added a creamy note. For a simple variation, we also created a version with cucumber, yogurt, and mint. Do not substitute quick-cooking or presteamed farro (read the ingredient list on the package to determine this) in this recipe. If using pearled farro, you will need to reduce the cooking time in step 2.

6 ounces asparagus, trimmed and cut into 1-inch lengths
6 ounces sugar snap peas, strings removed, cut into 1-inch lengths
¼ teaspoon table salt, plus salt for cooking vegetables and farro
1½ cups whole farro
3 tablespoons extra-virgin olive oil
2 tablespoons lemon juice
2 tablespoons minced shallot
1 teaspoon Dijon mustard
¼ teaspoon pepper
6 ounces cherry tomatoes, halved
3 tablespoons chopped fresh dill
2 ounces feta cheese, crumbled (½ cup), divided (optional)

1. Bring 4 quarts water to boil in Dutch oven. Add asparagus, snap peas, and 1 tablespoon salt and cook until crisp-tender, about 3 minutes. Using slotted spoon, transfer vegetables to large plate and let cool completely, about 15 minutes.

2. Add farro to water, return to boil, and cook until grains are tender with slight chew, 15 to 30 minutes. Drain farro, spread in rimmed baking sheet, and let cool completely, about 15 minutes.

3. Whisk oil, lemon juice, shallot, mustard, pepper, and salt together in large bowl. Add vegetables; farro; tomatoes; dill; and ¼ cup feta, if using, and toss gently to combine. Season with salt and pepper to taste. Transfer to serving platter; sprinkle with remaining ¼ cup feta, if using; and serve.

Farro Salad with Asparagus, Snap Peas, and Tomatoes

1. Bring 4 quarts water to boil in Dutch oven. Add farro and 1 tablespoon salt, return to boil, and cook until grains are tender with slight chew, 15 to 30 minutes. Drain farro, spread in rimmed baking sheet, and let cool completely, about 15 minutes.

2. Whisk oil, lemon juice, shallot, yogurt, pepper, and salt together in large bowl. Add farro, cucumber, tomatoes, arugula, and mint and toss gently to combine. Season with salt and pepper to taste. Serve.

Farro Risotto with Fennel and Radicchio
Serves 4 to 6   FAST

Why This Recipe Works Italians often prepare farro in a similar way as they cook rice for risotto to make a rich, creamy dish called farrotto. Here we adapted our almost hands-free risotto method, with a few modifications. Farro required more frequent stirring to ensure even cooking. We also found that we didn't need to warm the broth before adding it to the pot—the farro cooked through just fine without this extra step. Onion, garlic, thyme, and fennel flavored our farrotto. While it's traditional to finish risotto with butter and Parmesan, these masked the nutty flavors of this grain; we preferred fresh parsley and balsamic vinegar. Stirring in the radicchio at the end preserved its assertive flavor. Be sure to stir the farro often in step 2. Do not substitute pearled, quick-cooking, or presteamed farro (check the ingredient list on the package) for the whole farro.

  1 tablespoon extra-virgin olive oil
  1 onion, chopped fine
  1 fennel bulb, halved, cored, and chopped fine
  ¼ teaspoon table salt
  3 garlic cloves, minced
  1 teaspoon minced fresh thyme
1½ cups whole farro
  2 cups vegetable broth
1½ cups water
  ½ small head radicchio, sliced thin
  2 tablespoons minced fresh parsley
  2 teaspoons balsamic vinegar

1. Combine oil, onion, fennel, and salt in large saucepan. Cover and cook over medium-low heat, stirring occasionally, until vegetables are softened, 8 to 10 minutes. Stir in garlic and thyme and cook until fragrant, about 30 seconds.

VARIATION
Farro Salad with Cucumber, Yogurt, and Mint
Do not substitute quick-cooking or presteamed farro (read the ingredient list on the package to determine this) in this recipe. If using pearled farro, you will need to reduce the cooking time in step 2.

1½ cups whole farro
  ¼ teaspoon table salt, plus salt for cooking farro
  3 tablespoons extra-virgin olive oil
  2 tablespoons lemon juice
  2 tablespoons minced shallot
  2 tablespoons plain plant-based yogurt or dairy yogurt
  ¼ teaspoon pepper
  1 English cucumber, halved lengthwise, seeded, and cut into ¼-inch pieces
  6 ounces cherry tomatoes, halved
  1 cup baby arugula
  3 tablespoons chopped fresh mint

2. Stir in farro and cook until lightly toasted, about 2 minutes. Stir in broth and water and bring to simmer. Reduce heat to low and continue to simmer, stirring often, until farro is tender, 20 to 25 minutes.

3. Stir in radicchio, parsley, and vinegar. Season with salt and pepper to taste, and serve.

Farro and Broccoli Rabe Gratin
Serves 4 to 6

Why This Recipe Works Setting out to create a fresh, modern gratin, we chose Italian flavors, accenting nutty farro with creamy white beans and slightly bitter broccoli rabe. Toasting the farro first gave it extra nuttiness and jump-started the cooking process, making the end result more evenly cooked. Small white beans blended in nicely with the farro while adding creaminess and protein. Blanching the broccoli rabe in salted water tamed its bitterness. We then tossed it with garlic- and red pepper flake–infused olive oil for extra flavor. Sun-dried tomatoes gave us the extra pop of umami we were after in this dish, with their sweetness a counterpoint to the assertive broccoli rabe. Cheese is typically used to bind a gratin filling into a cohesive whole, but we found that miso paste created a supercreamy sauce when mixed with cooked grains, while adding a subtle backbone of flavor. A combo of bread crumbs and our own vegan Parm transformed into a burnished, crunchy topping after a quick spell under the broiler. Do not substitute pearled, quick-cooking, or presteamed farro (read the ingredient list on the package to determine this) for the whole farro in this recipe.

- 3 tablespoons extra-virgin olive oil, divided
- 1 onion, chopped fine
- ¼ teaspoon table salt, plus salt for cooking vegetables
- 1½ cups whole farro
- 2 cups vegetable broth
- 2 tablespoons white miso
- ½ cup panko bread crumbs
- ¼ cup Vegan Parmesan Substitute (page 27) or grated dairy Parmesan
- 1 pound broccoli rabe, trimmed and cut into 2-inch pieces
- 6 garlic cloves, minced
- ⅛ teaspoon red pepper flakes
- 1 (15-ounce) can small white beans or navy beans, rinsed
- ¾ cup oil-packed sun-dried tomatoes, chopped

Farro and Broccoli Rabe Gratin

1. Heat 1 tablespoon oil in large saucepan over medium heat until shimmering. Add onion and salt and cook until softened and lightly browned, 5 to 7 minutes. Stir in farro and cook until lightly toasted, about 2 minutes. Stir in 2½ cups water, broth, and miso; bring to simmer; and cook, stirring often, until farro is just tender and remaining liquid is thickened and creamy, 25 to 35 minutes.

2. Meanwhile, toss panko with 1 tablespoon oil in bowl and microwave, stirring occasionally, until golden brown, 1 to 2 minutes. Stir in vegan Parmesan substitute and set aside.

3. Bring 4 quarts water to boil in Dutch oven. Add broccoli rabe and 1 tablespoon salt and cook until just tender, about 2 minutes. Drain broccoli rabe and set aside. Combine remaining 1 tablespoon oil, garlic, and pepper flakes in now-empty pot and cook over medium heat until fragrant and sizzling, 1 to 2 minutes. Stir in broccoli rabe and cook until well coated, about 2 minutes. Off heat, stir in beans, sun-dried tomatoes, and farro. Season with salt and pepper to taste.

4. Adjust oven rack 10 inches from broiler element and heat broiler. Transfer bean-farro mixture to broiler-safe 3-quart gratin dish (or broiler-safe 13 by 9-inch baking dish) and sprinkle with panko mixture. Broil until lightly browned and hot, 1 to 2 minutes. Serve.

Freekeh Pilaf with Dates and Cauliflower

Serves 4 to 6

Why This Recipe Works Freekeh, a traditional grain popular in eastern Mediterranean and North African cuisines, is made from roasted durum wheat that's been harvested while the grains are still young and green. The grains are polished ("freekeh" is a colloquialization of "farik," which means "rubbed" in Arabic) and sold whole as well as cracked into smaller pieces. For a pilaf that accentuated freekeh's unique flavor and chew, we paired it with pan-roasted cauliflower, sweet dates, and warm spices and aromatics. We found that simply boiling the grain like pasta was the most foolproof cooking method to achieve an evenly chewy, firm texture. Allowing the cauliflower to soften and brown slightly before adding the remaining ingredients to the pan was essential. Finished with toasted pistachios and refreshing mint, our pilaf was a satisfying meal. We prefer the texture of whole, uncracked freekeh; cracked freekeh can be substituted, but you will need to decrease the freekeh cooking time in step 1.

- 1½ cups whole freekeh
- ½ teaspoon table salt, plus salt for cooking freekeh
- ¼ cup extra-virgin olive oil, divided, plus extra for serving
- 1 head cauliflower (2 pounds), cored and cut into ½-inch florets
- ¼ teaspoon pepper
- 3 ounces pitted dates, chopped (½ cup)
- 1 shallot, minced
- 1½ teaspoons grated fresh ginger
- ¼ teaspoon ground coriander
- ¼ teaspoon ground cumin
- ¼ cup shelled pistachios, toasted and chopped coarse
- ¼ cup chopped fresh mint
- 1½ tablespoons lemon juice

1. Bring 4 quarts water to boil in Dutch oven. Add freekeh and 1 tablespoon salt, return to boil, and cook until grains are tender, 30 to 45 minutes. Drain freekeh, return to now-empty pot, and cover to keep warm.

2. Heat 2 tablespoons oil in 12-inch nonstick skillet over medium-high heat until shimmering. Add cauliflower, salt, and pepper; cover; and cook until florets are softened and start to brown, about 5 minutes.

3. Remove lid and continue to cook, stirring occasionally, until florets turn spotty brown, about 10 minutes. Add remaining 2 tablespoons oil, dates, shallot, ginger, coriander, and cumin and cook, stirring frequently, until dates and shallot are softened and fragrant, about 3 minutes.

4. Reduce heat to low, add freekeh, and cook, stirring frequently, until heated through, about 1 minute. Off heat, stir in pistachios, mint, and lemon juice. Season with salt and pepper to taste, and drizzle with extra oil. Serve.

Freekeh Salad with Butternut Squash, Walnuts, and Raisins

Serves 4 to 6

Why This Recipe Works Freekeh has a grassy, slightly smoky flavor that deserves more recognition in America. Here, we pair it with subtly sweet butternut squash in a satisfying salad. Roasting the squash resulted in lightly charred, beautifully caramelized edges; to give the squash more dimension, we paired it with fenugreek, a nutty seed with a unique maple-like flavor. To bring the two elements together, we stirred in a rich yet bright tahini-lemon dressing. A little extra sweetness came in the form of plumped raisins. Toasted walnuts offered complementary crunch, and a generous amount—a whole cup—of chopped cilantro gave the salad freshness in spades. We prefer the texture of whole, uncracked freekeh; cracked freekeh can be substituted, but you will need to decrease the freekeh cooking time in step 1.

- 1½ cups whole freekeh
- ¾ teaspoon table salt, divided, plus salt for cooking freekeh
- 1½ pounds butternut squash, peeled, seeded, and cut into ½-inch pieces (4 cups)
- 5 tablespoons extra-virgin olive oil, divided
- ½ teaspoon ground fenugreek
- ¼ teaspoon pepper, divided
- ⅓ cup golden raisins
- 2½ tablespoons lemon juice
- 2 tablespoons tahini
- 1 garlic clove, minced
- 1 cup coarsely chopped cilantro
- ⅓ cup walnuts, toasted and chopped

1. Adjust oven rack to lowest position and heat oven to 450 degrees. Bring 4 quarts water to boil in Dutch oven. Add freekeh and 1 tablespoon salt, return to boil, and cook until grains are tender, 30 to 45 minutes. Drain freekeh, spread over rimmed baking sheet, and let cool completely, about 15 minutes.

2. Meanwhile, toss squash with 1 tablespoon oil, fenugreek, ⅛ teaspoon pepper, and ¼ teaspoon salt. Spread on rimmed baking sheet and roast until well browned and tender, 30 to 35 minutes, stirring halfway through roasting; let cool completely, about 15 minutes.

3. Combine raisins and ¼ cup hot tap water in small bowl and let sit until softened, about 5 minutes; drain.

4. Whisk lemon juice, tahini, 1 tablespoon water, garlic, remaining ½ teaspoon salt, and remaining ⅛ teaspoon pepper in large bowl until smooth. Whisking constantly, slowly drizzle in remaining ¼ cup oil. Add cooled freekeh, squash, plumped raisins, cilantro, and walnuts and toss to combine. Season with salt and pepper to taste, and serve.

Creamy Polenta
Serves 4 to 6

Why This Recipe Works Polenta makes a sturdy canvas for many meals. We tried various plant-based ingredients to enrich it instead of the typical butter and Parmesan, including miso, vegetable oil, olive oil, and plant-based creamers and butters, but we were unimpressed by the flavors and textures they imparted. Coconut oil was a surprising but excellent fix, easily emulsifying into the polenta and giving it a glossy sheen and a rich depth. A little nutritional yeast gave us just the right level of umami savoriness while keeping the polenta neutral enough to work with different toppings. We love this with Sautéed Mushrooms with Red Wine–Miso Reduction (recipe follows) or with Broccoli Rabe and Spicy Tomato Sauce (page 192). Coarse-ground degerminated cornmeal such as yellow grits (with couscous-size grains) works best here. Avoid instant and quick-cooking products. Do not omit the baking soda—it reduces the cooking time and makes for a creamier polenta. The polenta should do little more than release wisps of steam. If it bubbles or sputters even slightly after the first 10 minutes, the heat is too high and you may need a flame tamer, available at most kitchen supply stores.

Sautéed Mushrooms with Red Wine–Miso Reduction over Creamy Polenta

5 cups water
1 teaspoon table salt
   Pinch baking soda
1 cup coarse-ground cornmeal
3 tablespoons refined coconut oil
4 teaspoons nutritional yeast

1. Bring water to boil in large saucepan over medium-high heat. Stir in salt and baking soda. Slowly pour cornmeal into water in steady stream while stirring back and forth. Bring mixture to boil, stirring constantly, about 1 minute. Reduce heat to lowest possible setting and cover saucepan.

2. After 5 minutes, whisk polenta to smooth out any lumps, about 15 seconds. (Make sure to scrape down sides and bottom of saucepan.) Cover and continue to cook, without stirring, until grains of polenta are tender but slightly al dente, about 25 minutes longer. (Polenta should be loose and barely hold its shape but will continue to thicken as it cools.)

3. Off heat, stir in oil and nutritional yeast and season with pepper to taste. Let polenta stand, covered, for 5 minutes. Serve.

Sautéed Mushrooms with Red Wine–Miso Reduction

Serves 4

Deeply luscious, winey mushrooms sprinkled with peppery baby arugula elevate any grain from homey to sophisticated. Soy and miso boosted the umami power of the mushrooms even higher, and some sugar balanced the acidity of the wine. A touch of cornstarch thickened the reduction to a velvety consistency. We prefer a mix of mushrooms, including some wild ones. Stem portobellos and slice ¼ inch thick. Trim white or cremini; quarter them if large or medium or halve them if small. Tear trimmed oyster or maitake mushrooms into 1½-inch pieces. Stem shiitakes; quarter large caps and halve small caps.

  2 tablespoons extra-virgin olive oil
1½ pounds mixed mushrooms
  ¼ teaspoon table salt
  2 cups dry red wine
  1 cup vegetable broth
  1 tablespoon sugar
  1 teaspoon soy sauce
  2 tablespoons white miso
  1 tablespoon water
  ¾ teaspoon cornstarch
  2 teaspoons fresh thyme leaves
  1 cup baby arugula

1. Heat oil in 12-inch nonstick skillet over medium-high heat until shimmering. Add mushrooms and salt, cover, and cook, stirring occasionally, until mushrooms have released their liquid, 5 to 7 minutes. Uncover and continue to cook, stirring occasionally, until well browned, 10 to 12 minutes longer; transfer to bowl.

2. Bring wine, broth, sugar, and soy sauce to simmer in now-empty skillet over medium heat and cook until reduced to ¾ cup, 10 to 12 minutes. Off heat, whisk miso into wine reduction until combined. Whisk water and cornstarch together in small bowl, then whisk into sauce. Bring to simmer over medium heat, and cook until thickened, about 1 minute. Stir in cooked mushrooms and thyme and cook until heated through, about 1 minute. Garnish with arugula before serving.

Easy Baked Quinoa with Curry, Cauliflower, and Cilantro

Serves 4

Why This Recipe Works There are many ways to prepare quinoa, but this simple hands-off method delivers perfectly cooked grains—plus, its simplicity makes it easy to incorporate flavorful add-ins to turn it into a meal. For the cooking liquid, we chose vegetable broth, which we microwaved with curry powder until just boiling; we poured the hot liquid over the quinoa, which we had combined with olive oil and garlic in a baking dish, added the cauliflower, then covered the dish with foil and placed it in the oven. Lemon juice and cilantro stirred in before serving lent bright notes to this main dish. We like the convenience of prewashed quinoa; rinsing removes the quinoa's bitter protective coating (called saponin). If you buy unwashed quinoa, rinse it and then spread it out on a clean dish towel to dry for 15 minutes.

1½ cups prewashed white quinoa
  2 tablespoons extra-virgin olive oil
  2 garlic cloves, minced
1½ cups vegetable broth
  2 teaspoons curry powder
  ¼ teaspoon table salt
  2 cups small cauliflower florets
  2 tablespoons minced fresh cilantro
  1 teaspoon lemon juice

1. Adjust oven rack to middle position and heat oven to 450 degrees. Combine quinoa, oil, and garlic in 8-inch square baking dish.

2. Microwave broth, curry powder, and salt in covered bowl until just boiling, about 5 minutes. Pour hot broth over quinoa mixture, sprinkle with cauliflower florets, and cover dish tightly with double layer of aluminum foil. Bake quinoa until tender and no liquid remains, about 25 minutes.

3. Remove dish from oven, uncover, and fluff quinoa with fork, scraping up any quinoa that has stuck to bottom. Re-cover dish with foil and let sit for 10 minutes. Fold in cilantro and lemon juice and season with salt and pepper to taste. Serve.

VARIATION

Easy Baked Quinoa with Lemon, Garlic, and Parsley
Omit cauliflower. Substitute 1 teaspoon grated lemon zest for curry powder and fresh parsley for cilantro.

Quinoa Salad with Red Bell Pepper and Cilantro

Serves 4

Why This Recipe Works Bell peppers work especially well in room-temperature grain salads, lending a burst of crunchy, juicy sweetness and a pop of bright color. Here we chose red bell pepper, along with jalapeño and red onion for a spicy counterpoint and fresh cilantro for a bright herbal note. All these ingredients both tasted and looked great paired with the hearty, chewy quinoa (which happens to be high in protein). Before serving, we tossed the salad mixture with a bright dressing flavored with lime juice, mustard, garlic, and cumin. We like the convenience of prewashed quinoa; rinsing removes the quinoa's bitter protective coating (called saponin). If you buy unwashed quinoa, rinse it and then spread it out on a clean dish towel to dry for 15 minutes. To make this dish spicier, add the chile seeds.

- 1 cup prewashed white quinoa
- 1½ cups water
- ¼ teaspoon table salt
- ½ red bell pepper, chopped fine
- ½ jalapeño chile, minced
- 2 tablespoons finely chopped red onion
- 1 tablespoon minced fresh cilantro
- 2 tablespoons fresh lime juice
- 1 tablespoon extra-virgin olive oil
- 2 teaspoons Dijon mustard
- 1 garlic clove, minced
- ½ teaspoon ground cumin

1. Toast quinoa in large saucepan over medium heat, stirring frequently, until quinoa is lightly toasted and aromatic, about 5 minutes. Stir in water and salt and bring to simmer. Cover, reduce heat to low, and cook until water is mostly absorbed and quinoa is nearly tender, about 12 minutes. Spread quinoa out on rimmed baking sheet and set aside until tender and cool, about 20 minutes.

2. Transfer cooled quinoa to large bowl. Stir in bell pepper, jalapeño, onion, and cilantro. In separate bowl, whisk lime juice, oil, mustard, garlic, and cumin together, then pour over quinoa mixture and toss to coat. Season with salt and pepper to taste, and serve.

Quinoa Taco Salad

Serves 4

Why This Recipe Works Here's a taco salad for the 21st century. We've replaced the usual beef with protein-rich quinoa, which gets simmered in a flavorful vegetable broth doctored with chipotle chile in adobo, tomato paste, and cumin to give it deeply spiced flavor. We also added a riot of vegetables to our salad: corn sautéed until it deepened in flavor and browned, along with tomatoes, avocado, and scallions. Romaine lettuce made a perfect addition to give our rich plant-based taco salad plenty of crunch. A quick dressing of olive oil and lime juice brought everything together. We like the convenience of prewashed quinoa; rinsing removes the quinoa's bitter protective coating (called saponin). If you buy unwashed quinoa, rinse it and then spread it out on a clean dish towel to dry for 15 minutes. To make this dish spicier, add the chile seeds. Garnish with a little queso fresco, if you like.

- ¾ cup prewashed white quinoa
- ¼ cup extra-virgin olive oil, divided
- 1 small onion, chopped fine
- ½ teaspoon table salt, divided
- 2 teaspoons minced canned chipotle chile in adobo sauce
- 2 teaspoons tomato paste
- ½ teaspoon ground cumin
- 1¼ cups vegetable broth
- 1½ cups fresh or frozen corn
- 2 tablespoons lime juice
- ¼ teaspoon pepper
- 1 large head romaine lettuce (14 ounces), torn into bite-size pieces
- 1 (15-ounce) can black beans, rinsed
- 8 ounces cherry or grape tomatoes, quartered
- 1 ripe avocado, halved, pitted, and chopped
- 2 scallions, sliced thin
- ½ cup chopped fresh cilantro, divided

1. Toast quinoa in medium saucepan over medium-high heat, stirring frequently, until quinoa is very fragrant and makes continuous popping sound, 5 to 7 minutes; transfer to bowl. Heat 1 tablespoon oil in now-empty saucepan over medium heat until shimmering. Add onion and ¼ teaspoon salt and cook until onion is softened and lightly browned, 5 to 7 minutes.

Quinoa Taco Salad

Baked Quinoa with Roasted Kale and Chickpeas
Serves 4

Why This Recipe Works When developing this flavorful main-course casserole, we initially baked a simple mixture of quinoa, chickpeas, lemon zest, and scallions. Tasters liked the flavors but wanted more texture and vegetable volume. Kale was the perfect solution, and by roasting it briefly with olive oil before baking it with the quinoa, we boosted its earthy flavor and eliminated excess moisture to keep the casserole from becoming too heavy. Fresh tomatoes and a squirt of lemon juice, folded in toward the end of baking, ensured brightness. If you would like to incorporate cheese, sprinkling feta on top for the last few minutes of baking adds a warm, creamy element. We like the convenience of prewashed quinoa; rinsing removes the quinoa's bitter protective coating (called saponin). If you buy unwashed quinoa, rinse it and then spread it out on a clean dish towel to dry for 15 minutes.

- 6 ounces kale, stemmed and chopped
- 3 tablespoons extra-virgin olive oil, divided
- 1 (15-ounce) can chickpeas, rinsed
- 1 cup prewashed white quinoa
- ½ teaspoon table salt
- ¼ teaspoon dried oregano
- ¼ teaspoon pepper
  Pinch pepper flakes
- 1½ cups water
- 2 teaspoons grated lemon zest, divided, plus 1 tablespoon juice
- 2 plum tomatoes, cored and chopped fine
- 6 ounces feta cheese, crumbled (1½ cups) (optional)

1. Adjust oven rack to middle position and heat oven to 450 degrees. Toss kale with 1 tablespoon oil, spread in even layer on aluminum foil–lined rimmed baking sheet, and roast until crisp and lightly browned at edges, 6 to 8 minutes.

2. Toss roasted kale with chickpeas, quinoa, salt, oregano, pepper, pepper flakes, and 1 tablespoon oil and transfer to 8-inch square baking dish. Microwave water and 1 teaspoon lemon zest in covered bowl until just boiling, about 2 minutes. Pour hot water over quinoa mixture and cover dish tightly with foil. Bake until quinoa is tender and no liquid remains, 20 to 25 minutes.

3. Remove dish from oven and fluff quinoa with fork. Gently fold in tomatoes, lemon juice, remaining 1 tablespoon oil, and remaining 1 teaspoon lemon zest. Sprinkle with feta, if using, and continue to bake, uncovered, until warmed through, 6 to 8 minutes. Serve.

2. Stir in chipotle, tomato paste, and cumin and cook until fragrant, about 30 seconds. Stir in broth and toasted quinoa, increase heat to medium-high, and bring to simmer. Cover, reduce heat to low, and simmer until quinoa is tender and liquid has been absorbed, about 25 minutes, stirring once halfway through cooking. Remove pan from heat and let sit, covered, for 10 minutes. Spread quinoa onto rimmed baking sheet and let cool for 20 minutes.

3. Meanwhile, heat 1 tablespoon oil in 12-inch nonstick skillet over medium-high heat until shimmering. Add corn and cook, stirring occasionally, until kernels begin to brown and pop, 6 to 8 minutes. Transfer corn to bowl and season with salt and pepper to taste.

4. Whisk lime juice, pepper, remaining 2 tablespoons oil, and remaining ¼ teaspoon salt together in large bowl. Add romaine, beans, tomatoes, avocado, scallions, and ¼ cup cilantro and toss to combine. Transfer to serving platter and top with cooled quinoa, corn, and remaining ¼ cup cilantro. Serve.

Warm Wheat Berries with Zucchini, Red Pepper, and Oregano

Serves 4 to 6

Why This Recipe Works Since wheat represents new life and a bountiful harvest in Greek culture, we seized on that idea to create this Greek-inspired salad that capitalizes on summer vegetables. We cooked the wheat berries using the pasta method to ensure even cooking, but our standard ratio of salt to water (1 tablespoon to 4 quarts) prevented the grains from properly absorbing the water; they stayed crunchy no matter how long we cooked them. Reducing the amount of salt was a simple fix. Sautéing zucchini, red pepper, and red onion in batches was essential to achieving the deep sear we were after. We allowed the warm wheat berries to soak in our bold vinaigrette while the vegetables were cooking. Do not add more than 1½ teaspoons of salt when cooking the wheat berries; adding more will prevent the grains from softening. If using quick-cooking or presteamed wheat berries (read the ingredient list on the package to determine this), you will need to decrease the cooking time in step 1.

- 1½ cups wheat berries
- ½ teaspoon table salt, divided, plus salt for cooking wheat berries
- 3 tablespoons red wine vinegar
- 2 tablespoons extra-virgin olive oil, divided
- 1 tablespoon grated lemon zest
- 1 tablespoon minced fresh oregano or 1½ teaspoons dried
- 1 garlic clove, minced
- 1 zucchini, cut into ½-inch pieces
- 1 red onion, chopped
- 1 red bell pepper, stemmed, seeded, and cut into ½-inch pieces

1. Bring 4 quarts water to boil in Dutch oven. Add wheat berries and 1½ teaspoons salt, return to boil, and cook until tender but still chewy, 1 hour to 1 hour 10 minutes.

2. Meanwhile, whisk vinegar, 1 tablespoon oil, lemon zest, oregano, and garlic together in large bowl. Drain wheat berries, add to bowl with dressing, and toss gently to coat.

3. Heat 2 teaspoons oil in 12-inch nonstick skillet over medium-high heat until just smoking. Add zucchini and ¼ teaspoon salt and cook, stirring occasionally, until deep golden brown and beginning to char in spots, 6 to 8 minutes; transfer to bowl with wheat berries.

4. Return now-empty skillet to medium-high heat and add remaining 1 teaspoon oil, onion, bell pepper, and remaining ¼ teaspoon salt. Cook, stirring occasionally, until onion is charred at edges and pepper skin is charred and blistered, 8 to 10 minutes. Add wheat berry–zucchini mixture and cook, stirring frequently, until heated through, about 2 minutes. Season with salt and pepper to taste. Serve.

Wheat Berry Salad with Figs and Pine Nuts

Serves 4 to 6

Why This Recipe Works Delicately sweet and lightly juicy, fresh figs make a wonderful addition to a summery Mediterranean grain salad. Wheat berries provided the perfect nutty base, while toasted pine nuts and parsley leaves lent crunch and herbal fragrance. For the dressing, we made a zippy vinaigrette with balsamic vinegar, shallot, and mustard. If you would like to incorporate cheese, goat cheese will contribute a pleasantly tangy element. Do not add more than 1½ teaspoons of salt when cooking the wheat berries; adding more will prevent the grains from softening. If using quick-cooking or presteamed wheat berries (read the ingredient list on the package to determine this), you will need to decrease the cooking time in step 1.

- 1½ cups wheat berries
- ¼ teaspoon table salt, plus salt for cooking wheat berries
- 3 tablespoons balsamic vinegar
- 1 small shallot, minced
- 1 teaspoon Dijon mustard
- ¼ teaspoon pepper
- 3 tablespoons extra-virgin olive oil
- 8 ounces fresh figs, cut into ½-inch pieces
- ½ cup fresh parsley leaves
- ¼ cup pine nuts, toasted
- 2 ounces goat cheese, crumbled (½ cup) (optional)

1. Bring 4 quarts water to boil in Dutch oven. Add wheat berries and 1½ teaspoons salt, return to boil, and cook until tender but still chewy, 1 hour to 1 hour 10 minutes. Drain wheat berries, spread onto rimmed baking sheet, and let cool completely, about 15 minutes. (Cooled wheat berries can be refrigerated for up to 3 days.)

2. Whisk vinegar, shallot, mustard, pepper, and salt together in large bowl. Whisking constantly, slowly drizzle in oil. Add wheat berries, figs, parsley, and pine nuts and toss gently to combine. Season with salt and pepper to taste; sprinkle with goat cheese, if using; and serve.

Wheat Berry Salad with Blueberries and Endive

Serves 4 to 6

Why This Recipe Works Here's another hearty summer salad that pairs earthy, nutty, pleasingly chewy wheat berries with fruit and nuts—in this case, plump blueberries and buttery pecans. We found it easiest to cook the wheat berry kernels like pasta, simply simmering them in a large pot of water until they were tender but still chewy. For the dressing, we chose a simple bright vinaigrette made with white wine vinegar, shallot, chives, and mustard. Juicy fresh blueberries added the perfect amount of sweetness and tang to our chewy grains. Endive provided an interesting slightly bitter note. If you would like to add cheese, we found that goat cheese was the perfect rich complement to finish off this summery salad. Do not add more than 1½ teaspoons of salt when cooking the wheat berries; adding more will prevent the grains from softening. If using quick-cooking or presteamed wheat berries (read the ingredient list on the package to determine this), you will need to decrease the cooking time in step 1.

1½ cups wheat berries
½ teaspoon table salt, plus salt for cooking wheat berries
2 tablespoons white wine vinegar
1 tablespoon minced shallot
1 tablespoon minced fresh chives
1 teaspoon Dijon mustard
¼ teaspoon pepper
6 tablespoons extra-virgin olive oil
2 heads Belgian endive (4 ounces each), halved, cored, and sliced crosswise ¼ inch thick
7½ ounces (1½ cups) blueberries
¾ cup pecans, toasted and chopped coarse
4 ounces goat cheese, crumbled (1 cup) (optional)

1. Bring 4 quarts water to boil in Dutch oven. Add wheat berries and 1½ teaspoons salt, return to boil, and cook until tender but still chewy, 1 hour to 1 hour 10 minutes. Drain wheat berries, spread onto rimmed baking sheet, and let cool completely, about 15 minutes. (Cooled wheat berries can be refrigerated for up to 3 days.)

2. Whisk vinegar, shallot, chives, mustard, pepper, and salt together in large bowl. Whisking constantly, drizzle in oil. Add wheat berries, endive, blueberries, and pecans and toss to combine. Season with salt and pepper to taste; sprinkle with goat cheese, if using; and serve.

Warm Wheat Berries with Zucchini, Red Pepper, and Oregano

Wheat Berry Salad with Figs and Pine Nuts

BOUNTIFUL BEANS

■ FAST (45 minutes or less total time)
Photos: Baked Navy Beans; Thai Red Curry with Lentils and Tofu; Red Lentil Kibbeh

Southwestern Black Bean Salad

Serves 4 to 6 `FAST`

Why This Recipe Works Bean salads make for hearty and delicious quick meals anytime, especially when you take advantage of convenient canned beans. Although the ingredients are infinitely variable, it can be easy to fall into the trap of just piling on an endless array of ingredients. We've found that, generally, less is more. For this boldly flavored but balanced black bean salad, a judicious mixture of black beans, corn, avocado, tomato, and cilantro gave us just the right combination of varied textures and Southwestern flavors. Sautéing the corn (both fresh and frozen worked well in this recipe) until it was toasty and just starting to brown added a pleasant nuttiness to the kernels. We wanted a dressing with plenty of kick, so we made a concentrated mixture with lots of lime juice plus spicy chipotle chile. Raw onion was too harsh, but thinly sliced scallions lent a mild onion flavor. You will need three to four ears of corn in order to yield 2 cups of fresh kernels. If using frozen corn, be sure to thaw and drain it before cooking.

- ¼ cup extra-virgin olive oil, divided
- 2 cups fresh or thawed frozen corn
- 4 scallions, sliced thin
- ⅓ cup lime juice (3 limes)
- 1 tablespoon minced canned chipotle chile in adobo sauce
- ½ teaspoon table salt
- ½ teaspoon pepper
- 2 (15-ounce) cans black beans, rinsed
- 2 ripe avocados, halved, pitted, and chopped
- 2 tomatoes, cored and chopped
- ¼ cup minced fresh cilantro

1. Heat 2 tablespoons oil in 12-inch skillet over medium-high heat until shimmering. Add corn and cook until spotty brown, about 5 minutes; let cool slightly.

2. Whisk scallions, lime juice, chipotle, salt, and pepper together in large bowl. Slowly whisk in remaining 2 tablespoons oil until incorporated. Add toasted corn, beans, avocados, tomatoes, and cilantro and toss to combine. Season with salt and pepper to taste, and serve.

Black Bean Chilaquiles Verdes

Serves 4

Why This Recipe Works Nothing says Mexican comfort food quite like chilaquiles. Comprised of fried tortilla wedges tossed in a deeply flavored chile sauce, this dish is jam-packed with bright flavor and varying textures—and loaded with veggies. We started with the chips: Store-bought tortilla chips became instantly soggy after being tossed in our sauce, but by baking—not frying—our own, we got chips that gave us an irresistible "crunchewy" result. Rather than going down the classic red chile sauce route, we decided to go green with a salsa verde. To build a flavorful sauce base, we went heavy on aromatics: onions, mild poblanos, spicier jalapeño, and lots of garlic. Fresh tomatillos are delicious but not always easy to find, so we simplified the whole dish by using canned. In order to really up the "verde" factor, we added a hefty ½ cup of cilantro leaves. Shredded meat is a common addition, but for a plant-based protein boost we opted for black beans. (You could use whatever beans you have on hand.) We kept texture, aesthetics, and vegetables in mind when considering toppings: crispy radishes, creamy avocado, fresh cilantro, crunchy onions, and thinly sliced jalapeño. A final drizzle of yogurt (plant-based or dairy) woke everything up. To make this dish less spicy, remove the ribs and seeds from your jalapeño.

- ¼ cup plain plant-based yogurt or dairy yogurt
- 1 teaspoon grated lime zest
- 1 tablespoon plus 1 cup water, divided
- 12 (6-inch) corn tortillas, each cut into 8 wedges
- 3 tablespoons vegetable oil, divided
- 2 poblano chiles, stemmed, seeded, and chopped coarse
- 2 jalapeño chiles, stemmed (1 chopped coarse, 1 sliced thin)
- 1 onion, chopped fine, divided
- ½ teaspoon table salt
- 6 garlic cloves, minced
- 1½ teaspoons ground cumin
- 1 (26-ounce) can whole tomatillos, drained
- ¾ cup fresh cilantro leaves, divided
- 2 (15-ounce) cans black beans, rinsed
- 1 avocado, halved, pitted, and cut into ½-inch pieces
- 4 radishes, trimmed and sliced thin

1. Adjust oven racks to upper-middle and lower-middle positions and heat oven to 350 degrees. Combine yogurt, lime zest, and 1 tablespoon water together in small bowl; set aside until ready to serve.

Cuban-Style Black Beans and Rice

Cuban-Style Black Beans and Rice
Serves 6 to 8

Why This Recipe Works Beans and rice is a familiar combination the world over, with good reason: It's healthful, inexpensive, and flavorful. Cuban black beans and rice is unique in that the rice is cooked in the inky, concentrated liquid left over from cooking the dried black beans. For our own version, we brined the beans overnight before cooking. We reserved half of our sofrito ingredients (a combination of sautéed garlic, bell pepper, and onion) and added them to the cooking liquid to infuse the beans with aromatic flavor. Lightly browning the remaining sofrito vegetables along with spices and tomato paste added complex flavor to this simple dish. Once the beans were soft, we combined them with the sofrito and rice to finish cooking. Baking the rice and beans eliminated the crusty bottom that can form when the dish is cooked on the stovetop. You will need a Dutch oven with a tight-fitting lid for this recipe.

1½ tablespoons table salt for brining
1 cup dried black beans, picked over and rinsed
2 large green bell peppers, halved, stemmed, and seeded, divided
1 large onion, halved crosswise and peeled, root end left intact, divided
1 garlic head, 5 cloves minced, rest of head halved crosswise with skin left intact, divided
2 bay leaves
2½ teaspoons table salt, divided
2 tablespoons vegetable oil
4 teaspoons ground cumin
1 tablespoon minced fresh oregano or 1 teaspoon dried
1 tablespoon tomato paste
1½ cups long-grain white rice
2 tablespoons red wine vinegar
2 scallions, sliced thin
Lime wedges

2. Toss tortillas with 2 tablespoons oil, then spread over 2 rimmed baking sheets. Bake until brown and dried, 16 to 25 minutes, flipping tortillas halfway through baking; set aside to cool.

3. While tortillas bake, heat remaining 1 tablespoon oil in Dutch oven over medium heat until shimmering. Add poblanos, coarsely chopped jalapeño, ¾ cup onion, and salt and cook until vegetables are softened and lightly browned, 6 to 8 minutes.

4. Stir in garlic and cumin and cook until fragrant, about 30 seconds. Stir in canned tomatillos and remaining 1 cup water and cook until sauce is slightly thickened, about 10 minutes. Carefully transfer pepper mixture to blender, along with ½ cup cilantro, and process until smooth, about 1 minute.

5. Return sauce to now-empty pot and bring to simmer over medium heat. Add beans and cook, stirring frequently, until beans are warmed through, about 5 minutes. Stir in cooled tortillas and cook until they begin to soften, about 2 minutes. Season with salt and pepper to taste. Drizzle yogurt mixture over top and sprinkle with avocado, radishes, thinly sliced jalapeño, remaining ¼ cup onion, and remaining ¼ cup cilantro. Serve.

1. Dissolve 1½ tablespoons salt in 2 quarts cold water in large bowl or container. Add beans and soak at room temperature for at least 8 hours or up to 24 hours. Drain and rinse well.

2. In Dutch oven, combine drained beans, 4 cups water, 1 bell pepper half, 1 onion half (with root end), halved garlic head, bay leaves, and 1 teaspoon salt. Bring to simmer over medium-high heat, cover, and reduce heat to low. Cook until beans are just soft, 30 to 40 minutes.

3. Discard pepper, onion, garlic, and bay leaves. Drain beans in colander set over large bowl, reserving 2½ cups bean cooking liquid. (If you don't have enough cooking liquid, add water as needed to measure 2½ cups.) Do not wash pot.

4. Adjust oven rack to middle position and heat oven to 350 degrees. Cut remaining bell peppers and onion into 2-inch pieces and pulse in food processor until chopped into rough ¼-inch pieces, about 8 pulses, scraping down bowl as needed.

5. Add oil to now-empty pot and heat over medium heat until shimmering. Add processed peppers and onion, cumin, oregano, and tomato paste and cook, stirring often, until vegetables are softened and beginning to brown, 10 to 15 minutes. Stir in minced garlic and cook until fragrant, about 1 minute. Stir in rice and cook for 30 seconds.

6. Stir in beans, reserved bean cooking liquid, vinegar, and remaining 1½ teaspoons salt. Increase heat to medium-high and bring to simmer. Cover, transfer to oven, and cook until liquid is absorbed and rice is tender, about 30 minutes. Fluff rice with fork and let rest, uncovered, for 5 minutes. Serve with scallions and lime wedges.

Black-Eyed Pea Salad with Peaches and Pecans

Serves 4 to 6 FAST

Why This Recipe Works With their delicate skins and creamy interiors, black-eyed peas are great in salads and are especially popular in the South, so we looked to Southern cuisine for inspiration for this ultrasimple salad. We used canned black-eyed peas, which are convenient and have great flavor and texture. Peaches added sweet juiciness, while pecans lent crunch and richness. For a little spice, we chopped a jalapeño, removing its seeds to mellow its fruity heat. We felt greens were necessary, but we weren't interested in humdrum romaine. Instead, we turned to frisée, a delicate but slightly bitter-tasting lettuce. Finely chopped red onion added a nice bite, and basil added freshness. The tartness of our lime vinaigrette nicely counterbalanced the sweet peaches. If you can't find good ripe peaches, you can substitute 1 orange, peeled and chopped into ½-inch pieces.

- 1 teaspoon grated lime zest plus 2½ tablespoons juice (2 limes)
- 1 small garlic clove, minced
- ¾ teaspoon table salt
- 2 tablespoons extra-virgin olive oil
- 2 (15-ounce) cans black-eyed peas, rinsed
- 2 peaches, halved, pitted, and chopped coarse

- 3 ounces frisée, trimmed and chopped into 2-inch pieces
- ¼ cup red onion, chopped fine
- ¼ cup pecans, toasted and chopped
- ¼ cup fresh basil leaves, torn into ½-inch pieces
- 1 jalapeño chile, stemmed, seeded, and chopped fine

Whisk lime zest and juice, garlic, and salt together in large bowl. Slowly whisk in oil until incorporated. Add beans, peaches, frisée, onion, pecans, basil, and jalapeño and toss to combine. Season with salt and pepper to taste, and serve.

Black-Eyed Peas and Greens

Serves 6 to 8

Why This Recipe Works Southern tradition holds that if on New Year's Day you eat collards and black-eyed peas stewed with tomatoes, spices, and a hambone, you will experience greater wealth and prosperity in the coming year. With all respect to Southern tradition, we think this hambone-free version is lucky, too—and downright delicious. To get the jump on acquiring said prosperity, we decided to speed up this one-pot dish to make it more accessible on a regular basis. We swapped the more time-consuming dried legumes for a couple of convenient cans of black-eyed peas, and then gave the collards a 15-minute head start on the stove before adding the peas. For maximum good luck, be careful not to crush those black-eyed peas—stir them gently.

- 2 tablespoons extra-virgin olive oil
- 1 onion, halved and sliced thin
- 1¼ teaspoons table salt
- 4 garlic cloves, minced
- ½ teaspoon ground cumin
- ½ teaspoon pepper
- ¼ teaspoon red pepper flakes
- 1½ cups vegetable broth
- 1 (14.5-ounce) can diced tomatoes
- 1 pound collard greens, stemmed and cut into 2-inch pieces
- 2 (15-ounce) cans black-eyed peas, rinsed
- 1 tablespoon cider vinegar
- 1 teaspoon sugar

1. Heat oil in large Dutch oven over medium heat until shimmering. Add onion and salt and cook, stirring frequently, until golden brown, about 10 minutes. Stir in garlic, cumin, pepper, and pepper flakes and cook until fragrant, about 30 seconds.

Black-Eyed Pea Salad with Peaches and Pecans

flakes; the subtle spiciness balanced the sweetness of the beans and roasted peppers. Slicing the kale into thin ribbons and adding it to the skillet a handful at a time allowed it to wilt evenly. For the cooking liquid, we used equal parts water and white wine to add light body and acidity to the dish. We served it all with lemon wedges for squeezing over the top and a drizzle of extra-virgin olive oil. Swiss chard can be substituted for the kale, if you prefer.

¼ cup extra-virgin olive oil, plus extra for serving
4 garlic cloves, minced
¼ teaspoon red pepper flakes
1 small red onion, halved and sliced thin
¼ teaspoon table salt
1 cup jarred roasted red peppers, sliced thin lengthwise
1 pound kale, stemmed and sliced thin crosswise
2 (15-ounce) cans cannellini beans, rinsed
½ cup dry white wine
½ cup water
   Lemon wedges

1. Cook oil, garlic, and pepper flakes in 12-inch skillet over medium-high heat until garlic turns golden brown, about 2 minutes. Stir in onion and salt, reduce heat to medium, and cook until onion is softened, about 5 minutes. Stir in red peppers and cook until softened and glossy, about 3 minutes.

2. Stir in kale, 1 handful at a time, and cook until wilted, about 3 minutes. Stir in beans, wine, and water and bring to simmer. Reduce heat to medium-low, cover, and cook until flavors meld and kale is tender, 15 to 20 minutes. Season with salt and pepper to taste. Serve with lemon wedges and extra oil.

2. Stir in broth and tomatoes and their juice and bring to boil. Add collard greens, cover, and reduce heat to medium-low. Simmer until greens are tender, about 15 minutes.

3. Add black-eyed peas and cook, covered, stirring occasionally, until greens are silky and completely tender, about 15 minutes. Uncover, increase heat to medium-high, and cook until liquid is reduced by one-quarter, about 5 minutes. Stir in vinegar and sugar and serve.

Cannellini Beans with Roasted Red Peppers and Kale

Serves 4 to 6   FAST

Why This Recipe Works Some particularly inspired beans-and-greens dishes come from Italy, so for this full-flavored one-pot take on the classic combination, we chose Italian flavors, pairing cannellini beans and kale with roasted red peppers. Choosing canned beans and jarred red peppers meant this dish could come together quickly for a great weeknight meal. We sautéed garlic and onion with some hot red pepper

Chickpea Salad with Carrots, Arugula, and Olives

Serves 4 to 6   FAST

Why This Recipe Works Chickpeas are a no-brainer when it comes to making satisfying salads. For this rendition, we wanted to infuse each bean with bold flavor to the core. We discovered that the key was to warm the chickpeas before mixing them with our lemony and slightly spicy dressing ingredients. The seed coats that cover chickpeas are rich in pectin, which breaks down when exposed to heat and moisture, creating a more porous inner surface that a dressing could easily penetrate. Further, letting the dressed chickpeas rest for 30 minutes put the flavor over the top while allowing the

Chickpea Salad with Carrots, Arugula, and Olives

chickpeas to cool. For complementary add-ins, chopped arugula offset the mild chickpeas with peppery bite. A combination of sweet carrots and briny olives added more contrasting texture and flavor. And a variation featuring crunchy, anise-flavored fennel kept things interesting.

2 (15-ounce) cans chickpeas, rinsed
¼ cup extra-virgin olive oil
2 tablespoons lemon juice
¾ teaspoon table salt
½ teaspoon pepper
   Pinch cayenne pepper
3 carrots, peeled and shredded
1 cup baby arugula, chopped coarse
½ cup pitted kalamata olives, chopped coarse

1. Microwave chickpeas in medium bowl until hot, about 2 minutes. Stir in oil, lemon juice, salt, pepper, and cayenne and let sit for 30 minutes.

2. Add carrots, arugula, and olives and toss to combine. Season with salt and pepper to taste, and serve.

VARIATION

Chickpea Salad with Fennel and Arugula
Substitute 1 fennel bulb, stalks discarded, bulb halved, cored, and cut into ¼-inch pieces, for carrots and olives.

Chickpea Salad with Carrots, Raisins, and Mint
Serves 4 to 6 FAST

Why This Recipe Works This simple salad comes together in a flash using canned chickpeas. Often when a salad features a carrot-raisin combo, the dressing seems to be mayonnaise-based. But here, to enhance those two ingredients rather than mute them, we looked to flavor combinations used in North Africa, whisking up a simple lemony vinaigrette with cumin, paprika, and garlic. The mint adds an unexpected but uplifting fresh herbal element. Try this served over a bed of greens with pita wedges or pita chips.

1½ tablespoons lemon juice
1 small garlic clove, minced
½ teaspoon ground cumin
½ teaspoon paprika
2 tablespoons extra-virgin olive oil
2 (15-ounce) cans chickpeas, rinsed

Chickpeas with Garlic and Parsley

1 carrot, peeled and shredded
½ cup raisins
2 tablespoons minced fresh mint

Whisk lemon juice, garlic, cumin, and paprika together in large bowl. Slowly whisk in oil until incorporated. Add chickpeas, carrot, raisins, and mint and toss to combine. Season with salt and pepper to taste, and serve.

Chickpeas with Garlic and Parsley

Serves 4 to 6 `FAST`

Why This Recipe Works Sautéed with just a few flavorful ingredients, chickpeas become ultraversatile as a main dish served over grains or noodles or as part of a plate-sharing arrangement with any number of vegetables. In search of Mediterranean flavors that would easily transform our canned chickpeas, we reached for garlic and red pepper flakes. Instead of mincing the garlic, we cut it into thin slices and sautéed them in extra-virgin olive oil to mellow their flavor. The thin slivers nicely maintained their presence in the finished dish. We softened an onion along with this aromatic base, then added the chickpeas with vegetable broth, which imparted a rich, savory backbone to the dish. As final touches, parsley and lemon juice gave our warm chickpeas a burst of freshness.

¼ cup extra-virgin olive oil, divided
4 garlic cloves, sliced thin
⅛ teaspoon red pepper flakes
1 onion, chopped fine
¼ teaspoon table salt
2 (15-ounce) cans chickpeas, rinsed
1 cup vegetable broth
2 tablespoons minced fresh parsley
2 teaspoons lemon juice

1. Cook 3 tablespoons oil, garlic, and pepper flakes in 12-inch skillet over medium heat, stirring frequently, until garlic turns golden but not brown, about 3 minutes. Stir in onion and salt and cook until softened and lightly browned, 5 to 7 minutes. Stir in chickpeas and broth and bring to simmer. Reduce heat to medium-low, cover, and cook until chickpeas are heated through and flavors meld, about 7 minutes.

2. Uncover, increase heat to high, and continue to cook until nearly all liquid has evaporated, about 3 minutes. Off heat, stir in parsley and lemon juice. Season with salt and pepper to taste and drizzle with remaining 1 tablespoon oil. Serve.

VARIATIONS

Chickpeas with Bell Pepper, Scallions, and Basil
Add 1 chopped red bell pepper to skillet with onion. Substitute 2 tablespoons chopped fresh basil for parsley and stir in 2 thinly sliced scallions before serving.

Chickpeas with Smoked Paprika and Cilantro
Omit red pepper flakes. Add ½ teaspoon smoked paprika to skillet before chickpeas and cook until fragrant, about 30 seconds. Substitute 2 tablespoons minced fresh cilantro for parsley and 2 teaspoons sherry vinegar for lemon juice.

Spicy Braised Chickpeas and Turnips with Couscous

Serves 4 to 6

Why This Recipe Works The flavors in this dish were inspired by Tunisian cuisine, which is known for being quite hot and spicy. While the combination of chickpeas and braised turnips may sound unfamiliar, these two earthy ingredients actually work very well together. Turnips have a peppery bite akin to radishes when raw (they add great crunch to salads), but when cooked, their spiciness mellows and they develop a dense, creamy texture similar to potatoes but with less starch. Including the aquafaba—the starchy, seasoned liquid from the cans of chickpeas—in the dish instead of draining it away gave the braising liquid that became the sauce good body and flavor. Finally, a base of fluffy couscous allowed all of our ingredients along with our punchy sauce to shine through.

3 tablespoons extra-virgin olive oil, divided
2 onions, chopped
2 red bell peppers, stemmed, seeded, and chopped
¾ teaspoon table salt, divided
¼ teaspoon pepper
¼ cup tomato paste
1 jalapeño chile, stemmed, seeded, and chopped
5 garlic cloves, minced
¾ teaspoon ground cumin
¼ teaspoon cayenne pepper
2 (15-ounce) cans chickpeas
12 ounces turnips, peeled and cut into ½-inch pieces
2¼ cups water, divided, plus extra hot water as needed
1½ cups couscous
¼ cup chopped fresh parsley
2 tablespoons lemon juice, plus lemon wedges for serving

1. Heat 2 tablespoons oil in Dutch oven over medium heat until shimmering. Add onions, bell peppers, ½ teaspoon salt, and pepper and cook until softened and lightly browned, 5 to 7 minutes. Stir in tomato paste, jalapeno, garlic, cumin, and cayenne and cook until fragrant, about 30 seconds.

2. Stir in chickpeas and their liquid, turnips, and ¾ cup water. Bring to simmer and cook until turnips are tender and sauce has thickened, 25 to 35 minutes.

3. Meanwhile, heat remaining 1 tablespoon oil in medium saucepan over medium-high heat until shimmering. Add couscous and cook, stirring frequently, until grains are just beginning to brown, 3 to 5 minutes. Stir in remaining 1½ cups water and remaining ¼ teaspoon salt. Cover, remove saucepan from heat, and let sit until couscous is tender, about 7 minutes. Fluff couscous with fork.

4. Stir parsley and lemon juice into braised turnips. Season with salt and pepper to taste. Adjust consistency with hot water as needed. Serve chickpeas over couscous with lemon wedges.

Cranberry Beans with Fennel, Grapes, and Pine Nuts

Serves 6 to 8

Why This Recipe Works "Agrodolce" refers to an Italian sweet-and-sour sauce made by reducing vinegar and sugar. This boldly flavored condiment can accompany anything from pasta to beans to vegetables. Here we use this classic sauce in a flavorful cranberry bean dish. Since canned cranberry beans are difficult to find, we used dried, brining the beans overnight to ensure creamy texture and fewer blowouts before rinsing and simmering them until tender. Next, we sautéed chopped fennel until it softened and added fennel seeds to reinforce the fresh fennel's flavor. We reduced red wine vinegar and sugar until they thickened into the signature agrodolce glaze, which beautifully coated the beans. Grapes and pine nuts provided pops of sweetness and crunch. A sprinkling of fennel fronds underscored the fennel flavor. If cranberry beans are unavailable, you can substitute pinto beans.

Cranberry Beans with Fennel, Grapes, and Pine Nuts

  3 tablespoons table salt for brining
  1 pound (2½ cups) dried cranberry beans, picked over and rinsed
1¼ teaspoons table salt, divided
  3 tablespoons extra-virgin olive oil
  ½ fennel bulb, 2 tablespoons fronds chopped, stalks discarded, bulb cored and chopped
  ¼ teaspoon pepper
  1 cup plus 2 tablespoons red wine vinegar, divided
  ½ cup sugar
  1 teaspoon fennel seeds
  6 ounces seedless red grapes, halved (1 cup)
  ½ cup pine nuts, toasted

1. Dissolve 3 tablespoons salt in 4 quarts cold water in large container. Add beans and soak at room temperature for at least 8 hours or up to 24 hours. Drain and rinse well.

2. Bring beans, 4 quarts water, and 1 teaspoon salt to boil in Dutch oven. Reduce to simmer and cook, stirring occasionally, until beans are tender, 1 to 1½ hours. Drain beans and set aside.

3. Wipe Dutch oven clean with paper towels. Heat oil in now-empty pot over medium heat until shimmering. Add fennel bulb, pepper, and remaining ¼ teaspoon salt and cook until softened, about 5 minutes. Stir in 1 cup vinegar, sugar, and fennel seeds until sugar is dissolved. Bring to simmer and cook until liquid is thickened to syrupy glaze and edges of fennel are beginning to brown, about 10 minutes.

4. Add beans to vinegar-fennel mixture and toss to coat. Transfer to large bowl and let cool to room temperature. Add grapes, pine nuts, fennel fronds, and remaining 2 tablespoons vinegar and toss to combine. Season with salt and pepper to taste, and serve.

ALL ABOUT BEANS

Canned beans are undeniably convenient, and in many cases they work as well as or even better than dried beans. However, there are instances when dried beans are central to a recipe's success because their long cooking time adds thickness and body (and some beans, such as cranberry beans, are far more readily available dried).

Buying and Storing Dried Beans

When shopping, check packages for dates to select "fresh" dried beans. Buy those that are uniform in size and have a smooth exterior. Uncooked beans should be stored in a cool, dry place in a sealed plastic or glass container. Dried beans are less susceptible than rice and grains to pests and spoilage, but it is still best to use them within a month or two. When "fresh" dried beans are fully hydrated and cooked, they should be plump, with taut skins, and have creamy insides; spent beans will have wrinkled skins and a dry, almost gritty texture.

Rinsing Dried Beans

Before cooking dried beans, you should pick them over for any small stones or debris and then rinse them in a colander to wash away any dust. The easiest way to check for small stones is to spread the beans out over a large plate or rimmed baking sheet.

Brining Dried Beans

Brining dried beans means you need to plan ahead, since we suggest at least an 8-hour brine. But when you soak dried beans in salted water, they cook up with softer skins and are less likely to blow out and disintegrate during cooking. It has to do with how the sodium ions in salt interact with the cells of the bean skins. As the beans soak, the sodium ions replace some of the calcium and magnesium ions in the skins. Because sodium ions are more weakly charged than calcium and magnesium ions, they allow more water to penetrate into the skins, leading to a softer texture. During soaking, the sodium ions will filter only partway into the beans, so their greatest effect is on the cells in the outermost part of the beans. Softening the skins also makes them less likely to split as the beans cook, keeping the beans intact.

For a Regular Brine

For 1 pound of dried beans, dissolve 3 tablespoons table salt in 4 quarts cold water. Soak the beans at room temperature for 8 to 24 hours. Drain and rinse them well before using.

For a Quick Brine

If you are pressed for time, you can "quick-brine" your dried beans. Simply combine 3 tablespoons table salt with 4 quarts cold water and 1 pound beans in a large Dutch oven and bring to a boil over high heat. Remove the pot from the heat, cover, and let stand for 1 hour. Drain and rinse them well before using.

Substituting Canned Beans for Dried

Most recipes that call for dried beans require the beans to cook slowly with the other ingredients so that they release their starches and thicken the dish. When you replace the dried beans with canned beans and shorten the cooking time (canned beans are fully cooked and need to cook only long enough to warm through and soak up flavor), you sacrifice both the flavor and the texture of the finished dish. But if you're short on time and want to swap in canned beans for convenience, a general rule is that 1 cup dried beans equals 3 cups canned beans.

Canned Beans: To Rinse or Not to Rinse?

Canned beans are made by pressure-cooking dried beans directly in the can with water, salt, and preservatives. As the beans cook, starches and proteins leach into the liquid, thickening it. To find out whether rinsing away this starchy liquid mattered, we did side-by-side taste tests of both chickpea salad and bean chili made with rinsed and unrinsed beans. In the salad, tasters detected differences; the salad with rinsed chickpeas was noticeably brighter in flavor and less pasty than the one with unrinsed chickpeas. However, in the chili, which was stewy and had lots of bold flavors, rinsing the beans didn't make a difference. And in some recipes, like Spicy Braised Chickpeas and Turnips with Couscous (page 283), retaining the aquafaba (the chickpeas' starchy seasoned bean liquid) contributes additional flavor and body to the finished dish. Bottom line: Follow the recipe directions for whether or not to rinse the beans.

Cranberry Beans with Tequila, Green Chiles, and Pepitas

Serves 6 to 8

Why This Recipe Works Though they are found in many cuisines the world over, cranberry beans originated in South America. Since they have become popular in Mexico as well, we decided to pair them here with bold Mexican flavors—including tequila! Cranberry beans are rarely found canned, so we started with dried beans, soaking them overnight in salt water to help them cook up evenly tender and creamy. Then we sautéed some onion and garlic with lots of paprika, some cumin seeds, and dried oregano. Once the mixture was fragrant, we added a little tequila to the pot to give the beans some kick. (Cooking it until evaporated prevented the dish from tasting boozy.) Next we stirred in the brined beans and water and transferred the pot to the oven, where the beans cooked gently without the need for monitoring. Once the beans were tender, we stirred in some convenient canned chiles to give the dish great spice and some brightness and then we cooked the beans uncovered for 15 minutes more to allow the sauce to thicken. A garnish of rich plant-based (or dairy) sour cream, crunchy pepitas, and pickled shallots and radishes nicely balanced the rich, warm flavors of the cranberry beans. You may use plant-based or dairy yogurt in place of the sour cream, if you prefer. If cranberry beans are unavailable, substitute pinto beans.

- 3 tablespoons table salt for brining
- 1 pound (2½ cups) dried cranberry beans, picked over and rinsed
- ¼ cup extra-virgin olive oil
- 1 onion, chopped fine
- 1 teaspoon table salt
- 6 garlic cloves, minced
- 1 tablespoon paprika
- ½ teaspoon cumin seeds
- ½ teaspoon dried oregano
- ¼ cup tequila
- 1 tablespoon packed brown sugar
- 1 bay leaf
- ½ cup canned chopped green chiles
- ½ cup roasted pepitas
- ½ cup plant-based sour cream or dairy sour cream
- 1 recipe Quick Pickled Shallots and Radishes (recipe follows)

1. Dissolve 3 tablespoons salt in 4 quarts cold water in large container. Add beans and soak at room temperature for at least 8 hours or up to 24 hours. Drain and rinse well.

2. Adjust oven rack to middle position and heat oven to 325 degrees. Heat oil in Dutch oven over medium heat until shimmering. Add onion and salt and cook until onion is softened, about 5 minutes. Stir in garlic, paprika, cumin, and oregano and cook until fragrant, about 1 minute. Stir in tequila and cook until evaporated, about 30 seconds. Stir in 5 cups water, sugar, bay leaf, and cranberry beans; bring to simmer. Cover, transfer pot to oven, and cook until beans are tender, stirring once halfway through cooking, about 1¼ hours.

3. Add green chiles, stirring vigorously. Return pot to oven uncovered, and cook until sauce is thickened slightly, about 15 minutes. Season with salt and pepper to taste, and serve with pepitas, sour cream, and pickles.

Quick Pickled Shallots and Radishes
Makes about 1 cup

- ¼ cup lime juice (2 limes)
- 1 teaspoon sugar
- ¼ teaspoon table salt
- 6 large radishes, trimmed and sliced thin
- 1 shallot, sliced thin

Whisk lime juice, sugar, and salt in medium bowl until sugar and salt have dissolved. Stir in radishes and shallot and let sit for 15 minutes for flavors to blend (or refrigerate for up to 1 hour). Drain vegetables before serving.

Lentil Salad with Olives and Mint

Serves 4 to 6

Why This Recipe Works We love tiny French green lentils in salads, since they are small and firm and hold their shape better than standard green or brown lentils. A quick soak in salt water softened their skins before cooking, leading to fewer lentil blowouts and resulting in a faster cooking time. We then simmered them until tender, easily boosting their flavor by simply adding some crushed cloves of garlic and a bay leaf to the pot. With our cooked lentils in hand, we turned to the other ingredients. A simple, tart vinaigrette worked perfectly to balance the lentils. We chose several boldly flavored mix-ins to

French Lentils with Carrots and Parsley

2. Bring lentils, garlic, bay leaf, salt, and 1 quart water to boil in medium saucepan. Reduce heat to medium-low and simmer until the lentils are tender but still hold their shape, 8 to 10 minutes.

3. Drain lentils well; discard garlic and bay leaf. Whisk oil and vinegar together in large bowl. Add drained lentils, olives, mint, and shallot to dressing and toss to combine. Season with salt and pepper to taste, and sprinkle with feta, if using. Serve warm or at room temperature.

VARIATION

Lentil Salad with Spinach and Walnuts
Substitute 3 tablespoons sherry vinegar for white wine vinegar. Place 4 cups baby spinach and 2 tablespoons water in bowl. Cover and microwave until spinach is wilted to half its original volume, about 4 minutes. Remove bowl from microwave and keep covered for 1 minute. Transfer spinach to colander and gently press to release liquid. Transfer spinach to cutting board and chop coarse. Return to colander and press again. Substitute chopped spinach for olives and mint and ¼ cup Vegan Parmesan Substitute (page 27) or coarsely grated Parmesan cheese for feta, if using. Sprinkle salad with ¼ cup walnuts, toasted and chopped coarse, before serving.

French Lentils with Carrots and Parsley

Serves 4 to 6

Why This Recipe Works For a simple, versatile dish that would highlight the sweet-earthy flavors of lentilles du Puy, we took inspiration from their namesake and looked to France, slowly cooking the small, firm lentils with carrots, onion, and celery (a classic French combination called a mirepoix). We wanted a low, slow simmer so that the lentils could be infused with the aromatics, so we skipped the soaking step; they still held their shape nicely through cooking. Garlic and thyme added more aromatic flavors that complemented the lentils. Using water rather than broth let the pure flavors come through. Lentilles du Puy, also called French green lentils, are our first choice for this recipe, but brown, black, or regular green lentils are fine, too (note that cooking times will vary depending on the type used).

bring our salad to life: fresh mint, minced shallot, and chopped kalamata olives. If you would like to incorporate cheese, we like the richness of feta here. Lentilles du Puy, also called French green lentils, are our first choice for this recipe, but brown, black, or regular green lentils are fine, too (note that cooking times will vary depending on the type used).

- 1 teaspoon table salt for brining
- 1 cup dried lentilles du Puy (French green lentils), picked over and rinsed
- 5 garlic cloves, lightly crushed and peeled
- 1 bay leaf
- ½ teaspoon table salt
- 5 tablespoons extra-virgin olive oil
- 3 tablespoons white wine vinegar
- ½ cup pitted kalamata olives, chopped coarse
- ½ cup chopped fresh mint
- 1 large shallot, minced
- 1 ounce feta cheese, crumbled (¼ cup) (optional)

1. Dissolve 1 teaspoon salt in 1 quart warm water (about 110 degrees) in bowl. Add lentils and soak at room temperature for 1 hour. Drain well.

2 carrots, peeled and chopped fine
1 onion, chopped fine
1 celery rib, chopped fine
2 tablespoons extra-virgin olive oil, divided
½ teaspoon table salt
2 garlic cloves, minced
1 teaspoon minced fresh thyme or ¼ teaspoon dried
2½ cups water
1 cup dried lentilles du Puy (French green lentils), picked over and rinsed
2 tablespoons minced fresh parsley
2 teaspoons lemon juice

1. Combine carrots, onion, celery, 1 tablespoon oil, and salt in large saucepan. Cover and cook over medium-low heat, stirring occasionally, until vegetables are softened, 8 to 10 minutes. Stir in garlic and thyme and cook until fragrant, about 30 seconds.

2. Stir in water and lentils and bring to simmer. Reduce heat to low, cover, and simmer gently, stirring occasionally, until lentils are mostly tender, 40 to 50 minutes.

3. Uncover and continue to cook, stirring occasionally, until lentils are completely tender, about 8 minutes. Stir in remaining 1 tablespoon oil, parsley, and lemon juice. Season with salt and pepper to taste, and serve.

VARIATION
Curried French Lentils with Golden Raisins
Add 1 teaspoon curry powder to pot with onion. Stir ½ cup golden raisins into pot after uncovering in step 3. Substitute minced fresh cilantro for parsley.

Lentils with Roasted Broccoli and Lemony Bread Crumbs
Serves 4 to 6

Why This Recipe Works This supersavory dish elevates earthy French green lentils and humble broccoli to a whole new level. And although it's company-worthy, this comes together in less than an hour, making it achievable any day of the week. We opted for classic aromatics to create our flavorful base: onions, garlic, and herbaceous thyme. By preheating the sheet pan in a 500-degree oven and laying the broccoli on it in a single layer, we were able to impart deep, flavorful browning to the stalks and florets in a short amount of time. While the lentils cooked, we quickly made a bright, crispy, lemony bread crumb topping in a skillet. Using the same skillet, we reduced some balsamic vinegar, transforming its flavor from sharp and assertive to luxurious and sweet. We then assembled our bowls: lentils topped with broccoli and bread crumbs, all drizzled with balsamic reduction. Lentilles du Puy (or French green lentils) hold their shape quite well during cooking; we do not recommend substituting other types of lentils in this dish.

6 tablespoons extra-virgin olive oil, divided, plus extra for drizzling
1 onion, chopped fine
¾ teaspoon table salt, divided
2 garlic cloves, minced
1 teaspoon minced fresh thyme or ½ teaspoon dried
12 ounces (1¾ cups) dried lentilles du Puy (French green lentils), picked over and rinsed
3¾ cups water
½ cup panko bread crumbs
2 teaspoons grated lemon zest
½ cup balsamic vinegar
2 pounds broccoli, florets cut into 1-inch pieces, stalks peeled and sliced lengthwise into ½-inch thick planks

1. Adjust oven rack to lowest position, place aluminum foil–lined rimmed baking sheet on rack, and heat oven to 500 degrees. Heat 1 tablespoon oil in large saucepan over medium heat until shimmering. Add onion and ¼ teaspoon salt and cook until softened, about 5 minutes. Stir in garlic and thyme and cook until fragrant, about 30 seconds.

2. Stir in lentils and water and bring to simmer over high heat. Reduce heat to low, cover, and simmer, stirring occasionally, until lentils are just tender, about 25 minutes. Uncover, increase heat to medium and continue to cook until lentils are completely tender and most of liquid has evaporated, 10 to 15 minutes. Season with salt and pepper to taste, cover to keep warm, and set aside.

3. While lentils cook, combine panko and 2 tablespoons oil in 8-inch skillet, stirring to coat. Cook over medium-low heat, stirring frequently, until light golden brown, 5 to 7 minutes; transfer to bowl and stir in lemon zest. Wipe skillet clean with paper towels. Cook vinegar in now-empty skillet, scraping bottom of skillet with rubber spatula, until thickened and reduced to 2 tablespoons, about 5 minutes.

4. Toss broccoli with remaining 3 tablespoons oil and remaining ½ teaspoon salt in bowl. Working quickly, lay broccoli in single layer, flat sides down, on preheated sheet. Roast until florets are browned, 9 to 11 minutes. Divide lentils among individual serving bowls and top with broccoli mixture. Sprinkle with panko mixture, drizzle with balsamic reduction, and serve, drizzling with extra oil.

Koshari

Koshari
Serves 4 to 6

1 cup elbow macaroni
1 teaspoon table salt, divided, plus salt for cooking pasta and lentils
1 cup dried green or brown lentils, picked over and rinsed
1 recipe Crispy Onions, plus ¼ cup reserved oil, divided (page 290)
4 garlic cloves, minced, divided
1½ teaspoons ground coriander, divided
1½ teaspoons ground cumin, divided
¾ teaspoon ground cinnamon, divided
¼ teaspoon ground nutmeg, divided
¼ teaspoon cayenne pepper, divided
1 (28-ounce) can tomato sauce
1 (15-ounce) can chickpeas, rinsed
1 cup basmati rice
1 tablespoon red wine vinegar
3 tablespoons minced fresh parsley

Why This Recipe Works Considered the national dish of Egypt, koshari evolved as a way to use up leftovers and became a popular street food. This hearty dish usually features lentils, rice, pasta, and chickpeas smothered in a spiced tomato sauce and topped with crispy fried onions. Our tasters couldn't get enough of this comforting combination, and although the dish took some time to put together, each element was fairly simple. We cooked the lentils and the pasta in boiling water and drained them, then set them aside while we prepared the rice and sauce. Soaking the rice in hot water before cooking eliminated excess starch so it didn't clump. Tasters preferred a tomato sauce spiked with vinegar over spicier options. Using the same spices (coriander, cumin, cinnamon, nutmeg, and cayenne) in the sauce and the rice built a layered flavor profile. Adding the chickpeas directly to the sauce to simmer infused them with flavor. The finishing touch: a generous amount of ultrasavory, crunchy fried onions. Large green or brown lentils both work well in this recipe; do not use French green lentils, or lentilles du Puy. Long-grain white, jasmine, or Texmati rice can be substituted for the basmati.

1. Bring 2 quarts water to boil in Dutch oven. Add pasta and 1½ teaspoons salt and cook, stirring often, until al dente. Drain pasta, rinse with water, then drain again. Transfer to bowl and set aside.

2. Meanwhile, bring lentils, 4 cups water, and 1 teaspoon salt to boil in medium saucepan over high heat. Reduce heat to low and cook until lentils are just tender, 15 to 17 minutes. Drain and set aside.

3. Cook 1 tablespoon reserved onion oil, 1 teaspoon garlic, ½ teaspoon coriander, ½ teaspoon cumin, ¼ teaspoon cinnamon, ⅛ teaspoon nutmeg, ⅛ teaspoon cayenne, and ½ teaspoon salt in now-empty saucepan over medium heat until fragrant, about 1 minute. Stir in tomato sauce and chickpeas, bring to simmer, and cook until slightly thickened, about 10 minutes. Cover and keep warm.

4. While sauce cooks, place rice in medium bowl, cover with hot tap water by 2 inches, and let sit for 15 minutes. Using your hands, gently swish grains to release excess starch. Carefully pour off water, leaving rice in bowl. Repeat adding and pouring off cold water 4 or 5 times, until water runs almost clear. Drain rice in fine-mesh strainer.

5. Cook remaining 3 tablespoons reserved onion oil, remaining garlic, remaining 1 teaspoon coriander, remaining 1 teaspoon cumin, remaining ½ teaspoon cinnamon, remaining ⅛ teaspoon nutmeg, and remaining ⅛ teaspoon cayenne in now-empty pot over medium heat until fragrant, about 2 minutes. Add rice and cook, stirring occasionally, until grain edges begin to turn translucent, about 3 minutes. Stir in 2 cups water and remaining ½ teaspoon salt and bring to boil. Stir in lentils, reduce heat to low, cover, and simmer gently until all liquid is absorbed, about 12 minutes.

6. Off heat, sprinkle pasta over rice mixture. Cover, laying clean dish towel underneath lid, and let sit for 10 minutes.

7. Return sauce to simmer over medium heat. Stir in vinegar and season with salt and pepper to taste. Fluff rice and lentils with fork and stir in parsley and half of onions. Transfer to serving platter and top with half of sauce and remaining onions. Serve, passing remaining sauce separately.

Crispy Onions
Makes 1½ cups
It is crucial to thoroughly dry the microwaved onions after rinsing. Be sure to reserve enough oil to use in the Mujaddara or Koshari. The remaining oil may be refrigerated in an airtight container for up to four weeks; it tastes great in salad dressings, sautéed vegetables, and pasta sauces.

   2   pounds onions, halved and sliced crosswise
        into ¼-inch-thick pieces
   2   teaspoons table salt
   1½ cups vegetable oil

1. Toss onions and salt together in large bowl. Microwave for 5 minutes. Rinse thoroughly, transfer to paper towel–lined baking sheet, and dry well.

2. Heat onions and oil in Dutch oven over high heat, stirring frequently, until onions are golden brown, 25 to 30 minutes. Drain onions in colander set in large bowl. Transfer onions to paper towel–lined baking sheet to drain. Serve.

Mujaddara
Serves 4 to 6

Why This Recipe Works Essentially the "rice and beans" of the eastern Mediterranean, this classic Levantine dish is a spectacular example of how a few humble ingredients can add up to something that's satisfying and complex. Traditional versions consist of tender basmati rice and lentils seasoned with warm spices and minced garlic and topped with deeply savory fried onions. To give the onions the best crispy texture, we microwaved them to remove some of their liquid and then fried them in oil to a deep golden brown. To ensure that the rice and lentils were done at the same time, we parcooked the lentils and then set them aside while we prepared the rice. We soaked the rice in hot water to ensure that it turned out fluffy,

not sticky, and then toasted it along with the spices in some of the flavorful frying oil from the onions. Finished with a bracing garlicky yogurt sauce (equally delicious with plant-based or dairy yogurt), this pilaf is comfort food at its best. Large green or brown lentils both work well in this recipe; do not use French green lentils, or lentilles du Puy. Long-grain white, jasmine, or Texmati rice can be substituted for the basmati.

Yogurt Sauce
   1   cup plain plant-based yogurt or dairy yogurt
   2   tablespoons lemon juice
   ½   teaspoon minced garlic
   ½   teaspoon table salt

Rice and Lentils
   8¾ ounces (1¼ cups) dried green or brown lentils,
        picked over and rinsed
   1   teaspoon table salt, plus salt for cooking lentils
   1¼ cups basmati rice
   1   recipe Crispy Onions, plus 3 tablespoons reserved
        oil
   3   garlic cloves, minced
   1   teaspoon ground coriander
   1   teaspoon ground cumin
   ½   teaspoon ground cinnamon
   ½   teaspoon ground allspice
   ¼   teaspoon pepper
   ⅛   teaspoon cayenne pepper
   1   teaspoon sugar
   3   tablespoons minced fresh cilantro

1. For the yogurt sauce Whisk all ingredients together in bowl and refrigerate until ready to serve.

2. For the rice and lentils Bring lentils, 4 cups water, and 1 teaspoon salt to boil in medium saucepan over high heat. Reduce heat to low and cook until lentils are just tender, 15 to 17 minutes. Drain and set aside.

3. Meanwhile, place rice in medium bowl, cover with hot tap water by 2 inches, and let sit for 15 minutes. Using your hands, gently swish grains to release excess starch. Carefully pour off water, leaving rice in bowl. Repeat adding and pouring off cold water 4 or 5 times, until water runs almost clear. Drain rice in fine-mesh strainer.

4. Cook reserved onion oil, garlic, coriander, cumin, cinnamon, allspice, pepper, and cayenne in Dutch oven over medium heat until fragrant, about 2 minutes. Add rice and cook, stirring occasionally, until grain edges begin to turn translucent, about 3 minutes. Stir in 2¼ cups water, sugar, and salt and bring to boil. Stir in lentils, reduce heat to low, cover, and simmer gently until all liquid is absorbed, about 12 minutes.

5. Off heat, cover, laying clean dish towel underneath lid, and let sit for 10 minutes. Fluff rice and lentils with fork and stir in cilantro and half of onions. Transfer to serving platter and top with remaining onions. Serve with yogurt sauce.

Red Lentil Kibbeh

Serves 4 to 6

Why This Recipe Works Kibbeh is a popular Middle Eastern dish made from bulgur, minced onions, varying spices, and (traditionally) ground meat. During Lent, however, this common meal is often prepared with lentils in lieu of meat, as the texture of the two is similar. We wanted to take advantage of this flavor-packed plant-based mixture and develop it as something that could be served either on its own with some Bibb lettuce and yogurt or as a showstopping addition to a larger spread. We chose red lentils for their vibrant hue and enhanced both their color and flavor with two red pastes. Tomato paste brought sweetness and an umami quality, and harissa, a smoky, spicy chili paste, added complexity. We gave the bulgur a head start before adding the quick-cooking lentils to the same saucepan, which allowed both components to finish cooking at the same time. To balance the deep flavors from the aromatics and pastes, we stirred in lemon juice and fresh parsley at the end. This spoonable, delicious mixture would go great on a mezze platter alongside Whipped Cashew Dip with Roasted Red Peppers and Olives (page 349), Baba Ghanoush (page 345) or hummus, Spiced Roasted Chickpeas (page 355) or nuts, pickled radishes, and pita. You can use our Harissa or store-bought harissa, though spiciness can vary greatly by brand. If your harissa is spicy, omit the cayenne.

- 3 tablespoons extra-virgin olive oil, divided
- 1 onion, chopped fine
- 1 red bell pepper, stemmed, seeded, and chopped fine
- 1 teaspoon table salt
- 2 tablespoons Harissa (page 292)
- 2 tablespoons tomato paste
- ½ teaspoon cayenne pepper (optional)
- 1 cup medium-grind bulgur
- 4 cups water
- ¾ cup dried red lentils, picked over and rinsed
- ½ cup chopped fresh parsley
- 2 tablespoons lemon juice
- 1 head Bibb lettuce (8 ounces), leaves separated
- ½ cup plain plant-based yogurt or dairy yogurt
  Lemon wedges

Mujaddara

Red Lentil Kibbeh

1. Heat 1 tablespoon oil in large saucepan over medium heat until shimmering. Add onion, bell pepper, and salt and cook until softened, about 5 minutes. Stir in harissa; tomato paste; and cayenne, if using, and cook, stirring frequently, until fragrant, about 1 minute.

2. Stir in bulgur and water and bring to simmer. Reduce heat to low, cover, and simmer gently until bulgur is barely tender, about 8 minutes. Stir in lentils, cover, and continue to cook, stirring occasionally, until lentils and bulgur are tender, 8 to 10 minutes.

3. Off heat, lay clean dish towel underneath lid and let mixture sit for 10 minutes. Stir in 1 tablespoon oil, parsley, and lemon juice and stir vigorously until mixture is cohesive. Season with salt and pepper to taste. Transfer to platter and drizzle with remaining 1 tablespoon oil. Spoon kibbeh into lettuce leaves and drizzle with yogurt. Serve with lemon wedges.

Harissa
Makes ½ cup
This traditional North African condiment is great for flavoring soups, sauces, and dressings or dolloping on hummus, sandwiches, and eggs. If you can't find Aleppo pepper, you can substitute ¾ teaspoon paprika and ¾ teaspoon finely chopped red pepper flakes.

- 6 tablespoons extra-virgin olive oil
- 6 garlic cloves, minced
- 2 tablespoons paprika
- 1 tablespoon ground coriander
- 1 tablespoon ground dried Aleppo pepper
- 1 teaspoon ground cumin
- ¾ teaspoon caraway seeds
- ½ teaspoon table salt

Combine all ingredients in bowl and microwave until bubbling and very fragrant, about 1 minute, stirring halfway through microwaving; let cool to room temperature. (Harissa can be refrigerated for up to 4 days.)

Masoor Dal
Serves 4 to 6

Why This Recipe Works Dals are heavily spiced lentil stews common throughout India. Split red lentils give this dal a mild, slightly nutty taste, and as the stew slowly simmers, they break down to a smooth consistency. We wanted our red lentil dal to be simple yet still embody the complex flavors of Indian cuisine, so we started with the spices. We created a balanced blend of warm spices with just a subtle layer of heat. Blooming the spices in oil until they were fragrant boosted and deepened their flavors. Onion, garlic, and ginger rounded out the aromatics. Authentic dal should have a porridge-like consistency, bordering on a puree (without the need for a blender). Getting this consistency required cooking the lentils with just the right amount of water: We finally settled on 4 cups water to 1¼ cups lentils for a dal that was smooth but not thin. Before serving, we added cilantro for color and freshness and diced raw tomato for sweetness and acidity. A bit of coconut oil stirred in before serving added a rich finish. You cannot substitute other types of lentils for the red lentils here; they have a very different texture. Serve over rice or with pita bread.

- 3 tablespoons refined coconut oil, divided
- ½ teaspoon ground coriander
- ½ teaspoon ground cumin
- ½ teaspoon ground cinnamon
- ½ teaspoon ground turmeric
- ⅛ teaspoon ground cardamom
- ⅛ teaspoon red pepper flakes
- 1 onion, chopped fine
- ¾ teaspoon table salt
- 3 garlic cloves, minced
- 1½ teaspoons grated fresh ginger
- 4 cups water
- 8½ ounces (1¼ cups) dried red lentils, picked over and rinsed
- 1 pound plum tomatoes, cored, seeded, and chopped
- ½ cup minced fresh cilantro
  Lemon wedges

1. Melt 1 tablespoon oil in large saucepan over medium-high heat. Add coriander, cumin, cinnamon, turmeric, cardamom, and pepper flakes and cook until fragrant, about 10 seconds. Stir in onion and salt and cook until softened, about 5 minutes. Stir in garlic and ginger and cook until fragrant, about 30 seconds.

Masoor Dal

2. Stir in water and lentils and bring to boil. Reduce heat to low and simmer, uncovered, until lentils are tender and resemble coarse puree, 20 to 25 minutes.

3. Stir in tomatoes, cilantro, and remaining 2 tablespoons oil and season with salt and pepper to taste. Serve with lemon wedges.

VARIATION

Masoor Dal with Cauliflower and Cilantro

Omit tomatoes. Substitute 1 teaspoon garam masala for coriander, cumin, turmeric, cardamom, and pepper flakes. Substitute lime wedges for lemon wedges. While lentils cool, toss 1 head cauliflower, cut into 8 equal wedges, with 2 tablespoons extra-virgin olive oil and ¼ teaspoon salt. Place wedges cut side down on parchment paper–lined rimmed baking sheet. Cover tightly with aluminum foil and cook for 10 minutes. Remove foil. Continue to cook until bottoms of wedges are golden, 8 to 12 minutes. Remove from oven, flip wedges using spatula, and continue to cook until golden all over, 8 to 12 minutes. Serve cauliflower with lentils.

Misir Wot
Serves 4 FAST

Why This Recipe Works One of Ethiopia's most famous vegetarian dishes, misir wot is a deeply flavored lentil dish traditionally seasoned with the spice blend berbere. This unique blend delivers intense warmth followed by sweet and citrusy notes. Since it's not always easy to find in the grocery store, we made it ourselves. Pre-made berbere often contains powdered ginger, which has a strong peppery bite. However, we wanted to bring out the floral sweetness that comes with fresh ginger. To start, we incorporated lots of aromatics: red onion, umami-rich tomato paste, plus fresh ginger and garlic. Then we got to blooming our berbere blend: paprika, coriander, cardamom, cumin, and cayenne. Next came our quick-cooking red lentils and some plum tomatoes, which brought a necessary freshness and almost cooling effect to this complex dish. Finally, we finished with a drizzle of red wine vinegar, the acidity of which helped to cut through the many layers of delicious heat. Do not substitute other types of lentils for the red lentils here; they have a very different texture. Adjust the cayenne amount according to your taste. Be sure to bloom the spices for the full minute; otherwise, you'll be left with a raw, dusty texture in the dish.

- 3 tablespoons extra-virgin olive oil
- 1 red onion, chopped fine
- 2 tablespoons tomato paste
- 4 teaspoons grated fresh ginger
- 3 garlic cloves, minced
- 2½ teaspoons paprika
- 1¼ teaspoons ground coriander
- ¾ teaspoon ground cardamom
- ¾ teaspoon ground cumin
- ½–1 teaspoon cayenne pepper
- 2 cups water
- 1 cup dried red lentils, picked over and rinsed
- 4 plum tomatoes, cored and chopped fine
- 1 teaspoon table salt
  Red wine vinegar

1. Heat oil in large saucepan over medium-high heat until shimmering. Add onion and cook, stirring occasionally, until softened and lightly browned, 5 to 7 minutes. Add tomato paste, ginger, garlic, paprika, coriander, cardamom, cumin, and cayenne and cook until fragrant, about 1 minute.

2. Stir in water, lentils, tomatoes, and salt and bring to a simmer. Reduce heat to low and simmer, stirring occasionally, until lentils are tender and beginning to break down, 15 to 25 minutes. Season with salt, pepper, and vinegar to taste. Serve.

Thai Red Curry with Lentils and Tofu

Serves 4 to 6

Why This Recipe Works Thai curries embrace a delicate balance of flavors, textures, temperatures, and colors to produce lively, satisfying meals. Our Thai-style red curry features lentils and tofu for plenty of protein. We started by cooking the lentils in an aromatic red curry broth. When the lentils were tender but still slightly al dente and had absorbed most of the liquid, we incorporated a bit of coconut milk to create a rich, fragrant sauce. To contrast the nutty earthiness of the lentils, we added vibrant red bell pepper slices, snow peas, and cubes of tofu at the very end, simply warming them through to maintain the vegetables' color and crisp-fresh texture. A generous handful of fresh basil and a sprinkle of scallions gave the dish a brisk, heady finish. Lentilles du Puy, also called French green lentils, are our first choice, but brown, black, or regular green lentils are fine, too (cooking times will vary depending on the type used). Do not use light coconut milk. Not all Thai curry pastes are vegan, so check the labels carefully. You will need a 12-inch skillet with a tight-fitting lid.

Thai Red Curry with Lentils and Tofu

- 14 ounces extra-firm tofu, cut into ½-inch pieces
- ⅛ teaspoon table salt
  Pinch pepper
- 1 tablespoon vegetable oil
- 1 tablespoon Thai red curry paste
- 2½ cups water
- 2 tablespoons Fish Sauce Substitute (page 22)
- 1 cup dried lentilles du Puy (French green lentils), picked over and rinsed
- ½ cup canned coconut milk
- 1 red bell pepper, stemmed, seeded, and cut into ¼-inch strips
- 4 ounces snow peas, strings removed and halved crosswise
- ½ cup coarsely chopped fresh basil
- 1 tablespoon lime juice
- 2 scallions, sliced thin

1. Spread tofu on paper towel–lined baking sheet and let drain for 20 minutes. Gently press dry with paper towels and sprinkle with salt and pepper.

2. Heat oil in 12-inch skillet over medium heat until shimmering. Add curry paste and cook, stirring constantly, until fragrant, about 1 minute. Stir in water, fish sauce substitute, and lentils and bring to simmer. Cover, reduce heat to low, and simmer gently, stirring occasionally, until lentils are tender and two-thirds of liquid has been absorbed, 30 to 35 minutes.

3. Stir in coconut milk until well combined. Add bell pepper, snow peas, and tofu and increase heat to medium-high. Cover and cook, stirring occasionally, until tofu is warmed through and vegetables are crisp-tender, about 2 minutes.

4. Off heat, stir in basil and lime juice. Season with salt to taste, and sprinkle with scallions. Serve.

Baked Navy Beans

Serves 6 to 8

Why This Recipe Works Authentic Boston baked beans are always a hit, but classic versions aren't exactly vegan-friendly fare: Salt pork, and sometimes bacon as well, is often the first ingredient in the pot. To get the same creamy-textured beans in a meatless version, and in a lot less time to boot, we first simmered dried navy beans with a little baking soda. The alkaline baking soda weakened the cell structure of the beans, helping them to become tender more quickly and allowing us to shave the baking time down to 2 hours from the normal 5 to 6 hours. We started out by adding the usual traditional flavorings—molasses, brown sugar, mustard, and cider vinegar—but tasters still wanted more. To deepen the flavor and amp up the meatiness of the dish, we added soy sauce and smoked paprika; the umami-rich soy sauce gave the dish more deeply savory flavor, and the paprika added great smoky depth to our baked beans.

1 pound (2½ cups) dried navy beans, picked over and rinsed
1 tablespoon baking soda
1 tablespoon vegetable oil
1 onion, chopped fine
¼ cup molasses
2 tablespoons packed dark brown sugar
2 tablespoons soy sauce
4 teaspoons Dijon mustard, divided
2 teaspoons smoked paprika
¾ teaspoon table salt
¼ teaspoon pepper
2 teaspoons cider vinegar

1. Adjust oven rack to middle position and heat oven to 350 degrees. Bring 3 quarts water, beans, and baking soda to boil in Dutch oven over high heat. Reduce heat to medium-high and simmer vigorously for 20 minutes. Drain and rinse beans and pot. Dry pot.

2. Heat oil in now-empty pot over medium heat until shimmering. Add onion and cook until softened, about 5 minutes. Stir in 4½ cups water, rinsed beans, molasses, sugar, soy sauce, 1 tablespoon mustard, paprika, salt, and pepper and bring to boil. Cover pot, transfer to oven, and cook until beans are nearly tender, about 1½ hours.

3. Uncover and continue to bake until beans are completely tender, about 30 minutes. Stir in vinegar and remaining 1 teaspoon mustard. Season with salt and pepper to taste. Serve.

Pinto Bean and Swiss Chard Enchiladas

Serves 4 to 6

Why This Recipe Works Cheesy, meaty fillings are pretty typical for enchiladas, but this hearty, plant-forward version uses neither, while still delivering tons of flavor. We kept things green by wilting flavorsome Swiss chard and crisp, slightly bitter green peppers with garlic and onions. To add creamy cohesiveness and protein heft, we mashed half a can of pinto beans and mixed in our greens; we then stirred in the rest of the beans whole for contrasting texture. This clean-tasting

filling needed a robust sauce to round out the flavors; a quick simmer of convenient canned tomato sauce with aromatics and spices did the trick. Traditional recipes call for frying the tortillas one at a time, but we found that brushing them with oil and microwaving worked just as well—and without the mess of frying. If you would like to incorporate cheese, see the variation. A topping of a crema cilantro sauce (made from either plant-based or dairy mayo and sour cream) and chopped avocado was ideal: tangy, creamy, fresh-tasting, and rich.

Cilantro Sauce
¼ cup plant-based mayonnaise or egg-based mayonnaise
¼ cup plant-based sour cream or dairy sour cream
3 tablespoons water
3 tablespoons minced fresh cilantro
¼ teaspoon table salt

Enchiladas
¼ cup vegetable oil, divided
2 onions, chopped fine, divided
¾ teaspoon table salt, divided
3 tablespoons chili powder
2 teaspoons ground cumin
2 teaspoons sugar
6 garlic cloves, minced, divided
2 (8-ounce) cans tomato sauce
½ cup water
1 pound Swiss chard, stemmed and sliced into ½-inch-wide strips
2 green bell peppers, stemmed, seeded, and cut into ½-inch pieces
1 (15-ounce) can pinto beans, rinsed, divided
12 (6-inch) corn tortillas
1 avocado, halved, pitted, and cut into ½-inch pieces
¼ cup fresh cilantro leaves
Lime wedges

1. For the cilantro sauce Whisk all ingredients together in bowl. Cover and refrigerate until ready to serve.

2. For the enchiladas Adjust oven rack to middle position and heat oven to 450 degrees. Heat 1 tablespoon oil in large saucepan over medium heat until shimmering. Add half of onions and ½ teaspoon salt and cook until softened, about 5 minutes. Stir in chili powder, cumin, sugar, and half of garlic and cook until fragrant, about 30 seconds. Stir in tomato sauce and water, bring to simmer, and cook until slightly thickened, about 7 minutes. Season with salt and pepper to taste; set aside.

Pinto Bean and Swiss Chard Enchiladas

3. Heat 1 tablespoon oil in Dutch oven over medium heat until shimmering. Add remaining onions and remaining ¼ teaspoon salt and cook until softened and lightly browned, 5 to 7 minutes. Add remaining garlic and cook until fragrant, about 30 seconds. Add chard and bell peppers, cover, and cook until chard is tender, 6 to 8 minutes. Using potato masher, coarsely mash half of beans in large bowl. Stir in chard-pepper mixture, ¼ cup sauce, and remaining whole beans.

4. Grease 13 by 9-inch baking dish. Spread ½ cup sauce over bottom of prepared dish. Brush both sides of tortillas with remaining 2 tablespoons oil. Stack tortillas, wrap in damp dish towel, and place on plate. Microwave until warm and pliable, about 1 minute. Working with 1 warm tortilla at a time, spread ¼ cup chard filling across center. Roll tortilla tightly around filling and place seam side down in dish, arranging enchiladas in 2 columns across width of dish. Cover completely with remaining sauce.

5. Cover dish tightly with greased aluminum foil and bake until enchiladas are heated through, 15 to 20 minutes. Let enchiladas cool for 10 minutes. Drizzle with cilantro sauce and sprinkle with avocado and cilantro. Serve with lime wedges.

VARIATION
Pinto Bean, Swiss Chard, and Monterey Jack Enchiladas
At end of step 4, sprinkle 1 cup shredded Monterey Jack over top of sauce.

Red Beans and Rice with Okra and Tomatoes

Refried Pinto Beans
Serves 4 to 6 (**Makes** 2½ cups) `FAST`

Why This Recipe Works Authentic refried beans, or frijoles refritos, are leftover stewed beans cooked in a generous amount of lard until they are softened enough to mash. We wanted to achieve the same lush texture and rich, savory flavor without the lard. While we were at it, we figured we'd make them fast enough to prepare any night of the week. To start, we found that dried beans weren't essential—canned pinto beans worked just fine and saved us the time of cooking beans from scratch. For authentic flavor, we reached for smoky chipotle chile powder, cumin, oregano, and several cloves of garlic. Two tablespoons of umami-rich tomato paste added even more savory depth. Processing a portion of the beans with some water in the food processor created the silky, creamy "refried" texture we were after, and pulsing the remaining beans ensured some chunky bites remained in the final dish. Adding cilantro and lime juice at the end gave our beans some brightness.

2 (15-ounce) cans pinto beans, rinsed, divided
1 cup water, plus extra as needed
1 tablespoon vegetable oil
1 onion, chopped fine
½ teaspoon table salt
2 tablespoons tomato paste
3 garlic cloves, minced
1 teaspoon ground cumin
½ teaspoon chipotle chile powder
½ teaspoon dried oregano
1 tablespoon minced fresh cilantro
2 teaspoons lime juice

1. Process all but 1 cup of beans with water in food processor until smooth, about 30 seconds, scraping down sides of bowl as needed. Add remaining beans and pulse until coarsely ground, about 5 pulses.

2. Heat oil in 12-inch nonstick skillet over medium heat until shimmering. Add onion and salt and cook until onion is softened, about 5 minutes. Stir in tomato paste, garlic, cumin, chile powder, and oregano and cook until fragrant, about 1 minute. Stir in bean mixture and cook, stirring constantly, until well combined and thickened slightly, about 3 minutes. Off heat, stir in cilantro and lime juice and season with salt and pepper to taste. Add additional hot water as needed to adjust consistency and serve.

Red Beans and Rice with Okra and Tomatoes

Serves 6 to 8

Why This Recipe Works Boosting the flavor profile of classic New Orleans red beans and rice by adding okra and tomatoes creates a hearty, vegetable-packed meal. This Cajun dish traditionally calls for Camellia-brand dried red beans and tasso ham. An easy switch to a more readily available ingredient was to use small dried red beans, which we brined overnight. And naturally we skipped the tasso ham, but fine-tuning the proportions of sautéed green peppers, onions, and celery gave this dish flavor balance without the need for meat. To ensure that the okra retains some of its crunchy bite in the finished dish, toss the whole okra pods in salt and let sit for an hour before rinsing, cutting, and adding them to the beans and tomatoes for the final half hour of cooking. While we prefer the flavor and texture of fresh okra in this recipe, you can substitute frozen cut okra, thawed and thoroughly patted dry, for fresh. If using frozen, skip step 2.

Red Beans
3 tablespoons plus 1 teaspoon table salt, divided, for brining and salting
1 pound small red beans (2 cups), picked over and rinsed
1 pound okra, stemmed
1 tablespoon vegetable oil
1 onion, chopped fine
1 green bell pepper, stemmed, seeded, and chopped fine
1 celery rib, minced
3 garlic cloves, minced
1 teaspoon minced fresh thyme or ¼ teaspoon dried
1 teaspoon smoked sweet paprika
2 bay leaves
¼ teaspoon cayenne pepper
¼ teaspoon pepper
3 cups vegetable broth
2 (14.5-ounce) cans diced tomatoes, drained
1 tablespoon red wine vinegar, plus extra for seasoning
3 scallions, sliced thin
Hot sauce

Rice
1 tablespoon vegetable oil
2 cups long-grain white rice, rinsed
3 cups water
1 teaspoon table salt

1. For the red beans Dissolve 3 tablespoons salt in 4 quarts cold water in large bowl or container. Add beans and soak at room temperature for at least 8 hours or up to 24 hours. Drain and rinse well; set aside.

2. Toss okra with 1 teaspoon salt, and let sit for 1 hour, stirring halfway through. Rinse well, then cut into 1-inch pieces; set aside.

3. Heat oil in large Dutch oven over medium heat until shimmering. Add onion, bell pepper, and celery and cook until vegetables are softened, 5 to 7 minutes. Stir in garlic, thyme, paprika, bay leaves, cayenne, and pepper and cook until fragrant, about 30 seconds.

4. Stir in beans, 5 cups water, and broth and bring to boil over high heat. Reduce to vigorous simmer and cook, stirring occasionally, until beans are just softened and liquid begins to thicken, 45 minutes to 1 hour.

5. Stir in okra, tomatoes, and vinegar and cook until liquid is thickened and beans are fully tender and creamy, about 30 minutes.

6. For the rice Meanwhile, heat oil in large saucepan over medium heat until shimmering. Add rice and cook, stirring often, until edges begin to turn translucent, about 2 minutes. Stir in water and salt and bring to boil. Cover, reduce heat to low, and simmer until liquid is absorbed and rice is tender, about 20 minutes. Remove pot from heat, lay clean folded dish towel underneath lid, and let rice sit for 10 minutes. Fluff rice with fork.

7. Discard bay leaves from beans. Season with salt, pepper, and extra vinegar to taste. Top individual portions of rice with beans and sprinkle with scallions. Serve with hot sauce.

Tuscan White Bean and Fresh Corn Salad

Serves 4 to 6

Why This Recipe Works Fresh corn salad is a summery addition to a picnic or backyard-barbecue table. We wanted to turn this favorite side dish into a vegan meal option, so we added convenient canned cannellini beans. The most typical preparation method for preparing the fresh corn—stripping kernels off the cob, adding vegetables (usually tomatoes, onions, and/or peppers), and tossing with dressing—produced rather wan salads. Instead, we discovered that browning the kernels lightly in a skillet for a few minutes gave even inferior, out-of-season corn a complex, nutty flavor dimension. As for the dressing, it took equal parts oil and vinegar to create a piquant dressing that balanced the creamy beans and sweet corn. Be sure to let the toasted corn cool before adding the tomatoes, as otherwise the heat from the corn will partially cook them.

  2 tomatoes, cored and cut into ½-inch pieces
1¼ teaspoons table salt, divided
2½ tablespoons extra-virgin olive oil, divided
  5 ears corn, kernels cut from cobs (about 5 cups)
  2 scallions, sliced thin
1½ tablespoons red wine vinegar
  ½ teaspoon pepper
  1 (15-ounce) can cannellini beans, rinsed
  2 tablespoons chopped fresh basil

1. Toss tomatoes with ½ teaspoon salt in bowl, then transfer to colander. Set colander over bowl and let drain for 30 minutes.

2. Meanwhile, heat 1 tablespoon oil in 12-inch nonstick skillet over medium-high heat until shimmering. Add corn and cook, stirring occasionally, until spotty brown, 5 to 7 minutes. Transfer to large bowl and stir in scallions, vinegar, pepper, remaining ¾ teaspoon salt, and remaining 1½ tablespoons oil; let cool to room temperature, about 20 minutes.

3. Stir in drained tomatoes, beans, and basil. Let sit until flavors meld, about 30 minutes. Season with salt and pepper to taste. Serve.

CUTTING CORN KERNELS FROM THE COB

1. Using sharp chef's knife, cut cobs in half crosswise.

2. Stand cob halves on cut ends to stabilize, then slice kernels from cob halves.

Sicilian White Beans and Escarole

Serves 4   **FAST**

Why This Recipe Works White beans and escarole are a classic pairing in Italian cooking: Combining the buttery texture of cannellini beans with tender, slightly bitter escarole results in a simple but well-balanced dish. Canned beans made this dish speedy and convenient, and their creamy texture was a perfect counterpoint to the greens. Sautéed onions gave the dish a rich, deep flavor base without requiring too much time at the stove. Red pepper flakes lent a slight heat, and a combination of broth and water for cooking provided a flavorful backbone. We added the escarole and beans along with the liquid and then cooked the greens just until the leaves were wilted before cranking up the heat so the liquid would quickly evaporate. This short stint on the heat prevented the beans from breaking down and becoming mushy. Once we took the pot off the heat, we stirred in lemon juice for a bright finish and drizzled on some extra olive oil for richness. Chicory can be substituted for the escarole; however, its flavor is stronger.

Sicilian White Beans and Escarole

1 tablespoon extra-virgin olive oil, plus extra for serving
2 onions, chopped fine
½ teaspoon table salt
4 garlic cloves, minced
⅛ teaspoon red pepper flakes
1 head escarole (1 pound), trimmed and sliced 1 inch thick
1 (15-ounce) can cannellini beans, rinsed
1 cup vegetable broth
1 cup water
2 teaspoons lemon juice

1. Heat oil in Dutch oven over medium heat until shimmering. Add onions and salt and cook until softened and lightly browned, 5 to 7 minutes. Stir in garlic and pepper flakes and cook until fragrant, about 30 seconds.

2. Stir in escarole, beans, broth, and water and bring to simmer. Cook, stirring occasionally, until escarole is wilted, about 5 minutes. Increase heat to high and cook until liquid is nearly evaporated, 10 to 15 minutes. Stir in lemon juice and season with salt and pepper to taste. Drizzle with extra oil and serve.

White Beans with Broccoli Rabe
Serves 4   **FAST**

Why This Recipe Works Broccoli rabe has a big personality, with its spiky leaves and baby florets, but what makes this vegetable really stand out is its bright, faintly bitter flavor that shocks the palate awake. Italian cuisine often pairs cannellini beans with broccoli rabe, since the mellow, creamy, sweet beans complement the pleasantly sharp greens incredibly well. Our quick version of this Italian favorite can be on the table in less than half an hour. Cutting the broccoli rabe into 1-inch pieces meant that the pieces cooked evenly when quickly sautéed. Canned beans were the obvious choice to make this an easy weeknight meal. Adding the beans early in the cooking process gave them a little time to absorb the flavors of the garlic-infused olive oil. A shot of savory vegetable broth rounded out the dish.

¼ cup extra-virgin olive oil, divided
3 garlic cloves, sliced thin
¼ teaspoon red pepper flakes
1 pound broccoli rabe, trimmed and cut into 1-inch pieces
1 (15-ounce) can cannellini beans, rinsed
¼ cup vegetable broth
½ teaspoon table salt
Lemon wedges

Cook 2 tablespoons oil, garlic, and pepper flakes in Dutch oven over medium heat until garlic is golden brown, 2 to 4 minutes. Stir in broccoli rabe, beans, broth, and salt and cook, stirring occasionally, until broccoli rabe is tender, 4 to 6 minutes. Off heat, stir in remaining 2 tablespoons oil and season with salt and pepper to taste. Serve, passing lemon wedges separately.

White Bean and Mushroom Gratin
Serves 4 to 6

Why This Recipe Works Gratins don't need cheese or dairy to qualify as elevated comfort food. This rendition features creamy white beans, meaty cremini mushrooms, tender carrots, and a crisp, toasty bread layer. We got great flavor from the fond we developed by sautéing mushrooms and aromatics and deglazing the skillet with nutty dry sherry. A combination of flour and starchy bean liquid thickened the sauce. We baked the gratin in a low oven after topping it with seasoned bread cubes. As it baked, the lower portion of the bread merged with the beans, creating a lovely texture, while the upper portion dried out. Then, by flipping on the broiler for a few minutes, we browned and crisped the top. We prefer a round rustic loaf (also known as a boule) with a chewy, open crumb and a sturdy crust for this recipe. Cannellini or navy beans can be used in place of great Northern beans, if desired.

- ½ cup extra-virgin olive oil, divided
- 10 ounces cremini mushrooms, trimmed and sliced ½ inch thick
- ¾ teaspoon table salt
- ½ teaspoon pepper, divided
- 4–5 slices country-style bread, cut into ½-inch cubes (5 cups)
- ¼ cup minced fresh parsley, divided
- 1 cup water
- 1 tablespoon all-purpose flour
- 1 small onion, chopped fine
- 5 garlic cloves, minced
- 1 tablespoon tomato paste
- 1½ teaspoons minced fresh thyme
- ⅓ cup dry sherry
- 2 (15-ounce) cans great Northern beans
- 3 carrots, peeled, halved lengthwise, and cut into ¾-inch pieces

1. Adjust oven rack to middle position and heat oven to 300 degrees. Heat ¼ cup oil in 12-inch ovensafe skillet over medium-high heat until shimmering. Add mushrooms, salt, and ¼ teaspoon pepper and cook, stirring occasionally, until mushrooms are well browned, 8 to 12 minutes.

2. While mushrooms cook, toss bread, 3 tablespoons parsley, remaining ¼ cup oil, and remaining ¼ teaspoon pepper together in bowl. Set aside. Stir water and flour in second bowl until no lumps of flour remain. Set aside.

3. Reduce heat to medium, add onion to skillet, and continue to cook, stirring frequently, until onion is translucent, 4 to 6 minutes. Reduce heat to medium-low; add garlic, tomato paste, and thyme; and cook, stirring constantly, until bottom of skillet is dark brown, 2 to 3 minutes. Add sherry and cook, scraping up any browned bits.

4. Add beans and their liquid, carrots, and flour mixture. Bring to boil over high heat. Off heat, arrange bread mixture over surface in even layer. Transfer skillet to oven and bake for 40 minutes. (Liquid should have consistency of thin gravy.)

5. Leave skillet in oven and turn on broiler. Broil until crumbs are golden brown, 4 to 7 minutes. Remove gratin from oven and let sit for 20 minutes. Sprinkle with remaining 1 tablespoon parsley and serve.

Stir-Fried Tempeh with Orange Sauce

Stir-Fried Tempeh with Orange Sauce
Serves 4 `FAST`

Why This Recipe Works Because it is a firm, dense cake, tempeh is better at holding its shape when cooked than tofu, so we especially like it for stir-fries. And like tofu, it absorbs flavors easily. For this recipe, we had visions of golden-brown tempeh and crisp vegetables in a sweet-and-sour orange sauce. First we perfected the tempeh, searing it in a hot skillet with soy sauce to give it an umami flavor boost and a crisp brown crust. We added red bell pepper for sweetness and crunch. Broccoli florets also stood up well to the quick, high heat. As for the sauce, we knew we needed a sweeter sauce to stand up to the slightly bitter tempeh but were wary of adding sugar. A tangy, full-bodied sauce made with orange juice tamed the tempeh and contributed just enough sweetness. Sliced scallions gave our stir-fry a mild bite. Serve with rice and garnish with toasted sesame seeds.

Sauce

- ¼ cup Shaoxing wine or dry sherry
- ¼ cup water
- 2 tablespoons soy sauce
- 1 tablespoon cornstarch
- 1 tablespoon grated fresh ginger
- 3 garlic cloves, minced
- 1½ teaspoons toasted sesame oil
- ¼ teaspoon grated orange zest, plus ¾ cup juice (2 oranges)

Stir-Fry

- 2 tablespoons vegetable oil, divided
- 12 ounces tempeh, cut into ½-inch pieces
- 2 tablespoons soy sauce
- 1 pound broccoli, florets cut into ½-inch pieces, stalks peeled, halved, and sliced thin
- 1 red bell pepper, stemmed, seeded, and cut into ¼-inch-wide strips
- 6 scallions, sliced thin on bias

1. For the sauce Whisk all ingredients together in bowl.

2. For the stir-fry Heat 1 tablespoon oil in 12-inch non-stick skillet over high heat until just smoking. Add tempeh and soy sauce, and cook, stirring occasionally, until well browned, 4 to 6 minutes; transfer to plate.

3. Return now-empty skillet to high heat, add remaining 1 tablespoon oil, and heat until just smoking. Add broccoli and bell pepper, and cook, stirring occasionally, until vegetables are spotty brown and crisp-tender, about 4 minutes.

4. Stir in browned tempeh. Whisk sauce to recombine, then add to skillet and cook, stirring constantly, until sauce is thickened, about 30 seconds. Off heat, sprinkle with scallions and serve.

Crispy Tempeh with Sambal Sauce

Serves 4 FAST

Why This Recipe Works Sambals are hugely popular throughout Indonesia. These condiment sauces, which can be served cooked or raw, are typically made from chiles; aromatics such as onion, fresh herbs, and spices. Shrimp paste or fish sauce is frequently included, but we found our Anchovy Substitute to be just right for adding a savory, funky umami depth to this vegan version. Here we cooked a mouth-warming but not-too-hot sambal and tossed it with cubes of tempeh,

which we fried until they were golden brown and slightly crispy on the outside but still meaty-textured on the inside. Tempeh is often deep-fried for this preparation, but we found that a shallow fry in a cup of oil gave us similar results. We used a small portion of the remaining oil from frying the tempeh to cook the sambal, which partially tamed the fruity heat of the Fresno chiles and rendered the onion and garlic sweet and melting. Before cooking, we used a food processor to quickly combine all the sambal ingredients while maintaining a pleasingly coarse texture. Then it was just a matter of tossing the crispy tempeh in the sambal sauce and stirring in plenty of fresh basil. Lemon basil is traditional in Indonesia, but Thai and Italian basil are both excellent substitutes. It's worth seeking out kecap manis (Indonesian sweet soy sauce). If you can't find it, you can substitute a combination of 1½ tablespoons dark brown sugar and 1 teaspoon soy sauce. You will need a 12-inch nonstick skillet for this recipe. Serve with rice, if desired.

- 12 ounces Fresno chiles, stemmed, seeded, and chopped coarse
- 1 small onion, chopped coarse
- 5 garlic cloves, peeled
- 2 teaspoons Anchovy Substitute (page 23)
- ½ teaspoon table salt
- 1 cup vegetable oil
- 1 pound tempeh, cut into ½-inch pieces
- ½ cup water
- 2 tablespoons kecap manis
- 1½ cups fresh Thai or Italian basil leaves

1. Process chiles, onion, garlic, anchovy substitute, and salt in food processor until finely chopped, about 30 seconds, scraping down sides of bowl as needed; transfer to bowl.

2. Adjust oven rack to middle position and heat oven to 200 degrees. Set wire rack in rimmed baking sheet and line rack with triple layer of paper towels. Heat oil in nonstick skillet over medium-high heat to 375 degrees. Carefully add half of tempeh to hot oil and increase heat to high. Cook, turning as needed, until golden brown, 3 to 5 minutes. Adjust burner, if necessary, to maintain oil temperature between 350 and 375 degrees. Off heat, transfer tempeh to prepared rack and keep warm in oven. Return oil to 375 degrees over medium-high heat and repeat with remaining tempeh; transfer to rack.

3. Carefully pour off all but 2 tablespoons oil from skillet. Add chile mixture to oil left in skillet and cook over medium-high heat, tossing slowly but constantly, until darkened in color and completely dry, 7 to 10 minutes. Off heat, stir in water and kecap manis until combined. Add tempeh and basil and toss until well coated. Serve.

Pan-Seared Tempeh Steaks with Chimichurri Sauce

Serves 4

Why This Recipe Works Since tempeh has such a concentration of protein and is so good at absorbing flavor, we went all in and prepared it as a "meaty" steak with a classic serving condiment. Marinating the tempeh in a seasoned vinegar-and-water base infused it with flavor. Patting the marinated tempeh dry and pan-searing it created a delectably crisp edge and made the interior texture more cohesive. The tempeh's earthy flavor is well balanced by the bright herb sauce. Chimichurri sauce is a traditional steak sauce that combines parsley, wine vinegar, oil, lots of garlic, oregano, and a good dose of red pepper flakes. It paired perfectly with our tempeh, lending bright flavor and richness to the impressive seared steaks. Our variation uses chermoula, which employs cilantro, lemon, and lots of warm spices.

  5 tablespoons red wine vinegar, divided
  ¼ cup water
  4 garlic cloves, minced, divided
  1½ teaspoons dried oregano, divided
  ½ teaspoon red pepper flakes, divided
  1 pound tempeh, cut into 3½-inch-long by ⅜-inch-thick slabs
  1 cup fresh parsley leaves
  ½ cup extra-virgin olive oil, divided
  ½ teaspoon table salt

1. Combine ¼ cup vinegar, water, half of garlic, 1 teaspoon oregano, and ¼ teaspoon pepper flakes in 1-gallon zipper-lock bag. Add tempeh, press out air, seal, and toss to coat. Refrigerate tempeh for at least 1 hour or up to 24 hours, flipping bag occasionally.

2. Pulse parsley, ¼ cup oil, salt, remaining 1 tablespoon vinegar, remaining garlic, remaining ½ teaspoon oregano, and remaining ¼ teaspoon pepper flakes in food processor until coarsely chopped, about 10 pulses, scraping down sides of bowl as needed. Transfer to bowl and season with salt and pepper to taste.

3. Remove tempeh from marinade and pat dry with paper towels. Heat 2 tablespoons oil in 12-inch nonstick skillet over medium heat until shimmering. Add 4 pieces tempeh and cook until golden brown on first side, 2 to 4 minutes.

4. Flip tempeh, reduce heat to medium-low, and continue to cook until golden brown on second side, 2 to 4 minutes; transfer to platter. Wipe out skillet with paper towels and repeat with remaining 2 tablespoons oil and remaining tempeh. Serve with parsley sauce.

VARIATION
Pan-Seared Tempeh Steaks with Chermoula Sauce
Omit oregano. Substitute lemon juice for red wine vinegar, ¼ teaspoon cayenne pepper for red pepper flakes, and cilantro for parsley. Add ½ teaspoon ground cumin and ½ teaspoon paprika to tempeh marinade. Add ½ teaspoon ground cumin and ½ teaspoon paprika to sauce.

Indian Curried Tempeh with Cauliflower and Peas

Serves 4 to 6

Why This Recipe Works With its deep, intense flavors, Indian curry powder makes an excellent pairing for sturdy tempeh. To create truly complex curry flavor, we started by toasting curry powder and garam masala in a dry skillet. A serrano chile delivered the right combination of flavor and spice. Blooming glutamate-rich tomato paste with our seasonings added a savory umami element to our curry. Canned diced tomatoes pulsed in a food processor formed the base of the sauce. Simmering the tempeh in the curry for 15 minutes helped to infuse it with the curry's flavor. To round out our curry with vegetables, we added cauliflower, simmering it in the sauce until tender, and convenient frozen peas. Finishing our tempeh curry with a dash of coconut milk imparted a little extra richness. To make this sauce spicier, use the higher amount of chiles and/or add the seeds from the chile. We prefer our homemade Garam Masala (page 330), but you may use store-bought. Serve over rice.

  2 tablespoons curry powder
  1½ teaspoons garam masala
  1 (14.5-ounce) can diced tomatoes
  ¼ cup vegetable oil, divided
  2 onions, chopped fine
  3 garlic cloves, minced
  1 tablespoon grated fresh ginger
  1–1½ serrano chiles, stemmed, seeded, and minced
  1 tablespoon tomato paste
  ½ head cauliflower (1 pound), cored and cut into 1-inch florets
  8 ounces tempeh, cut into 1-inch pieces
  1¼ cups water
  1 teaspoon table salt
  1 cup frozen peas
  ¼ cup canned coconut milk
  2 tablespoons minced fresh cilantro

Pan-Seared Tempeh Steaks with
Chimichurri Sauce

1. Toast curry powder and garam masala in 10-inch skillet over medium-high heat, stirring constantly, until spices darken slightly and become fragrant, about 1 minute. Transfer to bowl. Pulse tomatoes and their juice in food processor until coarsely chopped, 3 to 4 pulses.

2. Heat 3 tablespoons oil in Dutch oven over medium-high heat until shimmering. Add onions and cook, stirring occasionally, until caramelized, about 10 minutes.

3. Reduce heat to medium. Clear center of pot and add remaining 1 tablespoon oil, garlic, ginger, serrano, toasted spices, and tomato paste. Cook, mashing mixture into pot, until fragrant, about 1 minute. Add cauliflower and tempeh and cook, stirring constantly, until well coated with spices.

4. Stir in processed tomatoes, water, and salt, scraping up any browned bits. Increase heat to medium-high and bring to simmer. Cover, reduce heat to medium, and cook, stirring occasionally, until vegetables are tender, 10 to 15 minutes. Stir in peas and coconut milk and cook until heated through, about 2 minutes. Off heat, season with salt to taste and sprinkle with cilantro. Serve.

Sweet Chili Glazed Tofu

Serves 4 to 6

Why This Recipe Works Crispy tofu fingers tossed with a bold sweet-and-spicy chili glaze can be served alongside your choice of rice or with vegetables ranging from steamed broccoli to Stir-Fried Asparagus with Shiitake Mushrooms (page 189). We wanted the coating for our tofu to be light, crisp, and nicely browned; to achieve this, we found that a combination of ¾ cup cornstarch and ¼ cup cornmeal was just right. Cutting our tofu into fingers gave us a greater coating-to-tofu ratio, which provided the right balance of crispy crust to creamy interior along with plenty of surface area for the clingy glaze to adhere to. Soft tofu gave us a lovely textural contrast between the crisp outside and the silky interior. To keep the light coating from getting greasy, we swapped the traditional skillet for nonstick so we could use less oil. Firm or extra-firm tofu will also work, but the finished dish will taste drier. To make the dish spicier, use the higher amount of Asian chili-garlic sauce.

Tofu
28 ounces soft tofu, cut into 3-inch-long by ½-inch-thick fingers
½ teaspoon table salt
¼ teaspoon pepper
¾ cup cornstarch
¼ cup cornmeal
¼ cup vegetable oil, divided

Glaze
½ cup water
½ cup rice vinegar
⅓ cup sugar
4 garlic cloves, minced
2–3 teaspoons Asian chili-garlic sauce
2 teaspoons cornstarch
¼ cup minced fresh cilantro

1. For the tofu Spread tofu over paper towel–lined baking sheet, let drain for 20 minutes, then gently press dry with paper towels and sprinkle with salt and pepper.

2. Adjust oven rack to middle position, place paper towel–lined plate on rack, and heat oven to 200 degrees. Combine cornstarch and cornmeal in shallow dish. Working with several tofu pieces at a time, coat thoroughly with cornstarch mixture, pressing gently to adhere; transfer to wire rack set in baking sheet.

3. Heat 2 tablespoons oil in 12-inch nonstick skillet over medium-high heat until shimmering. Cook half of tofu until crisp and lightly golden on all sides, 10 to 12 minutes. Lift tofu from oil, letting excess oil drip back into skillet, then transfer to plate in oven. Repeat with remaining 2 tablespoons oil and remaining tofu.

4. For the glaze Whisk water, vinegar, sugar, garlic, chili-garlic sauce, and cornstarch together in bowl. Wipe out now-empty skillet with paper towels, add glaze, and simmer over medium heat until syrupy and reduced to 1¼ cups, 2 to 3 minutes.

5. Off heat, stir in cilantro. Add tofu and turn to coat with glaze. Season with salt to taste, and serve.

DRYING TOFU

Spread tofu pieces evenly over rimmed baking sheet lined with paper towels, and let sit for 20 minutes to drain. Gently press tofu dry with paper towels.

Grilled Soy-Ginger Glazed Tofu

Grilled Soy-Ginger Glazed Tofu
Serves 4 to 6

Why This Recipe Works Tofu has a delicate, silky texture that contrasts beautifully with the crisp, browned crust that results from a quick stint on the grill, and its mild flavor gets a boost from the gingery, garlicky flavors of this glaze. First we made the glaze by simmering soy sauce, sugar, mirin, fresh ginger, garlic, and chili-garlic sauce. Some cornstarch helped to thicken the sauce so it would cling to the tofu. We found that the keys to successfully grilled tofu were cutting it to the right shape and handling it carefully on the grill. We tried grilling tofu that had been cut into planks, strips, and cubes, and found that tofu cut lengthwise into 1-inch-thick planks fared best. This shape maximized surface contact, and the larger pieces were easier to turn. Using two spatulas provided the best leverage for flipping the delicate tofu. You can use either firm or extra-firm tofu in this recipe. Dry sherry or white wine can be substituted for the mirin. Be sure to handle the tofu gently on the grill to prevent it from breaking apart.

Glaze
- ⅓ cup soy sauce
- ⅓ cup water
- ⅓ cup sugar
- ¼ cup mirin
- 1 tablespoon grated fresh ginger
- 2 garlic cloves, minced
- 2 teaspoons cornstarch
- 1 teaspoon Asian chili-garlic sauce

Tofu
- 28 ounces firm tofu, sliced lengthwise into 1-inch-thick planks
- 2 tablespoons vegetable oil
- ½ teaspoon table salt
- ¼ teaspoon pepper
- ¼ cup minced fresh cilantro

1. For the glaze Simmer soy sauce, water, sugar, mirin, ginger, garlic, cornstarch, and chili-garlic sauce in small saucepan over medium-high heat until thickened and reduced to ¾ cup, 5 to 7 minutes; transfer to bowl.

2. For the tofu Spread tofu over paper towel–lined baking sheet, let drain for 20 minutes, then gently press dry with paper towels. Brush tofu with oil and sprinkle with salt and pepper.

3A. For a charcoal grill Open bottom vent completely. Light large chimney starter filled with charcoal briquettes (6 quarts). When top coals are partially covered with ash, pour two-thirds evenly over half of grill, then pour remaining coals over other half of grill. Set cooking grate in place, cover, and open lid vent completely. Heat grill until hot, about 5 minutes.

3B. For a gas grill Turn all burners to high, cover, and heat grill until hot, about 15 minutes. Leave all burners on high.

4. Clean and oil cooking grate. Gently place tofu on grill, perpendicular to grate bars (on hotter part of grill if using charcoal). Cook (covered if using gas) until lightly browned on both sides, 6 to 10 minutes, gently flipping tofu halfway through cooking using 2 spatulas.

5. Turn all burners to medium if using gas, or slide tofu to cooler part of grill if using charcoal. Brush tofu with ¼ cup glaze and cook until well browned, 1 to 2 minutes. Flip tofu, brush with ¼ cup glaze, and cook until well browned, 1 to 2 minutes. Transfer tofu to platter, brush with remaining ¼ cup glaze, and sprinkle with cilantro. Serve.

CUTTING TOFU

To cut into planks:
Slice block of tofu crosswise into planks of desired width.

To cut into fingers:
Cut tofu crosswise into planks, then slice each plank into fingers of desired size.

To cut into cubes:
Cut tofu into fingers, then cut each finger into cubes of desired size.

Caramel Tofu
Serves 4

Why This Recipe Works This satisfying, surprisingly savory Vietnamese recipe will have even the most reluctant tofu skeptic coming back for more. We tossed cubes of tofu with cornstarch, lightly pan-fried them, and served them with a traditional salty-sweet caramel sauce. To achieve the tricky balance of sweet and savory in our sauce, we kept the caramel base simple with water and sugar and then added a healthy dose of garlic, fish sauce substitute, and pepper. To give the sauce more depth, we added a thinly sliced onion to caramelize and soften in the sauce. Tossing the tofu with cornstarch and pan-frying it gave it an appealingly crisp, browned exterior; we then drizzled it with the caramel sauce and topped it all with some chopped peanuts for textural contrast and a sprinkling of cilantro and scallions for a fresh finish. You can use either firm or extra-firm tofu in this recipe. The caramel can go from amber-colored to burnt quickly after the garlic is added, so it's important to have the measured water at the ready to stop the caramelization. Serve over rice.

- 21 ounces firm tofu, cut into ¾-inch cubes
- 1¼ teaspoons pepper, divided
- ½ teaspoon table salt
- 1¾ cups water, divided
- ⅓ cup sugar
- 6 tablespoons vegetable oil, divided
- 5 garlic cloves, minced
- 1 onion, halved and sliced thin
- 3 tablespoons Fish Sauce Substitute (page 22)
- 2 teaspoons plus ½ cup cornstarch, divided
- ½ cup fresh cilantro leaves
- ¼ cup dry-roasted peanuts, chopped
- 3 scallions, green parts only, sliced thin on bias

1. Spread tofu over paper towel–lined baking sheet, let drain for 20 minutes, then gently press dry with paper towels and sprinkle with ¼ teaspoon pepper and salt.

2. Meanwhile, pour ¼ cup water into medium saucepan, then sprinkle sugar evenly over top. Cook over medium heat, gently swirling pan occasionally (do not stir), until sugar melts and mixture turns color of maple syrup, 7 to 10 minutes.

3. Stir in 3 tablespoons oil and garlic and cook until fragrant, about 30 seconds. Off heat, slowly whisk in remaining 1½ cups water (sauce will sizzle). Stir in onion, fish sauce substitute, 2 teaspoons cornstarch, and remaining 1 teaspoon pepper. Return pan to medium-low heat and simmer vigorously until onion is softened and sauce has thickened, 10 to 15 minutes. Remove from heat and cover to keep warm.

4. Spread remaining ½ cup cornstarch in shallow dish. Working with several tofu pieces at a time, coat thoroughly with cornstarch, pressing gently to adhere; transfer to plate.

5. Heat remaining 3 tablespoons oil in 12-inch nonstick skillet over high heat until just smoking. Add tofu and cook, turning as needed, until all sides are crisp and well browned, 10 to 15 minutes; transfer to paper towel–lined plate to drain. Transfer tofu to platter, drizzle with sauce, and sprinkle with cilantro, peanuts, and scallions. Serve.

NOTES FROM THE TEST KITCHEN

CHOOSING THE RIGHT TOFU

Tofu is available in a variety of textures: extra-firm, firm, medium, soft, and silken. Reaching for the right variety will be key to the success of any given recipe. In general, firmer varieties hold their shape when cooking, while softer varieties do not, so it follows that each type of tofu is best when used in specific ways. Regardless of type, tofu is highly perishable and is best when it is fresh. To store an opened package, cover the tofu with water and refrigerate in a covered container, changing the water daily. Any hint of sourness means the tofu is past its prime.

Extra-Firm and Firm Tofu We prefer extra-firm or firm tofu for stir-fries and noodle dishes, as they hold their shape in high-heat cooking applications and when tossed with pasta. These two varieties of tofu are also great marinated (they absorb marinade better compared with softer varieties) or tossed raw into salads.

Medium and Soft Tofu Medium and soft tofu boast a creamy, custardy texture; we love to pan-fry these kinds of tofu, often coated with cornstarch, to achieve a crisp exterior, which makes a nice textural contrast to the silky interior. Soft tofu is also great scrambled like eggs.

Silken Tofu Silken tofu has a very soft, ultracreamy texture and is often used as a base for smoothies and dips, in desserts such as puddings, or as an egg replacement in vegan baked goods.

Chilled Marinated Tofu
Serves 4 to 6

Why This Recipe Works Marinated raw tofu is served throughout Japan during the hot summer months as a cool and refreshing appetizer or simply as a snack. In the best renditions, a flavorful marinade and a few choice garnishes amplify the tofu's delicate flavor. The marinade for this dish is typically a soy sauce–enhanced dashi, the ubiquitous Japanese broth prepared from kombu seaweed and bonito (skipjack tuna) flakes. We replaced the bonito with a glutamate-rich combination of wakame seaweed, fish sauce substitute, mirin, and sugar. This mixture produced a well-rounded marinade: sweet, salty, and robust—almost fishy in its intensity. A splash of rice wine vinegar, added off the heat after the broth had steeped, provided a bit of balance. To garnish our chilled tofu, we liked a sprinkle of crumbled nori, sliced scallions, and a drizzle of toasted sesame oil. A sprinkling of shichimi togarashi (a common Japanese spice mix) also tastes great here. For an accurate measurement of boiling water, bring a full kettle of water to a boil and then measure out the desired amount.

14 ounces firm tofu, halved lengthwise, then cut into ½-inch-thick squares
¼ teaspoon table salt
⅛ teaspoon pepper
2 cups boiling water
¼ cup Fish Sauce Substitute (page 22)
¼ cup mirin
4 teaspoons sugar
¼ ounce wakame seaweed
¼ ounce kombu seaweed
4 teaspoons rice vinegar
2 sheets toasted nori seaweed, crumbled
2 scallions, sliced thin on bias
Toasted sesame oil
Shichimi Togarashi (recipe follows)

1. Spread tofu over paper towel–lined baking sheet, let drain for 20 minutes, then gently press dry with paper towels and sprinkle with salt and pepper.

2. Meanwhile, combine boiling water, fish sauce substitute, mirin, sugar, wakame, and kombu in bowl. Cover and let sit for 15 minutes. Strain liquid through fine-mesh strainer, discarding solids, then return broth to now-empty bowl.

3. Add tofu and vinegar, cover, and refrigerate until cool, at least 2 hours or up to 2 days. To serve, use slotted spoon to transfer tofu to platter, top with nori and scallions, and drizzle with sesame oil and sprinkle with shichimi togarashi to taste.

Shichimi Togarashi

Makes about ¼ cup

This intriguing spice is savory from sesame seeds, spicy from cayenne, and aromatic from ginger and garlic. We microwaved the fragrant orange zest to dry it out before adding it to the blend.

1½   teaspoons grated orange zest
4   teaspoons sesame seeds, toasted
1   tablespoon paprika
2   teaspoons pepper
½   teaspoon garlic powder
½   teaspoon ground ginger
¼   teaspoon cayenne pepper

Microwave orange zest in small bowl, stirring occasionally, until dry and no longer clumping together, about 2 minutes. Stir in sesame seeds, paprika, pepper, garlic powder, ginger, and cayenne. (Shichimi togarashi can be stored in airtight container for up to 1 week.)

Chilled Marinated Tofu

Thai-Style Tofu and Basil Lettuce Cups

Serves 4

Thai-Style Tofu and
Basil Lettuce Cups

Why This Recipe Works We drew inspiration from the sweet, savory, and spicy flavors of Thai cuisine to develop a stir-fried tofu filling to serve in crisp, cool lettuce cups. The Thai method of stir-frying involves sautéing aromatics slowly over moderate heat. The aromatics infuse the oil as they cook, which gives the finished dish layers of complexity, so we thought this technique would be perfect for packing mild tofu with flavor. To give the tofu lots of surface area and to make it a cohesive filling, we pulsed it in a food processor to give it a texture akin to ground meat. We then combined garlic, basil, and Thai chiles, reserving a portion and adding to it fish sauce substitute, vegan oyster sauce, sugar, and vinegar to make a savory stir-fry sauce. Next, we added oil along with the remaining aromatics, sliced shallot, and tofu to a cold skillet and cooked everything until the tofu and shallots turned golden brown. At the end, we stirred in the sauce and more basil leaves until wilted and then added some crunchy peanuts. You can use either firm or extra-firm tofu. If fresh Thai chiles are unavailable, substitute two serranos or one jalapeño. For a milder dish, remove the seeds and ribs from the chiles.

14 ounces extra-firm tofu, cut into 2-inch pieces
¼ teaspoon table salt
⅛ teaspoon pepper
2 cups fresh basil leaves, divided
3 garlic cloves, peeled
6 green or red Thai chiles, stemmed
2 tablespoons Fish Sauce Substitute (see page 22), plus extra as needed
1 tablespoon mushroom oyster sauce
1 tablespoon sugar
1 teaspoon distilled white vinegar, plus extra as needed
3 shallots, halved and sliced thin
2 tablespoons vegetable oil
¼ cup dry-roasted peanuts, chopped
2 heads Bibb lettuce (1 pound), leaves separated
   Red pepper flakes

1. Spread tofu over paper towel–lined baking sheet and let drain for 20 minutes. Gently press dry with paper towels and sprinkle with salt and pepper.

2. Meanwhile, process 1 cup basil, garlic, and chiles in food processor until finely chopped, 6 to 10 pulses, scraping down sides of bowl as needed. Transfer 1 tablespoon basil mixture to small bowl and stir in fish sauce substitute, mushroom oyster sauce, sugar, and vinegar. Transfer remaining basil mixture to 12-inch nonstick skillet.

3. Pulse tofu in now-empty food processor until coarsely chopped, 3 to 4 pulses. Line baking sheet with clean paper towels. Spread processed tofu over prepared baking sheet and press gently with paper towels to dry.

4. Stir dried tofu, shallots, and oil into skillet with basil mixture and cook over medium heat, stirring occasionally, until tofu and shallots are browned, 10 to 15 minutes. (Mixture should start to sizzle after about 1½ minutes; adjust heat as needed.)

5. Add reserved basil mixture and continue to cook, stirring constantly, until well coated, about 1 minute. Stir in remaining 1 cup basil and cook, stirring constantly, until wilted, 30 to 60 seconds. Off heat, stir in peanuts. Transfer mixture to platter and serve with lettuce leaves, pepper flakes, extra fish sauce substitute, and extra vinegar.

Stir-Fried Tofu, Shiitakes, and Green Beans
Serves 4

Why This Recipe Works This dish is a great way to get started with stir-frying tofu because of its ease of preparation and its crowd-pleasing Chinese flavors. We sliced and drained extra-firm tofu and then coated it simply with cornstarch, which developed a slightly crunchy outer sheath as it browned in the skillet. After transferring the tofu to a bowl, we added sturdy green beans and meaty shiitake mushrooms to the skillet, covering them until they softened and then uncovering them to brown them. Don't overstir the tofu or vegetables while they're browning, or else you won't get that desired sear. Although we often stir-fry vegetables in batches, here we were able to stir-fry them at the same time; the moisture released from the mushrooms nicely steamed the green beans. For a classic brown sauce, we combined soy sauce, sesame oil, rice vinegar, and a touch of sugar and pepper flakes, and we thickened it with cornstarch. Serve over rice.

Sauce
¾ cup vegetable broth
3 tablespoons soy sauce
2 tablespoons rice vinegar
1 tablespoon packed brown sugar
2 teaspoons cornstarch
1 teaspoon toasted sesame oil
⅛ teaspoon red pepper flakes

Stir-Fry
14 ounces extra-firm tofu, cut into ¾-inch pieces
⅓ cup cornstarch
3 tablespoons vegetable oil, divided
2 scallions, white and green parts separated and sliced thin on bias
3 garlic cloves, minced
1 tablespoon grated fresh ginger
12 ounces green beans, trimmed and cut on bias into 1-inch lengths
12 ounces shiitake mushrooms, stemmed and quartered
1 tablespoon toasted sesame seeds (optional)

1. For the sauce Whisk all ingredients together in bowl.

2. For the stir-fry Spread tofu on paper towel–lined baking sheet and let drain for 20 minutes. Gently pat dry with paper towels. Toss drained tofu with cornstarch in bowl, then transfer to fine-mesh strainer and shake gently to remove excess cornstarch.

Stir-Fried Tofu, Shiitakes, and Green Beans

Thai Red Curry with Sweet Potatoes and Tofu
Serves 4 to 6

Why This Recipe Works For a simplified and streamlined skillet Thai curry, we used store-bought red curry paste, sautéing it in a little oil and adding coconut milk, fish sauce substitute, and brown sugar for a deep flavor without a lot of time or effort. Browning the drained tofu pieces before adding them to the simmering base paid off in texture and flavor. Snow peas and red pepper strips provided color and flavor as well as a crispness that complemented the yielding texture of the tofu. To make the dish spicier, use the higher amount of curry paste. Serve this satisfying curry on its own or with rice.

14 ounces extra-firm tofu, cut into ¾-inch pieces
¼ teaspoon table salt
⅛ teaspoon pepper
2 tablespoons vegetable oil, divided
1-1½ tablespoons red curry paste
1 (14-ounce) can coconut milk
2 tablespoons Fish Sauce Substitute (page 22)
4 teaspoons packed light brown sugar
¼ cup water
1½ pounds sweet potatoes, peeled and cut into ¾-inch pieces
1 red bell pepper, stemmed, seeded, and cut into ¼-inch-wide strips
½ pound snow peas, strings removed
½ cup coarsely chopped fresh basil leaves
1 tablespoon fresh lime juice

3. Combine 1 teaspoon oil, scallion whites, garlic, and ginger in bowl. Heat 2 tablespoons oil in 12-inch nonstick skillet over high heat until shimmering. Add tofu and cook, turning as needed, until crisp and well browned on all sides, 12 to 15 minutes; transfer to paper towel–lined plate to drain.

4. Add remaining 2 teaspoons oil to now-empty skillet and heat over medium-high heat until shimmering. Add green beans and mushrooms, cover, and cook until mushrooms release their liquid and green beans are bright green and beginning to soften, 4 to 5 minutes. Uncover and continue to cook until vegetables are spotty brown, about 3 minutes.

5. Push vegetables to sides of skillet. Add garlic mixture to center and cook, mashing mixture into pan, until fragrant, about 30 seconds. Stir garlic mixture into vegetables. Add browned tofu and stir to combine. Whisk sauce to recombine, then add to skillet and cook, stirring constantly, until sauce is thickened, about 30 seconds. Transfer to platter; sprinkle with scallion greens and sesame seeds, if using; and serve.

1. Spread tofu on paper towel–lined baking sheet and let drain for 20 minutes. Gently pat dry with paper towels and sprinkle with salt and pepper.

2. Heat 1 tablespoon oil in 12-inch nonstick skillet over medium-high heat until shimmering. Add tofu in single layer and cook until golden brown on 1 side, about 2 minutes. Gently stir tofu and cook until second side is golden brown, about 2 minutes. Transfer to plate and set aside.

3. Add remaining 1 tablespoon oil to skillet and return to medium heat until shimmering. Add curry paste and cook, stirring constantly, until fragrant, about 1 minute. Whisk in coconut milk, fish sauce substitute, sugar, and water. Add sweet potatoes and tofu; bring to simmer. Turn heat to low, cover, and cook until potatoes are tender, 15 to 20 minutes.

4. Add bell pepper and snow peas, increase heat to medium-low, and continue to cook, covered, until peas are crisp-tender, about 4 minutes. Off heat, stir in basil and lime juice. Season with salt to taste. Serve immediately.

CHAPTER 9
ELECTRIC PRESSURE-COOKER AND SLOW-COOKER DISHES

■ FAST (45 minutes or less total time)
Photos: Greek Chickpeas with Coriander and Sage; Braised Spring Vegetables; Vegetable and Chickpea Stew

Creamy Carrot Soup with Warm Spices

Serves 6 `FAST` `PRESSURE COOKER`

Why This Recipe Works Creamy, satiny-smooth vegetable soups made without cream are just as achievable in the pressure cooker as they are on the stovetop. Sturdy carrots and onions plus a few delicately balanced aromatics cooked for a mere 3 minutes under pressure to produce this luxurious yet simple soup. In many carrot soup recipes, additional vegetables are used, but tasters felt that this muted the clean brightness of the carrots, so we kept such extras to a minimum. Taking a flavor cue from the eastern Mediterranean, we added fresh ginger plus ground coriander, fennel, and cinnamon. A touch of baking soda helped break down the carrots, and after a quick spin in the blender we had a silken soup you'd never guess was cream-free. To finish, we topped individual portions with a drizzle of pomegranate molasses (to underscore the natural sweetness of the carrots), a small dollop of yogurt, toasted hazelnuts, and some fresh herbs. If you can't find pomegranate molasses, you can make your own (page 351).

- 2 tablespoons extra-virgin olive oil
- 2 onions, chopped
- 1 teaspoon table salt
- 1 tablespoon grated fresh ginger
- 1 tablespoon ground coriander
- 1 tablespoon ground fennel
- 1 teaspoon ground cinnamon
- 4 cups vegetable broth
- 2 cups water
- 2 pounds carrots, peeled and cut into 2-inch pieces
- ½ teaspoon baking soda
- 2 tablespoons pomegranate molasses
- ½ cup plain plant-based Greek yogurt or dairy Greek yogurt
- ½ cup hazelnuts, toasted, skinned, and chopped
- ½ cup chopped fresh cilantro or mint

1. Using highest sauté or browning function, heat oil in electric pressure cooker until shimmering. Add onions and salt and cook until onions are softened, about 5 minutes. Stir in ginger, coriander, fennel, and cinnamon and cook until fragrant, about 30 seconds. Stir in broth, water, carrots, and baking soda.

2. Lock lid in place and close pressure release valve. Select high pressure cook function and cook for 3 minutes. Turn off pressure cooker and quick-release pressure. Carefully remove lid, allowing steam to escape away from you.

3. Working in batches, process soup in blender until smooth, 1 to 2 minutes. Return processed soup to pressure cooker and bring to simmer using highest sauté or browning function. Season with salt and pepper to taste. Drizzle individual portions with pomegranate molasses and top with yogurt, hazelnuts, and cilantro before serving.

NOTES FROM THE TEST KITCHEN

The recipes in this chapter were developed to work in an electric pressure cooker—either a multicooker or a dedicated pressure cooker. They will not work with a stovetop pressure cooker. We recommend the **Instant Pot Duo Evo Plus 9-in-1 Electric Pressure Cooker, 8-QT**. It has a clear, intuitive digital interface, a lid that seals automatically, a pressure-release switch, and silicone pot handles. It sears and sautés evenly, and its stainless-steel pot is stovetop-friendly.

NOTES FROM THE TEST KITCHEN

The recipes in this chapter were developed to work in a traditional slow cooker; they will not work in a multicooker. Most of these recipes were designed for a 4- to 7-quart cooker. We recommend the **KITCHENAID 6-Quart Slow-Cooker with Solid Glass Lid**. Its control panel is simple to set and monitor. Its thick stoneware crock, insulated housing, and built-in thermal sensor are all well designed.

Fire-Roasted Tomato and Fennel Soup

Serves 6 SLOW COOKER

Cooking time 6 to 8 hours on low or 4 to 6 hours on high

Why This Recipe Works Fire roasting gives tomatoes even more umami power and depth of flavor. Canned fire-roasted tomatoes are a great pantry product and give this soup smoky undertones and a subtle, appealing charred quality. We also turned to fennel for its fresh, subtle anise flavor. Microwaving the fennel before adding it to the slow cooker ensured that it came out perfectly cooked. To reinforce the soup's smokiness, we added a little smoked paprika for an extra kick. Pureeing only a portion of the soup helped to thicken the base but left the finished soup appealingly chunky and rustic. Adding brown sugar at the end of cooking helped balance the acidity of the tomatoes, and tarragon brightened the soup with fresh herbal notes. A small drizzle of olive oil before serving added richness. You will need a 4- to 7-quart slow cooker for this recipe.

- 2 fennel bulbs, stalks discarded, bulbs halved, cored, and cut into ½-inch pieces
- 2 tablespoons plus 1 teaspoon extra-virgin olive oil, divided
- 4 garlic cloves
- 1 tablespoon tomato paste
- 2 teaspoons smoked paprika
- 2 (28-ounce) cans diced fire-roasted tomatoes
- 2 cups vegetable broth
- ¼ teaspoon table salt
- 2 tablespoons minced fresh tarragon
- 2 tablespoons packed brown sugar

1. Microwave fennel, 1 teaspoon oil, garlic, tomato paste, and paprika in bowl, stirring occasionally, until fennel is softened, about 5 minutes; transfer to slow cooker. Stir in tomatoes and their juice, broth, and salt. Cover and cook until fennel is tender, 6 to 8 hours on low or 4 to 6 hours on high.

2. Process 4 cups soup in blender until smooth, about 1 minute; return to slow cooker. Stir in tarragon and sugar and season with salt and pepper to taste. Drizzle each portion with 1 teaspoon oil before serving.

Creamy Cauliflower and Potato Soup

Creamy Cauliflower and Potato Soup

Serves 6 SLOW COOKER

Cooking time 6 to 8 hours on low or 4 to 6 hours on high

Why This Recipe Works Both cauliflower and potatoes break down as they cook for a long time to bring creamy qualities to soup, so we thought a slow cooker soup using both vegetables would be ultracreamy—and we were right. The long slow-cooking time coaxed out the sweet, nutty flavor and creamy texture of the cauliflower, and the Yukon Gold potatoes delivered a buttery taste and helped thicken the soup when pureed along with the cauliflower. Some plant-based creamer provided even more richness while still letting the pure vegetable flavors shine through. A pinch of nutmeg added depth and a pinch of cayenne lent warmth. Finally, for a hearty and flavorful finishing touch, we sautéed some reserved cauliflower florets until tender and browned. You will need a 4- to 7-quart slow cooker for this recipe.

1 onion, chopped fine

2 garlic cloves, minced

1 teaspoon vegetable oil

Pinch ground nutmeg

Pinch cayenne pepper

6 cups vegetable broth, plus extra as needed

1 large head cauliflower (3 pounds), cored and cut into 1-inch florets, divided

1 pound Yukon Gold potatoes, peeled and cut into ½-inch pieces

½ teaspoon table salt

2 tablespoons refined coconut oil or unsalted butter

½ teaspoon sherry vinegar

½ cup plant-based creamer or dairy half-and-half

2 tablespoons minced fresh chives

1. Microwave onion, garlic, oil, nutmeg, and cayenne in bowl, stirring occasionally, until onion is softened, about 5 minutes; transfer to slow cooker. Stir in broth, all but 2 cups cauliflower, potatoes, and salt. Cover and cook until vegetables are tender, 6 to 8 hours on low or 4 to 6 hours on high.

2. Meanwhile, melt oil in 12-inch skillet over medium heat. Add remaining 2 cups cauliflower and cook, stirring frequently, until florets are golden brown and tender, 8 to 10 minutes. Off heat, stir in vinegar and season with salt and pepper to taste.

3. Working in batches, process soup in blender until smooth, 1 to 2 minutes. Return soup to slow cooker, stir in creamer, and let sit until heated through, about 5 minutes. (Adjust soup consistency with extra hot broth as needed.) Season with salt and pepper to taste. Top individual portions with browned cauliflower mixture and sprinkle with chives before serving.

Wild Rice Soup with Coconut and Lime

Serves 6   PRESSURE COOKER

Why This Recipe Works Wild rice can be tricky and time-consuming to cook, even in a soup, so we took advantage of the pressure cooker to make it foolproof. Our Thai-inspired soup features tender wild rice and mushrooms in a vegetable broth enriched with coconut milk and brightened with lemongrass and cilantro. Initially we tried putting all of the broth ingredients in the pressure cooker along with the rice, but the flavor of the dish was dull. To make sure our soup turned out bright, we reserved half of the coconut milk to stir in after releasing the pressure, along with red curry paste and

Wild Rice Soup with Coconut and Lime

lime juice. We stirred the mushrooms in along with the reserved coconut milk mixture, so that their flavor stayed distinct and didn't turn muddy. We preferred a combination of mushrooms, but 12 ounces of any one type will work. Do not use quick-cooking or presteamed wild rice in this recipe. Not all Thai curry pastes are vegan, so read the labels carefully.

2 tablespoons vegetable oil

2 onions, chopped fine

6 garlic cloves, minced

2 tablespoons grated fresh ginger

4 cups vegetable broth

2 (14-ounce) cans coconut milk, divided

1 cup wild rice, picked over and rinsed

2 lemongrass stalks, trimmed to bottom 6 inches and smashed with back of knife

3 tablespoons Fish Sauce Substitute (page 22), divided, plus extra for seasoning

4 sprigs fresh cilantro, plus leaves for serving

3 tablespoons lime juice (2 limes), plus lime wedges for serving

1 tablespoon sugar

1 tablespoon Thai red curry paste
12 ounces cremini, shiitake, or white mushrooms, trimmed and sliced thin
Salt and pepper
2 scallions, sliced thin

1. Using highest sauté or browning function, heat oil in electric pressure cooker until shimmering. Add onions and cook until softened, 3 to 5 minutes. Stir in garlic and ginger and cook until fragrant, about 30 seconds. Stir in broth, 1 can coconut milk, rice, lemongrass, 1 tablespoon fish sauce substitute, and cilantro sprigs.

2. Lock lid in place and close pressure release valve. Select high pressure cook function and cook for 23 minutes. Turn off pressure cooker and quick-release pressure. Carefully remove lid, allowing steam to escape away from you.

3. Discard lemongrass and cilantro sprigs. Whisk remaining 1 can coconut milk, remaining 2 tablespoons fish sauce substitute, lime juice, sugar, and curry paste together in bowl. Stir coconut milk mixture and mushrooms into soup and cook using highest sauté or browning function until mushrooms are just tender, 3 to 5 minutes. Turn off pressure cooker. Season with extra fish sauce substitute and salt and pepper to taste. Top individual portions with cilantro leaves and scallions and serve, passing lime wedges separately.

TRIMMING LEMONGRASS

Trim stalk to bottom 6 inches and remove dry outer layers.

Farro and Butternut Squash Stew

Serves 6   `SLOW COOKER`
Cooking time 10 to 12 hours on low or 7 to 9 hours on high

Why This Recipe Works Nutty-sweet farro is a great source of plant-based protein in this hearty whole-grain vegetable stew, which also includes mushrooms for umami depth and butternut squash for satisfying substance. We cooked the squash in a foil packet right on top of the rest of the stew to make sure it would retain its sweet taste and bright color. Microwaving the mushrooms and aromatics with a little oil caused the mushrooms to soften, release some of their moisture, and become flavored by the aromatics. To give the vegetable broth a flavor boost, we stirred in white wine for complexity and brightness. At the end of cooking, we stirred the squash into the stew and added handfuls of peppery arugula. The arugula may seem like a lot at first, but it wilts down substantially. We prefer the flavor and texture of whole farro; pearled farro can be used, but the texture may be softer. Do not use quick-cooking or presteamed farro (the ingredient list on the package will specify the type) in this recipe. You will need a 4- to 7-quart slow cooker for this recipe.

1½ pounds cremini mushrooms, trimmed and quartered
1 onion, chopped fine
2 tablespoons tomato paste
3 garlic cloves, minced
1 tablespoon extra-virgin olive oil, plus extra for serving
1 teaspoon table salt, divided
6 cups vegetable broth, plus extra as needed
1 cup whole farro
¼ cup dry white wine
2 bay leaves
1½ pounds butternut squash, peeled, seeded, and cut into ½-inch pieces (4 cups)
¼ teaspoon pepper
5 ounces (5 cups) baby arugula
Vegan Parmesan Substitute (page 27) or grated dairy Parmesan (optional)

1. Microwave mushrooms, onion, tomato paste, garlic, oil, and ½ teaspoon salt in bowl, stirring occasionally, until vegetables are softened, 8 to 10 minutes; transfer to slow cooker.

2. Stir broth, farro, wine, and bay leaves into slow cooker. Sprinkle squash with pepper and remaining ½ teaspoon salt, wrap in aluminum foil packet, and place on top of stew. Cover and cook until farro is tender, 10 to 12 hours on low or 7 to 9 hours on high.

3. Carefully open foil packet and stir squash, along with any accumulated juices, into stew. Discard bay leaves. Stir in arugula, 1 handful at a time, and let sit until wilted, about 5 minutes. Adjust consistency with extra hot broth as needed. Season with salt and pepper to taste. Serve, passing vegan Parmesan substitute, if using, and extra oil separately.

Farro and Butternut Squash Stew

Wheat Berry and Wild Mushroom Stew

Wheat Berry and Wild Mushroom Stew

Serves 6   `SLOW COOKER`

Cooking time 8 to 9 hours on low or 5 to 6 hours on high

Why This Recipe Works Wheat berries, like farro, are naturally high in plant-based protein and are sturdy enough to maintain their satisfyingly chewy texture in this hearty slow-cooked stew. Including both fresh cremini mushrooms and dried porcini mushrooms ensured that our stew had tender bites of mushroom and intense, earthy flavor. To reinforce the woodsy notes of the mushrooms, we added dried thyme. We also stirred in some Madeira, adding an extra splash of the fortified wine at the end of cooking for brightness. Baby spinach provided color and freshness. The spinach may seem like a lot at first, but it wilts down substantially. If using quick-cooking or presteamed wheat berries (the ingredient list on the package specifies the type), you will need to decrease the cooking time in step 1. The wheat berries will retain a chewy texture once fully cooked. You can substitute dry sherry for the Madeira if desired. You will need a 4- to 7-quart slow cooker for this recipe.

> 2 pounds cremini mushrooms, trimmed and sliced thin
> ½ ounce dried porcini mushrooms, rinsed and minced
> 3 garlic cloves, minced
> 3 tablespoons extra-virgin olive oil, divided, plus extra for drizzling
> 2 teaspoons minced fresh thyme or ½ teaspoon dried
> ½ teaspoon table salt
> 6 cups vegetable broth, plus extra broth as needed
> 1½ cups wheat berries
> ½ cup dry Madeira, divided
> 6 ounces (6 cups) baby spinach
> Vegan Parmesan Substitute (page 27) or grated dairy Parmesan (optional)

1. Microwave cremini mushrooms, porcini mushrooms, garlic, 1 tablespoon oil, thyme, and salt in bowl, stirring occasionally, until mushrooms are softened, about 5 minutes; transfer to slow cooker. Stir in broth, wheat berries, and 6 tablespoons Madeira. Cover and cook until wheat berries are tender, 8 to 9 hours on low or 5 to 6 hours on high.

2. Stir in spinach, 1 handful at a time, and let sit until wilted, about 5 minutes. Adjust consistency with extra hot broth as needed. Stir in remaining 2 tablespoons oil and remaining 2 tablespoons Madeira and season with salt and pepper to taste. Serve, drizzling individual portions with extra oil and sprinkling with vegan Parmesan substitute, if using.

Moroccan Lentil Soup with Mustard Greens

Serves 6 `SLOW COOKER`

Cooking time 7 to 9 hours on low or 4 to 6 hours on high

Why This Recipe Works Even though lentils are more delicate and quicker-cooking than other beans, they still hold up well in the slow cooker. We found that French green or brown lentils did an especially good job of retaining their texture, shape, and flavor through the long simmer. We started our slow-cooker lentil soup by microwaving aromatics (garlic and onion) with Moroccan spices—coriander, garam masala, and cayenne—for a deep, round flavor. To finish, we wanted a new and interesting flavor that worked with our North African flavor spin. Dates are a common Moroccan ingredient, and we discovered that they imparted a rich sweetness to the broth. Mustard greens, also added at the end, offered the perfect peppery balance to all the warm spices. For a little tang, we topped the soup with a mixture of yogurt, parsley, and lemon juice. We prefer French green lentils, or lentilles du Puy, for this recipe, but it will work with any type of lentil except red or yellow. If you can't find mustard greens, you can substitute kale. You will need a 4- to 7-quart slow cooker for this recipe.

- 1 onion, chopped fine
- 2 garlic cloves, minced
- 1 teaspoon vegetable oil
- 1 teaspoon garam masala
- ¾ teaspoon ground coriander
- ⅛ teaspoon cayenne pepper
- 8 cups vegetable broth
- 1 cup French green lentils, picked over and rinsed
- ¼ teaspoon table salt
- 12 ounces mustard greens, stemmed and sliced ½ inch thick
- 4 ounces pitted dates, chopped (¾ cup)
- ½ cup plain plant-based Greek yogurt or dairy Greek yogurt
- ¼ cup chopped fresh parsley
- 1 tablespoon lemon juice
- ⅛ teaspoon pepper

1. Microwave onion, garlic, oil, garam masala, coriander, and cayenne in bowl, stirring occasionally, until onion is softened, about 5 minutes; transfer to slow cooker. Stir in broth, lentils, and salt. Cover and cook until lentils are tender, 7 to 9 hours on low or 4 to 6 hours on high.

2. Stir mustard greens and dates into soup, cover, and cook on high until greens are tender, 20 to 30 minutes. Season with salt and pepper to taste.

3. Combine yogurt, parsley, lemon juice, and pepper in bowl. Season with salt and pepper to taste. Top individual portions of soup with yogurt mixture before serving.

Vegetable and Chickpea Stew

Serves 6 `PRESSURE COOKER`

Why This Recipe Works Bold spices are an exciting contrast to the bounty of vegetables in this Lebanese-inspired stew. We wanted to streamline the lengthy list of spices included in many Lebanese recipes, so we turned to baharat, a potent Middle Eastern spice blend. Using the sauté or browning function of the pressure cooker, we started by browning the bell peppers and onion to develop depth of flavor. The baharat went in next, followed by a little garlic and tomato paste. After adding tomatoes and potatoes and cooking it all under pressure, we released the pressure and briefly simmered the delicate zucchini in the stew to ensure that it cooked through while remaining green and tender, adding convenient canned chickpeas to warm through at the same time. A little olive oil drizzled on at the end provided richness, while chopped mint added freshness. If you can't find baharat, you can substitute 1½ teaspoons ground nutmeg, 1½ teaspoons paprika, ½ teaspoon ground coriander, ½ teaspoon ground cinnamon, and ½ teaspoon ground cumin.

- ¼ cup extra-virgin olive oil, plus extra for drizzling
- 2 red bell peppers, stemmed, seeded, and cut into 1-inch pieces
- 1 onion, chopped fine
- ½ teaspoon table salt
- ½ teaspoon pepper
- 1½ tablespoons baharat
- 4 garlic cloves, minced
- 1 tablespoon tomato paste
- 4 cups vegetable broth
- 1 (28-ounce) can whole peeled tomatoes, drained with juice reserved, chopped
- 1 pound Yukon Gold potatoes, peeled and cut into ½-inch pieces
- 2 zucchini, quartered lengthwise and sliced 1 inch thick
- 1 (15-ounce) can chickpeas, rinsed
- ⅓ cup chopped fresh mint

1. Using highest sauté or browning function, heat oil in electric pressure cooker until shimmering. Add bell peppers, onion, salt, and pepper and cook until vegetables are softened and lightly browned, 5 to 7 minutes. Stir in baharat, garlic, and tomato paste and cook until fragrant, about 1 minute. Stirin broth and tomatoes and reserved juice, scraping up any browned bits, then stir in potatoes.

2. Lock lid in place and close pressure release valve. Select high pressure cook function and cook for 9 minutes. Turn off pressure cooker and quick-release pressure. Carefully remove lid, allowing steam to escape away from you.

3. Stir zucchini and chickpeas into stew and cook, using highest sauté or browning function, until zucchini is tender, 10 to 15 minutes. Turn off pressure cooker. Season with salt and pepper to taste. Drizzle individual portions with extra oil, and sprinkle with mint before serving.

Black Bean Chili
Serves 4 to 6   `PRESSURE COOKER`

Why This Recipe Works Chili becomes a cinch to make in the pressure cooker using dried beans. We chose black beans because of their robust flavor and dense, sturdy texture, and brined the dried beans in salted water before cooking to help them hold their shape and cook evenly. Naturally we wanted tocreate a hearty bean chili as deeply savory and satisfying as any meat version. Creating big flavor in chili without using meat can be tricky, but browning a hefty amount of aromatics and blooming spices in the cooker gave our chili depth. For bigvegetable flavor, we also added white mushrooms and bell peppers. A cup of vegetable broth and a can of crushed tomatoes provided enough liquid for our beans to cook evenly while still resulting in a thick, hearty finished dish. See page 285 for more information on brining beans. Serve with your favorite chili garnishes.

- 3 tablespoons table salt, for brining
- 1 pound (2½ cups) dried black beans, picked over and rinsed
- 3 tablespoons vegetable oil
- 1 onion, chopped fine
- 9 garlic cloves, minced
- 2 tablespoons ground cumin
- 1½ tablespoons chili powder
- 1 teaspoon minced canned chipotle chile in adobo sauce
- 1 (28-ounce) can crushed tomatoes
- 1 cup vegetable broth, plus extra as needed
- 1 pound white mushrooms, trimmed and halved if small or quartered if large
- 2 red bell peppers, stemmed, seeded, and cut into ½-inch pieces
- 2 bay leaves
- ½ cup minced fresh cilantro
  Lime wedges
  Plant-based sour cream or dairy sour cream

1. Dissolve 3 tablespoons salt in 4 quarts cold water in large container. Add beans and soak at room temperature for at least 8 hours or up to 24 hours. Drain and rinse well.

2. Using highest sauté or browning function, heat oil in electric pressure cooker until shimmering. Add onion and cook until softened, 3 to 5 minutes. Stir in garlic, cumin, chili powder, and chipotle and cook until fragrant, about 1 minute. Stir in tomatoes and broth, scraping up any browned bits, then stir in beans, mushrooms, bell peppers, and bay leaves.

3. Lock lid in place and close pressure release valve. Select high pressure cook function and cook for 40 minutes. Turn off pressure cooker and quick-release pressure. Carefully remove lid, allowing steam to escape away from you.

4. Discard bay leaves. Adjust consistency with extra hot broth as needed. Stir in cilantro and season with salt and pepper to taste. Serve with lime wedges and sour cream.

VARIATION
Black Bean Chili with Fried Eggs and Queso

- 2 teaspoons vegetable oil
- 4–6 large eggs
- 2–3 pinches table salt
- 2–3 pinches pepper
  Queso fresco

1. Heat oil in 12-inch nonstick skillet over low heat for 5 minutes. Meanwhile, crack 2 eggs into small bowl and sprinkle with pinch of salt and pinch of pepper. Repeat with remaining 2 eggs and second small bowl (if using 6 eggs, repeat with remaining 2 eggs and third small bowl).

2. Increase heat to medium-high and heat until oil is shimmering. Working quickly, pour 1 bowl of eggs in 1 side of pan and second bowl of eggs in other side. Cover and cook for 1 minute. Remove skillet from burner and let stand, covered, 15 to 45 seconds for runny yolks (white around edge of yolk will be barely opaque), 45 to 60 seconds for soft but set yolks, and about 2 minutes for medium-set yolks. Top each serving of chili with a fried egg and some queso fresco.

Thai Eggplant Green Curry

Serves 6 `SLOW COOKER`
Cooking time 2 to 4 hours on low

Why This Recipe Works Meaty-textured eggplant is the star of this vegetable-packed curry. Though we liked the hands-off element of using the slow cooker, our first attempts resulted in bland mush. To drive off excess moisture from the eggplant before adding it to the moist heat environment of the cooker, we gave it a quick spin under the broiler, deepening the eggplant's flavor in the process. For complex curry flavor without the need for gathering up a laundry list of ingredients, we turned to convenient store-bought green curry paste, which contained all the ingredients of classic Thai curries we wanted to incorporate. A combination of vegetable broth and coconut milk (added at the end) gave us a rich, creamy base, with instant tapioca helping to thicken it. Snow peas and red bell pepper were the perfect accents to the eggplant, and to ensure that they were perfectly crisp-tender, we simply microwaved them with a little water, then added them to the finished curry. Serve with Hands-Off Baked Coconut Rice (page 238). You will need a 4- to 7-quart slow cooker for this recipe.

Vegetable oil spray
2 pounds eggplant, cut into 1-inch pieces
4 shallots, minced
3 tablespoons Thai green curry paste
1 tablespoon sugar
4 cups vegetable broth
2 tablespoons Fish Sauce Substitute (page 22), plus extra for seasoning
2 tablespoons instant tapioca
¼ teaspoon table salt
1 pound snow peas, strings removed, cut into 1-inch pieces
1 red bell pepper, stemmed, seeded, and cut into 2-inch-long matchsticks
1 (14-ounce) can coconut milk
¼ cup chopped fresh cilantro
1 tablespoon lime juice, plus extra for seasoning

1. Adjust oven rack 6 inches from broiler element and heat broiler. Line rimmed baking sheet with aluminum foil and spray with oil spray. Toss eggplant, shallots, curry paste, and sugar together in bowl. Spread eggplant mixture evenly in prepared sheet and lightly spray with oil spray. Broil vegetables until softened and beginning to brown, 10 to 12 minutes, rotating sheet halfway through broiling; transfer to slow cooker. Stir in broth, fish sauce substitute, tapioca, and salt. Cover and cook until flavors meld and eggplant is tender, 2 to 4 hours on low.

Vegetable and Chickpea Stew

Thai Eggplant Green Curry

2. Microwave snow peas, bell pepper, and 1 tablespoon water in covered bowl, stirring occasionally, until crisp-tender, 4 to 6 minutes. Drain vegetables, then stir into curry. Microwave coconut milk in bowl until hot, about 2 minutes. Stir into curry and let sit until heated through, about 5 minutes. Stir in cilantro and lime juice. Season with salt, pepper, extra fish sauce substitute, and extra lime juice to taste. Serve.

Root Vegetable Tagine with Dried Cherries

Serves 6   `SLOW COOKER`
Cooking time 8 to 10 hours on low or 5 to 7 hours on high

Why This Recipe Works Tagine refers to both the conical cooking vessel and the stew-like dish (typically containing meat or poultry) that is prepared in this vessel throughout North Africa. For our plant-based take on tagine transplanted to the slow cooker, we chose root vegetables as the starting point, since we knew they would be able to stand up to a long, slow cooking time. Carrots were a must for their sweet, earthy flavor, as were parsnips. To round out the mix, we turned to an undersung hero of the vegetable world: the nutritional powerhouse rutabaga. Its flavor (similar to a mild turnip) helped offset the sweetness of the other root vegetables. To create just the right flavorful broth with warm spices, we microwaved an aromatic mixture of onions, garlic, and garam masala with fresh ginger. We then added dried cherries and fresh cilantro at the end of cooking to bring freshness and vibrancy to the dish. Topping individual portions with yogurt and toasted almonds tamed the spices of the stew and added contrast and crunch. Serve with rice or couscous. You will need a 4- to 7-quart slow cooker for this recipe.

- 2 **onions, chopped fine**
- 4 **garlic cloves, minced**
- 1½ **tablespoons garam masala**
- 2 **teaspoons vegetable oil**
- 2 **teaspoons paprika**
- 1½ **teaspoons grated fresh ginger**
  Pinch cayenne
- 1½ **pounds carrots, peeled, halved lengthwise, and sliced 1 inch thick**
- 1 **pound parsnips, peeled, halved lengthwise, and sliced 1 inch thick**
- 1 **pound rutabaga, peeled and cut into ½-inch pieces**
- 4 **cups vegetable broth**
- 2 **(2-inch) strips orange zest**

- 2 **tablespoons instant tapioca**
- ½ **teaspoon table salt**
- ½ **cup dried cherries, chopped**
- 2 **tablespoons minced fresh cilantro**
- ½ **cup plain plant-based Greek yogurt or dairy Greek yogurt**
- ⅓ **cup slivered almonds, toasted**

1. Microwave onions, garlic, garam masala, oil, paprika, ginger, and cayenne in bowl, stirring occasionally, until onions are softened, about 5 minutes; transfer to slow cooker. Stir carrots, parsnips, rutabaga, broth, orange zest, tapioca, and salt into slow cooker. Cover and cook until vegetables are tender, 8 to 10 hours on low or 5 to 7 hours on high.

2. Discard orange zest. Stir cherries and cilantro into tagine and season with salt and pepper to taste. Top individual portions with yogurt and almonds before serving.

Navy Bean and Bulgur Chili

Serves 6 to 8   `SLOW COOKER`
Cooking time 8 to 10 hours on high

Why This Recipe Works Meatless chilis frequently rely on a mixture of beans and vegetables for heartiness, but for this chili we wanted something even heartier and more savory. We started our chili with dried navy beans, which turned tender and creamy with the long slow-cooker simmer. After some experimentation with grains, it turned out that bulgur provided the satisfying textural dimension we sought, adding a meat-like texture but a deliciously different flavor all its own. After a quick rinse and a few minutes in the microwave, the grain needed just 5 to 10 minutes in the slow cooker to fully soften and absorb the other flavors. Finally, we ramped up the umami intensity of our chili with soy sauce, dried shiitake mushrooms, and tomato paste. When shopping, don't confuse bulgur with cracked wheat, which has a much longer cooking time and will not work in this recipe. Bulgur is made from cracked wheat that has been parboiled or steamed, whereas cracked wheat has had no processing other than milling. Serve with your favorite chili garnishes. You will need a 4- to 7-quart slow cooker for this recipe.

- 2 **onions, chopped fine**
- 3 **tablespoons chili powder**
- ¼ **cup tomato paste**
- 2 **tablespoons vegetable oil**
- 4 **teaspoons dried oregano**

Navy Bean and Bulgur Chili

Braised Spring Vegetables

Serves 4 to 6 `PRESSURE COOKER`

Why This Recipe Works This vibrant dish of quickly braised artichokes, asparagus, and peas captures springtime with fresh seasonal vegetables, varying vegetable textures, and verdant colors. As lovely and tasty as they are when combined, however, these vegetables don't cook at anywhere near the same rate. The pressure cooker came to the rescue, helping us to cook each to perfection and in just one pot. First, we pressure-cooked halved baby artichokes (in garlicky vegetable broth to infuse them with flavor). They came out tender and evenly cooked from leaf to stem. After releasing the pressure, we then added asparagus and shelled fresh peas, and simmered them until just crisp-tender. Shredded basil and mint and lemon zest gave the dish an extra bright, springy taste. If you can't find fresh peas, you can substitute 1 cup frozen.

    1 lemon, grated to yield 2 teaspoons zest and halved
    8 baby artichokes (4 ounces each)
    1 tablespoon extra-virgin olive oil, plus extra for
       serving
    3 garlic cloves, minced
    ¾ cup vegetable broth
    ½ teaspoon table salt
    1 pound asparagus, trimmed and cut on bias into
       2-inch lengths
    1 pound fresh peas, shelled (1¼ cups)
    2 tablespoons shredded fresh basil
    1 tablespoon shredded fresh mint

1. Squeeze zested lemon halves into container filled with 4 cups water, then add spent halves. Working with 1 artichoke at a time, trim stem to about ¾ inch and cut off top quarter of artichoke. Break off bottom 3 or 4 rows of tough outer leaves by pulling them downward. Using paring knife, trim outer layer of stem and base, removing any dark green parts. Cut artichoke in half and submerge in lemon water.

2. Using highest sauté or browning function, cook oil and garlic in electric pressure cooker until fragrant, about 1 minute. Remove artichokes from lemon water, shaking off excess liquid, and add to pressure cooker along with broth and salt.

3. Lock lid in place and close pressure release valve. Select high pressure cook function and cook for 4 minutes. Turn off pressure cooker and quick-release pressure. (If using Instant Pot, quick-release pressure immediately after multicooker reaches pressure.) Carefully remove lid, allowing steam to escape away from you.

    1   tablespoon ground cumin
    1¼ teaspoons table salt, divided
    1   pound (2½ cups) dried navy beans, picked over
        and rinsed
    3   tablespoons soy sauce
    ½   ounce dried shiitake mushrooms, rinsed and minced
    ⅔   cup medium-grind bulgur, rinsed

1. Microwave onions, chili powder, tomato paste, oil, oregano, cumin, and 1 teaspoon salt in bowl, stirring occasionally, until onions are softened, about 5 minutes; transfer to slow cooker. Stir in beans, 9 cups water, soy sauce, and mushrooms. Cover and cook until beans are tender, 8 to 10 hours on high.

2. Microwave bulgur, 2 cups water, and remaining ¼ teaspoon salt in covered bowl until bulgur is softened, about 5 minutes; drain bulgur and stir into chili. Cover and cook on high until bulgur is tender, 5 to 10 minutes. Adjust consistency with extra hot water as needed. Season with salt and pepper to taste. Serve.

Green Beans with Potatoes and Basil

4. Add asparagus and peas and cook using highest sauté or browning function, stirring occasionally, until crisp-tender, 4 to 6 minutes. Turn off pressure cooker. Stir in basil, mint, and lemon zest and season with salt and pepper to taste. Transfer vegetables to serving platter and drizzle with extra oil. Serve.

Green Beans with Potatoes and Basil

Serves 4 FAST PRESSURE COOKER

Why This Recipe Works Unlike crisp-tender green beans that have been steamed or sautéed, Greece's traditional braised green beans boast a unique texture that's meltingly soft without ever being mushy. Unfortunately, achieving this can require 2 hours of simmering. To get ultratender braised green beans in a fraction of the time, we loved the quick-cooking, even heat of the pressure cooker. To turn this into a substantial plant-based meal, we added chunks of buttery Yukon Gold potatoes, which turned tender in the same amount of time as the green beans. Canned tomatoes supplied sweetness, while their juice along with a little water provided just enough braising liquid for the beans and potatoes. A final drizzle of fruity extra-virgin olive oil and a sprinkling of toasted pine nuts added richness and textural contrast.

- 2 tablespoons extra-virgin olive oil, plus extra for drizzling
- 1 onion, chopped fine
- 2 tablespoons minced fresh oregano or 2 teaspoons dried
- 2 tablespoons tomato paste
- 4 garlic cloves, minced
- 1 (14.5-ounce) can whole peeled tomatoes, drained with juice reserved, chopped
- 1 cup water
- 1 teaspoon table salt
- ¼ teaspoon pepper
- 1½ pounds green beans, trimmed and cut into 2-inch lengths
- 1 pound Yukon Gold potatoes, peeled and cut into 1-inch pieces
- 3 tablespoons chopped fresh basil or parsley
- 2 tablespoons toasted pine nuts
  Vegan Parmesan Substitute (page 27) or shaved Parmesan (optional)

Beet and Watercress Salad with Orange and Dill

1. Using highest sauté or browning function, heat oil in electric pressure cooker until shimmering. Add onion and cook until softened, about 5 minutes. Stir in oregano, tomato paste, and garlic and cook until fragrant, about 30 seconds. Stir in tomatoes and their juice, water, salt, and pepper, then stir in green beans and potatoes. Lock lid in place and close pressure release valve. Select high pressure cook function and cook for 5 minutes.

2. Turn off pressure cooker and quick-release pressure. Carefully remove lid, allowing steam to escape away from you. Season with salt and pepper to taste. Sprinkle individual portions with basil, pine nuts, and vegan Parmesan substitute and drizzle with extra oil. Serve.

Beet and Watercress Salad with Orange and Dill

Serves 4 **FAST** **PRESSURE COOKER**

Why This Recipe Works Sweet, slightly earthy beets do double duty in this pretty magenta-and-green salad bursting with an unexpected combination of ingredients. After quickly cooking the unpeeled beets under pressure with caraway seeds and water (there was no need to peel the beets, since the intense heat of the pressure cooker made the skins undetectable in the finished dish), we stirred their potent and vibrantly colored cooking liquid into some Greek yogurt, turning it a spectacular shade of pink, perfect as a base for some peppery green watercress. Orange zest brightened up the beets, which we arranged on top of the greens. A sprinkling of fresh dill brought out the anise notes of the caraway seeds, and hazelnuts and coarse sea salt added a rich finishing crunch. Look for small or medium-size beets; large beets can be woody.

2 pounds beets, scrubbed, trimmed, and cut into ¾-inch pieces
½ cup water
1 teaspoon caraway seeds
½ teaspoon table salt
1 cup plain plant-based Greek yogurt or dairy Greek yogurt
1 small garlic clove, minced to paste
5 ounces (5 cups) watercress, torn into bite-size pieces
1 tablespoon extra-virgin olive oil, divided, plus extra for drizzling
1 tablespoon white wine vinegar, divided

1 teaspoon grated orange zest plus 2 tablespoons juice
¼ cup hazelnuts, toasted, skinned, and chopped
¼ cup coarsely chopped fresh dill
Coarse sea salt

1. Combine beets, water, caraway seeds, and table salt in electric pressure cooker. Lock lid in place and close pressure release valve. Select high pressure cook function and cook for 8 minutes. Turn off pressure cooker and quick-release pressure. Carefully remove lid, allowing steam to escape away from you.

2. Using slotted spoon, transfer beets to plate; set aside to cool slightly. Combine yogurt, garlic, and 3 tablespoons beet cooking liquid in bowl; discard remaining cooking liquid. In large bowl toss watercress with 2 teaspoons oil and 1 teaspoon vinegar. Season with table salt and pepper to taste.

3. Spread yogurt mixture over surface of serving platter. Arrange watercress on top of yogurt mixture, leaving 1-inch border of yogurt mixture. Add beets to now-empty large bowl and toss with orange zest and juice, remaining 2 teaspoons vinegar, and remaining 1 teaspoon oil. Season with table salt and pepper to taste. Arrange beets on top of watercress mixture. Drizzle with extra oil and sprinkle with hazelnuts, dill, and sea salt. Serve.

Braised Red Cabbage with Fennel and Orange

Serves 6 **SLOW COOKER**
Cooking time 5 to 6 hours on low or 3 to 4 hours on high

Why This Recipe Works Braised red cabbage is a favorite German side dish. It typically includes apples and warm spices—and plenty of lard or other animal fat. For an updated, plant-based spin and a dish worthy of being served on its own, we turned toward the Mediterranean, adding fresh fennel and using a minimal amount of fat in the form of vegetable oil. With its enclosed heat environment, the slow cooker was perfect for braising the cabbage while trapping the enticing aromas of the fennel. Adding the vegetables directly to the slow cooker left them too crunchy for our liking, so to get the texture just right, we precooked the cabbage and fennel in the microwave to soften them slightly. For a bright braising liquid that would add another flavor dimension, we chose sweet-tangy orange juice, enhancing it with fennel seeds, bay leaves, and thyme. A bit of sugar rounded out the sweetness, and vinegar perked up the flavors and added balance. You will need a 5- to 7-quart slow cooker for this recipe.

1 head red cabbage (2 pounds), cored and shredded

2 fennel bulbs, 2 tablespoons fronds minced, stalks discarded, bulbs halved, cored, and sliced ½ inch thick

1 onion, chopped fine

2 teaspoons vegetable oil

½ teaspoon table salt

1 cup orange juice (2 oranges)

2 tablespoons packed light brown sugar, divided, plus extra as needed

2 sprigs fresh thyme

½ teaspoon fennel seeds

3 bay leaves

2 tablespoons white wine vinegar, plus extra as needed

1. Microwave cabbage, fennel slices, onion, oil, and salt in covered bowl, stirring occasionally, until vegetables are softened, 15 to 20 minutes. Drain cabbage mixture and transfer to slow cooker. Stir in orange juice, 1 tablespoon sugar, thyme sprigs, fennel seeds, and bay leaves. Cover and cook until cabbage is tender, 5 to 6 hours on low or 3 to 4 hours on high.

2. Discard thyme sprigs and bay leaves. Stir in vinegar and remaining 1 tablespoon sugar. Season with salt, pepper, extra sugar, and extra vinegar to taste. (Cabbage can be held on warm or low setting for up to 2 hours.) Sprinkle with fennel fronds before serving.

Glazed Carrots

Serves 6 to 8   **SLOW COOKER**

Cooking time 5 to 6 hours on low or 3 to 4 hours on high

Why This Recipe Works Glazed carrots are a reliable side dish that we often turn to when hosting a crowd. Doing them on the stovetop involves some last-minute fussing that makes them less simple than we'd like, however. Using the slow cooker eliminated all the last-minute fuss involved and freed up a burner. Initially we tried cooking the carrots in vegetable broth, but tasters felt the broth was a distraction from the carrots' delicate sweetness. In the end, water seasoned with a little sugar and salt turned out to be the right choice for gently simmering these carrots. Once they were tender, we simply drained them and tossed them with coconut oil and tart orange marmalade. The marmalade and coconut oil (or butter) melted to form a ready-to-use glaze that conveniently did not need to be reduced on the stovetop. Simple, sweet, and

delicious—this is a plant-based side at its easiest. The variation makes it just a little fancier with parsnips, rutabaga, and celery root. You will need a 4- to 7-quart slow cooker for this recipe.

3 pounds carrots, peeled and sliced ¼ inch thick on bias

1 tablespoon sugar

¼ teaspoon table salt

½ cup orange marmalade

2 tablespoons refined coconut oil or unsalted butter, softened

1. Combine carrots, ¾ cup water, sugar, and salt in slow cooker. Cover and cook until carrots are tender, 5 to 6 hours on low or 3 to 4 hours on high.

2. Drain carrots and return to now-empty slow cooker. Stir in marmalade and oil. Season with salt and pepper to taste. Serve. (Carrots can be held on warm or low setting for up to 2 hours; loosen glaze with hot water as needed.)

VARIATION

Glazed Root Vegetables

Cooking time 5 to 6 hours on low or 3 to 4 hours on high

1 pound parsnips, peeled and cut into 1-inch pieces

1 pound rutabaga, peeled and cut into 1-inch pieces

1 celery root (14 ounces), peeled and cut into 1-inch pieces

½ teaspoon table salt

3 tablespoons orange marmalade

1 tablespoon refined coconut oil or unsalted butter, softened

2 teaspoons minced fresh parsley

2 teaspoons lemon juice

1. Combine parsnips, rutabaga, celery root, ¾ cup water, and salt in slow cooker. Press 16 by 12-inch sheet of parchment paper firmly onto vegetables, folding down edges as needed. Cover and cook until vegetables are tender, 5 to 6 hours on low or 3 to 4 hours on high.

2. Discard parchment. Drain vegetables and return to now-empty slow cooker. Stir in marmalade, oil, parsley, and lemon juice. Season with salt and pepper to taste. Serve. (Vegetables can be held on warm or low setting for up to 2 hours; loosen glaze with hot water as needed.)

Braised Whole Cauliflower with Tomatoes, Olives, and Ras el Hanout

Serves 2 as a main dish or 4 as a side dish

`FAST` `PRESSURE COOKER`

Why This Recipe Works A whole head of cauliflower is a showstopping sight to behold no matter how you prepare it. When done in the pressure cooker, it's also a super-speedy way to a vegetable-focused entrée. We started by making an intensely savory cooking liquid of garlic, our anchovy substitute, ras el hanout, and tomatoes. When the large cauliflower's fibrous core didn't always cook through during initial testing, we made deep cuts in the stem to allow the liquid and heat to reach the center, which rendered the whole head perfectly tender. After releasing the pressure, we removed the cauliflower, stirred in the sweet-savory, flavor-intense combo of golden raisins and green olives, and thickened the sauce using the sauté or browning function of the cooker before spooning it over the beautiful vegetable and finishing with cilantro and pine nuts. We prefer our homemade Ras el Hanout (page 174), but you may use store-bought; just be aware that different brands can vary in intensity.

- 2 tablespoons extra-virgin olive oil
- 6 garlic cloves, minced
- 1 tablespoon Anchovy Substitute (page 23) (optional)
- 2 teaspoons ras el hanout
- ⅛ teaspoon red pepper flakes
- 1 (28-ounce) can whole peeled tomatoes, drained with juice reserved, chopped coarse
- 1 large head cauliflower (3 pounds)
- ½ cup pitted brine-cured green olives, chopped coarse
- ¼ cup golden raisins
- ¼ cup fresh cilantro leaves
- ¼ cup pine nuts, toasted

1. Using highest sauté or browning function, cook oil, garlic, anchovy substitute, ras el hanout, and pepper flakes in electric pressure cooker until fragrant, about 3 minutes. Turn off pressure cooker, then stir in tomatoes and reserved juice.

2. Trim outer leaves of cauliflower and cut stem flush with bottom florets. Using paring knife, cut 4-inch-deep cross in stem. Nestle cauliflower, stem side down, into pot and spoon some of sauce over top. Lock lid in place and close pressure release valve. Select high pressure cook function and cook for 3 minutes.

Glazed Carrots

Braised Whole Cauliflower with Tomatoes, Olives, and Ras el Hanout

3. Turn off pressure cooker and quick-release pressure. Carefully remove lid, allowing steam to escape away from you. Using tongs and slotted spoon, transfer cauliflower to serving platter and tent with aluminum foil. Stir olives and raisins into sauce and cook, using highest sauté or browning function, until sauce has thickened slightly, about 5 minutes. Season with salt and pepper to taste. Cut cauliflower into wedges and spoon some of sauce over top. Sprinkle with cilantro and pine nuts. Serve, passing remaining sauce separately.

Turkish Eggplant Casserole

Serves 4 to 6 **SLOW COOKER**
Cooking time 3 to 4 hours on low or 2 to 3 hours on high

Why This Recipe Works Eggplant is often prepared with meat in Turkish cuisine. This versatile vegetable is also plenty satisfying and hearty on its own, paired with traditional Turkish spices (paprika, cumin, cayenne pepper, and cinnamon). For this plant-focused casserole, we included bulgur, which cooks perfectly in the steamy environment. Broiling the eggplant before adding it to the cooker drove off extra moisture and kept the slices firm. An herb-yogurt sauce added a welcome richness and tang to this well-spiced dish. When shopping, don't confuse bulgur with cracked wheat, which has a much longer cooking time and will not work here. You will need a 5- to 7-quart oval slow cooker for this recipe.

Sauce
- 1 cup plain plant-based yogurt or dairy yogurt
- ¼ cup chopped fresh parsley
- 2 tablespoons chopped fresh mint
- 1 garlic clove, minced

Bulgur
- 2 teaspoons paprika
- 1½ teaspoons ground cumin
- 1½ teaspoons table salt, divided
- ⅛ teaspoon cayenne pepper
- ⅛ teaspoon ground cinnamon
- 1½ pounds eggplant, sliced into ½-inch-thick rounds
- ¼ cup extra-virgin olive oil, divided
- 1 onion, chopped fine
- 4 garlic cloves, minced
- 1 tablespoon tomato paste
- 1 cup medium-grind bulgur, rinsed
- 1 cup vegetable broth
- 4 tomatoes, cored and sliced ½ inch thick

Turkish Eggplant Casserole

1. For the sauce Combine all ingredients in bowl and season with salt and pepper to taste. Refrigerate until ready to serve.

2. For the bulgur Adjust oven rack 6 inches from broiler element and heat broiler. Combine paprika, cumin, ¾ teaspoon salt, cayenne, and cinnamon in bowl. Arrange eggplant in single layer on aluminum foil–lined rimmed baking sheet, brush both sides with 3 tablespoons oil, and sprinkle with spice mixture. Broil eggplant until softened and beginning to brown, 10 to 12 minutes, flipping eggplant halfway through broiling.

3. Lightly coat slow cooker with vegetable oil spray. Microwave onion, garlic, tomato paste, remaining ¾ teaspoon salt, and remaining 1 tablespoon oil in bowl, stirring occasionally, until onion is softened, about 5 minutes; transfer to prepared slow cooker. Stir in bulgur and broth. Shingle alternating slices of eggplant and tomato into 3 tightly fitting rows on top of bulgur mixture. Cover and cook until eggplant and bulgur are tender and all broth is absorbed, 3 to 4 hours on low or 2 to 3 hours on high. Serve, passing sauce separately.

Braised Fennel with Radicchio and Pear

Serves 4 `FAST` `PRESSURE COOKER`

Why This Recipe Works Assertive greens and sweet pear make perfect companions to braised fennel in this brunch-worthy salad. When fennel is cooked quickly under pressure, it gently softens and its vegetal flavor mellows into something sweeter and almost caramelized. We started by cutting the fennel into wedges and browning them in the pressure cooker before cooking them under pressure for a mere 2 minutes. We whisked together a lemony dressing, assembled the salad, and topped it off with toasty, crunchy almonds. The optional Pecorino offered an additional salty, nutty note. Don't core the fennel before cutting it into wedges; the core helps hold the wedges together during cooking.

- 6 tablespoons extra-virgin olive oil, divided
- 2 fennel bulbs (12 ounces each), 2 tablespoons fronds chopped, stalks discarded, bulbs halved, each half cut into 1-inch-thick wedges
- ¾ teaspoon table salt, divided
- ½ teaspoon grated lemon zest plus 4 teaspoons juice
- 5 ounces (5 cups) baby arugula
- 1 small head radicchio (6 ounces), shredded
- 1 Bosc or Bartlett pear, quartered, cored, and sliced thin
- ¼ cup whole almonds, toasted and chopped
   Shaved Pecorino Romano cheese (optional)

1. Using highest sauté or browning function, heat 2 tablespoons oil in electric pressure cooker until just smoking, about 5 minutes. Brown half of fennel, about 3 minutes per side; transfer to plate. Repeat with 1 tablespoon oil and remaining fennel; do not remove from pot.

2. Return first batch of fennel to pot along with ½ cup water and ½ teaspoon salt. Lock lid in place and close pressure release valve. Select high pressure cook function and cook for 2 minutes. Turn off pressure cooker and quick-release pressure. Carefully remove lid, allowing steam to escape away from you. Using slotted spoon, transfer fennel to plate; discard cooking liquid.

3. Whisk lemon zest and juice, remaining 3 tablespoons oil, and remaining ¼ teaspoon salt together in large bowl. Add arugula, radicchio, and pear and toss to coat. Transfer arugula mixture to serving platter and arrange fennel wedges on top. Sprinkle with almonds; fennel fronds; and Pecorino, if using. Serve.

Mustard Greens and Sweet Potato Tacos

Serves 4 `SLOW COOKER`
Cooking time 3 to 4 hours on low or 2 to 3 hours on high

Why This Recipe Works Tacos in the slow cooker means you can set this out for a crowd and it will stay perfectly warm and juicy as people come back for more. And they will: Corn tortillas stuffed with seasoned mustard greens and sweet potatoes made even the most carnivorous among us in the test kitchen excited to eat meatless tacos. In order for the sweet potatoes to be a manageable size for folding into a taco and eating without having them fall out, we cut them into ½-inch pieces. But we discovered that these small pieces cooked quickly and lost their shape, so we wrapped the starchy tubers in foil to help tame the heat of the slow cooker and keep them from falling apart. We arranged the foil-wrapped potatoes right on top of the greens in the slow cooker, and then unwrapped them and stirred them into the greens at the end. The tender vegetables needed a crunchy counterpoint, so we put together some quickly pickled radishes. If you would like to include cheese, we recommend queso fresco. You can substitute an equal amount of Swiss chard for the mustard greens, if desired. You will need a 4- to 7-quart slow cooker for this recipe.

- 1 onion, chopped fine
- 2 tablespoons minced fresh oregano or 2 teaspoons dried
- 2 tablespoons extra-virgin olive oil, divided
- 4 garlic cloves, minced
- 1 teaspoon ground cumin
- 1 teaspoon ground coriander
- ¾ teaspoon table salt
- 1½ pounds mustard greens, stemmed and cut into 1-inch pieces
- 1 pound sweet potatoes, peeled and cut into ½-inch pieces
- 12 (6-inch) corn tortillas, warmed
- 1 recipe Spicy Pickled Radishes (recipe follows)
- 4 ounces queso fresco, crumbled (1 cup) (optional)

1. Lightly coat slow cooker with vegetable oil spray. Microwave onion, oregano, 1 tablespoon oil, garlic, cumin, coriander, and salt in bowl, stirring occasionally, until onion is softened, about 5 minutes; transfer to prepared slow cooker. Stir in mustard greens and ½ cup water. Season sweet potatoes with salt and pepper, wrap in aluminum foil packet, and place on top of greens. Cover and cook until greens and potatoes are tender, 3 to 4 hours on low or 2 to 3 hours on high.

2. Transfer foil packet to plate. Drain greens mixture and return to now-empty slow cooker. Carefully open foil packet and gently fold potatoes, along with any accumulated juices, into greens. Stir in remaining 1 tablespoon oil and season with salt and pepper to taste. Serve with tortillas; pickled radishes; and queso fresco, if using.

Spicy Pickled Radishes
Makes about 1¾ cups

- 10 radishes, trimmed and sliced thin
- ½ cup lime juice (4 limes)
- ½ jalapeño chile, stemmed and sliced thin
- 1 teaspoon sugar
- ¼ teaspoon table salt

Combine all ingredients in bowl, cover, and let stand at room temperature for 30 minutes. (Mixture can be refrigerated for up to 24 hours.)

MAKING FOIL PACKETS

1. Place vegetables on 1 side of large sheet of aluminum foil. Fold foil over vegetables and crimp 3 open edges to seal.

2. Place packet on top of ingredients in slow cooker, pressing it gently to fit.

Olive Oil Mashed Potatoes
Serves 6 **SLOW COOKER**
Cooking time 5 to 6 hours on low or 3 to 4 hours on high

Why This Recipe Works "Traditional" mashed potatoes are undeniably delicious, but they require loads of butter and dairy to achieve the expected flavor and texture. But cooking sliced russet potatoes in the moist environment of the slow cooker, using a sheet of parchment paper laid on top of them to trap steam and ensure even cooking, meant we didn't need to use either butter or cream to achieve mashed-potato nirvana. Cooking garlic alongside the potatoes in the cooker added a noticeable but mellow garlic flavor to our mash. And switching from butter to olive oil gave our slow-cooker mashed potatoes a luxuriously smooth texture and a deep, subtle peppery flavor all their own. You will need a 4- to 7-quart slow cooker for this recipe.

- 2 pounds russet potatoes, peeled and sliced ¼ inch thick
- 1 cup water, plus extra as needed
- 3 garlic cloves, lightly crushed and peeled
- 1 teaspoon table salt
  Vegetable oil spray
- 3 tablespoons extra-virgin olive oil
- 2 teaspoons lemon juice

1. Combine potatoes, water, garlic, and salt in slow cooker. Spray top layer of potatoes with oil spray. Press 16 by 12-inch sheet of parchment paper firmly onto potatoes, folding down edges as needed. Cover and cook until potatoes are tender, 5 to 6 hours on low or 3 to 4 hours on high.

2. Discard parchment. Mash potatoes with potato masher until smooth. Fold in oil and lemon juice and season with salt and pepper to taste. Serve. (Mashed potatoes can be held on warm or low setting for up to 2 hours; loosen with hot water as needed before serving.)

CREATING A PARCHMENT SHIELD

Press 16 by 12-inch sheet of parchment paper firmly onto vegetables, folding down edges as needed.

2 pounds fingerling potatoes
4 teaspoons extra-virgin olive oil, divided
2 scallions, white parts minced, green parts sliced thin, divided
3 garlic cloves, minced
1 teaspoon table salt
¼ teaspoon pepper
1 tablespoon chopped fresh parsley
1 teaspoon lemon zest plus 1 tablespoon juice

1. Combine potatoes, 1 teaspoon oil, scallion whites, garlic, salt, and pepper in slow cooker. Cover and cook until potatoes are tender, 5 to 6 hours on low or 3 to 4 hours on high.

2. Stir in parsley, lemon zest and juice, scallion greens, and remaining 1 tablespoon oil; season with salt and pepper to taste. Serve. (Potatoes can be held on warm or low setting for up to 2 hours.)

Indian-Spiced Mashed Butternut Squash

Serves 4   **SLOW COOKER**

Cooking time 5 to 6 hours on low or 3 to 4 hours on high

Why This Recipe Works Garam masala, golden raisins, and toasted cashews transform hearty and comforting but mild-tasting butternut squash into a flavor-packed dish. We simply slow-cooked seasoned sliced squash until tender, then mashed the squash right in the cooker using a potato masher. For luxurious creaminess and rich flavor and texture, we folded in plant-based creamer and coconut oil along with the raisins and nuts. We like our homemade Garam Masala (recipe follows) in this recipe, but you can use store-bought. You will need a 4- to 7-quart slow cooker for this recipe.

2 pounds butternut squash, peeled, halved lengthwise, seeded, and sliced ¼ inch thick
½ cup water, plus extra as needed
2 teaspoons packed brown sugar
¾ teaspoon table salt
½ teaspoon garam masala
  Vegetable oil spray
6 tablespoons plant-based creamer or dairy half-and-half, warmed
¼ cup golden raisins
¼ cup roasted cashews, chopped
1 tablespoon refined coconut oil or unsalted butter, melted

Herbed Fingerling Potatoes with Lemon

Herbed Fingerling Potatoes with Lemon

Serves 6   **SLOW COOKER**

Cooking time 5 to 6 hours on low or 3 to 4 hours on high

Why This Recipe Works Fingerling potatoes are creamy and dense and feel somehow special because of their small, narrow shape, making them an attractive alternative to standard white or red potatoes. So for a supereasy, company-worthy side dish, we turned to fingerlings, which require no prep work and turn perfectly tender in the slow cooker. They are traditionally roasted because boiling them dilutes their delicate flavor and turns them mushy, but we found that adding them to the slow cooker without any liquid whatsoever—just some olive oil, garlic, and scallions for flavor—allowed them to retain their earthy sweetness and cook through without a hint of mushiness. Before serving, we simply added chopped fresh parsley and lemon zest and juice for bright color and flavor. Use fingerling potatoes measuring approximately 3 inches long and 1 inch in diameter. You will need a 4- to 7-quart slow cooker for this recipe.

1. Combine squash, water, sugar, salt, and garam masala in slow cooker. Spray top layer of squash with oil spray. Press 16 by 12-inch sheet of parchment paper firmly onto squash, folding down edges as needed. Cover and cook until squash is tender, 5 to 6 hours on low or 3 to 4 hours on high.

2. Discard parchment. Mash squash with potato masher until smooth. Fold in plant-based creamer, raisins, cashews, and melted oil. Season with salt and pepper to taste. Serve. (Mashed squash can be held on warm or low setting for up to 2 hours; loosen with hot water as needed before serving.)

Garam Masala
Makes about ½ cup
For the best results, grind your own peppercorns.

- 1½ tablespoons black peppercorns
- 2 teaspoons cardamom pods
- 1½ teaspoons coriander seeds
- 1¼ teaspoons cumin seeds
- ¾ of 1 (3-inch) cinnamon stick

Process all ingredients in spice grinder until finely ground, about 30 seconds. Mixture can be stored at room temperature in airtight container for up to 1 year.

Mashed Butternut Squash with Sage and Toasted Hazelnuts

Mashed Butternut Squash with Sage and Toasted Hazelnuts
Serves 4 **FAST** **PRESSURE COOKER**

Why This Recipe Works The pressure cooker makes achieving this comforting autumnal mash fast and simple. Blooming garlic, onion, and cinnamon in coconut oil gave the dish a warm richness. We then stirred in cut-up squash and a chopped Granny Smith apple, which accented the sweetness of the squash with some brightness. A small amount of broth steamed the squash and apple to tenderness and boosted flavor, and then, after releasing the pressure, we simply switched to the sauté or browning function to quickly cook off any excess liquid, concentrating the flavors with minimal effort. Mashing the squash and apple with a potato masher gave the dish a pleasingly rustic texture. Maple syrup stirred in at the end enhanced sweetness, minced sage brought an herbal touch, and hazelnuts added a crunchy, toasty finish.

- 2 tablespoons refined coconut oil or unsalted butter
- ½ onion, chopped fine
- 1 teaspoon table salt
- ½ teaspoon pepper
- 1 garlic clove, minced
- ⅛ teaspoon ground cinnamon
- 2 pounds butternut squash, peeled, seeded, and cut into 1-inch pieces (5 cups)
- 1 Granny Smith apple, peeled, cored, and cut into 1-inch pieces
- ½ cup vegetable broth
- 2 tablespoons maple syrup
- 2 teaspoons minced fresh sage
- ¼ cup hazelnuts, toasted, skinned, and chopped coarse

1. Using highest sauté or browning function, melt oil in electric pressure cooker. Add onion, salt, and pepper and cook until onion is softened, 3 to 5 minutes. Stir in garlic and cinnamon and cook until fragrant, about 30 seconds. Stir in squash, apple, and broth.

2. Lock lid in place and close pressure release valve. Select high pressure cook function and cook for 6 minutes. Turn off pressure cooker and quick-release pressure. Carefully remove lid, allowing steam to escape away from you.

3. Using highest sauté or browning function, continue to cook squash mixture, stirring occasionally, until liquid is almost completely evaporated, 3 to 5 minutes. Turn off pressure cooker. Using potato masher, mash squash mixture until mostly smooth. Stir in maple syrup and sage and season with salt and pepper to taste. Transfer to serving bowl and sprinkle with hazelnuts. Serve.

1. Combine 1 cup water, orange juice, cloves, and cinnamon in slow cooker. Sprinkle squash with salt and pepper and shingle, cut side down, in slow cooker. Cover and cook until squash is tender, 3 to 4 hours on low or 2 to 3 hours on high.

2. Using tongs, transfer squash to serving platter. Brush away any cloves that stick to squash and discard cooking liquid and cinnamon stick. Microwave maple syrup, coriander, cayenne, and orange zest in bowl, stirring occasionally, until heated through, about 1 minute; season with salt and pepper to taste. Drizzle glaze over squash and sprinkle with hazelnuts and parsley. Serve.

Maple-Orange Glazed Acorn Squash

Serves 4   **SLOW COOKER**

Cooking time 3 to 4 hours on low or 2 to 3 hours on high

Why This Recipe Works Another quintessential fall and winter squash, acorn squash takes seemingly forever to roast in the oven and can sometimes emerge dry and a bit grainy when cooked that way. In the slow cooker, however, it turns tender easily without ever overcooking or drying out. Here we created a simple cooking base made up of water, orange juice, cloves, and cinnamon and placed the squash wedges cut side down in this flavorful mixture. And since we think a glaze greatly enhances both the look and flavor of acorn squash, we made a quick one in the microwave by combining maple syrup with coriander, cayenne pepper, and orange zest. This lively glaze elevated the humble squash, toasted hazelnuts provided flavorful crunch, and a sprinkling of fresh parsley added a bright herbal finish. You will need a 5- to 7-quart oval slow cooker for this recipe.

- 2 teaspoons grated orange zest plus ½ cup juice
- 5 cloves
- 1 cinnamon stick
- 2 (1-pound) acorn squashes, quartered pole to pole and seeded
- ¼ teaspoon table salt
- ⅛ teaspoon pepper
- ¼ cup maple syrup
- ⅛ teaspoon ground coriander
   Pinch cayenne pepper
- ¼ cup hazelnuts, toasted, skinned, and chopped coarse
- 1 tablespoon chopped fresh parsley

Spaghetti Squash with Fresh Tomato Sauce

Serves 2 as a main dish or 4 as a side dish

PRESSURE COOKER

Why This Recipe Works Spaghetti squash strands are a fun vegetable stand-in for pasta, and using a pressure cooker allowed us to cook a large spaghetti squash and make a simple fresh tomato sauce all together in one pot. First, we bloomed aromatic garlic, oregano, and pepper flakes with tomato paste to create an umami-rich base. We opted for plum tomatoes and chose not to peel them, and because they contain proportionally less juice than larger tomatoes, we didn't need to worry about seeding. Finally, we added the squash, halved and seeded, to the pressure cooker and cooked it until it was tender. The liquid from the tomatoes was enough to steam our squash to perfection. To rid the final dish of excess moisture, we drained the shredded squash in a strainer and reduced and concentrated the tomato sauce using the sauté or browning function. Fresh basil and Parmesan (vegan or dairy) completed our plant-based plate.

- 3 tablespoons extra-virgin olive oil
- 3 garlic cloves, minced
- 1 tablespoon tomato paste
- 1 teaspoon minced fresh oregano or ½ teaspoon dried
- ½ teaspoon table salt
   Pinch red pepper flakes
- 2 pounds plum tomatoes, cored and cut into 1-inch pieces
- 1 (4-pound) spaghetti squash, halved lengthwise and seeded
- 2 tablespoons chopped fresh basil
   Vegan Parmesan Substitute (page 27) or shaved dairy Parmesan

1. Using highest sauté or browning function, heat oil in electric pressure cooker until shimmering. Add garlic, tomato paste, oregano, salt, and pepper flakes and cook, stirring frequently, until fragrant, about 30 seconds. Stir in tomatoes. Season squash halves with salt and pepper and nestle cut side down into pressure cooker.

2. Lock lid in place and close pressure release valve. Select high pressure cook function and cook for 10 minutes. Turn off pressure cooker and quick-release pressure. Carefully remove lid, allowing steam to escape away from you.

3. Transfer squash to cutting board, let cool slightly, then shred flesh into strands using 2 forks; discard skins. Transfer squash to fine-mesh strainer and let drain while finishing sauce.

4. Cook sauce using highest sauté or browning function until tomatoes are completely broken down and sauce is thickened, 15 to 20 minutes. Transfer squash to serving platter, spoon sauce over top, and sprinkle with basil and vegan Parmesan substitute. Serve.

Spaghetti Squash with Fresh Tomato Sauce

All-Purpose Fresh Tomato Sauce

Braised Sweet Potatoes with Cilantro-Lime Dressing

Serves 4   **SLOW COOKER**

Cooking time 3 to 4 hours on low or 2 to 3 hours on high

Why This Recipe Works Highly nutritious, hearty, and versatile, sweet potatoes should be a mainstay in any diet, plant-based or otherwise. Though they can be prepared many different ways, they take beautifully to slow cooking since they are dense and take a while to cook through, even when sliced, as they are here. We chose to braise the sweet potatoes in an Asian-inspired liquid infused with lemongrass, star anise, and ginger, which gave this superfood super flavor. After the sweet potatoes were tender, we tossed the aromatic potato slices with a fresh cilantro and lime vinaigrette, which provided a bright and spicy contrast and herbaceous note to the sweet potatoes. You will need a 5- to 7-quart oval slow cooker for this recipe.

- 1 lemongrass stalk, trimmed to bottom 6 inches and bruised with back of knife
- 2 star anise pods
- 1 tablespoon grated fresh ginger, divided
- ½ teaspoon table salt
- 2 pounds sweet potatoes, peeled and sliced ½ inch thick
- 1 tablespoon chopped fresh cilantro

1 tablespoon packed brown sugar
1 tablespoon toasted sesame oil
1 teaspoon grated lime zest plus 4 teaspoons juice
¼ teaspoon Fish Sauce Substitute (page 22)
    Pinch cayenne

1. Combine 1 cup water, lemongrass, star anise, 2 teaspoons ginger, and salt in slow cooker. Nestle potatoes into slow cooker, cover, and cook until potatoes are tender, 3 to 4 hours on low or 2 to 3 hours on high.

2. Using slotted spoon, transfer potatoes to serving platter. Brush away any lemongrass or star anise that sticks to potatoes and discard cooking liquid. Whisk cilantro, sugar, oil, lime zest and juice, fish sauce substitute, cayenne, and remaining 1 teaspoon ginger together in bowl; season with salt and pepper to taste. Drizzle dressing over potatoes and serve.

Garlicky Swiss Chard

Serves 4   FAST   PRESSURE COOKER

Why This Recipe Works Sturdy Swiss chard takes well to braising, which turns it meltingly tender and tempers its assertive flavor. So using a pressure cooker to prepare an abundant amount of Swiss chard in a flash was a no-brainer. We decided on simple flavorings to keep the chard in the spotlight: A healthy dose of garlic and a pinch of red pepper flakes made for a punchy base. We made sure to use the chard stems as well as the leaves to add textural contrast (and minimize waste). Using vegetable broth to braise the greens infused them with extra savory flavor, and the garlicky chard turned out tender with just the right amount of chew. A splash of lemon juice at the end lightened the finished dish. Make this a meal by serving it over the cooked grains of your choice.

¼ cup extra-virgin olive oil, divided
5 garlic cloves, sliced thin
⅛ teaspoon red pepper flakes
½ cup vegetable broth
¼ teaspoon table salt
2 pounds Swiss chard, stems cut into 2-inch lengths, leaves sliced into 2-inch-wide strips
1 tablespoon lemon juice, plus extra for seasoning

1. Using highest sauté or browning function, cook 2 tablespoons oil, garlic, and pepper flakes in electric pressure cooker until fragrant, about 1 minute. Stir in broth and salt, then stir in chard stems and leaves, 1 handful at a time.

2. Lock lid in place and close pressure release valve. Select high pressure cook function and cook for 5 minutes. Turn off pressure cooker and quick-release pressure. Carefully remove lid, allowing steam to escape away from you.

3. Stir in lemon juice and remaining 2 tablespoons oil. Season with salt, pepper, and extra lemon juice to taste. Serve.

All-Purpose Fresh Tomato Sauce

Makes about 8 cups; enough for 2 pounds pasta
SLOW COOKER
Cooking time 8 to 10 hours on low or 5 to 7 hours on high

Why This Recipe Works The beauty of this recipe is that you can put a bounty of fresh tomatoes into a slow cooker along with a little salt, walk away for up to 10 hours, and end up with a brightly flavored, endlessly versatile tomato sauce. This is the recipe to turn to when your local farmers' markets are overflowing with their late summer crops of field-grown tomatoes (and aromatic stalks of freshly picked basil). It makes enough to serve a crowd—or plenty to freeze for later use, when summer is long gone and you need a reminder of what a fresh tomato tastes like. This is a lighter-bodied sauce, so if serving with pasta, don't dilute the sauce with pasta-cooking water as you normally might. Be sure to leave the lid slightly ajar—about ½ inch—to allow steam to escape and help concentrate the intense tomato flavor. You will need a 4- to 7-quart slow cooker for this recipe.

8 pounds plum tomatoes, cored and halved crosswise
1½ teaspoons table salt
¼ cup extra-virgin olive oil
¼ cup chopped fresh basil

1. Working over bowl, squeeze each tomato half to expel seeds and excess juice. Discard seeds and juice. Combine tomatoes and salt in slow cooker. Cover, leaving lid about ½ inch ajar, and cook until tomatoes are very soft, 8 to 10 hours on low or 5 to 7 hours on high.

2. Transfer tomatoes to colander and let excess liquid drain (do not press on tomatoes). Working in batches, process tomatoes in blender until smooth, about 1 minute; return to now-empty slow cooker. Stir oil into sauce and season with salt and pepper to taste. Before serving, stir in basil. (Sauce can be refrigerated for 1 week or frozen for up to 3 months.)

Classic Marinara Sauce

Makes about 10 cups; enough for 2 pounds pasta

`SLOW COOKER`

Cooking time 8 to 10 hours on low or 5 to 7 hours on high

Why This Recipe Works The long simmering time that comes from using a slow cooker renders classic marinara sauce rich and flavorful. Our biggest hurdle in creating a marinara that was neither watery nor too thick was choosing the right tomato products. Our solution was a combination of three different tomato products (paste, crushed, and puree). The concentrated products (paste and puree) added complex, umami-rich flavor to the canned crushed tomatoes without unwanted dilution, so there was no need to evaporate excess liquid. We microwaved onions, garlic, and oregano along with the tomato paste to create a flavor-packed sauce base with a classic marinara taste profile. Fresh basil added at the end provided an aromatic finishing touch. In addition to serving this with pasta, we like to use it as a dipping sauce for fried vegetables or spoon it onto Italian sandwiches. You will need a 4- to 7-quart slow cooker for this recipe.

- 2 onions, chopped fine
- 6 garlic cloves, minced
- 2 tablespoons tomato paste
- 2 tablespoons extra-virgin olive oil
- 2 tablespoons minced fresh oregano or 2 teaspoons dried
- 1 teaspoon table salt
- 2 (28-ounce) cans crushed tomatoes
- 1 (28-ounce) can tomato puree
- ½ cup dry red wine
- 2 teaspoons sugar, plus extra for seasoning
- ¼ cup chopped fresh basil

1. Microwave onions, garlic, tomato paste, oil, oregano, and salt in bowl, stirring occasionally, until onions are softened, about 5 minutes; transfer to slow cooker. Stir in tomatoes, tomato puree, and wine. Cover and cook until sauce is deeply flavored, 8 to 10 hours on low or 5 to 7 hours on high.

2. Stir sugar into sauce. Season with salt, pepper, and extra sugar to taste. Before serving, stir in basil. (Sauce can be refrigerated for 1 week or frozen for up to 3 months.)

Tomatoes with Olive Oil

Serves 4 to 6   `SLOW COOKER`

Cooking time 5 to 6 hours on low or 3 to 4 hours on high

Why This Recipe Works Whether you have an overabundance of just-picked August tomatoes or you are just looking for a way to improve average supermarket tomatoes, slow roasting is a beautiful way to go. We were after a foolproof slow-cooker "roasting" method that would deliver a sweet, intense flavor and melt-in-your-mouth texture. We gently tossed halved tomatoes with just enough olive oil to infuse them with flavor as they released their juices into the slow cooker, creating a flavorful cooking liquid. The addition of smashed garlic cloves, which mellowed and softened during the cooking time, lent a rich, nutty flavor to the oil. Aside from a little thyme, salt, and pepper, no other seasoning was needed. We recommend serving these tomatoes alongside plenty of crusty bread for dipping into the extra cooking liquid. You can also use this seriously flavorful cooking liquid to make a salad dressing. These tomatoes are great on sandwiches, or spread whole-grain toast with ricotta or goat cheese and top with the roasted tomatoes. You will need a 5- to 7-quart slow cooker for this recipe.

- 6 ripe tomatoes, cored and halved lengthwise
- ½ cup extra-virgin olive oil
- 6 garlic cloves, peeled and smashed
- 2 teaspoons minced fresh thyme or ¾ teaspoon dried
- ¾ teaspoon table salt
- ¼ teaspoon pepper

1. Combine all ingredients in slow cooker. Cover and cook until tomatoes are tender and slightly shriveled around edges, 5 to 6 hours on low or 3 to 4 hours on high.

2. Let tomatoes cool in oil for at least 15 minutes or up to 4 hours. Season with salt and pepper to taste. Serve.

CORING TOMATOES

Remove core of tomato using paring knife.

Ratatouille

Serves 4 `FAST` `PRESSURE COOKER`

Why This Recipe Works The pressure cooker is tailor-made for traditionally long-cooked stews, but it doesn't allow for any evaporation—and this Provençal classic is chock-full of watery vegetables. Cooking off some of their moisture before and after pressure-cooking did the trick. Sautéing the peppers also concentrated their flavor. We found that pretreating the eggplant with salt wasn't necessary—cutting it small ensured it would break down and help create a thicker sauce (it also helped shorten the cooking time). Canned whole tomatoes and zucchini rounded out the vegetable medley. Garlic, pepper flakes, and herbes de Provence added a zesty spice backbone characteristic of this dish, and a splash of sherry vinegar to finish woke up the flavors of the sweet vegetables. We prefer to make our Vegan Pesto, but a store-bought variety (vegan or dairy) will work.

- 2 tablespoons extra-virgin olive oil
- 2 red or yellow bell peppers, stemmed, seeded, and cut into 1-inch pieces
- 1 onion, chopped fine
- 1 teaspoon table salt
- 4 garlic cloves, minced
- 1 teaspoon herbes de Provence
- ¼ teaspoon red pepper flakes
- 1 (28-ounce) can whole peeled tomatoes, drained with juice reserved, chopped
- 1 pound eggplant, cut into ½-inch pieces
- 1 pound zucchini, quartered lengthwise and sliced 1 inch thick
- 1 tablespoon sherry vinegar
- ¼ cup basil Vegan Pesto (page 23), plus extra for serving

1. Using highest sauté or browning function, heat oil in electric pressure cooker until shimmering. Add bell peppers, onion, and salt and cook until vegetables are softened, about 5 minutes. Stir in garlic, herbes de Provence, and pepper flakes and cook until fragrant, about 30 seconds. Stir in tomatoes and reserved juice, eggplant, and zucchini. Lock lid in place and close pressure release valve. Select high pressure cook function and cook for 1 minute.

2. Turn off pressure cooker and quick-release pressure. Carefully remove lid, allowing steam to escape away from you. Using highest sauté function, continue to cook vegetable mixture until zucchini is tender and sauce has thickened slightly, 3 to 5 minutes. Stir in vinegar and season with salt and pepper to taste. Dollop individual portions with pesto and serve, passing extra pesto separately.

Tomatoes with Olive Oil

Ratatouille

Brown Rice with Shiitakes and Edamame

Serves 4   PRESSURE COOKER

Why This Recipe Works Using a pressure cooker makes perfect brown rice completely foolproof. (If you're using a multicooker, although many multicookers now have preset "rice" buttons, we discovered that we got more consistent results by manually setting the pressure-cook time ourselves.) While stovetop rice is usually cooked using the absorption method (in which the rice soaks up all the liquid it's cooked in), we cooked ours in plenty of liquid (similar to pasta) and then drained away the extra after cooking. This resulted in more evenly cooked rice, since all of the grains were completely submerged in liquid for the entire cooking time. To turn our brown rice into a satisfying main dish, we sautéed meaty shiitake mushrooms, fragrant scallions, and grated fresh ginger in the cooker after the rice was done, then stirred in edamame for satisfying protein and rice vinegar and mirin for brightness.

- 1½ cups short-grain brown rice, rinsed
- ¼ teaspoon table salt, plus salt for cooking rice
- 1 tablespoon vegetable oil
- 4 ounces shiitake mushrooms, stemmed and sliced thin
- 4 scallions, white parts minced, green parts sliced thin on bias
- 2 teaspoons grated fresh ginger
- 1 cup frozen edamame, thawed
- 4 teaspoons rice vinegar, plus extra for seasoning
- 1 tablespoon mirin, plus extra for seasoning
- 1 teaspoon toasted sesame oil

1. Combine 12 cups water, rice, and 2 teaspoons salt in electric pressure cooker.

2. Lock lid in place and close pressure release valve. Select high pressure cook function and cook for 8 minutes. Turn off pressure cooker and let pressure release naturally for 15 minutes. Quick-release any remaining pressure, then carefully remove lid, allowing steam to escape away from you.

3. Drain rice and transfer to large bowl. Wipe out pressure cooker with paper towels. Using highest sauté or browning function, heat vegetable oil in now-empty pressure cooker until shimmering. Add mushrooms, scallion whites, ginger, and salt and cook until mushrooms are softened, 5 to 7 minutes. Transfer to bowl with rice, then add edamame, vinegar, mirin, sesame oil, and scallion greens and gently toss to combine. Season with extra vinegar and mirin to taste. Serve.

Warm Wild Rice Salad with Pecans and Cranberries

Serves 6   FAST   PRESSURE COOKER

Why This Recipe Works Using a pressure cooker to cook wild rice turned this healthy grain, which can take up to an hour on the stovetop, into a hands-off, any-night possibility. When prepared well, wild rice has a pleasantly chewy outer husk and a nutty, savory flavor; we found that the pressure cooker produced perfect wild rice every time as long as we cooked it pasta-style: that is, in enough water to keep it submerged. The pressure cooker's ability to moderate the temperature of the cooking liquid meant that every grain turned out tender and intact. A handful of thyme sprigs and a couple of bay leaves added to the water infused the rice with flavor. To transform the nutty rice into a finished dish with contrasting flavors and textures, we added sweet-tart dried cranberries, crunchy pecans, fresh parsley, and bright apple cider vinegar. Do not use quick-cooking or presteamed wild rice in this recipe (read the ingredient list on the package to determine this).

- 2 cups wild rice, picked over and rinsed
- 8 sprigs fresh thyme
- 2 bay leaves
- ½ teaspoon table salt, plus salt for cooking rice
- 1 cup fresh parsley leaves
- ¾ cup dried cranberries
- ¾ cup pecans, toasted and chopped coarse
- 3 tablespoons refined coconut oil or unsalted butter, melted
- 1 shallot, minced
- 2 teaspoons apple cider vinegar

1. Combine 12 cups water, rice, thyme sprigs, bay leaves, and 1 tablespoon salt in electric pressure cooker.

2. Lock lid in place and close pressure release valve. Select high pressure cook function and cook for 18 minutes. Turn off pressure cooker and quick-release pressure. Carefully remove lid, allowing steam to escape away from you.

3. Discard thyme sprigs and bay leaves. Drain rice and transfer to large bowl. Add parsley, cranberries, pecans, melted oil, shallot, vinegar, and salt and gently toss to combine. Season with salt and pepper to taste. Serve.

Warm Wild Rice Salad with Pecans and Cranberries

1 onion, chopped fine
1½ cups pearl barley, rinsed
2 tablespoons extra-virgin olive oil, divided
2 teaspoons grated fresh ginger
½ teaspoon table salt
⅛ teaspoon ground cinnamon
⅛ teaspoon ground cardamom
3½ cups vegetable broth
3 ounces pitted dates, chopped (½ cup)
⅓ cup chopped fresh parsley
2 teaspoons lemon juice

1. Lightly coat slow cooker with vegetable oil spray. Microwave onion, barley, 1 tablespoon oil, ginger, salt, cinnamon, and cardamom in bowl, stirring occasionally, until onion is softened and barley is lightly toasted, about 5 minutes; transfer to prepared slow cooker. Stir in broth, cover, and cook until barley is tender and all broth is absorbed, 3 to 4 hours on low or 2 to 3 hours on high.

2. Fluff barley with fork, then gently fold in dates, parsley, lemon juice, and remaining 1 tablespoon oil. Season with salt and pepper to taste. Serve.

Beet and Wheat Berry Salad with Arugula and Apples

Serves 4   SLOW COOKER
Cooking time 6 to 8 hours on low or 4 to 5 hours on high

Why This Recipe Works Nutty wheat berries, earthy beets, crisp apples, and peppery arugula combine forces in this hearty salad. The wheat berries simmered in the slow cooker right alongside the beets, which we wrapped in foil to keep the cooking even and the deep color from bleeding. Minced garlic and thyme provided an aromatic backbone. Once the wheat berries were tender, we drained and dressed them with a lively vinaigrette. Tasters felt that a creamy counterpoint was desirable to balance the flavors, so we added a dollop of cashew ricotta before serving (crumbled goat cheese also worked well). To ensure even cooking, we recommend using beets that are roughly 3 inches in diameter. If using quick-cooking or presteamed wheat berries (the ingredient list on the package specifies the type), you will need to decrease the cooking time. The wheat berries will retain a chewy texture once fully cooked. You will need a 4- to 7-quart slow cooker for this recipe.

Spiced Barley Pilaf with Dates and Parsley

Serves 6   SLOW COOKER
Cooking time 3 to 4 hours on low or 2 to 3 hours on high

Why This Recipe Works Barley's high protein content and appealingly nutty flavor make it a boon to the plant-based pantry. This distinctive barley pilaf features a potent blend of Indian-inspired spices—ginger, cinnamon, and cardamom—plus dates for sweetness and texture. To cook it properly in the slow cooker, we needed to find the right liquid-to-barley ratio. After a few tests, we found that 3½ cups broth to 1½ cups barley produced barley that was cooked through once all the broth had been absorbed, though the texture was on the soft side. Reducing the amount of liquid wasn't an option because it resulted in unevenly cooked barley. To maintain a bit of the grains' structure and ensure even cooking, we briefly toasted the barley in the microwave before adding it to the slow cooker—which also created deeper flavor. Do not substitute hulled, hull-less, quick-cooking, or presteamed barley (read the ingredient list on the package to determine this) in this recipe. You will need a 4- to 7-quart slow cooker for this recipe.

1 cup wheat berries
2 garlic cloves, minced
2 teaspoons minced fresh thyme or ½ teaspoon dried
1 teaspoon table salt, divided
1 pound beets, trimmed
1 Granny Smith apple, peeled, cored, halved, and sliced ¼ inch thick
4 ounces (4 cups) baby arugula
3 tablespoons extra-virgin olive oil
3 tablespoons red wine vinegar
Pinch pepper
Pinch sugar
½ cup Cashew Ricotta (page 26) or 4 ounces goat cheese, crumbled (1 cup)

1. Combine 5 cups water, wheat berries, garlic, thyme, and ½ teaspoon salt in slow cooker. Wrap beets individually in aluminum foil and place in slow cooker. Cover and cook until wheat berries and beets are tender, 6 to 8 hours on low or 4 to 5 hours on high.

2. Transfer beets to cutting board, open foil, and let sit until cool enough to handle. Rub off beet skins with paper towels and cut beets into ½-inch-thick wedges.

3. Drain wheat berries, transfer to large serving bowl, and let cool slightly. Add beets, apple, arugula, oil, vinegar, remaining ½ teaspoon salt, pepper, and sugar and toss to combine. Season with salt and pepper to taste. Dollop with cashew ricotta and serve.

Freekeh Pilaf with Dates and Pistachios

Serves 4 to 6 `FAST` `PRESSURE COOKER`

Why This Recipe Works Freekeh, a protein-packed grain often used in eastern Mediterranean and North African cooking, is made from durum wheat that's been harvested while the grains are still young and green; the grains are roasted and then sold whole or cracked. For a pilaf that accentuates freekeh's smoky earthiness, we cooked it with warm spices including coriander, cumin, pepper. A quick sauté in the pressure cooker softened a shallot and bloomed the spices, and then we just had to add the freekeh and water and cook under pressure. Studded with sweet dates and toasted pistachios and topped with aromatic fresh mint and a drizzle of olive oil, our pilaf was hearty and healthful. You can find freekeh in the grain aisle or natural foods section of most well-stocked supermarkets. Whole freekeh requires a different cooking method and will not work in this recipe.

Freekeh Pilaf with Dates and Pistachios

2 tablespoons extra-virgin olive oil, plus extra for drizzling
1 shallot, minced
1½ teaspoons grated fresh ginger
½ teaspoon table salt
¼ teaspoon ground coriander
¼ teaspoon ground cumin
¼ teaspoon pepper
1¾ cups water
1½ cups cracked freekeh, rinsed
3 ounces pitted dates, chopped (½ cup)
¼ cup shelled pistachios, toasted and chopped coarse
1½ tablespoons lemon juice
¼ cup chopped fresh mint

1. Using highest sauté or browning function, heat oil in electric pressure cooker until shimmering. Add shallot, ginger, salt, coriander, cumin, and pepper and cook until shallot is softened, about 2 minutes. Stir in water and freekeh.

2. Lock lid in place and close pressure release valve. Select high pressure cook function and cook for 4 minutes. Turn off pressure cooker and quick-release pressure. Carefully remove lid, allowing steam to escape away from you.

3. Add dates, pistachios, and lemon juice and gently fluff freekeh with fork to combine. Season with salt and pepper to taste. Transfer to serving platter, sprinkle with mint, and drizzle with extra oil. Serve.

Greek Chickpeas with Coriander and Sage
Serves 6 `PRESSURE COOKER`

Why This Recipe Works Chickpeas capture the spotlight in this satisfying dish inspired by a traditional Greek preparation of slow-baked chickpeas. The dish is little more than chickpeas, caramelized onions, and some carefully chosen herbs and spices in a superflavorful broth, but it adds up to far more than the sum of its parts. The chickpeas paired beautifully with some lemony coriander seeds that kept their distinctive character but softened into little bursting pockets of flavor. Sage leaves, mellowed by low-pressure cooking, transformed into tender, mild greens that lent subtle floral notes to the dish. See page 285 for more information on brining beans. To crack coriander, place the seeds on a cutting board and rock the bottom edge of a skillet over them until they crack. For a spicier dish, use the higher amount of pepper flakes. Serve these chickpeas with rice or pita bread.

1½ tablespoons table salt, for brining
1 pound (2½ cups) dried chickpeas, rinsed
2 tablespoons extra-virgin olive oil, plus extra for drizzling
2 onions, halved and sliced thin
¼ teaspoon table salt
1 tablespoon coriander seeds, cracked
¼–½ teaspoon red pepper flakes
2½ cups vegetable broth
¼ cup fresh sage leaves
2 bay leaves
1½ teaspoons grated lemon zest plus 2 teaspoons juice
2 tablespoons minced fresh parsley

1. Dissolve 1½ tablespoons salt in 2 quarts cold water in large container. Add chickpeas and soak at room temperature for at least 8 hours or up to 24 hours. Drain and rinse well.

2. Using highest sauté or browning function, heat oil in electric pressure cooker until shimmering. Add onions and ¼ teaspoon salt and cook until onions are softened and well browned, 10 to 12 minutes. Stir in coriander and pepper flakes and cook until fragrant, about 30 seconds. Stir in broth, scraping up any browned bits, then stir in chickpeas, sage, and bay leaves.

3. Lock lid in place and close pressure release valve. Select low pressure cook function and cook for 10 minutes. Turn off pressure cooker and let pressure release naturally for 15 minutes. Quick-release any remaining pressure, then carefully remove lid, allowing steam to escape away from you.

4. Discard bay leaves. Stir lemon zest and juice into chickpeas and season with salt and pepper to taste. Sprinkle with parsley. Serve, drizzling individual portions with extra oil.

Smoky Braised Chickpeas
Serves 6 `SLOW COOKER`
Cooking time 9 to 11 hours on low or 6 to 8 hours on high

Why This Recipe Works Chickpeas are prized for their high fiber content as well as for being an excellent source of plant-based protein. But they also have a great buttery texture and an adaptable flavor, so they easily soak up the flavors of other ingredients they're cooked with, making them ideal for slow cooking in a flavor-packed broth. We infused vegetable broth with distinctive smoked paprika and a sliced red onion for flavor and texture. Once our chickpeas were perfectly tender and creamy, we drained away all but a cup of the cooking liquid, using what we reserved to create a simple, smoky sauce. Mashing a portion of the beans enhanced the creamy consistency of the dish without adding any extra fat, and citrusy cilantro added brightness and color. The Garlicky Yogurt Sauce adds a pungent yet creamy finishing touch. You will need a 4- to 7-quart slow cooker for this recipe.

1 red onion, halved and sliced thin
1 tablespoon extra-virgin olive oil, divided
1 tablespoon sweet or hot smoked paprika
3 cups vegetable broth
3 cups water
1 pound (2½ cups) dried chickpeas, picked over and rinsed
1 teaspoon table salt
¼ cup chopped fresh cilantro
Garlicky Yogurt Sauce (recipe follows) (optional)

1. Microwave onion, 1 teaspoon oil, and paprika in bowl, stirring occasionally, until onion is softened, about 5 minutes; transfer to slow cooker. Stir in broth, water, chickpeas, and salt. Cover and cook until chickpeas are tender, 9 to 11 hours on low or 6 to 8 hours on high.

2. Drain chickpeas, reserving 1 cup cooking liquid. Return one-third of chickpeas to now-empty slow cooker and mash with potato masher until smooth. Stir in reserved cooking liquid, cilantro, remaining chickpeas, and remaining 2 teaspoons oil. Season with salt and pepper to taste. Serve with yogurt sauce, if using.

Garlicky Yogurt Sauce
Makes about 1 cup

1 cup plain plant-based yogurt or dairy yogurt
2 tablespoons chopped fresh mint
1 garlic clove, minced

Combine plant-based yogurt, mint, and garlic in bowl; cover and refrigerate until ready to serve.

INGREDIENT SPOTLIGHT

SMOKED PAPRIKA
Smoked paprika is the Spanish cousin to the more widely used Hungarian paprika. Smoked paprika can be either sweet or hot, and it is made from a different variety of red pepper than regular paprika is made from. The peppers are dried over oak embers and then ground, and the resulting spice has a woodsy smokiness. Sprinkle smoked paprika over hummus, mashed potatoes, or Blistered Shishito Peppers (page 358).

Braised White Beans with Olive Oil and Sage
Serves 6   SLOW COOKER
Cooking time 9 to 11 hours on low or 6 to 8 hours on high

Why This Recipe Works These slow-cooked beans deliver rich flavor and creamy, tender texture. We found that dried small white beans worked well here, and they required no prep other than being picked over and rinsed. To ensure that the beans took on robust flavor during their long stint in the slow cooker, we simmered them with onion, a hefty amount of garlic, and a little sage. Once the beans were perfectly cooked, we drained the mixture and reserved a cup of the flavorful

cooking liquid to stir back into the beans. We then mashed a portion of the beans to thicken the sauce and enhance the creamy consistency of the dish. To serve, we dressed them up with some good-quality olive oil. Extra fresh sage stirred in at the end enhanced the herbaceous flavors. You will need a 4- to 7-quart slow cooker for this recipe. Serve these over whole grains or with crusty bread.

1 onion, chopped fine
5 garlic cloves, minced
2 tablespoons extra-virgin olive oil, divided
2 teaspoons minced fresh sage, divided
3 cups vegetable broth
3 cups water
1 pound (2½ cups) dried small white beans, picked over and rinsed
1 teaspoon table salt

1. Microwave onion, garlic, 1 teaspoon oil, and 1 teaspoon sage in bowl, stirring occasionally, until onion is softened, about 5 minutes; transfer to slow cooker. Stir in broth, water, beans, and salt. Cover and cook until beans are tender, 9 to 11 hours on low or 6 to 8 hours on high.

2. Drain beans, reserving 1 cup cooking liquid. Return one-third of beans to now-empty slow cooker and mash with potato masher until smooth. Stir in reserved cooking liquid, remaining beans, remaining 5 teaspoons oil, and remaining 1 teaspoon sage. Season with salt and pepper to taste. Serve.

French Lentils with Swiss Chard
Serves 6   PRESSURE COOKER

Why This Recipe Works Versions of beans and greens are found all over the world, and we think you can't have too many plant-based versions of this dish in your cooking arsenal. This sophisticated, Mediterranean-inspired rendition of beans and greens comes together quickly and easily in the pressure cooker. The quick, even cooking of the pressure cooker ensured that the lentils kept their shape and firm-tender texture after cooking in a garlic-and-thyme-bolstered liquid. After releasing the pressure, we stirred in Swiss chard leaves until just wilted, letting them maintain their fresh bite. A bit of mustard stirred in off the heat added a tangy kick, while almonds added richness and parsley countered with freshness. We prefer French green lentils, or lentilles du Puy, for this recipe, but it will work with any type of lentil except red or yellow.

French Lentils with Swiss Chard

pressure cooker and let pressure release naturally for 15 minutes. Quick-release any remaining pressure, then carefully remove lid, allowing steam to escape away from you.

3. Stir chard leaves into lentils, 1 handful at a time, and let cook in residual heat until wilted, about 5 minutes. Stir in mustard and lemon zest and juice. Season with salt and pepper to taste. Transfer to serving platter, drizzle with extra oil, and sprinkle with almonds and parsley. Serve.

Warm Lentil Salad with Radishes and Mint

Serves 4   `SLOW COOKER`

Cooking time 4 to 5 hours on low or 3 to 4 hours on high

Why This Recipe Works We chose tiny green lentils for this tasty warm salad, for their earthy, complex flavor and tender-firm texture. With a ratio of 2½ cups vegetable broth to 1 cup lentils, we were able to produce perfectly cooked legumes. We flavored them with garlic, thyme, and paprika and stirred in sliced radishes and chopped mint to bring crunch and bright freshness to our warm salad. We prefer French green lentils, or lentilles du Puy, for this recipe, but it will work with any type of lentil except red or yellow. For a heartier salad, serve this over mixed greens. If you would like to add cheese, we suggest feta. You will need a 4- to 7-quart slow cooker for this recipe.

- 2 tablespoons extra-virgin olive oil, plus extra for drizzling
- 12 ounces Swiss chard, stems chopped fine, leaves sliced into ½-inch-wide strips
- 1 onion, chopped fine
- ½ teaspoon table salt
- 2 garlic cloves, minced
- 1 teaspoon minced fresh thyme or ¼ teaspoon dried
- 2½ cups water
- 1 cup lentilles du Puy (French green lentils), picked over and rinsed
- 3 tablespoons whole-grain mustard
- ½ teaspoon grated lemon zest plus 1 teaspoon juice
- 3 tablespoons sliced almonds, toasted
- 2 tablespoons chopped fresh parsley

1. Using highest sauté or browning function, heat oil in electric pressure cooker until shimmering. Add chard stems, onion, and salt and cook until vegetables are softened, about 5 minutes. Stir in garlic and thyme and cook until fragrant, about 30 seconds. Stir in water and lentils.

2. Lock lid in place and close pressure release valve. Select high pressure cook function and cook for 11 minutes. Turn off

- 1 tablespoon extra-virgin olive oil, divided
- 2 garlic cloves, minced
- 1½ teaspoons minced fresh thyme or ¼ teaspoon dried
- 1 teaspoon paprika
- 2½ cups vegetable broth
- 1 cup lentilles du Puy (French green lentils), picked over and rinsed
- 2½ tablespoons red wine vinegar, divided
- ¼ teaspoon table salt
- 6 radishes, trimmed, halved, and sliced thin
- ¼ cup chopped fresh mint
- 1 shallot, halved and sliced thin
- 1 ounce feta cheese, crumbled (¼ cup) (optional)

1. Microwave 1 teaspoon oil, garlic, thyme, and paprika in bowl, stirring occasionally, until fragrant, about 30 seconds; transfer to slow cooker. Stir in broth, lentils, 1 tablespoon vinegar, and salt. Cover and cook until lentils are tender, 4 to 5 hours on low or 3 to 4 hours on high.

2. Stir in radishes; mint; shallot; feta, if using; remaining 2 teaspoons oil; and remaining 1½ tablespoons vinegar. Season with salt and pepper to taste. Serve.

CHAPTER 10
SMALL BITES AND SNACKS

■ FAST (45 minutes or less total time)
Photos: Beet Chips; Meaty Loaded Nacho Dip; Spiced Roasted Chickpeas; Smoky Shishito Peppers with Espelette and Lime

Sweet Potato Hummus

Serves 8 (Makes 2 cups)

Why This Recipe Works Vegetables can be used to make hummus just like beans. While we love traditional chickpea hummus, we thought it would be fun to create a new rendition that turned hummus on its head, keeping the hallmark flavorings (tahini, olive oil, garlic, and lemon juice) but switching out the legumes for a vegetable. So in their place, we turned to earthy, vibrant sweet potatoes. We aimed to bring out the sweet potatoes' flavor by figuring out the best cooking method as well as the ideal balance of complementary ingredients. To keep things speedy, we opted to microwave rather than bake the sweet potatoes—after all, dip shouldn't take more than an hour to make. Happily, microwaving the potatoes resulted in flavor that was nearly as intense as when we roasted them. Just ¼ cup of tahini was enough to stand up to the spuds without overwhelming the hummus. To round out the flavor of the hummus, we added warm spices: paprika, coriander, and cumin. The addition of chipotle and a clove of garlic curbed the sweetness and accented the spices, while some lemon juice brought the flavors into focus. We liked this hummus so much we developed a variation with another root vegetable: earthy-floral parsnips.

- 1 pound sweet potatoes, unpeeled
- ¼ cup tahini
- 3 tablespoons extra-virgin olive oil, plus extra for drizzling
- ¾ cup water
- 2 tablespoons lemon juice
- ¾ teaspoon table salt
- 1 garlic clove, minced
- 1 teaspoon paprika
- ½ teaspoon ground coriander
- ¼ teaspoon ground cumin
- ¼ teaspoon chipotle chile powder
- 1 tablespoon toasted sesame seeds (optional)

1. Prick sweet potatoes several times with fork, place on plate, and microwave until very soft, about 12 minutes, flipping potatoes halfway through microwaving. Let potatoes cool for 5 minutes. Combine tahini and oil in small bowl.

2. Slice potatoes in half lengthwise and scoop flesh from skins; discard skins. Process sweet potato, water, lemon juice, salt, garlic, paprika, coriander, cumin, and chile powder in food processor until completely smooth, about 1 minute, scraping down sides of bowl as needed. With processor running, add tahini mixture in steady stream and process until hummus is smooth and creamy, about 15 seconds, scraping down bowl as needed. Season with salt and pepper to taste.

3. Transfer hummus to bowl, cover with plastic wrap, and let sit at room temperature until flavors meld, about 30 minutes. Drizzle with oil and sprinkle with sesame seeds, if using. Serve. (Hummus can be refrigerated for up to 5 days; stir in 1 tablespoon warm water to loosen if necessary before serving.)

VARIATION
Parsnip Hummus
Look for tender, thin parsnips; large parsnips can taste bitter.

Substitute 1 pound parsnips, peeled and cut into 1-inch lengths, for sweet potatoes. Microwave parsnips in covered bowl until tender, about 10 minutes. Transfer parsnips to food processor and proceed with recipe.

Artichoke and White Bean Dip

Serves 10 (Makes 2½ cups)

Why This Recipe Works Bean dips are often offered as the healthy alternative on a party spread, but they tend to disappoint unless they are loaded with cheese. We wanted to create a dairy-free bean dip that was healthy but still had our guests coming back for more, so we took it in a Mediterranean direction. We processed cannellini beans with just enough extra-virgin olive oil for richness and binding, along with a shallot, lemon juice, and water. We stirred in water-packed jarred artichokes, which gave our dip a nicely chunky texture. Some lemon zest and parsley further brightened our zesty dip. Be sure to puree the beans to a smooth texture before stirring in the artichokes.

- 1 (15-ounce) can cannellini beans, rinsed
- 3 tablespoons extra-virgin olive oil
- 1 shallot, minced
- 1 tablespoon water
- 1½ teaspoons grated lemon zest plus 1½ tablespoons juice, divided, plus extra juice for seasoning
- 1 garlic clove, minced
- ½ teaspoon table salt
- ⅛ teaspoon pepper
  Pinch cayenne pepper, plus extra for seasoning
- 9 ounces jarred artichoke hearts packed in water, rinsed, patted dry, and chopped fine
- 1 tablespoon minced fresh parsley or mint

Process beans, oil, shallot, water, lemon zest and juice, garlic, salt, pepper, and cayenne in food processor until smooth, about 30 seconds, scraping down sides of bowl as needed. Transfer dip to medium serving bowl and stir in artichokes and parsley. Cover and refrigerate until flavors meld, about

1 hour. Season with extra lemon juice and cayenne to taste before serving. (Dip can be refrigerated for up to 2 days; bring to room temperature before serving.)

Baba Ghanoush

Serves 8 (**Makes** 2 cups)

Why This Recipe Works When roasted, eggplant turns creamy and soft, making it the perfect base for the beloved Middle Eastern dip baba ghanoush. Before roasting the eggplants, we pricked their skin to encourage moisture to evaporate and to prevent the skin from splitting open, then roasted them whole in a very hot oven until the flesh was meltingly tender. To avoid a watery dip, we scooped the hot pulp into a colander to drain before putting it into the food processor with the other ingredients. We kept the flavorings true to tradition: lemon juice, olive oil, garlic, and tahini. A drizzle of olive oil and a sprinkle of parsley finished our baba ghanoush. In addition to serving as a dip, this makes a great sandwich spread (or filling). Look for eggplants with an even shape for this recipe, as bulbous eggplants won't cook evenly.

- 2 eggplants (1 pound each), pricked all over with fork
- 2 tablespoons tahini
- 2 tablespoons extra-virgin olive oil, plus extra for serving
- 4 teaspoons lemon juice
- 1 small garlic clove, minced
- ¾ teaspoon table salt
- ¼ teaspoon pepper
- 2 teaspoons chopped fresh parsley

1. Adjust oven rack to middle position and heat oven to 500 degrees. Place eggplants on aluminum foil–lined rimmed baking sheet and roast, turning eggplants every 15 minutes, until uniformly soft when pressed with tongs, 40 minutes to 1 hour. Let eggplants cool for 5 minutes on sheet.

2. Set colander over bowl. Trim top and bottom ¼ inch of eggplants, then halve eggplants lengthwise. Using spoon, scoop hot pulp into colander (you should have about 2 cups pulp); discard skins. Let pulp drain for 3 minutes.

3. Transfer drained eggplant to food processor. Add tahini, oil, lemon juice, garlic, salt, and pepper. Pulse mixture to coarse puree, about 8 pulses. Season with salt and pepper to taste.

4. Transfer to serving bowl, cover tightly with plastic wrap, and refrigerate until chilled, about 1 hour. Season with salt and pepper to taste, drizzle with extra oil to taste, and sprinkle with parsley before serving. (Dip can be refrigerated for up to 24 hours; bring to room temperature before serving.)

Sweet Potato Hummus

Baba Ghanoush

Super Guacamole

Fresh Tomato Salsa

Super Guacamole

Serves 6 to 8 (**Makes** about 2 cups) `FAST`

Why This Recipe Works Everyone loves buttery avocados, as
healthful as they are rich. For a supercharged guac that would
never become tired on a party spread, we incorporated pomegranate seeds and pepitas for a lively interplay of flavors and
textures. First, we minced our seasonings to a paste to ensure
that the flavors would be evenly distributed. Mashing three
diced avocados with a whisk until cohesive but still chunky
gave our guacamole the perfect creamy yet rustic texture. We
combined the pomegranate seeds and pepitas with scallions
and cilantro leaves and scattered the mixture over the top.
The result was a creamy guacamole punctuated with pops of
bright fruit and earthy crunch. For more spice, mince the ribs
and seeds from the chile with the other ingredients. A mortar
and pestle can be used to process the aromatics.

3 tablespoons pomegranate seeds
2 scallions, sliced thin
2 tablespoons roasted pepitas
2 tablespoons fresh cilantro leaves plus 2 tablespoons
  chopped
2 tablespoons finely chopped onion
1 serrano chile, stemmed, seeded, and chopped fine
¼ teaspoon grated lime zest plus 5 teaspoons juice,
  divided
1 teaspoon kosher salt
3 ripe avocados, halved, pitted, and cut into ½-inch
  pieces
1 plum tomato, cored, seeded, and minced
1 teaspoon extra-virgin olive oil

1. Combine pomegranate seeds, scallions, pepitas, and
cilantro leaves in bowl.

2. Chop onion, chile, and lime zest with salt until very
finely minced and homogeneous. Transfer to second bowl and
stir in 1½ tablespoons lime juice. Add avocado and, using
sturdy whisk, mash and stir mixture until well combined with
some ¼- to ½-inch chunks remaining. Stir in tomato and
chopped cilantro and season with salt to taste.

3. Toss pomegranate-pepita mixture with oil and remaining
½ teaspoon lime juice. Transfer guacamole to serving bowl and
top with pomegranate-pepita mixture. Serve.

CUTTING AVOCADO

1. Strike pit with chef's knife. Twist blade to remove pit. Use wooden spoon to knock pit off blade.

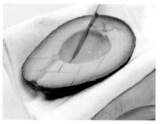

2. Secure avocado half with dish towel and use paring knife to make ½-inch crosshatch slices into flesh without cutting into skin.

3. Insert spoon between skin and flesh to separate them. Gently scoop out avocado cubes.

Fresh Tomato Salsa

Serves 12 (**Makes** about 3 cups) `FAST`

Why This Recipe Works A fresh, chunky salsa emphasizing the tomatoes is a simple but great accompaniment to a big bowl of tortilla chips. To solve the problem of watery salsa, we diced the tomatoes and let them drain in a colander. This put all our tomatoes, regardless of ripeness or juiciness, on a level playing field. Next, we chose red onion over yellow or white for its pretty color and milder flavor, and jalapeño chile for its slight vegetal flavor and moderate heat. Lime juice lent some acidity and tasted more authentic (and better) than vinegar or lemon juice. We found that the best, and simplest, way to combine the ingredients was to layer each chopped ingredient on top of the tomatoes while they drained. Once the tomatoes were ready, we gave the mixture a few stirs before finishing the salsa with the lime juice, salt, pepper, and sugar. The amount of sugar and lime juice you will need depends on the ripeness of the tomatoes. To make this salsa spicier, add the seeds from the chile. The salsa can be made 2 to 3 hours in advance; add the lime juice, salt, and sugar just before serving.

1½ pounds tomatoes, cored and cut into ½-inch pieces
½ cup finely chopped red onion
¼ cup chopped fresh cilantro
1 large jalapeño chile, stemmed, seeded, and minced
1 small garlic clove, minced
2 teaspoons lime juice, plus extra to taste
½ teaspoon table salt
    Pinch pepper
    Sugar

1. Place tomatoes in colander set over large bowl and let drain 30 minutes. As tomatoes drain, layer onion, cilantro, jalapeño, and garlic on top.

2. Shake colander to drain excess tomato juice. Discard juice, wipe out bowl, and transfer tomato mixture to bowl. Stir in lime juice, salt, and pepper. Season with sugar and extra lime juice to taste before serving.

Toasted Corn and Black Bean Salsa

Serves 8 (**Makes** about 2 cups)

Why This Recipe Works When you're in the mood for a different kind of salsa, try this tomato-free one (which is still chock-full of vegetables). In addition to serving it with tortilla chips, you can pile this satisfying salsa onto rice or even use it as a taco filling. The combo of fresh toasted corn kernels and chopped red bell pepper gives the salsa bright color and contrasting vegetable flavor, and the black beans bring hearty texture and protein, while jalapeño, scallion, and garlic add pops of spicy intensity. In keeping with the Mexican theme, we rounded out this salsa with lime juice, cilantro, and cumin. Do not substitute frozen corn for the fresh corn here. Be sure to use a nonstick skillet when toasting the corn. To make this salsa spicier, add the seeds from the chile.

1½ tablespoons extra-virgin olive oil, divided
1 ear corn, kernels cut from cob
1 red bell pepper, stemmed, seeded, and chopped fine
¾ cup canned black beans, rinsed
½ jalapeño chile, stemmed, seeded, and minced
1 scallion, sliced thin
2 garlic cloves, minced
2 tablespoons lime juice, plus extra for seasoning
2 tablespoons minced fresh cilantro
½ teaspoon ground cumin
¼ teaspoon table salt
⅛ teaspoon pepper

1. Heat 1½ teaspoons oil in 10-inch nonstick skillet over medium-high heat until shimmering. Add corn and cook, stirring occasionally, until golden brown, about 4 minutes.

2. Transfer corn to medium serving bowl and stir in remaining 1 tablespoon oil, bell pepper, beans, jalapeño, scallion, garlic, lime juice, cilantro, cumin, salt, and pepper. Cover and refrigerate until flavors meld, about 1 hour. Season with extra lime juice to taste before serving. (Salsa can be refrigerated for up to 2 days; bring to room temperature before serving.)

Carrot-Habanero Dip

Serves 10 (**Makes 2½ cups**)

Why This Recipe Works This highly seasoned dip is packed with vibrant carrot flavor. To really bring out the fruity-earthy flavor qualities of the carrots, the addition of a little spicy heat in the form of habanero chiles worked wonders. Cooking the carrots in a saucepan over an initial blast of heat quickly broke down their cell walls and released their sugars. To maintain their brilliant color, we avoided browning and instead added water after the initial cooking, simmering the carrots until perfectly tender. We tossed in some Moroccan-inspired spices that stood up well to the intensely sweet carrot flavor, and minced habanero chile provided a surprise kick (use one or two depending on your preference). Processing the mixture at the end produced a smooth, spreadable dip that's reminiscent of hummus. With a healthy drizzle of olive oil and some crunchy pepitas on top, this is an unexpected but simple dip that's a definite crowd-pleaser. To make this dip spicier, add the seeds from the chile.

 3 tablespoons extra-virgin olive oil, divided, plus extra for serving
 2 pounds carrots, peeled and sliced ¼ inch thick
 ½ teaspoon table salt
1–2 habanero chiles, seeded and minced
 2 garlic cloves, minced
 ¾ teaspoon ground coriander
 ¾ teaspoon ground cumin
 ¾ teaspoon ground ginger
 ⅛ teaspoon chili powder
 ⅛ teaspoon ground cinnamon
 ⅓ cup water
 1 tablespoon white wine vinegar
 1 tablespoon roasted, salted pepitas
 1 tablespoon minced fresh cilantro

1. Heat 1 tablespoon oil in large saucepan over medium-high heat until shimmering. Add carrots and salt and cook until carrots begin to soften, 5 to 6 minutes. Stir in habanero,

garlic, coriander, cumin, ginger, chili powder, and cinnamon and cook until fragrant, about 30 seconds. Add water and bring to simmer. Cover, reduce heat to low, and cook, stirring occasionally, until carrots are tender, 15 to 20 minutes.

2. Transfer carrots to bowl of food processor, add vinegar, and process until smooth, scraping down sides of bowl as needed, 1 to 2 minutes. With processor running, slowly add remaining 2 tablespoons oil until incorporated. Transfer to serving bowl, cover, and refrigerate until chilled, 30 minutes to 1 hour. Season with salt and pepper to taste. Sprinkle with pepitas and cilantro and drizzle with extra oil. Serve.

Meaty Loaded Nacho Dip

Serves 8 (**Makes 2 cups**) `FAST`

Why This Recipe Works Creamy, gooey, and tangy, this dip is downright cheesy and meaty in every way, except it doesn't contain dairy cheese or meat! We experimented with the familiar cast of characters used to develop cheese-like sauces—including cashews, nutritional yeast, and miso—but tasters were distracted by their textures and flavors. The most neutral ingredient we found was potato, and we had a breakthrough when we broke a cardinal kitchen rule: We whirred boiled potatoes in the blender at high speed to release as much of their starch as possible. While this would make awful mashed potatoes, the sticky mixture was ideal for a cheese-like sauce. We blended in carrot for color, chipotle chile for smoky spiciness, nutritional yeast for funky flavor depth, and vegetable oil for richness and fluidity and ended up with a flavorful, ultracreamy yellow-orange dip. To top it off in style, we sautéed poblano pepper, onion, garlic, and spices and added plant-based beef to crumble and brown. We loved the dip garnished with chopped red onion, tomatoes, and fresh cilantro, but you can also finish with chopped avocado, fresh or pickled jalapeños, sliced scallions, or Quick Sweet-and-Spicy Pickled Red Onions (page 99). Serve with tortilla chips or crudités. To rewarm cooled dip, microwave, covered, in 30-second bursts, whisking at each interval and thinning with water as needed, or rewarm on the stovetop, whisking occasionally, and thinning with water as needed.

12 ounces russet potatoes, peeled and cut into 1-inch pieces
 1 small carrot, peeled and cut into ½-inch pieces (⅓ cup)
 3 tablespoons vegetable oil, divided
1½ tablespoons nutritional yeast
1½ teaspoons distilled white vinegar
 1 teaspoon minced canned chipotle chile in adobo sauce, divided

Meaty Loaded Nacho Dip

2. Meanwhile, heat remaining 1 tablespoon oil in 10-inch nonstick skillet over medium-high heat until shimmering. Add two-thirds of onion, poblano, and remaining ⅛ teaspoon salt and cook until softened and lightly browned, 5 to 7 minutes. Stir in garlic, cumin, coriander, and remaining ½ teaspoon chipotle and cook until fragrant, about 30 seconds. Add plant-based beef and cook, breaking up meat with wooden spoon, until lightly browned, 3 to 5 minutes.

3. Transfer dip to serving bowl and top with plant-based beef mixture. Sprinkle with tomatoes, cilantro, and remaining onion. Serve.

VARIATION

Naked Nacho Dip

To rewarm cooled dip, follow instructions for rewarming Loaded Nacho Dip.

Omit plant-based beef, cherry tomatoes, and cilantro. Cook all of onion with poblano mixture in step 2. After cooking garlic, cumin, and coriander in step 2, transfer poblano mixture to serving bowl and stir in potato mixture to combine. Serve. (Nacho dip can be refrigerated for up to 24 hours.)

Whipped Cashew Dip with Roasted Red Peppers and Olives

Serves 8 (Makes 2 cups)

Why This Recipe Works A big bowl of this creamy, flavorful nut-based dip will be as crowd-pleasing at your next party as any dairy-based dip. Cashews were the ideal starting point: Soaked and pureed, they turned creamy and neutral-tasting. We found that we needed to soak the raw cashews for at least 12 hours; any less, and the dip turned out grainy. Next, we turned to a variety of simple pantry ingredients to amp up the flavor of the dip. Tasters loved the mildly smoky flavor of roasted red peppers with the briny, salty depth of chopped kalamata olives. A bit of olive oil and lemon juice boosted the flavor further and thinned the dip to a perfect consistency. Some parsley, stirred in with the olives after processing, provided welcome freshness. Since our dip had come together so quickly and easily, we decided to create two flavorful variations, one using smoky chipotle chile powder, tangy lime juice, and fresh cilantro, and another with sweet sun-dried tomatoes and earthy fresh rosemary. You can substitute an equal amount of slivered almonds for the cashews; however, the dip will have a slightly coarser consistency.

1⅛ teaspoons table salt, divided
⅛ teaspoon mustard powder
1 small red onion, chopped fine, divided
⅓ cup minced poblano chile
1 garlic clove, minced
⅛ teaspoon ground cumin
⅛ teaspoon ground coriander
4 ounces plant-based beef (page 9)
2 ounces cherry or grape tomatoes, quartered
2 tablespoons chopped fresh cilantro

1. Bring 2 quarts water to boil in medium saucepan over high heat. Add potatoes and carrot and cook until tender, about 12 minutes; drain well. Combine cooked vegetables, ⅓ cup water, 2 tablespoons oil, nutritional yeast, vinegar, ½ teaspoon chipotle, 1 teaspoon salt, and mustard powder in blender. Pulse until chopped and combined, about 10 pulses, scraping down sides of blender jar as needed. (You will need to stop processing to scrape down sides of blender jar several times for mixture to come together.) Process mixture on high speed until very smooth, about 2 minutes. Season with salt and pepper to taste.

1½ cups raw cashews
½ cup jarred roasted red peppers, rinsed, patted dry, and chopped
3 tablespoons extra-virgin olive oil
3 tablespoons lemon juice
¾ teaspoon table salt
½ teaspoon pepper
1 garlic clove, minced
½ cup minced fresh parsley
½ cup pitted kalamata olives, chopped

1. Place cashews in bowl and add cold water to cover by 1 inch. Let sit at room temperature for at least 12 hours or up to 24 hours. Drain and rinse well.

2. Process soaked cashews, red peppers, 3 tablespoons water, oil, lemon juice, salt, pepper, and garlic in food processor until smooth, about 2 minutes, scraping down sides of bowl as needed.

3. Transfer cashew mixture to bowl, stir in parsley and olives, and season with salt and pepper to taste. Cover with plastic wrap and let sit at room temperature until flavors meld, about 30 minutes. Serve. (Dip can be refrigerated for up to 5 days; stir in 1 tablespoon warm water to loosen dip if necessary before serving.)

VARIATIONS

Whipped Cashew Dip with Chipotle and Lime

Omit red peppers and olives. Add ½ teaspoon chipotle chile powder and ½ teaspoon ground cumin to processor with soaked cashews and increase water to 6 tablespoons in step 2. Substitute ¼ cup lime juice (2 limes) for lemon juice and ⅓ cup minced fresh cilantro for parsley.

Whipped Cashew Dip with Sun-Dried Tomatoes and Rosemary

Omit red peppers and parsley. Add 2 teaspoons minced fresh rosemary to processor with soaked cashews and increase water to 6 tablespoons in step 2. Substitute ½ cup finely chopped oil-packed sun-dried tomatoes for olives.

Creamy Turkish Nut Dip

Serves 4 (Makes 1 cup)   `FAST`

Why This Recipe Works Traditionally made by pureeing nuts, bread, and olive oil to create a velvety-smooth dip without dairy, Turkish tarator is a rich accompaniment to pita wedges, Falafel (page 94), or other meze platter foods. We made the base by mashing torn pieces of white bread and

Creamy Turkish Nut Dip

water into a paste. We then pulsed this in the blender with nuts, olive oil, lemon juice, and garlic. A pinch of cayenne contributed welcome heat. With our simple method in place, we turned to choosing our dip's flavor profile. Many traditional recipes call for hazelnuts, but our research turned up versions made with almonds, walnuts, and pine nuts. We tried all four nuts and found that they worked quite well, so use whichever you prefer. No matter the nut, toasting was essential, since it brought out deep flavor complexity and created a welcome contrast with the lemon and garlic.

1 slice hearty white sandwich bread, crusts removed, torn into 1-inch pieces
¾ cup water, plus extra as needed
1 cup blanched and skinned almonds, toasted
¼ cup extra-virgin olive oil
2 tablespoons lemon juice, plus extra as needed
1 small garlic clove, minced
½ teaspoon table salt
⅛ teaspoon pepper
Pinch cayenne pepper

1. With fork, mash bread and water together in bowl into paste. Process bread mixture, almonds, oil, lemon juice, garlic, salt, pepper, and cayenne in blender until smooth, about 2 minutes. Add extra water as needed until sauce is barely thicker than consistency of heavy cream.

2. Season with salt, pepper, and extra lemon juice to taste. Serve at room temperature. (Dip can be refrigerated for up to 2 days; bring to room temperature before serving.)

Beet Muhammara

Serves 8 (**Makes** 2 cups)

Why This Recipe Works Traditional muhammara is a sweet-smoky blend of roasted red peppers, toasted walnuts, pomegranate molasses, and spices popular in Turkish and Syrian cuisine. A true multi-use recipe bursting with flavor, it makes a delicious dip, a spread for sandwiches, and even a sauce for roasted vegetables. Our simple version incorporates beets, which gives the already veggie-packed mixture a splendid color and earthier flavor. We tested several methods of preparing the beets, steering away from roasting to minimize kitchen time. Some tasters loved the flavor and texture imparted by raw grated beets, but for optimal creaminess we found that microwaving grated beets softened them just enough to blend into the mixture while preserving their bright, fresh flavor. Some recipes thicken muhammara with bread, but we opted for protein-rich walnuts to do the job. Jarred roasted peppers added smokiness without any hassle. A touch of pomegranate molasses gave the dip its hallmark sweet yet slightly bitter flavor. If you can't find pomegranate molasses, you can make your own (recipe follows). You can use the large holes of a box grater or a food processor fitted with a shredding disk to shred the beets.

- 8 **ounces beets, trimmed, peeled, and shredded**
- 1 **cup jarred roasted red peppers, rinsed and patted dry**
- 1 **cup walnuts, toasted**
- 1 **scallion, sliced thin**
- 2 **tablespoons extra-virgin olive oil, plus extra for drizzling**
- 2 **tablespoons pomegranate molasses**
- 2 **teaspoons lemon juice**
- ¾ **teaspoon table salt**
- ½ **teaspoon ground cumin**
- ⅛ **teaspoon cayenne pepper**
- 2 **tablespoons minced fresh parsley**

1. Microwave beets in covered bowl, stirring often, until beets are tender, about 4 minutes. Transfer beets to fine-mesh strainer set over bowl and let drain for 10 minutes.

2. Process drained beets, peppers, walnuts, scallion, oil, pomegranate molasses, lemon juice, salt, cumin, and cayenne together in food processor until smooth, about 1 minute, scraping down sides of bowl as needed.

3. Transfer mixture to serving bowl. Season with salt to taste. Drizzle with extra oil to taste, and sprinkle with parsley before serving. (Dip can be refrigerated for up to 3 days; bring to room temperature before serving.)

Pomegranate Molasses
Makes ⅔ cup
If you over-reduce the syrup in step 2, you can slowly whisk in warm water as needed to measure ⅔ cup.

- 2 **tablespoons water**
- 1 **tablespoon sugar**
- 4 **cups unsweetened pomegranate juice, divided**
- 2 **teaspoons lemon juice**

1. Stir water and sugar in medium saucepan until sugar is completely moistened. Bring to boil over medium-high heat and cook until sugar begins to turn golden, 2 to 3 minutes, gently swirling saucepan as needed to ensure even cooking. Continue to cook until sugar begins to smoke and is color of peanut butter, about 1 minute. Off heat, let caramel sit until mahogany brown, 45 to 60 seconds. Carefully swirl in 2 tablespoons pomegranate juice until incorporated; mixture will bubble and steam. Slowly whisk in remaining pomegranate juice and lemon juice, scraping up any caramel.

2. Bring mixture to boil over high heat and cook, stirring occasionally, until tight, slow-popping bubbles cover surface and syrup measures ⅔ cup, 30 to 35 minutes. Let cool slightly, then transfer to container and continue to cool to room temperature. (Pomegranate Molasses can be refrigerated for up to 1 month.)

CRUDITÉS

A well-thought-out platter of crudités can be a beautiful and versatile centerpiece for plant-based entertaining. For perfect crudités, you simply need to prep fresh vegetables properly: Some vegetables must first be blanched and then shocked in ice water; others benefit from being cut in a particular manner. To store crudités, refrigerate raw vegetables wrapped in damp paper towels in a zipper-lock bag and blanched vegetables in an airtight container for up to two days.

Asparagus To remove tough, fibrous ends of asparagus, bend thick end of each stalk until it snaps off. Blanch asparagus for 30 to 60 seconds.

Broccoli and Cauliflower Cut broccoli and cauliflower florets into bite-size pieces by slicing down through stem. Blanch broccoli and cauliflower (separately) for 1 to 1½ minutes.

Carrots and Celery Slice both celery and peeled carrots lengthwise into long, elegant lengths rather than short, stumpy pieces.

Endive Gently pull off leaves one at a time, continuing to trim root end as you work your way toward heart of endive.

Green Beans Line beans up in a row and trim off inedible stem ends with just 1 cut. Blanch beans for 1 minute.

Peppers Slice off top and bottom of pepper and remove seeds and stem. Slice down through side of pepper, unroll it so that it lies flat, then slice into ½-inch-wide strips.

Radishes Choose radishes with green tops still attached so that each half has a leafy handle for grasping and dipping. Slice each radish in half through stem.

> **BLANCHING DIRECTIONS**
> Bring 6 quarts water and 2 tablespoons table salt to boil in large pot over high heat. Cook vegetables, 1 variety at a time, until slightly softened but still crunchy at core, following times given for individual vegetables above. Transfer blanched vegetables immediately to bowl of ice water until completely cool, then drain and pat dry.

Kale Chips

Serves 4

Why This Recipe Works Store-bought versions of kale chips typically try to mimic potato chips: that is, they're deep fried and loaded with salt. We didn't want to try to mimic a greasy potato chip; rather, we wanted to create a light-as-air vegetable chip that would remain crispy from cooking right through to consumption. We discovered three keys to getting them to the perfect texture. First, we started with completely dry leaves, blotted between dish towels after washing to make sure no water was left clinging to them. Next, we baked the kale on wire racks to allow the oven air to circulate above and beneath the leaves. Finally, we used a long cooking time and low oven temperature to mimic the effects of a food dehydrator. Tossed with olive oil and seasoned with crunchy kosher salt, these ultracrisp kale chips were a super-satisfying snack. Our variations offer a ranch seasoning as well as an Asian-inspired combination. We prefer to use Lacinato kale in this recipe, but curly-leaf kale can be substituted; chips made with curly-leaf kale will taste a bit chewy at the edges and won't keep as well. We prefer the larger crystal size of kosher salt here; if using table salt, reduce the amount by half.

12 ounces Lacinato kale, stemmed and torn into 3-inch pieces
1 tablespoon extra-virgin olive oil
½ teaspoon kosher or flake sea salt

1. Adjust oven racks to upper-middle and lower-middle positions and heat oven to 200 degrees. Set wire racks in 2 rimmed baking sheets. Dry kale thoroughly between dish towels, transfer to large bowl, and toss with oil and salt.

2. Arrange kale on prepared racks, making sure leaves overlap as little as possible. Bake kale until very crisp, 45 minutes to 1 hour, switching and rotating sheets halfway through baking. Let kale chips cool completely before serving. (Chips can be stored in airtight container for up to 1 day.)

VARIATIONS

Ranch-Style Kale Chips
Combine 2 teaspoons dried dill, 1 teaspoon garlic powder, and 1 teaspoon onion powder with salt before tossing with kale.

Spicy Sesame-Ginger Kale Chips
Substitute 1 tablespoon sesame oil for olive oil. Combine 2 teaspoons toasted sesame seeds, 1 teaspoon ground ginger, and ¼ teaspoon cayenne pepper with salt before tossing with kale.

MAKING KALE CHIPS

1. Stem kale, then tear leaves into rough 3-inch pieces.

2. Wash and dry kale using salad spinner, then dry thoroughly between dish towels. Transfer to large bowl and toss with oil and seasonings.

3. Bake on prepared racks until very crisp, 45 minutes to 1 hour, switching and rotating sheets halfway through baking.

Beet Chips

Serves 2

Why This Recipe Works A snack chip made from beets has become another popular healthful alternative to potato chips, but we were skeptical about getting truly crisp results without any special equipment. Indeed, many of the recipes we tested produced chips that were leathery and floppy or overcooked and bitter. We knew that crisp chip texture depended on extracting as much moisture as possible from the beets. To do this without overcooking the chips, we tried lightly salting the raw beets to draw out some water—and it worked, extracting almost 2 tablespoons. To cook them, we first tried microwaving, which is a popular alternative to frying, but the process was inconsistent at best: The difference between perfection and burnt was mere seconds. So we took a cue from our kale chip method and slow-baked our beets in a 200-degree oven. It took a couple of hours but was hands-off and produced chips with a concentrated beet flavor, light crunch, and deep color. Be careful to not let the beet chips turn brown, as they will become bitter. Thinly sliced beets are key to crispy beet chips—use a mandoline, V-slicer, or the slicing disk on a food processor.

1 pound beets, peeled, trimmed, and sliced
   ¹⁄₁₆ inch thick
½ teaspoon table salt

1. Adjust oven racks to upper-middle and lower-middle positions and heat oven to 200 degrees. Set wire racks in 2 rimmed baking sheets and spray with canola oil spray. Combine beets and salt in colander set over bowl and let drain for 25 minutes. Pat beets dry with paper towels.

2. Arrange beet slices on prepared racks, making sure slices overlap as little as possible. Bake beets until shrunken slightly and crisp throughout, 2 to 3 hours, switching and rotating sheets halfway through baking. Let beet chips cool completely before serving. (Beets will continue to crisp as they cool). (Chips can be stored in airtight container for up to 2 weeks.)

Sesame Nori Chips
Serves 12 `FAST`

Why This Recipe Works Our nori chips are ethereally light in texture and delicately crisp. To create this great chip with fresh-from-the-sea flavor, we focused on a few simple elements. First, we tested various oven temperatures and times and found that a moderately hot oven consistently produced the best chips. A low oven temperature resulted in floppy chips (even with a longer time), while a high temperature produced and unpleasantly burnt taste. To highlight the clean nori flavor, we added only sesame seeds, which toasted nicely while the chips baked, and salt. Vegetable oil brushed on the chips pulled double duty, helping the sesame seeds to adhere while helping to further crisp up the chips. For a sturdier chip, we folded the nori sheets to double their thickness; water brushed between the folded sheets kept them together. Finally, we cut each sheet into uniform strips. After a few minutes in the oven, these toasty dark green treats were ready to enjoy. You can use either toasted or untoasted nori sheets for this recipe.

10 sheets nori
1¼ teaspoons vegetable oil
 5 teaspoons sesame seeds

1. Adjust oven racks to upper-middle and lower-middle positions and heat oven to 350 degrees. Line 2 rimmed baking sheets with parchment paper. Working with 1 nori sheet at a time, brush bottom half liberally with water. Fold top half toward you and press firmly until sealed. Brush top of folded nori with ⅛ teaspoon oil, sprinkle with ½ teaspoon sesame seeds, and season with kosher or flake sea salt to taste. Cut nori into 1-inch strips.

2. Arrange nori strips in single layer, spaced evenly apart on prepared baking sheets. Bake until nori is very crisp and sesame seeds are golden, about 8 minutes, switching and rotating sheets halfway through baking (nori strips should be dark and shriveled slightly). Let cool completely on sheets, 8 to 10 minutes. Serve. (Chips can be stored in airtight container for up to 1 week.)

Whole-Wheat Seeded Crackers
Serves 12

Why This Recipe Works While many store-bought crackers are free of animal products, they are also loaded with refined flours, saturated fat, preservatives, and excess salt or sugar. For a crisp, flavorful, whole-grain cracker, we chose as a starting point the Mediterranean lavash cracker, typically made with a mix of white, wheat, and semolina flours. For our version, we preferred using all whole-wheat flour. To boost their plant power and give them texture and flavor, we added omega-3-rich flaxseeds and sesame seeds to the dough along with a touch of turmeric for its warm flavor. We let the dough rest for an hour to make it easier to roll out, then rolled it between sheets of parchment paper. We pricked it with a fork to prevent air bubbles, brushed it with olive oil, and sprinkled it with chia seeds, sea salt, and pepper. Finally, we baked the giant crackers until deep golden brown and let them cool before breaking them up. We prefer golden flaxseeds for their milder flavor, but brown flaxseeds can be used. We prefer the larger crystal size of sea salt or kosher salt for sprinkling on the crackers; if using table salt, reduce the amount by half.

3 cups (16½ ounces) whole-wheat flour
2 tablespoons ground golden flaxseeds
2 tablespoons sesame seeds
1 teaspoon ground turmeric
¾ teaspoon table salt
1 cup warm water
⅓ cup extra-virgin olive oil, plus extra for brushing
2 tablespoons chia seeds, divided
2 teaspoons flake sea salt or kosher salt, divided

1. Using stand mixer fitted with dough hook, mix whole-wheat flour, ground flaxseeds, sesame seeds, turmeric, and table salt together on low speed. Gradually add water and oil and knead until dough is smooth and elastic, 7 to 9 minutes. Turn dough out onto lightly floured counter and knead by hand to form smooth, round ball. Divide dough into 4 equal pieces, brush with oil, and cover with plastic wrap. Let rest at room temperature for 1 hour.

Whole-Wheat Seeded Crackers

Spiced Roasted Chickpeas
Serves 6

Why This Recipe Works Tossed with an appealing spice mix, roasted chickpeas have a crisp, airy texture that makes them a most poppable (and healthy) snack—or salad topper or roasted vegetable accompaniment or hummus garnish. Chickpeas are used throughout India, so a version with spices from the region—coriander, turmeric, allspice, and cumin— seemed appropriate. We achieved crispiness by first micro- waving the chickpeas for about 10 minutes to burst them open at the seams so they released interior moisture. We then baked them in a 350-degree oven. To prevent burning, we crowded them toward the center of the pan near the end of roasting. We finished with our dusting of spices and liked the result so much that we came up with two variations. You will need a 13 by 9-inch metal baking pan for this recipe; a glass or ceramic baking dish will result in uneven cooking.

- 2 (15-ounce) cans chickpeas
- 3 tablespoons extra-virgin olive oil
- 2 teaspoons paprika
- 1 teaspoon ground coriander
- ½ teaspoon ground turmeric
- ½ teaspoon ground allspice
- ½ teaspoon ground cumin
- ½ teaspoon sugar
- ⅛ teaspoon table salt
- ⅛ teaspoon cayenne pepper

1. Adjust oven rack to middle position and heat oven to 350 degrees. Place chickpeas in colander and drain for 10 minutes. Line large plate with double layer of paper towels. Spread chickpeas over plate in even layer. Microwave until exteriors of chickpeas are dry and many have ruptured, 8 to 12 minutes.

2. Transfer chickpeas to 13 by 9-inch metal baking pan. Add oil and stir until evenly coated. Using spatula, spread chickpeas into single layer. Transfer to oven and roast for 30 minutes. Stir chickpeas and crowd them toward center of pan. Continue to roast until chickpeas appear dry, slightly shriveled, and deep golden brown, 20 to 40 minutes. (To test for doneness, remove a few paler chickpeas and let cool briefly before tasting; if interiors are soft, return to oven and test again in 5 minutes.)

3. Combine paprika, coriander, turmeric, allspice, cumin, sugar, salt, and cayenne in small bowl. Transfer chickpeas to large bowl and toss with spice mixture to coat. Season with salt to taste. Let cool fully before serving, about 30 minutes. (Chickpeas can stored in airtight container for up to 7 days.)

2. Adjust oven racks to upper-middle and lower-middle positions and heat oven to 400 degrees. Roll 1 piece of dough (keep remaining dough covered with plastic) between 2 large sheets of parchment paper into 15 by 11-inch rectangle (about ⅛ inch thick). Remove top sheet of parchment and slide parchment with dough onto baking sheet. Repeat with second piece of dough and second baking sheet.

3. Using fork, poke holes in doughs at 2-inch intervals. Brush each dough with 1½ teaspoons oil, then sprinkle each with 1½ teaspoons chia seeds, ½ teaspoon sea salt, and pepper to taste. Press gently on seeds and seasonings to help them adhere.

4. Bake crackers until golden brown, 15 to 18 minutes, switching and rotating sheets halfway through baking. Transfer crackers to wire rack and let cool completely. Let baking sheets cool completely before rolling out, brushing, topping, and baking remaining 2 pieces of dough. Break cooled crackers into large pieces and serve. (Crackers can be stored in airtight container for up to 2 weeks.)

Barbecue-Spiced Roasted Chickpeas
Omit allspice and cumin. Increase sugar to 1½ teaspoons. Substitute 1 tablespoon smoked paprika for paprika, garlic powder for coriander, and onion powder for turmeric.

Spanish-Spiced Roasted Chickpeas
Omit turmeric, allspice, and sugar. Decrease coriander to ½ teaspoon and cumin to ¼ teaspoon. Substitute 1 tablespoon smoked paprika for paprika.

Orange-Fennel Spiced Almonds

Serves 8 (**Makes** about 2 cups) `FAST`

Why This Recipe Works Like Spiced Roasted Chickpeas (page 355), protein-rich spiced nuts are a great cocktail snack and also make a wonderful gift when packaged in an attractive container. They're satisfying and easy to prepare and are more healthful and less expensive than packaged seasoned nuts. This version has a sweet-salty flavor profile from the orange zest, fennel seeds, and salt. The variation takes the almonds in a spicier Southwestern direction with cumin, chipotle chile powder, and garlic. Watch the nuts carefully during toasting, as they go from golden and fragrant to burnt very quickly.

    1   tablespoon extra-virgin olive oil
    1   teaspoon grated orange zest
    1   teaspoon fennel seeds
    1   teaspoon table salt
    ¼   teaspoon pepper
    2   cups raw whole almonds

Adjust oven rack to middle position and heat oven to 350 degrees. Combine oil, orange zest, fennel seeds, salt, and pepper in bowl. Toss almonds with oil mixture until well coated, then spread into single layer on rimmed baking sheet. Bake, stirring often, until fragrant and lightly browned, about 10 minutes. Transfer almonds to serving bowl and let cool completely before serving. (Almonds can be stored at room temperature for up to 1 week.)

VARIATION
Spicy Chipotle Almonds
Substitute 1 teaspoon ground cumin, ¾ teaspoon chipotle chile powder, and ½ teaspoon garlic powder for orange zest and fennel seeds.

Chewy Granola Bars with Hazelnuts, Cherries, and Cacao Nibs

Chewy Granola Bars with Hazelnuts, Cherries, and Cacao Nibs

Serves 24 (**Makes** 24 bars)

Why This Recipe Works Most store-bought granola bars contain far too much sugar and lots of filler ingredients; and they are soft and mushy rather than pleasingly chewy. They're also prone to falling apart—not a plus if you're eating them on the go, as so many of us do with granola bars. For bars that were wholesome, satisfyingly chewy, and neat to eat, we combined toasted oats, nuts, and seeds with a mixture of pureed apricots, brown sugar, oil, and water and pressed the mixture firmly into a baking pan before baking it. Small chunks of dried fruit provided pops of bright flavor and extra chew, while airy rice cereal provided a crisp texture that lightened the bars. The nuts, seeds, and fruit can be swapped out according to your preference to make bars that suit a variety of tastes (see the variations for a couple of our favorites). Be sure to use apricots that are soft and moist, or the bars will not hold together well. Avoid using extra-thick rolled oats here.

1½ cups blanched hazelnuts
2½ cups (7½ ounces) old-fashioned rolled oats
1 cup raw sunflower seeds
1 cup dried apricots
1 cup packed (7 ounces) brown sugar
¾ teaspoon table salt
½ cup vegetable oil
3 tablespoons water
1½ cups (1½ ounces) crisped rice cereal
1 cup dried cherries
½ cup cacao nibs

1. Adjust oven rack to middle position and heat oven to 350 degrees. Make foil sling for 13 by 9-inch baking pan by folding 2 long sheets of aluminum foil; first sheet should be 13 inches wide and second sheet should be 9 inches wide. Lay sheets of foil in pan perpendicular to each other, with extra foil hanging over edges of pan. Push foil into corners and up sides of pan, smoothing foil flush to pan. Lightly spray foil with vegetable oil spray.

2. Pulse hazelnuts in food processor until finely chopped, 8 to 12 pulses. Spread hazelnuts, oats, and sunflower seeds on rimmed baking sheet and toast until lightly browned and fragrant, 12 to 15 minutes, stirring halfway through toasting. Reduce oven temperature to 300 degrees.

3. While oat mixture is toasting, process apricots, sugar, and salt in food processor until apricots are very finely ground, about 15 seconds. With processor running, add oil and water. Continue to process until homogeneous paste forms, about 1 minute. Transfer paste to large, wide bowl.

4. Add warm oat mixture to bowl and stir with rubber spatula until well coated. Add cereal, cherries, and cacao nibs and stir gently until ingredients are evenly mixed. Transfer mixture to prepared pan and spread into even layer. Place 14-inch sheet of parchment or waxed paper on top of granola and press and smooth very firmly with your hands, especially at edges and corners, until granola is level and compact. Remove parchment and bake granola until fragrant and just beginning to brown around edges, about 25 minutes. Transfer pan to wire rack and let cool for 1 hour. Using foil overhang, lift granola out of pan. Return to wire rack and let cool completely, about 1 hour.

5. Discard foil and transfer granola to cutting board. Using chef's knife, cut granola in half crosswise to create two 6½ by 9-inch rectangles. Cut each rectangle in half to make four 3¼ by 9-inch strips. Cut each strip crosswise into 6 equal pieces. (Granola bars can be stored at room temperature for up to 3 weeks.)

VARIATIONS

Chewy Granola Bars with Walnuts and Cranberries
Omit cacao nibs. Substitute walnuts for hazelnuts and pulse until finely chopped, 8 to 10 pulses. Substitute chopped dried cranberries for cherries.

Nut-Free Chewy Granola Bars
Omit hazelnuts, cherries, and cacao nibs. Toast 1 cup raw pepitas, ¼ cup sesame seeds, and ¼ cup chia seeds with oats in step 2. Increase cereal to 2 cups.

Popcorn with Olive Oil
Serves 14 (Makes 14 cups) `FAST`

Why This Recipe Works You might think that popcorn isn't popcorn without a generous drizzle of butter, but we're here to prove that notion wrong. This universally popular snack is just as munchable made with olive oil. Looking for the healthiest way to make popcorn, we discovered an interesting trick: You can actually cook popcorn on the stovetop without any fat at all. Just adding a small amount of water to the pot along with the kernels was enough to do the trick. But we didn't want to abandon a classic popcorn profile altogether, so we found that a modest amount of olive oil and salt tossed with the popcorn before serving gave us just the flavor we craved. The garlicky variation and the cinnamon-sugar variation will also both keep you reaching into the bowl for more. When cooking the popcorn, be sure to keep the lid on tight and shake the pot vigorously to prevent scorching.

1 tablespoon water
½ cup popcorn kernels
2 tablespoons extra-virgin olive oil
½ teaspoon table salt
½ teaspoon pepper

Heat Dutch oven over medium-high heat for 2 minutes. Add water and popcorn, cover, and cook, shaking frequently, until first few kernels begin to pop. Continue to cook, shaking vigorously, until popping slows to about 2 seconds between pops. Transfer popcorn to large serving bowl and toss with oil, salt, and pepper. Serve.

VARIATIONS

Popcorn with Warm Spices and Garlic

Heat oil, 2 teaspoons garlic powder, ½ teaspoon ground coriander, and ½ teaspoon ground cumin in small skillet over medium-low heat until fragrant, about 1 minute; toss spiced oil with popcorn, salt, and pepper.

Popcorn with Spicy Cinnamon Sugar

Substitute vegetable oil for olive oil and omit pepper. Heat oil, 2 tablespoons sugar, 1 teaspoon cinnamon, and ½ teaspoon ground chile powder in 8-inch skillet over medium-low heat until warm and fragrant, about 1 minute. Toss spiced oil with popcorn and salt.

Tomato, Olive, and Basil Skewers

Serves 8 (**Makes** 24 skewers) `FAST`

Why This Recipe Works Meaty kalamata olives replace mini mozzarella balls in these elegant, flavor-packed mini skewers that require no cooking and can be made ahead for serving al fresco to guests while you're firing up the grill on a warm evening. We made a dressing with lemon, garlic, mustard, and fennel seeds and tossed halved grape tomatoes and the olives in the dressing. We then skewered them on toothpicks along with fresh, anise-y basil leaves (which were complemented by the fennel in the dressing), creating an hors d'oeuvre that was far more than the sum of its parts. You will need about 24 sturdy wooden toothpicks for this recipe; avoid using very thin, flimsy toothpicks here. Placing a halved tomato, with its flat side facing down, on the bottom of the toothpick is a clever way to stand the skewers upright on a serving platter. Once assembled, the skewers can be held at room temperature for up to 4 hours.

- ¼ teaspoon grated lemon zest plus ½ tablespoon juice
- 1 small garlic clove, minced
- ¼ teaspoon Dijon mustard
- ⅛ teaspoon fennel seeds, chopped
- ⅛ teaspoon table salt
- ⅛ teaspoon pepper
- 3 tablespoons extra-virgin olive oil
- 8 ounces grape tomatoes, halved
- ½ cup pitted kalamata olives
- ½ cup fresh basil leaves

1. Whisk lemon zest and juice, garlic, mustard, fennel, salt, and pepper together in large bowl. Whisking constantly, drizzle in oil. Gently stir in tomatoes and olives.

Blistered Shishito Peppers

2. Skewer ingredients onto toothpicks in this order: tomato half, olive, basil leaf (folded if large), and tomato half with flat side facing down. Stand skewers upright on serving platter, drizzle with some of remaining dressing, and serve.

Blistered Shishito Peppers

Serves 4 to 6 `FAST`

Why This Recipe Works Mild little chile peppers, fried until blistered, that you pick up by the stems and pop into your mouth whole fly out of the kitchen wherever trendy bar snacks are sold. Shishitos are what you usually find at Asian restaurants; they are the Japanese cousin to Spain's Padrón chiles, which are common at tapas restaurants. These bright-tasting, citrusy, mild green chiles are thin-skinned and crisp-textured and totally craveable. Restaurants often deep-fry the whole shishitos, but we've found that cooking them in a small amount of oil works just as well. They are delicious simply salted, but we've also offered three variations: two that amp up the chiles with dried ground peppers, and a third that adds a touch of herbal sweetness with dried mint and orange zest. We prefer the larger crystal size of flake sea salt or kosher salt for sprinkling on the peppers, but you can use regular table salt instead. It's said that only one in 10 shishito peppers is truly spicy, so happy hunting!

2 tablespoons vegetable oil
8 ounces shishito peppers

Heat oil in 12-inch skillet over medium-high heat until just smoking. Add peppers and cook, without stirring, until skins are blistered, 3 to 5 minutes. Using tongs, flip peppers and continue to cook until blistered on second side, 3 to 5 minutes. Transfer to serving bowl, season with flake sea salt or kosher salt to taste, and serve.

VARIATIONS

Smoky Shishito Peppers with Espelette and Lime
Combine 1 teaspoon ground dried Espelette pepper, 1 teaspoon smoked paprika, ½ teaspoon flake sea salt or kosher salt, and ¼ teaspoon grated lime zest in small bowl. Sprinkle over peppers in serving bowl. Serve with lime wedges.

Shishito Peppers with Fennel Pollen, Aleppo, and Lemon
Combine 1 teaspoon Aleppo pepper, 1 teaspoon fennel pollen, ½ teaspoon flake sea salt or kosher salt, and ¼ teaspoon grated lemon zest in small bowl. Sprinkle over peppers in serving bowl. Serve with lemon wedges.

Shishito Peppers with Mint, Poppy Seeds, and Orange
Combine 1 teaspoon dried mint, 1 teaspoon poppy seeds, ½ teaspoon flake sea salt or kosher salt, and ¼ teaspoon grated orange zest in small bowl. Sprinkle over peppers in serving bowl. Serve with orange wedges.

Bruschetta with Artichoke Hearts and Basil

Serves 8 to 10   FAST

Why This Recipe Works As we tested our way through various vegan bruschetta toppings, this combination of tangy, tender jarred artichoke hearts with our funky, punchy vegan Parmesan substitute—brightened with a hefty dose of aromatic fresh basil—was a runaway hit. (For a vegetarian version, it's as simple as swapping in dairy Parmesan for the plant-based variety.) A food processor quickly transformed our ingredients into a rustic, spreadable mixture that stayed in place on top of our garlic-scented toasted bread. For an elegant finish, we sprinkled on vegan Parmesan substitute and chopped fresh basil along with a generous drizzle of extra-virgin olive oil. We prefer jarred whole baby artichoke hearts, but you can substitute 6 ounces frozen, thawed and patted dry.

1 cup jarred whole baby artichoke hearts packed in water, rinsed and patted dry
3 tablespoons chopped fresh basil, divided
¼ cup Vegan Parmesan Substitute (page 27) or grated dairy Parmesan cheese, divided
2 tablespoons extra-virgin olive oil, plus extra for drizzling
2 teaspoons lemon juice
¼ teaspoon table salt
¼ teaspoon pepper
1 recipe Toasted Bread for Bruschetta (recipe follows)

Pulse artichoke hearts, 2 tablespoons basil, 3 tablespoons vegan Parmesan substitute, oil, lemon juice, salt, and pepper in food processor until coarsely ground, 6 to 8 pulses, scraping down sides of bowl as needed; season with salt and pepper to taste Spread artichoke mixture evenly over toasts, then sprinkle with remaining 1 tablespoon basil and remaining 1 tablespoon vegan Parmesan. Drizzle with extra oil to taste. Serve.

Toasted Bread for Bruschetta
Serves 8 to 10
Toast the bread just before assembling the bruschetta.

1 (10 by 5-inch) loaf country bread with thick crust, ends discarded, sliced crosswise into ¾-inch-thick pieces
1 garlic clove, peeled
Extra-virgin olive oil

Adjust oven rack 4 inches from broiler element and heat broiler. Arrange bread in single layer on aluminum foil–lined baking sheet. Broil until bread is deep golden and toasted on both sides, 1 to 2 minutes per side. Lightly rub 1 side of each toast with garlic (you will not use all of garlic). Brush with oil and season with salt to taste.

CHILES

Chiles don't just make foods hot; they also add nuanced layers of flavor to a dish. And if they're mild, they can be dishes on their own, as with the Blistered Shishito Peppers (page 358). Since everyone's taste buds are different (one person can enjoy Scotch bonnets while another can't even go near jalapeños), let your preferences be your guide. Here's a quick primer.

FRESH

1 Shishitos

Shishitos are very mild medium-size Japanese chiles that are long, skinny, and shiny bright green, with a grassy, citrusy flavor. Substitute Padrón chiles. **Heat:** ◖○○○○

2 Poblanos

Poblanos are mild, large, triangular chiles that are green to red-brown in color, with a crisp, vegetal flavor. Substitute Anaheim chiles. **Heat:** ●○○○○

3 Anaheims

Anaheims are mild to medium-hot large chiles that are long and skinny, yellow-green to red, and mildly tangy and vegetal. Substitute poblanos. **Heat:** ●●○○○

4 Jalapeños

Jalapeños are medium-hot small green or red chiles that are smooth and shiny, with a bright, grassy flavor. Substitute serranos. **Heat:** ●●○○○

5 Serranos

Serranos are medium-hot small dark green chiles with a bright, citrusy flavor. Substitute jalapeños. **Heat:** ●●●○○

6 Thai chiles

Thai chiles are hot, bright red or green, narrow, and petite, with a clean flavor similar to black peppercorns. Substitute a half-dose of habaneros. **Heat:** ●●●◖

7 Habaneros

Habaneros are very hot, bulbous, bright orange to red, deeply floral, and fruity. Substitute a double dose of Thai chiles. **Heat:** ●●●●

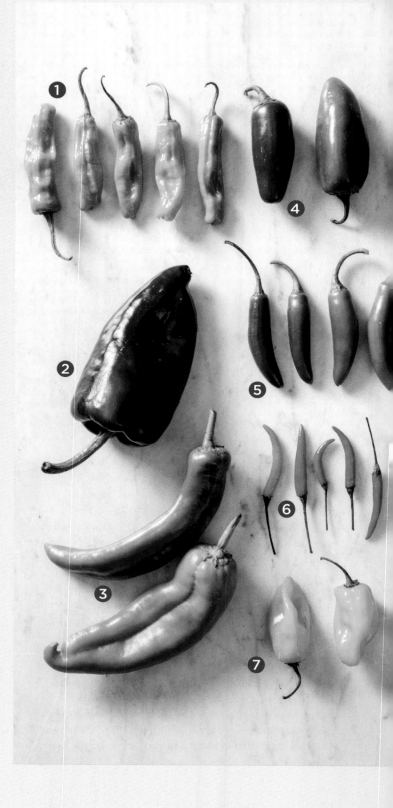

DRIED

1 Guajillos

Guajillos are mild to medium-hot, with a fruity flavor and subtle natural smokiness. Substitute anchos or pasillas. **Heat:** ●○○○○

2 Anchos

Anchos are mild to medium-hot. These dried poblanos have deep, earthy flavors that evoke chocolate, coffee, raisins, and licorice. Substitute mulatos or pasillas. **Heat:** ●○○○○

3 Chipotles

Chipotles are medium-hot. These dried, smoked jalapeños have charred wood, tobacco, and barbecue flavors balanced by subtle sweetness. Substitute anchos. Chipotles are also available canned in tangy red adobo sauce. **Heat:** ●●○○○

4 New Mexican chiles

New Mexican chiles are medium-hot, with a sweet, earthy flavor reminiscent of roasted red peppers, tomatoes, and cherries. Substitute guajillos or cascabels. **Heat:** ●●○○○

5 Calabrian peperoncini

Calabrian peperoncini are hot, tiny, and a bit smoky, with a mildly fruity flavor. They are available as flakes and whole. Arbol chiles are a better substitute than regular red pepper flakes. **Heat:** ●●●○○

Bruschetta with Smashed Minty Peas, Chili, and Lemon Zest

Serves 8 to 10 **FAST**

Why This Recipe Works Sweet, delicate peas mashed with baby spinach, pungent mint, and bright lemon zest makes a simple and delightfully unexpected topping for bruschetta. The topping seemed simple enough, but early versions we tried fell flat with pasty consistency and underwhelming flavor. To ensure the best texture, we cooked the peas on their own until just tender. A quick whiz in the food processor along with some key additions—spinach for body and deeper green vegetal flavor, mint for unbeatable freshness and aroma, lemon zest and red pepper flakes for zing, olive oil for richness, and just enough water to tie it all together—gave us just the right balance of flavors and textures. A bit of flake sea salt made for an elegant and punchy finish. Be careful not to overprocess the peas. They can go from smashed to pureed in seconds. If you don't have almonds, you can substitute any toasted nut, or top with Vegan Parmesan Substitute (page 27) or grated or shaved dairy Parmesan.

8 ounces frozen peas
¼ cup water
1 cup baby spinach
2 tablespoons chopped fresh mint
2 tablespoons extra-virgin olive oil, plus extra for drizzling
1 teaspoon grated lemon zest
½ teaspoon red pepper flakes, divided
¼ teaspoon table salt
¼ teaspoon pepper
1 recipe Toasted Bread for Bruschetta (page 359)
2 tablespoons sliced almonds, toasted

1. Bring peas and water to simmer in medium saucepan over medium heat. Cover, reduce heat to medium-low, and cook until peas are tender, 8 to 10 minutes. Transfer peas (and any remaining water) to food processor. Add spinach, mint, oil, lemon zest, ¼ teaspoon pepper flakes, salt, and pepper and pulse until coarsely ground, 8 to 10 pulses; season with salt and pepper to taste.

2. Spread pea mixture evenly over toasts, then sprinkle with almonds and remaining ¼ teaspoon pepper flakes. Sprinkle with flake sea salt, if desired, and drizzle with extra oil to taste. Serve.

Bruschetta with Smashed Minty Peas, Chili, and Lemon Zest

Crispy Polenta Squares with Olives and Sun-Dried Tomatoes

Serves 12 (**Makes** 24 squares)

Why This Recipe Works With their crispy crust and creamy interior, bite-size polenta squares serve as an excellent base for a hearty appetizer that goes beyond the usual things-on-bread recipes. And to make these elegant little bites even more convenient for serving a crowd, we started with instant polenta. After cooking the polenta on the stovetop, we poured it into a loaf pan and let it firm up in the refrigerator. Once firm, it was easy to slice into bite-size squares. Broiling the polenta on a preheated baking sheet proved to be the best (and most hands-off) method for achieving a nicely browned exterior. We topped the crispy squares with a quick tapenade of sun-dried tomatoes and kalamata olives, brightened with a dash of red wine vinegar. A sprinkle of basil added the perfect herbal and aesthetic finishing touch. Be sure to use instant or quick-cooking polenta; traditional polenta will not work in this recipe.

2 tablespoons plus 1 teaspoon extra-virgin olive oil, divided
4 garlic cloves, minced
½ teaspoon minced fresh rosemary
2 cups water
½ teaspoon table salt
½ cup instant polenta
¼ teaspoon pepper, divided
⅓ cup pitted kalamata olives, chopped fine
⅓ cup oil-packed sun-dried tomatoes, patted dry and chopped fine
½ teaspoon red wine vinegar
1 tablespoon minced fresh basil

1. Line 8½ by 4½-inch loaf pan with parchment paper and lightly coat with vegetable oil spray. Cook 4 teaspoons oil and three-quarters of garlic in 8-inch nonstick skillet over low heat, stirring often, until garlic is golden and fragrant, about 10 minutes. Off heat, stir in rosemary; set aside.

2. Bring water to boil in large saucepan. Reduce heat to low and stir in salt. Slowly add polenta while whisking constantly in circular motion to prevent clumping. Continue to cook, stirring often, until polenta is soft and smooth, 3 to 5 minutes. Off heat, stir in oil-garlic mixture and ⅛ teaspoon pepper.

3. Pour polenta into prepared pan, smooth top, and let cool to room temperature, about 2 hours. Wrap pan tightly in plastic wrap and refrigerate until polenta is very firm, at least 2 hours or up to 24 hours.

4. Combine olives, tomatoes, vinegar, remaining 1 tablespoon oil, remaining garlic, and remaining ⅛ teaspoon pepper in bowl; set aside.

5. Run small knife around edge of polenta, then flip onto cutting board; discard parchment. Trim polenta loaf as needed to create uniform edges. Cut loaf in half lengthwise, then cut each strip crosswise into 6 pieces. Slice polenta pieces in half to form ¼-inch-thick squares. (You should have 24 squares.)

6. Adjust oven rack 3 inches from broiler element. (If necessary, set overturned rimmed baking sheet on oven rack to get closer to broiler element.) Place rimmed baking sheet on rack and heat broiler for 10 minutes. Carefully remove sheet from oven. Spray vegetable oil spray evenly on hot sheet and arrange squares in single layer. Broil polenta until spotty brown and crisp, 8 to 10 minutes. Transfer polenta to serving platter, top each square with olive mixture, sprinkle with basil, and serve.

MAKING POLENTA SQUARES

1. Cut trimmed loaf in half lengthwise, then cut each strip crosswise into 6 pieces.

2. Slice polenta pieces in half to form ¼-inch-thick squares.

Stuffed Mushrooms

Serves 6 to 8 (**Makes** 24 stuffed mushrooms)

Why This Recipe Works Mushrooms are loaded with umami, so it's no deception to say that these stuffed mushrooms are impressively meaty bites loaded with great savory flavor. To get rid of excess moisture before stuffing, we roasted the mushrooms gill side up until their juice was released and they were browned; we then flipped them gill side down to let the liquid evaporate and the mushrooms brown. To create the filling, we chopped the mushroom stems in the food processor and sautéed them with garlic, shallot, and wine. Our Vegan Parmesan Substitute bound the filling together (dairy Parm also works), and a final hit of acidity from lemon juice brightened the earthy, savory flavor. We stuffed our mushroom caps, sprinkled on a panko topping, and baked them to golden-brown finger-food perfection. You can substitute cremini mushrooms for the white mushrooms.

2 tablespoons panko bread crumbs
7 tablespoons Vegan Parmesan Substitute (page 27) or grated dairy Parmesan cheese
3 tablespoons extra-virgin olive oil, divided, plus extra for drizzling
24 large white mushrooms (1¾ to 2 inches in diameter), stems removed and reserved
¼ teaspoon table salt
¼ teaspoon pepper, divided
1 small shallot, minced
2 garlic cloves, minced
¼ cup dry white wine
1 teaspoon minced fresh thyme
1 teaspoon lemon juice
1 tablespoon minced fresh parsley

1. Adjust oven rack to middle position and heat oven to 425 degrees. Line rimmed baking sheet with aluminum foil. Combine panko, 1 tablespoon vegan Parmesan substitute, and 1 tablespoon oil in bowl; set aside.

2. Toss mushroom caps with 1 tablespoon oil, salt, and ⅛ teaspoon pepper and arrange gill side up on prepared sheet. Bake until mushrooms release their moisture and shrink in size, about 15 minutes. Flip caps and continue to bake until well browned, about 5 minutes; remove from oven and set aside.

3. Meanwhile, pulse reserved mushroom stems, shallot, garlic, and remaining ⅛ teaspoon pepper in food processor until finely chopped, 10 to 14 pulses. Heat remaining 1 tablespoon oil in 10-inch nonstick skillet over medium heat until shimmering. Add stem mixture and cook until golden brown, about 5 minutes. Stir in wine and cook until evaporated and mixture is thickened slightly, about 2 minutes. Transfer to bowl and stir in thyme, lemon juice, and remaining 6 tablespoons Parmesan.

4. Flip mushroom caps gill side up. Divide stuffing evenly among caps, then sprinkle evenly with panko mixture. Bake until stuffing is warmed through and topping is deep golden brown, about 10 minutes. Transfer to serving platter, drizzle with extra oil to taste, and sprinkle with parsley. Serve.

Buffalo Cauliflower Bites with Vegan Ranch Dressing

Buffalo Cauliflower Bites with Vegan Ranch Dressing

Serves 4 to 6   FAST

Why This Recipe Works Deemed "better than wings" by our tasters, these tangy, spicy, munchable cauliflower bites will be the new star of your game day table. For a flavorful, ultracrisp coating that would hold up under the buffalo sauce, a mixture of cornstarch and cornmeal gave us the ideal exterior. But because cauliflower is not naturally moist (like chicken), the mixture didn't adhere; so we dunked the florets in canned coconut milk first, which had the right viscosity. We got decent results when we baked our bites, but we absolutely flipped over the crackly crust and tender interior we achieved through frying. An herby ranch dressing was a cooling foil to the kick of the bites. We used Frank's Red Hot Original Cayenne Pepper Sauce, but other hot sauces can be used. Use a Dutch oven that holds 6 quarts or more for this recipe.

Buffalo Sauce
- ¼ cup refined coconut oil
- ½ cup hot sauce
- 1 tablespoon packed dark brown sugar
- 2 teaspoons cider vinegar

Cauliflower
- 1–2 quarts peanut or vegetable oil
- ¾ cup cornstarch
- ¼ cup cornmeal
- ½ teaspoon table salt
- ¼ teaspoon pepper
- ⅔ cup canned coconut milk
- 1 tablespoon hot sauce
- 1 pound cauliflower florets, cut into 1½-inch pieces
- 1 recipe Vegan Ranch Dressing (recipe follows)

1. For the buffalo sauce Melt coconut oil in small saucepan over low heat. Whisk in hot sauce, brown sugar, and vinegar until combined. Remove from heat and cover to keep warm; set aside.

2. For the cauliflower Line platter with triple layer of paper towels. Add oil to large Dutch oven until it measures about 1½ inches deep and heat over medium-high heat to 400 degrees. While oil heats, combine cornstarch, cornmeal, salt, and pepper in small bowl. Whisk coconut milk and hot sauce together in large bowl. Add cauliflower; toss to coat well. Sprinkle cornstarch mixture over cauliflower; fold with rubber spatula until thoroughly coated.

3. Fry half of cauliflower, adding 1 or 2 pieces to oil at a time, until golden and crisp, gently stirring as needed to prevent pieces from sticking together, about 3 minutes. Using slotted spoon, transfer fried cauliflower to prepared platter.

4. Return oil to 400 degrees and repeat with remaining cauliflower. Transfer ½ cup sauce to clean large bowl, add fried cauliflower and gently toss to coat. Serve immediately with dressing and remaining sauce.

Vegan Ranch Dressing
Makes about ½ cup

We strongly prefer our favorite vegan mayonnaise, Just Mayo, or our homemade Vegan Mayonnaise (page 27).

- ½ cup plant-based mayonnaise or egg-based mayonnaise
- 2 tablespoons plain plant-based yogurt or dairy yogurt
- 1 teaspoon white wine vinegar
- 1½ teaspoons minced fresh chives
- 1½ teaspoons minced fresh dill
- ¼ teaspoon garlic powder
- ⅛ teaspoon table salt
- ⅛ teaspoon pepper

Whisk all ingredients in bowl until smooth. (Dressing can be refrigerated for up to 4 days.)

Cashew Ricotta Tartlets with Celery-Olive Topping

Serves 4 to 6 (**Makes** 15 tartlets) `FAST`

Why This Recipe Works These elegant, delectable hors d'oeuvres combine the satisfying creaminess of ricotta—either our homemade Cashew Ricotta (page 26) or dairy ricotta—with an exquisitely perfumed mixture of crunchy celery, briny black olives, and aromatic fresh marjoram. What's more, they're so easy to make, you may be tempted to skip the party and whip up a batch as a light meal for two. For ease of preparation, we started with store-bought mini phyllo cups, which we crisped briefly in the oven before filling

them with ricotta that we brightened with a combination of lemon zest, olive oil, salt, and pepper. Making the topping was simply a matter of combining and lightly seasoning our trio of ingredients. Once filled and topped, these tartlets were ready for the festivities! For our variation, we chose a classic Italian flavor profile of tomatoes and basil to complement our ricotta. We found that a standard (2.1-ounce) box of frozen mini phyllo cups contains 15 pieces. Use two teaspoons to distribute the filling among the phyllo cups. We prefer the tender inner ribs and leaves of the celery heart in this recipe. If you can't find fresh marjoram, you can substitute fresh oregano or parsley. If using dairy ricotta in this recipe, do not use fat-free ricotta; we prefer the rich flavor of whole-milk ricotta, but part-skim ricotta can be substituted.

- ¼ cup minced celery
- 2 tablespoons pitted kalamata olives, chopped
- 1 tablespoon minced fresh marjoram or oregano
- 1 tablespoon extra-virgin olive oil, divided, plus extra for drizzling
- 15 frozen mini phyllo cups
- ½ cup Cashew Ricotta (page 26) or whole-milk dairy ricotta
- 1 teaspoon grated lemon zest
- ⅛ teaspoon table salt
- ⅛ teaspoon pepper

1. Adjust oven rack to middle position and heat oven to 350 degrees. Combine celery, olives, marjoram, and 1 teaspoon oil in bowl; season with salt and pepper to taste and set aside.

2. Arrange phyllo cups on rimmed baking sheet and bake until golden and crisp, 3 to 5 minutes; transfer to wire rack to cool completely.

3. Whisk ricotta, lemon zest, salt, pepper, and remaining 2 teaspoons oil together in bowl. Divide ricotta mixture evenly among cooled phyllo cups then top with celery mixture. Drizzle with extra oil to taste. Serve.

VARIATION

Cashew Ricotta Tartlets with Tomato-Basil Topping
Substitute 1 cored, seeded, and chopped tomato for the celery, 1 minced small shallot for the olives, and shredded fresh basil for the marjoram.

Butternut Squash Tartlets with Almonds, Pomegranate, and Mint

Serves 4 to 6 (**Makes** 15 tartlets) `FAST`

Why This Recipe Works An enticing and beautiful addition to any party spread, these exquisite little tartlets—like our cashew ricotta tartlets (page 365)—are a cinch to make and require only a handful of carefully balanced elements. We started with store-bought mini phyllo cups, which we crisped briefly in the oven before filling with a delicately sweet and smoky, ultravelvety butternut squash puree. (Steaming the squash in the microwave yielded a puree in less than 15 minutes!) For the topping, we combined bright, juicy pomegranate seeds with toasty sliced almonds and fresh mint, and we finished with a drizzle of tangy, bittersweet pomegranate molasses and smooth, rich olive oil. We found that a standard (2.1-ounce) box of frozen mini phyllo cups contains 15 pieces. Use two teaspoons to distribute the filling among the phyllo cups. If you can't find pomegranate molasses, you can make your own (page 351).

- 2 tablespoons sliced almonds, toasted
- 2 tablespoons pomegranate seeds
- 1 tablespoon chopped fresh mint
- 1 pound butternut squash, peeled, seeded, and cut into 1-inch pieces (3½ cups)
- 1 tablespoon extra-virgin olive oil, plus extra for drizzling
- ½ teaspoon table salt
- ¼ teaspoon smoked paprika
- 15 frozen mini phyllo cups
  Pomegranate molasses

1. Adjust oven rack to middle position and heat oven to 350 degrees. Combine almonds, pomegranate seeds, and mint in bowl; season with salt and pepper to taste and set aside.

2. Microwave squash in covered bowl, stirring occasionally, until tender, 10 to 12 minutes; drain well. Process squash, oil, salt, and paprika in food processor until smooth, about 30 seconds, scraping down sides of bowl as needed; season with salt and pepper to taste and set aside to cool slightly.

3. Arrange phyllo cups on rimmed baking sheet and bake until golden and crisp, 3 to 5 minutes; transfer to wire rack to cool slightly. Divide squash mixture evenly among phyllo cups then top with almond mixture. Drizzle with pomegranate molasses and extra oil to taste. Serve warm or at room temperature.

Butternut Squash Tartlets with Almonds, Pomegranate, and Mint

Stuffed Grape Leaves

Serves 12 (**Makes** 24 stuffed leaves)

Why This Recipe Works Although they can include meat, stuffed grape leaves (known in Greece as dolmathes) are traditionally a naturally vegan dish, made with rice, herbs, lemon, and other ingredients. We love them served as small bites, but they also make a great hearty addition to salads. To develop a foolproof recipe, we started with the leaves themselves. Not wanting to be restricted by seasonality, we chose to use jarred grape leaves. Since the jarred leaves were packed in brine, we needed to figure out a way to tame their flavor before using them; blanching them briefly in boiling water did the trick. As for the filling, tasters preferred the slight stickiness of short-grain rice to the texture of long-grain rice. Parcooking the rice ensured that it would cook to the perfect doneness as the rolled leaves simmered. We cooked the stuffed grape leaves in a skillet since they fit nicely in a single layer; a bit of lemon juice added to the steaming water gave the leaves citrusy flavor. Lining the bottom of the skillet with the extra, unused grape leaves ensured that the stuffed leaves were not in direct contact with the heat, preventing scorching.

We've had good luck using Peloponnese and Krinos brand grape leaves. Larger grape leaves can be trimmed to 6 inches, and smaller leaves can be overlapped to achieve the correct size. Take care when handling the grape leaves; they can be delicate and easily tear. Long-grain rice can be substituted for short-grain in this recipe, but the filling will not be as cohesive.

1 (16-ounce) jar grape leaves
2 tablespoons extra-virgin olive oil, plus extra for serving
1 large onion, chopped fine
½ teaspoon table salt
¾ cup short-grain white rice
⅓ cup chopped fresh dill
¼ cup chopped fresh mint
1½ tablespoons grated lemon zest plus 2 tablespoons juice

1. Reserve 24 intact grape leaves, roughly 6 inches in diameter; set aside remaining leaves. Bring 6 cups water to boil in medium saucepan. Add reserved grape leaves and cook for 1 minute. Gently drain leaves and transfer to bowl of cold water to cool, about 5 minutes. Drain again, then transfer leaves to plate and cover loosely with plastic wrap.

2. Heat oil in now-empty saucepan over medium heat until shimmering. Add onion and salt and cook until softened and lightly browned, 5 to 7 minutes. Add rice and cook, stirring frequently, until grain edges begin to turn translucent, about 2 minutes. Stir in ¾ cup water and bring to boil. Reduce heat to low, cover, and simmer gently until rice is tender but still firm in center and water has been absorbed, 10 to 12 minutes. Off heat, let rice cool slightly, about 10 minutes. Stir in dill, mint, and lemon zest.

3. Place 1 blanched leaf smooth side down on counter with stem facing you. Remove stem from base of leaf by cutting along both sides of stem to form narrow triangle. Pat leaf dry with paper towels. Overlap cut ends of leaf to prevent any filling from spilling out. Place heaping tablespoon filling ¼ inch from bottom of leaf where ends overlap. Fold bottom over filling and fold in sides. Roll leaf tightly around filling to create tidy roll. Repeat with remaining blanched leaves and filling.

4. Line 12-inch skillet with single layer of remaining leaves. Place rolled leaves seam side down in tight rows in prepared skillet. Combine 1¼ cups water and lemon juice, add to skillet, and bring to simmer over medium heat. Cover, reduce heat to medium-low, and simmer until water is almost completely absorbed and leaves and rice are tender and cooked through, 45 minutes to 1 hour.

5. Transfer stuffed grape leaves to serving platter and let cool to room temperature, about 30 minutes; discard leaves in skillet. Drizzle with extra oil before serving.

VARIATION
Stuffed Grape Leaves with Currants and Pine Nuts
Omit dill and lemon juice. In step 2, add 1½ teaspoons ground allspice and ¼ teaspoon ground cinnamon to cooked onions, and add ¼ cup toasted pine nuts and ¼ cup currants to cooked rice. Increase water in step 4 to 1⅓ cups.

ASSEMBLING GRAPE LEAVES

1. Place 1 leaf, smooth side down, on counter. Remove any thick stem from base of grape leaf by cutting along both sides of rib to form narrow triangle.

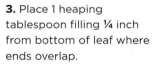

2. Overlap ends of leaf to prevent any filling from spilling out.

3. Place 1 heaping tablespoon filling ¼ inch from bottom of leaf where ends overlap.

4. Fold bottom over filling and fold in sides. Roll leaf tightly around filling to create tidy roll. Repeat with remaining filling and reserved leaves.

PLANT-POWERED DESSERTS

■ FAST (45 minutes or less total time)
Photos: Tropical Fruit Pavlova; French Apple Tart; Grilled Fruit

Melon, Plums, and Cherries with Mint and Vanilla

Melon, Plums, and Cherries with Mint and Vanilla

Serves 4 to 6 `FAST`

Why This Recipe Works This elegant fresh fruit salad is equally at home on a dessert table as it is at brunch. We chose a combination of cantaloupe, plums, and cherries, which not only offered a range of complementary flavors but also looked gorgeous. A small amount of sugar encouraged the fruit to release its juices. We balanced that sweetness with fresh lime juice, but tasters wanted even more complexity. Mashing the sugar with fresh mint before stirring it into the fruit worked perfectly and ensured even distribution of bright minty flavor. Since our fruit salad had come together so easily, we decided to apply the same techniques to a variation with peaches and berries, using fresh basil in place of the mint and a small amount of pepper to bring the flavors to life. Blueberries can be substituted for the cherries.

- 4 teaspoons sugar
- 1 tablespoon minced fresh mint
- 3 cups ½-inch cantaloupe pieces
- 2 plums, halved, pitted, and cut into ½-inch pieces
- 8 ounces fresh sweet cherries, pitted and halved
- ¼ teaspoon vanilla extract
- 1 tablespoon lime juice, plus extra for seasoning

Combine sugar and mint in large bowl. Using rubber spatula, press mixture into side of bowl until sugar becomes damp, about 30 seconds. Add cantaloupe, plums, cherries, and vanilla and gently toss to combine. Let sit at room temperature, stirring occasionally, until fruit releases its juices, 15 to 30 minutes. Stir in lime juice and season with extra lime juice to taste. Serve.

VARIATION
Peaches, Blackberries, and Strawberries with Basil and Pepper
Serves 4 to 6

Nectarines can be substituted for the peaches.

- 2 tablespoons chopped fresh basil
- 4 teaspoons sugar
- ½ teaspoon pepper
- 1½ pounds peaches, halved, pitted, and cut into ½-inch pieces
- 10 ounces (2 cups) blackberries
- 10 ounces strawberries, hulled and quartered (2 cups)
- 1 tablespoon lime juice, plus extra for seasoning

Roasted Pears with Dried Apricots and Pistachios

Combine basil, sugar, and pepper in large bowl. Using rubber spatula, press mixture into side of bowl until sugar becomes damp, about 30 seconds. Add peaches, blackberries, and strawberries and gently toss to combine. Let sit at room temperature, stirring occasionally, until fruit releases its juices, 15 to 30 minutes. Stir in lime juice and season with extra lime juice to taste. Serve.

Cider Baked Apples with Dried Cranberries

Serves 4

Why This Recipe Works Fresh apples stuffed with dried fruit, nuts, and spices and baked until tender make a dessert that's simultaneously cozy enough to snack on in front of the TV and sophisticated enough to serve to company. We preferred baking the apples uncovered instead of wrapping them in foil because the fruit caramelized better when exposed to the oven's heat. To allow steam to escape and thereby keep the apples from bursting, we found that removing a strip of skin around the apple's stem end with a vegetable peeler did the trick. Use Golden Delicious, Cortland, or Baldwin apples here. To keep all the flavorful fillings from leaking out, take care not to puncture the blossom end (opposite the stem end) of the apples when coring them.

- 4 large apples (8 ounces each)
- ½ cup dried cranberries or cherries
- ¼ cup (1¾ ounces) sugar
- ¼ teaspoon ground cinnamon
- 1½ cups apple cider
- 2 cinnamon sticks
- ¼ cup walnuts, toasted and chopped (optional)

1. Adjust oven rack to middle position and heat oven to 350 degrees. Using vegetable peeler, remove strip of apple peel from top of each apple, then use melon baller to remove stem and core of apple, being careful not to cut all the way through blossom end.

2. Place apples in 8-inch square baking dish. Spoon 1 tablespoon dried cranberries into each apple. Combine sugar and ground cinnamon, then sprinkle in and around apples in dish. Add remaining ¼ cup dried cranberries, cider, and cinnamon sticks around apples in dish.

3. Bake apples until tender when pierced with fork or skewer, 45 to 55 minutes, brushing apples with cider several times during baking. (Be careful not to overbake apples or skins will split.)

PREPARING APPLES FOR BAKING

After removing strip of peel from stem end of apple with vegetable peeler, use melon baller to scoop out core, being careful not to puncture blossom end.

4. Transfer apples to individual bowls and tent with aluminum foil while making sauce. Pour cooking liquid with cranberries and cinnamon sticks into small saucepan, bring to simmer over medium-high heat, and cook until liquid has reduced to 1 cup, 7 to 10 minutes.

5. Discard cinnamon sticks. Spoon some of sauce over each apple; sprinkle with walnuts, if using; and serve, passing remaining sauce separately.

VARIATIONS
Cider Baked Apples with Ginger and Orange
Substitute one 3-inch-long strip orange peel and one 1-inch piece fresh ginger, peeled and sliced into ¼-inch-thick rounds, for cinnamon sticks. Before serving, discard orange peel and ginger.

Cider Baked Apples with Rum and Golden Raisins
Substitute golden raisins for dried cranberries and add ¼ cup dark rum to dish with cider in step 2. Before serving, stir 2 tablespoons dark rum into sauce.

Roasted Pears with Dried Apricots and Pistachios

Serves 4 to 6

Why This Recipe Works Pears are often poached, but when they're roasted until bronzed and adorned with a few simple embellishments, they make a lovely after-dinner treat. Since pears contain a lot of liquid, we needed to drive off some moisture before we could achieve browning, so we jump-started cooking the pears on the stovetop. Transferring the skillet to the oven for the rest of the cooking time ensured even and consistent browning and fork-tender fruit. A quick pan sauce made the most of the flavorful browned bits left in the pan. White wine, lemon juice, and cardamom offered an aromatic flavor profile. A small amount of sugar and some dried apricots brought balanced sweetness. For textural contrast, we sprinkled on a handful of toasted pistachios just before serving. We prefer Bosc pears in this recipe, but Comice and Bartlett pears also work. Use a medium-bodied dry white wine such as Sauvignon Blanc or Pinot Grigio.

  2 tablespoons extra-virgin olive oil
  4 ripe but firm Bosc pears (7 to 8 ounces each),
    peeled, halved, and cored
1¼ cups dry white wine
  ½ cup dried apricots, quartered
  ⅓ cup (2⅓ ounces) sugar
  ¼ teaspoon ground cardamom
  ⅛ teaspoon table salt
  1 teaspoon lemon juice
  ⅓ cup shelled pistachios, toasted and chopped

1. Adjust oven rack to middle position and heat oven to 450 degrees. Heat oil in 12-inch ovensafe skillet over medium-high heat until shimmering. Place pears cut side down in skillet and cook, without moving, until just beginning to brown, 3 to 5 minutes.

2. Transfer skillet to oven and roast pears for 15 minutes. Being careful of hot skillet handle, flip pears and continue to roast until toothpick slips easily in and out of pears, 10 to 15 minutes.

3. Being careful of hot skillet handle, remove skillet from oven and carefully transfer pears to serving platter. Add wine, apricots, sugar, cardamom, and salt to now-empty skillet and bring to simmer over medium-high heat. Cook, whisking to scrape up any browned bits, until sauce is reduced and has consistency of maple syrup, 7 to 10 minutes. Off heat, stir in lemon juice. Pour sauce over pears and sprinkle with pistachios. Serve.

VARIATIONS
Roasted Apples with Dried Figs and Walnuts
Use a medium-bodied dry red wine such as Pinot Noir.
    Substitute Gala apples for pears, dry red wine for white wine, dried figs for apricots, ¾ teaspoon pepper for cardamom, and walnuts for pistachios.

Roasted Plums with Dried Cherries and Almonds
Substitute unpeeled plums for pears, dried cherries for apricots, ground cinnamon for cardamom, and sliced almonds for pistachios. Reduce oven roasting time in step 2 to 5 minutes per side.

Peaches and Cherries Poached in Spiced Red Wine
Serves 6 FAST

Why This Recipe Works Poaching fruit makes for an elegant dessert presentation, allowing the shape and texture of the fruit to remain intact while rendering it tender and enhancing its pure, fresh flavor. Sweet cherries and floral peaches made a perfect pair when poached in a red wine syrup. We found that a 2:1 ratio of wine to sugar was necessary to achieve a glossy syrup that would nicely coat the fruit. Poaching the delicate fruit over the heat directly in the syrup caused it to break down too much; instead, we boiled the syrup first to dissolve the sugar completely, then allowed the fruit to cook gently by pouring the hot syrup over it and letting it poach off the heat. Slicing the peaches thin ensured that they would cook at the same rate as the cherries. To infuse the fruit with flavor as it cooled in the syrup, we added half a cinnamon stick (a whole one was overpowering) and a couple of whole cloves. Serve this compote as is or spooned over plant-based or dairy yogurt, frozen yogurt, or ice cream.

  1 pound fresh sweet cherries, pitted and halved
  1 pound ripe but firm peaches, peeled, halved, pitted,
    and sliced ¼ inch thick
  ½ cinnamon stick
  2 whole cloves
  2 cups dry red wine
  1 cup sugar

Combine cherries, peaches, cinnamon stick, and cloves in large bowl. Bring red wine and sugar to boil in small saucepan and cook, stirring occasionally, until sugar has dissolved, about 5 minutes. Pour syrup over fruit, cover with plastic wrap, and let cool to room temperature. Discard cinnamon stick and cloves. Serve.

NOTES FROM THE TEST KITCHEN

PITTING CHERRIES
For neater cherry pitting, place a large bowl of water in the sink. Add cherries and then pit them at the bottom of the bowl. Pits float to the surface for easy removal, the cherries are rinsed in the process, and your hands (and the kitchen walls) aren't bright red.

Plum-Blackberry Compote

Strawberry-Rhubarb Compote

Serves 6 `FAST`

Why This Recipe Works Peak-season fruit is transformed into the simplest of desserts, to be served as is or spooned over plant-based or dairy yogurt or ice cream or our Greek Lemon Rice Pudding (page 387). We followed up this classic duo of strawberries and rhubarb with a couple of colorful stone fruit and berry combinations. Gentle cooking released the juices of the rhubarb or stone fruit without turning them into jam. Adding the delicate berries at the end prevented an overly soft compote, as did transferring the compote to a bowl to cool. Do not overcook the rhubarb or it will become stringy. You may substitute 1 teaspoon vanilla extract for the vanilla bean; stir it in with the coconut oil in step 2.

½ vanilla bean
6 tablespoons sugar
¼ cup water
Pinch table salt
8 ounces rhubarb, peeled and cut into 1-inch lengths
20 ounces strawberries, hulled and quartered (4 cups)
1 tablespoon refined coconut oil or unsalted butter

1. Cut vanilla bean in half lengthwise. Using tip of paring knife, scrape out seeds and reserve bean. Bring vanilla seeds and bean, sugar, water, and salt to simmer in 12-inch nonstick skillet over medium heat. Stir in rhubarb and cook until rhubarb begins to soften and sauce thickens slightly, 4 to 6 minutes.

2. Off heat, gently stir in strawberries and oil and let sit until oil has melted. Discard vanilla bean, transfer compote to bowl, and let cool to room temperature, 10 to 15 minutes. Serve. (Compote can be refrigerated for up to 1 day; return to room temperature before serving.)

VARIATIONS
Plum-Blackberry Compote
Try to buy plums of similar ripeness so that they cook evenly.

½ vanilla bean
6 tablespoons water
¼ cup sugar
Pinch table salt
1½ pounds plums, pitted, sliced ⅓ inch thick, then halved crosswise
10 ounces (2 cups) blackberries
1 tablespoon refined coconut oil or unsalted butter

1. Cut vanilla bean in half lengthwise. Using tip of paring knife, scrape out seeds and reserve bean. Bring vanilla seeds and bean, water, sugar, and salt to simmer in 12-inch nonstick skillet over medium heat. Stir in plums and cook until plums begin to soften and sauce thickens slightly, 5 to 7 minutes.

2. Stir in blackberries and continue to cook until blackberries begin to soften, about 1 minute. Off heat, stir in oil and let sit until melted. Discard vanilla bean, transfer compote to bowl, and let cool to room temperature, 10 to 15 minutes. Serve. (Compote can be refrigerated for up to 1 day; return to room temperature before serving.)

REMOVING SEEDS FROM A VANILLA BEAN

1. Use paring knife to cut vanilla bean in half lengthwise.

2. Scrape vanilla seeds out of bean using blade of knife.

Blueberry-Nectarine Compote

Try to buy nectarines of similar ripeness so that they cook evenly.

½ vanilla bean
3 tablespoons sugar
2 tablespoons water
Pinch table salt
1½ pounds nectarines, pitted, sliced ⅓ inch thick, then halved crosswise
10 ounces (2 cups) blueberries
1 tablespoon lemon juice
1 tablespoon refined coconut oil or unsalted butter

1. Cut vanilla bean in half lengthwise. Using tip of paring knife, scrape out seeds and reserve bean. Bring vanilla seeds and bean, sugar, water, and salt to simmer in 12-inch nonstick skillet over medium heat. Stir in nectarines and cook until nectarines begin to soften and sauce thickens slightly, 3 to 5 minutes. Stir in blueberries and continue to cook until blueberries begin to release their juice, 2 to 4 minutes.

2. Off heat, stir in lemon juice and oil and let sit until oil has melted. Discard vanilla bean, transfer compote to bowl, and let cool to room temperature, 10 to 15 minutes. Serve. (Compote can be refrigerated for up to 1 day; return to room temperature before serving.)

Grilled Fruit
FAST

Why This Recipe Works Grilled fruit makes a simple but fantastic al fresco dessert, either on its own or alongside a scoop of our Lemon Ice (page 391). The natural sweetness of the fruit is intensified by the caramelization that happens on the grill. In the chart below, we have included those fruits that we believe do best on the grill. Use smaller plums, peaches, apples, and pears when grilling, since larger fruits may burn on the outside before heating through to the center. All fruit to be grilled should be ripe but still firm. Grill delicate fruits with their skins intact, as the skins keep the fruit from falling apart on the grill. To prevent sticking, be sure to clean your cooking grate thoroughly before adding the fruit. Grilled fruit is also delicious served with plant-based or dairy yogurt, frozen yogurt, or ice cream.

Prepared fruit (see chart)
Vegetable oil

1A. For a charcoal grill Open bottom vent completely. Light large chimney starter three-quarters filled with charcoal briquettes (4½ quarts). When top coals are partially covered with ash, pour evenly over grill. Set cooking grate in place, cover, and open lid vent completely. Heat grill until hot, about 5 minutes.

NOTES FROM THE TEST KITCHEN

PREPPING FRUIT FOR THE GRILL

FRUIT	PREPARATION	GRILLING DIRECTIONS
Banana	Leave skin on; cut in half lengthwise using sharp paring knife.	Grill skin side up for 2 minutes; turn and grill skin side down for 2 minutes.
Mango	Peel, pit, and cut into 4 pieces.	Grill larger pieces for 5 minutes, smaller pieces for 4 minutes, turning all pieces once halfway through cooking time.
Peach	Cut in half and remove pit.	Grill skin side up for 4 minutes; turn and grill skin side down for 3 to 4 minutes.
Apple	Cut in half through core. Remove core with melon baller. Use paring knife to cut out stem.	Grill skin side up for 5 to 6 minutes; turn and grill skin side down for 5 to 6 minutes.
Pear	Cut in half lengthwise. Remove core with melon baller. Use paring knife to cut out stem.	Grill skin side up for 5 minutes; turn and grill skin side down for 5 minutes.
Pineapple	Cut into half-circles.	Grill for 6 minutes, turning once halfway through cooking time.
Plum	Cut in half and remove pit.	Grill skin side up for 4 minutes; turn and grill skin side down for 2 minutes.

1B. For a gas grill Turn all burners to high, cover, and heat grill until hot, about 15 minutes. Turn all burners to medium-high.

2. Clean and oil cooking grate. Lightly brush prepared fruit with oil. Grill fruit as directed in chart. Fruit is done when it is marked on exterior and just barely softened and heated through at center.

No-Bake Cherry-Almond Crisp
Serves 6

Why This Recipe Works Most fruit crisps are baked, but oven versions we tried of this sweet cherry crisp either emerged with stodgy fillings or the filling boiled up over the topping in the oven, making it soggy. So we migrated to the stovetop. After browning a topping of almonds, sugar, flour, and coconut oil (or butter) in a skillet on the stovetop, we used the same pan to cook the filling, sprinkling on the crispy cooked topping at the end. Starting with frozen pitted cherries is superconvenient, making this a great year-round dessert, and they were luscious once combined with sugar, lemon juice, and almond and vanilla extracts. Adding dried cherries soaked up excess moisture from the frozen fruit while adding texture, and cornstarch thickened the filling to a syrupy consistency. You will need a 10-inch nonstick skillet with a tight-fitting lid for this recipe. Serve with Coconut Whipped Cream (page 378) or dairy whipped cream.

Topping
- ¾ cup sliced almonds, divided
- ⅔ cup (3⅓ ounces) all-purpose flour
- ¼ cup packed (1¾ ounces) light brown sugar
- ¼ cup (1¾ ounces) granulated sugar
- ½ teaspoon vanilla extract
- ½ teaspoon ground cinnamon
- ¼ teaspoon table salt
- 6 tablespoons refined coconut oil or unsalted butter, melted
- 1 tablespoon water

Filling
- 5 tablespoons (2¼ ounces) granulated sugar, divided
- 1 tablespoon cornstarch
- 2 pounds frozen sweet cherries
- 1 tablespoon lemon juice
- 1 teaspoon vanilla extract
- ½ teaspoon table salt
- ¼ teaspoon almond extract
- ⅔ cup dried cherries

No-Bake Cherry-Almond Crisp

1. For the topping Finely chop ¼ cup almonds. Combine flour, brown sugar, granulated sugar, vanilla, cinnamon, salt, and chopped almonds in bowl. Stir in melted oil and water until mixture resembles wet sand and no dry flour remains.

2. Toast remaining ½ cup almonds in 10-inch nonstick skillet over medium-low heat until just beginning to brown, about 4 minutes. Add flour mixture and cook, stirring constantly, until lightly browned, 8 to 10 minutes; transfer to plate to cool. Wipe out skillet with paper towels.

3. For the filling Combine 2 tablespoons sugar and cornstarch in small bowl; set aside. Combine cherries, lemon juice, vanilla, salt, almond extract, and remaining 3 tablespoons sugar in now-empty skillet. Cover and cook over medium heat until cherries thaw and release their juice, about 7 minutes, stirring halfway through cooking. Uncover, stir in dried cherries, and simmer until cherries are very tender, about 3 minutes.

4. Stir in cornstarch mixture and simmer, stirring constantly, until thickened, 1 to 3 minutes. Off heat, sprinkle topping evenly over filling. Return skillet to medium-low heat and cook until filling is bubbling around edges, about 3 minutes. Let cool for at least 30 minutes before serving.

Apple Crumble

4 pounds Golden Delicious apples, peeled, cored, and cut into ¾-inch pieces
2 tablespoons packed brown sugar, plus ½ cup packed (3½ ounces)
2 tablespoons lemon juice
¾ teaspoon ground cinnamon
½ teaspoon table salt, divided
1 cup (5 ounces) all-purpose flour
½ cup sliced almonds, chopped fine
6 tablespoons refined coconut oil or unsalted butter, melted
2 teaspoons vanilla extract
2 teaspoons water

1. Adjust oven racks to upper-middle and lowest positions and heat oven to 400 degrees. Toss apples, 2 tablespoons sugar, lemon juice, cinnamon, and ¼ teaspoon salt together in large bowl. Transfer to 8-inch square baking pan with at least 2-inch tall sides and press into even layer. Cover pan tightly with aluminum foil and place on foil-lined rimmed baking sheet. Transfer sheet to oven and bake on lower rack for 35 minutes.

2. While apples bake, whisk flour, almonds, remaining ½ cup sugar, and remaining ¼ teaspoon salt in medium bowl until combined. Add melted coconut oil, vanilla, and water and stir with spatula until clumps form and no dry flour remains.

3. Remove sheet from oven and smooth top of apples with spatula. If apples have not collapsed enough to leave at least ¼ inch of space below rim of pan, replace foil, return sheet to oven, and continue to bake 5 to 15 minutes longer.

4. Sprinkle topping evenly over apples, breaking up any clumps larger than a marble. Transfer sheet to upper rack and bake until topping is evenly browned and filling is just bubbling at edges, 20 to 30 minutes. Let cool for at least 45 minutes before serving.

Apple Crumble
Serves 6 to 8

Why This Recipe Works This is an apple lover's apple crumble: By dialing back the sweetness and packing in as much fruit as possible, we allowed all the bright, tart flavor of the apples to shine through without blanketing it under a mountain of sugar and streusel. Parbaking the apples before adding the topping meant that we could pack the baking dish to the top with raw fruit. After it softened and collapsed in the oven's heat, we added our lightly sweetened topping and finished baking the crumble to golden perfection. Waiting to add the topping also prevented it from becoming soggy. For the best texture, we chose Golden Delicious, an apple variety that offers near-universal availability, plus balanced sweet-tart flavor and enough structural integrity that it wouldn't turn to mush. You can use Braeburn or Honeycrisp apples in place of the Golden Delicious or a combination of all three. Serve with plant-based or dairy frozen yogurt or ice cream, if you like.

Peach Crumble

Serves 4 to 6

Why This Recipe Works Peaches are certainly juicier than apples, but they can also vary quite a bit more than apples in terms of juiciness and sweetness. To get a great peach crumble every time with fickle peaches, we let peeled, sliced peaches macerate in sugar for half an hour before draining them and measuring out the amount of peach juice that would be added back to the filling: always ¼ cup. This both concentrated the peaches' flavor and controlled their moisture content. To ensure that the crumble topping would stay crisp on top of the delicate peaches, we parbaked it separately first (while the peaches were macerating) and then added it to the fruit in the baking dish to bake until browned and bubbling. We recommend fresh peaches in this recipe. Serve with plant-based or dairy frozen yogurt or ice cream, if you like.

Filling
- 3½ pounds ripe but firm peaches, peeled, pitted, and cut into ¾-inch-thick wedges
- ⅓ cup (2⅓ ounces) granulated sugar
- 1 tablespoon lemon juice
- 1¼ teaspoons cornstarch
-   Pinch table salt
-   Pinch ground cinnamon
-   Pinch ground nutmeg

Topping
- 1 cup (5 ounces) all-purpose flour
- ¼ cup (1¾ ounces) granulated sugar
- ¼ cup packed (1¾ ounces) brown sugar
- 2 teaspoons vanilla extract
- ⅛ teaspoon table salt
- 6 tablespoons refined coconut oil or unsalted butter, melted
- ½ cup sliced almonds, divided
- 1 tablespoon water

1. Adjust oven racks to lower-middle and upper-middle positions and heat oven to 350 degrees. Line rimmed baking sheet with parchment paper.

2. **For the filling** Gently toss peaches and sugar together in large bowl and let sit for 30 minutes, tossing occasionally. Drain peaches in colander set over large bowl. Whisk ¼ cup drained peach juice, lemon juice, cornstarch, salt, cinnamon, and nutmeg together in small bowl; discard excess peach juice. Toss juice mixture with peaches and transfer to 8-inch square baking dish.

Peach Crumble

3. **For the topping** While peaches are macerating, pulse flour, granulated sugar, brown sugar, vanilla, and salt in food processor until combined, about 5 pulses. Add melted oil, ¼ cup almonds, and water and process until combined, about 30 seconds, scraping down sides of bowl as needed. Add remaining ¼ cup almonds and pulse until combined, about 2 pulses. Transfer mixture to prepared sheet, pinch into rough ½-inch chunks with some smaller, loose bits, and spread into even layer. Bake on upper rack until lightly browned and firm, 15 to 19 minutes.

4. Sprinkle topping evenly over peaches and spread into even layer with spatula, packing down lightly and breaking up any very large pieces. Place dish on lower rack and increase oven temperature to 375 degrees. Bake until topping is well browned and juices are bubbling around edges, 20 to 30 minutes. Let cool for at least 45 minutes before serving.

Strawberry Shortcakes with Coconut Whipped Cream

Strawberries
2 pounds strawberries, hulled and quartered (6⅓ cups)
6 tablespoons (2⅔ ounces) granulated sugar

Shortcakes
2 cups (10 ounces) all-purpose flour
2 tablespoons granulated sugar
2 teaspoons baking powder
½ teaspoon baking soda
½ teaspoon table salt
1 cup plant-based milk or dairy milk, chilled
½ cup refined coconut oil or 8 tablespoons unsalted butter, melted and cooled slightly
1 tablespoon lemon juice
1 tablespoon turbinado sugar

1 recipe Coconut Whipped Cream

1. For the strawberries Using potato masher, mash one-third of strawberries with sugar in bowl. Stir in remaining strawberries, cover, and let sit while making shortcakes, at least 30 minutes or up to 2 hours.

2. For the shortcakes Adjust oven rack to middle position and heat oven to 475 degrees. Set rimmed baking sheet in second baking sheet and line with parchment paper. Whisk flour,

Strawberry Shortcakes with Coconut Whipped Cream

Serves 8

Why This Recipe Works Strawberry shortcakes, with their rustic biscuits, juicy berries, and fluff of whipped cream, capture the casual fun of summer days. But this treat is a three-part dessert, and only one—the fruit filling—is naturally vegan. We tested through vegan shortcakes with tough, crumbly biscuits and soupy, bland dairy-free cream before hitting on this winning combination. For the biscuits, we melted and slightly cooled coconut oil before adding it to cold milk (plant-based or dairy). The oil acted similarly to butter (which also works here), instantly solidifying into tiny clumps that added richly flavorful fat pockets, making for tender biscuits. Some lemon juice added a buttermilk-style tang. For the whipped cream, canned coconut milk whipped perfectly into velvety billows, and its mild coconut flavor beautifully complemented the sweet strawberries and rich biscuits. You will need to chill the unopened cans of coconut milk for at least 24 hours before use. You may serve this with dairy whipped cream instead, if you like.

Coconut Whipped Cream
Makes about 2 cups
The cream from canned coconut milk easily whips into delicately flavored soft-peaked billows.

4 (14-ounce) cans coconut milk
2 tablespoons granulated sugar
2 teaspoons vanilla extract

Refrigerate unopened cans of coconut milk for at least 24 hours to ensure that 2 distinct layers form. Skim top layer of cream from each can and measure out 2 cups of cream (save any extra cream and milky liquid for another use). Using stand mixer fitted with whisk attachment, whip coconut cream, sugar, and vanilla on low speed until well combined, about 30 seconds. Increase speed to high and whip until mixture thickens and soft peaks form, about 2 minutes. (Coconut whipped cream can be refrigerated for up to 4 days.)

granulated sugar, baking powder, baking soda, and salt together in large bowl. Whisk milk, melted oil, and lemon juice together (oil will clump) in second bowl. Stir milk mixture into flour mixture until just incorporated.

3. Using greased ⅓-cup dry measuring cup, drop level scoops of batter 1½ inches apart on prepared sheet. Sprinkle evenly with turbinado sugar. Bake until tops are golden, 12 to 14 minutes, rotating sheet halfway through baking. Transfer biscuits to wire rack and let cool completely, about 30 minutes.

4. Split each biscuit in half and place bottoms on individual plates. Using slotted spoon, portion strawberries over biscuit bottoms, then top with dollop of coconut whipped cream. Top shortcakes and serve immediately.

Tropical Fruit Pavlova

Serves 8

Why This Recipe Works Pavlova is a gorgeous dessert featuring a meringue that's a little crispy on the outside and a little chewy on the inside. Piled with whipped cream and fresh fruit, it's a showstopper. Since aquafaba, the liquid in canned chickpeas, is a magical egg-replacing ingredient, we figured that creating a vegan pavlova by whipping aquafaba and sugar into a stiff, fluffy foam would be a cinch. But were we wrong. The first hurdle was sugar: Confectioners' sugar had too much starch, and we were better able to achieve a glossy sheen from granulated sugar. The second hurdle was color: The bottoms of our meringues turned spotty brown, which signified sugar crystals sinking to the bottom, so we heated the aquafaba mixture to ensure that the sugar dissolved properly. The third hurdle was appearance: We had mottled meringues from too many air bubbles. Although aquafaba takes longer than egg whites to whip, there was a point when the meringue went from dense and glossy to aerated and cottony—a sign of overwhipping. Chilling the mixture before whipping helped us achieve the proper stage faster, preventing the likelihood of mottling. Last, though propping the oven door open for cooling is typical for egg white meringues, this caused our vegan meringues to deflate, so we left the door closed. Finally, we were ready to celebrate with our creamy and fruity toppings! You will need to refrigerate the unopened cans of coconut milk for the coconut whipped cream for at least 24 hours before use. You may use sweetened dairy whipped cream instead of the coconut whipped cream, if you like. If you can't find Thai basil, you can use Italian basil. These are a bit crisper than egg white meringues, so we let the assembled pavolvas sit for a short time before serving to let them soften.

Tropical Fruit Pavlova

Meringues

- ⅔ cup (4⅔ ounces) sugar
- 4 ounces (½ cup) aquafaba (page 16)
- ½ teaspoon vanilla extract
- ¼ teaspoon cream of tartar

Fruit Topping

- 1 mango, peeled, pitted, and cut into ¼-inch pieces
- 2 kiwis, peeled, quartered lengthwise, and sliced crosswise ¼ inch thick
- 1½ cups ½-inch pineapple pieces
- 1 tablespoon sugar
- ⅓ cup chopped fresh Thai basil

- 1 recipe Coconut Whipped Cream
- ½ cup unsweetened coconut, toasted

1. For the meringues Adjust oven rack to upper-middle and lower-middle positions and heat oven to 250 degrees. Heat sugar and aquafaba in small saucepan over medium-low heat, whisking until sugar is dissolved, about 5 minutes (mixture should not be bubbling). Transfer to bowl of stand mixer and refrigerate until chilled, about 1 hour.

2. Fit stand mixer with whisk attachment and whip chilled aquafaba mixture, vanilla, and cream of tartar on high speed until stiff peaks form and mixture is dense and bright white, 7 to 9 minutes, scraping down the bowl halfway through. (Do not overwhip.)

3. Spoon about ¼ teaspoon meringue onto each corner of 2 rimmed baking sheets. Line sheets with parchment paper, pressing on corners to secure. Spoon ⅓ cup meringue into 4 evenly spaced piles on each prepared sheet. Evenly distribute any remaining meringue among piles and spread each with back of spoon or spatula from center outward, building 4-inch disks that are slightly higher around edges.

4. Bake meringues for 50 minutes. Without opening oven door, turn off oven and let meringues cool in oven for 1 hour (meringues will still be soft to the touch, but will firm as they continue to cool). Remove meringues from oven and let cool completely before topping, about 15 minutes. (Cooled meringues can be wrapped tightly in plastic wrap and stored at room temperature for up to 2 days.)

5. For the fruit topping Gently toss mango, kiwis, and pineapple with sugar in bowl. Let sit at room temperature until sugar has dissolved and fruit is juicy, about 30 minutes. Just before serving, stir basil into fruit mixture.

6. To assemble, place meringue shells on individual plates and spoon heaping ¼ cup coconut whipped cream into each. Top with about ½ cup fruit (some fruit and juice will fall onto plate) and let sit for about 15 minutes. Sprinkle with toasted coconut and serve.

Trail Mix Cookies
Makes 24

Why This Recipe Works Chock-full of oats, nuts, seeds, dried fruit, and chocolate chips, these cookies are perfect for tucking into your backpack for a hike, sneaking into a lunch box, or simply nibbling on for an afternoon or bedtime snack. To create them, we tweaked the test kitchen's classic recipe for chocolate chip cookies, removing the eggs (no substitute needed!) and using all brown sugar, which gave the cookies richer flavor and a softer center. We substituted part of the flour with toasted rolled oats, which added nuttiness and wholesome texture, and added almond butter to stand in for the toffee-like richness usually provided by butter. Letting the mixed dough rest for 1 to 4 hours at room temperature created a chewier cookie (which we preferred): The proteins and starches in the flour start breaking down and the sugar dissolves, hydrates, and later retains this moisture better during baking, preventing the cookie from becoming brittle. Then we turned to the mix-ins: We knew we wanted dried fruit, nuts, and seeds—trail mix classics—to add texture, crunch, and richness. Pepitas added nice pops of color and texture, and pecans added rich, sweet crunchiness. Sweetened dried cranberries gave us bites of tangy fruitiness, and chocolate chips were a must. Not all chocolate chips are vegan, so check ingredient lists carefully. Do not use quick or instant oats in this recipe.

  1 cup (3 ounces) old-fashioned rolled oats
1⅔ cups (8⅓ ounces) all-purpose flour
1½ teaspoons baking powder
  ½ teaspoon baking soda
  ½ teaspoon table salt
1⅓ cups packed (9⅓ ounces) light brown sugar
  ½ cup refined coconut oil or 8 tablespoons unsalted butter, melted and cooled slightly
  6 tablespoons water, room temperature
  ⅓ cup unsalted creamy almond butter
  2 teaspoons vanilla extract
  ½ cup (3 ounces) bittersweet chocolate chips
  ½ cup dried cranberries, chopped
  ½ cup pecans, toasted and chopped
  ¼ cup raw pepitas

1. Adjust oven rack to middle position and heat oven to 350 degrees. Spread oats on rimmed baking sheet and bake until fragrant and lightly browned, about 10 minutes, stirring halfway through baking; let cool completely.

2. Whisk flour, baking powder, baking soda, and salt together in bowl. Whisk sugar, melted oil, water, almond butter, and vanilla together in large bowl until smooth. Using rubber spatula, stir flour mixture into oil mixture until just combined, then fold in toasted oats, chocolate chips, cranberries, pecans, and pepitas.

3. Cover bowl with plastic wrap and let sit at room temperature for at least 1 hour or up to 4 hours. (Dough can be refrigerated for up to 24 hours; let sit at room temperature for 30 minutes before portioning.)

4. Line 2 rimmed baking sheets with parchment paper. Working with 3 tablespoons dough at a time, roll into balls and space them evenly on prepared sheets. Press dough to 2-inch width using bottom of dry measuring cup.

5. Bake cookies, 1 sheet at a time, until edges are light golden and have begun to set but centers are still soft, about 14 minutes, rotating sheet halfway through baking. Let cookies cool completely on sheet. Serve. (Cookies can be stored at room temperature for up to 3 days.)

French Apple Tart

Serves 8

Why This Recipe Works This showstopping dessert is little more than apples artfully arranged in a pastry crust and baked until golden. We used our foolproof recipe for vegan tart dough and cooked half of the apples into a concentrated puree to fill the shell; we sliced the remaining apples and parcooked them until they were pliable enough to adorn the top with concentric circles in a rosette shape. A thin coat of apricot preserves and a run under the broiler provided a shiny, caramelized finish. You may have extra apple slices after arranging the apples in step 5. If you don't have a potato masher, you can puree the apples in a food processor. To ensure that the outer ring of the pan releases easily, avoid getting apple puree or apricot glaze on the edge of the crust.

- 10 Golden Delicious apples (8 ounces each), peeled and cored, divided
- 3 tablespoons refined coconut oil or unsalted butter, divided
- 1 tablespoon water
- ½ cup apricot preserves
- ¼ teaspoon table salt
- 1 recipe Vegan Tart Dough, fully baked

1. Adjust oven rack to lowest position and heat oven to 350 degrees. Cut 5 apples lengthwise into quarters and cut each quarter lengthwise into 4 slices. Melt 1 tablespoon oil in 12-inch skillet over medium heat. Add apple slices and water and toss to combine. Cover and cook, stirring occasionally, until apples begin to turn translucent and are slightly pliable, 3 to 5 minutes. Transfer apples to large plate, spread into single layer, and set aside to cool. Do not clean skillet.

MAKING THE APPLE ROSETTE

1. Starting at outer edge of tart, arrange apple slices, tightly overlapping, in concentric circles.

2. Bend 5 thinnest slices of sautéed apple to fit in center.

Vegan Tart Dough

Makes one 9-inch tart crust

While tart crusts typically get their shortbread-like texture from butter, we achieved the same effect using melted coconut oil plus a little water. The water replaced the moisture that butter contains and prevented a crumbly crust.

- 1¾ cups (8¾ ounces) all-purpose flour
- 3 tablespoons sugar
- ¼ teaspoon table salt
- ½ cup refined coconut oil, melted and cooled slightly
- 3 tablespoons water

1. Whisk flour, sugar, and salt together in bowl. Add melted oil and water and stir with rubber spatula until dough forms. Roll dough into 12-inch circle between 2 large sheets of parchment paper. Remove top sheet of parchment and, working quickly, gently invert dough (still on bottom sheet parchment) onto 9-inch tart pan with removable bottom. Center dough over pan letting excess dough hang over edge and remove remaining parchment. Ease dough into pan by gently lifting edge of dough with your hand while pressing into corners and fluted sides of pan with your other hand. Run rolling pin over top of pan to remove any excess dough. Prick dough all over with fork, then wrap pan loosely in plastic wrap and refrigerate for 30 minutes. (Dough-lined tart pan can be refrigerated for up to 24 hours or frozen for up to 1 month).

2. Adjust oven rack to middle position and heat oven to 350 degrees. Line chilled tart shell with double layer of aluminum foil and fill with pie weights. Bake on rimmed baking sheet until tart shell is evenly pale and dry, 30 to 35 minutes, rotating sheet halfway through baking.

3. Remove foil and weights and continue to bake tart shell until light golden brown and firm to touch, about 20 minutes, rotating pan halfway through baking. Set aside to cool completely. (Cooled crust can be wrapped in plastic wrap and stored at room temperature for up to 24 hours. Do not refrigerate or crust will become hard.)

2. While apples cook, microwave apricot preserves until fluid, about 30 seconds. Strain preserves through fine-mesh strainer into small bowl, reserving solids. Set aside 3 tablespoons strained preserves for brushing tart.

3. Cut remaining 5 apples into ½-inch-thick wedges. Melt remaining 2 tablespoons oil in now-empty skillet over medium heat. Add remaining apricot preserves, reserved apricot solids, apple wedges, and salt. Cover and cook, stirring occasionally, until apples are very soft, about 10 minutes.

4. Mash apples to puree with potato masher, then continue to cook, stirring occasionally, until puree is reduced to 2 cups, about 5 minutes.

5. Set baked tart shell on wire rack in rimmed baking sheet. Transfer apple puree to tart shell and smooth surface. Select 5 thinnest slices of sautéed apple and set aside. Starting at outer edge of tart, arrange remaining slices, tightly overlapping, in concentric circles. Bend reserved slices to fit in center. Bake tart for 30 minutes. Remove from oven and heat broiler.

6. While broiler heats, warm reserved preserves in microwave until fluid, about 20 seconds. Brush evenly over surface of apples, avoiding tart crust. Broil tart, checking every 30 seconds and turning as necessary, until apples are browned in spots, 1 to 3 minutes. Let tart cool for at least 1½ hours. Remove outer metal ring of tart pan, slide thin metal spatula between tart and pan bottom, and carefully slide tart onto serving platter. Cut into wedges and serve.

Chocolate-Espresso Tart

Chocolate-Espresso Tart

Serves 10 to 12

Why This Recipe Works "Showstopping" and "dead-easy" are terms rarely used to describe the same dessert. But this pull-out-all-the-stops chocolate tart with a dreamy espresso "meringue" is so elegant and sophisticated, yet so simple, that even we science-based test cooks thought it must be magic. We started with our vegan tart dough, which we rolled out to fit the tart pan; docking it and baking it with pie weights kept it in good shape. Next, we made the simplest "water ganache," an emulsion of chocolate and hot water (instead of the usual heavy cream) that became smooth and silky with a little whisking, set up beautifully glossy at room temperature, and sliced like a dream. Finally, the crowning touch: a three-ingredient espresso "meringue" inspired by Dalgona coffee. Instant espresso crystals, when dissolved in water with sugar and then whipped, created a billowy, glossy foam that could be piped or dolloped as an elegant decoration. Not all brands of bittersweet chocolate are vegan, so check ingredient lists carefully. We used bittersweet chocolate with 60 to 70 percent cacao for the filling (higher-percentage cacao will set faster).

We had the best results using a stand mixer to whip the topping; you can skip the topping if you like and just dust the tart with cocoa powder or confectioners' sugar, or add a dollop of Coconut Whipped Cream (page 378) or dairy whipped cream. For an accurate measurement of boiling water, bring a full kettle of water to a boil and then measure out the desired amount.

1 recipe Vegan Tart Dough (page 381), fully baked and cooled

Filling
10½ ounces bittersweet chocolate, chopped fine
¼ cup (1¾ ounces) sugar
¼ teaspoon table salt
¾ cup boiling water

Topping (optional)
6 tablespoons (2⅔ ounces) sugar
¼ cup ice water
4 teaspoons instant espresso powder

Unsweetened cocoa powder (optional)

FITTING TART DOUGH INTO THE PAN

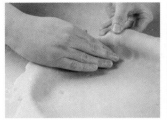 

1. Ease dough into tart pan by lifting dough and gently pressing it into corners and fluted sides of pan.

2. Run rolling pin over top of pan to remove any excess dough.

Pecan Pie

1. For the filling Place chocolate, sugar, and salt in bowl. Pour boiling water over chocolate mixture and let sit for 30 seconds, then whisk until mixture is completely smooth. Transfer filling to cooled tart shell, popping any large bubbles that form with a toothpick, and let tart sit at room temperature until chocolate is set, at least 2 hours and up to 24 hours. (Do not refrigerate or crust will become hard.)

2. For the optional topping Using stand mixer fitted with whisk attachment, whip sugar, ice water, and espresso powder on high speed until soft peaks form, 2 to 3 minutes. Transfer mixture to pastry bag fitted with star tip and pipe decoratively over filling (or use zipper-lock bag with corner snipped off). Dust with cocoa powder, if using, and serve.

Pecan Pie
Serves 8

Why This Recipe Works Classic pecan pie relies heavily on butter and eggs to get the texture of the sweet filling right, so we knew it would be a challenge to develop a hallmark vegan version. Things seemed promising when we tried our favorite recipe and simply omitted the dairy and eggs, but the filling never set up, even long after cooling, with a result more like a sticky caramel-nut pie—good, but not a true pecan pie. Eventually we struck upon using a classic French technique usually reserved for savory sauces: a roux. By cooking a little flour in hot coconut oil and whisking in some maple syrup, sugar, and water, we were able to create a thick emulsion that gave our pie filling body and cohesion. However, by the time we had incorporated enough of the roux to hold our pie together after slicing, the cooked filling felt too heavy. By changing our tactic and baking the pie in a very low oven until it puffed, we cooked off some of the extra moisture, and our

filling assumed the light custardy texture and glossy sheen we were looking for with less roux. Plus, the low temperature meant the parbaked crust never got too dark.

- ⅓ cup refined coconut oil
- ⅓ cup (1⅔ ounces) all-purpose flour
- 1¼ cups maple syrup
- ¾ cup water
- ⅔ cup packed (4⅔ ounces) dark brown sugar
- ½ teaspoon table salt
- 2½ cups (10 ounces) pecans, toasted and chopped
- 4 teaspoons vanilla extract
- 1 recipe Vegan Single-Crust Pie Dough (page 384), fully baked and cooled

1. Adjust oven rack to middle position and heat oven to 275 degrees.

2. Heat oil in large saucepan over medium heat until shimmering. Whisk in flour and cook, whisking constantly, until combined and pale honey-colored, about 2 minutes. Whisking constantly, add maple syrup, water, sugar, and salt and cook until combined and sugar is dissolved, about 1 minute. Bring to boil, then reduce heat to medium-low and simmer, stirring occasionally, until rubber spatula leaves trail when dragged across bottom of saucepan, 3 to 5 minutes. Off heat, stir in pecans and vanilla.

3. Transfer pecan mixture to pie shell and spread evenly with rubber spatula. Bake until edges of filling are slightly puffed and few small bubbles appear around edges, 45 to 55 minutes. Let pie cool completely on wire rack until filling has set, about 4 hours, before serving.

Vegan Single-Crust Pie Dough

Makes one 9-inch pie crust

We typically favor all-butter pie dough in the test kitchen, finding dough with all shortening to be tender but greasy and lacking structure. And vegetable oil dough is an out-and-out failure. We'd hesitated to try coconut oil, because it hardens when chilled—too hard to roll. But when we substituted room-temperature coconut oil for chilled butter (and passed on chilling the dough itself), we achieved a flaky, nicely browned crust. However, it crumbled when sliced. So, for structure we turned to a test-kitchen-standard method: We mixed only half the flour with the coconut oil; we then pulsed in the remaining flour before folding in our water. This managed the hydration level for dough that was tender and rich yet also structured enough to support the filling. This dough will be more moist than most pie doughs.

1½ cups (7½ ounces) all-purpose flour, divided
1 tablespoon sugar
½ teaspoon table salt
½ cup plus 1 tablespoon refined coconut oil
¼ cup ice water, plus extra as needed

1. Process ¾ cup flour, sugar, and salt in food processor until combined, about 5 seconds. Pinch off ½-inch pieces of oil into flour mixture and pulse until sticky and dough begins to come together, 10 to 16 pulses. (If dough clumps around blade, redistribute around workbowl.) Add remaining ¾ cup flour and pulse until just incorporated, 3 to 6 pulses; transfer to large bowl.

2. Sprinkle ice water over top of dough, then, using rubber spatula, fold and press dough to fully incorporate water and bring dough together, being careful not to overmix. If dough doesn't come together, add up to 1 tablespoon ice water, 1 teaspoon at a time. Form dough into 4-inch disk. (Dough can be wrapped tightly in plastic wrap and refrigerated for up to 2 days or frozen for up to 1 month. Let dough sit at room temperature to soften completely before rolling out, about 2 hours if refrigerated or 4 hours if frozen.)

3. Roll dough between 2 large sheets parchment paper into 12-inch circle. Remove top parchment and gently flip into 9-inch pie plate; discard second sheet parchment. Ease dough into plate by gently lifting edge of dough with your hand while pressing into plate bottom with your other hand.

4. Trim overhang to ½ inch beyond lip of plate. Tuck overhang under itself so that folded edge is flush with edge of plate. Crimp dough evenly around edge of plate using your fingers. Wrap dough-lined plate loosely in plastic and refrigerate until dough is firm, about 45 minutes. (Dough-lined plate can be refrigerated for up to 24 hours.)

5. Adjust oven rack to lowest position and heat oven to 400 degrees. Set rimmed baking sheet in second rimmed baking sheet. Line chilled pie shell with double layer of aluminum foil, covering edges to prevent burning, and fill with pie weights. Bake on prepared sheet until pie dough looks dry and is pale in color, about 30 minutes, rotating plate halfway through baking. Remove foil and weights and continue to bake crust until light golden brown, 10 to 15 minutes, rotating plate halfway through baking. Let crust cool completely in plate on wire rack. (Cooled crust can be wrapped with plastic wrap and stored at room temperature for up to 24 hours.)

Blueberry Pie
Serves 8

Why This Recipe Works For a blueberry pie with a firm, glistening filling of still-plump berries bursting with bright flavor, we favored tapioca as a thickener, which allowed the fresh berry flavor to shine through. Too much of it, though, and we had a congealed mess. Cooking and reducing half of the berries helped us cut down on the tapioca, but not enough. Another inspiration came when we remembered that apples are high in pectin. Along with a modest 2 tablespoons of tapioca, a peeled and shredded Granny Smith apple thickened the filling to a soft, even consistency. To vent the steam from the berries, we used a biscuit cutter to cut out circles in the top crust. We thought a pie wouldn't be complete without the glistening, bronzed top that comes from an egg wash. But we successfully borrowed a technique sometimes used when baking rye breads: We painted a hot cornstarch slurry over the crust when we pulled it from the oven. Once dried, it gave the pie the gleaming, golden finish we wanted. Use the large holes of a box grater to shred the apple. Measure the tapioca, which may be sold as "minute tapioca," before grinding it. Grind the tapioca to a powder in a spice grinder or a mini food processor.

30 ounces (6 cups) blueberries, divided
1 recipe Vegan Double-Crust Pie Dough
1 Granny Smith apple, peeled, cored, and shredded
¾ cup (5¼ ounces) plus 1 tablespoon sugar, divided
2 tablespoons instant tapioca, ground
2 teaspoons grated lemon zest plus 2 teaspoons juice
    Pinch table salt
2 tablespoons refined coconut oil or unsalted butter
⅔ cup water
2 teaspoons cornstarch

1. Place 3 cups blueberries in medium saucepan. Cook over medium heat, stirring and mashing occasionally with potato masher, until half of blueberries are broken down and mixture measures 1½ cups, 7 to 10 minutes. Transfer to large bowl and let cool completely, about 20 minutes.

2. Meanwhile, adjust oven rack to lowest position and heat oven to 400 degrees. Line rimmed baking sheet with aluminum foil. Roll 1 disk of dough between 2 large sheets parchment paper into 12-inch circle. Remove parchment on top of dough round and gently flip into 9-inch pie plate; peel off second sheet parchment. Ease dough into plate by gently lifting edge of dough with your hand while pressing into plate bottom with your other hand. Roll other disk of dough between 2 large sheets parchment paper into 12-inch circle.

MAKING THE TOP CRUST OF BLUEBERRY PIE

Using 1¼-inch round cookie cutter, cut round from center of dough. Cut 6 more rounds from dough, 1½ inches from edge of center hole and equally spaced around center hole.

Vegan Double-Crust Pie Dough
Makes enough for 1 double-crust 9-inch pie

3 cups (15 ounces) all-purpose flour, divided
2 tablespoons sugar
1 teaspoon table salt
1 cup plus 2 tablespoons refined coconut oil
½ cup ice water, plus extra as needed

1. Process 1½ cups flour, sugar, and salt in food processor until combined, about 5 seconds. Pinch off ½-inch pieces of oil into flour mixture and pulse until sticky and dough just begins to clump, 12 to 15 pulses. Redistribute dough around workbowl, add remaining 1½ cups flour, and pulse until just incorporated, 3 to 6 pulses; transfer to large bowl.

2. Sprinkle ice water over top of dough, then, using rubber spatula, fold and press dough to fully incorporate water and bring dough together, being careful not to overmix. If dough doesn't come together, add up to 2 tablespoons ice water, 1 teaspoon at a time. Divide dough in half and form each half into 4-inch disk. (Dough can be wrapped tightly in plastic wrap and refrigerated for up to 2 days or frozen for up to 1 month. Let dough sit at room temperature to soften completely before rolling out, about 2 hours if refrigerated or 4 hours if frozen.)

3. Place shredded apple in center of dish towel. Gather ends together and twist tightly to drain as much liquid as possible. Transfer apple to bowl with cooked blueberry mixture and stir in remaining 3 cups uncooked blueberries, ¾ cup sugar, tapioca, lemon zest and juice, and salt until combined. Spread mixture into dough-lined pie plate. Pinch ½-inch pieces of coconut oil and disperse evenly over top of blueberries.

4. Using 1¼-inch round cookie cutter, cut out single round in center of 12-inch dough circle. Cut out 6 more rounds from dough, 1½ inches from edge of center hole and equally spaced around center hole. Loosely roll dough circle around rolling pin and gently unroll it onto filling.

5. Trim overhang to ½ inch beyond lip of plate. Pinch edges of top and bottom crusts firmly together. Tuck overhang under itself; folded edge should be flush with edge of plate. Crimp dough evenly around edge of plate using your fingers. Sprinkle surface evenly with remaining 1 tablespoon sugar.

6. Set pie on prepared baking sheet and bake until crust is light golden brown, about 25 minutes. Reduce oven temperature to 350 degrees, rotate sheet, and continue to bake until juices are bubbling and crust is golden brown, 40 to 50 minutes.

7. Whisk water and cornstarch together in small saucepan. Whisking constantly, bring to boil over high heat; remove pot from heat. Working quickly, brush surface of pie with cornstarch mixture, being careful to avoid pooling. Let pie cool completely on wire rack, about 4 hours, before serving.

Pumpkin Cashew Cheesecake
Serves 12 to 16

Why This Recipe Works In pursuing a plant-based cheesecake that would be as irresistibly creamy as any dairy rendition, we first focused on creating a thick, creamy base. So we looked to cashews: Soaked and pureed, the mild nuts made a velvety ricotta-like mixture. However, once unmolded from the pan, the cake slumped into a mound of pumpkin mousse. We tried fortifying the base with silken tofu, but it turned out rubbery. Blotting the pumpkin puree with paper towels before mixing it with the other ingredients helped eliminate some moisture, but the cake still lacked the dense, set-up structure of true cheesecake. So we tried some melted coconut oil. Because coconut oil becomes solid at or below room temperature, the cheesecake set up into a sliceable dessert after some refrigeration time. A small amount of cream cheese (plant-based or dairy) provided tanginess. Not all graham crackers are vegan, so check ingredient lists carefully. For the best results, chill the cheesecake for the full 24 hours. Don't let the cheesecake sit at room temperature for more than 1 hour; it will soften too much.

Filling
 4 cups (1¼ pounds) raw cashews
 1 (15-ounce) can unsweetened pumpkin puree
 ⅔ cup refined coconut oil, melted and hot
 2 tablespoons lemon juice

 1½ tablespoons vanilla extract
 1⅓ cups (10⅓ ounces) sugar
 1 teaspoon ground cinnamon
 ¾ teaspoon table salt
 ½ teaspoon ground ginger
 ¼ teaspoon ground nutmeg
 ¼ teaspoon allspice
 8 ounces plant-based cream cheese, softened

Crust
 8 whole graham crackers, broken into 1-inch pieces
 1 tablespoon sugar
 ⅓ cup refined coconut oil, melted

1. For the filling Place cashews in bowl and add water to cover by 1 inch. Soak at room temperature for at least 12 hours or up to 24 hours.

2. For the crust Adjust oven rack to lower-middle position and heat oven to 325 degrees. Spray bottom and sides of 9-inch springform pan with vegetable oil spray. Line pan bottom with parchment paper and grease parchment.

3. Process graham crackers and sugar in food processor to fine, even crumbs, about 30 seconds. Sprinkle melted oil over top and pulse to incorporate, about 5 pulses. Sprinkle crumbs into prepared pan and press into even layer with bottom of dry measuring cup. Bake until fragrant and edges begin to darken, about 13 minutes. Let cool completely on wire rack, about 1 hour.

4. While crust cools, line baking sheet with triple layer of paper towels. Spread pumpkin puree on paper towels into even layer. Cover pumpkin with second triple layer of paper towels and press firmly until paper towels are saturated. Discard top layer of towels, then transfer pumpkin puree to now-empty food processor bowl.

5. Rinse and drain soaked cashews well. Add cashews, hot melted oil, lemon juice, and vanilla to food processor and process until thoroughly combined and cashews are finely chopped, 2 to 3 minutes, scraping down sides of bowl as needed. Add sugar, cinnamon, salt, ginger, nutmeg, and allspice. Continue to process until thoroughly combined, about 1 minute. Add cream cheese and process until very smooth and creamy, about 3 minutes, scraping down sides of bowl as needed (mixture will be grainy like ricotta cheese).

6. Pour filling into cooled crust and, using offset spatula dipped in hot water and wiped dry, smooth top. Refrigerate for at least 6 hours or up to 24 hours.

7. To unmold cheesecake, run thin knife between cake and sides of pan, then remove sides of pan. Slide thin metal spatula between parchment and crust and carefully slide cheesecake onto plate. To slice, dip sharp knife in hot water and wipe dry between cuts. Serve immediately.

**Dark Chocolate
Avocado Pudding**

1 cup water
¾ cup (5¼ ounces) sugar
¼ cup (¾ ounce) unsweetened cocoa powder
1 tablespoon vanilla extract
1 teaspoon instant espresso powder (optional)
¼ teaspoon table salt
2 large ripe avocados (8 ounces each), halved and pitted
3½ ounces bittersweet chocolate, chopped

1. Combine water; sugar; cocoa; vanilla; espresso powder, if using; and salt in small saucepan. Bring to simmer over medium heat and cook, stirring occasionally, until sugar and cocoa dissolve, about 2 minutes. Remove saucepan from heat and cover to keep warm.

2. Scoop flesh of avocados into food processor bowl and process until smooth, about 2 minutes, scraping down sides of bowl as needed. With processor running, slowly add warm cocoa mixture in steady stream until completely incorporated and mixture is smooth and glossy, about 2 minutes.

3. Microwave chocolate in bowl at 50 percent power, stirring occasionally, until melted, 2 to 4 minutes. Add to avocado mixture and process until well incorporated, about 1 minute. Transfer pudding to bowl, cover, and refrigerate until chilled and set, at least 2 hours or up to 24 hours. Serve.

Dark Chocolate Avocado Pudding

Serves 6

Why This Recipe Works Making a luscious chocolate pudding by substituting avocados for the cream and eggs has become an established vegan trend. But more often than not, these puddings are a far cry from the silky-smooth, ultra-chocolaty pudding we crave, as they yield a grainy texture and lackluster chocolate flavor that doesn't conceal the vegetal notes. We knew we could do better without making the recipe too complicated. Rather than simply blending everything together, we started by creating a simple hot cocoa syrup in a saucepan (with a touch of espresso powder, vanilla, and salt to enhance the chocolate flavor). Meanwhile, we processed the flesh of two large avocados for a full 2 minutes, until it was absolutely smooth. Next, with the food processor running, we carefully streamed in the cocoa syrup until the mixture was velvety and glossy. We finished by blending in a moderate amount of melted dark chocolate to give our pudding additional richness and wonderfully full chocolate flavor.

Greek Lemon Rice Pudding

Serves 8

Why This Recipe Works Rice puddings are found in cuisines all over the world, from India to Mexico. We especially love Greek-style rice pudding, which uses short-grain rice and is distinguished by its custardy and velvety-smooth texture and a hit of bright lemon flavor. We were delighted to discover that swapping in plant-based milk for dairy milk did not detract from our pudding's texture or taste. For the most appealing rice flavor and satisfyingly rich consistency, we cooked starchy short-grain Arborio rice in water and then added milk (plant-based or dairy) to make the pudding. Bay leaves, a traditional addition to Greek rice pudding, offered a balanced floral note. Adding the lemon zest off the heat ensured that its citrus notes weren't dulled by cooking. We adjusted the texture of the pudding just before serving so that it would be nicely thick≈and creamy but not heavy and to accommodate for the differences in texture and thickness among the different types of plant-based milks.

2 cups water
  1 cup Arborio rice
  ½ teaspoon table salt
  1 vanilla bean
4½ cups plant-based milk or dairy whole milk, plus extra as needed
  ½ cup (3½ ounces) sugar
  ½ cinnamon stick
  2 bay leaves
  2 teaspoons grated lemon zest

1. Bring water to boil in large saucepan over medium-high heat. Stir in rice and salt. Reduce heat to low, cover, and simmer until water is almost fully absorbed, 15 to 20 minutes.

2. Cut vanilla bean in half lengthwise. Using tip of paring knife, scrape out seeds. Stir vanilla bean and seeds, milk, sugar, cinnamon stick, and bay leaves into rice. Increase heat to medium-high and bring to simmer. Cook, uncovered, stirring often, until rice is soft and pudding has thickened to consistency of yogurt, 35 to 45 minutes.

3. Off heat, discard bay leaves, cinnamon stick, and vanilla bean. Stir in lemon zest. Transfer pudding to large bowl and let cool, about 2 hours. Stir pudding to loosen and adjust consistency with extra milk as needed. Serve at room temperature or chilled. (Pudding can be refrigerated for up to 2 days.)

Semolina Pudding with Almonds and Dates

Semolina Pudding with Almonds and Dates

Serves 6 to 8

Why This Recipe Works Describing this as a porridge-type pudding makes it sound rather humble, but the saffron, cardamom, and dates flavoring this dessert make it anything but ordinary. Sweetened grain puddings are popular throughout the Middle East, flavored with a variety of aromatic ingredients including rose water, orange blossom water, and more. As with our rice pudding (page 387), swapping in plant-based milk for dairy milk worked perfectly. Traditional semolina flour, which is made from durum wheat, thickened the pudding nicely and gave it a pleasantly coarse texture; toasting the semolina added flavor depth. Almonds brought a nutty crunch, and dates offered a contrasting honeyed sweetness. Traditional recipes often call for chilling the pudding, but we preferred to serve it warm so the texture was creamy rather than firm. We adjusted the texture of the pudding just before serving so that it would be nicely thick but not heavy and to accommodate for the differences in texture and thickness among the different types of plant-based milks.

  1 tablespoon extra-virgin olive oil
  ¾ cup fine semolina flour
4½ cups plant-based milk or dairy whole milk, plus extra as needed
  ½ cup (3½ ounces) sugar
  ½ teaspoon ground cardamom
  ⅛ teaspoon saffron threads, crumbled
  ⅛ teaspoon table salt
  ½ cup slivered almonds, toasted and chopped
  3 ounces pitted dates, sliced thin (½ cup)

1. Heat oil in 12-inch skillet over medium heat until shimmering. Add semolina and cook, stirring occasionally, until fragrant, 3 to 5 minutes; transfer to bowl.

2. Bring milk, sugar, cardamom, saffron, and salt to simmer in large saucepan over medium heat. Whisking constantly, slowly add semolina, 1 tablespoon at a time, and cook until mixture thickens slightly and begins to bubble, about 3 minutes. Remove saucepan from heat, cover, and let pudding rest for 30 minutes.

3. Stir pudding to loosen and adjust consistency with extra warm milk as needed. Sprinkle individual portions with almonds and dates before serving warm.

Coconut Ice Cream

Serves 8 (Makes 1 quart)

Why This Recipe Works Developing a recipe for ice cream without milk, cream, or eggs seemed like a pretty tall order, but we were determined to make a thick, creamy plant-based frozen treat with the dense texture of the premium ice creams we love. Tasters enjoyed the clean coconut flavor and silky texture of canned coconut milk for the base. In addition to sugar, we added corn syrup, which minimized unpleasant ice crystal formation. Cornstarch also prevented ice crystal formation while acting as a stabilizer. But tasters noticed a persistent grainy, starchy texture—and it wasn't caused by the cornstarch. As it turned out, it came from unemulsified bits of coconut fat. To solve this, we blended our hot mixture after cooking so that the fat became fully emulsified. The lightly coconutty base was the perfect backdrop for flavor variations—we liked one version with lime and another with warm spices. We prefer to make this recipe in a canister-style ice cream maker; the ice cream was grainy when made in self-refrigerating models. Be sure to freeze the empty canister for at least 24 hours and preferably for 48 hours before churning. Make sure your blender is only two-thirds full or less, open the lid vent, and hold in place with a dish towel in step 2. Do not use light coconut milk in this recipe.

Coconut Ice Cream

- 2 (14-ounce) cans coconut milk, divided
- 2 tablespoons cornstarch
- ½ cup (3½ ounces) sugar
- ¼ cup light corn syrup
- 1 teaspoon vanilla extract
- ¼ teaspoon table salt

1. Shake unopened cans of coconut milk to form homogeneous mixture. Whisk ¼ cup coconut milk and cornstarch together in small bowl and set aside. Combine remaining coconut milk, sugar, corn syrup, vanilla, and salt in large saucepan. Cook over medium-high heat, whisking often to dissolve sugar and break up any clumps, until small bubbles form around edge of saucepan and mixture registers 190 degrees, 5 to 7 minutes. Reduce heat to medium. Whisk cornstarch mixture to recombine, then whisk into coconut milk mixture in pan. Cook, constantly scraping bottom of pan with rubber spatula, until thickened slightly, about 30 seconds.

2. Carefully transfer mixture to blender, let cool slightly, about 1 minute, then process on high speed for 1 minute. Pour ice cream base into large bowl and let cool until no longer steaming, about 20 minutes. Cover with plastic wrap and refrigerate for at least 6 hours or up to 24 hours. (Alternatively,

place bowl over ice bath of 6 cups ice, ½ cup water, and ⅓ cup table salt and chill base to 40 degrees, stirring occasionally, about 1½ hours.)

3. Whisk chilled ice cream base until recombined and smooth, then transfer to ice cream machine and churn until mixture has consistency of soft-serve ice cream and registers 22 to 23 degrees. Transfer to airtight container, cover, and freeze until firm, at least 6 hours. Serve. (Ice cream is best eaten within 2 weeks.)

VARIATION
Coconut-Horchata Ice Cream
Add ¾ teaspoon ground cinnamon and ⅛ teaspoon ground cloves to coconut milk mixture in saucepan before cooking in step 1. Serve topped with toasted sliced almonds.

Coconut-Lime Ice Cream
Substitute 1 tablespoon lime juice for vanilla extract. Add 2 teaspoons grated lime zest to coconut milk mixture with lime juice in step 1.

Banana Ice Cream

Serves 8 (**Makes** 1 quart)

Why This Recipe Works This supersimple, silky-smooth ice cream ditches the ice cream machine altogether, instead using only standard kitchen equipment. Bananas were a perfect choice for the base: Their high pectin content allowed them to remain creamy when frozen and their natural sweetness meant that we didn't even need to add any sugar. We started by simply freezing whole peeled bananas and then sliced them and processed them into a smooth puree. Letting the bananas come to room temperature for 15 minutes before slicing made them easier to cut through and kept the processing time to only 5 minutes. The end result had good banana flavor but wasn't as creamy as tasters wanted. We thought about adding plant-based creamers, but these are typically lower in fat than dairy heavy cream, and since there is no added sugar here, the fat component was important. So instead, we added canned coconut milk to reach the goal of our desired creamy consistency. (And likewise, if you make this with dairy, we recommend heavy cream.) Lemon juice and cinnamon gave the ice cream more dimension, while vanilla rounded out the other flavors. Be sure to use very ripe, heavily speckled (or even black) bananas in this recipe. You can skip the freezing in step 3 and serve the ice cream immediately, but the texture will be softer.

   6 very ripe bananas
   ½ cup canned coconut milk or dairy heavy cream
   1 tablespoon vanilla extract
   1 teaspoon lemon juice
   ¼ teaspoon table salt
   ¼ teaspoon ground cinnamon

1. Peel bananas, place in large zipper-lock bag, and press out excess air. Freeze bananas until solid, at least 8 hours.

2. Let bananas sit at room temperature to soften slightly, about 15 minutes. Slice into ½-inch-thick rounds and place in food processor. Add coconut milk, vanilla, lemon juice, salt, and cinnamon and process until smooth, about 5 minutes, scraping down sides of bowl as needed.

3. Transfer mixture to airtight container and freeze until firm, at least 2 hours or up to 5 days. Serve.

VARIATIONS
Banana–Peanut Butter Ice Cream
Reduce amount of coconut milk to ¼ cup. Add ¼ cup peanut butter to food processor with bananas in step 2.

Banana-Chocolate Ice Cream with Walnuts
Add ½ cup unsweetened cocoa powder to food processor with bananas in step 2. Before removing ice cream from processor, add 1 cup walnuts, toasted and chopped, and pulse to combine, about 5 pulses.

Raspberry Sorbet

Serves 8 (**Makes** 1 quart)

Why This Recipe Works Raspberry sorbet is mouth-wateringly fruity—but it's often too icy to be worth eating. For smooth, velvety scoops without the jagged ice crystals that often develop on homemade sorbets, we froze a small portion of the base separately, adding it back to the rest before churning. Because this small amount froze so rapidly, there wasn't enough time for large ice crystals to grow; mixing this superchilled mixture into the larger base encouraged the growth of similarly small crystals, for a fine-textured result. Using corn syrup in addition to sugar also contributed to the smooth texture. We added store-bought pectin to boost the berries' natural amount and give the sorbet stability in and out of the freezer. If using a canister-style ice cream machine, be sure to freeze the empty canister for at least 24 hours and preferably 48 hours before churning. For self-refrigerating machines, prechill the canister by running the machine for 5 to 10 minutes before pouring in the sorbet mixture. Let the sorbet sit at room temperature for 5 minutes to soften before serving. Fresh or frozen berries may be used. If using frozen berries, thaw them before proceeding. Don't use regular Sure-Jell here.

   1   cup water
   1   teaspoon Sure-Jell for Less or No Sugar Needed Recipes
   ⅛   teaspoon table salt
   1¼ pounds (4 cups) raspberries
   ½   cup plus 2 tablespoons (4⅓ ounces) sugar
   ¼   cup light corn syrup

1. Heat water, pectin, and salt in medium saucepan over medium-high heat, stirring occasionally, until pectin is fully dissolved, about 5 minutes. Remove saucepan from heat and let cool slightly, about 10 minutes.

2. Process raspberries, sugar, corn syrup, and cooled water mixture in food processor until smooth, about 30 seconds. Strain puree through fine-mesh strainer into bowl, pressing on solids to remove seeds and pulp (you should have about 3 cups

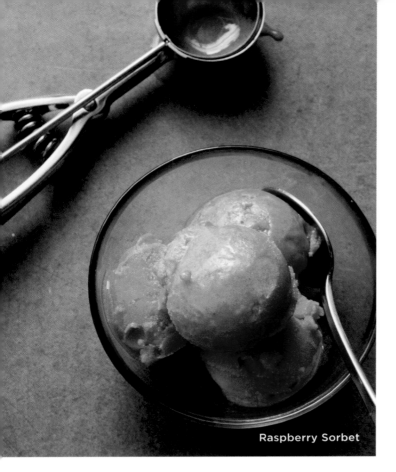
Raspberry Sorbet

Lemon Ice
Serves 8 (Makes 1 quart)

Why This Recipe Works Perfect lemon Italian ice is tart and sweet and never bitter and always supremely refreshing on a hot summer day. A cup of sugar gave our lemon ice the ideal amount of sweetness; less sugar left it with a pronounced bitterness, and more sugar made our ice taste too much like frozen lemonade. Using spring water might seem fussy, but we found that it really made a difference in this recipe, with a cleaner, less metallic flavor than tap water. We opted to add a bit of vodka to ensure a soft, slightly slushy texture (softer than our Raspberry Sorbet) and a pinch of salt to boost the flavor. To achieve a fluffy ice with a pleasingly coarse-grained texture and crystalline crunch, we froze the mixture in ice cube trays and then pulsed the cubes in the food processor right before serving. For even more refreshment, try the variation with mint. Or for a softer-edged Italian ice, try the orange version.

2¼ cups water, preferably spring water
1 cup lemon juice (6 lemons)
1 cup (7 ounces) sugar
2 tablespoons vodka (optional)
⅛ teaspoon table salt

1. Whisk all ingredients together in bowl until sugar has dissolved. Pour mixture into 2 ice cube trays and freeze until solid, at least 3 hours or up to 5 days.

2. Place medium bowl in freezer. Pulse half of ice cubes in food processor until creamy and no large lumps remain, about 18 pulses. Transfer mixture to chilled bowl and return to freezer. Pulse remaining ice cubes; transfer to bowl. Serve immediately.

puree); discard solids. Transfer 1 cup puree to small bowl and place remaining puree in large bowl; cover both bowls with plastic wrap. Place large bowl in refrigerator and small bowl in freezer and chill for at least 4 hours or up to 24 hours. (Small bowl will freeze solid.)

3. Remove puree from refrigerator and freezer. Using tines of fork, scrape frozen puree into large bowl with chilled puree. Stir occasionally until frozen puree has fully dissolved.

4. Transfer mixture to ice cream machine and churn until mixture resembles thick milkshake and lightens in color, 15 to 25 minutes. Transfer to airtight container and freeze until firm, at least 2 hours or up to 5 days. Serve.

VARIATION
Raspberry Sorbet with Ginger and Mint
Substitute ginger beer for water in step 1. Add 2-inch piece of peeled and thinly sliced ginger and ¼ cup mint leaves to food processor with raspberries. Decrease amount of sugar to ½ cup.

VARIATIONS
Minted Lemon Ice
Bring 1 cup water, sugar, and salt to simmer in small saucepan over medium-high heat, stirring occasionally. Off heat, stir in ½ cup torn fresh mint leaves and let steep for 5 minutes. Strain mixture through fine-mesh strainer into medium bowl. Stir in remaining 1¼ cups water, lemon juice, and vodka and let cool to room temperature, about 15 minutes. Freeze and pulse ice cubes as directed.

Orange Ice
Reduce lemon juice to 2 tablespoons and sugar to ¾ cup. Add ¾ cup orange juice (2 oranges) to mixture in step 1.

GLUTEN-FREE RECIPES IN THIS BOOK

CHAPTER 11: PLANT-POWERED DESSERTS

NUTRITIONAL INFORMATION FOR OUR RECIPES

To calculate the nutritional values of our recipes per serving, we used The Food Processor SQL by ESHA research. When using this program, we entered all the ingredients, using weights wherever possible. We also used our preferred brands in these analyses. Any ingredient listed as "optional" was excluded from the analyses. If there is a range in the serving size, we used the highest number of servings to calculate nutritional values.

Total sugars are natural sugars found in ingredients and are calculated in net carbs.
Net Carbs = Total Carbs - (Fiber + Sugar Alcohols)

	Cal	Total Fat (g)	Sat Fat (g)	Chol (mg)	Sodium (mg)	Total Carbs (g)	Fiber (g)	Total Sugars (g)	Protein (g)
INTRODUCTION									
Traditional Vegetable Broth (per cup)	70	1	0	0	360	15	4	6	4
Slow-Cooker Vegetable Broth (per cup)	45	1.5	0	0	130	8	2	3	2
Vegetable Broth Base (per tablespoon)	10	0	0	0	350	2	0	1	0
Umami Broth (per cup)	30	0.5	0	0	240	4	1	0	3
Fish Sauce Substitute (per teaspoon)	0	0	0	0	380	0	0	0	0
Anchovy Substitute (per teaspoon)	10	0	0	0	160	2	0	1	1
Vegan Pesto (per 2 tablespoons)	220	22	3	0	160	3	1	0	2
Crispy Tempeh (serves 4)	150	9	1	0	95	10	0	0	8
Almond Butter (per tablespoon)	100	9	0.5	0	35	4	2	1	4
Almond Milk (per cup)	260	23	2	0	80	8	4	2	9
Soy Milk (per cup)	100	4.5	0.5	0	75	7	2	2	8
Oat Milk (per cup)	80	2.5	0	0	80	13	2	0	2
Oat Milk with Ginger and Turmeric (per cup)	80	2.5	0	0	80	13	2	0	2
Rice Milk (per cup)	30	1	0	0	80	5	0	0	1
Brown Rice Milk (per cup)	25	1	0	0	80	4	0	0	0
Almond Milk Yogurt (per cup)	35	2.5	0	0	170	2	0	0	1
Cashew Ricotta (per 2 tablespoons)	110	10	1.5	0	75	4	1	1	3
Cheez Sauce (per ¼ cup)	70	3.5	0	0	300	9	1	1	2
Vegan Parmesan Substitute (per tablespoon)	50	3.5	0.5	0	115	3	0	0	2
Vegan Mayonnaise (per tablespoon)	180	20	3	0	75	0	0	0	0
BRUNCH									
Tofu Frittata with Mushrooms	160	10	1	0	370	7	1	2	10
Tofu Rancheros with Avocado	510	25	3	0	1610	61	7	17	17
Huevos Rancheros with Avocado	480	30	10	395	1720	32	3	16	24

BRUNCH (CONT.)	Cal	Total Fat (g)	Sat Fat (g)	Chol (mg)	Sodium (mg)	Total Carbs (g)	Fiber (g)	Total Sugars (g)	Protein (g)
Tofu Scramble with Bell Pepper, Shallot, and Basil	100	6	0	0	440	4	1	1	8
Tofu Scramble with Tomato and Scallions	100	6	0	0	440	4	1	1	8
Sweet Potato Red Flannel Hash with Tempeh	370	19	2	0	830	38	10	9	15
Brussels Sprouts Hash	280	15	5	0	800	34	8	7	6
Brussels Sprouts Hash with Poached Eggs	420	24	8	370	1090	35	8	7	19
Hash Brown Omelet with Kimchi	200	13	1	0	320	21	2	1	3
Classic Hash Browns	150	7	7	0	150	21	1	1	2
Avocado Toast	280	22	3.5	0	230	19	7	1	4
Avocado Toast with Fried Eggs	420	30	5	185	460	28	7	2	11
Black Beans on Toast with Tomato and Avocado	290	13	1.5	0	860	37	4	3	8
Sautéed Grape and Almond Butter Toast	450	25	6	0	390	50	5	24	12
Banana-Hazelnut Toast	480	25	4.5	0	340	60	5	26	8
Chocolate-Hazelnut Spread	200	16	1	0	25	15	2	10	4
Almond Granola with Dried Fruit	340	16	2	0	70	43	5	21	7
Quinoa Granola with Sunflower Seeds and Almonds	340	20	6	0	70	35	5	17	7
Three-Grain Breakfast Bowl	310	4	0.5	0	340	61	6	16	10
Carrot Spice Steel-Cut Oatmeal	300	5	0.5	0	490	58	6	24	7
Millet Porridge with Maple Syrup	250	3	0	0	105	48	4	10	7
Hot Quinoa Cereal with Blueberries and Almonds	210	8	0.5	0	65	27	4	6	8
Hot Quinoa Cereal with Raspberries and Sunflower Seeds	200	8	1	0	65	26	5	4	7
Hot Quinoa Cereal with Golden Raisins and Pistachios	240	7	1	0	70	37	4	16	8
Pepita, Almond, and Goji Berry Muesli	320	11	1.5	0	110	48	7	22	10
Sunflower Seed, Hazelnut, and Cherry Muesli	330	12	1	0	70	49	6	23	8
Chia Pudding with Fresh Fruit and Coconut	250	12	4	0	190	31	11	12	8
Blueberry Muffins	290	10	1	0	320	44	0	21	4
Cherry, Orange, and Rosemary Muffins	360	10	1.5	0	320	61	0	32	6
Currant Scones	270	11	8	0	330	40	1	11	4
Lemon-Glazed Ginger Scones	370	10	8	0	330	66	0	37	4
Spiced Sweet Potato Scones with Chocolate and Pepitas	320	15	10	0	340	43	3	10	6
Maple-Glazed Spiced Sweet Potato Scones	370	13	9	0	340	60	2	25	6
Savory Drop Biscuits	260	15	13	0	410	27	0	1	5
Classic Pancakes	300	9	8	0	650	47	0	11	6
100-Percent Whole-Wheat Pancakes	330	12	9	0	590	52	6	13	8
Carrot Cake Pancakes	510	24	8	0	680	64	2	23	10
Belgian Waffles	460	16	13	0	740	67	0	7	11
Crunchy Cinnamon French Toast	400	12	0.5	0	480	62	0	13	9
Banana Bread	360	17	2	0	210	50	2	22	6
Zucchini Bread	280	9	1.5	0	530	49	2	27	4
Coffee Cake	370	15	11	0	340	56	2	30	5

	Cal	Total Fat (g)	Sat Fat (g)	Chol (mg)	Sodium (mg)	Total Carbs (g)	Fiber (g)	Total Sugars (g)	Protein (g)
SOUPS, STEWS, AND CHILIS									
Creamy Curried Cauliflower Soup	180	14	5	0	640	13	4	5	4
Creamy White Bean Soup	310	22	11	0	500	22	5	2	7
Carrot-Ginger Soup	160	5	0	0	1020	29	5	16	2
Sweet Potato Soup	200	9	9	0	660	27	4	10	2
Creamy Kohlrabi Soup	190	16	10	0	570	12	6	5	4
Chickpea Noodle Soup	200	6	0	0	1000	29	5	4	7
Black Bean Soup	400	8	1	0	680	65	4	13	17
Classic Tuscan White Bean Soup	320	19	2.5	35	970	31	5	5	8
Classic Tuscan White Bean Soup with Egg	340	20	3	75	970	31	5	5	9
Butternut Squash and White Bean Soup with Parsley-Sage Pesto	460	34	11	0	700	34	8	5	10
Lentil and Escarole Soup	250	10	1.5	0	410	32	9	4	10
Red Lentil Soup with North African Spices	280	11	1.5	0	730	36	9	2	12
Mushroom Barley Soup	180	6	10	0	510	23	4	4	8
Turkish Tomato, Bulgur, and Red Pepper Soup	140	4	0.5	0	840	21	4	5	3
Tortilla Soup	190	6	0	0	1090	30	1	2	5
French Onion Soup	410	18	2.5	0	1100	50	7	21	12
French Onion Soup with Gruyère Croutons	550	29	9	40	1360	49	7	21	21
Vegetable Tagine with Chickpeas and Olives	500	20	2.5	0	1880	72	14	22	12
Rustic Leek and Potato Soup	1130	108	99	0	230	49	6	10	5
Eggplant and Kale Soup	290	26	3.5	0	340	13	5	6	4
Roasted Eggplant and Tomato Soup	230	15	2	0	920	21	5	12	3
Moroccan Lentil and Chickpea Soup	280	11	1.5	0	370	38	8	6	11
Spring Vegetable Soup	180	1.5	0	0	340	37	7	9	7
Tuscan Tomato and Bread Soup	230	10	1.5	0	950	28	3	8	5
Thai Coconut Soup with Tofu	170	12	8	0	510	8	0	4	8
Chickpea Curry	300	17	8	0	1470	30	7	7	8
Watercress and Shiitake Mushroom Soup with Tofu	110	4	0	0	480	8	1	2	10
Shiitake Ramen	310	5	0.5	0	1290	55	2	9	11
Ultimate Vegan Chili	450	13	1	0	1210	69	15	10	19
Weeknight Meaty Chili	240	10	3.5	0	960	26	7	8	13
Roasted Poblano and White Bean Chili	300	9	0.5	0	650	46	11	10	13
Butternut Squash Chili with Quinoa and Peanuts	620	40	16	0	1390	61	10	11	14
Black Bean Chili	430	9	0.5	0	510	69	6	19	20
Everyday Chili Powder	10	0	0	0	0	2	1	0	0
Italian Vegetable Stew	200	11	1.5	0	810	24	3	8	4
Caribbean-Style Swiss Chard and Butternut Squash Stew	310	20	11	0	570	35	7	8	6
Celeriac, Fennel, and Apple Chowder	180	6	4.5	0	710	27	4	7	3
Green Gumbo	240	15	1	0	860	22	6	3	6
Green Gumbo with Fresh Okra	240	15	1	0	880	22	6	3	6
Vegan Mapo Tofu	370	28	2	0	1510	17	2	4	13

SANDWICHES, BURGERS, PIZZA, AND MORE	Cal	Total Fat (g)	Sat Fat (g)	Chol (mg)	Sodium (mg)	Total Carbs (g)	Fiber (g)	Total Sugars (g)	Protein (g)
Philly-Style Broccoli Rabe, Portobello, and Cheez Sandwiches	480	26	3.5	0	1130	54	7	12	16
MLTs	420	15	2	0	690	59	7	13	12
Chickpea Salad Sandwiches	450	18	1.5	0	880	58	5	6	11
Curried Chickpea Salad Sandwiches	490	18	1.5	0	870	58	6	16	11
Cilantro-Mint Chutney	10	0	0	0	35	1	0	1	0
Cilantro Sauce	40	4	0.5	0	95	0	0	0	0
Tomato-Chile Sauce	60	5	0.5	0	400	4	1	1	1
Herbed Yogurt Sauce	70	5	1	0	0	2	0	2	2
Romesco Sauce	50	4.5	0.5	0	85	1	0	1	1
Avocado Crema	25	2	0	0	0	1	1	0	0
Summer Rolls with Tofu and Spicy Almond Butter Sauce	290	10	1.5	0	670	39	4	9	15
Korean Barbecue Tempeh Wraps	580	21	3	0	1730	79	1	40	21
Tofu Banh Mi	500	28	3.5	0	910	50	1	9	15
Falafel	500	30	4	0	1020	57	1	2	16
Quick Pickled Turnips and Carrots with Lemon and Coriander	20	0	0	0	95	4	1	2	0
Sizzling Saigon Crepes	280	11	3.5	0	1140	42	4	8	6
Mumbai Frankie Wraps	630	29	9	0	1340	83	9	7	16
Whole-Wheat Wraps (Chapati)	300	14	2	0	580	40	3	0	7
Baja-Style Cauliflower Tacos	460	28	17	0	750	50	4	6	8
Black Bean and Sweet Potato Tacos	400	12	1.5	0	770	68	6	22	8
Quick Sweet-and-Spicy Pickled Red Onions	20	0	0	0	55	5	0	5	0
Jackfruit Tinga Tacos	260	10	1	0	430	42	7	7	5
Plant-Based Beef Tacos	280	16	5	0	610	25	6	2	12
Double Smashie Burgers	590	38	9	0	1350	44	3	11	20
Classic Burger Sauce	110	10	1	0	170	4	0	3	0
Pub Burger Sauce	150	15	1.5	0	380	2	0	2	1
Barbecue Sauce	30	0	0	0	140	7	0	6	0
Caramelized Onion Jam	50	2.5	0	0	75	7	1	4	0
Quick Pickle Chips	5	0	0	0	0	1	0	0	0
Shoestring Onion Rings	40	2.5	0	0	95	4	0	0	1
Spiced Cauliflower Burgers	430	20	3	0	590	51	5	17	13
Grilled Portobello Burgers	530	42	6	0	430	32	2	7	7
Lentil and Mushroom Burgers	410	17	2.5	0	440	53	4	7	12
Curried Millet Cakes with Peach-Ginger Chutney	420	18	3.5	0	760	60	8	16	8
Black Bean Burgers	320	12	2	0	700	46	0	4	10
Chickpea Cakes	260	16	2	0	330	24	5	1	6
Pinto Bean–Beet Burgers	430	19	2.5	0	840	55	5	7	12
Thin-Crust Pizza with Broccoli and Sun-Dried Tomatoes	410	8	1	0	1010	70	4	7	13
Thin-Crust Pesto Pizza with Fennel and Cauliflower	580	27	3.5	0	920	69	5	7	14
Thin-Crust Pizza Dough	320	2.5	0	0	580	61	2	4	11

	Cal	Total Fat (g)	Sat Fat (g)	Chol (mg)	Sodium (mg)	Total Carbs (g)	Fiber (g)	Total Sugars (g)	Protein (g)
SANDWICHES, BURGERS, PIZZA, AND MORE (CONT.)									
Thin-Crust Pizza with Mushrooms and Cashew Ricotta	620	29	4.5	0	1210	73	4	8	16
Whole-Wheat Pizza Dough	280	6	1	0	680	49	5	2	9
Lavash with Romesco, Tomatoes, and Spinach	420	31	3.5	0	880	26	3	4	9
Lavash with Tahini Sauce, Cauliflower, and Fennel	350	22	3	0	530	33	6	7	10
Pide with Eggplant and Tomatoes	390	15	2	0	740	52	4	5	10
Mushroom Musakhan	890	43	6	0	1920	109	15	20	22
Red Pepper Coques	580	26	3.5	0	1390	72	3	12	11
Scallion Pancakes with Dipping Sauce	310	19	3	0	500	29	0	3	5
Savory Fennel-Apple Tarte Tatin	740	46	19	5	600	76	6	23	16
Tomato Tart with Cashew Ricotta	660	42	28	0	740	61	2	6	13
Socca with Swiss Chard, Pistachios, and Apricots	460	30	3.5	0	630	40	11	10	13
VEGETABLE SALADS									
Pomegranate Vinaigrette	70	3.5	0	0	150	10	0	8	0
Apple Cider–Sage Vinaigrette	60	3.5	0	0	150	8	0	7	0
Orange-Ginger Vinaigrette	60	3.5	0.5	0	150	7	0	5	1
Roasted Garlic Dressing	80	3.5	0.5	0	210	9	1	0	2
Balsamic-Mustard Vinaigrette	110	11	1.5	0	135	1	0	1	0
Walnut Vinaigrette	100	11	1	0	90	0	0	0	0
Tahini-Lemon VInaigrette	170	18	2.5	0	290	3	0	0	1
Creamless Creamy Dressing	50	4	0.5	0	180	3	0	1	2
Creamless Creamy Green Goddess Dressing	40	3	0.5	0	110	2	0	0	1
Creamless Creamy Roasted Red Pepper and Tahini Dressing	50	4	0.5	0	280	3	0	1	1
Creamless Creamy Ginger-Miso Dressing	60	4	0.5	0	180	4	0	1	2
Avocado-Grapefruit Salad	270	20	2.5	0	220	24	11	11	3
Raw Beet and Carrot Noodle Salad with Almond-Sesame Dressing	200	11	1.5	0	240	24	6	13	6
Roasted Beet and Carrot Salad with Cumin and Pistachios	190	11	1.5	0	400	20	6	11	4
Rainbow Salad with Crispy Tempeh	560	29	3.5	0	490	57	11	23	21
Broccoli Salad with Creamy Avocado Dressing	210	14	1.5	0	320	22	6	12	4
Brussels Sprout and Kale Slaw with Herbs and Peanuts	220	12	2	0	330	25	6	13	7
Tangy Apple-Cabbage Slaw	160	9	0.5	0	170	21	3	17	1
Warm Cabbage Salad with Crispy Tofu	480	31	2.5	0	630	35	4	8	16
Roasted Cauliflower Salad with Golden Raisins and Almonds	310	21	3	0	810	26	7	15	7
Roasted Cauliflower Salad with Apricots and Hazelnuts	350	23	3	0	810	34	8	21	7
Roasted Cauliflower Salad with Cranberries and Pistachios	360	22	3.5	0	810	38	7	25	7
Cucumber Salad with Chile, Mint, and Basil	80	5	0.5	0	510	7	2	4	3
Fattoush	230	17	2.5	0	260	17	2	3	3
Endive, Beet, and Pear Slaw	280	19	2.5	0	760	26	5	19	2
Bitter Greens, Carrot, and Chickpea Salad	400	21	4	10	630	45	9	25	10
Escarole and Orange Salad with Green Olive Vinaigrette	220	19	2	0	180	13	5	6	4
Roasted Fennel and Mushroom Salad with Radishes	170	11	1.5	0	540	15	4	9	4

	Cal	Total Fat (g)	Sat Fat (g)	Chol (mg)	Sodium (mg)	Total Carbs (g)	Fiber (g)	Total Sugars (g)	Protein (g)
VEGETABLE SALADS (CONT.)									
Crisp and Creamy Kale Salad	430	38	5	15	490	14	6	3	13
Kale Caesar Salad	300	23	2.5	0	560	20	3	3	6
Cheese Frico	100	8	5	25	340	0	0	0	7
Orange-Jicama Salad with Sweet and Spicy Peppers	230	14	2	0	240	26	8	12	2
Classic Croutons	40	2.5	0	0	50	3	0	0	1
Crispy Tortilla Strips	80	3	0	0	10	14	0	2	2
Crispy Shallots	90	9	0.5	0	0	2	0	1	0
Spiced Pepitas or Sunflower Seeds	60	5	1	0	75	1	1	0	2
Pistachio Dukkah	30	2.5	0	0	150	2	1	0	1
Umami Croutons	50	3	0	0	80	5	0	0	1
Quick Pickled Grapes	15	0	0	0	30	4	0	4	0
Pea Green Salad with Warm Apricot-Pistachio Vinaigrette	180	10	1	0	150	18	6	10	5
French Potato Salad with Dijon Mustard and Fines Herbes	210	10	1.5	0	310	27	4	3	3
French Potato Salad with Fennel, Tomato, and Olives	210	10	1.5	0	310	27	4	3	3
Hard-Cooked Eggs	70	5	1.5	185	70	0	0	0	6
Green Goodness Salad with Tofu	380	27	4	0	400	18	7	3	20
Spinach Salad with Carrots, Oranges, and Sesame	110	7	0.5	0	110	10	3	5	2
Spinach Salad with Frisée and Strawberries	100	8	1	0	100	6	2	3	1
Potato, Green Bean, and Tomato Salad	460	29	4	0	900	45	5	7	8
Roasted Butternut Squash Salad with Za'atar and Parsley	230	13	2	0	500	27	5	7	4
Peach and Tomato Salad	110	7	1	0	390	12	2	9	2
Peach, Tomato, and Mozzarella Caprese	270	21	9	40	420	12	2	9	12
Cherry Tomato Salad with Mango and Lime-Curry Vinaigrette	140	10	1	0	105	14	3	5	3
Panzanella	600	32	4	0	1070	66	3	9	12
Panzanella with Garlic and Capers	610	32	4	0	1170	66	3	9	12
Panzanella with Peppers and Arugula	610	32	4	0	1070	67	3	10	12
Grilled Vegetable Salad	180	14	2	0	530	12	4	7	2
Moroccan Tempeh Salad	680	40	5	0	690	62	7	27	21
Tofu Salad with Vegetables	220	12	1	0	460	14	3	6	15
Mediterranean Chopped Salad	370	28	7	25	1070	20	5	7	11
Chopped Winter Salad with Butternut Squash	400	28	5	15	460	35	7	13	8
THE PASTA AND NOODLE BOWL									
Penne with Roasted Cherry Tomato Sauce	390	11	1.5	0	400	64	2	7	11
Pasta alla Norma	440	12	1.5	0	640	72	3	10	13
Fiery Macaroni	730	34	4.5	0	670	91	0	2	15
Penne with Red Pepper Pesto	430	14	2	0	660	65	2	7	14
Gemelli with Pesto, Potatoes, and Green Beans	540	23	3	0	350	73	3	5	14
Whole-Wheat Spaghetti with Greens, Beans, and Tomatoes	440	12	1.5	0	970	65	5	5	17
Farfalle and Summer Squash with Tomatoes, Basil, and Pine Nuts	460	18	2	0	160	65	2	8	13
Campanelle with Roasted Cauliflower, Garlic, and Walnuts	580	27	3.5	0	870	72	4	6	17
Orecchiette with Broccoli Rabe and White Beans	610	26	3.5	0	820	76	5	4	23

	Cal	Total Fat (g)	Sat Fat (g)	Chol (mg)	Sodium (mg)	Total Carbs (g)	Fiber (g)	Total Sugars (g)	Protein (g)
THE PASTA AND NOODLE BOWL *(CONT.)*									
Spaghetti with Spring Vegetables	490	19	2.5	0	610	66	4	6	15
Pasta e Ceci	470	20	3	0	1200	58	8	5	17
Fideos with Chickpeas	400	11	1.5	0	720	60	3	6	11
Fettuccine with Walnut Sauce	610	34	3	0	710	64	3	3	18
Cashew e Pepe e Funghi	450	16	2.5	0	360	63	1	4	14
Creamy Cashew Mac and Cheese	600	29	14	0	1040	69	2	4	19
Fettuccine Alfredo	510	23	13	0	810	66	2	5	15
Mushroom Bolognese	460	9	1	0	820	73	1	11	15
Spaghetti and Meatless Meatballs	620	11	1.5	0	1670	98	5	16	29
Big-Batch Meatless Meat Sauce with Chickpeas and Mushrooms	180	11	1.5	0	690	16	2	6	4
Hearty Vegetable Lasagna	410	26	4	0	620	37	3	10	11
Baked Ziti with Creamy Leeks, Kale, and Sun-Dried Tomatoes	560	16	2	0	930	89	4	8	15
Pasta Salad with Asparagus and Red Peppers	440	22	3	0	630	50	3	5	12
Orzo Salad with Arugula and Sun-Dried Tomatoes	640	35	4.5	0	900	68	2	7	18
Toasted Orzo Pilaf with Fennel, Orange, and Olives	360	9	1	0	460	56	2	5	11
Spiced Vegetable Couscous	350	15	2	0	760	45	6	5	9
Ras el Hanout	20	0.5	0	0	0	4	2	0	1
Moroccan-Style Couscous with Chickpeas	340	10	1.5	0	730	50	6	4	10
Hearty Pearl Couscous with Eggplant, Spinach, and White Beans	370	12	1.5	0	650	55	5	5	11
Spicy Peanut Rice Noodle Bowl	490	25	3	0	530	58	2	6	12
Tofu Pad Thai	680	28	3	95	470	94	2	16	17
Spicy Basil Rice Noodles with Crispy Tofu, Snap Peas, and Bell Peppers	530	20	1.5	0	1190	75	2	13	12
Thai Curry Rice Noodles with Crispy Tofu and Broccoli	510	22	7	0	1050	65	2	4	15
Sweet Potato Noodles with Shiitakes and Spinach	220	11	1	0	670	27	3	12	4
Sweet Potato Noodles with Shiitakes, Spinach, and Eggs	250	14	2	60	690	27	3	12	6
Vegetable Lo Mein	480	11	1.5	0	720	83	4	11	15
Mee Goreng	500	15	1.5	5	1180	75	2	27	18
Sesame Noodles with Sweet Peppers and Cucumbers	390	14	2	10	1220	56	3	9	14
Udon Noodles with Mustard Greens and Shiitake-Ginger Sauce	360	6	0	0	880	60	3	6	17
Soba Noodles with Roasted Eggplant and Sesame	710	27	3.5	0	1810	108	9	33	15
Chilled Soba Noodles with Cucumbers, Snow Peas, and Radishes	220	6	0.5	220	6	0.5	0	540	36
VEGETABLE DISHES BIG AND SMALL									
Roasted Artichokes with Lemon and Basil	170	11	1.5	0	390	13	9	1	3
Roasted Artichokes with Fennel, Mustard, and Tarragon	190	12	1.5	0	500	17	10	3	4
Roasted Artichokes with Olives, Bell Pepper, and Lemon	190	13	1.5	0	450	15	9	2	4
Stir-Fried Asparagus with Shiitake Mushrooms	80	4.5	0	0	140	8	2	5	3
Roasted Asparagus with Mint-Orange Gremolata	80	6	1	0	190	5	3	2	3
Roasted Asparagus with Cilantro-Lime Gremolata	80	6	1	0	190	5	3	2	3
Roasted Asparagus with Tarragon-Lemon Gremolata	80	6	1	0	190	5	3	2	3

	Cal	Total Fat (g)	Sat Fat (g)	Chol (mg)	Sodium (mg)	Total Carbs (g)	Fiber (g)	Total Sugars (g)	Protein (g)
VEGETABLE DISHES BIG AND SMALL (CONT.)									
Braised Asparagus, Peas, and Radishes with Tarragon	140	9	1.5	0	390	10	4	4	4
Braised Beets with Lemon and Almonds	120	6	0	0	350	14	4	9	4
Braised Beets with Lime and Pepitas	110	5	1	0	350	12	3	8	5
Braised Beets with Orange and Walnuts	100	6	0.5	0	350	12	3	8	3
Steamed Broccoli with Lime-Cumin Dressing	140	11	1.5	0	40	8	3	2	3
Roasted Broccoli with Garlic	90	7	1	0	220	6	2	2	2
Roasted Broccoli with Shallots and Fennel Seeds	120	10	1.5	0	220	8	3	3	3
Broccoli Rabe and Spicy Tomato Sauce	120	6	1	0	480	14	5	6	7
Broiled Broccoli Rabe	120	11	1.5	0	240	3	2	0	3
Skillet-Roasted Brussels Sprouts with Pomegranate and Pistachios	270	22	3	0	170	16	5	6	5
Skillet-Roasted Brussels Sprouts with Mustard and Brown Sugar	220	18	2.5	0	260	13	4	6	3
Skillet-Roasted Brussels Sprouts with Gochujang and Sesame Seeds	220	19	2.5	0	260	12	4	3	4
Stir-Fried Bok Choy with Soy Sauce and Ginger	60	5	0	0	370	3	1	2	2
Curry Roasted Cabbage Wedges with Tomatoes and Chickpeas	490	29	2.5	0	1230	45	16	10	14
Roasted Carrots and Shallots with Chermoula	310	24	9	0	690	23	6	11	3
Pan-Roasted Cauliflower with Capers and Pine Nuts	160	14	2	0	690	9	3	3	4
Pan-Roasted Cauliflower with Cumin and Pistachios	160	12	2	0	340	10	4	3	4
Grilled Cauliflower	80	5	1	0	95	8	3	3	3
Cauliflower Rice	90	4	1	0	510	13	5	5	5
Curried Cauliflower Rice	130	7	1	0	510	14	6	5	6
Buddha Bowl with Cauliflower, Sweet Potatoes, and Avocados	500	30	4.5	0	880	54	18	11	12
Whipped Cauliflower	150	11	10	0	360	11	5	4	4
Whipped Cauliflower with Fennel, Garlic, and Lemon	150	11	10	0	360	12	5	4	5
Cauliflower Steaks with Salsa Verde	320	29	4.5	0	500	14	6	5	5
Thai Red Curry with Cauliflower	260	17	9	0	1000	23	7	11	9
Thai Red Curry with Bell Peppers and Tofu	310	20	9	0	840	21	1	7	12
Whole Pot-Roasted Cauliflower with Tomatoes and Olives	240	11	1.5	0	1150	30	6	16	9
Quick Collard Greens	100	8	1	0	115	6	4	1	3
Sesame-Hoisin Braised Escarole	180	13	1.5	0	410	12	7	3	4
Grilled Eggplant with Cherry Tomatoes and Cilantro Vinaigrette	230	21	3	0	100	9	4	5	2
Walkaway Ratatouille	210	12	1.5	0	530	24	7	12	4
Stir-Fried Japanese Eggplant	140	7	0.5	0	290	13	3	6	3
Fennel Confit	280	28	4	0	120	7	3	4	1
Horta	110	8	1	0	160	10	4	1	3
Mediterranean Braised Green Beans	170	12	1.5	0	680	13	4	6	3
Roasted Green Beans	70	3.5	0.5	0	300	8	3	4	2

	Cal	Total Fat (g)	Sat Fat (g)	Chol (mg)	Sodium (mg)	Total Carbs (g)	Fiber (g)	Total Sugars (g)	Protein (g)
Braised Leeks	190	14	2	0	170	14	2	4	2
Grilled Onions with Balsamic Vinaigrette	360	28	4	0	880	25	4	13	3
Sautéed Mushrooms with Shallots and Thyme	130	7	3.5	0	105	9	0	7	3
Stir-Fried Portobellos with Soy-Maple Sauce	290	14	1.5	0	740	33	4	23	8
Mushroom Bourguignon	300	15	2	0	290	21	4	10	7
Madras Okra Curry	250	22	8	0	125	13	4	4	3
Roasted Okra with Fennel and Oregano	100	7	1	0	105	8	4	1	2
Roasted Okra with Sesame and Cumin	110	9	1	0	105	8	3	1	2
Greek Stewed Okra with Tomatoes	200	14	2	0	600	16	5	6	3
Sautéed Parsnips with Ginger, Maple, and Fennel Seeds	210	9	0.5	0	480	32	7	11	3
Simple Pureed Parsnips	150	4.5	2.5	10	15	26	7	7	2
Sautéed Snow Peas with Lemon and Parsley	70	3.5	0	0	150	7	0	4	2
Sautéed Snow Peas with Garlic, Cumin, and Cilantro	70	3.5	0	0	150	8	0	4	3
Sautéed Snow Peas with Lemongrass and Basil	70	3.5	0	0	150	7	0	4	2
Mechouia	170	12	1.5	0	210	14	5	7	3
Grilled Peppers with Sherry Vinegar, Green Olives, and Capers	70	6	0.5	0	115	5	2	3	1
Grilled Potatoes with Garlic and Rosemary	200	10	1.5	0	320	26	3	2	3
Roasted Smashed Potatoes	350	21	0	0	330	36	4	3	4
Potato Galette	170	5	5	0	300	26	0	0	3
Plant-Based Shepherd's Pie	340	12	1.5	0	520	42	6	5	16
Spinach with Garlic and Lemon	130	11	1.5	0	110	5	3	0	3
Grilled Radicchio	130	14	2	0	0	0	0	0	0
Saag Tofu	250	16	2	0	590	17	4	4	12
Overstuffed Sweet Potatoes with Tofu and Thai Curry	560	34	2.5	0	790	51	7	13	15
Vindaloo-Style Sweet Potatoes	210	5	0	0	980	38	5	10	5
Sweet Potato Curry with Eggplant, Chickpeas, and Herb Chutney	280	13	4.5	0	560	37	10	12	7
Potato Curry with Cauliflower, Chickpeas, and Herb Chutney	290	13	4.5	0	550	37	8	8	9
Vegetable Pot Pie	480	31	28	0	720	48	3	8	7
Green Shakshuka	230	15	2	0	990	20	8	5	8
Green Shakshuka with Eggs	380	24	5	370	1200	21	8	6	21
Garlicky Swiss Chard	90	7	1	0	390	6	2	2	3
Gingery Swiss Chard	130	10	1.5	0	600	8	3	2	5
Roasted Delicata Squash	160	13	6	0	220	11	2	2	1
Chile-Rubbed Butternut Squash Steaks with Vegan Ranch Dressing	480	35	4.5	0	1130	44	8	10	4
Roasted Butternut Squash with Radicchio	210	15	7	0	230	19	3	4	2
Spaghetti Squash with Garlic	120	8	1	0	200	11	2	4	2
Mexican-Style Spaghetti Squash Casserole	360	21	3	0	780	40	11	9	8
Grilled Tomatoes	50	2.5	0	0	200	6	2	4	1
Roasted Tomatoes	320	29	4	0	85	14	4	9	3

	Cal	Total Fat (g)	Sat Fat (g)	Chol (mg)	Sodium (mg)	Total Carbs (g)	Fiber (g)	Total Sugars (g)	Protein (g)
VEGETABLE DISHES BIG AND SMALL (CONT.)									
Sautéed Summer Squash	170	15	2	0	310	9	2	5	3
Sautéed Summer Squash with Mint and Pistachios	190	17	2.5	0	310	9	3	6	4
Summer Vegetable Gratin	430	29	4.5	0	760	35	6	14	10
Braised Zucchini	80	7	1	0	300	4	1	3	1
Greek Stewed Zucchini	100	6	1	0	420	10	2	6	3
Grilled Zucchini with Red Pepper Sauce	190	17	2.5	0	500	7	2	4	3
GREAT GRAINS									
Basmati Rice Pilaf	180	3	0	0	100	34	0	0	3
Basmati Rice Pilaf with Peas, Scallion, and Lemon	190	3	0	0	100	37	1	1	4
Basmati Rice Pilaf with Currants and Toasted Almonds	220	5	0	0	100	40	1	5	4
Hands-Off Baked White Rice	240	3.5	0	0	300	48	0	0	5
Hands-Off Baked Coconut Rice	330	13	9	0	330	49	0	0	6
Hands-Off Baked Curried Rice	280	3.5	0	0	300	56	0	7	6
Coconut Rice with Bok Choy and Lime	240	8	5	0	810	39	1	1	5
Jeweled Rice	310	10	1	0	600	51	3	13	6
Spiced Basmati Rice with Cauliflower and Pomegranate	180	6	1	0	200	28	3	3	4
Spiced Baked Rice with Roasted Sweet Potatoes and Fennel	360	16	2	0	650	48	4	6	4
Rice Salad with Oranges, Olives, and Almonds	270	9	1	0	540	44	2	5	6
Rice Salad with Pineapple, Jícama, and Pepitas	260	8	1	0	440	43	2	4	6
Dolsot Bibimbap with Tempeh	590	21	2	0	2050	87	8	15	20
Vegan Nasi Goreng	460	14	1	0	1560	72	3	18	9
Nasi Goreng with Eggs	520	19	2	125	1700	74	4	19	13
Faux Leftover Rice	870	75	5	0	0	47	0	0	4
Vegetable Fried Rice with Broccoli and Shiitake Mushrooms	390	15	1	0	650	56	2	5	6
Vegetable Fried Rice with Broccoli, Shiitake Mushrooms, and Eggs	430	19	2	60	670	56	2	5	8
Cauliflower Biryani	340	14	2	0	430	48	4	9	8
Soy Dipping Sauce	10	0	0	0	330	1	0	1	1
Za'atar Yogurt Sauce	15	1.5	0	0	0	1	0	1	1
Chile Sauce	50	3.5	0	0	180	6	0	3	0
Creamy Chipotle Sauce	60	6	1	0	70	1	0	0	0
Citrus Sauce	15	0	0	0	440	2	0	2	0
Tahini Sauce	35	3	0	0	0	2	0	0	1
Tahini-Yogurt Sauce	70	6	1	0	220	3	0	0	2
Classic Mexican Rice	260	9	0.5	0	690	40	1	2	5
Almost Hands-Free Mushroom Risotto	400	11	1.5	0	1130	62	3	6	11
Almost Hands-Free Fennel Risotto	390	11	1.5	0	1160	63	4	7	9
Baked Brown Rice with Roasted Red Peppers and Onions	220	4.5	0.5	0	610	41	2	3	4
Baked Brown Rice with Black Beans and Cilantro	250	5	0.5	0	700	48	2	2	7
Baked Brown Rice with Peas, Mint, and Feta	260	7	2.5	10	630	41	3	3	7
Brown Rice Burrito Bowl	450	23	3.5	0	630	54	6	4	8

	Cal	Total Fat (g)	Sat Fat (g)	Chol (mg)	Sodium (mg)	Total Carbs (g)	Fiber (g)	Total Sugars (g)	Protein (g)
GREAT GRAINS *(CONT.)*									
Brown Sushi Rice Bowl with Tofu and Vegetables	620	16	1	0	910	94	3	10	19
Brown Rice Salad with Asparagus and Lemon	290	12	1.5	0	390	41	4	3	7
Brown Rice Salad with Jalapeño, Tomatoes, and Avocado	290	12	1.5	0	390	41	4	3	7
Brown Rice Salad with Fennel, Mushrooms, and Walnuts	280	13	1.5	0	300	44	6	4	4
Brown Rice Onigiri with Spinach, Edamame, and Sesame	370	20	2.5	0	610	44	4	4	8
Vegetable Paella	200	7	0.5	0	820	29	3	2	8
Vegetable Paella in a Paella Pan	450	16	2	0	1330	66	4	6	11
Wild Rice Pilaf with Pecans and Cranberries	460	16	2	0	1360	67	4	6	11
Wild Rice Pilaf with Scallions, Cilantro, and Almonds	370	11	1	0	470	64	4	13	8
Red Rice and Quinoa Salad	310	8	1	0	470	53	3	2	9
Black Rice Salad with Snap Peas and Ginger-Sesame Vinaigrette	350	11	1.5	0	100	59	5	24	6
Herbed Barley Pilaf	270	13	1.5	0	250	37	4	2	5
Barley Bowl with Roasted Carrots and Snow Peas	250	8	1	0	200	41	8	1	5
Barley with Lentils, Mushrooms, and Tahini-Yogurt Sauce	440	22	3	0	240	53	12	5	11
Bulgur Salad with Carrots and Almonds	430	15	2	0	670	63	15	3	16
Bulgur with Chickpeas, Spinach, and Za'atar	300	17	2	0	330	35	7	3	7
Tabbouleh	300	12	1.5	0	620	42	8	3	8
Garlicky Tofu Tabbouleh	190	14	2	0	210	14	3	2	3
Warm Farro with Lemon and Herbs	210	13	2	0	410	16	3	2	10
Warm Farro with Mushrooms and Thyme	240	9	1	0	200	39	1	3	6
Farro Salad with Asparagus, Snap Peas, and Tomatoes	250	9	1	0	200	39	0	4	7
Farro Salad with Cucumber, Yogurt, and Mint	260	9	1	0	310	41	2	5	8
Farro Risotto with Fennel and Radicchio	260	9	1.5	0	200	40	1	4	7
Farro and Broccoli Rabe Gratin	190	2.5	0	0	400	36	5	3	7
Freekeh Pilaf with Dates and Cauliflower	400	13	1.5	0	880	61	5	5	15
Freekeh Salad with Butternut Squash, Walnuts, and Raisins	350	13	2	0	280	52	11	13	10
Creamy Polenta	410	20	2.5	0	400	53	10	9	9
Sautéed Mushrooms with Red Wine–Miso Reduction	120	8	7	0	410	14	2	0	2
Easy Baked Quinoa with Curry, Cauliflower, and Cilantro	240	8	1	0	670	17	0	10	4
Easy Baked Quinoa with Lemon, Garlic, and Parsley	320	11	1.5	0	450	46	6	3	10
Quinoa Salad with Red Bell Pepper and Cilantro	310	11	1.5	0	430	43	5	2	9
Quinoa Taco Salad	200	6	1	0	230	29	3	2	6
Baked Quinoa with Roasted Kale and Chickpeas	480	25	3.5	0	780	56	12	7	13
Warm Wheat Berries with Zucchini, Red Pepper, and Oregano	230	5	0.5	0	250	39	7	3	7
Wheat Berry Salad with Figs and Pine Nuts	300	12	1.5	0	170	44	8	8	7
Wheat Berry Salad with Blueberries and Endive	400	24	2.5	0	260	43	9	4	8
BOUNTIFUL BEANS									
Southwestern Black Bean Salad	320	21	2.5	0	550	33	6	5	9
Black Bean Chilaquiles Verdes	570	24	3	0	920	86	8	15	16
Cuban-Style Black Beans and Rice	270	4	0.5	0	740	50	2	6	9

	Cal	Total Fat (g)	Sat Fat (g)	Chol (mg)	Sodium (mg)	Total Carbs (g)	Fiber (g)	Total Sugars (g)	Protein (g)
BOUNTIFUL BEANS (CONT.)									
Black-Eyed Pea Salad with Peaches and Pecans	170	9	1	0	300	20	5	5	6
Black-Eyed Peas and Greens	120	4	0.5	0	800	16	5	2	5
Cannellini Beans with Roasted Red Peppers and Kale	220	10	1.5	0	480	24	7	5	8
Chickpea Salad with Carrots, Arugula, and Olives	190	12	1.5	0	620	17	5	2	5
Chickpea Salad with Fennel and Arugula	190	11	1.5	0	580	18	6	2	6
Chickpea Salad with Carrots, Raisins, and Mint	180	7	1	0	280	25	5	10	5
Chickpeas with Garlic and Parsley	180	11	1.5	0	490	16	5	1	5
Chickpeas with Bell Pepper, Scallions, and Basil	180	11	1.5	0	490	16	5	1	5
Chickpeas with Smoked Paprika and Cilantro	180	11	1.5	0	490	16	5	1	5
Spicy Braised Chickpeas and Turnips with Couscous	370	9	1.5	0	700	59	9	7	12
Cranberry Beans with Fennel, Grapes, and Pine Nuts	370	12	1.5	0	160	53	15	17	15
Cranberry Beans with Tequila, Green Chiles, and Pepitas	370	14	3	0	540	42	15	3	17
Quick Pickled Shallots and Radishes	5	0	0	0	40	1	0	1	0
Lentil Salad with Olives and Mint	230	13	1.5	0	290	23	6	1	8
Lentil Salad with Spinach and Walnuts	290	19	2.5	0	290	23	6	2	9
French Lentils with Carrots and Parsley	180	6	0.5	0	30	25	6	3	8
Curried French Lentils with Golden Raisins	210	5	0.5	0	220	33	7	12	8
Lentils with Roasted Broccoli and Lemony Bread Crumbs	420	16	2	0	340	55	12	11	16
Koshari	450	8	1	0	1080	81	12	10	17
Crispy Onions	25	1	0	0	25	3	1	1	0
Mujaddara	410	10	1.5	0	400	69	9	9	15
Red Lentil Kibbeh	300	12	2	0	510	40	8	3	10
Harissa	110	11	1.5	0	150	2	1	0	1
Masoor Dal	220	8	7	0	310	30	8	4	10
Masoor Dal with Cauliflower and Cilantro	290	13	7	0	440	34	10	5	12
Misir Wot	290	12	1.5	0	660	37	10	5	12
Thai Red Curry with Lentils and Tofu	260	11	4.5	0	550	27	6	3	16
Baked Navy Beans	260	2.5	0	0	970	47	9	14	13
Pinto Bean and Swiss Chard Enchiladas	480	26	3.5	0	1240	57	10	11	11
Pinto Bean, Swiss Chard, and Monterey Jack Enchiladas	490	28	4.5	5	1280	57	10	11	12
Refried Pinto Beans	140	3.5	0	0	460	23	6	2	7
Red Beans and Rice with Okra and Tomatoes	440	3.5	0.5	0	980	82	12	5	18
Tuscan White Bean and Fresh Corn Salad	170	7	0.5	0	610	24	5	6	7
Sicilian White Beans and Escarole	140	4	0.5	0	700	22	8	4	7
White Beans with Broccoli Rabe	220	15	2	0	560	15	6	2	8
White Bean and Mushroom Gratin	430	21	3	0	820	48	6	8	11
Stir-Fried Tempeh with Orange Sauce	300	12	2	0	980	31	3	7	16
Crispy Tempeh with Sambal Sauce	580	11	1.5	0	520	79	1	7	28
Pan-Seared Tempeh Steaks with Chimichurri Sauce	440	32	4.5	0	340	23	1	0	16
Indian Curried Tempeh with Cauliflower and Peas	230	13	3.5	0	560	22	5	6	9
Sweet Chili Glazed Tofu	310	14	1.5	0	270	32	0	11	10
Grilled Soy-Ginger Glazed Tofu	230	11	1.5	0	1040	19	0	15	14

	Cal	Total Fat (g)	Sat Fat (g)	Chol (mg)	Sodium (mg)	Total Carbs (g)	Fiber (g)	Total Sugars (g)	Protein (g)
BOUNTIFUL BEANS *(CONT.)*									
Caramel Tofu	510	32	4.5	0	1020	41	2	19	17
Chilled Marinated Tofu	100	3	0	0	800	9	1	6	7
Shichimi Togarashi	10	0.5	0	0	0	1	0	0	0
Thai-Style Tofu and Basil Lettuce Cups	270	17	2.5	0	760	15	3	7	16
Stir-Fried Tofu, Shiitakes, and Green Beans	320	17	2.5	0	850	30	4	8	15
Thai Red Curry with Sweet Potatoes and Tofu	330	18	10	0	630	31	4	12	11
ELECTRIC PRESSURE-COOKER AND SLOW-COOKER DISHES									
Creamy Carrot Soup with Warm Spices	170	10	1.5	0	830	21	5	9	3
Fire-Roasted Tomato and Fennel Soup	170	6	1	0	1010	26	7	14	4
Creamy Cauliflower and Potato Soup	180	7	4.5	0	990	24	2	2	4
Wild Rice Soup with Coconut and Lime	480	33	25	0	1100	41	3	5	9
Farro and Butternut Squash Stew	250	4	0	0	1010	46	3	8	8
Wheat Berry and Wild Mushroom Stew	320	8	1	0	980	48	7	5	10
Moroccan Lentil Soup with Mustard Greens	210	2.5	0.5	0	1130	41	8	14	9
Vegetable and Chickpea Stew	200	8	1	0	860	27	4	6	5
Black Bean Chili	420	8	0.5	0	540	66	5	17	20
Black Bean Chili with Fried Eggs and Queso	500	15	2.5	185	680	67	5	17	26
Thai Eggplant Green Curry	260	15	13	0	1110	305	13	13	6
Root Vegetable Tagine with Dried Cherries	260	6	1	0	800	48	9	18	5
Navy Bean and Bulgur Chili	300	5	0	0	870	51	12	5	16
Braised Spring Vegetables	90	2.5	0	0	350	14	6	4	5
Green Beans with Potatoes and Basil	270	10	1.5	0	880	39	6	10	8
Beet and Watercress Salad with Orange and Dill	180	10	2.5	0	470	21	5	12	5
Braised Red Cabbage with Fennel and Orange	120	2	0	0	270	25	5	16	3
Glazed Carrots	150	4	3.5	0	190	29	4	21	1
Glazed Root Vegetables	110	2	1.5	0	200	22	4	10	2
Braised Whole Cauliflower with Tomatoes, Olives, and Ras el Hanout	300	15	2	0	690	36	8	19	10
Turkish Eggplant Casserole	250	13	2.5	0	780	32	7	6	5
Braised Fennel with Radicchio and Pear	210	17	2.5	0	340	13	4	7	3
Mustard Greens and Sweet Potato Tacos	380	10	1	0	590	67	10	10	10
Spicy Pickled Radishes	20	0	0	0	170	5	1	3	0
Olive Oil Mashed Potatoes	170	7	1	0	400	25	2	1	3
Herbed Fingerling Potatoes with Lemon	160	3	0	0	400	28	0	0	4
Indian-Spiced Mashed Butternut Squash	160	6	2.5	0	310	25	3	9	2
Garam Masala	0	0	0	0	0	0	0	0	0
Mashed Butternut Squash with Sage and Toasted Hazelnuts	250	12	7	0	690	37	5	15	4
Maple-Orange Glazed Acorn Squash	170	4.5	0	0	150	33	3	18	3
Spaghetti Squash with Fresh Tomato Sauce	240	13	2	0	390	32	7	15	4
Braised Sweet Potatoes with Cilantro-Lime Dressing	190	3.5	0.5	0	420	38	6	14	3
Garlicky Swiss Chard	120	10	1.5	0	460	6	2	2	3
All-Purpose Fresh Tomato Sauce	90	5	0.5	0	300	11	3	7	2

	Cal	Total Fat (g)	Sat Fat (g)	Chol (mg)	Sodium (mg)	Total Carbs (g)	Fiber (g)	Total Sugars (g)	Protein (g)
ELECTRIC PRESSURE-COOKER AND SLOW-COOKER DISHES *(CONT.)*									
Classic Marinara Sauce	90	2.5	0	0	480	19	4	12	4
Tomatoes with Olive Oil	200	19	2.5	0	300	6	2	3	1
Ratatouille	440	34	4.5	0	1120	28	8	15	8
Brown Rice with Shiitakes and Edamame	240	5	0	0	200	42	2	2	7
Warm Wild Rice Salad with Pecans and Cranberries	480	18	7	0	300	74	7	18	12
Spiced Barley Pilaf with Dates and Parsley	280	6	0.5	0	630	53	10	10	6
Beet and Wheat Berry Salad with Arugula and Apples	450	23	3.5	0	720	54	9	12	11
Freekeh Pilaf with Dates and Pistachios	280	8	1	0	200	46	9	10	8
Greek Chickpeas with Coriander and Sage	190	6	0.5	0	410	41	1	2	11
Smoky Braised Chickpeas	310	7	0	0	780	49	14	9	15
Garlicky Yogurt Sauce	20	1.5	1	0	35	2	0	0	0
Braised White Beans with Olive Oil and Sage	310	6	1	0	780	51	19	2	16
French Lentils with Swiss Chard	190	8	1	0	460	23	6	2	9
Warm Lentil Salad with Radishes and Mint	210	4.5	0.5	0	630	32	8	2	11
SMALL BITES AND SNACKS									
Sweet Potato Hummus	140	9	1.5	0	250	12	2	3	2
Parsnip Hummus	140	9	1.5	0	230	12	3	3	2
Artichoke and White Bean Dip	70	4	0.5	0	260	7	1	1	2
Baba Ghanoush	80	6	1	0	220	8	3	4	2
Super Guacamole	140	13	2	0	150	8	6	2	2
Fresh Tomato Salsa	15	0	0	0	100	3	1	2	1
Toasted Corn and Black Bean Salsa	60	3	0	0	160	8	1	2	2
Carrot-Habanero Dip	80	5	0.5	0	180	8	2	4	1
Loaded Meaty Nacho Dip	120	7	2	0	380	11	2	1	4
Naked Nacho Dip	90	5	1	0	340	10	1	1	2
Whipped Cashew Dip with Roasted Red Peppers and Olives	210	17	3	0	290	9	1	2	5
Whipped Cashew Dip with Chipotle and Lime	200	17	3	0	210	9	1	2	5
Whipped Cashew Dip with Sun-Dried Tomatoes and Rosemary	210	18	3	0	230	10	1	2	5
Creamy Turkish Nut Dip	190	17	2	0	180	6	2	1	4
Beet Muhammara	160	13	1.5	0	320	9	2	5	3
Pomegranate Molasses	60	0	0	0	0	15	0	13	0
Kale Chips	60	4	0.5	0	160	5	2	1	3
Ranch-Style Kale Chips	70	4	0.5	0	170	7	2	1	3
Spicy Sesame-Ginger Kale Chips	70	5	0.5	0	170	6	2	1	3
Beet Chips	70	0	0	0	700	15	4	10	2
Sesame Nori Chips	30	1.5	0	0	65	2	1	0	2
Whole-Wheat Seeded Crackers	230	11	1.5	0	330	30	5	0	6
Spiced Roasted Chickpeas	150	9	1	0	310	14	5	0	5
Barbecue-Spiced Roasted Chickpeas	70	4	0.5	0	140	7	2	0	2
Spanish-Spiced Roasted Chickpeas	150	9	1	0	330	13	4	0	5

	Cal	Total Fat (g)	Sat Fat (g)	Chol (mg)	Sodium (mg)	Total Carbs (g)	Fiber (g)	Total Sugars (g)	Protein (g)
SMALL BITES AND SNACKS *(CONT.)*									
Orange-Fennel Spiced Almonds	230	20	1.5	0	290	7	0	2	7
Spicy Chipotle Almonds	230	20	1.5	0	290	8	5	2	8
Chewy Granola Bars with Hazelnuts, Cherries, and Cacao Nibs	260	14	2	0	90	31	3	19	4
Chewy Granola Bars with Walnuts and Cranberries	240	12	1.5	0	90	31	3	20	3
Nut-Free Chewy Granola Bars	230	12	2	0	90	27	4	16	5
Popcorn with Olive Oil	45	2	0	0	85	5	1	0	1
Popcorn with Warm Spices and Garlic	45	2	0	0	85	5	1	0	1
Popcorn with Spicy Cinnamon Sugar	50	2	0	0	85	7	1	2	1
Tomato, Olive, and Basil Skewers	60	6	0.5	0	75	3	0	0	0
Blistered Shishito Peppers	50	4.5	0	0	0	2	1	1	0
Smoky Shishito Peppers with Espelette and Lime	80	7	0.5	0	290	3	1	1	1
Shishito Peppers with Fennel Pollen, Aleppo Pepper, and Lemon	50	5	0	0	95	2	1	1	0
Shishito Peppers with Mint, Poppy Seeds, and Orange	50	5	0	0	95	2	1	1	0
Bruschetta with Artichoke Hearts and Basil	210	9	1	0	420	27	2	1	6
Toasted Bread for Bruschetta	160	5	0.5	0	160	230	1	0	4
Bruschetta with Smashed Minty Peas, Chili, and Lemon Zest	210	9	1	0	220	27	2	2	6
Crispy Polenta Squares with Olives and Sun-Dried Tomatoes	90	5	0.5	0	180	0	0	1	1
Stuffed Mushrooms	100	8	1	0	160	5	0	2	2
Buffalo Cauliflower Bites	530	47	16	0	780	26	2	4	2
Vegan Ranch Dressing	120	14	1.5	0	160	0	0	0	0
Cashew Ricotta Tartlets with Celery-Olive Topping	150	12	1.5	0	140	9	0	1	3
Cashew Ricotta Tartlets with Tomato-Basil Topping	160	12	1.5	0	130	10	1	2	3
Butternut Squash Tartlets with Almonds, Pomegranate, and Mint	110	4.5	0	0	220	16	2	2	2
Stuffed Grape Leaves	70	2.5	0	0	220	11	1	1	1
Stuffed Grape Leaves with Currants and Pine Nuts	100	4.5	0	0	220	14	1	3	2
PLANT-POWERED DESSERTS									
Melon, Plums, and Cherries with Mint and Vanilla	70	0	0	0	15	18	2	16	1
Peaches, Blackberries, and Strawberries with Basil and Pepper	90	0.5	0	0	0	22	5	16	2
Cider Baked Apples with Dried Cranberries	310	5	0.5	0	15	70	7	58	2
Cider Baked Apples with Rum and Golden Raisins	250	5	0	0	15	40	1	37	2
Cider Baked Apples with Ginger and Orange	300	5	0.5	0	10	67	6	56	2
Roasted Pears with Dried Apricots and Pistachios	280	8	1	0	50	43	5	31	2
Roasted Apples with Dried Figs and Walnuts	260	9	1	0	55	38	5	30	2
Roasted Plums with Dried Cherries and Almonds	220	7	1	0	55	29	1	23	2
Peaches and Cherries Poached in Spiced Red Wine	270	0	0	0	0	55	3	49	2
Strawberry-Rhubarb Compote	110	2.5	2	0	25	21	3	17	1
Plum-Blackberry Compote	140	2.5	2	0	25	31	4	27	1
Blueberry-Nectarine Compote	120	3	2	0	25	25	3	20	1

	Cal	Total Fat (g)	Sat Fat (g)	Chol (mg)	Sodium (mg)	Total Carbs (g)	Fiber (g)	Total Sugars (g)	Protein (g)
PLANT-POWERED DESSERTS *(CONT.)*									
No-Bake Cherry-Almond Crisp	510	20	13	0	300	78	5	55	6
Apple Crumble	370	14	10	0	150	61	6	39	4
Peach Crumble	460	19	13	0	75	72	5	49	6
Strawberry Shortcakes with Coconut Whipped Cream	620	27	25	0	380	92	2	62	5
Tropical Fruit Pavlova	440	15	14	0	30	76	2	66	2
Trail Mix Cookies	210	11	6	0	105	26	1	15	3
French Apple Tart	500	20	18	0	160	79	7	42	4
Vegan Tart Dough	250	14	13	0	75	27	0	5	3
Chocolate-Espresso Tart	340	19	14	0	100	42	2	14	4
Vegan Single-Crust Pie Dough	230	16	15	0	150	21	0	2	3
Vegan Double-Crust Pie Dough	470	32	29	0	290	42	0	3	5
Pecan Pie	780	51	25	0	300	80	3	50	7
Blueberry Pie	660	35	33	0	310	83	3	36	6
Pumpkin Cashew Cheesecake	440	32	17	0	180	35	1	23	7
Dark Chocolate Avocado Pudding	310	18	6	0	105	41	7	31	3
Greek Lemon Rice Pudding	160	1.5	0	0	240	33	1	13	2
Semolina Pudding with Almonds and Dates	210	7	0.5	0	130	34	2	20	4
Coconut Ice Cream	280	21	19	0	95	25	0	21	2
Coconut-Horchata Ice Cream	280	21	19	0	95	26	0	21	2
Coconut-Lime Ice Cream	280	21	19	0	95	26	0	21	2
Banana Ice Cream	230	15	13	0	75	27	3	17	1
Banana–Peanut Butter Ice Cream	210	12	7	0	110	29	3	18	3
Banana-Chocolate Ice Cream with Walnuts	330	25	14	0	75	32	4	17	4
Raspberry Sorbet	130	0	0	0	50	32	5	27	1
Raspberry Sorbet with Ginger and Mint	130	0.5	0	0	55	33	5	27	1
Lemon Ice	100	0	0	0	40	27	0	26	0
Minted Lemon Ice	110	0	0	0	40	27	0	26	0
Orange Ice	80	0	0	0	40	21	0	21	0

CONVERSIONS AND EQUIVALENTS

The recipes in this book were developed using standard U.S. measures following U.S. government guidelines. The charts below offer equivalents for U.S. and metric measures. All conversions are approximate and have been rounded up or down to the nearest whole number.

EXAMPLE

1 teaspoon = 4.9292 milliliters, rounded up to 5 milliliters
1 ounce = 28.3495 grams, rounded down to 28 grams

VOLUME CONVERSIONS

U.S.	Metric
1 teaspoon	5 milliliters
2 teaspoons	10 milliliters
1 tablespoon	15 milliliters
2 tablespoons	30 milliliters
¼ cup	59 milliliters
⅓ cup	79 milliliters
½ cup	118 milliliters
¾ cup	177 milliliters
1 cup	237 milliliters
1¼ cups	296 milliliters
1½ cups	355 milliliters
2 cups (1 pint)	473 milliliters
2½ cups	591 milliliters
3 cups	710 milliliters
4 cups (1 quart)	0.946 liter
1.06 quarts	1 liter
4 quarts (1 gallon)	3.8 liters

WEIGHT CONVERSIONS

Ounces	Grams
½	14
¾	21
1	28
1½	43
2	57
2½	71
3	85
3½	99
4	113
4½	128
5	142
6	170
7	198
8	227
9	255
10	283
12	340
16 (1 pound)	454

CONVERSIONS FOR COMMON BAKING INGREDIENTS

Because measuring by weight is far more accurate than measuring by volume, and thus more likely to produce reliable results, in our recipes we provide ounce measures in addition to cup measures for many ingredients. Refer to the chart below to convert these measures into grams.

Ingredient	Ounces	Grams
Flour		
1 cup all-purpose flour*	5	142
1 cup cake flour	4	113
1 cup whole-wheat flour	5½	156
Sugar		
1 cup granulated (white) sugar	7	198
1 cup packed brown sugar (light or dark)	7	198
1 cup confectioners' sugar	4	113
Butter		
4 tablespoons (½ stick or ¼ cup)	2	57
8 tablespoons (1 stick or ½ cup)	4	113
16 tablespoons (2 sticks or 1 cup)	8	227

* U.S. all-purpose flour, the most frequently used flour in this book, does not contain leaveners, as some European flours do. These leavened flours are called self-rising or self-raising. If you are using self-rising flour, take this into consideration before adding leaveners to a recipe.

† In the United States, butter is sold both salted and unsalted. We recommend unsalted butter. If you are using salted butter, take this into consideration before adding salt to a recipe.

OVEN TEMPERATURE

Fahrenheit	Celsius	Gas Mark
225	105	¼
250	120	½
275	135	1
300	150	2
325	165	3
350	180	4
375	190	5
400	200	6
425	220	7
450	230	8
475	245	9

CONVERTING TEMPERATURES FROM AN INSTANT-READ THERMOMETER

We include doneness temperatures in many of the recipes in this book. We recommend an instant-read thermometer for the job. Refer to the table above to convert Fahrenheit degrees to Celsius. Or, for temperatures not represented in the chart, use this simple formula:

Subtract 32 degrees from the Fahrenheit reading, then divide the result by 1.8 to find the Celsius reading.

To convert 160°F to Celsius:
160°F – 32 = 128°
128° ÷ 1.8 = 71.11°C, rounded down to 71°C

Blistered Shishito Peppers

INDEX

Note: Page references in *italics* indicate photographs.

Key: FAST   SLOW COOKER   PRESSURE COOKER